Marketing

CONCEPTS AND APPLICATIONS

McGraw-Hill Series in Marketing

CONSULTING EDITOR

Charles D. Schewe, *University of Massachusetts*

Marketing

CONCEPTS AND APPLICATIONS

Second Edition

Charles D. Schewe
University of Massachusetts

Reuben M. Smith
National Life and Accident Insurance Company

McGraw-Hill Book Company

New York St. Louis San Francisco Auckland Bogotá Hamburg
Johannesburg London Madrid Mexico Montreal New Delhi
Panama Paris São Paulo Singapore Sydney Tokyo Toronto

MARKETING: Concepts and Applications

34567890KGPKGP8987654

ISBN 0-07-055251-7

This book was set in Souvenir Light by Black Dot, Inc. (ECU).
The editors were Beth A. Lewis, Barbara Brooks, and Jonathan Palace;
the designer was Joseph Gillians;
the production supervisor was Dominick Petrellese.
New drawings were done by Fine Line Illustrations, Inc.
The cover photograph was taken by Martin Bough.
Kingsport Press, Inc., was printer and binder.

Library of Congress Cataloging in Publication Data

Schewe, Charles D., date
    Marketing: concepts and applications.

    (McGraw-Hill series in marketing)
    Includes bibliographies and index.
    1. Marketing.   2. Marketing—Problems, exercises, etc.
I. Smith, Reuben M. II. Title. III. Series.
HF5415.S3238   1983   658.8   82-17300
ISBN 0-07-055251-7

ABOUT THE AUTHORS

CHARLES D. SCHEWE, Professor of Marketing at the University of Massachusetts in Amherst, received his Ph.D. from Northwestern University. He has contributed articles to many journals, including *The Journal of Marketing, The Journal of Marketing Research, Public Opinion Quarterly, Academy of Management Journal,* and *The Journal of Business Research.* Professor Schewe has worked for and consulted with such companies as General Motors, National Can Corporation, United Airlines, Data Resources, and Field Enterprises, and he is currently serving as Consulting Editor for McGraw-Hill's Series in Marketing. In the spring of 1979, Professor Schewe lectured as a Fulbright Scholar at the University of Lund, Sweden.

REUBEN M. SMITH is a Vice President of Advertising/Public Relations at National Life and Accident Insurance Company in Nashville. He was Marketing Editor for *Business Week* from 1975 to 1979, after serving as *BW* Bureau Chief in Atlanta for 5 years. He has worked for R. J. Reynolds Industries as Director of Media Relations, and his background as a journalist includes staff positions on *The Knoxville Journal, The Atlanta Times,* and *The Atlanta Constitution.* Mr. Smith's cover stories for *Business Week* dealt with corporations as diverse as Warner-Lambert, Eastman Kodak, and the Coca-Cola Company. His area of special interest is consumer and package goods.

To our wives, Anne Schewe and Shirley Jane Smith, for their patience and encouragement.

To our parents, Ralph and Marion Schewe and Guy L. and Thelma Smith, for their sacrifices.

Contents

PART TWO

Marketing as Decision Making and Information Gathering

PART THREE

Programming the Marketing Mix

PART FOUR

Marketing Today

List of Applications

Preface

Effective marketing forms the foundation of all successful business and nonbusiness transactions. Our objective for the second edition of *Marketing: Concepts and Applications,* as it was for the first edition, has been to define marketing by describing its day-to-day activities. We believe that a textbook for the introductory marketing course should convey the excitement and usefulness of the discipline, making it come alive for the student. The salient features of the first edition—its readability and real-world examples—continue in this new edition as an aid in presenting fundamental marketing principles and examining their application to a wide variety of exciting real-world situations.

With currency in mind, we have included virtually all new Applications and woven a multitude of new and relevant real-world examples into the body of the text. The cases are completely new, focusing on decision making rather than on describing marketing activities.

Topical Coverage

We retained the basic structure of the first edition, but we have deepened the topic coverage in a number of areas. We revised Chapter 2 to place substantial emphasis on the uncontrollable variables that influence marketing decisions. Throughout the 1970s these environmental conditions played havoc with marketers and the effectiveness of their decision making. Our thoroughly updated coverage of these key areas reflects the state of marketing in the 1980s. We then introduce the concept of strategic planning as the guiding framework for marketing decisions. After fully developing the marketing process and the marketing mix in the next two parts, we integrate the discussion of the marketing mix and thoroughly explain the strategic planning process in the completely new Chapter 18.

Most students confront marketing at the middle-management level, and this is the perspective of the text, even though senior management designs the groundwork that guides middle managers. Integrating the material previously discussed in the book, Chapter 18 covers the following new material: corporate mission; business definition; corporate culture; product portfolio analysis; and the strategic alternatives of leader, challenger, follower, and nicher. As with all chapters, extensive real-world examples are interwoven to make the material come to life for the reader.

The sections on industrial goods and services in Chapter 8 have been substantially revised and expanded. A solid treatment of industrial buying behavior has been added to round out discussion of industrial marketing. Many not-for-profit examples appear throughout the second edition. Following is a sampling of some other topics that have been added throughout the book to provide a more comprehensive treatment of marketing:

Our own, more "managerial" definition of marketing appears in Chapter 1.

Post-exchange servicing has been added as a controllable variable in Chapter 2.

Chapter 4, "Marketing Research," includes a greatly expanded appendix of secondary sources.

All pertinent statistics that describe markets have been updated in Chapter 5.

The subculture section of Chapter 6 now includes an examination of Hispanic markets, the fastest growing ethnic market segment in the United States today, as well as the very contemporary area of situational factors in marketing.

A section on low-involvement learning has been added to Chapter 7.

Venture teams and other organizational forms of new-product development have been added to Chapter 9.

The product management strategy of brand extension has been added to the treatment of the problem of cannibalism in Chapter 10.

Chapter 14 has updated coverage on the deregulation circumstances surrounding commercial trucking and railroads.

A discussion of cost-per-thousand now appears in Chapter 16 along with new advertising approaches.

Chapter 19 contains new coverage of the various stages of managerial philosophy and orientation in international marketing.

Up-to-date treatment of consumer issues in marketing, including the effects of the Reagan administration, appears in Chapter 20.

The organization of the text remains traditional. Part One shows marketing's place in society—and in the firm—and outlines the actual tasks of marketers. Part Two describes the types of information that marketers need and how they obtain it. Part Three looks in detail at the major marketing activities: product development, pricing, distribution, and promotion, including strategic marketing planning and the integration of activities to form the marketing mix. Part Four describes international marketing, consumerism, and careers in marketing.

As this overview of the book's structure shows, we have attempted to present basic marketing concepts comprehensively; but we have done it without being long-winded. The resulting text is sufficiently brief to allow room for individual instructors to amplify those topics which they feel are most important, most interesting, and most valuable. We believe that the resultant balance between topic "width" and "depth" will satisfy the needs of your introductory marketing course.

Acknowledgments

There are a number of individuals who, at various stages of this project, offered able assistance. Sincere thanks go to Bertil Liander, who contributed Chapter 19, "International Marketing," and to Marc Weinberger, who contributed Chapter 20, "Consumer Issues in Marketing," to the first edition. Our special appreciation goes to Michael Sorkin and Thomas Madden, who provided valuable input for the Instructor's Manual. Special thanks also go to Candida Johnson, who shared her thoughts and efforts about pedagogy, and to Barton Macchiette for his help on the marketing to minorities section. Bonnie Webster typed and retyped many drafts of the manuscript without complaint. A number of research assistants performed the legwork necessary to put this text into your hands, and they deserve special thanks: Stuart Hotchkiss, Benjamin Carr, Elizabeth Kempisty, Robert Palladino, Lynn Pijar, Katherine Scholberg, and Kenny Chan.

We are especially grateful for the critiques of our professional colleagues who reviewed portions of the manuscript in its various stages:

Professor Chris T. Allen
University of Massachusetts

Professor Sam Carter
Michigan State University

David Diamond
Journalist

Professor Ralph Gaedeke
California State, Sacramento

Professor James Gammel
Pace University

Professor David Georgoff
Florida Atlantic University

Professor Mark Jones
Chabot College

Professor J. Daniel Lindley
Ohio University

Professor Gerald Manning
Des Moines Area Community College

Professor James McNeal
Texas A&M University

Professor Donald Nagourney
New York Institute of Technology

Professor Michael Nobel
California Polytechnical

Professor Constantine Petrides
Borough of Manhattan Community College

Dr. Kent Pinney
University of Nevada, Las Vegas

Professor Peter Shaffer   Professor Jerry Wheat
Western Illinois University   Indiana University

We would like also to thank the group we worked with at the McGraw-Hill Book Company. We are indebted to James Walsh, who seeded the idea that grew into this textbook; to William Kane and John Carleo, who saw it through its first edition; and to Carol Napier, Beth Lewis, Jon Palace, and Mary Ferrandino, who supervised the second edition. Special thanks are due Robert Weber and Mary Drouin, veritable magicians with words, who are most responsible for the ease with which this book reads. We are perhaps most indebted to Barbara Brooks, whose enthusiasm and encouragement throughout the development of the second edition provided us with the inspiration and devotion to provide the quality text that you are about to read.

Finally, an enthusiastic declaration of thanks to our wives, Anne Schewe and Shirley Jane Smith.

Charles D. Schewe
Reuben M. Smith

Marketing

CONCEPTS AND APPLICATIONS

PART ONE

Marketing: An Overview

At the Chicago headquarters of Esmark, Inc., the multibillion-dollar holding company, things are changing. The company is finally breaking away from its traditional production orientation, a business philosophy that was carried over from the days of Swift & Company, the old-line meat-packing firm that became Esmark. While meat packing is still Esmark's major subsidiary, the company now boasts a product line that includes gasoline, fertilizer, girdles, and peanut butter. Swift had long been fingered for its lack of marketing shrewdness. As one Swift veteran told *Business Week,* "We had a purely manufacturing mentality of moving the highest possible volume of meat out the back door and worrying later about how to sell it."

For many years Swift had little trouble in selling, but in the late 1960s, a new generation of meat processors with more efficient plants in better locations and with cheaper labor rates created heavy competition for Swift. Swift failed to react. "We should have moved quickly to match them, to make it hard for them to grow," recalled Esmark's president. "Instead, we sat back and read the 1913 annual report and didn't change anything." Not until 1976 did the company begin to assume a marketing orientation.

In each of the company's subsidiaries, Esmark is striving to develop marketing muscle. Esmark installed a marketing-oriented executive, the former head of Colgate-Palmolive Co.'s domestic consumer divisions, as head of Swift & Company. In all, Esmark recruited more than forty managers from strong marketing companies between 1977 and 1979. And nowhere is Esmark's sudden fascination with marketing more evident than in the company's advertising and sales promotion budgets, soaring from $30 million in 1974 to more than $200 million in 1979.

This transformation from production to marketing is having its greatest impact at Swift. To convert the meat company (more than 150 years old) into a strong marketer of food products, the company is now beginning to institute conventional marketing strategies. "I really want to know what we are going to do with the product after it's produced," Swift's president told *Business Week.* "My mind begins in the kitchen and works its way back to the question of building a plant." And, as the head of Swift's Consumer Products Division added, "Certain marketing fundamentals apply whether you're in girdles or food. You find out what the consumer needs, develop a product, and give it a good trial before making a huge commitment."

Source of data: "A Meatpacker Discovers Consumer Marketing," *Business Week,* May 28, 1979, pp. 164–172.

Chapter

1

Marketing and Society

Looking Ahead

This chapter describes the nature of marketing and discusses its place in society. We will see that marketing provides satisfaction to various parts of society through exchanges. Then we will look at the place and function of marketing within a business organization.

Key Topics

The major objective of marketing: to provide satisfaction to individuals within the economic system

How to conduct activities that match the goods and services offered with those desired

How satisfaction in society comes about through the exchange process

The four types of satisfaction or utility that can result from the exchange process

The history of marketing

The recent development of marketing as seen through a series of definitions

Why the study of marketing is valuable for all daily activities, not only for business activities

How the business system is directed toward providing satisfaction

Why marketing, one of several basic business functions, is actually the key to success

Why the marketing concept is so vital a philosophy, both socially and economically

Chapter Outline

Marketing and Exchange in Society
The Nature of Marketing
An Economist's View of the
    Exchange Process

A Historical Approach to Marketing
The Production Era
The Sales Era
The Marketing Era

A Definitional Approach to Marketing
The Quality-of-Life Approach
The Managerial Approach
The Societal Approach
The Broadening of the Marketing
    Approach
Our Definition of Marketing

Marketing and the Organization
Business as a Satisfaction System
The Processing Activities of
    Business
The Marketing Concept

Looking Back

Marketing and Exchange in Society

To understand the nature of marketing, it will be helpful for you to put yourself into the shoes of an economist, someone who looks at how the economy works and considers its effects on society. Later in the chapter we will ask you to put on another pair of shoes, those of someone who runs an organization that must operate within the economy. But first, just think of yourself as a person who is looking at the world's economic activities and wants to understand how they work. From that vantage point, you can see what marketing is—and what it is *not*.

The Nature of Marketing

Each of us comes into contact daily with some aspect of marketing—advertising, selling, promotion, merchandising, or distribution, for example. But none of these activities, alone, is marketing. Only when they are all brought together—along with others such as research, product development, and pricing—can the result be called marketing. All the commercials on television are but one part of the overall marketing process. Though we may think of advertising as being the same as marketing, it no more represents the total concept than a keg of nails and a load of lumber represent a house. A house results only when a contractor brings all its materials together. In the same way, marketing results only when its many activities are coordinated. The study of marketing will convince you that it is much, much more than the sum of its parts.

Types of Satisfaction

Economists often talk about goods and services providing a "bundle of utility." When they use the term *utility,* they basically mean *satisfaction*. As we'll see, marketing is closely involved with the exchange process that provides satisfaction to people within society.

When we lay out cold, hard cash for a product, we expect to get some satisfaction in return. The satisfaction we receive, however, comes from many different facets of what we buy. Satisfaction certainly results from the function, or use, of a product. In buying a car, for example, we get transportation. But, besides this *functional* satisfaction, we often get *psychological* satisfaction as well. That is, we may gain some intangible (nonphysical) benefits in buying a product. Besides providing transportation, a car can also enhance a person's feelings of importance and self-worth (a Mercedes-Benz has long been a status symbol). A car can bring a feeling of power or provide a sense of freedom and independence. Owning an automobile may be especially important in the life of teenagers; it may give them greater prestige within their peer group and symbolically "cut the apron strings." Sometimes the psychological satisfaction is more important to the buyer than the functional satisfaction.

Satisfaction, then, comes from both functional and psychological facets of a good or service. But it also can be seen to include four types of utility: form utility, time utility, place utility, and possession utility. *Form utility* is the satisfaction buyers receive from the tangible (physical) characteristics of a good—its shape, function, or style. Form utility involves both functional and psychological satisfaction. A suit, for

Application 1-1
Functional and Tangible Satisfaction—
From a Novelty to an Essential

The video screen and the computer are technological marvels that until a few years ago were shrouded in a deep mystique, but these space-age devices are becoming down-to-earth, everyday appliances.

Soon, the video screen and the computer will be essential parts of the automobile; in a few years, they will be as common as the odometer is today. Cathode ray tubes (CRT) will in the future replace the traditional instrument panel on automobiles and trucks.

Already, some luxury-model cars are equipped with small computers which provide the driver with fuel data—miles per gallon, the number of miles left in the tank, and elapsed time on a trip. And to aid in maintenance, Cadillac has a system which flashes a number to indicate to a mechanic the exact system or part which needs attention.

(Courtesy Zenith Radio Corporation)

The applications of the computer in the automobile are almost limitless. Soon, some think, the computer and the CRT will tell the driver when oil is needed, that tire pressure is low, and even remind drivers of appointments or special occasions like a spouse's birthday. Although the computer/video combination may seem like a novelty today, in the not-so-distant future, this technology will be a functional, tangible satisfaction feature as essential as the automatic transmission.

Source of data: "TV Sets in Auto Dashboards May Soon Be Aiding Drivers," *The Wall Street Journal,* March 6, 1981, p. 21.

example, can provide warmth as well as symbolic and aesthetic appeal. An exclusive label may provide status, and a particular design may be more appealing and more fashionable than others. (See Application 1-1.)

But consumers do not get all their satisfaction from the physical characteristics of a product. For instance, although most men's and women's garments are produced in New York City, people throughout the country—from California to Florida, from Alaska to Texas—have needs for clothing. Surely they don't want to take the time to travel to New York to make their purchases and satisfy their needs. Another element of satisfaction, then, comes from being able to buy a suit or a dress at a particular time and in an easily accessible place. Thus, satisfaction includes both *time utility* and *place utility,* which result from moving goods closer to consumers in terms of time and place.

Merely having clothing on a rack in a store is not totally satisfying, either. Consumers also want to really own the article themselves. The satisfaction derived from learning that a product is available and then gaining ownership is called *possession utility.* It gives the owner the right to actually consume the good.

Thus, the total satisfaction that comes from an item—or its *bundle of satisfaction* —is a combination of its form, time, place, and possession utilities. And these aspects provide both functional and psychological satisfaction to consumers. (See Applications 1-2 and 1-3.)

Levels of Satisfaction

Besides the different types of satisfaction that a product may bring, there are different levels of satisfaction. One product may provide far greater satisfaction to a consumer than another product. On the whole, it is far more satisfying to buy a house than it is to purchase a necktie or a hairbrush.

Marketing takes place because consumers are faced with problems: It's a hot day, and you are thirsty; or your car tires are wearing out, causing you to skid on wet roads; or you have a job interview on Monday and want something new to wear. Generally, in facing such problems, you pick the solution that you think will give you the most

Application 1-2
Psychological and Intangible Satisfaction—Sending Up Signals

Throughout the ages, many methods of showing affection or of conjuring up ways to celebrate have been devised. The newest is with a bouquet of balloons. In almost every major city across the United States, balloons are a growth industry. A cluster of two dozen balloons costs about $25, and you get more than just balloons. Included in the tab is delivery by a messenger dressed as a magician, a mime, a clown, Big Bird, the Mad Hatter, or Groucho Marx . . . or you can spring for a little more cash and get an entire chorus line. Sometimes champagne is included.

These helium-filled, nonflammable balloons are in demand for almost all occasions—wedding anniversaries, birthdays, bar mitzvahs, Valentine's Day and Mother's Day. A Los Angeles balloonery, the Red Balloon, reports many requests for clusters of black balloons inscribed with hand-painted messages such as "I Don't Love You Any More."

The balloon business is booming. Balloons over Boston, begun in 1979, grossed $100,000 in its first year. Another Boston-based concern, Balloon Bouquests, plans to offer franchises nationwide.

Success seems to depend on knowledge of the roots of the business one is in. As the operator of the Chicago Balloonery told *Time* magazine: "We are in the business of selling magic, and our return is joy."

Source of data: "Balloonacy Blooms and Booms," *Time,* Sept. 8, 1980. pp. 60–61.

Application 1-3
Psychological and Functional Satisfaction—
"Worth Its Weight in Gold"

(Jim Cron/Monkmeyer)

While some American makers of luxury automobiles have had to resort to rebates, Mercedes-Benz officials worry about how to reduce the 2- and 3-year waiting time for several models— especially the fuel-efficient diesel-engine cars. "Mercedes is in a class by itself," one observer commented.

Unquestionably, part of Mercedes' success is due to snob appeal; a relatively small number of persons intent on impressing their friends buy the cars.

Most certainly, Mercedes benefits to a degree from snob appeal, but its main appeal is quality. As one satisfied customer, a physician, told *The Wall Street Journal*, "A Mercedes is pure gold. The longer you drive it, the more it appreciates. . . . It's the safest car on the road. I had a patient who totaled his Mercedes and walked away with only minor scratches. . . . A Mercedes lasts and lasts. You take an American car . . . after 150,000 miles, it's a piece of junk. A Mercedes is just getting broken in after 150,000 miles."

Mercedes believes it could easily double its United States sales to 100,000 per year, but the scarcity factor heightens the vehicle's status and hence its psychological appeal.

Source of data: "As U.S. Auto Makers Worry, the Mercedes Just Rolls Right Along," *The Wall Street Journal,* Sept. 11, 1979. p. 1.

total satisfaction. So it is with all consumers. Given the need for something to drink, a consumer can choose water; but that's not as nutritious as milk, which, perhaps, doesn't taste as good as a grape soda. To solve the problem of thirst, then, a consumer often will opt for the greatest taste satisfaction—in this case, a soft drink.

But then there is the choice to be made among all the available brands that solve the problem. The brand that gives the greatest amount of "good taste" is the logical solution. But what if a potential buyer considers all brands of grape soda to be similar or equal in terms of taste (equal in terms of functional satisfaction)? Then other sources of satisfaction may enter the decision process. This type of reasoning led Crush International (Evanston, Illinois) to the following strategy with its soft drinks: The company noticed that its competitors' cans of soft drinks featured labels with pictures of fresh strawberries, grapes, or orange slices. To counter this visual appeal and add a greater degree of satisfaction to its own product, Crush began to use symbols on its cans. To convey purity, Crush's new label used strong, deep colors—red for strawberry, purple for grape, and orange, of course, for orange. Four clusters of bubbles were grouped to suggest four fruit-tree blossoms and to communicate the idea of freshness and effervescence. When the new label was tried in two test markets, Orange Crush sales jumped more than 40 percent, while national sales of soda in the regular cans were up only 7 percent—attesting to the additional psychological satisfaction consumers received from the new labeling. In short, while the product provides a sizable amount of satisfaction by quenching thirst and tasting good, it also provides an additional degree of utility or satisfaction through its labeling. And it's the product or brand which is seen to have the greatest *total* utility that gets selected. The bundle of satisfaction, then, is the sum total of the types and levels of satisfaction that are perceived by potential consumers.

Consider another example. Disposable diapers now come with adhesive tapes to fit them snugly to the shape of the baby. Yet often parents, believing the child to be ''wet,'' pull off the taped diaper only to find it dry—consequently losing the use of that diaper. To reduce such waste, and thereby increase the level of satisfaction, in 1978 Kimberly-Clark introduced Kleenex Super Dry diapers with the slogan ''so dry we added wetness indicators.'' The wetness indicator is a toy block design on the diaper: its colored letters lighten as the inside of the diaper goes from dry to very wet.

Satisfying Our Needs and Wants through Exchange

Marketing, then, involves activities that provide satisfaction to consumers. It is a matching process. Marketers must recognize and understand consumers' needs and wants and then must determine how best to satisfy them. But *need* is our lack of something that is *necessary* for our physical or psychological well-being. A *want* is less critical to us; it is our lack of something that we would *like* to have because we believe it is desirable or useful. The greater the match between what is offered to us and what we want or need, the greater our satisfaction. In many cases, what we lack is basic: we *need* transportation, or food, or a drink, or cleanliness. We *want* a car, a steak, a milkshake, or a sauna. In other cases, what we lack is entirely in our minds: we *want* excitement, or acclaim, or great success, or novelty. While our basic needs can be met by *any* product that solves a particular problem, our wants are met through products that offer additional degrees of personal satisfaction in solving the problem. (Application 1-4 shows how Frank Perdue satisfies wants as well as nutritional needs.)

Satisfaction becomes available through the process of exchange in society. And marketing, with its emphasis on satisfaction, exists because society has needs that must be met and wants that must be satisfied. The goal of marketing is to facilitate exchange so that satisfaction is increased for all parties involved.

Exchange requires two or more individuals or groups that have certain wants and certain want-satisfying products. In order for exchange to come about, each party must want what will be received more than what will be given up. That is, both parties must feel that their total satisfaction will be enhanced as a result of the exchange. As Figure 1-1 shows, an exchange involves two parties with unsatisfied wants and/or needs, each with something to exchange, and some means for the parties to communicate their willingness to exchange.

While the exchange process between individuals or between buyers and sellers is the focal point of the study of marketing, some other exchanges are crucial for the effective and efficient running of our economy. We will now examine the exchange process from an economist's point of view.

Application 1-4
Increasing the Level of Satisfaction—
"It Takes a Tough Man to Make a Tender Chicken"

Until the 1970s chickens were treated pretty much like any other commodity—like potatoes, soybeans, or pork bellies. The consumer perceived no real difference in chickens. That was, of course, before a fellow by the name of Frank Perdue arrived on the scene from Maryland and shook up the chicken industry.

What Perdue did was to make his chickens a household word—one that the homemaker would call for by name in supermarkets. He accomplished this feat through aggressive and heavy advertising on radio and in newspapers and magazines. His advertising is also clever: "My chickens eat better than you do." The advertising copy took off in other ads, as in "Ladies, Please Squeeze the Chicken." To liven the ads even more, Frank Perdue stars in his own ads, providing personal testimony to his product with his nasal twang: "It takes a tough man to make a tender chicken." Scrawny, baldish, with an egg-shaped head and a nose like a beak, Perdue accounts for much of the impact of the ads through his appearance. As one

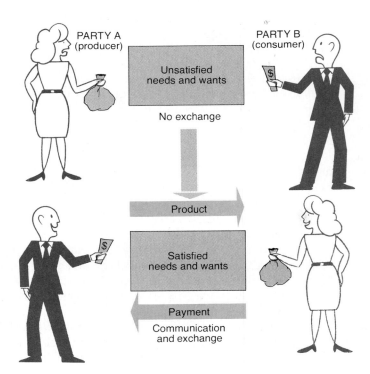

Figure 1-1 The communication and exchange process.

envious competitor told *TV Guide,* "Perdue not only has his name on every chicken, he looks like one too."

Clever ads have given the Perdue bird an aura of increased satisfaction in terms of purity, freshness, and tenderness. By increasing the consumer's perception of the level of satisfaction via advertising, Frank Perdue is able to command a premium for his chickens in the marketplace, although the superiority of Perdue's chickens is, of course, debatable. Generally, a Perdue-tagged chicken will fetch upward of 20 cents more per pound than any other bird. This differential, Frank Perdue would claim, is due to the lusciousness of the large breasts of his yellow-skinned chickens (they are fed marigold petals). Yet, quite obviously, something is also attributable to the appeal of his advertising. After 9 years and over 130 TV commercials, Frank Perdue's business has grown about 500 percent.

Sources of data: "Not Just Chicken Feed," *Time,* Sept. 6, 1976, p. 54; and "It Helps if You Look like a Chicken," *TV Guide,* Feb. 21, 1981, pp. 20–23.

(Courtesy R. C. Auletta and Company, Inc.)

An Economist's View of the Exchange Process
Stage 1: Obtaining Resources

As depicted in Figure 1-2, there are four stages in the provision of satisfaction in our economy: (1) obtaining resources; (2) producing goods and services; (3) making intermediate exchanges; and (4) consuming goods and services.

Raw materials, such as lumber, ore, and farm goods, provide little or no satisfaction when in their natural states. The greatest amount of satisfaction comes from their actual use or consumption (stage 4). To reach that end, natural resources must be

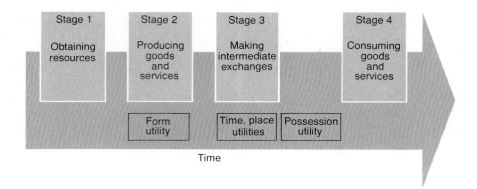

Figure 1-2 Four stages in the provision of satisfaction.

procured or extracted. Trees must be cut down; ore must be mined; and agricultural goods must be farmed. But even these acts are not enough. Trees that have been cut and are lying in a forest have a long way to go before they yield satisfaction to consumers. Those who farm these natural resources exchange them with producers and receive their income in return. Note, too, that services go through these stages—surgeons give little satisfaction without the proper resources such as training, cobblers need the skills to repair shoes, and so on.

Stage 2: Producing Goods and Services

The manufacturing stage involves the processing of resources and the production of products. This stage, by putting resources into consumable condition, provides form utility (as, for example, when a cabinet is made from timber, or a surgeon performs a diagnosis). At this point, the producer exchanges the product with retailers or wholesalers and receives money that in turn can be exchanged backward for more resources.

Stage 3: Making Intermediate Exchanges

Intermediaries, or middlemen, accomplish the next step in providing satisfaction. Wholesalers and retailers buy and sell products in their own exchange process and move them closer in time and place to ultimate consumers. These intermediate exchanges provide time and place utility. But they also set the stage for purchase by consumers, and in this way they provide possession utility for products. Furniture stores, for example, allow buyers who have a need for cabinets to come in and choose the one that best matches their needs; surgeons suggest getting more than one opinion. This stage results in an exchange with the consumer who gives money to obtain the goods.

Stage 4: Consuming Goods and Services

Only when a product can be owned and consumed does it fully deliver the potential satisfaction that has been developing throughout this four-stage process. As the time line in Figure 1-2 indicates, additional satisfaction is added to the raw materials in each stage until total satisfaction is produced. Over time, the utilities of form, time, place, and possession are added to the resources and offered to consumers. The cabinet is brought home and put to use; the needed surgery is performed.

Now that we've examined the exchange process and how it provides satisfaction, we can look at it in historical terms to see how modern marketing developed.

A Historical Approach to Marketing

In history books, considerable space is devoted to the early merchants who traveled the known world selling and buying goods—making exchanges. Evidence shows that as far back as 2100 B.C., people specialized in different trades. Eventually, towns grew larger and developed marketplaces, common areas where the members of society would meet and exchange wares. Artisans built shops in which to practice their specialties—woodworking, pottery making, leathercrafts, woolens, wines, and so on. The benefits of such specialization were noted, and people became confident that it would work to their increased satisfaction.

The Middle Ages brought a greater demand for goods than had been known before. With the growing trade between nations, the seeds of organized industry were sown. While craftworkers could satisfy the local needs of a town, the enlarged trading area demanded more goods and greater variety. Thus, the need for specialization of labor grew critical.

The industrial revolution began about 1750, and its impact was soon felt throughout the civilized world. Its labor specialization and mass production techniques resulted in increased productivity and more goods at lower prices. But before new possibilities for trade could be realized, new markets had to be found to absorb the greater output. America provided at least a partial solution to the problem.

The Production Era

In the early 1700s, the American Colonies were dependent on England for everything from china to tea to clothing. The industrial revolution did not reach the United States until the early 1800s. With the break between the Colonies and Great Britain in 1776, the newborn United States became more self-sufficient.

Mass production industries began to develop—textile plants, tobacco factories, meat packers, and armament plants. The advent of these industries spawned wholesalers who settled near rivers and on the coast, since large-scale transportation was limited to the waterways that connected the large industrial cities with the smaller towns and communities. The wholesalers fed supplies to the retailers, who then sold finished products to consumers.

With the coming of the railroads, goods could be moved faster and farther. Inland towns grew larger, and the United States economy came into its own. People now had more money to spend for goods that were not actually necessary for life; soon manufacturers began producing *discretionary goods*, items chosen through want rather than simple need. In the past, the sale of needed goods had required little more than moving them to consumers, but discretionary goods presented another situation.

Manufacturers now found that they had to create demand for their discretionary products and send people into the field to sell them personally.

Until this time, manufacturers had been interested only in providing for basic needs—food, drink, clothing. In most cases, they sold what they produced, for the market would buy whatever was turned out. The concept of satisfying consumers' wants was yet to come.

The Sales Era

In the 1930s, the United States moved from a production economy to a sales economy. Competition evolved in almost every industry. Manufacturers who had enjoyed virtual monopolies now found that they had to improve the quality and variety of goods. Competition also forced companies to "sell" their products. No longer could a manufacturer simply produce goods and be assured that they would be bought. Now competition in the marketplace slightly favored consumers: there was more product than demand.

Even so, companies still paid little attention to satisfying consumers' wants. The production lines ran, and the sales forces tried to sell their products. Little effort was given to finding out what consumers wanted. With the exception of World War II and the immediate postwar period, the available supply of goods and services far surpassed the demand for them. There was little or no difficulty in producing goods; the real problem lay in marketing them.

The Marketing Era

For most companies, the sales era continued until the 1950s. Then some manufacturers began to realize that pushing goods onto the marketplace was not as effective as focusing on the provision of satisfaction. The marketing era emerged as manufacturers finally adopted the sensible philosophy that they should examine the needs and wants of consumers and produce to match those factors. They realized that simply getting people to buy a product—even though it might not meet their needs and wants—would not ensure repeat purchasing. And repeat purchasing is the foundation of any successful business. In short, during the marketing era, a company's total effort is guided by consumers' demands for satisfaction.

It would be foolish, of course, to believe that all companies now subscribe to this marketing philosophy and follow through with it in performing their tasks. Certainly, many top corporate executives spend too much time worrying about profits when they might be thinking about how to provide customer satisfaction. If people like what they buy, not only will they buy again, but they will probably tell friends about purchases that made them happy. The result is increased sales and—assuming an efficient, effectively run organization—increased profits.

A review of the top companies in the United States shows that, with some exceptions, the ones which strive to satisfy consumers are the most successful year after year. On the other hand, many companies which have ignored consumer wants have failed. With that sobering thought in mind, let's look at how effective marketing can make the difference between success and failure.

A Definitional Approach to Marketing

We have seen that marketing is intimately involved with providing satisfaction. It's now time to examine some definitions of marketing to learn what that entails. (As an overview to this section, read the definitions of marketing given in Table 1-1. By reviewing these definitions, we can see how marketing has evolved from the end of World War II to its present form.)

The Quality-of-Life Approach

The first definition in Table 1-1 is old but certainly not outdated. In 1947 Paul Mazur said that marketing is "the delivery of a standard of living to society."[1] The term *standard of living* relates to the quality of life. And since it is marketing's job to recognize unmet needs and wants and to satisfy them, marketing improves consumers' quality of life.

Consider the invention of the electronic calculator. Until this product became available, people were confronted with time-consuming mathematical computations. Now, a product is available which frees consumers from lengthy calculations and contributes to their general happiness. The dishwasher is another product suited to the needs of our time. It is a space-saver and an organizer, and it eliminates a tedious job. While some advances in products and services are more significant than others, it is the planned effort to satisfy people's needs—i.e., marketing—which provides a better standard of living.

The Managerial Approach

In 1960 the American Marketing Association defined marketing as "the performance of business activities that direct the flow of goods and services from producer to

---

[1]Paul Mazur, "Does Distribution Cost Enough?" *Fortune,* November 1947, p. 138.

TABLE 1-1   Some Definitions of Marketing

MARKETING

—is the delivery of a standard of living to society. *(Mazur, 1947)*
—is the performance of business activities that direct the flow of goods and services from producer to consumer or user. *(AMA, 1960)*
—is a total system of interacting business activities designed to plan, price, promote, and distribute want-satisfying goods and services to present and potential customers. *(Stanton, 1971)*
—is a set of activities necessary and incidental to bringing about exchange relationships in our economic system. *(Holloway and Hancock, 1973)*
—encompasses exchange activities conducted by individuals and organizations for the purpose of satisfying human wants. *(Enis, 1977)*
—is managing human and organizational exchange activities directed at satisfying human wants and needs. *(Schewe and Smith, 1983)*

Figure 1-3 During the late 1970s, American auto manufacturers began to realize that the era of the "gas guzzler" had come to an end. (Norman Hurst/Stock, Boston)

consumer or user."[2] This definition reflects a more managerial emphasis. It notes that marketing is a set of activities which business performs to promote the flow of products and services between companies and people.

During the 1950s, businesses recognized that they could improve the movement of their goods and services by performing a specific set of activities both inside and outside the firm. Essentially, these activities attempt to stimulate sales, which are a measure of the firm's success in matching consumers' needs and wants. The much-discussed failure of Ford Motor Company's Edsel in the late 1950s told the company that its product did not provide satisfaction. Similarly, the midiskirt did not satisfy consumers' fashion wants in the early 1970s, and it did not gain acceptance at that time. And in the late 1970s and on to the 1980s, the resounding rejection of domestically made "gas guzzlers" proved again the reluctance of United States automobile manufacturers to meet America's wants and needs. (See Figure 1-3.)

More than a decade after the AMA defined marketing, that definition was amended to say that marketing is "a total system of interacting business activities designed to plan, price, promote, and distribute want-satisfying goods and services to present and potential customers."[3] Stanton explicitly noted the activities of planning, pricing, promoting, and distributing goods and services. He stressed that these marketing activities are interrelated in a system. The term *system* means that a set of elements are related to one another by some common objective. In the marketing system, the activities Stanton identified are the related elements, and satisfaction is the common objective.

Each of the marketing activities reinforces the others, and no one element is particularly effective without the others. For example, if a product's price is out of line with its perceived value, the promotion and distribution of that product are likely to be

---

[2]American Marketing Association, Committee on Definitions, *Marketing Definitions: A Glossary of Marketing Terms,* Chicago, 1960, p. 15.

[3]William J. Stanton, *Fundamentals of Marketing,* 4th ed., McGraw-Hill, New York, 1971, p. 5.

affected negatively. In similar fashion, the activities of planning a product and promoting it essentially reinforce one another. While it would be difficult to convince people through television advertising that castor oil has a delightful taste, the marketers of toothpaste *can* promote its flavor because they have planned a product that satisfies this want. Stanton's definition of marketing stresses the importance of the "want-satisfying" aspect of goods and services. It also notes that marketing must be future-oriented by concerning itself with present *non*buyers as well as buyers.

The Societal Approach

So far, our definitions of marketing have focused on the internal management of a business firm. But business is only one facet of society. In the late 1960s and early 1970s, marketers came to recognize publicly their responsibility to serve society.

Society can regulate a business through laws and governmental actions, but it also can affect business through activities in the marketplace. Simply put, people can refuse to buy a company's products. By this means, undesirable firms—that is, firms which do not meet society's wants and needs—can be eliminated from the economy. Thus, today's marketers must recognize their place within society and the economy. Holloway and Hancock underscored this basic fact by pointing out that marketing is "a set of activities necessary and incidental to bringing about exchange relationships in our economic system."[4]

The Responsibilities of Marketers

In recent years, business generally has come under close scrutiny. Various social and consumer groups are raising important questions and are demanding legislation to regulate business activities. Marketers now realize that they must satisfy not only their customers but also society at large. They recognize that business is only one facet of society, and that marketing activities affect many other aspects of our lives as well.

Marketing has been criticized, especially in recent years, for providing and promoting products that offer only superficial satisfaction. For example, many people believe that nonreturnable bottles lead to more problems than they solve. Obviously, such bottles provide some satisfaction in that consumers do not have to return them. For their users, at least, the bottles seem more convenient. But what about the effects on society at large—the litter, pollution, and costs of waste removal? In some states, society has challenged marketers' use of nonreturnable bottles by banning them outright; in other cases, recycling programs and local regulations seek to make marketers (and consumers) responsive to society's overall needs.

The societal approach to marketing can also be illustrated by the kinds of automobiles we drive. Cars without safety features or fuel-saving engines perhaps satisfy individual buyers who want lower prices and faster cars. But society's greater needs are not met if death and injury rates soar and if energy is not conserved. As a result, society has demanded, through Congress and government agencies, that automobile manufacturers provide safety equipment and improved gas mileage.

---

[4]Robert J. Holloway and Robert S. Hancock, *Marketing in a Changing Environment,* Wiley, New York, 1973, p. 10.

Figure 1-4 Consumer protection in the form of product labeling and warnings mark the emergence of the societal approach to marketing. (Randy Matusow)

Another aspect of the societal approach to marketing is the emphasis on ensuring that individual consumers' interests will be protected. Advertising is examined closely by government agencies such as the Federal Trade Commission (FTC). For example, the FTC ruled that the Warner-Lambert Company, the maker of Listerine mouthwash, was falsely advertising its product when it claimed that Listerine "kills germs by millions on contact, for . . . colds and resultant sore throats." As a penalty, Warner-Lambert was ordered to run $10 million of corrective advertisements stating that Listerine would *not* help prevent colds or sore throats or lessen their severity.

Product safety has also become a concern of society, and thus of marketers also. Toy companies are monitored constantly by consumer groups and government agencies to make sure that their products are not dangerous to children. (See Figure 1-4.) Such groups have also forced manufacturers to recall defective automobiles. Most notably, pressures from consumer groups and government forced General Motors to discontinue its rear-engine Corvair. Similarly, society has demanded that products be priced in terms of units of measurement—in dollars or cents per ounce or gallon. And food products now must carry labels that list their ingredients.

All these examples show marketers that "Let the buyer beware" is no longer a socially good and acceptable means of exchanging. The societal approach to marketing serves the interests of individuals, but, more important, it stresses the interests of society.

Marketing in Crisis: Demarketing

During this period of the societal approach to marketing, the United States was struck with an energy crisis. For the first time since World War II, the public was faced with shortages of products. The petroleum needed to produce many goods, such as plastics, did not exist in full supply. Some companies lacked the raw materials they needed to make their products. At times, in some regions, gasoline was scarce or unavailable. In addition, many by-products of petroleum were scarce—antifreeze, electricity, etc.—and, if available, were extremely expensive.

During this period many companies were forced to *demarket;* that is, they had to encourage customers to use less of their product, namely, power. For many reasons, the idea of demarketing was contrary to the previous efforts of these companies. Their petroleum-related resources had always been plentiful, and the companies had done an excellent job of satisfying consumers' demands for more and more power. Before the energy crunch, their efforts had been aimed at convincing homeowners to switch to totally electric houses. Now, suddenly, demarketing was necessary instead in order to reduce their sales and yet continue to provide satisfaction.

Even under such adverse conditions, the marketing orientation of such companies was not lost. Rather, the demarketing approach became a useful part of marketing efforts since the idea of demarketing is to *de*stimulate or reduce sales, yet to do so without losing sight of the provision of satisfaction.[5] In short, marketers must try to keep customers happy while not selling to them.

---

[5]Philip Kotler and Sidney J. Levy, "Demarketing, Yes, Demarketing," *Harvard Business Review,* November–December 1971, pp. 74–80.

The concept of demarketing has found many non-energy-related applications. In an effort to curb inflation in 1980, for instance, the Federal Reserve imposed consumer credit restrictions to reduce consumers' "buy today—pay tomorrow" habits. In addition to adding a $20 card membership fee, Interbank conducted broadcast advertising to MasterCard holders to limit use of the card to "necessities and emergencies." And, on a different front, *The Wall Street Journal,* the daily newspaper with the largest circulation in the United States found its printing and delivery capacity strained because of shortage of newsprint. As a result, the daily wanted to reduce its circulation by 100,000 copies per day. To help cut back on circulation, the company reduced its radio and TV advertising, increased its subscription term from 20 to 26 weeks, and raised its newsstand price by 5 cents. Demarketing, then, has become a useful activity to help marketers reach their goals.

The Broadening of the Marketing Approach

While the 1960s brought into focus the necessity of marketing to satisfy society, the decade was also notable for beginning the transfer of marketing concepts to fields other than business.[6] Throughout the 1970s, the territory of marketing was expanded to not-for-profit organizations like hospitals, museums, colleges, unions, and charitable institutions such as the United Fund and the American Cancer Society. Even the armed services discovered that marketing techniques could help them gain recruits. Countries also market themselves to one another through diplomatic relations. (In this context, our secretary of state can be seen as a sales representative.)

Traditionally, marketing focused on the exchange of goods and services. But as the role of marketing broadened to more than purely economic exchanges, the product exchanged broadened to include ideas and social causes. For example, individuals participating in an election may exchange their votes for a candidate's promise to enact a particular political platform. Clearly, this situation involves exchange, and marketing has its impact on the political process. Special-interest groups use marketing techniques. "Stop smoking" organizations, for example, sponsor informational seminars, distribute special products designed to alleviate the desire to smoke in those who want to quit smoking, and initiate publicity aimed at the general public regarding the disadvantages of smoking. Marketing activities have been applied to such other causes as energy conservation, drug abuse, family planning, safer driving, improved nutrition, and preventive health care.

It's clear, then, that marketing has many applications—and not only in the performance of business activities. This broadened approach to marketing is noted in Table 1-1 in the definition by Enis, who says that marketing "encompasses exchange activities conducted by individuals and organizations for the purpose of satisfying

---

[6]Philip Kotler and Sidney J. Levy, "Broadening the Concept of Marketing," *Journal of Marketing,* vol. 33, no. 1 (January 1969), pp. 10–15; Philip Kotler and Gerald Zaltman, "Social Marketing: An Approach to Planned Social Change," *Journal of Marketing,* vol. 35, no. 3 (July 1971), pp. 3–12; and Philip Kotler, "A Generic Concept of Marketing," *Journal of Marketing,* vol. 36, no. 2 (April 1972), pp. 46–54.

TABLE 1-2   Nonprofit Organizations and the Four Utilities

Form utility	To gain more maternity patients, a Philadelphia hospital offered a steak-and-champagne candlelight dinner to parents of a newborn child the night before mother and child were to leave the hospital.
Time utility	Drake University (in Des Moines) advertised on a billboard near Chicago's O'Hare Airport that "Drake is only 40 minutes from Chicago." (By plane, that is.)
Place utility	Wingate College, a small private institution in North Carolina, offered within the normal cost of tuition a two-week trip abroad for sophomores.
Possession utility	The admissions office at North Kentucky State University released 103 balloons filled with scholarship offers, and Bard College offered a same-day admission system for students who walked into its offices and qualified.

human wants."[7] While the main emphasis in this book is on business marketing efforts, we will also offer many examples of noncommercial products and marketing applications. Table 1-2 shows how the utilities we have discussed are applicable to nonprofit organizations.

Our Definition of Marketing

As the 1970s began drawing to a close, marketers realized the impact of some extreme environmental pressures affecting their exchange efforts. The energy crisis, shortages of natural resources, unabating high levels of inflation, concern for polluting our natural environment, and social forces such as changing sex roles and consumerism all forced marketers to retrench to a more managerial focus on marketing. While marketers have not lost sight of their social responsibility and of the broadened applications of marketing activities, their concern returned to the basics of marketing management—understanding the forces that change the wants and needs of consumers and undertaking the activities necessary to react properly to those changes. Thus our broadened yet managerial definition of marketing and the emphasis that floods this entire book is: "Marketing is *managing* human and organizational exchange activities directed at satisfying human wants and needs."

Thus marketing becomes a conscious effort at bringing satisfaction to exchanges. From a broadened perspective, teachers market themselves and their course material to their students, and students market themselves to their teachers; their exchange revolves around the students' giving back the teacher's knowledge in return for a grade. Yet, contemporary marketers realize that this exchange activity is better performed when a well-informed, planned effort—rather than a haphazard, random attempt—takes place.

---

[7]Ben M. Enis, *Marketing Principles: The Management Process,* 2d ed., Goodyear, Pacific Palisades, Calif., 1977, p. 17.

Marketing and the Organization

Having looked at marketing and society from an economist's point of view, you are now ready to view it from the perspective of someone who heads a firm or organization that operates within the economy. Consider yourself to be an entrepreneur; put yourself in the shoes of a corporate president or the head of some organization. How does marketing fit into your entire organization's operation and goals?

Business as a Satisfaction System

As an economist, you viewed a business firm as being organized for the sole purpose of producing and distributing something of economic value, something that has want-satisfying capabilities which fit within the overall goals of society. This something is called a *social good*. From a business person's perspective, however, the firm is engaged in production primarily to serve an area of marketing opportunity *most profitably*. While these two views have different priorities, when a business recognizes that profits most likely will flow from providing a good or service which properly matches consumers' needs and wants, the two viewpoints converge.

As shown in Figure 1-5, a business can be seen to comprise five elements: inputs, processing, outputs, objectives, and feedback. The management of a business or any organization involves the planning, organizing, and controlling of a combination of inputs to achieve a desired set of outputs. Thee *inputs* include the tangible resources of capital, machines, raw materials, and labor, as well as the intangible factors of technology, information, time, and effort. The expected *outputs* of the processing are tangible goods or services that can be transformed through a sale into money (sales volume or revenue); market share (the percentage of the total industry's sales that a

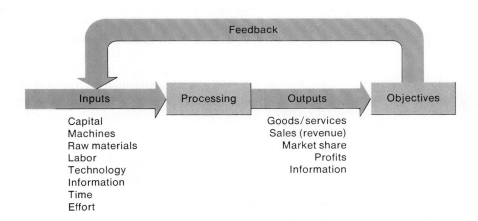

Figure 1-5   The five elements of a business system.

Feedback				
Inputs	Processing		Outputs	Objectives
Capital			Goods/services	
Machines			Sales (revenue)	
Raw materials			Market share	
Labor			Profits	
Technology			Information	
Information				
Time				
Effort				

given company holds); and profit (when costs are subtracted from sales). These outputs can be compared with the company's *objectives,* or goals—what the organization wants to achieve over a certain period of time. By comparing the actual outputs of processing with what was expected in terms of objectives, the company gains information called *feedback;* this allows the organization to adjust its inputs so that the outputs will be more in line with objectives.

The Processing Activities of Business

For a moment, let's focus on the processing activities of a firm or organization. To combine and use inputs in a way that achieves desired outputs, a company's processing activities must perform the following functions:

1 *Marketing*—assessing the want-satisfying opportunities and all activities directed toward stimulating exchange.

2 *Research and development*—the technical activities associated with product and service improvement and new-product or service development

3 *Financing*—raising the necessary capital and managing corporate investments

4 *Personnel*—recruiting the people needed to perform the business activities

5 *Purchasing*—acquiring the raw materials and supplies needed for production and other business activities

6 *Production*—processing the resources to produce the finished goods and services

7 *Accounting*—the control activity that provides information about sales, costs, and profits

In order to compete effectively and realize its profit potential, a firm must emphasize its overall operations, rather than any one function. In this sense, the firm's marketing function is no more important than any other of its activities. No matter how effectively the firm matches its product to customers' desires, no matter how many able people it employs, no matter how efficient its production units are—if the organization lacks the necessary capital, the venture will never get off the ground.

To carry this further, imagine that the processing component in the business system is a pipeline through which inputs flow to result in outputs. (The inputs are processed to provide satisfaction to ultimate buyers of finished products.) As depicted in Figure 1-6, this pipeline may be visualized as having a series of valves through which inputs flow; each valve represents one of the functions listed above, with the marketing function at both the beginning and the end of the process. Every one of the valves must be fully open. If any valve is closed, or only partly open, the whole profit pipeline becomes clogged. An example will clarify these points.

Fluctuating earnings, declining market shares, and management problems all

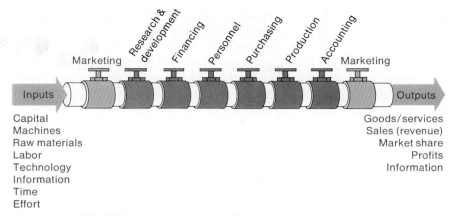

Figure 1-6   Functions in the satisfaction system. *(Adapted from Thomas A. Staudt and Donald A. Taylor, A Managerial Introduction to Marketing, 2d ed., Prentice-Hall, Inc., Englewood Cliffs, N.J., 1970, p. 20)*

combined in 1981 to give the Scott Paper Company cause for concern. At the heart of the 101-year-old company's problems was the antiquated manufacturing equipment Scott used to produce sanitary paper products. Traditionally a high-quality and high-price marketer, Scott's troubles began in the 1960s when a diversification binge resulted in management's losing sight of its core business. Instead of reinvesting its profits in new technology, Scott paid out earnings in dividends. The result was that in 1981, 70 percent of Scott's capacity was "old technology," compared with 50 percent at Kimberly Clark and just 20 percent at Procter & Gamble, its major competitors. The end result of this situation was that the packaged products division, which accounted for 70 percent of 1980 sales, decided to concentrate on products its machinery could make efficiently. Scott's management looked to this tactic to shore up its declining market share. By concentrating on the efficient use of existing machinery, Scott hoped to prevent further erosion of its market share.

Scott's decision to produce what it was geared to manufacture most efficiently regardless of consumers' wants or needs is a reversal of the traditional marketing approach of discovering consumers' needs and then satisfying them. As Scott's chairman and chief executive officer told *Business Week:* "We have a major challenge to become the low-cost producer in the industry."[8] Scott's troubles came about through clogs in the production area. The capabilities needed to carry out the successful delivery of a want-satisfying product were not available. A business organization, like a chain, is an interdependent system that is only as strong as its weakest link.

---

[8]"Scott Paper Fights Back, At Last," *Business Week,* Feb. 16, 1981, p. 108.

The Marketing Concept

While marketing is only one processing activity of a business firm, it is the activity that comes first and last in the pipeline, or satisfaction system. We know from the American Marketing Association's definition that marketing directs the flow of goods and services from producers to ultimate consumers. Obviously, then, marketing comes last. But marketing also uncovers the opportunities that exist to satisfy wants and needs.

As we have seen, the objective of marketing is to ensure satisfaction in the exchange behavior of society. And this goal can be reached only through a proper understanding of consumers' wants and needs, both present and future. From this knowledge base, marketing directs the performance of other activities within the firm. There is no sense in raising capital or hiring a sales force or producing a product if no market exists. So marketing comes first, directing the other activities by virtue of its understanding of the market.

This point—that marketing comes first in a successful satisfaction system—is summed up by the term *marketing concept:* the philosophy of business, or attitude of management, which maintains that the focal point of the entire firm is the consumer. The adage "The consumer is king" is the embodiment of this approach to conducting business. Today's successful companies realize that they are in existence to serve their customers rather than their own self-interests. Slogans like McDonald's "We do it all for you," United Airlines' "You're the boss," and Holiday Inn's "Chosen #1 in People Pleasin'" catch the spirit of the marketing concept. (See Application 1-5 and find out how Coors forgot this basic philosophy.)

Still, the profit motive is not out of line with the marketing concept. It is far easier to sell a good or a service that properly matches the needs or wants of buyers than it is to sell a product that does not. And since sound knowledge of consumers' needs and wants provides the information base to effect this match, application of the marketing concept should result in greater sales, which—assuming efficient and effective management of costs—should result in greater profits. Thus, the provision of satisfaction in the marketplace is the key to profitability; and the marketing concept bridges the gap between the economist's and the business owner's viewpoints.

The marketing concept is a philosophy that has application in all exchanges, not only in profit-oriented business transactions. Simple, everyday exchanges can benefit from the marketing concept, too. By recognizing the needs and wants of other people in day-to-day activities, we can make even our social exchanges more satisfying. For instance, borrowing a book from a classmate is an exchange. But if the borrower is sensitive to the lender's needs for that book and returns it in good time, then the exchange leads to greater satisfaction than if the book is returned late. This, too, is an example of the marketing concept.

To return to the economic system, however, we find that the marketing concept is efficient in bringing a balance to the exchanges within the system. Earlier in this chapter we saw the four stages of providing satisfaction in exchanges. To review, the stages are interrelated in the following fashion:

Application 1-5
The Marketing Concept—Coors Learns Its Marketing Lesson

During the early 1970s, the Adolph Coors Company was smugly content. Its beer—the nation's fifth biggest seller—was all manufactured in one brewery in Golden, Colorado. So bright was the outlook, Coors had the good fortune of having to ration rather than to market.

Five years later, however, the situation abruptly changed, and Coors found itself pulled into the world of marketing. One of the problems that confronted the company was intense product competition from the likes of giant Anheuser-Busch, Inc., and marketing-oriented Miller Brewing Company, both shrewd competitors. Their "light beer" innovation and aggressive marketing stole much thunder from Coors—well known to be a light-tasting beer but with a full complement of calories.

Competition, though, was only part of Coors' problems. Coors introduced a container that, although hailed by environmentalists (it didn't include a poptop opener), was soundly rejected by the beer drinker who found it impossible to open. Said a senior vice president, "We were so arrogant then. We thought people would buy Coors if they had to open it with their teeth."

The result of all these problems was that Coors' market share, sales, and net earnings tumbled. Its 41 percent market share in California plunged to 23 percent in 1979. What was once paradise in Colorado had suddenly evolved into a corporate nightmare.

Without question, Coors learned a lesson, and now the company has joined the fold of its competitors—relying on sound marketing techniques to get Coors on a growth track.

In the late 1970s, Coors was spending less than $1 per barrel for advertising, a pittance compared with its competitors. Now, the company has committed $1.80 per barrel in an effort to recapture its market share.

In addition, Coors has reorganized and revitalized its moribund sales force, and has for the first time pulled away from being a one-product company with the introduction of a low-calorie light beer. And, on the drawing boards are plans for a premium brew to compete with beers like Busch's Michelob and Miller's Lowenbrau.

To top off its new image, the company has moved aggressively into the East with its products and is even considering building a second brewery in the Southeast.

Sources of data: "Men at Coors Beer Find the Old Ways Don't Work Anymore," *The Wall Street Journal,* Jan. 19, 1979, pp. 1, 29; and "Adolph Coors: Brewing Up Plans for an Invasion of the East Coast," *Business Week,* Sept. 29, 1980, pp. 122, 124, 126, 127.

1 *Originators* provide raw materials to manufacturers in exchange for money (income).

2 *Manufacturers* then exchange finished goods with wholesalers and retailers for money.

3 These *intermediaries,* in turn, exchange the goods with consumers for money.

4 *Consumers* provide input to the procurement process as labor, and they exchange their time and energy for income.

The key to all these exchanges is *information,* and consumers are the initial source of information that keeps the exchanges in balance. By accepting or rejecting goods and services offered, consumers communicate their needs and wants to retailers and other intermediaries. If the offerings are mismatched, no sales occur, and products are not reordered from manufacturers. Similarly, those items which fit the needs of the market are sought by the intermediaries (middlemen) in greater abundance. In this way, consumers dictate to producers what they demand to satisfy their needs and wants. Manufacturers then gear production to consumers' desires as communicated through the intermediaries. Manufacturers also adjust their purchasing of raw materials to meet this demand. Raw materials that are not wanted in finished products will not be extracted, mined, or cut. In this sense, then, consumers are the key to keeping economic exchanges in balance through communication. This backward communication from consumers to producers is essentially what the marketing concept is about. A successful and healthy organization is one that recognizes consumers' desires and adjusts its activities to meet those needs and wants.

Application 1-6
Consumers Keeping Exchanges in Balance—
"From Health Comes Farmer's Wealth"

For years and years, the farmers in the Red River Valley of North Dakota and Minnesota planted acre upon acre of wheat. Now the wheat shares its space with the region's best new cash crop—the sunflower, which brings the farmer a 25 percent higher return than wheat.

The recent surge in health foods and consumer consciousness about health has given the age-old sunflower new popularity, pushing it into the role of an invaluable cash crop for the agriculture industry.

Although sunflower oil costs 10 to 15 percent more than oil made from corn or soybeans, it has a much lower cholesterol content than either. Consumer demand for low cholesterol oil has

(Randy Matusow)

brought new life to the sunflower. Hunt-Wesson has started national distribution of a flower oil called Sunlite, Procter & Gamble is offering a blend of flower and soybean oil named Puritan, and Lever Bros. is marketing a part-flower margarine under the label of Promise.

So in demand is the sunflower that farmers have doubled plantings in the span of one year. The sunflower was expected to increase farm incomes by $800 million in 1979 alone.

Sources of data: "Flower Power on the Plains," *Time,* Nov. 26, 1979, p. 87; and "Sunflower Growers," *The Wall Street Journal,* March 29, 1979. p. 1.

Thus, the economy as a whole benefits from the marketing concept, since resources are not obtained and goods and services are not produced unless they will flow efficiently through the economic system. The marketing concept increases the efficiency of the economic system by providing information to keep it in balance. This information reduces the amount of mismatching that firms engage in as they perform the activities of the exchange process. (See Application 1-6.)

As yet, we have not looked at the specific activities that make up marketing. Marketing is a many-faceted function. We shall examine each of these functions briefly in the next chapter—and in much greater detail as we move through the book.

Looking Back

In this chapter we wore two pairs of shoes—those of an economist and those of an entrepreneur. From these viewpoints, we saw that marketing provides satisfaction of needs and wants through the exchange process. We examined the historical development of marketing up to the present time, the marketing era. We saw how marketing fits into society in general, as well as how it fits into an organization's activities. Finally, we concluded that the marketing concept is important to the effective functioning of both business organizations and the entire economic system.

In the next chapter we will wear still another pair of shoes, those of the marketing manager, to look closely at what marketing is all about. But first, let's review the main points covered in this chapter:

1 A product's bundle of satisfaction is made up of various types and levels of satisfaction.

2 Buyers select the product or brand that provides the greatest satisfaction.

3 Form, time, place, and possession utilities are provided through the exchange process.

4 Exchanges take place only when both parties will be more satisfied after the exchange than before the exchange.

5 The industrial revolution marked the beginning of what we know as modern marketing, which developed through the production era and the sales era to arrive at the marketing era.

6 Marketing has recently come to publicly recognize its many responsibilities to society.

7 Marketing activities are useful throughout the economic system, as well as in profit-oriented business firms.

8 The provision of satisfaction in society and the profit motive are not inconsistent.

9   A business is a system consisting of five elements: inputs, processing, outputs, objectives, and feedback.

10 Marketing is no more and no less important than the other business activities; however, it is the first activity necessary for a successful business.

11 The marketing concept, which focuses on consumers, should be understood and practiced in all exchanges.

12 The marketing concept helps to keep the entire economy in balance by keeping exchanges in the economy in line with consumer wants and needs.

Key Terms

If you aren't sure what each of the following words means, look back at the text. Numbers refer to pages on which the words are defined. Additional information can be found by checking the index and the glossary at the end of the book.

marketing 5
form utility 5
time utility 7
place utility 7
possession utility 7
bundle of utility 7

exchange process 9
discretionary products 13
demarketing 18
inputs 21
outputs 21
processing activities 21
marketing concept 24

Questions for Review

1 What is marketing's major objective?
2 What are the prerequisites for exchange?
3 What are the four exchange stages in the provision of satisfaction in the economy? What type of utility is provided in each of these stages?
4 What are the four definitional approaches to marketing? Explain each.
5 How do the economist and the head of an organization differ in their viewpoints of the exchange process?
6 What are the seven processing activities necessary for achieving desired output in the organization?

Questions for Thought and Discussion

1 At Christmas, in Dayton's department store in Minneapolis, Santa's helpers are computers. Shoppers tell the machines what age group they're buying presents for and how much they want to spend, and the computer provides a suggested shopping list. What concepts from this chapter are being used by Dayton's?
2 Why would it be more difficult to market a *want* than a *need*?
3 In 1978, the "Treasures of Tutankhamun" were exhibited at New York's Metropolitan Museum of Art. All 1.3 million tickets were sold out before the opening day, and mobs of people waited up to 12 hours to gain admission to the exhibit. With such vast waiting lines, what could the museum do to increase its attendees' satisfaction?
4 Marketing has sometimes been said to have "veto power" in the profit pipeline. Explain.

Suggested Project

Find two magazine or newspaper advertisements which reflect each of the definitional approaches to marketing.

Suggested Readings

Andresan, Alan R., and Arthur Best: "Consumers Complain—Does Business Respond?" *Harvard Business Review,* vol. 55, no. 4 (July–August 1977), pp. 93–101. A survey discloses much dissatisfaction among purchasers of goods and services and mediocre work by business in handling their complaints.

Bartels, Robert : *The History of Marketing Thought,* 2d ed., Grid, Inc., Columbus, Ohio, 1976. This book traces the development of marketing from the turn of the twentieth century to modern times.

Bloom, Paul N., and William D. Novelli: "Problems and Challenges in Social Marketing," *Journal of Marketing,* vol. 45, no. 2 (Spring 1981), pp. 79–88. The authors review the problems that arise in attempting to use conventional textbook approaches in social marketing programs.

Bogozzi, Richard P.: "Marketing as Exchange," *Journal of Marketing,* vol. 39, no. 4 (October 1975), pp. 32–39. In this article the exchange concept is shown to be a key factor in understanding the role of contemporary marketing.

Fox, Karen F. A., and Philip Kotler: "The Marketing of Social Causes: The First Ten Years," *Journal of Marketing,* vol. 44, no. 4 (Fall 1980), pp. 24–33. The authors position social marketing as an approach to social change, describe its evolution, and review social marketing applications and assess their impact.

Kotler, Philip: "The Generic Concept of Marketing," *Journal of Marketing,* vol. 38, no. 2 (April 1972), pp. 46–54. This article expands the nature of marketing activities to all transactions that take place in modern-day society.

Kotler, Philip: "Strategies for Introducing Marketing into Nonprofit Organizations," *Journal of Marketing,* vol. 43, no. 1 (January 1979), pp. 37–44. This article, instead of simply suggesting confusing marketing advertising and selling, offers nonprofit institutions some innovative ways to bring a marketing orientation into their organizations.

McNamara, Carlton P.: "The Present Status of the Marketing Concept," *Journal of Marketing,* vol. 36, no. 1 (January 1972), pp. 50–57. This article shows the extent to which the marketing concept has been accepted and implemented by firms in the United States.

Westbrook, Robert A., Joseph W. Newman, and James R. Taylor: "Satisfaction/ Dissatisfaction in the Purchase Decision Process," *Journal of Marketing,* vol. 42, no. 4 (October 1978), pp. 54–60. This study suggests that consumers find enjoyment and satisfaction in buying durables more often than they experience difficulty and discontent.

Chapter 2

The Uncontrollable and Controllable Variables of Marketing

Looking Ahead

In the last chapter, we examined marketing within society and then within the firm. In this chapter, we will look at the role of the marketing manager. From this perspective, we explore the ever-changing environment that heavily influences the decisions that marketing managers make. Then we focus on the specific activities marketers perform to provide satisfaction in the marketplace.

Key Topics

The influence of the uncontrollable environmental forces on marketing decisions

Specific marketing activities that make up the bundle of satisfaction: the controllable tasks of marketing

The 4 P's: product, price, place, and promotion

What the marketing mix is

One word that best describes marketing activities: *communication*

How marketers program their activities

Introduction and Overview

In Chapter 1, we saw that marketing provides satisfaction of society's needs and wants and that it does so through the exchange process. It is marketing's job to identify the needs and wants of consumers. But marketing also guides other activities of the firm so that products can be developed to provide satisfaction. The marketing concept dictates that the consumer is the focal point of a business. That is, when the needs of consumers are satisfied through the practice of the marketing concept, the economy runs more efficiently than when firms put their own interests before those of consumers.

We have already looked at marketing from the perspectives of an economist and the head of a business. In this chapter, we will look at marketing from the viewpoint of a key person within the organization—the marketing manager. A marketing manager's main responsibility is to determine what opportunities exist in the marketplace in terms of consumers' wants and needs and to meet those opportunities with appropriate products or services. Production, finance, personnel, and other activities focus on the

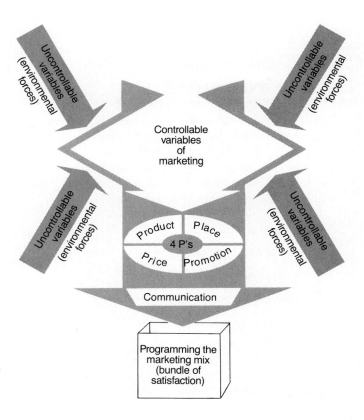

Figure 2-1   Relationships of the topics in this chapter.

actual running of a business organization, but it is marketing that directs how these activities will be conducted.

Marketing managers must make many decisions concerning the market—what it is in relation to the firm, where it is, and where it is headed. But the market is subject to many variables over which the marketing manager has virtually no control. This chapter will explore these uncontrollable environmental elements of marketing, particularly in regard to how they affect marketing decisions. Marketing managers, while unable to control environmental variables, must be fully aware of them and their effects in making decisions and planning their marketing programs.

Having reviewed the external marketing environment, we will focus on the internal controllable variables—namely, the activities that marketing managers must plan and perform to satisfy the wants and needs of the consumers they serve. These controllable decisions and activities will be collapsed into the 4 P's, four main decision areas that go into developing the bundle of satisfaction: product, price, place, and promotion. Figure 2-1 presents an overview of the elements of marketing into an overall framework that will show the step-by-step sequence of task undertaking—the marketing program. This framework will provide the structure for the remainder of this book.

The Uncontrollable Variables of Marketing: Its Environment

Marketers must operate in an environment of external forces which greatly influence what they are able to do. Building customer satisfaction is not a simple matter. The many forces that shape and direct a marketer's operations are not controllable by the marketer, and often they control the marketer. Marketers adapt to these external variables as they carry out their activities. And the marketers' success or failure is largely determined by how well they adjust to these forces. These outside forces are:

The social environment

The political and legal environment

The competitive environment

The technological environment

The economic environment

The natural environment

The objective of marketing is the satisfaction of wants and needs, but wants and needs are not static. Rather, they are ever-changing. Why? Because consumers are

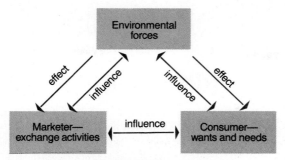

Figure 2-2   Interrelationships with the environment.

subject to the same uncontrollable environmental forces. For example, as a result of the drought that ravaged the Midwest and the South in 1980 and the East in the winter of 1980–1981, consumers became very much concerned with water conservation. As a consequence, Transcontinental Energy Saving Products Inc.'s Shower Saver, a $15.95 showerhead promising to cut water use by as much as 75 percent, enjoyed sales of about 1 million units in 1981, a sevenfold increase over the previous year.

So we see that these environmental forces have an impact on both marketers and their markets, their consumers. No individual marketer or single consumer can make a substantial impact on these environmental variables; yet, acting together as a totality, organizations and individuals shape many of the environmental forces. Clearly, we as consumers, acting through our legislative representatives, carve out the legal environment that surrounds our business and personal actions. (See Figure 2-2.) At the same time, individual marketers clearly *influence* these environmental forces. Businesses, for instance, such as Exxon and General Motors, have large staffs of lobbyists in Washington (and at state levels) to make known to legislators their views on energy conservation and automotive safety. Yet influence is certainly *not* control. A lobbyist can talk a lot, but the senator or representative need not listen.

Changes in these environmental forces can have both positive and negative effects on different marketers. Improvements in the fidelity quality of cassette-tape cartridges created an opportunity for that industry but became a barrier for the record industry. With 40 percent of 1979 American households owning some kind of cassette recording machine, blank cassette-tape sales doubled between 1973 and 1979 while record sales dipped slightly during that 6-year period.

The same external environmental variables affect different marketers in different ways. Consequently, each individual marketer is confronted with a *unique set* of opportunities and barriers to providing satisfaction. This unique combination represents the concerns—both positive and negative—that must be reflected in the marketer's activities. (See Figure 2-3.) The marketer must scan the environment and recognize all important forces, forecast their direction and intensity, and adjust or adapt decisions to them, which is no easy job. Now let's take a closer look at each of the major uncontrollable variables marketers face.

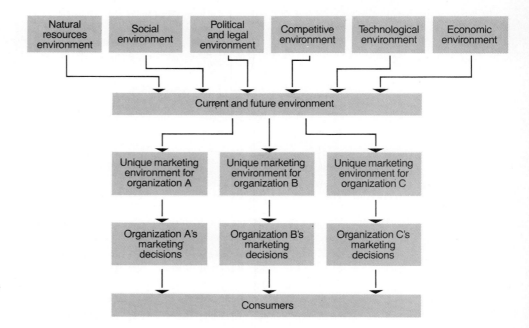

Figure 2-3   Setting the unique environment for the marketing organization.

The Social Environment

Marketers exchange with consumers, and these consumers are people. Marketers cannot control the quantity or the behavior of the people with whom they market. But they certainly can monitor the trends in the population and the values that govern its behavior. This is why marketers are keenly interested in the world's population—its growth pattern, geographical distribution, density, and mobility trends; age distribution; birth, marriage, and death rates; and the racial, ethnic, and religious structures.

In recent years, the boundaries of the markets served by marketers have greatly expanded. The world's population growth has been explosive. In 1981, it stood at 4.5 billion. It is expected to grow by another 1½ billion people by the end of the century. Currently, 70 percent of all the world's people live in undeveloped countries—and this figure will grow to 80 percent by 2000. This large part of the world market is undeveloped in terms of satisfaction of needs and wants, too—a situation that creates substantial opportunities for some marketers.

Nabisco, for example, received 17 percent of its total 1980 income from foreign markets, compared with 11 percent in 1976. To keep this momentum, Nabisco is accelerating a drive into some less-developed Latin American countries. The company will invest $250 million between 1980 and 1985 to expand foreign cookie and cracker production. The company feels international sales will be the fastest-growing part of its operations.

While marketers such as Nabisco look with pleasure at the expanding opportunities abroad, the static population of the United States is a concern. In 1980, it stood at 225 million persons, a 10 percent increase over 1970. But the rate of population growth has been declining, and in 1977 the birthrate dropped below the replacement rate. As a result, the complexion of the United States population is drastically changing. The post-World War II babies have reached adulthood. Today, there are fewer babies and teenagers, but many more young adults, and a growing population of the elderly. While more on the demographics of the national market will be discussed in Chapter 5, suffice it to say that these changes have resulted in changes for marketers. Gerber's slogan of "Babies Are Our Only Business" has been revamped to "Babies Are Our Business" as the company diversifies into such products as printing, prepackaged meals for single diners, and life insurance. To appeal to adults, Walt Disney World near Orlando, Florida, is opening a new section entitled EPCOT ("Experimental Prototype Community Of Tomorrow") Center. Instead of merry-go-rounds, Mickey Mouse, and haunted houses, visitors will learn about many forms of technology in "Future World" or about the history and arts and crafts of nine countries in "World Showcase." And this reduction in the younger population has led to a slowing in demand for records, jeans, soda pop, school supplies, and teachers.

The changing values of people, too, shape many of the other environmental forces. In short, there is an interrelationship among these environmental forces. For instance, the public outcry for less pollution has redirected *technological* resources toward the development of catalytic converters and political efforts toward government regulation of industrial pollution. These changing values are accelerating much faster than in any other time in history, which only adds to the monitoring problems facing marketers. The changing roles of women in society, the pleasure-seeking value of self-gratification, the preference for leisure over work, all shape the behavior of consumers and, therefore, marketers. Much of Chapter 6 will focus on these cultural values.

As we look into the future, there is little doubt that the consumer movement and the expectations for social justice will continue. Consumers have the right to expect safe products, to receive all pertinent information and protection from fraud and deception, to choose from a reasonable level of variety, and to be heard when inequities exist. From the positive side, being socially responsible can enhance the satisfaction offered to the consuming public. Consider Quaker Oats Company's Marx toy subsidiary market entrant, Krazy Kar, a hand-propelled riding toy similar to a Big Wheel. After keeping the toy 3 years on the shelves, the company announced that it was being discontinued. But a letter from a therapist who worked with handicapped children showed the therapeutic value of the toy, and Quaker Oats had a change of heart. The company began notifying children's hospitals and clinics that the Krazy Kar was still available to them on special order. Quaker Oats sold Krazy Kar for cost. No profit resulted, but the company—besides helping people—definitely gained a favorable image.

The Political and Legal Environment

Society recognizes that inequities develop when the economic and social systems are left to their own devices. Government, in theory at least, represents the wants and needs of its citizens, and it passes laws in their behalf. Just as citizens are responsible for knowing and obeying traffic laws, marketers, too, must be aware of the laws and regulations affecting their products and businesses. Violation not only subjects

Application 2-1
International Politics—
Getting Red Ink Instead of the Gold Medals

The Russian invasion of Afghanistan resulted in an American boycott of the 1980 Summer Olympics in Moscow. The political tactic not only dashed the hopes of scores of American athletes but also was devastating to many United States companies who had hoped to cash in on the Olympics through tie-ins with the games.

Companies such as Coca-Cola, Levi Strauss, McDonald's, Burger King, Gillette, and Wrigley lost nonrefundable fees they had paid for the rights to use the Olympics in their advertising. Some had paid fees of $50,000 to the U.S. Olympic Committee for the rights to use the Olympiad symbol in ad campaigns and to bill their companies as "official" suppliers to the U.S. team." Others had paid a $250,000 fee for the right to run consumer promotions tied to the games.

Chicago-based VPI, Inc., was left with 28,000 mugs and 15,000 key rings adorned with the Olympiad symbol or Misha the bear, the official mascot of the games. NBC bid $87 million for broadcasting rights to the games. While insurance paid for a large portion of the investment loss, the network lost $6 million to $13 million in potential advertising revenue. Levi Strauss lost the fee it paid to be allowed to supply $2.5 million worth of athletes' uniforms free and was set back in its negotiations to build a blue jeans plant in the Soviet Union. The Olympic Boycott Recovery Coalition, a group of thirty-four small companies, says its members lost $5.4 million in unrecoverable costs and $10 million in lost sales.

Some companies, however, made the best of the boycott. R. Dakin & Company, a San Francisco firm that had bought the rights to produce Misha bears, took the Olympic belts off and had perfectly salable teddy bears. And Gym-kin, a Pennsylvania manufacturer, left with 24,000 sport leotards embossed with the Olympic logo, recouped its loss by printing "Boycott Moscow" across the leotards.

Sources of data: "Busted Bonanza," *Time,* March 31, 1980, p. 53; and "Some Firms Are Jolted by Olympics Boycott, But Most Adjust to It," *The Wall Street Journal,* March 7, 1980, p. 1.

management to prosecution but also is costly in terms of the adverse publicity received.

The political and legal environment includes international boundaries as well as domestic ones. As marketers continue to look outside the United States for both markets and products to market, international political situations, trade agreements, and international laws shape and direct marketing activities. The international environment can present opportunities and also raise barriers to exchanges. The seizure of American hostages in Iran and the Soviet invasion of Afghanistan created a mood of patriotism among many Americans that translated into a business problem for many companies which engaged in trade with these countries. The Afghanistan crisis affected a myriad of companies, large and small, as well as individuals. The Trader Vic chain of 20 restaurants wired all members forbidding them to buy or sell

Russian vodka or caviar. And the five Fairmont hotels throughout the country would not stock Russian vodka or caviar from the Soviet Union or Iran.

In addition, the invasion resulted in President Carter's imposing a complete embargo on the sale of high technological goods to the Soviet Union. The President's Executive order disrupted the activities of hundreds of companies, large and small. (See Application 2-1.)

Government regulation generally has two purposes: to protect companies from one another and to protect individuals and society at large from unethical practices of businesses. Most laws up until the mid-1900s focused on maintaining a proper level of competitive activity. The Sherman Antitrust Act (1890), the Federal Trade Commission Act (1914), the Clayton Act (1914), and the Robinson-Patman Act (1936) were four major laws that attempted to ensure a competitive atmosphere within industries. (See Table 2-1 for more details on these and some other important laws.)

TABLE 2-1   Major Legislation Affecting Marketing

Sherman Antitrust Act (1890)
Prohibited (a) "monopolies or attempts to monopolize" and (b) "contracts, combinations, or conspiracies in restraint of trade" in interstate and foreign commerce.

Federal Food and Drug Act (1906)
Forbade the manufacture, sale, or transport of adulterated or fraudulently labeled foods and drugs in interstate commerce. Supplanted by the Food, Drug, and Cosmetic Act, 1938; amended by Food Additives Amendment in 1958 and the Kefauver-Harris Amendment in 1962. The 1962 amendments dealt with pretesting of drugs for safety and effectiveness and labeling of drugs by generic names.

Meat Inspection Act (1906)
Provided for the enforcement of sanitary regulations in meat-packing establishments, and for federal inspection of all companies selling meats in interstate commerce.

Federal Trade Commission Act (1914)
Established the commission, a body of specialists with broad powers to investigate and to issue cease and desist orders to enforce Section 5, which declared that "unfair methods of competition in commerce are unlawful." (Amended by Wheeler-Lea Act, 1938, which added the phrase "and unfair or deceptive acts or practices.")

Clayton Act (1914)
Supplemented the Sherman Act by prohibiting certain specific practices (certain types of price discrimination, tying clauses and exclusive dealing, intercorporate stockholdings, and interlocking directorates) "where the effect . . . may be to substantially lessen competition or tend to create a monopoly in any line of commerce." Provided that corporate officials who violate the law could be held individually responsible; exempted labor and agricultural organizations from its provisions.

Robinson-Patman Act (1936)
Amended the Clayton Act. Added the phrase "to injure, destroy, or prevent competition." Defined price discrimination as unlawful (subject to certain defenses) and provided the FTC with the right to establish limits on quantity discounts, to forbid brokerage allowances except to independent brokers and to prohibit promotional allowances or the furnishing of services or facilities except where made available to all "on proportionately equal terms."

(continued)

Miller-Tydings Act (1937)

Amended the Sherman Act to exempt interstate fair-trade (price fixing) agreements from antitrust prosecution. (The McGuire Act, 1952, reinstated the legality of the non-signer clause.)

Antimerger Act (1950)

Amended Section 7 of the Clayton Act by broadening the power to prevent intercorporate acquisitions where the acquisition may have a substantially adverse effect on competition.

Automobile Information Disclosure Act (1958)

Prohibited car dealers from inflating the factory price of new cars.

National Traffic and Safety Act (1966)

Provided for the creation of compulsory safety standards for automobiles and tires.

Fair Packaging and Labeling Act (1966)

Provided for the regulation of the packaging and labeling of consumer goods. Required manufacturers to state what package contains, who made it, and how much it contains. Permitted industries' voluntary adoption of uniform packaging standards.

Child Protection Act (1966)

Banned sale of hazardous toys and articles. Amended in 1969 to include articles that pose electrical, mechanical, or thermal hazards.

Federal Cigarette Labeling and Advertising Act (1967)

Required that cigarette packages contain the statement, "Warning: The Surgeon General Has Determined That Cigarette Smoking Is Dangerous to Your Health."

Consumer Credit Protection Act (1968)

Required lenders to state the true costs of a credit transaction, outlawed the use of actual or threatened violence in collecting loans, and restricted the amount of garnishments. Established a National Commission on Consumer Finance.

National Environmental Policy Act (1969)

Established a national policy on the environment and provided for the establishment of the Council on Environmental Quality. The Environmental Protection Agency was established by "Reorganization Plan No. 3 of 1970."

Consumer Product Safety Act (1972)

Established the Consumer Product Safety Commission and authorized it to set safety standards for consumer products as well as to exact penalties for failure to uphold the standards.

Magnuson-Moss Warranty/FTC Improvement Act (1975)

Authorized the FTC to determine rules concerning consumer warranties and provided for consumer access to means of redress, such as the "class action" suit. Also expanded FTC regulatory powers over unfair or deceptive acts or practices.

Other Laws

Many other federal laws affect business competition and regulate practices found in specific industries. A multitude of state and local laws also regulate competition and specific practices within each state and legally designated locality.

Consumer Goods Pricing Act (1975)

Repealed federal antitrust exemptions which permitted states to enact fair trade (resale price maintenance) laws. These state laws had legalized price fixing at the retail level.

Consumer Leasing Act (1976)

Amended Consumer Credit Protection Act to require meaningful disclosure of lease terms and ultimate liability in connection with leased products.

Consumer Education Act (1978)

Established the Office of Consumer Education. It is responsible for supporting research projects which are designed to provide consumer education to the public.

Reprinted by permission from Kotler, Philip, *Marketing Management,* 4th ed., Prentice-Hall, Inc., Englewood Cliffs, N.J., 1980, pp. 118–119; and Cunningham, William H., and Isabella C. M. Cunningham, *Marketing: A Managarial Approach,* South Western Publishing Co., Cincinnati, 1981, pp. 81–82.

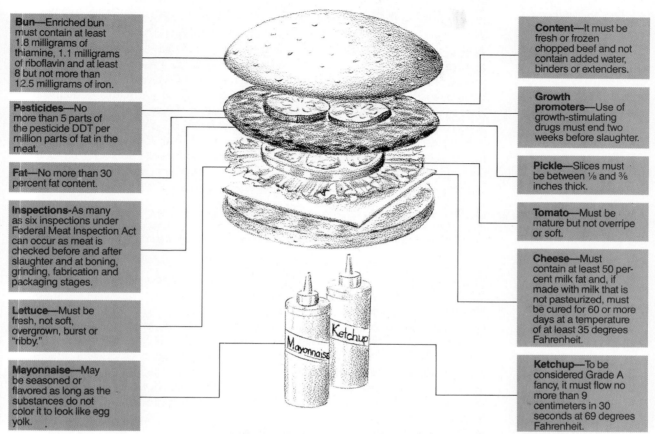

Bun—Enriched bun must contain at least 1.8 milligrams of thiamine, 1.1 milligrams of riboflavin and at least 8 but not more than 12.5 milligrams of iron.

Pesticides—No more than 5 parts of the pesticide DDT per million parts of fat in the meat.

Fat—No more than 30 percent fat content.

Inspections-As many as six inspections under Federal Meat Inspection Act can occur as meat is checked before and after slaughter and at boning, grinding, fabrication and packaging stages.

Lettuce—Must be fresh, not soft, overgrown, burst or "ribby."

Mayonnaise—May be seasoned or flavored as long as the substances do not color it to look like egg yolk.

Content—It must be fresh or frozen chopped beef and not contain added water, binders or extenders.

Growth promoters—Use of growth-stimulating drugs must end two weeks before slaughter.

Pickle—Slices must be between ⅛ and ⅜ inches thick.

Tomato—Must be mature but not overripe or soft.

Cheese—Must contain at least 50 percent milk fat and, if made with milk that is not pasteurized, must be cured for 60 or more days at a temperature of at least 35 degrees Fahrenheit.

Ketchup—To be considered Grade A fancy, it must flow no more than 9 centimeters in 30 seconds at 69 degrees Fahrenheit.

Figure 2-4   The hamburger, staple of the quick, inexpensive meal, is the subject of 41,000 federal and state regulations. This chart gives just a sampling of the rules and regulations governing the burger you buy. (Reprinted from U.S. News & World Report, Copyright 1980, U.S. News & World Report, Inc.)

As the consumer movement picked up its pace in the mid-1960s, a rash of consumer protection laws came into being. This body of laws focused on reducing injustices to consumers and focused on product safety, labeling and packaging, warranties, and the preservation of our environment. To emphasize the magnitude of consumer-related regulation, in 1976 alone, the federal government took action in the following areas: food labels, nursing homes, real estate, color additives, prescription drugs, automobile odometers, housing, consumer information, energy, credit leasing, product safety, medical devices, warranties, airline overbooking, product recalls, and several others.[1] Clearly, then, the regulations set up by the government have a substantial influence over the activities undertaken by marketers. (See Figure 2-4.) No dimension of the bundle of satisfaction offered is untouched by legislation.

[1]"Federal Consumer Actions in 1976," *Consumer News,* Dec. 15, 1976, pp. 1–4.

In addition to the laws themselves, marketers must be aware of regulatory forces. While the laws exist, they must realize that the real effects of these provisions depend largely on how marketers and the courts interpret these laws—and how they are enforced.[2] Federal, state, and local governments all have agencies to enforce regulations and set guidelines that influence the decisions of marketers. Most notable have been the Federal Trade Commission and the Food and Drug Administration. Throughout the 1970s, such agencies had considerable clout in regulating business practices. For instance, when the FDA in 1970 banned the use of cyclamates, scores of companies saw their marketing strategies disrupted. But, as the 1980s began, the mood seemed to be shifting away from giving substantial power to regulatory agencies. With the advent of the Reagan administration comes a clear political strategy of massive deregulation. As President Reagan stated,

Government regulations impose an enormous burden on large and small business in America, discourage productivity, and contribute substantially to our current economic woes. . . . It is my intention to curb the size and influence of the federal establishment.[3]

Marketers are also influenced by various industry-written and -unwritten codes. These codes create problems for some marketers and opportunities for others.

In 1972, the National Association of Broadcasters (NAB, a private organization) lifted the ban on television advertising for women's hygiene products. This decision caused every company in the field to change its marketing strategy, since the NAB's decree opened up television as an advertising medium for the products. While the ban was in effect, companies were limited to advertising hygiene products in magazines and in other print media. But after the ban was lifted, competition became fierce—and, for some, humbling. Tampax in 1972 had 80 percent of the tampon market. By 1980, the company's market share had dropped to 42 percent, while International Playtex had climbed to second place with a 24 percent share, followed by Procter & Gamble, with a 17 percent share.

The Competitive Environment

No environmental factor is more pervasive than competition. Marketers must constantly watch for competitive activity that may invade their market and erode their market share. No matter who you are, someone is likely trying to build a bigger and better bundle of satisfaction to "out-compete" you. No marketer is immune.

Competition comes in many forms. Basically, any alternative satisfier of a want or need is competition. Take jogging shoes, for example. The need felt by most of the 20 million joggers in the United States is one of exercise. Thus Nike, the industry leader, must consider bicycles (bicycling), weights (weight lifting), arobic dance classes (dancing), yoga, exercise salons, and other exercise alternatives as competitors. These

---

[2]See Werner, Ray O., "Marketing and the U.S. Supreme Court," *Journal of Marketing,* vol. 41, no. 1 (January 1977), pp. 32–43.

[3]"Deregulation—A Fast Start for the Reagan Strategy," *Business Week,* March 9, 1981, p. 62.

are called *generic* competitors. Additionally, within one of those alternatives, say running shoes, there are alternative *form* competitors—leather shoes versus nylon fabric shoes, waffle trainers versus flat-soled shoes, and so on. And within each of these forms there are *brand* competitors—Nike, Adidas, Brooks, New Balance, Pony, and Tiger.

Marketers must know the number and size of competitors as well as the tools they are using to build their bundles of satisfaction. When only a few competitors exist to serve a market, the competition generally is not as strong as when many competitors exist. When new products hit the market, competitors are few. As the product's attractiveness grows, many competitors enter to get a piece of the action—each trying to outdo the existing competitors with some new aspect of satisfaction. Personal computers have advanced from being little more than adult toys to being essential tools for small businesses. Aided by advancing technology and lower cost, sales of personal computers were increasing at a rate of 50 to 60 percent a year as the decade of the 1980s opened. In 1981, about 75 percent of the personal computer industry's sales were controlled by just three companies—Tandy, the Fort Worth–based manufacturer and owner of 8012 Radio Shack stores; Apple, the firm started by two college dropouts who launched their company with only $1300; and Commodore International, which has concentrated its marketing efforts in Europe. Behind these three are some corporate giants who are eyeing the small computer market; firms like Hewlett-Packard, Texas Instruments, and Zenith. But the small computer industry's biggest concern in 1981 was the possible entry of International Business Machines, the computer giant with $26 billion in annual sales. Few believe that IBM will ignore this market. In 1980, the company opened retail stores in Baltimore and Philadelphia. These stores could be the beginning of a network of stores for the sale of small computers. In addition to IBM, the small computer pioneers will face heavy competition from the Japanese, who brought their first machines into the United States in 1981.

There has been a notable change in the nature of competition in the United States. As demographics change the nature of markets, the competition has intensified in traditional industries. Too, marketers are feeling strong competition from abroad—most notably from Japanese and West German marketers.

Consider the situation in the watch industry. After only 7 years on the market, 23 percent of all watches sold were digital. In the mid-1970s, United States manufacturers and marketers of digital watches were expected to dominate the digital watch industry. But throughout the last half of the 1970s, American companies—Texas Instruments, Timex, and Fairchild Camera and Instrument, to name a few—repeatedly showed their ineptness both in learning to sell to the consumer and in mastering the new manufacturing technology. As a result, the Japanese, armed with a powerful electronics industry, came strongly into the United States watch market with such brands as Seiko, Citizen, and Casio. Their strategy was to sell their watches in a great number of outlets at a price slashed to the bone. By 1979, Japanese watchmakers had gained 21 percent of the market share of the 175 million watches sold throughout the world. (See Figure 2-5.)

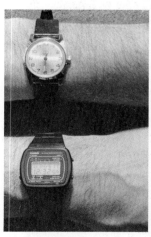

Figure 2-5 The wristwatch is one traditional market which has changed dramatically, mainly because of foreign competition. Can you name others? (Randy Matusow)

The Technological Environment

Closely allied to the competitive environment is the technological environment. Technology fosters opportunities to increase satisfaction and gain a competitive edge over other marketers. Today, many products exist that were not available a few years ago—computers, communication satellites, chemical fibers, and birth-control pills, to name a few. These are big developments, but let's not forget some of the smaller developments—freeze-dried coffee, ice-makers, antiperspirant deodorants, erasable pens, and so on. And often an improvement in a vital component can be the difference needed to create large market opportunities and spur on competition. Take the big-screen TV market. Throughout the 1970s, the relatively poor quality of big-screen, or "projection," TV discouraged most companies. But their interest was revived when they noticed a marked improvement from a new plastic lens made by a small company in Cincinnati, U.S. Precision Lens. The result: In 1981, firms such as RCA, Sony, Quasar, General Electric, and Magnavox spent about $60 million to promote big-screen TV in American homes.

Technology has been called the process of "creative destruction" in that new developments in the environment create new markets but destroy many existing markets. Where are the slide-rule companies after the advent of the pocket calculator? Television has altered marketers' promotional campaigns; electronic funds transfer has altered the banking industry; electronics have altered the toy market. Thus, marketers must continually watch the technological front or face the prospect of perishing. (See Figure 2-6.) Again, the watch industry serves as a poignant example. Prior to World War II, 90 percent of the world's watches were made in Switzerland. By 1980, that world market share dropped to 22 percent. The main villain proved to be the inflexibility of Swiss watchmakers. They simply refused to adjust to one of the biggest technological changes in the history of timekeeping, the development of an electronic

Figure 2-6 Technology and toys: Will the electronics revolution destroy markets for "traditional" toys? (Randy Matusow)

watch. The lapse was all the more surprising because the Swiss Watch Federation research center developed the first prototype quartz watch back in 1968. Swiss companies were so tied to traditional technology that they couldn't—or wouldn't—see the opportunities offered by the electronic revolution. It was a classic case of vested interests blocking innovation.

The growth rate of the economy is closely tied to the volume of new *major* technologies. Generally, large advances do not come frequently, and, while waiting for a major technological development, economies can flounder. America is still the world leader in innovative technology. The transistor, the laser, the semiconductor, aerography, and instant photography were all invented in the United States. But America's command of technical innovation is threatened. In the 1950s, 82 percent of all major inventions brought to the market were American. That share had dropped to 55 percent by the late 1960s. (Meanwhile, Japan and West Germany pumped more and more money into their own research and development.)

The microprocessor—the tiny silicon chip packed with information—probably ranks at the most important innovation of the 1970s. Introduced in 1971 by Intel of Santa Clara, California, this chip of silicon smaller than a child's fingernail performed the data processing functions of 5000 transistors. Since then, the race has been to pack more and more information onto the chips. In 1980, the state of the art is a microprocessor packing 64,000 bits of random access memory.

Another discovery, genetic engineering, may change the way of life itself. In 1972, two California scientists found a way to "splice" genes from one organism to another—and produce new traits in the host. This process has already produced both human insulin for the 1.5 million diabetics and the antiviral agent interferon, a possible weapon with which to combat cancer. In the future, it may produce vaccines against hepatitis and malaria; miracle products like low-calorie sugar; hardy, self-fertilizing food crops that could usher in a new "green revolution"; fuels, plastics, and other industrial chemicals out of civilization's wastes; and refining processes to relieve anxieties about a future without sufficient raw materials. (See Application 2-2.)

The Economic Environment

The economy reflects the gross level of exchanges that occur in a social system. In the United States, we are characterized as a "free enterprise" system in that exchanges are not highly regulated, but rather, are left to the mechanisms of society's demand and businesses' ability to respond to that demand. In that context, the United States embraces the concept of "consumer sovereignty" and relies on the ability of consumers to select from the variety of goods offered by competing suppliers. This, of course, is the foundation of the marketing concept.

While the ways in which all these rather complicated mechanisms operate are left to the study of economics, the outcome of the state of the economy is of extreme concern to marketers. Such indicators as the gross national product, inflation, interest rates, personal income, and savings-to-debt ratios allow marketers to get a feel for how well the economy is functioning. Basically, when the economy prospers, times are good and people buy. When the economy turns down, consumers' buying habits change.

Application 2-2
Laws and Competition—A Chill in the Air for Large Airlines

For years the Civil Aeronautics Board regulated the airline industry with an iron fist—controlling 95 percent of all decisions affecting airlines. Then came the 1978 Airline Deregulation Act, and the CAB's decision-making role dropped to a mere 5 percent.

Deregulation has suddenly changed the entire complexion of the United States airline industry. An airline can now, with only 90 days' notice, add or delete any city from its route structure and likewise can raise or lower fares by as much as 30 percent by simply filing a declaration with the CAB. In the past, either of these actions required long, drawn-out

examination by the CAB.

The consequences of deregulation have been considerable. Competition intensified as the carriers rejuggled routes and engaged in price cutting to gain a foothold on the lucrative long-haul routes. As a result, many of the big carriers have seen their earnings plummet. Surprisingly, the winners of deregulation appear to be the second-tier lines like Ozark, USAir, and Piedmont. These smaller carriers have been winning passengers at a much higher rate than the big carriers.

Piedmont Airlines, for example, followed the strategy of serving the small cities, bypassing

such hub airports as Atlanta, where delays are frequent and costs high.

Deregulation has also opened up new markets for the commuter lines (such as Midway Airlines, New York Air, and People Express), once the stepchildren of the industry. In 1980, the major carriers increased the number of passengers they carried by 6.3 percent, while the commuter lines recorded an 11 percent increase.

Sources of data: "The Airlines Are Flying in a Fog," *Fortune*, Oct. 20, 1980, pp. 50–56; "Friendly Skies for Little Airlines," *Fortune*, Feb. 9, 1981, pp. 45–53; and "Piedmont Rises by Landing in Small Cities," *The Wall Street Journal*, April 9, 1981, p. 27.

Basically, the 1960s was a time of prosperity. The decade was marked by optimism that the United States would continue as the dominant world economic power. The decade of the 1970s was quite different, a time of lowered expectations and rising anxieties about the future. It was a roller-coaster decade, one that recorded two recessions and the beginning of a third, a decade when energy shortages and persistent inflation presented constant problems. It was a high-risk decade for consumers. Interest rates, most notably home mortgage rates, hit all-time highs. Consumers, expecting prices to rise, fueled the fire of inflation by using credit with a "buy now—pay later" philosophy.

In short, as the 1970s drew to a close, the American standard of living was shrinking. So deeply ingrained is the American promise of "more" that many refused to accept the idea of a lowered standard of living.

In times of recession, especially with inflation added, consumption patterns change. Consumers generally put off buying durables and other big-ticket items such as cars, homes, vacations, television sets, and clothing. Consumers tend to econo-mize: to trade down to lower-cost foods, to shop at discount stores, to look for cut-rate grooming and health services, to avoid buying tickets for sporting and entertainment events, to reduce dry cleaning, and to patronize restaurants less often. At the same time, consumers tend toward staying at home, and thus to give rise to sales of yarn and hobby supplies, pets, do-it-yourself fix-it kits, inexpensive books, and garden supplies.

The Natural Environment

Marketers must contend with the natural resources—or lack of them. They must be aware of the challenges and opportunities that the natural environment provides. Changes in the environment can have positive effects on some marketers and, at the same time, negative effects on others.

There are three types of natural resources surrounding us. The first are resources that are in infinite supply. Water and air are logical examples—yet even with them there can be temporary changes. A drought had its impact on the Midwest in 1980 and the East in 1981. Irrigation equipment sales were running 30 percent higher in 1981 over 1980; and bottled water for personal consumption was running 50 percent ahead of 1980, according to Poland Springs, a Source Perrier subsidiary. Furthermore, while the air we breathe is infinite as a resource, even the air can cause marketers problems. Researchers said the fluorocarbon gases used in aerosol sprays could impair the atmosphere's ability to screen out excess ultraviolet radiation. Consumers turned away from aerosol cans. As a result, roll-ons increased their share of underarm products to about 34 percent from 10 percent. Gillette watched its Right Guard deodorant, then reformulated without fluorocarbons, slip to second place with about 14 percent of the market. (See Figure 2-7.)

The second type of natural resources are finite, renewable resources, such as forests and food. Yet, the 1980 volcano eruption at Mount St. Helens desecrated nearly 70,000 acres of Weyerhaeuser's timberland, while the hard freeze of January 1981 caused a 20 percent wipeout of the Florida orange crop (translated into 49 million fewer gallons of frozen juice concentrate). So, while some resources can be renewed, their supply is subject to fluctuations. Our nation's vulnerability in other natural resources is becoming more and more obvious.

Clearly, the most critical resources are those which are finite and nonrenewable. The most notable, of course, is energy. Much of the economic and political environment of the current decade is affected by the problems of the oil cartel—the Organization of Petroleum Exporting Countries (OPEC). Market barriers, as a result, have been created—high gasoline prices and high fuel oil prices for heating being the most notable.

But these barriers have created new opportunities. Coal—in abundant supply in the United States—is becoming increasingly popular, and solar energy is becoming economically feasible.

Another result of the oil crisis has been the redirection of the oil companies, reducing the number of service stations from 280,000 in 1973 to fewer than 230,000 some 5 years later. In addition, the companies have opted to concentrate on just selling fuel and eliminating service. This change in marketing direction has resulted in a new market for automobile service. The change in conditions is reflected by Midas International, which, since 1973, has seen its sales of exhaust systems, shock absorbers, and brakes double. And companies like Firestone have expanded service stores to include more automobile repairs.

Figure 2-7 The movement by manufacturers away from fluorocarbon sprays is a marketing response to environmental concerns. (Randy Matusow)

Application 2-3
The Natural Environment—Up and Down with the Weather

In December 1978, the United States supply of snow throwers was sold out. The snowfall of the previous winter resulted in a 50 percent increase in sales and caused a surge in snowblower production for the 1978–1979 winter. At the Toro Company, which holds 50 percent of the snow thrower market, production was boosted by 50 percent and by Christmas 1978 the Company's stock was depleted. At Ariens Company, a major producer of a larger type of snow thrower, dealers reportedly were 90 percent sold out before October. The abnormally high snowfall in many parts of the snow belt the previous winter was blamed for the surge in demand. "We've found that the snow of one winter carries over in the mind of the consumer to the next winter," a Toro spokesperson told *Advertising Age.*

Perhaps thinking the wretched weather would continue, Toro in 1979 again doubled its production of snowblowers. But the virtually snowless winter of 1979–1980 in the Northeast and Midwest forced Toro to offer $30 rebates to lure buyers. Buyers were offered the same deal by producers of Jacobsen and Deere machines—and both these manufacturers are sharing the

(© *The Toro Company*)

costs of financing inventories with their dealers. "It hurts dealers' attitudes if they feel the pinch," a Jacobsen vice president told *Business Week.* His understatement expresses what producers fear the most—dealers, hurt severely this season, will cut

back orders for next year and cut down on promotional efforts, further shrinking the market, even if snow is plentiful.

Sources of data: "Snowthrower Sell-out," *Advertising Age,* Dec. 25, 1978, p. 24; and "Struggling to Cope Without Snow," *Business Week,* Feb. 18, 1980, p. 66.

In addition to resources, marketers must reckon with natural phenomena that affect their markets. Earthquakes, hurricanes, rain, snow (or lack thereof), tornadoes, extreme heat, and severe cold all have consequences for marketers. Some marketers find ways of adding to their bundles of satisfaction by virtue of environmental circumstances. United Airlines, knowing that skiers purchase its profitable ski packages to the Rockies because they expect excellent ski conditions, offered "snow guarantee" flights in 1978. If fewer than half the lifts at their destination resorts were operating, buyers could claim a free flight home within 48 hours. And in 1980, Canada's Wardair International guaranteed warm weather in Florida. For each day the thermometer fell below 72 degrees, this air charter concern refunded $5 to each passenger. (See Application 2-3.)

The Controllable Variables of Marketing: The Marketing Tasks

While marketers have no control over the environmental forces, they do control the set of activities that go together to form their bundles of satisfaction. Just as we noted in Chapter 1 when we talked of the pipeline and all business processing activities acting together for maximum success, marketers must combine their activities to form the biggest and best bundles of satisfaction possible. This combination often puts emphasis on one activity over others, as we shall see. And, of course, the decisions about these tasks of marketing must reflect the environmental forces. Let us now take a look at these controllable tasks of marketing.

Marketing Research

Marketing must begin from a base of good information in order to learn as much as possible about the wants and needs of the market. *Marketing research* is gathering, recording, and analyzing facts about any problem facing marketers.

Marketing research can be conducted by analyzing sales and other in-company information, by studying government data, by conducting surveys, or by buying information from outside companies. For example, A. C. Nielsen monitors television audiences and sells information about them to television networks and other subscribers. Additionally, companies conduct their own surveys to determine such things as who their customers are and what motivates them to buy.

The first step in marketing is to know who is likely to buy what you are considering offering. But just knowing *who* will buy is not enough. Marketers need to identify as many characteristics of potential buyers as possible: *where* they live, *when* they buy, *how often* they buy, in *what quantities* they buy, and *why* they buy.

Some of the answers to these questions may be obvious. For example, people under 25 years of age are the largest cereal consumers; mothers with children are the most frequent buyers of cereal. And they tend to buy it on routine shopping trips. Yet not all descriptions of markets are so obvious. For instance, Hanes Corporation, the marketer of L'eggs panty hose, found that women make 85 percent of the purchases of men's underwear and buy a large percentage of their socks. As a result of this consumer study, Hanes tested lines of men's underwear and socks that were distributed through food and drug outlets where the company sells its panty hose. Another example is After Six, the largest marketer of tuxedos. The company found that women exert a tremendous influence on the need for male formal apparel by planning social occasions that require men to purchase tuxedos. As a result of this finding, the company advertises heavily in women's magazines, such as *Bride's* and *Cosmopolitan.*

Knowing who potential customers are and when, how, and where they buy is not enough to make good marketing decisions. Astute marketers must find out *why* consumers buy and must *understand* the influences that motivate or inhibit exchange behavior.

Some reasons why consumers buy are evident and easy to determine. Gillette Company markets Right Guard deodorant by correctly assuming that people have a fear or dislike of body odor. Makers of smoke detectors rely on the terror of fire to make their products desirable. And Goodyear markets tires on the basis of providing safety and durability. But not all purchase motivations are as obvious as these.

Coca-Cola's research found that children of working-class parents prefer to gulp their drinks, and therefore developed Mello Yello, a low-carbonated beverage for fast chug-a-lugging. Their advertising called it "The World's Fastest Soft Drink."

Whether the product is cereal, underwear, tuxedos, or soft drinks, marketers have to learn about the people who are likely to buy their product—their ages, their incomes, their education level, and as many descriptors as possible—and especially *why* they are likely to buy. The more a company knows about prospective customers, the better are its chances for success in delivering satisfaction. Marketing research, then, is the activity aimed at determining the identifying characteristics of potential customers.

This marketing research activity is controllable in two respects. First, marketers themselves decide whether or not to conduct research; second, they can control the quality and quantity of the research. Most successful companies conduct extensive marketing research to obtain accurate and relevant information to guide them in making marketing decisions.

The Product

The product is the major controllable variable in that it is the focal point for the other controllable activities. We've noted that the product is the means by which form utility is provided to the market. But a product is not only the item or service that is offered for exchange; it also includes intangible characteristics that buyers purchase. Often, the intangible features have the overriding appeal. Ford Motor Company sells status with its Lincoln, Saks Fifth Avenue sells the assurance of quality with all its merchandise, and the New York Metropolitan Opera sells culture with each of its performances.

The benefits and functions of a product result from the marketer's decisions.

Thus, the marketer controls the product's ability to provide satisfaction. And, since the whole idea of developing a product is to match consumers' needs and wants, the closer a product comes to providing satisfaction, the more successful it will be.

There's an adage that you can be sure of two things in this world—death and taxes. To that we add a third—that consumers' tastes change. Products preferred today will not necessarily be popular tomorrow. With this in mind, marketers must continually monitor changes in consumers' tastes and develop products to meet their latest wants and needs. (See Application 2-4.)

Application 2-4
Product— Adjusting the Product to Changes in Demand

The United States auto industry has unquestionably had its share of difficulties. By 1981, the Big Three all reported losses and Chrysler remained on the brink of bankruptcy. The root of their problems is their inability to properly forecast the rapid changes in the desires of fickle American auto buyers. With the Arab oil embargo in 1974 came the long gas line and increased prices. Consumers clamored for small cars. Since it takes the auto industry 3 years to retool, it responded with lines of small, compact cars in 1976. But by then the consumer had forgotten the energy crisis and was again demanding larger cars. Profitwise, this shift delighted the auto industry since it makes about $1000 profit on a large car and only $200 to $300 on a small car. So the auto industry continued to put its major efforts into larger cars on the traditional assumption that America will always want the larger car—and halfheartedly concerned itself with retooling for smaller cars. As the president of Ford told *Business Week,* "After the oil embargo in 1974, we went back to big cars as if nothing had happened." General Motors even considered a proposal for converting a compact car plant into a facility to produce full-size Oldsmobiles. Meanwhile, Chrysler fretted that the slimmed-down New Yorker would leave it behind in the renewed big-car battle.

Detroit's philosophy was expressed by GM's president: "We thought—rightly or wrongly—that we had to move down in an evolutionary way to better fuel economy." The revolution in Iran and the subsequent gasoline price surge made that choice completely incorrect. The market share of big cars plummeted from 42 percent to 33 percent between 1979 and 1980.

As an industry analyst told *Business Week,* "Detroit's dilemma is that it must sell cars no one wants to get the cash to make the cars that people will buy." And it will take billions to catch up—and time too. Many feel it will take Detroit until 1985 to produce small cars in sufficient quantity and quality. Meanwhile, the imports are capturing 25 to 30 percent of the market. For an industry that has always prided itself on its marketing skills, this loss of market share is most humiliating. At the root of all these woes is the consumer. As a Chrysler executive remarked to *Business Week,* "Ten years ago you could tell market changes three years ahead, but in today's world, you're really tossing a coin."

Sources of data: "Losing a Big Segment of the Market—Forever," *Business Week,* March 24, 1980, pp. 78–88; and "Detroit's New Sales Pitch," *Business Week,* Sept. 22, 1980, pp. 78–88.

The liquor industry reflects well the changing of consumer tastes. In 1970, bourbon, according to *Business Week,* controlled 22.9 percent of the total spirits market. By 1980, it had lost favor and accounted for only 13.9 percent of the market. Meanwhile, in 1980 vodka had soared to the favorite—holding a 29 percent market share, up from 12.4 percent in 1970.

Besides managing the controllable variable of product, marketers must develop their products within the constraints of the uncontrollable variables. The sale of certain products—pelts of endangered species, guns, and in many states, liquor on Sunday—is prohibited by law. Other product alternatives may be limited by the available technology or by social concerns. The important point is that a product must be developed within the boundaries defined by the uncontrollable variables.

Brands and Trademarks

Marketers identify and distinguish their products through the use of brands and trademarks. A *brand* is a name, term, symbol, or design, or a combination of these, which distinguishes a marketer's goods or services from others that are similar. A *trademark* is a brand that is given legal protection by being registered at the U.S. Patent Office.

Brands and trademarks are among a company's most valuable assets. They can provide a unique property to a product that has very little glamor in itself, as Church & Dwight's trademark—a muscular arm holding a hammer—does for Arm & Hammer sodium bicarbonate. But brand names can be a liability, too, as Cities Service (now Citgo) found out. A marketing research study showed that most people thought of Cities Service as a tired old company whose gasoline was not powerful enough to support the big engines of the late 1960s. As a result, the Cities Service signs came down and were replaced by Citgo signs—and consumers' images of the products changed.

Packaging

Figure 2-8 Packaging often influences sales. What would animal crackers be without the box? (Randy Matusow)

Packaging is the activity in product planning that involves designing and producing the container or wrapper for a product. Packaging serves to protect the product and to provide information about its use.

Crush-proof cigarette packages are an example of functional packaging. The packs serve a purpose that incidentally reflects contemporary fashion: More people are wearing jeans and casual clothes, and this type of package can be carried in a pocket without being crushed. But packaging also gives information. It tells customers what is in the package and how to use it so that the product will give satisfaction. (See Figure 2-8.)

Packaging changes constantly. Often, in fact, companies that switch packaging reduce the total satisfaction in the bundle of satisfaction offered. One of the most successful packages has been the Camel cigarette pack, which shows a camel, two pyramids, and three palm trees. An executive at R. J. Reynolds some years ago decided that the package would be more striking if the pyramids and trees were removed. The surgery was performed, but the public howled. Camel sales fell off instantly, and, not surprisingly, Reynolds quickly returned the camel's props.

Pricing

Buyers pay to receive a bundle of satisfaction in an exchange. Marketers can control the *price* variable, but only within a given range. The *ceiling,* or top price, that can be put on a product is set by consumers, who rate the value or worth of the product—which translates into the level of demand for an item. The *floor,* or lowest price that can be chosen, is the cost to the manufacturer. Pricing below cost for any long period is a quick road to bankruptcy. So the consumer demand and the manufacturing cost set the price range.

In the end, the price is equated with the value or worth of the product. If the two are not in line, then exchange does not happen and potential satisfaction is not realized. Although the uncontrollable forces must be considered in settling on a price, pricing is really more of an art than a science—as we'll see later.

Discounts

A *discount* is a deduction from the list price, and it is controlled by the marketer. This deduction may be in the form of cash (usually figured as a percentage of the price), or it may be some other concession, such as free merchandise. The idea underlying discounts is that the buyer will in turn perform some service that is of value to the seller. Such services provided by the buyer include buying in large quantities, paying cash rather than charging the item, and buying goods that are out of season.

In 1981, interest rates had soared to 18 percent and higher, scaring off potential automobile buyers. To combat the higher cost to the consumer caused by the auto loan, Ford and Chrysler at one point offered in effect a 6 percent discount on all new cars and thereby established a 12 percent ceiling on auto loans for buyers of selected automobiles. Ads proclaimed, "New Chrysler Corp. fights interest rates with 6 percent off all new 1981 U.S. built cars . . . get $325 to $1000 directly from Chrysler."

Channels of Distribution

As shown in Figure 2-9, marketers can take a number of routes in moving goods and services to their market. They can move products directly to consumers, or through retailers to consumers, or through wholesalers *and* retailers to consumers. These routes are called the *channels of distribution;* they are the paths products take in moving from the producer to the ultimate consumer.

Lumber, for example, originates with the timber processor, who sells it to a wholesaler; in turn, the wholesaler sells it to a retail lumberyard, which then sells it to carpenters and to builders. Clothing, however, usually does not pass through a wholesaler but, instead, goes straight from the manufacturer to the retail store. Hoover vacuum cleaners once were sold directly to consumers through house-to-house selling, but Hoover altered its channel of distribution to sell through retail outlets.

Within the distribution channel, marketers also can choose which type of outlet will handle their product.

In the spring of 1981, RCA Corp. began marketing SelectaVision, a video disc system, through 5000 retail outlets in seventy-four locations around the country. To offer large-scale time and place utility, RCA used mass retailers, including Sears, J.C. Penney, and Montgomery Ward, and secured dealers responsible for 60 percent of all color TV sales in the country.

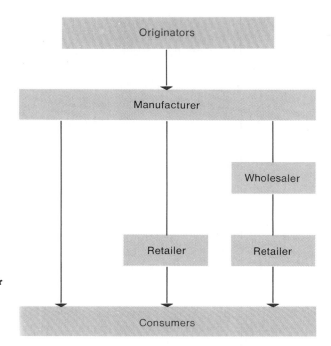

Figure 2-9   Three major routes from manufacturer to consumers. (This simplified structure will be enlarged in Chapter 13.)

Physical Distribution

Once the channels of distribution have been determined, the marketer can direct attention to the physical distribution of products through the channels. *Physical distribution* involves the range of activities that move the right quantity of products to the right place at the right time. Thus, physical distribution provides time and place utility and sets the stage for possession utility.

A marketer's decision about the channel of distribution directs physical distribution activities. In this sense, physical distribution "supports" the channel-of-distribution decision and includes decisions about the number, type, and location of warehouses to store goods along the way to buyers; about the level of inventory or goods stored to ensure that buyers can get the items when they want them; and about choosing a means of transporting goods from one place to another.

One of the increments of satisfaction in Frank Perdue's chickens (see Application 1-4) comes from their being sold in supermarkets fresh—never having been frozen. This practice creates distribution difficulties for the company since each chicken must be packed in ice and delivered quickly. Each chicken arrives at the food store no more than 6 hours after slaughter.

Advertising

Advertising, another controllable variable, is part of the promotion function. *Promotion* is a broad term used to describe the entire field of sales communication—

advertising, personal selling, and sales promotion. We'll look at these three controllable variables now.

Advertising is *nonpersonal* communication that is paid for by the marketer to promote a product or service through the mass media. It is nonpersonal communication in the sense that the marketer does not personally see or talk with buyers; there is no face-to-face confrontation. Also, the marketer *pays* for advertising. (If no payment is involved, the activity is called *publicity.*) Advertising uses *mass media* such as newspapers, television, radio, magazines, billboards, direct mail, and display cards in mass transit vehicles.

The two objectives of advertising are to expose a product to a large market and to encourage buyers to accept the product. The mass media give marketers the opportunity to accomplish these goals by communicating with large numbers of people.

To show how rewarding this activity can be, consider Nabisco. By mixing heavy television commercials and store promotions, Nabisco effectively communicated the slogan "Everything tastes great when it sits on a Ritz" to create a new awareness of its product among consumers, increasing sales by 16 percent in a single year.

Personal Selling

Personal selling is individual-to-individual communication. It has some advantages over advertising. Personal selling provides the human touch that is lacking in advertising. People prize communication with others, and personal selling often has a greater impact in encouraging exchange. Also, through personal selling, marketers can tailor their presentation to fit the needs, wants, motives, and behavior of individual customers. Salespeople can see the immediate reaction of customers to a particular sales approach and then can adjust their approach instantly. Personal selling often results in a purchase, while advertising usually only arouses interest and desire without the immediate purchase. The disadvantage of personal selling is its very high cost. Each contact with a customer is expensive.

Sales Promotion

Sales promotion is a controllable variable that includes everything normally thought of as advertising, but it does not involve mass media. Sales promotion techniques include trading stamps, cents-off coupons, mail-in refunds, calendars, trade shows, free demonstrations, samples, and displays at retail counters. More formally, *sales promotion* involves "those marketing activities, other than personal selling, advertising, and publicity, that stimulate consumer purchasing and dealer effectiveness."[4]

Public Relations

Public relations is a controllable variable that marketers use to promote their product or company in a favorable image. Public relations personnel attempt to get favorable

---

[4]American Marketing Association, Committee on Definitions, *Marketing Definitions: A Glossary of Marketing Terms,* Chicago, 1960, p. 20.

publicity by providing news stories and other information to the mass media. It is their responsibility, for example, to keep the news media informed about new products, corporate social concerns, financial results, and community involvement. While marketers must pay fees or salaries to those who disseminate such information, the public relations staff does not pay the mass media for communicating the information.

Services

In addition to the basic functions of a product, services can increase the bundle of satisfaction presented to buyers. *Services* are "activities, benefits, or satisfactions which are offered for sale, or are provided in connection with the sales of goods."[5] Services include free home delivery, free installation, trade-ins, credit extension, and gift wrapping. The basic idea is to build a total bundle of satisfaction that best satisfies buyers. When Rich's department store in Atlanta agrees to let customers buy merchandise under a long-term credit plan, it is offering an extra service that adds to the bundle of satisfaction.

Warranties

A *warranty* assures buyers that the product will live up to their reasonable expectations. The type of warranty offered and its duration are under the control of the marketer.

One of Midas Muffler's major marketing approaches has been to offer a lifetime warranty with any muffler it installs. Similarly, automobile manufacturers have long used warranties to stimulate sales. (See Application 2-5.)

Post-Exchange Servicing

Even after an exchange has been made, the marketer's job is not complete. Since the provision of satisfaction is a marketer's main objective, that responsibility remains even after the product or service has been consumed. The success of any marketing effort depends on repeated exchanges, and so it makes good business sense to follow up on sales.

Post-exchange servicing is illustrated by this sign in a Chicago supermarket: "Our meat is not sold until it is consumed." The store is telling shoppers, "If you don't like our meat, bring it back, and we'll exchange it or return your money." Automobile companies, too, have long practiced post-exchange activities, ranging from warranties to toll-free telephone numbers that customers can call to voice complaints.

Post-exchange servicing, then, consists of the activities that ensure satisfaction with a product. In addition to building repeated sales, this servicing provides marketers with information enabling their companies to improve products. Frequently, this activity is a forgotten part of marketing, but it is a critical function if satisfaction is to result from an exchange. (See Application 2-6.)

---

[5]Ibid., p. 21.

Application 2-5
Warranties—Even the "Ultimate in Guarantees" Doesn't Help

Chrysler's sales have been on the skids for some time, partly because its products had acquired a reputation for being unreliable and partly because some consumers feared the company might go bankrupt and not be available to stand behind its cars with parts and service. Full of optimism, Chrysler announced in early 1980 a 30-day, money-back guarantee on all new cars. This was accompanied by an offer of $50 for anyone who would test-drive a Chrysler and then buy it or a comparable competing make. Eager for something to jolt car sales, company officials dreamed of buyers lining up at showrooms to drive away a new Chrysler. Dealers, however, envisioned slightly used Chryslers flooding back into showrooms as unscrupulous motorists seized upon the opportunity to drive a new car free for 4 weeks.

While the unscrupulous did not respond, neither did the buyers. Paying about $10 million a month to fund the program, Chrysler found its sales dismal at best. Sales were off 26 percent from the previous year. The cars that did sell were the smaller models for which there was already a demand. The bottom line on this extraordinary offer can be summed up by an industry sales analyst's statement to *The Wall Street Journal:* "It is slowing down what would otherwise be a much steeper decline."

We build and back our cars to guarantee your satisfaction.

When you buy a new car from The New Chrysler Corporation, there is no risk. If you're not happy, for any reason, we'll take the car back...and give you your money back. That's the most powerful guarantee in the business. And only Chrysler has it. Not Ford. Not GM. Not the Imports. Only Chrysler.

Our satisfaction guarantee works for you in other ways, too. It makes us, and our dealers, work harder to make sure you're satisfied. Everybody, from top management to the man on the line, is dedicated to improving our quality.

We have new training programs for our salesmen. They've been schooled in demonstrating every vehicle, so you know exactly what you're getting. And we have new training methods for our service managers, because a good product with poor service is not satisfaction. We want our service to be the best in the industry.

Last, but not least, you're the final judge of our product. If you don't like it, you'll never have to live with it.

If you're looking for guaranteed satisfaction when you buy a car, there's only one car company to look for. The New Chrysler Corporation. **For more information, call this toll-free number:**

800-521-7270 or 7271.
In Michigan, 800-482-0415. Or ask your participating dealer for full details.

⭐ **The New Chrysler Corporation**

(Courtesy Chrysler Corporation)

Source of data: "Chrysler's Money-Back Plan Doesn't Lift Sales but Does Prevent a Steeper Decline," *The Wall Street Journal,* March 7, 1980, p. 40.

Application 2-6
Post-Exchange Servicing—Making Sales after Sales

Consumers have reached the realization that most manufacturers are not much excited about repairing the products they make and sell. Most manufacturers agree that good service is essential to keeping consumers happy, but the costs of equipment and salaries of qualified repairers (if they can be found) have skyrocketed and products themselves have become more complex. An official of Magic Chef told *The Wall Street Journal,* "You used to be able to take a kid out of high school and teach him a few fundamentals, and he could repair, say, a gas range just fine. But now the kid's got to know electronics and circuitry and microwaves and a lot of other things."

To provide the necessary service, many companies contract with independent service centers to make authorized repairs. Thus, many small shops abound and offer repairs on several brands of similar products.

Some manufacturers, however, see the repair business as a profitable venture. Firestone Tire & Rubber Company, for instance, plans to double its repair business without expanding its 1400 tire stores and 4700 independent dealers. The company believes tire stores now hold less than 10 percent of the automotive service business and is looking to double its repair business. Firestone is even considering producing a line of auto parts. Black & Decker Manufacturing Company has standardized its electrical tool products so that once a repair worker is trained, he or she can fix almost any company product.

And a number of companies, like General Electric, have tried to improve the cost efficiency of their repair operations by offering extended warranty coverage after a product's original warranty expires.

Astute marketers see the value of post-exchange servicing. As a Whirlpool executive told *The Wall Street Journal,* "If we can make repair service easier, we think people will appreciate that. And the next time they buy an appliance, they'll think of us."

Source of data: "Most Manufacturers Prefer Not to Repair the Goods They Make," *The Wall Street Journal,* Jan. 19, 1981, p. 1.

The 4 P's

The controllable tasks of marketing can be categorized into four major sets of activities that make up the bundle of satisfaction. These factors are most often referred to as the 4 P's: product, price, place, and promotion. Table 2-2 shows how the controllable variables relate to the 4 P's (only marketing research, a support activity that helps to fashion the 4 P's, does not have a place in this arrangement).

TABLE 2-2 How the Controllable Variables Fit into the 4 P's	
4 P's	*Controllable variables*
1 Product	The product
	Brand name, trademark
	Packaging
	Services
	Warranties
	Post-exchange servicing
2 Place	Channels of distribution
	Physical distribution
3 Price	Pricing
	Discounts
4 Promotion	Advertising
	Personal selling
	Sales promotion
	Public relations
	Brand name, trademark
	Packaging

Communication

The goal of managing the 4 P's can be summarized in one word that perhaps best describes all marketing activity: *communication*. The *product* communicates form utility; *place* communicates time and place *utility; price* communicates value and quality; and *promotion,* by its very nature, is a communicative activity concentrating on benefits. In short, we can boil down the business of marketing to communication. Note, though, that the communication goes two ways. The market communicates its wants and needs to help the marketer fashion the bundle of satisfaction; the marketer then creates that bundle and communicates how it will satisfy the market's desires.

The Marketing Mix

When seen from the viewpoint of a marketer, an organization's bundle of satisfaction also has another name: the *marketing mix*. This is the unique combination of controllable variables that a given marketer offers to consumers. A marketer's objective is to create a marketing mix that provides greater satisfaction than a competitor's does.

United Airlines, for instance, provides airplane service between cities (product) as well as baggage shipping (service) for a fare (price), sold through travel agents (personal selling). In these respects, United is no different from its competitors. But, hoping to make its bundle of satisfaction different and more satisfying than competitors', the company calls itself United (brand name), uses a distinctive mark on the tail of its planes and in its advertisements, has well-trained flight attendants (service), and uses distinctive promotional phrases such as "Fly the Friendly Skies of United" and "This Land Is Your Land" (advertising).

The key to building the best marketing mix is knowing the desires of the people to be served. And the key to success lies in applying the philosophy of the marketing concept to the development of the marketing mix.

The Perrier Story: Matching the Market with the Marketing Mix

Until the late 1970s, Perrier was an obscure bottled water coming from mineral springs in southern France. It was purchased by a few trendy consumers who generally found it at out-of-the-way gourmet shops. In 1976, United States sales of Perrier stood at only 3 million bottles, a mere 8 percent of Perrier's sales. But this lackluster performance was not to continue. Two years later, Perrier was on its way to becoming the biggest new drink since Miller Brewing introduced its Lite beer.

Source Perrier, to capitalize on the United States market, set up an American subsidiary, Great Waters of France, Inc., and installed well-recognized marketer Bruce Nevins as president. Having long expected a greater thirst for Perrier to emerge in America, Nevins secured a $2 million advertising budget to back up his strategy of appealing to affluent adults, particularly those with a growing health consciousness. Perrier was marketed as a noncaloric, chic alternative to soft drinks and alcoholic beverages, all designed to match the health and diet-consciousness atmosphere of the late 1970s.

Product: Perrier's major product distinction is naturally carbonated spring water, whereas most competing alternatives are produced by injecting human-made carbon dioxide. Perrier maintains that its smaller bubbles give the consumer a less bloated feeling.

Price: The initial gourmet store price was dropped by a third but kept at a premium niche (69 cents or more for a 23-ounce bottle). This price made it 50 percent more costly than the average soft drink and kept it aimed at adults.

Distribution: The channel of distribution was completely changed by replacing over 75 percent of the distributors to gain access to supermarkets and convenience stores—and to move away from gourmet shops. In 1979, supermarkets accounted for 70 percent of Perrier's distribution, up from 10 percent in 1976. Perrier also carefully expanded into new geographic markets. Using demographic data, the product was first put into twenty-six affluent, fashionable markets with high consumption of beers, wines, and health foods. Then it was further expanded to twenty-five metropolitan markets to give the product distribution in two-thirds of the country.

Promotion: The initial promotion was a $2 million advertising campaign directed to the well-heeled older market. The campaign consisted of print ads placed in high-fashion women's magazines and of TV commercials narrated by Orson Welles. In 1979, the advertising expenditure was raised to $7 million to promote the product nationwide.

The result: Sales dollars rose thirtyfold in just 2 years and unit volume went to 200 million bottles in 1979.[6]

The Marketing Program

Having examined the uncontrollable environment and controllable activities that marketers must contend with or manage, we now will look at the steps marketers take in developing and controlling their marketing mix, or bundle of satisfaction. A *marketing program* involves a listing of events or tasks that marketers perform to provide the satisfaction they wish to exchange in the marketplace. These tasks can be organized into four phases: (1) strategic planning and information gathering; (2) developing the marketing mix; (3) integrating the marketing mix; and (4) controlling the marketing mix, as shown in Figure 2-10. A formal marketing program lists and describes the details and tasks that are involved in each of these phases. The following review of these marketing tasks will provide an overview of how our study of marketing will proceed throughout this book.

Strategic Planning and Information Gathering

The marketing program begins with strategic planning. Earlier in this chapter, we saw how the environment surrounding the marketer changes. Planning is the process of anticipating the future and determining courses of action to ensure that the organization will achieve its goals. These courses of action are called *strategies*. The strategies chosen provide a blueprint for the marketing organization's activities. Thus, *strategic planning* is the process of deciding upon a distinct set of strategies that will reflect the predicted future environment and will meet the objectives or goals of the organization. Strategic plans tend to be long-term, often covering the next 5-year period. Central, then, to strategic planning are goals. While the overall goal of any marketing organization is the provision of satisfaction to the market, this objective is not totally sound because it is difficult to measure. Good objectives must be relevant, feasible,

---

[6]"Perrier: The Astonishing Success of an Appeal to Affluent Adults," *Business Week,* Jan. 22, 1979, pp. 64–65; and "The Selling of H$_2$O," *Consumer Reports,* September 1980, pp. 531–538.

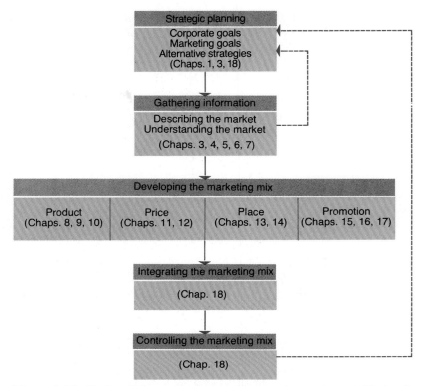

Figure 2-10   Tasks of the marketing program and overview of this book.

and measurable. Marketers need more to guide them than the vague objective of providing satisfaction. Of course, the organization that employs the marketers has its own goals, but these tend to emphasize profitability; marketing goals tend to be more sales-oriented. Marketers strive for increases in sales and improvements in share of market over previous periods, since sales are an indicator of the level of satisfaction provided. Therefore, strategic planning needs the specification of a set of appropriate goals.[7]

To establish good marketing objectives, it is necessary to gather information about the market. Most organizations have their own internal records, and these can be of substantial help in providing an information base. Companies also collect information from outside sources, such as customers, dealers, and the general public. Once this information has been obtained, the marketer must evaluate it. Often, information gathering can show weaknesses in the goals and lead to readjustment of

---

[7]Goals and objectives are used interchangeably in our discussion.

objectives, strategies, or both. In short, this information helps marketers describe and understand their market.

Developing the Marketing Mix

The information-gathering phase of the marketing program allows for the effective development of the marketing mix. The marketing mix represents the outcome of the *tactical planning* of marketing and reflects those activities specified by the strategic plans. Tactical plans are short-term, specifying current activities and the allocation of resources needed to implement the strategies. The nature of the *product* to be offered must be established. The product must be developed to meet the needs of the market, and it must be managed over time. These are important tasks that must be controlled from the time the product is brought out to the time it is retired from the market. Additionally, the marketer must determine brand names, trademarks, packaging, and warranties.

Once the product is developed, its *price* can be determined. The nature of pricing and its importance to buyers must be considered. A base or list price can be set, and decisions can be made about adjusting that price to meet unique circumstances in the marketplace.

Next, decisions must be made about *distribution*—the channel of distribution desired, the type of wholesalers and retailers needed, the physical distribution activities required to support the movement of the goods, and the means by which the cooperation of intermediaries within the channel can be obtained.

In the area of *promotion,* the marketer first must decide which combination of personal selling, advertising, and sales promotion to use and how much emphasis to place on each. Then, individual decisions about each promotional activity can be dealt with—size of budgets, appeals to be used, media to be emphasized, size of sales force, and the like.

Integrating the Marketing Mix

Marketing mix decisions cannot be made independently, since each activity affects the others. The decisions must be integrated in order to provide a coordinated bundle of satisfaction. The sales force must know which new products are coming out, and the advertising appeals should reflect the pricing and distribution decisions. In short, the entire marketing program must be integrated in order to be effective. Once the planning is completed, the decisions are carried out in the real world—making the product, stamping the price on it, distributing it, and implementing the promotional program.

Controlling the Marketing Program

But the marketing job is still not complete. The results of these decisions and their implementation should be *reviewed* to determine whether the objectives set out in the strategic plan are being met. If they are not, the marketer must determine how to change the marketing program so that it does meet the objectives. In short, the program must be controlled. And this control activity provides feedback so that the marketer can match the product to consumers' satisfaction.

These are the steps that marketers go through in putting together their marketing programs. This view sets the stage for our study. The remaining chapters will explore each step in detail to show how marketers actually go about the job of providing satisfaction to the market.

Looking Back

In this chapter, we have looked closely at the nature of marketing. You have seen that the marketer's job is essentially one of making decisions about the activities that will provide the best bundle of satisfaction to the market. In the next chapter, we will examine how marketers make their decisions and how they get the information they need. Before going further, though, review the following important points:

1 Marketers can influence their external environment, but they cannot control it.

2 The external environment greatly constrains and sets limits on marketers' decisions.

3 Markets change constantly, and marketers must adjust to these changes.

4 Knowledge about the nature and motivation of the market is required for effective marketing management.

5 One critical marketing activity occurs after the exchange, when the marketer's emphasis shifts to ensuring that expected satisfaction is actually received.

6 The bundle of satisfaction offered is the combination of controllable variables of marketing that the marketer chooses to provide.

7 The marketing mix is that unique combination of controllable variables which a given marketer uses to provide the bundle of satisfaction.

8 The four major categories of marketing activities center on product, place, price, and promotion.

9 If marketing can be boiled down to one word, that word is communication.

10 Marketers go through a specific set of activities, called the marketing program, to provide their bundle of satisfaction.

11 The marketing program begins with strategic planning and ends with reviewing performance to see whether the objectives have been reached.

Key Terms

If you aren't sure what each of the following words means, look back at the text. Numbers refer to pages on which the words are defined. Additional information can be found by checking the index and the glossary at the end of the book.

uncontrollable environment 32
the social environment 34
the political and legal environment 35
the competitive environment 40
the technological environment 42
the economic environment 43
the natural environment 45
marketing research 47
brand 50

trademark 50
promotion 52
sales promotion 53
marketing mix 57
marketing program 59
strategic planning 59
planning 59
strategy 59
tactical planning 61

Questions for Review

1 Why are the environmental forces outside the control of the marketer?

2 What types of competition are there?

3 What is the major controllable variable and why?

4 Is the marketer's job complete after the post-exchange activity? Explain.

5 What is the marketer's objective in developing a marketing mix?

6 What are the four phases of the marketing program? Explain each.

Questions for Thought and Discussion

1 "Space Invaders" is the video game in which players pit themselves against descending rows of little creatures who march across the screen and drop "bombs" on the player. The player's objective is to "bump off" the invaders with a laser beam. In 1980, this game set off an explosion of sales in the video game industry. What environmental forces might have accounted for this phenomenon?

2 A study by the Environmental Protection Agency, done in 1978, found that on 67 percent of cars built since 1973 with antipollution devices, consumers had had these devices disconnected. If the consumer is king, why do automobile companies put such devices on cars?

3 In 1980, Ford Motor Company proclaimed itself a *foreign* auto maker and advertised that it was the producer of the first "world cars"—the Ford Escort and the Mercury Lynx. The claim of being a world manufacturer is justified since Ford has made cars in Europe since 1912, and it exported to the European market before then. What do you think motivated this marketing approach?

4 To describe how a "boy-meets-girl exchange" can be thought of as marketing, what would be the product, price, place, and promotion activities?

Suggested Project

Find magazine and newspaper advertisements that reflect each of the controllable variables as their major focus. Put them in a folder and label each according to the controllable variable represented.

Suggested Readings

Abell, Derek F.: "Strategic Windows," *Journal of Marketing,* vol. 42, no. 3 (July 1978), pp. 21–26. The author emphasizes the importance of anticipating and responding to environmental changes in the marketplace.

Cox, Keith K.: "Marketing in the 1980s—Back to Basics," *Business,* vol. 30, no. 3 (May–June 1980), pp. 19–23. To adapt to some of the difficult environmental trends in the 1980s, the author suggests that marketing managers will need more than "business as usual" attitudes.

Drucker, Peter F.: *Management,* Harper & Row, New York, 1973. This excellent reference book focuses on the role and scope of the manager's job and keys on the importance of marketing.

Hall, William K.: "Survival Strategies in a Hostile Environment," *Harvard Business Review,* vol. 58, no. 5 (September–October 1980), pp. 75–85. This in-depth study of sixty-four companies reveals the best avenues to success when the environment is not friendly.

Kotler, Philip: "The Major Tasks of Marketing Management," *Journal of Marketing,* vol. 37, no. 4 (October 1973), pp. 42–49. This article identifies eight different marketing strategies, each arising out of a unique state of demand.

Laczniak, Gene R., Robert F. Lusch, and Jon G. Udell: "Marketing in 1985: A View from the Ivory Tower," *Journal of Marketing,* vol. 41, no. 4 (October 1977), pp. 47–56. Leading marketing scholars assess the effect on marketing strategy of some fifty technological, ecological, legal, economic, and resource dimensions, forecast to 1985.

vanDam, Andre: "Marketing in the New International Economic Order," *Journal of Marketing,* vol. 41, no. 1 (January 1977), pp. 19–23. This article shows the new challenges for marketing managers as the world economy emphasizes developing nations.

Welch, Joe L.: *Marketing Law,* PPC, Tulsa, Okla., 1980. This

book is an excellent reference source on the legal environment of marketing.
Werner, Ray O.: "Marketing and the U.S. Supreme Court," *Journal of Marketing,* vol. 41, no. 1 (January 1977), pp. 32–43. The restrictions on marketing decision making imposed by Supreme Court rulings are cataloged.

Cases For Part One

Case 1   Swift & Company

When Joseph P. Sullivan assumed the presidency of Swift & Company in 1980, he faced some significant problems. By frequently changing corporate strategies throughout the decade of the 1970s, the giant food company had confused both its customers and its employees and caused its profits to be very erratic. Furthermore, Donald P. Kelly, the chief executive officer of Swift's parent company, Esmark Inc., had decreed that by 1984 the Swift subsidiary must boost its profitability to that of Esmark's other chemical and consumer products businesses. That objective is a 15 percent return on assets. Failure to meet that goal would result in either reorganization of Swift or its sale to some other firm. In mid-1982, Sullivan was wondering whether his actions were the appropriate ones and what he should do in the future.

Many of the company's troubles were inherited from Sullivan's predecessor, William S. Watchman, Jr., who had emphasized marketing at Swift. He had brought out new products, such as Soup Starter, Sizzlean, frozen dinners, and some new turkey products. Yet these new-product programs were poorly executed and were given insufficient marketing support. The company hired new marketing-oriented managers, but

friction developed between them and the older, more staid managers. The new-product additions were very costly, and cash from the company's mainstay business of fresh meat was too low to finance the new sales, distribution, and accounting costs.

When Sullivan took over, he instituted some drastic cost reductions. The corporate staff was cut in half, eliminating 340 jobs. Purchasing procedures were instituted that decreased cheese inventories by $15 million. More efficient systems for inventory control and accounting reduced working capital needs to $163 million, a saving of 23 percent. And in the turkey business, greater procurement efficiencies and lower production cut inventory in half to $36 million. The turkey business had been a particular problem in the late 1970s under Watchman. Despite substantial efforts at Swift, consumers were not persuaded that turkey should be served much more frequently than at Thanksgiving and Christmas. While in 1982 Swift held a 24 percent share of the turkey market, Sullivan believed the company should cut costs rather than increase sales through greater marketing expenditures.

Sullivan's early results were impressive. In 1981, his first full year, he turned the company around from a 1980 loss of $9.8

million to a profit of $38.4 million on an increase of sales from $1.3 billion to $1.5 billion. Swift's return on assets (ROA) jumped to 10 percent compared with less than 4 percent in each of the previous five years. While this increase is substantial, it is still less than the 16.4 average return of other Esmark divisions. In the first six months of 1982, Swift's earnings jumped 35 percent on a sales increase of merely 2 percent. Sullivan believed the return on assets in 1982 would hit 14.4 percent, which would be a sizable advance toward reaching Kelly's corporate mandate of 15 percent ROA by 1984.

In mid-1982, Sullivan was reviewing his performance and setting plans for the future. He assessed his approach of cutting costs and product lines as a quick fix to move toward the top-priority 1984 deadline. His immediate growth plans were to add some high-profit new products— processed ham, salami, and pastrami, as well as a specialty cheese and several frozen dinner entrées. Such additions, Sullivan felt, would provide $40 million in 1983 sales and $10 million in 1983 profits. Additionally, he was considering acquiring other businesses that would build on Swift's strong goodwill with consumers and supermarkets. Poultry firms and companies handling grocery products or processed meats might be logical acquisitions, he believed, if their sales were in the $20-million to $50-million range.

1 Evaluate Swift's managerial philosophy.

2 What would you suggest that Sullivan do in the future?

Source of data: "Swift: Cutting Costs and Adding Products to Beat a Profit Deadline," *Business Week*, June 21, 1982, pp. 65–68.

Case 2   The United Way

When Dr. Thomas Frist, chairman of the Hospital Corporation of America, headed the 1981 United Way Drive in Nashville, Tennessee, he faced some difficult problems. Nashville's economy was confronted with high unemployment and high inflation. Many of the city's largest employers, such as Du Pont and Ford, were shut down. Other large employers had mandated hiring freezes. In addition, the city had increased business taxes and the general atmosphere in the business community was very gloomy.

To counter these problems, Dr. Frist began the campaign by going directly to the chairpersons of the city's top companies. These high-level executives agreed in turn to assign their high-level internal managers to heavily promote their individual company United Way campaigns. In addition, the public relations staffs of these companies were requested to assist the doctor's fund-raising efforts. The public relations executives were asked to come up with promotional ideas for their company's own campaign and for the United Way Drive in general.

Next, to raise some advertising funds, Dr. Frist asked each company to shift a portion of its advertising dollars to the United Way campaign. As a result, ample funds became available for television, radio, billboard, and brochure advertising. He also persuaded many companies to mention the United Way in their local advertising. Shoney's Incorporated, a large restaurant chain, tagged its TV spots with the United Way logo. NLT Corporation, a large insurance holding company, included United Way messages on its busboards.

Then three Nashville-based advertising agencies were recruited to donate their creative, production, and media-buying services. Next, Dr. Frist convinced the city's top two public relations companies to handle publicity at no charge. Finally, at his request, Barbara Mandrell, the country-and-western singer from Nashville, agreed to serve as spokesperson in a series of commercials, donating her time and thus saving United Way thousands of dollars in talent fees. But still Dr. Frist wondered whether there weren't some other marketing actions that he might undertake to help the United Way reach its goal.

1 What is the bundle of satisfaction that is being marketed by the United Way?

2 What additional actions would you recommend that Dr. Frist take to improve his campaign?

Case 3 Oxford Industries Inc.

Throughout most of the 1970s, Oxford Industries Inc., the Atlanta-based apparel firm, was content to realize consistent, although not substantial, profits from supplying large retailers with mid-priced clothes. J. C. Penney Co. and Sears, Roebuck & Co. were major customers. But between 1977 and 1982, the firm recorded the sharpest growth in its history. While most apparel competitors were severely hurt by the recession, Oxford flourished. Earnings for 1982 were $15 million on sales of $430 million, in contrast to 1981 profits of $8.8 million on sales of $334 million. This growth was attributed to Oxford's successful addition of designer-label clothes.

J. Hicks Lanier, Oxford's chief executive officer, was stating his philosophy to Vice President of Finance R. William Lee, Jr: "Fashion is the lifeblood of the industry. We don't want to be in the commodity replacement market." But at the same time, Lee was reminding him of some of the high risks of this strategy. Designer clothes are fashion-oriented and consequently a volatile business. Such product lines are subject to fast-changing trends in consumer taste. Furthermore, many designer markets, especially the designer jeans market, seem to be approaching saturation.

Oxford's strategy, Lanier argued, had been sound so far. In 1978, the company contracted with designer Ralph Lauren to produce Lauren's Polo line of children's apparel, which Oxford sold to exclusive retailers such as Bloomingdale's and Nieman-Marcus. Lanier also added other successful brand names, including John Henry and Lightning Bolt. His selection of designers has been particularly effective in maintaining consumer staying power. In 1982, the Polo line was still selling briskly.

To add to Oxford's growth, Lanier acquired Merona Corporation's Sport Division in 1981 and planned to offer new designer lines of Jeffrey Banks and Robert Stock in late 1982. As his hedge against risk, Lanier planned to target these designer clothes toward fast-growing markets. Most of the company's products are pitched at the high-growth children's market. Additionally, Lanier noticed an advancing trend among large retailers to offer higher-priced clothes carrying celebrity names. Sears, for example, introduced its own Cheryl Tiegs line in 1981. With Oxford's heritage as a manufacturer of unbranded apparel for large chains, this market seemed to be a logical source of future growth. Reflecting on Vice President Lee's cautionary comments, however, Lanier wondered whether he should consider some other, less risky alternatives for the future.

1 In the designer line of products, which uncontrollable variables should Oxford be particularly concerned with?

2 What strategic advice would you offer to Hicks Lanier?

Source of data: "Oxford: A Venture into Designer-Label Clothes Spruces Up Earnings by 90%," *Business Week*, June 21, 1982, pp. 68–71.

Case 4   Visa USA

In the spring of 1982, Charles Russell, president of San Francisco-based Visa USA, was reflecting on some of the many problems that were facing his worldwide bank card company. Russell had just cause not only to consider the problems, but also to make decisions that would greatly impact his bank card company in the years ahead.

Since the 1960s, Visa and its competitor MasterCard had dominated the charge card industry. In the process, they had forced many smaller card companies out of business and also had taken sales from entertainment and business card companies like American Express, Diners, and Carte Blanche. But in the 1980s, conditions were different.

Russell was most concerned with the acceptance of automatic teller machines (ATM) by the banking industry and, through the use of these machines, the building of a nationwide electronic network for funds transfer. ATMs accomplish much that bank cards, initially designed as consumer credit instruments, fail to provide. For example, ATMs provide customers with the ability to transfer funds from their checking to their savings accounts, make bank deposits, and withdraw cash from their accounts. A bank's ATM system can be linked directly to a retailer's machine that allows

retailers to make instant credit verifications and to transfer funds immediately from the customers' accounts to their own accounts. When Visa cards are used, funds are not transferred immediately to retailers' accounts, since the process requires a period of days. Thus, retailers lose their use of the customer's money for that length of time.

Groups of banks have begun assembling their own ATM regional networks. Member banks' ATMs are linked together to enlarge the bank customer's usage opportunities. Bank customers can withdraw funds at all member banks' ATMs in various geographic regions. In 1982, Plus Systems Inc., for example, was the largest such network, spanning 14 states and including 260 member banks. About 100 such linking networks were in operation in 1982.

Russell had attempted to counter this ATM networking with Visa's own ATM system. Rather than start their own network, banks could subscribe to Visa's network. But the banks rejected Visa's system. The banking industry believes that Visa has greatly blurred its image with its customers. In response, the banks are searching for a system that enhances their own image. A Visa ATM system could well further cloud a local bank's image. Banks want the ability to compete in

electronic-based products and delivery systems, and the bank card associations are not giving them that opportunity. Visa proposed a money market fund that would have channeled funds back to member banks for investment in money market certificates. However, Visa required member banks first to sign up with its own ATM system. Most banks immediately became annoyed and refused Visa's program.

To counter some of his company's difficulties, Russell was planning the introduction of a new premium credit card aimed at upper-income card users. Such cards, similar to the American Express Gold Card, would offer special privileges. Banks would be allowed to design the physical appearance of the cards as they wished and to downplay the familiar Visa service mark. Competitor MasterCard, meanwhile, was also planning a premium card but would demand that banks leave their MasterCard design intact.

1 What uncontrollable environmental influences must Charles Russell contend with?

2 What actions should he consider?

Source of data: "Visa's Bid to Keep Banks on Board," *Business Week*, April 26, 1982, pp. 101–102; "Electronic Banking," *Business Week*, Jan. 18, 1982, pp. 70–80.

PART TWO

Marketing as Decision Making and Information Gathering

Cases

"There's no doubt in my mind that we wouldn't be the company we are if we didn't have our close contact with consumers. We've never added it up, but I'm sure the feedback we get from consumers saves us many millions of dollars a year."

With this brief statement to *The Wall Street Journal,* an executive of Procter & Gamble summed up much of the extraordinary success of the Cincinnati-based company that had its beginning with a bar of soap and that now markets eighty brands which yield annual revenues of nearly $10 billion.

Without question, much of P&G's success is attributed to its market research. P&G's research is almost all-encompassing; consumers are quizzed constantly; researchers track housewives around as they do the laundry, noting how they sort the clothes, how many loads they do, and many other seemingly minor details. But, over time, this meticulous research uncovers consumer behavior trends that suggest products to P&G.

During the 1960s, for example, P&G's researchers found that the average household's loads of laundry increased from 6.4 to 7.6 a week, and that the temperature of the water fell an average of 15 degrees because clothes were made of more kinds of synthetic and synthetic-natural blends fabrics which required washing separately in cold or lukewarm, rather than hot, water.

As a result, P&G developed a detergent designed to work at all temperature levels on many different fabrics. This new product was marketed as Cheer and was aimed at people who wanted one detergent able to handle virtually all their laundry.

P&G conducts market research on each of its products at least once a year. Often, the research uncovers consumer attitudes that prompt P&G to modify even its best-selling products—perhaps because consumers don't like something specific about the P&G brand or because they prefer a competing product. One of P&G's biggest sellers, Tide detergent, has been altered fifty-seven times since it was introduced in 1946.

Sometimes a consumer complaint about a product can't be solved, but indicates a new need. P&G's research on its Downy fabric softener indicated that people disliked having to run to their washing machine on every rinse cycle to add fabric softener. P&G couldn't solve the problem by changing Downy, so it developed Bounce instead, a softener sheet that is tossed into the dryer with the clothes.

"In our business, we are forever trying to see what lies around the corner," P&G's chairman told *The Wall Street Journal.* "We study the ever-changing consumer and try to identify new trends in tastes, needs, environment, and living habits. We study changes in the marketplace and try to assess their likely impact on our brands. We study our competition. Competitive brands are continually offering new benefits and new ideas to the customer, and we must stay ahead of this."

Source of data: "At Procter & Gamble, Success Is Largely Due to Heeding Consumer," *The Wall Street Journal,* April 29, 1980, p. 1.

Chapter 3

Management of Marketing Information

Looking Ahead

In Chapter 2 we explored the marketing mix and saw how marketers must deal with the controllable variables and respond to the uncontrollable variables. We found that the job of marketing manager is essentially one of decision making. To make decisions, of course, marketers must have information. This chapter looks at and describes how marketers make these decisions and obtain the information they need for making decisions.

Key Topics

The difference between problem solving and decision making

How marketers make decisions

Why information is the key to good decisions

How data and information differ

What sources of information marketers use

Description of a marketing information system (MIS)

How the MIS differs from marketing research

How the MIS helps in the decision-making process

Chapter Outline

Problem Solving and Decision Making

Marketers are designers: they create a marketing program that focuses on the marketing mix, thereby offering the bundle of satisfaction to the market. Satisfaction develops as business firms provide services and change materials into goods that meet society's needs and wants.

Thus, marketers essentially make decisions to solve society's problems. But the problem-solving process really occurs on two levels because (1) the solution of societal problems (2) creates problems for marketers. That is, given society's need to solve a particular problem, marketers must find solutions. For instance, the dwindling supply of energy resources creates a social need for energy conservation. Marketers, then, must meet society's needs by creating energy-efficient products and promoting energy conservation through advertising. It is the second level of problem solving, that is, discussion about marketing activities, that we will focus on now and in the rest of the book.

The Problem-Solving Process

Marketers solve problems throughout the strategic planning, implementing, and controlling phases of their work. While problem solving happens only if decisions are carried out, marketers face two key prior problems: (1) determining goals and (2) developing tactical plans to achieve them. Since companies and marketers have limited resources, not all problems can be solved. Consequently, priorities must be set, and only certain problems can be selected for solution. Once the most important problems have been identified, it's up to the marketers to find the best solutions.

But, before marketing executives can even attempt to find a solution, they must recognize that a problem exists. This is not always an easy job. Often, symptoms are mistaken for the problem. For example, a marketer who is concerned with declining sales may describe the decline as a marketing problem. In reality, the decline may be only a symptom. The problem may lie in poor service, overpricing, ineffective advertising, or a combination of these. (See Application 3-1.)

Greyhound Corporation encountered just such a situation in the late 1970s. Deluged by consumer and employee complaints about customer service problems including filthy conditions and poor security at bus terminals, bus breakdowns, faulty bus air conditioning, and poor employee morale, the company's top management realized the underlying cause of its problem. Having diversified in the 1970s into such areas as computer and car leasing, food processing, mortgage financing, and personal-care products, Greyhound had clearly neglected the company's original business, its bus line. Changes were quickly made.

Effective marketers don't wait for problems to arise; instead, they try to anticipate them. For example, before the Ford Motor Company, Gulf Oil Corporation, and other multinational firms make a commitment to foreign investment, they often seek the advice of a political analyst within their corporate headquarters. Confronted with revolutions and rising patriotism within host countries as well as economic woes, more

Application 3-1
Solving Problems Before They Cause Lasting Pain—
Kroger Uses 250,000 Free Consultants

Kroger Company, the large supermarket chain, believes so strongly in the value of the consumer's ideas that the company conducted nearly a quarter of a million in-depth interviews with shoppers in 1981. It even welcomes complaints. As Kroger's chairman told *Forbes:* "The fundamental strength of this company is in listening to what customers are telling us."

The beginning of the 1970s found deteriorating sales growth and profits. But consumer research has turned that around. Customers have talked and Kroger has listened—resulting in such adjustments as developing superstores for one-stop shopping, adding high-profit specialty departments such as delicatessens, flower shops, and cheese counters, designing pick-and-choose produce departments instead of plastic-wrapped fruit and vegetable packages, and offering around-the-clock store hours.

The thoroughness of Kroger's research efforts has uncovered some finer points as well. Consumers indicated that obtaining cooking tips from store clerks in the highly profitable produce department would enhance their buying—and thus

(Bill Grimes/Black Star)

raise Kroger's sales. So the company trained its assistants. To show the impact: In 1976 Kroger did not sell avocados; in 1981, it sold close to 12 million pounds. The market Kroger serves essentially was taught how to use them.

Being human, Kroger's management has missed the boat occasionally along the way. But customer complaints were loud and clear—and problems were quickly rectified. For example, due to high labor costs, bagger and carryout services were avoided. "We could excuse ourselves because we were an organized company and therefore paid high wages, so we couldn't afford to have baggers and sackers," said

the chairman. "Well, that's an excuse but not a very good reason. Today we provide the baggers and sackers that our customers expect. Working with our people and with the unions, we have gotten it done."

Listening to customers and solving problems apparently pay off. Kroger's earnings growth has shot upward and has been topped only by Supermarket General in recent years. And over the decade of the 1970s, the company's return on investment has more than doubled—to 17 percent.

Source of data: "250,000 Unpaid Consultants," *Forbes,* Sept. 14, 1981, pp. 147–148.

companies are systematically assessing the political and economic risks of investing abroad. While analysts, many of whom are political scientists and former Foreign Service officers, do not pretend to be seers, they reflect a corporation's concern for the nation's current governmental policies and the country's opposition to such issues as local ownership of foreign investments, price controls, seizure of profits, and currency devaluation. As a Black & Decker Manufacturing Company representative told *The Wall Street Journal,* "Our strategic evaluation of an area is incomplete unless we take some look at political risks."[1]

The solution of a problem is usually the result of searching for and sifting through raw information. If possible, marketers, like most human beings, avoid expending energy, time, and money to create an original solution to a problem. Instead, it is far more economical to avoid the problem, to locate someone who already has a satisfactory solution, or to find a published solution to the problem. This pragmatic approach has value, since the creation of new solutions when simple, obtainable solutions already exist would be a duplication of effort and resources. Marketers face many, varied problems, and efficient use of resources is crucial.

However, not all problems lend themselves to this practical approach. When a problem is novel, or when no one is available to help, the marketer must become the expert and discover the answer. Borg-Warner Chemicals, for instance, used a unique and innovative approach to solve a marketing problem by creating the rolling sales floor. The company found that it was having difficulty reaching its customers engineers and designers. None of the traditional marketing approaches was working. To remedy this problem, Borg-Warner outfitted several tractor-trailer trucks with displays of its plastic products and sent them around the country to major manufacturing plants. During lunch hours, the vans were open to engineers and others who influence buying, and salespeople were available to answer questions. The result was that Borg-Warner created an awareness of its plastic products among people who influence what companies buy.

The Decision-Making Process

Decision making is closely related to problem solving, but a distinction should be made between the two. Whereas problem solving deals with searching for an answer, decision making actually *stops* further consideration of possible solutions and makes a commitment to one specific alternative. Problem solving involves a chain of further problems, or subproblems, each of which leads to new alternative courses of action. Likewise, each decision typically leads to another subproblem and the need for additional decisions. The process can be seen as a series of subproblems and resulting decisions. When Coca-Cola Company decided to add plastic bottles to its product line, for instance, some obvious subproblems came into play—such as where to buy the plastic needed and how to promote plastic bottles to consumers, who over the

---

[1]"More Firms Are Hiring Own Political Analysts to Limit Risks Abroad," *The Wall Street Journal,* March 30, 1981, p. 1.

years had become accustomed to glass bottles and metal cans for soft drinks. Thus, one decision led to the need for additional decisions.

Decisions are made at a number of points during the problem-solving process. For example, decisions are needed about goals and objectives, about the data needed for analysis, and about which alternative to choose as a possible solution to the problem. However, when we think of managerial decision making, we are usually referring to the initial determination of goals or objectives and to the selection of a general strategy for reaching these goals.

The decision-making process is undertaken by individuals, small groups, and large organizations. Sometimes scores of people try to solve a problem before a decision can be reached. For instance, when General Motors seeks raw materials, hundreds of people may be involved in the purchasing process, and their concerns utlimately affect decisions. Engineers, production managers, automobile designers, and purchasing agents all influence specifications, approvals, and other activities. Even so, our primary concern here is with individual marketing managers as decision makers. What guides their work in making decisions, and how do they reach solutions to marketing problems?

A Model of Decision Making

Numerous scholars have attempted to determine what mental process actually results in a decision. Essentially, a decision maker can be seen as a ''black box'' into which information flows and out of which a decision flows. Much of what goes on between the input and the output stages is unknown (hence the term *black box*) and is a subject of controversy. But great strides have been made in correctly identifying this decision-making procedure.

Figure 3-1 is a general model of what goes on inside the black box; it represents an individual's decision-making process. Basically, the first step is formulating the objectives that the decision must meet. Then criteria are determined so that the

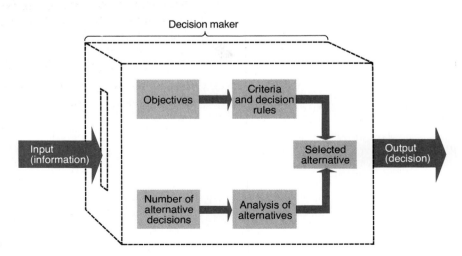

Figure 3-1   Inside the black box: the decision-making process.

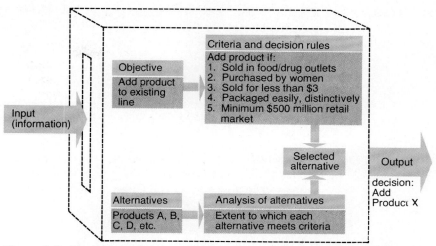

Figure 3-2   Decision making: a marketing example—Hanes Corporation.

decision maker can judge whether the perceived alternative courses of action satisfy the objectives. This provides *decision rules,* the guidelines for making a choice. Various alternatives are noted and considered by the decision maker, and each is analyzed with an eye toward predicting its outcome. The predicted outcome is then weighed against the established criteria, and one alternative is selected for action. To give more meaning to this conceptual approach, we'll consider a real marketing example.

In the early 1970s, Hanes Corporation revolutionized the panty-hose market by distributing its L'eggs panty hose through food markets and drugstores. While its problem solving and decision making resulted in a resounding success, sales began peaking and Hanes began to search for new products to add future growth to their revenues. As shown in Figure 3-2, the company used a set of criteria against which to measure and judge new ventures. The company will add a new product if (1) it can be sold through food and drug outlets; (2) it will be purchased primarily by women; (3) it will sell for less than $3; (4) it can be packaged easily and distinctively; and (5) it will comprise at least a $500 million retail market not already dominated by other major producers.

After considerable searching, Hanes, in the late 1970s, entered the highly competitive $1.6 billion cosmetics market with its line of L'erin cosmetics. Although cosmetics did not fit into Hanes' manufacturing capabilities, the product met their decision criteria in the following ways:

The cosmetics could be sold from open displays that appeal to impulse shoppers. Hanes would want the displays placed near checkout counters.

The packaging could be distinctive from that of any other cosmetic brand on the supermarket shelves. Each cosmetic item would be packaged in a burgundy-colored box with small plastic windows. (See Figure 3-3.)

Hanes' own sales force could stock displays and keep them in good order. This would provide Hanes with control at the retail level.

The cosmetic line could be distributed through supermarkets, drugstores, and discount stores. Thus, Hanes could piggyback on its existing L'eggs distribution system.

The market was not dominated by any competitors. In 1977, only Maybelline (Schering-Plough Corporation) and Cover Girl (Noxell Corporation) had any market share—while giants Avon and Chesebrough-Pond's had not entered the competitive fray.

Types of Decisions

In considering these models of the decision-making process, we must distinguish between two types of decisions: programmed and unprogrammed. In the computer field, the term *program* refers to a series of instructions that, when followed exactly, will lead to an automatic solution of an assignment or task. *Programmed decisions* are routine and repetitious and can be used for situations in which the problem is not new. Examples are found within the clerical area, such as filling orders, checking credit, and allocating costs. *Unprogrammed decisions* are unstructured decisions and can be used for situations that involve complex new problems. Such decisions are often of major importance, and usually they involve a large commitment of time, money, and effort. Decisions about new products or an advertising appeal fall into this category.

Within an organization, top management's main concern is with unprogrammed decisions, while first-level management (clerical staff and salespeople, for instance) is generally concerned with programmed decisions. Middle managers such as those making decisions about brand introduction and advertising campaigns concentrate on both programmed decisions and unprogrammed decisions.

A programmed decision lends itself to the decision-making process outlined above in situations where rules can be developed to allow quick, easy, and virtually automatic decisions. But we also must realize that the decision-making process is often much more complicated than the simplified picture presented in Figures 3-1 and 3-2.

Marketers as Problem Solvers and Decision Makers

The performance of the marketing function, then, can be viewed as being concerned essentially with problem solving and decision making. This occurs throughout the three sequential stages of strategic planning, implementing, and controlling.

As we entered the 1980s, the process of *strategic planning* became a key activity

Figure 3-3 While cosmetics does not fit into Hanes' traditional manufacturing setup, the L'Erin line fits their decision criteria perfectly. *(Randy Matusow)*

within marketing organizations. Throughout the 1970s, the environment became more and more difficult to predict; marketers grew more concerned with their greater failures to meet their own objectives. Clearly, environmental changes create problems for marketers. And strategic planning, by viewing the total marketing environment, anticipating changes in this environment, and then developing plans or strategies to cope with these changes, is a major problem-solving approach employed by marketers. As they make decisions about which strategies to undertake, at least some of their problems are solved.

NLT Corporation, a financial holding company with significant interests in insurance, undertook an in-depth strategic plan in 1980. The result was that NLT was able to identify clearly the many diverse markets within the insurance industry and the markets which best matched the capabilities of its insurance companies.

It was determined that the three NLT insurance companies would concentrate in definite, well-defined, demographic markets. For instance, National Life and Accident Insurance Company now concentrates in the lower- to middle-income markets; its life policies are offered in face amounts of $10,000 to $25,000. Great Southern Life Insurance Company, meanwhile, offers life policies to the upper-middle to the upper-income market; and Guardsman Life Insurance Company provides coverage for certain types of risk. Simultaneously with the implementation of the plan, NLT created NLT Marketing Services Corporation, which offers the policies of the three companies to the insurance brokerage industry.

It was also determined that the investment function of the three life insurance companies would be shifted from the individual companies to the parent NLT. "This enables the insurance companies to concentrate on marketing and provides us with a consistent investment strategy which is conducted by one department," said Russell L. Wagner, chairman of NLT.

Marketing *implementation* is the carrying out of marketing decisions made to enact the strategies and to solve marketing problems. In Chapter 2 we referred to these decision areas as the marketing mix, which is made up of the 4 P's (product, price, place, and promotion). These decision areas are the means by which marketers match wants and needs and stimulate demand; these are the tactical decisions of marketing.

During the *controlling* stage, results are compared with desired objectives. This process reveals deviations between expected and actual outcomes, and it is closely allied to problem solving. The control aspect of marketing uncovers problems that must be recognized and dealt with. Only then can marketers sort and evaluate solutions and select one for action.

Marketing, then, can be characterized as consisting of problem solving and decision making. Marketing problems abound, and their solution requires decisions. Furthermore, marketing decisions are among the most crucial made in business, for they determine the firm's environment, they affect its image, and they have a critical influence on its sales and profits. Even more important, though, is the tremendous impact that marketing decisions have on the solution of society's problems.

Marketing Decision Making and Information

Probably the most significant recent change in the business environment is the recognition that information gathering is crucial. And since the primary function of marketing is to assess want-satisfying opportunities and match resources to them, the knowledge which flows from information is extremely important for marketing.

Today, the need for efficient management of information is greater than ever—especially in marketing, which virtually charts the entire course of a business firm. Thus, information is the foundation and major source for the problem solving and decision making that marketing executives confront daily. But to grasp the nature of information fully, we need to distinguish between information and data.

The Nature of Information and Data

The dictionary defines *information* as "knowledge acquired in any manner."[2] Information is related intimately to the acquisition and transmission of meaning. In most cases, the transfer of information results in some sort of reaction on the part of the receiver. That is, information *affects behavior.* The receiver's behavior may be observable (such as movement or speech) or unobservable (such as remembering the information or changing an attitude because of it). At the very least, however, some sort of mental activity takes place when information is transmitted.

Because information affects behavior, a useful distinction can be drawn between it and *data,* which can be described as bits and pieces of fact. Data usually take the form of recorded observations, and they do *not* affect behavior. Data may *become* information, but only when they take on meaning for an individual and consequently affect behavior.

In short, data are *potential* information. When meaning is given to them, they become information. To illustrate this difference, consider the job of news reporters. They gather data from various sources—people, studies, and observations. Then they assemble these data (give them meaning) and write a story that communicates information to the readers.

Marketers do much the same thing. First they gather data from numerous sources; then they assemble and analyze the data to obtain information that can lead to decisions and, ultimately, the solution to a problem.

For example, Procter & Gamble phones or visits some 1.5 million people a year in conjunction with about a thousand research projects. People are questioned extensively about their likes and dislikes about P&G products, including their names, packaging, and product features. This is all in addition to P&G's basic research into

---

[2]*Webster's New World Dictionary of the American Language,* College Edition, World Publishing Company, New York, 1972, p. 749.

how people go about washing clothes, doing dishes, making meals, and performing other household tasks. Having generated this mountain of data, the marketers make sense out of the numbers and conversations and funnel the information monthly to every major segment of the company—including the board room. There it is sifted and resifted for implications on P&G marketing, advertising, and research and development operations.

Information, then, is the vital input to effective decision making and problem solving in marketing. Yet, while information is so important to marketers, we must note the following complaints that come from marketing managers.[3]

1 There is too much marketing information of the wrong kind.

2 There is not enough marketing information of the right kind.

3 Marketing information is so dispersed throughout the company that usually a great effort must be made to locate simple facts.

4 Important marketing information is sometimes suppressed by subordinates if they believe it will reflect unfavorably on their performance.

5 Important information often arrives too late to be useful.

6 Information often arrives in a form that leaves no idea of its accuracy, and there is no one to turn to for confirmation.

In short, the basic reality is that most companies have not adapted to the intensified information requirements necessary for effective competition in our contemporary economy. Yet, as markets expand from local and national to international, as buyers' *wants* become more the focus than buyers' *needs,* and as marketers shift from price to nonprice competition, the need for effective information management becomes all the more critical. The challenge of today's marketers is more to manage an *overabundance* of information than to manage the search for more and different sources. (See Application 3-2.)

Sources of Marketing Information

Marketers are exposed constantly to numerous sources of information, both on and off the job. (See Figure 3-4.) Some of these sources provide formal, written information, such as reports and computer printouts. Other sources are transient and less formal, sometimes providing information only through spoken words or gestures. But whatever its form and however it is obtained, all information pertinent to marketing decisions should be considered by marketers. Table 3-1 shows some frequently neglected informal sources of marketing information.

---

[3]Philip Kotler, *Marketing Management: Planning, Analysis, and Control,* 4th ed., Prentice-Hall, Inc., Englewood Cliffs, N.J., 1980, p. 601.

Application 3-2
Helping Marketers Cope with the Deluge of Information—"Just Push the Button"

(Catherine Ursillo/Photo Researchers)

"So much material is being printed that it's impossible to keep up with it," an information service representative told *Fortune.* "Either you have to put the data in a form in which they can be made useful, or else there is no need to keep printing so much."

It wasn't too long ago that a retailer who planned a new store had to sort through mounds of printed data or act largely on gut instincts. Not anymore. Since the computer age has arrived for even the general masses, a retailer who wants to open a store at a specific address can simply subscribe to an on-line vendor service which specializes in providing data to subscribers.

The on-line vendor buys raw data and then loads the data onto its own systems after reorganizing them to conform to the computer software being used. The vendor is then ready to market his or her data. Customers, many with their own terminals, are connected to the data base via telephone or through a special data communications network.

With the simple typing of a zip code, the computer will instantly provide the retailer with a complete demographic breakdown of a neighborhood—its population, home values, family income, education levels, and even the number of cars and appliances per household. These important data, which have been around for years but were not readily accessible unless a person had vast resources of time, money, and employees, are now available virtually instantaneously.

What once took marketers perhaps months and months to gather now can be on hand within minutes with the touch of a button.

Source of data: "Everything You Always Wanted to Know May Soon Be On Line," *Fortune,* May 5, 1980, pp. 226–240.

There are formal sources of marketing information as well. We use the word *formal* here to differentiate certain information sources which follow rigid procedures in securing information. For instance, both the marketing research department and the marketing information system (our next subject for discussion) supply information, but only after a set procedure has been followed, beginning with a specific request for information. Information from the coffee shop, periodical reading, and the like does not follow any set procedure. In addition, formal information sources emphasize analysis. As was pointed out earlier, data have no meaning until they are transformed into information.

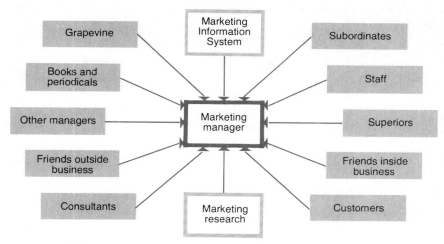

Figure 3-4   Sources of marketing information.

TABLE 3-1	Some Often-Missed Informal Sources of Information
Source	*Application*
Government patent filings	Watching such data discloses potential technological advancement within a firm's industry.
Competitors' annual reports	In an attempt to enhance stockholders' image of the firm, the annual report may express a new technology in research and development.
Competitors' employment ads	Such ads may suggest the technical and marketing directions of a competitor.
Professional associations and meetings	The competitor's products, research and development, and management philosophy are often disclosed in displays, brochures, scientific papers, and speeches.
Various governmental agencies	Under the 1966 Freedom of Information Act, many federal agencies must openly provide requested documents, files, or other records of a federal agency, such as Federal Drug Administration's inspection reports of competitors' plants, competitors' cost data in a competitive bid, and reports filed with the Federal Trade Commission to support advertising claims.

For more such sources, see David B. Montgomery and Charles B. Weinberg, ''Toward Strategic Intelligence Systems,'' *Journal of Marketing*, vol. 43, no. 4 (Fall 1979), pp. 41–52.

Application 3-3
The Sales Force as an Information Source—
"Filling the Products Gap"

At Minnesota Mining & Manufacturing Company, or 3M, as it is more widely called, continual new-product innovation has been the key to corporate success. In fact, so intent on new products is the company that its corporate edict is to derive 25 percent of sales in a given year from products that did not exist 5 years before. From its very beginning to the present, the company has counted on the sales force as a source for new-product ideas.

The company began almost by accident just after the turn of the century when several investors defaulted on the purchase of a mine that was found to have a low-grade abrasive useful only in making ordinary sandpaper. The creditors figured the only way to survive was to market offshoots that had higher value added. "The salesmen would go from smokestack to smokestack knocking on doors," the company chairman told *Fortune*. "But they didn't stop at the purchasing agent's office. They went into the back shop to talk . . . and see what was needed that nobody else was making."

When the sales force saw that workers in automobile factories were choking on the dust produced by dry sandpaper, 3M developed a sandpaper that could be used wet. When auto workers painting new two-tone cars had trouble keeping the colors from running together, 3M invented masking tape.

Shortly after World War II, a group of Cleveland doctors came to St. Paul with the need for a tape that would reduce infection. While the original concept did not work, a research team did develop a tape that resisted allergic reactions; later, the team developed a surgical drape to be used in surgery to form a barrier between the surgeon's incision and possible germs in the environment.

While in the operating room, in a manner of speaking, 3M salespeople looked to see what else doctors might need. As a result of their observations, 3M came up with Steri-Strip, a tape for closing incisions, and disposable surgical staplers that replace sutures in holding an incision closed.

The strategy at 3M has been to find the product areas overlooked by other firms and to fill the gaps. Being so close to the customer, the 3M sales force is in an excellent position for locating these gaps and diagnosing the needs of the marketplace. The salespeople report their findings to headquarters and the company manufactures needed products. And 3M has pretty well lived up to its "25 percent of sales from new products" goal. At last count, 3M makes more than 40,000 products—from tape to electrical outlets to artificial hips to traffic lights.

This method of marketing research is, of course, critical and necessary in any business, but 3M has made it a near science.

Source of data: "The Lures and Limits of Innovation," *Fortune,* Oct. 20, 1980, pp. 84–94.

Information can itself be combined in different ways to provide even better information. Eastman Kodak uses market information in a variety of ways. Every week, sales personnel receive a computer printout that tells them not only how many units of each product they sold the previous week but also the size of the dealer that bought it. Such information is useful to salespeople. At the same time that the field staff is receiving printouts about sales activities, the marketers are studying similar

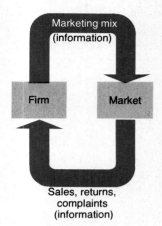

Figure 3-5 The flow of information between market and firm.

printouts that combine all staff reports. This information helps to identify problems with products as well as with sales personnel. Thus, the printouts provide product and sales information that marketers can use in making decisions. (See Application 3-3.)

To further underscore the value of this kind of formal marketing information, we will look at one particular conceptualization of the marketing process. (See Figure 3-5.) In this view, a firm exists to serve a market. This service is performed by means of an interaction between the firm and the market; the goal is the mutual satisfaction of each. Their interaction can be seen as a flow of information. (The product communicates form utility; distribution communicates time and place utility; price communicates perceived value; and promotion is by nature a communicative process.) In return, the market transmits information to the firm—in the form of sales, returns, and complaints—about its satisfaction with the marketing mix. Marketers must analyze this information and use it in making marketing decisions. None of the informal information sources provides enough of this essential feedback, nor are they as reliable as formal sources in meeting the needs of modern marketing managers. (See Application 3-4.)

Application 3-4
Marketers and Informal Information Sources— "Keeping an Eye Out, as well as an Ear"

Gaining customer feedback on product quality and service goes far beyond formal surveys and sophisticated statistical research. Often the most valuable feedback is gathered by firsthand observation by corporate executives and employees. Many companies periodically dispatch top executives into the field with instructions to remain anonymous and mingle with customers.

Some of the companies that do this are United Airlines, Southern Airways, and Montgomery Ward, and all cite positive examples of the practice. Coffee is now hotter on Southern's flights because an executive found his was lukewarm when served; United provides better flight information because an executive overheard passengers complaining; and customers at Montgomery Ward are paying less for some items because the chairman of the parent company, Marcor, went shopping in a K mart store. The chairman found, much to his surprise and dismay, many old-time employees of Montgomery Ward also shopping there. He examined their shopping bags and noted that the prices were less than Montgomery Ward's. As a result, he ordered that prices be reduced.

And McDonald's executives eat at company outlets frequently—and with impact. When Ray Kroc, McDonald's founder and chairman, stopped at a New England franchise, he found a sign requesting people to move to the "next position" at the counter. Soon afterward, a McDonald's policy statement was issued. All stores were instructed to take down such signs "because it's up to us to move to the customer, not them to us."

Source of data: "Top Executives Keep Tabs on the Consumer—Or Contend They Do," *The Wall Street Journal,* July 1, 1976, p. 10.

Marketing Information System (MIS)

The recognition that successful marketing requires useful information has given rise to the design and implementation of what is called a *marketing information system* (MIS): "a set of procedures and methods for regular, planned collection, analysis, and presentation of information for use in making marketing decisions."[4] While an MIS often uses a computer, that is not a requirement. What *is* necessary is the *planned, orderly,* and *continuous* collection, analysis, and presentation of the *right information* for marketing decisions. Thus an employee armed with a file cabinet or a library with its reference sources can be considered a marketing information system.

The concept of an MIS can be used by all marketers—not only a Procter & Gamble or an American Airlines but also a local grocery store or a small restaurant. The purpose of an MIS is to provide information needed for decisions so that reliance on intuition can be reduced. The point is that marketers must recognize the need for information and must make an effort to ensure that the information will be obtained and used.

Four Subsystems of the MIS

The MIS bridges the gap between marketers and their environment. As we noted in Chapter 2, marketers are confined by the uncontrollable environmental variables. But information about these constraining variables can be used to make effective decisions. Figure 3-6 shows that the MIS consists of four subsystems for gathering, processing, and utilizing data: (1) the internal accounting system, (2) the marketing intelligence system, (3) the marketing management science system, and (4) marketing research.

Internal Accounting System

The function of the *internal accounting system* is to supply marketers with measures of current activity and performance—sales, costs, cash flows, and accounts receivable and payable. An internal accounting system focuses primarily on meeting the demands of the business community for accurate profit and loss reports, as well as on preparing information for controlling all business activities. However, marketers can also glean useful data from the internal accounting system. The data may not be as complete as desired, but—in combination with other data—they may result in useful marketing information. While the accounting department possesses and provides much information that is suitable for marketing, many informational needs of marketers are unique. Thus, accounting information may have to be adapted to fit marketers' needs.

---

[4]Donald F. Cox and Robert E. Good, "How to Build a Marketing Information System," *Harvard Business Review,* vol. 45, no. 3 (May–June 1967), p. 145.

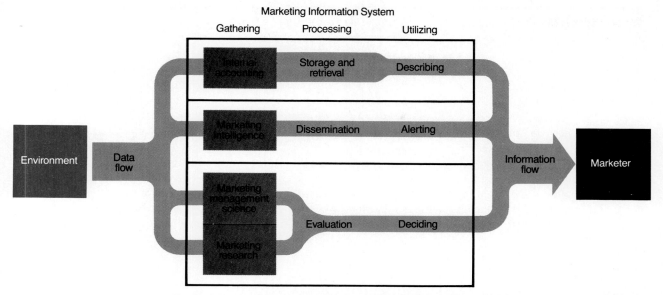

Figure 3-6 **The four subsystems of the marketing information system.** *(Adapted from Philip Kotler,* **Marketing Management: Analysis, Planning, and Control,** *4th ed., Prentice-Hall, Englewood Cliffs, N.J., 1980, p. 603)*

Marketing Intelligence System

The second subsystem of an MIS is the *marketing intelligence system,* a set of procedures that monitors developments in the market and circulates this information to the proper executives. Many companies assign personnel to comb periodicals and journals and relay pertinent information to appropriate managers. In addition, some companies use their sales force to record competitive information and channel it to decision makers. Without such an intelligence system, useful information about such things as competitive new products and customer dissatisfaction will almost certainly not reach the right people. Many marketers even purchase and analyze competitors' products in order to improve their own. (Application 3-5 discusses the intelligence systems in some major firms.)

Marketing Management Science System

The third subsystem of an MIS is the *marketing management science system,* which assists marketers in solving complex problems through the use of advanced quantitative (statistical) methods. The objective of this activity is to find the best solution to a problem through the employment of mathematics and analytical techniques. Although many companies do not have such systems, some of the larger firms are using them more and more.

Application 3-5
Marketing Intelligence—"Corporate Intrigue"

Corporations, like countries, have been gathering information about one another for years. While many companies are apt to call their "spying" marketing research or commercial analysis, these efforts have become more and more sophisticated—especially in highly competitive industries such as computers and semiconductors.

International Business Machines will not talk about its commercial analysis department—regarded by many as the model of corporate intelligence operations. Yet it is known that much of its information comes from the thousands of branch office representatives who keep close tabs on and report on competitors' installations. Such information is primarily used to identify areas that require marketing attention or to spot gaps in IBM's product line.

Texas Instruments, former

employees point out, keeps "fairly formal" files on competitors and even had one employee analyze government contracts to learn the technological strengths of competitors. And employees of New York's Chase Manhattan Bank open accounts at competing banks and feed back information to their management on how other banks service accounts.

In the high-technology field of semiconductors, it has become common practice for competitors to dive on new products and have them "reverse-engineered," stripped down to analyze how they work and possibly to learn a few things to improve performance in their own present and future products. Mostek Corporation's 16K memory chip, introduced in 1976, has been copied by Texas Instruments, Fairchild Camera & Instrument, and, in Europe, by International Telephone & Telegraph. Copies of

chips by Intel and Mostek have been found as far away as the Soviet Union and Japan.

Yet, in most companies, the process of intelligence is more informal. Information from trade publications, industry associations, and scientific meetings is combined with news from many other sources. "It's up to each product manager to keep up with what the competition is doing," says the vice president of Mostek Corporation. "Personnel looks at what kinds of engineers they're hiring. You start seeing aggressive quotations for parts. We talk about these things every Monday at staff meetings."

Sources of data: "Business Sharpens Its Spying Techniques," *Business Week,* Aug. 4, 1975, p. 60; "How 'Silicon Spies' Get Away with Copying," *Business Week,* April 21, 1980, pp. 180–188; and "Semiconductor Firms Are Plagued by Thefts of 'Hi-Tech' Materials," *The Wall Street Journal,* April 28, 1981, p. 1.

Marketing Research   The final subsystem of an MIS is *marketing research.* In Chapter 4 we will examine the research process at greater length, but here we must note how it differs from an MIS. Marketing information systems and marketing research differ in a number of ways. First, marketing research generally focuses on one particular problem at a time. Information is collected for the sole purpose of solving that problem. In contrast, an MIS continuously collects and stores data relevant to many and varied marketing problems and decisions. As problems arise, this information can be retrieved and used for making decisions. And sometimes more important, the MIS provides information that alerts marketers to future problems. In this sense, the MIS functions as a "crisis preventer" as well as a "crisis solver." In short, an MIS is used to uncover and solve potential and existing problems, while marketing research usually focuses on solving a single problem.

Another difference between marketing research and the MIS arises from how data are collected. In most instances, data for marketing research come from external sources, such as consumers, competitors, and the government. The MIS, however, relies heavily on data that are generated within the firm. Much of the original data in the MIS are gathered from sources outside the firm, but they remain raw (in the strict sense of the term) until combined or analyzed in some meaningful manner. Then the information is presented to decision makers. In many cases, the information that is compiled through marketing research is stored in the MIS.

Thus, the four subsystems of the MIS—internal accounting, marketing intelligence, marketing management science, and marketing research—provide for the gathering, processing, and utilization of data.

Evolution of the MIS

In recent years, computers have assumed a major role in the MIS but their use in marketing—as in other business functions—did not occur overnight.

As we noted in our discussion of programmed and unprogrammed decisions, certain tasks, because of their systematic nature, are especially suited to computer technology. Inventory tasks are a good example. Sales reports are also developed more easily by a computer than by marketers. Many kinds of computer-based reports are useful to managers and are issued regularly—for example, sales recorded by personnel, sales recorded by territory, inventory levels, and competitive activity. Additionally, computers give marketers the opportunity to request special reports that meet specific needs. Marketing executives determine which reports will be issued, since the reports are developed to facilitate decision making. But companies often provide so many reports that the data are never transformed into information; that is, marketers simply do not have the time needed to read and digest all the data that a computer can make available.

Over a period of time, in many companies, the computer-based MIS is upgraded to what is called an *interactive system,* one which allows marketers to communicate directly with the system. In this way, special needs can be handled almost immediately. A marketer can sit down at a teletype or a televisionlike cathode ray tube (CRT), type out instructions, and receive answers almost instantly.

Components of the MIS

An MIS brings marketers closer to the marketing environment. The environment provides the data. The MIS transforms the data into information that marketing managers can use to make decisions. Most modern information systems rely heavily on the use of a computer to store and process information. But how does an MIS work? What goes on inside that computer?

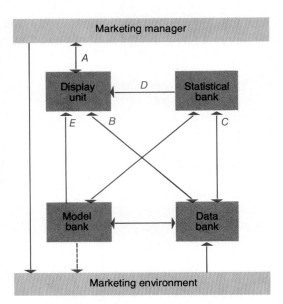

Figure 3-7 Components of a computer-based MIS. [*Adapted from David B. Montgomery and Glen L. Urban, "Marketing Decision-Information Systems: An Emerging View," Journal of Marketing Research, vol. 7, no. 2 (May 1970), p. 227*]

Figure 3-7 is a good example of a computer-based system. It is made up of four components: a display unit, a data bank, a statistical bank, and a model bank. The *display unit* is the means by which a user communicates with the system; it may involve a card reader and printer, a teletype, or a CRT. The *data bank* houses the raw data to be analyzed. The *statistical bank* is a collection of procedures used in analyzing the data. These procedures may involve simply adding or subtracting numbers, or they may be much more complex techniques, such as multivariate statistical and mathematical programming procedures. The *model bank* has within it mathematical representations of the marketing environment. These models can show relationships among various marketing mixes within the computer to see what might happen before actually implementing the mix in the marketplace. The better the model, of course, the better the prediction of the outcome.

Using the MIS

How do marketers use an MIS? Well, suppose the marketers at Procter & Gamble wanted to know how Tide detergent sold in Minneapolis during January 1982. They might very well sit down at a CRT and type instructions to the computer, which would go directly to the data bank and retrieve the data and then display it (see arrows *A* and *B* in Figure 3-7). Or the marketers might ask for Tide sales in both Minneapolis and St. Paul for January 1982. The computer would go to the data bank and retrieve sales for both cities, then go to the statistical bank (arrow *C*) and pull out a program that would add the two sales figures together, and then display the total sales on the screen (arrow *D*).

Perhaps the marketers want to test various marketing programs before making a final decision. In this case, they would type in appropriate data for various marketing mixes—say, $2 million for prime-time television advertising, a price of $1.19 for the detergent, and the inclusion of a 10-cents-off coupon in each box. The computer would go to the model bank (arrow *E*) and enter those figures into the mathematical model, which would determine and display information about sales, unit volume, market share, profit, and return on investment. This marketing mix could be compared with alternative mixes to determine which one appears most likely to produce desired results.

These three uses of the MIS could be refined in various ways. But the system basically revolves around the computer, which processes and presents data that are helpful in making marketing decisions. In doing this job, the MIS should perform the following six functions:

1 *Assembly*—searching for and gathering marketing data

2 *Processing*—editing, tabulating, and summarizing data

3 *Analysis*—computing percentages and ratios, combining sales and cost data, and various other mathematical tasks

4 *Storage and retrieval*—indexing, filing, and locating data

5 *Evaluation*—determining the quality (accuracy) of information

6 *Dissemination*—routing useful information to appropriate decision makers

The four components of the MIS perform these functions and thus support the marketing decision process. The model bank determines which information will be assembled and processed. The techniques stored in the statistical bank are used to analyze and evaluate data. And the data bank stores, retrieves, and disseminates the actual information through use of the display unit.

Fitting the MIS into the Marketing Decision Process

Marketing is primarily a decision-making job, and it is the marketing managers who are the decision makers. They develop plans for the marketing program, and they carry out those plans in the marketplace. But it is the MIS that helps the marketers to perform their decision-making function. Figure 3-8 shows how marketers and the MIS relate.

Suppose, for instance, that the product manager at Wrigley's decides to test a new package design for spearmint gum for the next 6 months in Seattle, Washington. Within a short time, Wrigley's will get data about whether consumers liked the package. But the marketplace is affected by other influences, too, such as competition, inflation, and consumers' tastes. Data about the market's reactions to this new

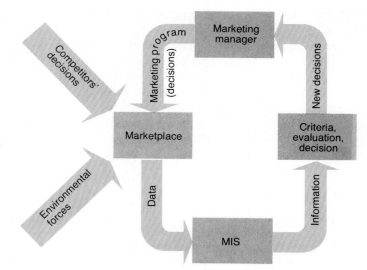

**Figure 3-8
Decision making and the
MIS. The MIS, a key
component in the
feedback activity of an
organization, provides
the information base for
decisions that result in
better bundles of
satisfaction being
delivered to the market.**

package and price are relayed to the company and become input for the MIS. To determine whether the new package adds to the bundle of satisfaction, the marketers turn to the information system to evaluate the test-market results. Sales figures for the old packaging in other cities are gathered, as are sales for the new package in Seattle. The marketers then receive this and other information from the MIS, analyze it, and evaluate their decision.

Note that the marketers' decisions are based on an evaluation of how the available alternatives compare with the objectives set for the product. The MIS simply provides the input for the decision-making process. All this activity leads to yet another decision—either to continue with the new packaging or to choose an alternative strategy. The end result is the generation of a new decision, which is implemented in the marketplace; then the process begins all over again.

Again, marketing can be seen as a series of decisions, and marketers are the decision makers. But a well-designed MIS plays an important role in the decision-making process by providing information to the marketers. The MIS gives marketers the information base on which to build decisions—and this is usually far more effective than guessing or relying on intuition. (See Application 3-6.)

Looking Back

In Chapters 1 and 2, we viewed the business firm and marketing in broad terms. We saw that a firm performs a number of business functions and that marketing holds a prominent position within an organization. A firm was looked upon as basically a

Application 3-6
Real World Marketing Information Systems—
From the Simple to the Sublime

The earlier a company spots a sales weakness, the faster it can move to remedy what could develop into a full-blown debacle. To help, Eastman Kodak has developed an MIS. The company sends out weekly computer printouts to all its field sales staff. These printouts tell the sales force how hundreds of products are selling in their sales territories—providing sales increases and decreases for each product. Thus a product category that is slipping in a certain area receives immediate attention from the Kodak representative or the supervisor. The printouts are also useful to the company in measuring the effectiveness of advertising and of sales promotions. Perhaps Kodak will try a certain sales display in one region and another display in another. Differences in purchase patterns can then be spotted.

Another company which formally monitors sales is R. J. Reynolds. Nightly, forty or more part-time workers enter the Reynolds building and spend the next few hours calling wholesalers across the country and obtaining the number of cartons of cigarettes sold that day. Overnight, a report is prepared on each brand and how it fared that day across the country. The next morning, each executive has on his or her desk an up-to-date sales report. Any weakness can instantly be tended to.

The Coca-Cola Company utilizes a worldwide information system. Coca-Cola executives around the world can tie by telephone into a central computer located in Cleveland and store and access the data they need. In addition, within Coca-Cola U.S.A.'s Marketing Intelligence Center, microfilm is being pushed as a data storage vehicle. Over one-half million frames can be stored in a single drawer. Any document can be located on film in a minute or two, and, if desired, a hard copy can be made. In addition, with the use of microfiche, one can obtain a postcard-sized duplicate (containing as many as seventy-two pages of data) which never has to be returned. Simple, cheap readers are utilized for reading documents.

problem-solving unit in which managers continuously face problems that require solutions.

In this chapter, we viewed the problem-solving process as a series of decisions that result from the process itself. The effectiveness of this process revolves around information. Marketing managers are exposed to many and varied sources of information. Two sources—marketing research and the MIS—stand out as formal means for transmitting information to marketers. Their relationship to other topics in this chapter is depicted in Figure 3-9. Note in this model that the two formal information sources are separated from the informal ones. But informal sources can also provide data for the MIS and for marketing research. As the arrows show, both internal and external information sources enter the MIS while only external information is used in marketing research.

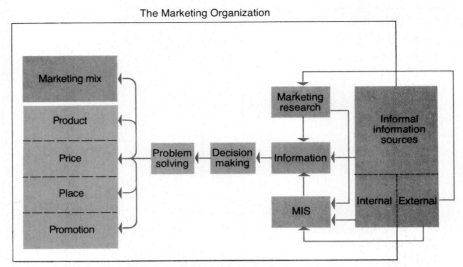

The Marketing Organization

Figure 3-9   Marketing and its information environment.

The place and importance of the MIS can thus be seen both within the context of a business and within the field of marketing. An effective MIS is a good first step toward the efficient operation of the marketing function and, consequently, of the entire firm. In Chapter 4, we will explore the second formal information source—marketing research. But first, let's review the following important points:

1   Marketing is essentially a problem-solving and decision-making process.

2   Problem solving is the process of searching for a solution to a problem; decision making is the choosing of an alternative solution.

3   Unprogrammed decisions are more difficult to make than programmed decisions.

4   The quantity of information surrounding marketers is exploding, and the flow of information has not yet been controlled.

5   Information is the vital input to effective decision making.

6   Formal sources of information are usually more effective than informal sources because they rely on analysis rather than intuition.

7   An MIS emphasizes the planned, orderly, and continuous collection, analysis, and presentation of the right information for marketing decisions.

8 An MIS does not require a computer, though computer technology has greatly expanded the uses of an MIS.

9 Accounting information and marketing research are parts of the MIS.

10 The MIS should perform six functions: assembly, processing, analysis, storage and retrieval, evaluation, and dissemination.

11 The MIS is used for planning the marketing mix as well as for controlling it.

Key Terms

If you aren't sure what each of the following words means, look back at the text. Numbers refer to pages on which the words are defined. Additional information can be found by checking the index and the glossary at the end of the book.

problem solving 73
decision making 75
decision rules 77
programmed decisions 78
unprogrammed decisions 78

information 80
data 80
formal information 81
informal information 81
marketing information system 86
interactive system 89

Questions for Review

1 Is marketing intertwined with problem solving *or* decision making? Explain.

2 How do data and information differ?

3 Should informal sources of marketing information be considered by marketers in the decision-making process?

4 What is the basic purpose of a marketing information system?

5 Cite the two major differences between marketing information systems and marketing research.

6 What role does an MIS play in the decision-making process?

Questions for Thought and Discussion

1 Having drunk drivers on the road creates problems for society. Viewing the government as a marketer, solving this social problem in turn creates problems and ultimately forces marketing decisions. What types of marketing problems would the government face?

2 What are some of the programmed and unprogrammed decisions that you believe the Hanes Corporation would have to make in developing a line of cosmetics?

3 What are some sources of information that Hanes Corporation would likely use in making a decision to add the L'erin line of cosmetics to its line of panty hose?

4 If a marketing organization decided that it wanted to begin to build a formal marketing information system, what should be the first step in its construction?

Suggested Project

Visit a local retailer and explore the programmed decisions made by that marketer.

Suggested Reading

Adler, Lee: "Systems Approach to Marketing," *Harvard Business Review,* vol. 45, no. 3 (May–June 1967), pp. 105–118. This classic article integrates decision-making information systems and research needs of marketing.

Hershey, Robert: "Commercial Intelligence on a Shoestring," *Harvard Business Review,* vol. 58, no. 5 (September–October 1980), pp. 22–48. Small companies are shown how to apply numerous monitoring techniques to keep tabs on their competitors.

Little, John D. C.: "Decision Support Systems for Marketing Managers," *Journal of Marketing,* vol. 43, no. 3 (Summer 1979), pp. 9–26. This article defines and illustrates the concept of a marketing decision support system and shows its effects on problem solving and marketing practice.

Montgomery, David B., and Charles B. Weinberg: "Toward Strategic Intelligence Systems," *Journal of Marketing,* vol. 43, no. 4 (Fall 1979), pp. 41–52. After presenting an overview of strategic intelligence systems, the authors discuss the collection, analysis, and processing of strategic intelligence.

Robertson, Dan H.: "Sales Force Feedback on Competitors' Activities," *Journal of Marketing,* vol. 38, no. 2 (April 1974), pp. 69–71. This study shows some of the weaknesses of sales-force feedback and suggests its implications for marketing management.

Rosenberg, Larry J., and Priscilla A. LaBarbera: "How Marketing Can Better Understand Consumers," *MSU Business Topics,* vol. 28, no. 4 (Winter 1980), pp. 29–36. The authors contend that conventional sources of information are becoming insufficient as consumers grow more sophisticated and demanding in judgments about products and firms.

Rummel, R. J., and David A. Heenan: "How Multinationals Analyze Political Risk," *Harvard Business Review,* vol. 56, no. 1 (January–February 1978), pp. 67–76. The authors demonstrate an approach to combining insight and wisdom with management science to evaluate a foreign investment.

Schewe, Charles D.: *Marketing Information Systems: Selected Readings,* American Marketing Association, Chicago, 1976. This collection of the major readings on marketing information systems stresses the benefits and design of such systems.

Chapter 4

Marketing Research

Looking Ahead

Chapter 3 described marketers as decision makers who must secure the best possible information in order to manage the controllable variables and solve their marketing problems. We saw that information is the key to successful decision making and problem solving. We also examined the marketing information system (MIS), a formal source of information that has become increasingly important to marketing managers. In this chapter, we will look at the other formal source of information for decision making: marketing research.

Key Topics

The nature of the marketing research process

The types of research that most marketers conduct

The importance in marketing research of defining the problem

The steps in the marketing research process

How data are collected, processed, and analyzed

The importance of eliminating error from the research process

Chapter Outline

Overview of the Marketing Research Process

So far, we have explored the general nature of marketing by examining its place within society and the firm (Chapter 1) and by describing its managerial activities (Chapter 2). Basically, the task of marketing is one of making decisions regarding the controllable variables. We saw that the key to this decision-making process is information (Chapter 3). Marketers who secure accurate, relevant information can make more effective decisions than those who use poor information or simple guesswork.

In Chapter 3, we noted many informal sources of information that are available to marketers and examined one formal source—the marketing information system (MIS). Now we are ready to focus on marketing research, the other formal information source. Chapter 3 outlined some of the main differences between the MIS and marketing research. Let's review them briefly. First, the MIS deals with a continuous flow of information for planning and control purposes, while marketing research is usually employed for a "one-shot," specific purpose. Second, the MIS is concerned with preventing problems, whereas marketing research is oriented toward solving problems. (In a way, the MIS aims at fire prevention, while marketing research is a fire-fighting tool.) Third, the MIS uses both internal and external sources of information, while marketing research tends to use sources outside the organization. Finally, marketing research is one of four elements *within* the MIS (look again at Figure 3-6); that is, information obtained through marketing research is often stored in the MIS for later use.

With these main differences in mind, we can move toward an understanding of how marketing research is used to meet marketers' needs for information.

The Nature of Marketing Research

Marketing research is usually associated with the survey process. The types of problems that marketing research helps to solve often require the use of a questionnaire to secure information. In examining marketing research, then, we will emphasize the survey process and the problems it raises for marketers. We can begin with a definition: *Marketing research* is a systematic, objective approach to the development and provision of information for marketing decision making.

Note that this definition emphasizes four elements.

1 The collection and provision of information by marketing research is *systematic;* it is a planned, well-organized process.

2 The method of obtaining information is *objective;* the information is not biased by the interviewer or by the interviewing process.

3 You'll recall from Chapter 3 that data are pieces of information; it is through the research process that data take on meaning and become *information.*

4 Information is gathered through marketing research for a purpose; it is used by marketers to make accurate *decisions.*

Marketing research, then, is systematic and objective. It provides information that marketers can use to make effective decisions. But what kinds of decisions and what types of marketing research are appropriate to these decisions?

Table 4-1 shows the results of a 1978 study conducted by the American Marketing Association to determine the kinds of research companies are engaged in. As the table shows, a very high percentage of the companies questioned were involved in "sales and market research," particularly in determining the characteristics of the market and in measuring market potentials. Many companies were also engaged in "business economics and corporate research," especially in regard to the study of business trends, and over 80 percent of the companies conducted short-range forecasting, with almost as many involved in long-range forecasting. A large

TABLE 4-1 Types of Research Activities Conducted by 798 Respondent Companies

	Companies doing research, %	Done by marketing research dept., %	Done by another dept., %	Done by outside firm, %
Advertising Research				
Motivation research	48	28	3	17
Copy research	49	22	6	21
Media research	61	24	11	26
Studies of ad effectiveness	67	38	5	24
Business Economics and Corporate Research				
Short-range forecasting (up to 1 year)	85	52	31	2
Long-range forecasting (over 1 year)	82	50	30	2
Studies of business trends	86	61	21	4
Pricing studies	81	36	44	1
Plant and warehouse location studies	71	30	38	3
Acquisition studies	69	29	38	2
Export and international studies	51	24	25	2
MIS (management information system)	72	26	44	2
Operations research	60	17	42	1
Internal company employees	65	18	41	6

(continued)

	Companies doing research, %	Done by marketing research dept., %	Done by another dept., %	Done by outside firm, %
Corporate Responsibility Research				
Consumers' "right to know" studies	26	11	12	3
Ecological impact studies	33	5	25	3
Studies of legal constraints on advertising and promotion	51	12	34	5
Social values and policies studies	40	18	17	5
Product Research				
New-product acceptance and potential	84	71	7	5
Competitive product studies	85	71	9	5
Testing of existing products	75	49	20	6
Packaging research: design or physical characteristics	60	36	16	8
Sales and Market Research				
Measurement of market potentials	93	82	7	4
Market share analysis	92	80	9	3
Determination of market characteristics	93	83	6	4
Sales analysis	89	64	24	1
Establishment of sales quotas, territories	75	27	48	—
Distribution channel studies	69	31	37	1
Test markets, store audits	54	38	9	7
Consumer panel operations	50	32	5	13
Sales compensation studies	60	14	43	3
Promotional studies of premiums, coupons, sampling, deals, etc.	52	34	15	3

*The total of the percentages "done by market research department," "done by other departments," and "done by outside firm" is greater than "companies doing research" because some firms have studies done by both inside departments and outside firms.
Source: D. W. Twedt (ed.), *1978 Survey of Marketing Research,* American Marketing Association, Chicago, 1978.

percentage of the companies also were involved in "product research," with the majority engaged in studies of competitive products. On the other hand, far fewer companies conducted "corporate responsibility research," particularly in regard to consumers' "right to know" studies. Another interesting highlight of this AMA study is the fact that most companies used their own research departments to gather the information needed. Outside research firms were involved primarily in studies of media, advertising effectiveness, and, to a lesser extent, motivation.

The usage of marketing research grew substantially throughout the 1970s. The AMA study found that 34 percent of the reporting companies who had formal market research reported that their research departments had been formed in the past 5 years. Moreover, the use of marketing research had spread to many not-for-profit organizations: political parties, candidates, and government agencies such as the Federal Trade Commission. (See Application 4-1 for an example of how marketing research worked on a college campus.) And services were expanding their use of research. In 1970, for instance, marketing research was rare among financial service companies. The 1978 AMA study found 71 percent of those businesses engaging in research, accounting for 13 percent of all market research activities. Even movie studios now widely use research. While in the past few years, it has been used primarily for comparative testing of advertising materials, it has been creeping into the evaluation of movie concepts, casting options, and postproduction editing as well.

From the rapid growth of marketing research, we can see that there is very little which does not interest marketers and, therefore, their researchers. The variables of marketing are such that all information has the potential to help marketers solve their problems through effective decisions. The information that is collected through research must be accurate, however, if it is to be useful. What can marketers do to keep errors from creeping into their research process?

Eliminating Error: The Scientific Approach

It is essential that marketing managers understand the research process. They must have a grasp of the pitfalls and problems that researchers face in order to evaluate the research effectively. Marketers receive an enormous amount of research information; in using it, they must be sure it is as "error-free" as is humanly possible. In fact, obtaining *accurate* information is the major goal of the research process. Marketing researchers constantly strive to eliminate the errors that can creep into their work. The purpose of the research process is to reach conclusions and to make recommendations that the marketing manager can use in solving a problem. Obviously, if the researchers err in collecting information and in drawing conclusions, the marketing manager is likely to be given incomplete or inaccurate information. As a result, he or she may make the wrong decision.

To avoid this situation, marketing researchers attempt to apply the scientific method in conducting their assignments. That is, they emphasize *objectivity* and *accuracy* in collecting information to solve a problem. And the stronger their emphasis is, the better their information will be. Beginning chemistry students know that by combining 2 parts hydrogen with 1 part oxygen they will get water. This process can be repeated again and again, and the result is always water. Unfortunately, though, applying the scientific method with such confidence to marketing research is not

Application 4-1
Marketing Research for a Service—
"Profitably Applying Research at a Not-For-Profit Institution"

Without a business school, a small, staid Northfield, Minnesota, liberal arts college has been showing quite sophisticated marketing techniques—and setting itself apart from most other schools. Its wrinkle—marketing research!

In the mid-1970s, student entry applications to Carleton decreased from about 1600 a year in the late 1960s to 1400 or so annually. This decline forced Carleton to accept a greater proportion of applicants—peaking at 82 percent in 1975 from a low of 40 to 50 percent in the 1960s. School officials began worrying about the academic reputation of the school.

In 1978, Carleton began mailing questionnaires to students who planned to enroll or who were interested in the college. The responses revealed that prospective students thought the location in southeastern Minnesota was cold and isolated, that Carleton's atmosphere was too

(Courtesy Carleton College)

cerebral and didn't leave time for socializing, and that the library was too small.

To counter this image, Carleton undertook the following marketing activities within its recruiting materials sent to high school students:

Instead of avoiding mentioning Minnesota winters, its brochures showed a photograph of cross-country skiers and indicated that bundling up "makes even the coldest days bearable and most days comfortable."

New literature stressed that Carleton is just a 50-minute bus ride from Minneapolis-St. Paul, and that, while the academic demands are steep, there's plenty of time for having fun.

Photographs of the library showed the rear of the four-story library—whereas earlier brochures showed the front side where only two stories were visible.

The results:

In 1980, applications rose to about 1850 from 1470 in 1977. The response rate to its mailings increased from 5.9 percent in 1978 to more than 14 percent.

Source of data: "College Learns to Use Fine Art of Marketing," *The Wall Street Journal,* Feb. 23, 1981, p. 25.

possible. A marketer has to deal with human beings, and they are not so predictable as chemical elements, nor can they be manipulated so easily or observed so closely. The fact that a person is being observed can affect his or her behavior. Thus, marketing researchers often find it difficult to apply a purely scientific method in their work. Even so, they can reduce the chance of error by emphasizing objectivity and accuracy when they collect data. This is the goal at which the scientific method aims.

Research Stages: Exploratory and Conclusive

Before we examine the specific steps in conducting marketing research, we must recognize two stages in the research process—the exploratory stage and the conclusive stage. In the *exploratory stage,* the marketing manager discusses and outlines the problem with the researchers. They make a preliminary investigation of the problem by defining it carefully and reviewing the alternative solutions available. The main objective of exploratory research is to gather as much information as possible about the problem—with minimal costs and delay. During the exploratory stage, marketers and researchers truly "explore" the limits and solutions to their problem.

Once the researchers decide that enough information has been gathered to define the problem properly, the *conclusive stage* of research can begin. At this point, the research objectives are developed and stated so the researchers know what kind of information is needed. They are now able to develop a plan for collecting information that will help the marketers reach a decision and solve the problem. Conducting conclusive research can be a very expensive and time-consuming process. As a result, this stage may be bypassed if the problem at hand is not important enough to justify the cost, or if the information gathered in the exploratory stage meets the needs of the marketing manager.

Steps in the Research Process

Now that we have a general view of the nature and types of marketing research, we can look more closely at how it is actually performed. The research process may be divided into the following seven steps:

1 Formulate the problem.

2 Determine information needs and sources.

3 Design the questionnaire.

4 Design the sample.

5 Collect the data.

6 Process and analyze the data.

7 Reporting the information.

The rest of this chapter examines each of these steps in detail.

1 Formulate the Problem

The most important—and most difficult—task in the research process is formulating the problem. If researchers do not know what the problem facing the marketing decision maker is, the research process cannot be conducted correctly. Many times, marketers have only a vague notion of what their problems are, but researchers need to work with a concrete definition of the problem. This definition will guide the conduct of the entire research process.

Defining the Problem

A marketing research organization was approached by Spalding, the sporting goods company, to conduct a survey. A marketing research consultant was asked to learn what people thought of Spalding tennis rackets and whether the endorsements of tennis stars made any difference to potential buyers. But, when the researcher met with marketers from Spalding to determine why the company wanted to investigate these areas, he found the manager's superior had suggested doing "some kind of study." At first, the marketers were concerned only with Spalding's tennis rackets. But the problem formulation session showed the marketers that they had to consider competitors' rackets, too. The session also made them realize that the same questions should be asked about their tennis balls. (See Figure 4-1.)

Problem formulation and definition require that the marketing manager explain the specific situation which surrounds a given request for information. After this in-depth analysis, the problem can be clearly defined and specific objectives can be set for the research.

Figure 4-1 Product endorsements by celebrities such as tennis star Tracy Austin, pictured here, are widely used by companies. Do celebrity endorsements affect your opinion of products? *(Courtesy of ProServ, Inc.)*

**Setting
Objectives**

When the marketer and the researcher have defined the problem, the marketer must determine the objectives of the research project. Such goals should be stated in precise terms. Moreover, they should be goals that the researcher can meet and the objectives should be stated so that specific action can be taken. In the Spalding survey, for example, the team of researchers and managers determined the following set of specific objectives for its study of how consumers evaluate tennis equipment:

1 To determine the product characteristics that consumers use in evaluating tennis rackets and balls for possible purchase

2 To determine the relative importance of each characteristic in the purchase of tennis rackets and balls

3 To determine the influence that endorsements have on the purchase of tennis rackets and balls

As the research progresses, each objective will be broken down into specific goals with target dates for their completion.

When a research project was begun at the House of Seagram, the vice president of marketing first requested "a survey of the U.S. wine market." After considerable discussion, the research team determined and stated four more precise objectives: (1) to uncover specific consumer groups as targets of advertising; (2) to learn the Seagram brand image vis-à-vis the images of competitor brands; (3) to develop an advertising strategy; and (4) to determine the appropriate media for the campaign. As the firm's market researcher told *Marketing News:*[1]

It's fundamental, but I think we would have not done anybody involved any favor if we had just done a survey when we were asked to do a survey. It is up to the marketing and research people involved to, up front, build action intentions or objectives into the research.

2   Determine Information Needs and Sources

Once the problem is formulated by defining it and setting research objectives, the second step in the research process is to determine (1) the information that is needed and (2) the sources of such information.

**Information
Needs**

The research objectives can be used to identify which specific sets of information are needed. For instance, to reach objective 1 of the Spalding example, the researcher would have to know the various characteristics that consumers might consider in

---

[1]"Action-Oriented Research Spells Success for New Seagram Wine," *Marketing News,* vol. 16, no. 14 (Jan. 9, 1981), p. 7.

choosing a tennis racket (such as grip, weight, string tension, color) and tennis balls (bounce, weight, color, durability, and so on). Similarly, to reach objective 3, the researcher would have to know whether buyers actually identify Tracy Austin as the endorser of Spalding tennis rackets and Jimmy Connors as the endorser of Wilson rackets. Furthermore, objective 3 requires information about the relationship between an endorsement and price: Does the endorsement of a tennis racket lead consumers to expect a higher price, or higher quality, or neither? These are the kinds of information needed that flow from research objectives.

After determining objectives and some of the information needs, the researchers then do further exploratory research to understand more fully the nature of the problem and identify information needs. In effect, they talk with anyone who might shed light on the problem. In the Spalding project, the researcher talked with the managers of sporting goods stores, with tennis pros, and with tennis players at public courts. By asking what caused people to choose one racket over another and how they saw the role of the endorser, the researcher better understood the buying process and learned more about what information should be sought. For example, tennis pros pointed out that advanced players are concerned with the stiffness of the racket's frame. Without talking to such people, the need to focus on this product characteristic might not have emerged. This vital step is overlooked too often, but the perspective of individual users of a product can provide important insight into a research problem and its information needs.

Secondary Sources

Marketing researchers sometimes forget that an incredible amount of information is collected and published regularly by existing sources both inside and outside the organization. Such information collected for another purpose, and already available, is referred to as a *secondary source.* Such secondary sources also should be combed by the researcher. For instance, a company's own sales records for the past few years may yield valuable data. Outside the company, researchers should look for reports that are obtained easily from industrial associations or the government. For the Spalding project, the National Sporting Goods Association provided data about the tennis industry that offered more information on the problem areas (though it did not satisfy the specific research objectives). Marketers can also purchase data from professional research companies such as A. C. Nielsen, Market Research Corporation of America, Audits and Surveys, and Brand Rating Index (see the chapter appendix). Professional research companies regularly collect data (about television audiences, shelf space for food products, and so on) and sell their findings to marketers for their use. (See the chapter appendix for information about selected secondary sources.)

However, in using information published by secondary sources—helpful though it may be—researchers must ask four questions:

1 Is it *relevant?* Some secondary sources may not provide the exact information desired, or it may have to be adapted to fit the researchers' needs.

2   Is it *obsolete?* Reports can become outdated quickly, and what was true yesterday may be completely untrue today.

3   Is it *accurate?* Some secondary sources are more careful than others in preparing, analyzing, and reporting data; researchers must be able to appraise the methods of the source they are using.

4   Is it *credible?* Again, researchers have to evaluate the source they are using in order to determine whether the information was collected in a reliable way and was reported honestly.

After tapping all useful secondary sources and talking with as many concerned people as possible, the researcher should review the objectives and determine whether it is necessary to revise them. All research activities up to this point have been exploratory. Now a specific and final set of objectives can be stated, and the researcher can decide whether or not conclusive research should be conducted. As noted earlier, it's possible (though unusual) that the secondary sources can provide enough information to solve the problem at hand satisfactorily; if so, no further research is necessary, and no further costs are incurred.

3   Design the Questionnaire

If researchers decide there is not enough information at hand to solve the problem, and if the problem is worth the extra costs in time and money, they may themselves collect data for their specific purpose. The collection of such *primary data* requires researchers to develop an overall plan for conducting the remainder of the research project.

Types of Research Methods

The Observational Approach

There are three main types of research methods: the observational approach, the experimental approach, and the questionnaire (survey) approach.

Using the *observational approach,* researchers simply observe and record behavior; that is, they watch and take notes regarding behavior. For example, if the research objective is to determine which brand of tennis racket is most attractive to consumers, researchers may merely observe and count the number of times each brand is picked out of a store's display. However, an obvious problem with this approach is that it doesn't tell researchers what people are thinking and feeling, or what their motives are. People may be picking a racket because of its brand, its visual impact, or its location in the display. If the research objective requires motivational information, the observational method is not practical.

With some types of research problems, observation is very effective. Toy companies, for example, often employ the observational method in determining whether to market products. For instance, Fisher-Price, one of the leaders in toys for preschool children, runs an on-site nursery school where designers observe children through one-way mirrors. Observers watch the children and toys for such things as general interest, safety features, and ease of play. The true test for a toy is its "play value," whether the child plays with a new toy for a few minutes and then goes back to his or her old favorites or whether the new toy is sufficiently fascinating and interesting to use over and over. At Kenner Toys in Cincinnati, a new toy is mixed in with older toys to see whether the child picks it out and plays with it. (See Application 4-2.)

The Experimental Approach

Another method of collecting marketing information is that of controlled experiments. Here the researcher makes changes with a test group or groups (usually consumers) with respect to a variable of interest (say, amount or type of advertising). The results, then, are compared with those of a control group that did not receive the change in order to determine the effect of the change. While such experiments are commonplace in the physical sciences, they are much more difficult to conduct properly when

Application 4-2
Observational Method—"I've Got Your Number"

(Ray Ellis/Photo Researchers, Inc.)

Data sources are often so available that they are overlooked. Now, from the obvious comes perhaps one of the most reliable sources available. Two Detroit companies, Urban Science Applications and R. L. Polk, are employing license plates as a research technique.

Urban Science researchers collect a sample of license-plate numbers from shopping center parking lots. Then the license numbers are fed into a computer and paired with auto registration information maintained by Polk, a directory publisher. This procedure produces a map that shows customers' homes by census tracts of ZIP codes.

By adding other demographic data, the maps assist developers, retailers, fast-food operations, and banks pick new locations. This technique is being tried by General Motors dealers to aid in determining billboard locations, what local advertising media to use, and where to prospect for customers. License research also showed Taubman Co., a shopping center developer, which shoppers were being missed. A direct-mail campaign to these shoppers increased sales by 40 percent in one year at a San Francisco area center.

License-plate surveys cost $5,000 to $25,000. Those who use them say they're less expensive, quicker, and more reliable than such traditional research methods as interviews with shoppers or analysis of credit card records.

Source of data: "License Plates Locate Customers," *The Wall Street Journal*, Feb. 5, 1981, p. 23.

Application 4-3
An Experimental Approach—
"Electronics Make a Laboratory out of a Supermarket"

The supermarket scanner which identifies products by optically reading the bar code printed on each item has the potential of being a revolutionary method for detecting buying behavior in supermarkets.

Information Resources Inc. is one of the first companies to attempt to harness this research tool. The company has invested $2 million in scanning equipment and provided it free to fifteen supermarkets in two carefully chosen towns—Marion, Indiana, and Pittsfield, Massachusetts. These two cities are perfect test markets because of their demographics—the makeup of their populations. IRI created a service called Behaviorscan which used 4000 households in Marion and Pittsfield. Identification cards were sent to each household to be used at the grocery store every

time items were purchased. The card alerted the point-of-sale terminal to relay an item-by-item record of the customer's purchase to IRI's computer. Another research method used by IRI involved the cable television systems in each of the test markets. A "black box" was installed on the TV set in each test household so that certain commercials could be sent to target families on a house-by-house basis. This technique allowed the researchers to try out different TV spots on selected households and compare the buying reactions. "We can send Duncan Hines cake mix commercials to only Betty Crocker customers and then find out if they switch," the research firm's president told *Business Week*.

In one test, researchers wanted to test the effectiveness of

a product sample for a children's food product as an alternative or an accompaniment to TV advertising. It divided its test households into four equal groups and varied the combinations of samples and advertising that each group received. In all the groups receiving samples, sales doubled during the 4-week period samples were distributed. But the group that was also exposed to TV commercials was more loyal to the product in the weeks following.

"It's the closest thing to a controlled laboratory that has ever come along," said a grocery products client. "We can experiment with new precision the impact of our promotional programs for existing products."

Source of data: "Market Research by Scanner," *Business Week*, May 5, 1980, pp. 113–116.

working with human subjects. People are less amenable to control than beakers of chemicals. For this reason, experimentation is less frequently used in marketing research.

The major use of the experimental method has been in test markets. Here, cities found to be representative of the national population are subjected to some variation in the marketing mix—some cities, for example, get a product with a new improvement, others do not. All other marketing activities are conducted similarly in both test and control cities. The differences in sales are compared and attributed to the one marketing difference between the two cities. (See Application 4-3.)

The Questionnaire (Survey) Approach

When researchers require information of a personal nature—such as consumers' feelings, attitudes, and motivations—they turn to the *questionnaire,* or *survey, approach.* There are three types of surveys: the personal interview, the telephone interview, and the mail survey. Each method has different benefits and costs.

The *personal interview* is the most expensive survey method because researchers must hire, train, and supervise interviewers to go out and talk with respondents. But

---

1–3

Number _____

Name _____

Address _____

4–5

Phone _____

Sex

(1) Male _____

(2) Female _____

6

Hello. Is this _____? My name is _____ and I'm from the University of _____ .

We are hoping to be of benefit to you through a study we are making of your theater preferences and those of other representative people in _____ like yourself.

Would you help me by taking about 10 minutes to answer some questions? Thank you.

7

1 Did you attend any stage productions in the last year?

(1) Yes (Go to #2) _____

(2) No (Go to #3) _____

8

(3) Don't know (Go to #3) _____

2 How often did you attend stage productions in the last year?

(1) 1 or 2 times _____   (2) 3 to 5 times _____

9

                  (3) 6 or more times _____

35

3 Please tell me, is there anything you don't like about going to the theater in _____ which keeps you from going more often?

_____

_____

_____

4 Do you now go more often, less often, or about as often as you did 3 or 4 years ago?

(1) More often _____

(2) Less often _____

(3) Same _____

5 If "more" or "less" often, why do you go more (less) often?

_____

_____

_____

_____

_____

9

6 How about movies? Do you now go more often, less often, or about as often as you did 3 or 4 years ago?

(1) More often _____

(2) Less often _____

10

(3) Same _____

Figure 4-2   Sample telephone questionnaire. Numbers along the left column reflect the coding system used by the researcher.

this method is also the most flexible, because questions can be phrased and rephrased to ensure that the needed information is obtained. The questionnaire used in a personal interview can be longer than that used for mail and telephone surveys, since this face-to-face situation makes it difficult for people to cut the interview short. We are basically social animals, and few people will run the risk of insulting an interviewer by saying, "Look, I don't want to talk with you any longer."

The *telephone interview* is the fastest of the survey methods. (Figure 4-2 shows a sample telephone questionnaire.) Within a short time, and for a flat rate, interviewers can call many people and get immediate answers to complete their questionnaire. However, it is relatively easy to hang up on a telephone interviewer. In addition, not everyone has a phone, and some of those who do have unlisted numbers. These factors may bias the survey results.

The *mail survey* is the least flexible data collection approach because its questionnaire has to contain a set of specific questions that must be standardized. (See Figure 4-3.) It provides no opportunity for the researchers to clarify the questions. In

Figure 4-3   Sample mail questionnaire.

Section VI—Media Usage

As an aid to knowing more about you and your likes and dislikes, we would like you to answer the following questions about some of your reading, listening, and viewing habits. "X" the appropriate line.

1   I read a newspaper

Every day	_____1	Rarely	_____4
Just Sundays	_____2	Never	_____5
Almost every day	_____3		

2   When I read the newspaper, I read the following sections:

	Never	Occasion- ally	Fre- quently	Always
a) News (national & international)	_____1	_____2	_____3	_____4
b) News (local)	_____1	_____2	_____3	_____4
c) Sports	_____1	_____2	_____3	_____4
d) Comics	_____1	_____2	_____3	_____4
e) Women's pages	_____1	_____2	_____3	_____4
f) Business financial	_____1	_____2	_____3	_____4
g) TV/Amusements	_____1	_____2	_____3	_____4

3   Please check those magazines which a member of your household receives regularly. (You can "X" more than one.)

a) Time ___	h) Ladies Home Journal ___	o) Business Week ___
b) Newsweek ___	i) Holiday ___	p) Motor Trend ___
c) U.S. News & World Report ___	j) Leisure Time ___	q) True ___
d) Sports Illustrated ___	k) New Yorker ___	r) Outdoor Life ___
e) Reader's Digest ___	l) Playboy ___	s) National Geographic ___
f) TV Guide ___	m) Redbook ___	t) Esquire ___
g) Cosmopolitan ___	n) House and Garden	

4   On weekdays, I usually listen to the radio   Less than 1 hour _____1
1–2 hours _____2   3–4 hours _____3   5–10 hours _____4
More than 10 hours _____5

addition, the response rate for mail surveys is typically low. Often less than 50 percent of the public respond to mail surveys,[2] and researchers have to guess whether the nonrespondents would respond similarly. Thus, it is easy to get biased results. Another problem with mail surveys is that researchers cannot really specify who will answer the questionnaire. The responses of a specific type of person may be sought—say, the male head of the household—and the questionnaire may state as much. But it's possible that one of the children will fill out the questionnaire, and researchers have no way of knowing this.

These three survey methods each have their own problems and benefits. In deciding which approach to use, researchers must determine what their information needs are, as specified by their research objectives. When they have selected the survey method that will be most useful in solving their problem, they can design the questionnaire.

Principles of Questionnaire Design

Designing a questionnaire is far from being a science; the creativity of the researchers is often involved. Basically, researchers want to obtain the information they need, and they want it to be accurate. Fortunately, there are some definite principles to follow in developing a successful questionnaire.

Designing the Questions

First, *only necessary questions* should be asked. It is self-defeating to present a respondent with more questions than necessary. Researchers should use as few questions as possible to satisfy their information needs. In designing a question, they should ask: "What are we going to do with this information? Is it really needed? Do we have to have it in order to meet our objectives?" If the information will not be used, the question should not be asked.

After deciding what questions to ask, researchers should make the questionnaire as *easy* to *answer* as possible. The use of checklists is more convenient than asking people to write out long answers. And researchers should avoid asking personal questions that involve exact figures for income or ages. People are more likely to respond to such things when they can check boxes that reflect ranges. Researchers also must be careful to use simple words that can be understood easily. After all, the point of the questionnaire is to get answers, not to test vocabulary levels.

In asking questions, researchers must *be specific* and avoid such generalizations as "On the whole, do you think . . . ?" Leading questions also should be avoided. For instance, if respondents are asked a series of questions about a specific brand of coffee and then are asked to name the best-known brand, they are likely to choose the one they have just been questioned about, since it's the one that's on their minds. Such questions can hardly result in accurate information.

Ordering the Questions

After deciding what to ask and how to ask it, researchers must choose an order in which to ask the questions. In using a questionnaire, they are after three main types of information. First, of course, is the *basic information* needed to reach the research

---

[2]Fred N. Kerlinger, *Foundations of Behavioral Research,* 2d ed., Holt, New York, 1973, p. 414.

objectives. But researchers also want *classification data,* which place respondents into groups by such categories as age, sex, or occupation. Finally, they may want *identification information:* the respondent's name and address, for example.

Generally, researchers position the most important questions—those asking for basic data—first on the questionnaire. Then they ask the classification and identification questions. The reasoning is simple. Unless they get the basic information, the researchers have nothing. The most important thing to them is the basic information that satisfies their objectives. Even if a respondent cuts the interviewer off or only partially completes a questionnaire, the most important information has still been obtained and can often be used.

In developing the sequence of questions, researchers should lead off with those which will get the respondents' attention. The opening questions should be interesting. If respondents will be asked about the color of a product and its technical characteristics, the question about color should come first. This will draw respondents into the questionnaire; once they pass the first few questions, there is a greater tendency for them to finish. Difficult questions should be placed within the body of the questionnaire, not at the beginning. For example, if a complicated rating system is used—as in the Spalding study, which asked people to rate six different brands according to twelve different characteristics—it should not appear at the beginning of the questionnaire. (See Figure 4-4.) Rating the weight, size, and price of competing tennis rackets is difficult. Such questions should be "hidden" in the middle of the questionnaire.

Now consider *only those brands* with which you *definitely* have had some *experience. Rate* each of the brands that you have used in the last *12 months* with respect to the following features.

1 = extremely bad; 2 = mildly bad; 3 = neither good nor bad; 4 = mildly good;
5 = extremely good
CIRCLE one (1 2 3 4 5).

	Bancroft	Davis	Dunlop	Head	Spalding	Wilson
Balance of racquet	1 2 3 4 5	1 2 3 4 5	1 2 3 4 5	1 2 3 4 5	1 2 3 4 5	1 2 3 4 5
Weight	1 2 3 4 5	1 2 3 4 5	1 2 3 4 5	1 2 3 4 5	1 2 3 4 5	1 2 3 4 5
Texture of grip	1 2 3 4 5	1 2 3 4 5	1 2 3 4 5	1 2 3 4 5	1 2 3 4 5	1 2 3 4 5
Quality of manufacture	1 2 3 4 5	1 2 3 4 5	1 2 3 4 5	1 2 3 4 5	1 2 3 4 5	1 2 3 4 5
Size	1 2 3 4 5	1 2 3 4 5	1 2 3 4 5	1 2 3 4 5	1 2 3 4 5	1 2 3 4 5
Flexibility of racquet	1 2 3 4 5	1 2 3 4 5	1 2 3 4 5	1 2 3 4 5	1 2 3 4 5	1 2 3 4 5
Quality of strings	1 2 3 4 5	1 2 3 4 5	1 2 3 4 5	1 2 3 4 5	1 2 3 4 5	1 2 3 4 5
Price	1 2 3 4 5	1 2 3 4 5	1 2 3 4 5	1 2 3 4 5	1 2 3 4 5	1 2 3 4 5
Color	1 2 3 4 5	1 2 3 4 5	1 2 3 4 5	1 2 3 4 5	1 2 3 4 5	1 2 3 4 5
Durability	1 2 3 4 5	1 2 3 4 5	1 2 3 4 5	1 2 3 4 5	1 2 3 4 5	1 2 3 4 5
Power delivering capacity	1 2 3 4 5	1 2 3 4 5	1 2 3 4 5	1 2 3 4 5	1 2 3 4 5	1 2 3 4 5
Appearance	1 2 3 4 5	1 2 3 4 5	1 2 3 4 5	1 2 3 4 5	1 2 3 4 5	1 2 3 4 5

Figure 4-4   A complicated rating system.

Design of the Questionnaire

The next step is designing the physical aspects of the questionnaire. Particularly with mail surveys, the layout and readability of a questionnaire can greatly affect its success. However, the physical design should be consistent with the type of survey being conducted. The respondents to a telephone interview do not see the questionnaire, and only the interviewer can be affected by its design. But appearance is very important if respondents will actually see and handle the questionnaire. It must look attractive. Compare the formats of the questionnaire in Figures 4-2 and 4-3. Such things as typesetting, printing method, and paper stock are all important. So is the way the questions are arranged. They should not be jammed together, nor should the type be so small that the questionnaire is difficult to read.

Pretesting the Questionnaire

Before the questionnaire is distributed widely, the researchers must pretest it. This task involves finding people like the subjects who later will answer the questionnaire in greater numbers. The test group should go through each questionnaire item by item and explain to the researcher what each one means to them. Many hidden wording problems can be uncovered in this way. After the questionnaire has been pretested, it can be revised to eliminate potential problems. Consider a soup company wanting to find what soup flavors its market desires. It may design its questionnaire item to ask, "What kind of soup do you like?" Instead of naming beef barley or chicken noodle, respondents are likely to give answers such as (1) Mom's; (2) homemade; (3) hot; (4) any kind I don't have to make; (5) Jim's Diner's; and so on.

Techniques for Collecting Behavioral Data

As part of the questionnaire design process, researchers must decide which *questioning technique* to use. If they are seeking very simple information—such as whether the respondent is male or female—they can use a simple, direct question. But when they need to learn about human feelings, attitudes, opinions, intentions, or motivations, they may find that simple, direct questions will not secure the desired information. In that case, the researchers must use an indirect approach.

The indirect questioning techniques that are used in marketing research can be divided into two kinds: structured and unstructured. Figures 4-5 and 4-6 give examples of each technique.

Structured Techniques

Structured questions ask for brief, specific answers. They usually limit respondents to a specific set of replies (see Figure 4-5). Examples include multiple-choice questions and simple checklists with a question such as "Which of the following brands of detergent do you think clean well?" Structured questions are easier to administer than unstructured questions. They require less skilled interviewers, and the data they yield are more easily tabulated and compared.

Unstructured Techniques

Unstructured questions give respondents more freedom in framing their answers. They often place no limit on the length of responses, and they may not provide specific directions for replies. (See Figure 4-6.) Some unstructured questions are designed only to get respondents to talk about the subject of interest. In using such

Likert Scale	Semantic Differential	Word Association	Sentence Completion
Presents respondents with a number of provocative statements and asks them the extent to which they agree or disagree with each statement. Quantitatively measures respondents' attitudes toward different products, brands, and so on.	Determines the connotative meanings of words and the intensity of those meanings as perceived by respondents. A scale is inscribed between two bipolar words (such as *good/bad* and *hot/cold*); respondents select the point that represents the direction and intensity of their feelings. Identifies words with favorable or unfavorable connotations.	Respondents are given a list of words and are asked to match each word with one of their own choosing. Answers are usually timed. Provokes quick, unrestrained answers that reveal strongest attitudes. First answer is important.	Respondents are shown the first parts of incomplete sentences and are asked to complete them. Requires respondents to take a position or express an attitude. Provokes an unrestrained response; first answer is considered most revealing.

Example	*Example*	*Example*	*Example*
Following are a series of statements about tennis rackets. Please indicate the extent of your agreement or disagreement with each statement. Be sure to "X" one number for each statement.	Spalding Tennis Racket Durable X: _: _: _: _: _: _: Nondurable Bad _: _: _: _: _: X: _: Good Stylish _: _: _: X: _: _: _: Nonstylish Inexpensive _: _: _: _: X: _: _: Expensive	What is the first word that comes to mind when you hear the following? Spalding ——————— Pressureless tennis ball ——————— Tracy Austin ——————— Steel tennis racket ———————	1 When I purchase a can of tennis balls, the most important consideration in that decision is ——————— ——————— 2 If I were given a Spalding tennis racket as a gift, I would feel like ——————— ———————

Definitely disagree	Generally disagree	Moderately disagree
1	2	3

Moderately agree	Generally agree	Definitely agree
4	5	6

1 I spend a lot of time shopping for price when I buy a tennis racket. 1 2 3 4 5 6

2 I believe gut strings give better control than nylon strings. 1 2 3 4 5 6

3 No racket priced below $39.00 will last long. 1 2 3 4 5 6

Figure 4-5 Structured questioning techniques.

Story completion	Picture frustration	Thematic apperception tests (TAT)
An extension of the sentence-completion approach (Figure 4-4), but less structured. Respondents are given the beginning of a story and are asked to complete it. Details of the story may be vague to avoid influencing responses. In completing the story, respondents reveal concerns, preferences, attitudes, and other important aspects of purchasing behavior.	Respondents are asked to identify with cartoon characters by supplying dialogue that reflects their feelings about the situation pictured. Gets at deep-seated, subconscious feelings. Analysis requires well-trained, skillful interpreter.	An extension of the picture-frustration approach. Respondents are shown an even more ambiguous picture or series of pictures and are asked to explain the scene, tell what is happening, and describe the characters. Sometimes respondents are asked to make up a story about what is happening now and what may happen in the future. Reveals hidden feelings and suppressed desires. Requires a skilled technician to give the test, which must be interpreted by a psychologist.
Example	*Example*	*Example*
Last Tuesday, I ran into Jenny as I was heading towards the tennis court. She noticed that I didn't have my usual tennis racket and, looking closer, saw I had a new Spalding "Big Bow" racket. *Now you complete the story.*	*Fill in the empty balloon.* 	*Now make up a story about what these two people are doing. Make up any kind of story you want.* 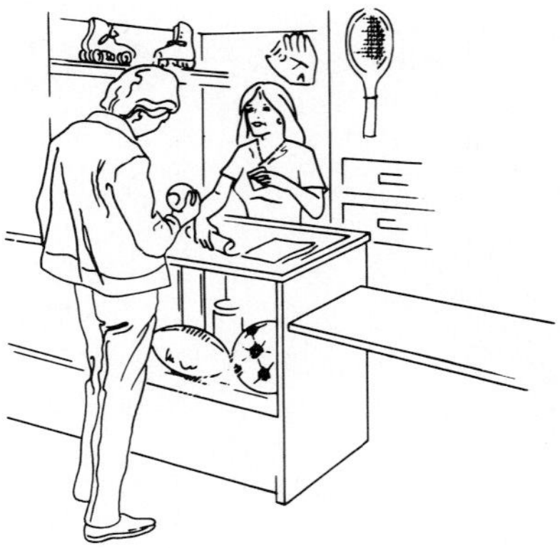

Figure 4-6 Unstructured questioning techniques.

questions, however, skilled questionnaire designers are required, and it is difficult to tabulate and compare the data.

In deciding what kind of questioning technique to use, researchers must examine their problem and the objectives of their research project. If they need to learn about the psychological aspects of respondents, then the techniques listed in Figures 4-5 and 4-6 will be useful. But if the research focuses on market description, the researchers usually can use simple, direct techniques such as checklists and multiple-choice questions.

4   Design the Sample

In settling the many questions relating to questionnaire design and construction, researchers must decide to whom the questionnaire will be directed. The choice of respondents may influence the type of questions asked, as well as the way they are asked. It usually is unrealistic and unnecessary to include *every* possible respondent in a survey. Instead, researchers select a *sample* of respondents who represent the entire population being surveyed. (A *population* includes all possible individuals who share the appropriate characteristic.) We are all familiar with the idea of sampling: The A. C. Nielsen Company asks a sample of the population about their TV viewing habits and then infers from the responses the TV tastes of the whole audience.

Marketing researchers use statistics to provide numerical descriptions of data. *Statistics* is a primary tool in marketing research because it turns raw data into information that is accessible for study. Statistics utilizes three distinct and important numbers: the mode, the median, and the mean. The *mode* is simply the most frequently occurring number. If you counted the number of cans of tennis balls sold in each of six brand categories, for example, the highest seller would be the mode. The *median* is the middle number. Like the grassy strip in the middle of a highway, the median divides a list of numbers in half: 50 percent are above the median, and 50 percent are below it. The *mean* is the sum of all the numbers divided by the number of scores. It is the term people usually refer to as the average. For example, if you wanted to know the mean (average) of a class test, you would simply add the total number of scores and then divide by the number of people who took the test. The researcher needs to consider the statistical measure that is most useful to the research. (See Table 4-2.)

The mean is used with the standard deviation (a measurement of how far away individual scores are from the mean) to make probability statements. Probability falls within the realm of inferential statistics, which simply means that researchers make statements about a population based on sample findings. Now, inferences from the sample to the population are valid only if the sample accurately reflects the population.

Sampling offers researchers a number of benefits that would be unavailable if the entire population were surveyed. In conducting personal interviews, for example, researchers can save both time and money through sampling, since fewer respondents are interviewed. The costs of printing questionnaires, training interviewers, and analyzing final data are thus reduced. Moreover, sampling can actually be *more accurate*. It is virtually impossible to interview an entire population—think about talking to all the tennis players in the United States—and respondents may change over that time.

While researchers can select a sample in many ways, there are two basic kinds of sampling procedures: (1) *probability sampling,* in which all members of a population have a known chance of being included in the sample; and (2) *nonprobability sampling,* in which respondents are selected in some part on the basis of researchers' judgment.

TABLE 4-2   An Example where the Mean, Median, and Mode Give Varying Results

Research on family size in a local suburb

Question:	How many children do you have?

1   2   3   4   5   6 or more

Results: (Population of 200 families)

1	2	3	4	5	6 or more
55	45	50	35	10	5

Mode: 1 child

Median: Between 2 and 3—50 percent have 2 or fewer and 50 percent have 3 or more

Mean:
$$55 \times 1 = 55$$
$$45 \times 2 = 90$$
$$50 \times 3 = 150$$
$$35 \times 4 = 140$$
$$10 \times 5 = 50$$
$$5 \times 6 = 30$$
$$515 \div 200 = 2.575 \text{ children per family}$$

Probability Sampling

In *probability sampling,* each member of the population has a known chance of being selected for the sample. This is done according to statistical rules that leave no room for judgment on the part of the researcher or interviewer. (Note that we said each member of the population has a *known* chance of being selected for the sample. This is not the same as having an *equal* chance. With a "known" chance, the researcher can at least calculate the probability of a certain person's being selected.)

The distinguishing feature of probability sampling is that, by using a chance mechanism to select population units for inclusion in the sample, researchers can use the mathematical theory of probability to determine the degree of sampling error in their data and thereby estimate the accuracy of the results. Probability sampling is complex. We will look at three probability techniques: simple random sampling, stratified random sampling, and area (cluster) sampling.

Simple Random Sampling

In this procedure, researchers begin with a complete list of all members of the population and then choose sample units in a random fashion. For example, the names of all population members might be written on cards and mixed thoroughly in a barrel. Researchers then choose sample units by pulling names without looking. This gives every population member not only a known but also an *equal* chance of being chosen for the sample.

Stratified Random Sampling	In this technique, the total population is divided into subgroups, or strata, each of which then is treated like a simple random sample. This approach is often followed when certain subgroups of the population have very high or very low values concerning the topic being measured. For instance, suppose the research objective is to determine the average amount of time spent playing tennis. Those who have higher incomes than the general tennis-playing population are more likely to play year-round and do so indoors. Thus, to ensure that the sample does not reflect too many year-round players, the researchers might divide all players into groups, depending on income or indoor-club membership. They then could use simple random sampling to select members from each of the strata.
Area (Cluster) Sampling	In many cases, it is difficult to secure a precise list of the total population, but data about specific geographic areas are easy to obtain from the United States Census Bureau. Everyone lives somewhere. As long as researchers begin with blocks or geographical territories that place people in a definite way, census information can be used to select a random sample. The sample, then, is chosen simply by taking a random sample of the geographical areas on the list.
Nonprobability Sampling	In *nonprobability sampling,* the selection of population members to be included in the sample is based in some part on the judgment of researchers. There is no known chance of any particular segment's being selected from the population. Therefore, researchers cannot calculate the sampling error and have no way of knowing how accurate their estimates are. Nonprobability sampling is used where probability sampling is not possible; that is, where no list of the population exists, where the population is not stable over time, and the like. Consider sampling tourists to the state of Florida in the month of March. We will look at three kinds of nonprobability techniques: convenience sampling, judgment sampling, and quota sampling.
Convenience Sampling	As the name implies, these samples are selected on the basis of convenience to the researchers. Examples include (1) asking people to volunteer to test products, (2) stopping people in a shopping mall to get their opinions, (3) using students or church groups as subjects in an experiment, (4) conducting ''on the street'' interviews on television, and so on. In all these cases, either the sample members volunteer out of interest in the project, or researchers select them because they are easily available. However, with such samples it is unclear as to what population they truly represent. A television interviewer may state that a particular sample represents the community, but the statement is clearly false. Only members of the community who happen to be ''in the right place at the right time'' have a chance of being selected; at 10:30 A.M. on a working day, individuals engaged in business would not have an equal or known chance of being selected.

Judgment Sampling

With this nonprobability technique, samples are selected on the basis of what an "expert" thinks is a group that is representative of the population and that can answer the research question at hand. In test marketing a new product, for example, researchers may make a judgment about which cities to use. And in industrial marketing research, they may decide to interview a company's purchasing agent as being representative of the entire company. Other examples of judgment sampling include an instructor's choice of a particular student to start a class discussion, the use of expert witnesses in a courtroom, and the selection of specific stores in which to test a line of merchandise.

Quota Sampling

In this special type of judgment sampling, researchers take explicit steps to obtain a sample that is like the overall population in terms of some specified control characteristics. For example, an interviewer may be instructed to select half the sample from people 30 years old or older and half from people under 30 years of age. In this case, the control characteristic is the age of respondents. Note, though, that with this particular control the researcher must know that the population of interest actually *is* divided in half at the 30-year mark. In addition, this simple example uses only one control characteristic; to get a realistic representative sample of a population, researchers have to use a number of control characteristics. Such factors make effective quota sampling very difficult.

Sampling Accuracy and Costs: A Trade-Off

The objective of any sampling process is to be as accurate as possible but at the lowest possible cost. There is a trade-off involved here. Generally, the larger the sample, the more accurate the conclusions drawn—yet also the greater the cost of surveying, in terms of time and money. With probability samples, researchers usually compromise at a *reasonable* level of confidence about the accuracy of the sample estimates. Of course, to be 100 percent sure about the results, they would have to interview 100 percent of the population. But to be 90 percent confident, they can sample far less than 90 percent because of the laws of inferential statistics. Obviously, time and money are saved.

With nonprobability sampling, researchers cannot apply the laws of probability to measure the degree of error. Yet, in so many marketing research situations, probability sampling is not feasible because a list of the population's membership does not exist. Consider the task of trying to take a random sample of tourists to a given state. They come and go so fast that their whereabouts cannot be monitored. Nor is there any way to obtain a list of all tourists. Nonprobability sampling must be employed. In designing such a nonrandom sample, the rule is to choose sample members who best approximate the characteristics of the population as a whole. Thus, the selected sample will closely represent the entire population.

The objective of the sampling process is to ensure representativeness. In designing their sample, researchers must consider whether probability or nonprobability methods best meet their needs and budget. In the end, accuracy is the most important consideration. Marketing decisions are only as good as the information upon which they are based. More accuracy means better information.

5   Collect the Data

Up to this point, the researchers and marketers have defined their problem and designed their questionnaire and sample. Now, to collect their data, they must contact the members of the population they are sampling and obtain the needed information.

When *personal interviews* are used to collect data, researchers must hire, train, and supervise people. Interviewers, especially, must be reliable; and once they are trained, they must be supervised in a way that ensures the proper collection of data. Interviewers have been known to fill out questionnaires themselves, rather than contact all sample members. Needless to say, such "results" are useless. (See Figure 4-7 and Application 4-4.)

Figure 4-7 Gathering marketing information in a personal interview. *(Ray Ellis/Photo Researchers, Inc.)*

Application 4-4
Data Collection Problem—
Countering the Perils of Personal Interviewing

Finding out how people feel about a certain product, a particular advertising campaign, or a public issue is not easy. The most perfectly constructed survey means nothing if the subjects will not cooperate. Researchers find that the greatest difficulty in getting cooperation in personal interview surveys is with two diverse groups—the affluent and the poor. The rich shun surveys, claiming they are a bother—and they are often not at home. Meanwhile, ghetto dwellers are reluctant to talk with strangers and are suspicious of almost all questions. And interviewers are reluctant to enter slum and low-income areas, especially after dark when most people are at home. Many companies logically

have emphasized mail and phone interviews. Yet some interesting countermeasures for personal interviewing have been taken by researchers.

Many companies have resorted to keeping the questionnaire exceptionally short—so interviewers can cover many respondents quickly. Taking surveys in the springtime when daylight is extended has been helpful. And some researchers even send interviewers out in teams to reduce interviewer fears. But perhaps the most extensive effort was undertaken by Audits and Surveys, a large research company. As their president told *Business Week* about an urban renewal survey conducted in New York City: "We sent supervisors to

schools, churches, and other organizations in the neighborhoods and asked them to recommend interviewers who would be known in the area. Then we trained the interviewers in both English and Spanish. We notified the schools and churches of the dates when the surveyors would be coming and had them pass the word on. We gave out instructions that told people to watch for the red badges the interviewers wore, and we set up a telephone headquarters where people could call to ask questions about the survey."

Source of data: "The Public Clams Up on Survey Takers," *Business Week,* Sept. 15, 1973, pp. 216–220.

When *telephone interviews* are the method of data collection, the questionnaire should be as brief as possible, and the interviewer should have a pleasant voice. The opening questions should be designed to catch the respondent's interest. Before starting to ask questions, the interviewer should indicate how long the interview will take so that the respondent will not grow impatient and end the call too soon.

When data are collected by *mail survey,* a cover letter should be included with the questionnaire. This letter should carry a letterhead to identify the firm conducting the research. The letter also should encourage the recipients to complete the questionnaire by telling them how the survey will benefit them. A postage-paid return envelope will help to ensure responses, as will the offering of incentives (money or gifts).(See Application 4-5.)

Application 4-5
Collecting Information— "Welcome VOXBOX"

Informative . . . Excellent . . . Dumb . . . Zap! VOXBOX, a toaster-sized console that rates TV quality, is creating a stir in Seattle. Marketers have high hopes that this computerized system will give them a boost into understanding the likes and dislikes of the consumer.

VOXBOX, in effect, is the hooking up of a television set and a computer with buttons so that the viewers can instantly rate their likes, dislikes, and preferences for programs, political figures, and product commercials.

The innovation works something like this. A program is shown on TV and Coca-Cola Co. tests one of its new commercials within that program. Viewers then are given the opportunity to rate both the show and the

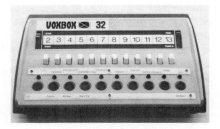

(Courtesy R. D. Percy & Co.)

commercial, with eight choices ranging from "excellent" to "dumb."

VOXBOX differs from the Nielsen rating system, which measures how many sets are tuned into a particular show, because VOXBOX can record how the viewers feel about what they are seeing. It can answer the question of whether a hit show attracts viewers because they like it or because they dislike it less

than other programs being shown at the same time.

Besides Coca Cola, United Airlines and Sears and Roebuck are testing viewer reactions to their messages and to the shows with which they appear through VOXBOX. The results may help to determine whether an advertising message is better received when the viewer is enjoying a program. Being receptive to a show may make the viewer more receptive to its sponsor's message. Corporate clients want the answers to these questions and are paying up to $10,000 a month for computerized VOXBOX reports.

Source of data: "Talking Back to the Tube," *Newsweek,* Feb. 25, 1980, p. 83.

6 Process and Analyze the Data

Before the data can be processed and analyzed, the questionnaires must be scanned to see whether there are obvious errors or incomplete responses. Faulty questionnaires are ignored, since they serve no useful purpose. Then—if a computer will be used in the analysis—the questionnaires are coded. Sometimes researchers use questionnaires that are already coded along the edge, where it is not obvious and will not confuse respondents. (See Figure 4-2.) With such precoded questionnaires, responses can be keypunched directly into the computer. Then the data can be tabulated and analyzed.

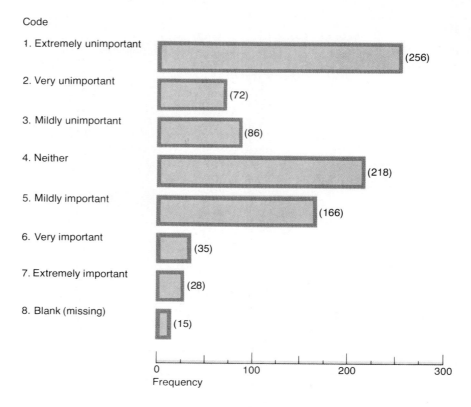

Figure 4-8   Importance of appearance in tennis racket purchase.

Tabulation refers to the counting of frequency of responses by respondents as well as cross-classifying the data (looking at frequencies of responses by different categories of respondents). Figure 4-8 shows a frequency of the importance ratings for the appearance of tennis rackets. Many respondents found appearance very unimportant; some respondents were noncommittal; some respondents said appearance was fairly important.

This same data could be broken down or cross-classified by age group, income level, etc. Table 4-3 shows the importance to buyers of various qualities, pricing, and packaging of tennis balls, broken down by United States region. The numbers in the cells are means on the 7-point importance scale. Apparently, little difference exists across regions.

Finally, more sophisticated analytical techniques can be used to extract further information from the data. These techniques can be complex, and special training in data analysis is needed to use the information properly.

TABLE 4-3 Importance of Tennis Ball Characteristics by Region of the United States

	Mean		
Factors	East	Midwest	West
Consistency of bounce	6.2	6.3	6.3
Pressure	4.9	5.1	5.1
Price	6.1	6.2	6.2
Endorsement	4.1	4.3	4.2
Type of cover	3.4	3.4	3.8
Brand name	6.5	6.5	6.4

7 Report the Information

The final step in the research process is putting together the report. It is important that researchers explain their research process and document what they have learned. The report should be simple and straightforward and should be written for the marketing managers who will use it to solve their problem. The first part of the report should present a summary of its highlights so that marketing managers can quickly see what conclusions have been reached. Generous use of graphs and tables is helpful in conveying the information. Recommendations should be offered for managerial action. The report should also mention any limitations that the study might have and any problems that were identified as data were collected.

Sources of Error in Marketing Research

Throughout our discussion of the research process, we have emphasized the dangers of error. Unclear questions, improper sampling methods, and poor identification of objectives can all lead to error; so can the mishandling of data, or faulty computer instructions. Since the purpose of research in the first place is to eliminate guesswork and error in decision making, marketers are especially concerned that researchers perform their duties properly.

There are three major types of error in marketing research: interviewer error, respondent error, and statistical error. Interviewers and researchers can introduce error in many ways—by using the wrong questions, by improper sequencing, or by not following the principles of research that ensure accurate, relevant information. These problems can be controlled through careful planning and supervision. Respondent error, however, is extremely difficult to control. People sometimes lie, and very often they don't know the answer but will give one anyway. Researchers can do little about this—they are interested in recording human nature, not in changing it. Finally, statistical error can occur when a sample is not representative. Conclusions will not be valid in such a case, since the sample is different from the overall population.

Above all else, then, researchers must be concerned with eliminating all sources of error from the research process. Millions of dollars may hang on their success in providing accurate information to marketing decision makers. In Chapter 5, we will look at the specific types of information researchers gather in order to describe a market's makeup and needs.

Looking Back

This chapter has presented an overview of the goals, techniques, and problems of marketing researchers. Their chief goal, of course, is achieving accuracy, since marketers will base decisions on researchers' conclusions. Marketing research is a complex process. Before going further, review the following important points:

1 Marketing research must be *systematic* (not haphazard) and *objective* (not subjective); its aim is to present *information* that is oriented toward *decision making*.

2 Problem formulation is the crucial first step in the marketing research process.

3 Exploratory research aims to refine problem definition, research objectives, and information needs.

4 The research objectives guide each of the subsequent decisions in the research process.

5 The use of secondary data is faster and less expensive than collecting primary data, but secondary sources must be relevant, up to date, accurate, and credible.

6 The design of a questionnaire is determined by the overall research design and by the type of survey approach it employs.

7 The kinds of questions used—their approach and sequencing—depend on the research objectives of the study.

8 An indirect questioning approach is useful in obtaining information about psychological aspects of respondents.

9 Using a sample of the population can lead to greater accuracy than it is possible to obtain by interviewing everyone.

10 Market researchers use statistics to make probability statements from samples to populations.

11 The mean, median, and mode are tools for interpreting research data.

12 A research report should be written with its users in mind, rather than for researchers.

13 The objective of the research process is accuracy; interviewer error, respondent error, and statistical error must be eliminated or controlled throughout the process.

Key Terms

If you aren't sure what each of the following words means, look back at the text. Numbers refer to pages on which the words are defined. Additional information can be found by checking the index and the glossary at the end of the book.

marketing research 98
scientific approach 101
exploratory research 103

conclusive research 103
secondary data source 106
primary data source 107
observational approach 107
experimental approach 108
survey approach 110
basic data 112
classification data 113
identification data 113
population 117
mean 117
mode 117

median 117
probability sampling 118
nonprobability sampling 119
simple random sample 118
stratified random sample 119
area (or cluster) sample 119
convenience sample 119
judgment sample 120
quota sample 120
interviewer error 125
respondent error 125
statistical error 125

Questions for Review

1 What is considered "the root of all evil" in conducting marketing research?

2 What are the two major types, or stages, of research design? How do they differ?

3 What is the most important task in the research process? Why?

4 What four criteria must be established in analyzing the usefulness of secondary information sources?

5 Identify the three probability sampling techniques.

6 Assuming that the steps in the research process are sequentially related, what steps must you perform once the sample has been designed?

Questions for Thought and Discussion

Below is a questionnaire that appeared in the daily newspaper of a large New England university.

1 What do you believe is the researcher's objective(s) in conducting this research project?

2 Which principles of questionnaire design do you see being violated?

3 Evaluate the sample design.

4 What types of error do you feel will result from this research project?

The Athlete Council would like to represent the varied opinions of both the women and the men here on campus. To get an idea of how the women feel about the existing spending of their Athletic Fee and what kinds of changes they would like to see in Women's Athletics, this questionnaire has been designed. We would appreciate the cooperation of University women in this survey. Please drop completed forms in Student Senate boxes in the Student Union or the Campus Center, or mail them as campus mail to the Women's Committee, Student Senate Office, Campus Center. Thank-you.

1 Do you want the Athletic Fee optional?
( ) Yes ( ) No ( ) Neutral

2 Do you resent paying 44% of the Athletic Fee and getting 2% back for Women's Activities?
( ) Yes ( ) No ( ) Neutral

3 Do you want less money spent on men's sports and more on women's sports?
( ) Yes ( ) No ( ) Neutral In what way?

4 Do you want to go big time and, thus, raise the Athletic Fee? That is, do you want the football team to get out of the Yankee Conference and play more audience drawing teams?
( ) Yes ( ) No ( ) Neutral

5 Are you aware of the existence of the women's intercollegiate varsity and junior varsity teams?
( ) Yes ( ) No

6 Would you like more information about these teams?
( ) Yes ( ) No ( ) Neutral

7 Would you like more write-ups in the Collegian of women's athletic activities?
( ) Yes ( ) No ( ) Neutral

8 Have you heard of any women's athletic activities which lacked or lack sufficient funds?
( ) Yes ( ) No Which?

9 Do you have any gripes about women's sport facilities here?
( ) Yes ( ) No What are they?

10 Do you have any suggestions concerning the expenditure of the Athletic Fee related to Women's Athletics?
( ) Yes ( ) No What are they?

Suggested Project

What are the major considerations that influence a student in deciding which college to attend? Identify the information needed to answer this question, and begin the design of a questionnaire to collect the necessary data.

Suggested Readings

Boyd, Harper W., Jr., Ralph Westfall, and Stanley F. Stasch: *Marketing Research: Text and Cases,* 5th ed., Irwin, Homewood, Ill., 1981. This is an easy-to-read basic text in marketing research.

Cox, Keith K., and Ben M. Enis (eds.): *Readings in the Marketing Research Process,* Goodyear Publishing, Pacific Palisades, Calif., 1973. This anthology presents twenty-eight articles that increase the reader's understanding of contemporary marketing research and the marketing decision-making environment.

Fouss, James H., and Elaine Solomon: "Salespeople as Researchers: Help or Hazard?" *Journal of Marketing,* vol. 44, no. 3 (Summer 1980), pp. 36–39. The authors' study demonstrates that it is difficult for sales representatives to collect unbiased information. *Journal of Marketing Research,* vol. 14, no. 3 (August 1977). The entire issue of this highly professional journal is devoted to survey research—especially sampling, question formulation, and data collection. The footnotes will key the reader to even more sources.

Kanuk, Leslie, and Conrad Berenson: "Mail Surveys and Response Rates: A Literature Review," *Journal of Marketing Research,* vol. 12, no. 4 (November 1975), pp. 440–453. This literature review systematically looks at research studies comparing different methods of increasing response rates in mail surveys.

Kinnear, Thomas C., and James Taylor: *Marketing Research: An Applied Approach,* McGraw-Hill, New York, 1979. This excellent, detailed text presents a systematic procedure for conducting marketing research.

Tarpey, Lawrence X., James H. Donnelly, and J. Paul Peter: *A Preface to Marketing Management,* Business Publications, Inc., Dallas, Texas, 1979, pp. 227–234. The appendix of this book provides an excellent list of secondary sources.

Tyebjee, Tyzoon T.: "Telephone Survey Methods: The State of the Art," *Journal of Marketing,* vol. 43, no. 3 (Summer 1979), pp. 68–77. This article presents the advantages and disadvantages of telephone interviewing.

Webb, Eugene, Donald Campbell, Richard Schwartz, and Lee Secrest: *Unobtrusive Measures: Nonreactive Research in the Social Sciences,* Rand McNally, Chicago, 1966. This interesting book provides some useful approaches to obtaining information through some usually neglected observation techniques.

Appendix Secondary Sources

I GOVERNMENT PUBLICATIONS

Census of Population Provides information on the characteristics of the population for states, counties, cities, etc., in a series of reports. In addition, several series of short *Current Population Reports* are published. These provide summaries of population trends by age group, income, sex, etc., with extended forecasts of population growth.

County and City Data Book Compiled about three times a decade. Its primary purpose is to provide a selection of recent statistical information for counties, cities, and other small geographic areas. More than 160 statistical items are presented for each county and city of 25,000 or more. These are also shown for regions, divisions, states, and SMSAs (standard metropolitan statistical areas). Descriptive text and sources are included. Provides data on population, education, employment, aggregate and median income, housing, bank deposits, employment and payrolls in manufacturing, retail sales, size of farms, value of products sold, etc. It is also available on computer tape or computer cards.

County Business Patterns This volume, issued annually, shows county, state, and U.S. summary statistics on employment, number and employment size of reporting business units, and taxable payrolls for approximately fifteen broad industry categories. The statistics are particularly suited to analyzing market potential, establishing sales quotas, and locating facilities.

Guide to Industrial Statistics A locator guide to published data, and illustrations of types of data presented. The book describes the industry, commodity, and materials reference lists available, and the availability of unpublished material and special services undertaken by the Bureau of the Census. It also includes a chapter on other important industrial statistics published by the federal government.

Marketing Information Guide A monthly annotated bibliography of marketing information prepared by the Bureau of Domestic Commerce. It covers governmental and nongovernmental publications in the field of marketing and is perhaps the most comprehensive listing available.

Monthly Catalog of United States Government Publications Contains an alphabetical listing of documents issued by each government agency. The list is compiled each month and indexed for access by author, title, subject, and series/report. The catalog also includes a stock number index and title key word index.

Statistical Abstract of the United States This publication is updated annually to reflect changes. Items of value in the marketing field include such information as salaries in industry, income of the aged population, mergers and acquisitions in manufacturing and mining, income of white and black families, reasons for retirement, and migration of population.

U.S. Industrial Outlook Contains narrative forecast analyses and a statistical appendix of projections of industrial activity. Covers various individual industries or industry groups including manufacturing, construction, trade and service activities, and provides data on production, sales, shipments, employment, productivity, imports, new products, developments, regulations and financing.

II TRADE PUBLICATIONS

Advertising Age A weekly publication that offers several annual surveys and special features. The following are examples: "Marketing Reports," providing information on sales and earnings, leading product lines and brands, advertising expenditures, and ad agencies used by each of the top 100 national advertisers; "100 Leading National Advertisers"; "National Expenditures in Newspapers"; and "Profiles of the Top 100 Markets in the U.S."

Merchandising Week A weekly journal with two issues of special importance: "Annual Statistical and Marketing Report," issued each February, presents dollar and unit sales for major household appliances and products over the last 10 years; and "Annual Statistical and Marketing Forecast," issued each May, surveys industry estimates of household appliance and product sales.

Product Management A monthly with two reports of particular note: "Advertising Expenditures for Health and Beauty Aids," a July publication listing industry predictions of advertising expenditures; and "Top Health and Beauty Aid Promotions," a trimonthly series of articles that cite the top marketing promotions of the drug and cosmetic industry.

Sales & Marketing Management A widely read magazine published monthly except in February, April, July, and October, when it appears twice a month. Noted for its four annual statistical issues: (1) "Survey of Buying Power" (late July issue), which offers current estimates of United States and Canadian population, income, and retail business; (2) "Survey of Buying Power, Part II" (late October

issue), which contains two marketing surveys: "Metropolitan Market Projections" and "Annual Surveys of TV, Newspaper, and Media"; (3) "Survey of Industrial Purchasing Power" (April Issue); and (4) "Survey of Selling Costs" (January issue).

III BUSINESS GUIDES

Funk & Scott Index of Corporations and Industries An index of company, product, and industry information that has appeared in over 750 business-related publications. It is divided into an Industries & Products section arranged by SIC number and a Companies section arranged alphabetically by company name.

Moody's Industrial Manual Annually revised information on the history of companies, their operations, subsidiaries, products, and financial position. Company names are indexed in alphabetical order.

Reference Book of Corporate Management Provides an alphabetical listing of companies and their principal officers. Biographical data covering age, education, experience, and principal business affiliations are shown for each officer.

Standard Directory of Advertisers Lists over 17,000 advertiser companies with annual appropriations for national or regional advertising campaigns. Includes two editions: Classified (arranged in fifty-one product

classifications) and Geographical (companies arranged by state or city). Also includes a trademark index.

Standard Directory of Advertising Agencies Lists information (annual billing, breakdown by media, account executives) on approximately 4,400 advertising agencies in the United States and overseas. Includes a geographical index of agencies as well as an alphabetical listing.

Standard & Poor's Industry Survey Includes thirty-three industry segments which are divided into a Current Analysis and a Basic Analysis section. Each Basic Analysis section includes an examination of the prospects for the industry, an analysis of trends and problems, and a comparative company analysis. The Current Analysis section provides latest industry developments, industry, market and company statistics, and an appraisal of the investment outlook.

Standard & Poor's Register of Corporations, Directors and Executives A 3-volume set which includes addresses of companies, names, titles, and functions of executives and officers, SIC code, annual sales, subsidiaries, and divisions.

Survey of Buying Power Data Service Includes statistical information on population and household characteristics, total retail sales, effective buying income, and TV market data. Data are divided into three volumes.

IV PERIODICALS INDICES

Business Periodicals Index   A subject index to approximately 150 business-related periodicals. Articles about specific companies are indexed by company name.

Journal of Marketing, Marketing Abstracts Section
Each issue of the journal contains an annotated bibliography describing selected articles and special studies. Arranged according to major subject areas.

Wall Street Journal Index   An index of all articles published in *The Wall Street Journal.* Entries are arranged alphabetically into two sections: Corporate News (by company name) and General News (by subject).

New York Times Index   Indexes all issues of *The New York Times* from 1851 to date. Entries are made under subject headings and briefly describe article contents.

V SPECIAL GUIDES

Predicasts   Includes short- and long-range forecasts for numerous industries and product categories, with each abstract indicating both the size of the individual forecasts and a reference as to their source.

Topicator   A subject index to about twenty journals in the fields of advertising, communications, and marketing.

VI PRIVATE SOURCES

A. C. Nielsen Company, Chicago, publisher of:
Retail Index Services   Data on products sold through retail outlets.
Media Research Services   Data on television audiences.
Neodata Services, Inc.   Magazine circulation data.
Nielsen Clearing House
Coupon-processing service and promotion service.
Nielsen Special Research
Custom-designed service for individual clients.

Market Research Corporation of America (MRCA), New York, publisher of:
National Consumer Panel   Data on weekly family purchases of consumer products.
National Menu Census   Data on home food consumption.
Metro Trade Audits   Survey of 3000 retail, drug, and discount retailers in various geographic areas. Data must be purchased from MRCA.

Selling Areas-Marketing, Inc., New York, publisher of: *SAMI Reports*
Reports warehouse withdrawals to food stores in selected market areas. Thirteen reports, 4 weeks after the end of the reporting period. Better than 85 percent of the total market volume is represented.

Simmons Market Research Bureau, Inc., New York, publisher of: *Selective Markets and Media Reaching Them*   Annual series of reports covering television markets, sporting goods, proprietary drug, smoking products, food wraps, soft drinks, magazines, alcoholic beverages, etc. Excellent reports giving demographic data by sex, income, age, and brand preferences.

For more on these and other sources, see Goeldner, Charles R., and Laura M. Dirks, ''Business Facts: Where to Find Them,'' *MSU Business Topics,* Summer 1976, pp. 23–36; and Peter, J. Paul, James H. Donnelly, Jr., and Lawrence X. Tarpey, *A Preface to Marketing Management,* rev. ed., Business Publications, Inc., 1982, Plano, Texas, pp. 251–259.

Chapter 5

Looking at the Market

Looking Ahead

Chapters 3 and 4 focused on how marketers gather marketing information. Now we will examine some ways in which they use that information to help them describe and understand their markets effectively.

People are all different, but marketers obviously cannot keep track of all their differences. Consequently, to develop a marketing program, marketers often divide people into groups, or segments, according to some common thread. Then they try to match the needs and wants of the people within each market segment.

The first section of this chapter covers the strategies used by marketers to define their markets. If they assume all consumers to be alike in some important way, they may appeal to them in the aggregate—as one large market. Otherwise, they will use the segmentation approach to divide the market into groups of similar consumers. We will examine that process in detail. Finally, we will turn our attention to that enigma called "the consumer" in order to see how various population and income trends affect marketing.

Key Topics

The benefits and costs of two marketing strategies: aggregation and segmentation

The criteria for effective use of market segmentation

How marketers divide consumers into market segments

Some trends in population growth

Changes taking place in the makeup of American households

Geographic shifts of the United States population

Current trends and expected changes in consumers' purchasing power

Defining the Market

Marketers quickly realize that no two consumers are alike and that it is extremely difficult—at times impossible—to satisfy all consumers in the same way. To meet the many diverse needs in the marketplace, marketers target their efforts toward smaller groups, or *segments,* within the larger marketplace. Consumers within segments tend to have similarities that hold them together. These similarities can be based on personal characteristics, buying behavior, or psychological makeup. Most marketers try to appeal to only some segments of the consuming public and to develop different marketing mixes that best match each segment's wants and needs.

In exploring this concept of selective marketing, we will look at some criteria for effective segmentation and at how marketers identify target markets. Then we will examine some population factors and income trends that show why the process of describing the market is so important and why it should come before other marketing activities.

Before going into the details of market segmentation, however, we need to consider a broader approach sometimes used by marketers. Instead of subdividing the overall market into smaller, more homogeneous (similar) segments, they may approach all consumers in the aggregate—as one large group. Thus there are two overall strategies available to marketers: market aggregation and market segmentation. We will now study the objectives, methods, costs, and benefits of each marketing strategy.

Market Aggregation—The Practice of Undifferentiated Marketing

When marketers follow the strategy of *market aggregation,* also called *undifferentiated marketing,* the overall market is *not* subdivided into segments. Rather, a single marketing program is used to offer a single product to all consumers. Because of the diversity of wants and needs among consumers, however, marketers know that the market aggregation approach will not perfectly satisfy everyone's wants and needs. Yet they use this strategy when they believe that there are enough consumers who will compromise and buy the product to make it a profitable venture. The market aggregation strategy has been used in the past by marketers dealing in mass-appeal, basically standardized items such as beer, cigarettes, coffee, household cleansers, and gasoline.

With the undifferentiated marketing approach, the products offered are such that little or no differences can be perceived by consumers. That is, competing products are virtually the same physically and chemically. In such cases, marketers use promotion to make their product seem different from and better than competitors' products. Often, only the brand or packaging is different. While the marketers realize that consumers may have different wants and needs, they also believe that a sufficient number of consumers are similar enough to be approached as a homogeneous group. In short, consumers are expected to conform to the will of supply; they are expected to compromise by accepting a product that may not perfectly match or satisfy their wants and needs.

The basic advantage of the market aggregation strategy is that it results in lower costs for both production and marketing. Production runs can make maximum use of the principles of mass production, since only one product is made and assembly techniques do not have to be altered for variations. This is very efficient. And on the marketing side, media discounts can be realized when only one large-scale advertising campaign is employed. Johnson & Johnson follows an aggregation strategy in marketing its baby shampoo, oil, and powder: To increase its market while gaining production efficiencies, the company uses the same products for both the baby market and the adult market. To the adult market, the company stresses the gentleness of its baby shampoo for those who wash their hair frequently and the versatility of its baby oil as a cosmetic. For its baby powder, J&J emphasizes its use to promote staying "cool, dry and comfortable" during sticky weather. The results: In 1981, Johnson & Johnson's shampoo, oil, and powder had more adult than infant users. (See Figure 5-1.)

Figure 5-1 Market aggregation has been a successful strategy for Johnson & Johnson. (Reproduced with permission of Johnson & Johnson Baby Products Co.)

Despite the advantages in terms of costs and efficiencies, however, there are built-in dangers in an aggregation strategy. In taking an approach that may leave some consumers' needs unfulfilled, marketers expose themselves to challenges from competitors. This is especially true when serving large markets. In trying to match the entire market's needs reasonably well, marketers are vulnerable to competitors who match the needs more precisely. Consider the case of Zippo, a manufacturer of cigarette lighters. For years the company followed an aggregation strategy and was immensely successful. But when Gillette and Bic entered the market with cheap, disposable lighters, the bother of fluid-filled lighters caused Zippo's share of the market to falter. Obviously, the competitors had discovered and capitalized on a consumer need that was not being satisfied. Additionally, undifferentiated marketing focuses on the largest segment of the market. Yet, because of size, this segment also attracts intense competition. Thus, markets can erode from invasion of the largest segment as well as from the flanks (the unfilled wants) being left unattended. (See Application 5-1.)

Because of these weaknesses in the market aggregation strategy, marketers often pursue the alternative strategy of market segmentation.

Market Segmentation

In following a strategy of *market segmentation,* marketers view the overall market as being made up of many smaller parts whose elements have common characteristics and resemble one another more than they resemble the total market. Market segmentation, then, breaks the larger heterogeneous market into smaller, more homogeneous segments. The elements of each smaller segment are more similar in terms of wants, needs, or behavior than the total market is. Separate marketing programs are developed to best match each segment's individual needs and wants.

Like the market aggregation strategy, a segmentation strategy has its advantages and disadvantages. Market segmentation takes the opposite approach to market aggregation: It bends supply to meet the will of demand. Thus, products more precisely match each segment's wants and needs. Promotional expenditures can be allocated more appropriately to the most profitable market segments within the total market, and promotional appeals and media campaigns can be varied for each segment. As a result, market segmentation results in a better match between what the marketer does and what the market desires. In the end, the effect is more total sales than those produced by undifferentiated marketing.

But all this is not without greater costs. Research expenditures increase as more and more market segments are investigated. Production costs rise because runs are shorter, and variations are introduced into the assembly process. Finally, sales in one market segment may be sacrificed as another segment is served (for instance, Gillette's addition of disposable razors may cut into its sales of regular blades). On the whole, then, market segmentation provides a better match, but not without substantial costs.

Application 5-1
Undifferentiated Marketing—
Showing that "All Chicken Isn't Created Equal"

After years of dominating the fast fried chicken market, Kentucky Fried Chicken (KFC) in the late 1970s saw its position threatened. Revenues and profits were declining, along with morale among franchisees and employees. Many KFC outlets were dirty and the food was unappetizing. Even the late Colonel Harland Sanders, the founder and chain spokesperson, announced, to the chagrin of parent Heublein, that KFC served "the worst chicken I've ever seen," and that the gravy resembled "wallpaper paste."

In 1977, Heublein declared it was taking KFC back to "the basics." To fortify its return to yesteryear, KFC emphasized the acronym "quascvoofamp"— quality, service, cleanliness, value, other operating factors, advertising merchandising, and promotion. Marketing research indicated that consumers were concerned about

the nutritional value of fast food, so a campaign was designed to reassure mothers who felt guilty about feeding take-out fried chicken and mashed potatoes to their families. The theme of the campaign was, "It's so nice to feel so good about a meal." These promotion efforts, along with improved management, proved to be effective. The more than 4200 KFC outlets registered 33 consecutive months of sales gains.

In 1981, KFC's primary problem was competition. In 1977, the company competed against 6400 fast-food restaurants that specialized in fried chicken. In 1981, there were about 7800. In addition, it faced strong competition from other major fast-food operators. Burger King and McDonald's introduced chicken sandwiches, and most other fast-food chains broadened their menus to include such products as steak sandwiches and

salad bars.

Yet KFC refused to compete by offering new products, a tactic it had tried years earlier, and one that had concluded with disaster. Instead, to differentiate itself from rival chicken restaurants as well as the hamburger chains, the company stayed with its basic product: it promoted KFC heavily with a $60 million campaign with the theme "We do chicken right."

One of the commercials showed a frazzled counter employee taking orders for a super cheesburger, super fish sandwich, and super roast beef, while holding the "super pickle." An announcer says that KFC "concentrates on just one thing. Maybe that's why it's so good."

Source of data: "At Kentucky Fried Chicken, It's Time to Set Itself Apart," *The Wall Street Journal,* March 19, 1981, p. 29.

Approaches to Market Segmentation

Once the marketer determines that a segmentation strategy rather than an aggregation strategy will be more profitable, marketers can take three approaches. They can aim their efforts toward a single market segment, they can try to treat each consumer as an individual, or they can take the middle ground and try to serve several of the market segments at once.

Concentrated Marketing

When marketers attempt to serve a single market segment, the approach is called *concentrated marketing*. Companies that (at some point) have employed this segmentation strategy include Volkswagen, The Seven-Up Company, Hallmark, and U.S. Time (Timex). Concentrated marketing is also the segmentation strategy followed by Rolls-Royce, which correctly pinpoints its market as being affluent consumers. A Rolls-Royce automobile costs over $100,000; obviously, not everyone can afford to own one. But Rolls-Royce knows its market and how to reach it. The company advertises in such publications as *The New Yorker* and *The Wall Street Journal—* periodicals that serve affluent readerships. Meanwhile, Volkswagen also recognizes that automobile buyers can be segmented into groups of consumers, depending on whether they demand small-car economy, dependability, status, speed, or large-car luxury. But Volkswagen has concentrated its marketing efforts only on the small-car market, ignoring the other market segments. Thus, Rolls-Royce and Volkswagen both practice concentrated marketing, but the market segments for which they aim are made up of consumers with different needs and wants. Concentrated marketing has many of the same advantages and disadvantages of market aggregation.

Market Atomization

Alternatively, marketers may pursue a policy of *market atomization,* a segmentation strategy that treats each consumer uniquely. This approach is especially popular among firms that market industrial goods. In such transactions, there are no common market segments to serve; each customer has unique needs and concerns that the marketers must satisfy. This ultimate form of market segmentation is also used for many consumer goods. Companies that market custom-built homes, tailor-made suits and shirts, and furniture reupholstering are all practicing market atomization.

Differentiated Marketing

In following an extreme strategy of market segmentation, then, marketers focus either on a single group of consumers (concentrated marketing) or on a single buyer (atomization). But most marketers find it more profitable to select and *appeal to several market segments.* When they do this, they are practicing differentiated marketing. This strategy involves variations in the marketing mix through different products, different prices, different promotional efforts, different distribution arrangements, or a combination of them. Because so many marketers use a differentiated strategy, individual consumers have a wealth of products to choose from. Automobiles, laundry detergents, and soft drinks are just three examples of products that are available in every size, description, and price range. Political candidates, too, come in as many forms as there are market segments to support them. Similarly, airplane manufacturers provide their market segments with commercial models, military equipment, and jets for personal use. Textbook publishers engage in market segmentation, publishing materials for every educational level, as well as magazines, newsletters, and business periodicals.

Some Questions to Ask

The use of market segmentation is not always the sure-fire best strategy to employ. For it to work profitably, the following questions should all be resoundingly answered with a "Yes!"

Can the Market Be Identified and Measured?

Marketers must be able to identify which consumers are members of a particular market segment. There must be some common characteristic that includes or excludes a consumer from the group. And this characteristic must be measurable, which is often a problem. How can marketers identify and measure consumers whose vision is poor or whose scalps itch? These are difficult, perhaps impossible, traits for marketers to measure—yet marketers of contact lenses and shampoos may well wish they could do so.

General Foods, for example, markets Cycle dog food on the basis of identifying different market segments. The company correctly found that many dog owners consider their pets (the "consumers") to be four-footed humans. Such dog owners respond favorably to Cycle because it's formulated specifically to match their animal's age and activity pattern. Four products are marketed under the Cycle label, and each is designed to meet the needs of an identifiable age segment: Cycle 1 for puppies, Cycle 2 for young adult dogs, Cycle 3 for overweight dogs, and Cycle 4 for older dogs.

Not all marketers find segments so identifiable. Consider the $12.5 billion "newlywed" market. In 1980, some 2.4 million people got married. Yet Eastern Air Lines spent only $100,000 on advertising aimed at honeymooners, and concentrated this advertising in bride magazines and travel agent brochures. United Air Lines has dropped most honeymoon-type advertising altogether. "We can't identify the market clearly," a UAL executive told *Forbes,* "so we don't know if the advertising is accomplishing anything." Retailers also have a problem. "You can't tell when a bride comes walking into your store," said the publisher of *Modern Bride.* "She isn't wearing a wedding gown and veil yelling, 'I'm getting married.' "[1]

Is the Market Substantial?

Unless a market is large enough to generate a sales volume that ensures profitability, it is not economical to design unique marketing mixes. We have seen that market segmentation can be costly and that a market must be able to support these costs. While some segments are small, they still have a substantial purchasing power that makes them profitable. Consider the market segment for men's fur coats. While only about 10 percent of all fur coats are sold to males, that small segment's profit potential is very high. (See Figure 5-2.)

The success of Cycle dog food triggered competitive activity. To compete with Cycle 3 (the diet blend), Ralston Purina introduced its own low-calorie dog food called Fit and Trim. Why did Ralston choose to market to the diet segment? Because its research showed that this market was substantial: 41 percent of dog owners think their pets are overweight, and 62 percent say their animals are inactive. (See Application 5-2.)

Is the Market Accessible?

In following a segmentation strategy, marketers also must be able to communicate effectively and efficiently with each market segment. Some segments, even though identified as substantial, cannot be reached properly because no medium matches the characteristics of the market. For instance, potential buyers of inexpensive watches are

---

[1] "The High Cost of Living," *Forbes,* June 22, 1981, p. 88.

THE FURS OF NEIMAN-MARCUS FOR MEN.

Photographed at the Gaudi Gardens, Barcelona, Spain.

On site. Globe-hopping jackets from N-M's adventurous collection
of men's furs. Rugged raccoon pieces from the U.S.A., 595.00.
And leather-trimmed, brown-dyed rabbit from Spain, 295.00. Both hip-length.
Fur-imagination for your wardrobe with hardly a dent in your finances.
Fur Salon
To order by mail, write:
Neiman-Marcus Fur Salon, Dallas, Texas 75201 or the N-M store nearest you.
Order jackets according to your suit size.

Neiman-Marcus

Dallas   Fort Worth   Houston   Bal Harbour   Atlanta   St. Louis   Chicago   Washington, D.C.   Beverly Hills   Newport Beach   White Plains, N.Y.

Figure 5-2 Market segmentation works in areas like men's furs because, even though the segment itself is small, the profit potential per unit is high. *(Reprinted with permission of Neiman-Marcus)*

not likely to read any one magazine or view any one television program. Thus, much of the promotional expenditure would be wasted in contacting people who are not really interested in the product. Compare that situation with the ability of furniture companies, such as Baker, Thomasville, and Knapp and Tubbs, to reach their market through magazines like *Metropolitan Life* and *Better Homes and Gardens*.

Is the Market Responsive?

Unless market segments are willing to react to the marketing programs developed, there is little reason to develop a unique program for each segment. Clearly, market segments must be defined on the basis of their willingness to purchase the product in response to variations in the marketing mix. For example, diet colas and soft drinks found a ready market segment when they were introduced in the 1960s, while the

Application 5-2
Meeting the Substantial Criterion—and Not Coming Up on the Short End

For years, men's specialty clothiers have catered to the oversized man—flattering the gangling and corpulent with such reassuring terms as "tall" and "big." Largely ignored has been the short man. As one retailing expert told *The Wall Street Journal,* "It's not too profitable for the general merchant to carry the odd size." But in 1981, a number of merchants began giving full attention to the short-man market segment when research revealed that 25 percent of American males are 5 feet 7 or under. (Average male height is 5 feet, 9 inches.)

Most of these specialty retailers name their shops so as not to offend, but some have been more bold, tagging their stores with such names as "Napoleon's Closet" and "The Short Shop." Many of the stores have also attended to the unique needs of their customers. Mirrors are short, checkout counters are closer to the floor, and coat racks are lower than usual. Suit sizes include short, extra short, extra-extra short, and "portly cadet." Even neckties are shortened.

Obtaining merchandise for the smaller man has not always been easy for retailers. General merchants just haven't bought sufficient quantities to attract manufacturers. To help solve this problem, in 1981 a dozen retailers formed a Small Man's Association of America with plans to buy in large quantities. These twelve association stores estimate their combined sales to reach $5 million a year. Clearly, one market segment has reason to rejoice.

Source of data: "Little Guys' Shops Separate the Men from the Boys Dept.," *The Wall Street Journal,* Feb. 23, 1981, p. 1.

response was poor for beard softeners that came in the form of a gel rather than a foamy cream.

Often, even the most careful analysis of consumers cannot guarantee success. Several years ago, Ideal Toy Corporation introduced a Jesus doll. Preliminary research had indicated that the market for such a product was considerable, and the doll was received favorably by department store buyers at the annual Toy Fair. Yet sales results were dismal. The reason, Ideal learned, was that people considered Jesus so sacred that they could not bear to have children mishandle the doll. While the first reactions of consumers were positive, most had second thoughts. Ideal was left with an inventory worth millions of dollars because the marketers had not identified the religious feelings that made the market unresponsive.

Bases for Market Segmentation

In meeting the above four criteria for effective market segmentation, marketers must choose some means of dividing the total market into segments. The most common ways of doing this are on the basis of (1) demographics, (2) geographics, (3) product usage, (4) perceived product benefits, and (5) lifestyle, or psychographics. We will further categorize these bases into two groups: *consumers' characteristics* and *consumers' behavior.*

Analyzing Consumers' Characteristics

This approach to segmentation measures various characteristics of consumers (such as age, income, location, and the like) and then determines the extent to which these characteristics relate to buying behavior. The analysis of consumers' characteristics includes demographic and geographic market segmentation.

Demographic segmentation involves the analysis of characteristics that provide a profile or picture of consumers. Demographics encompass such variables as age, income, marital status, sex, size of household, and education. (We will look closely at such variables later in the chapter.) Demographic variables are most helpful in describing market segments and in directing the development of marketing programs for each segment. Simple examples of this process can be found among cigarette manufacturers, who are major users of demographic segmentation. For instance, Philip Morris has promoted masculine symbols of cowboys and tattoos to direct Marlboro cigarettes primarily toward the male population, while the Liggett Group has created Eve cigarettes to appeal to female smokers. And marketers have found that women are buying an increasing share of wine now that wine distribution has spread to supermarkets. The departments are laid out attractively, but not so opulently that the shopper might be scared off by what appears to be a "luxury" department, with wines priced above family budget limits.

Geographic segmentation divides the market according to consumer's locations, which affect buyers' needs and wants. For example, locational differences form segments for RJR Foods, manufacturers of Chun King products, Patio brand Mexican dishes, College Inn Broths, and Hawaiian Punch. The Patio brand is marketed only in the Southwest; Chun King is sold on the East and West coasts; College Inn is distributed in the Northeast; and only Hawaiian Punch is marketed nationally. The company discovered that consumers' preferences for Mexican food were strong in the western part of the United States but that it was much more difficult to try to market Mexican dishes elsewhere. In the same way, Southerners do not list Chinese foods among their favorites, but Easterners and Westerners do.

While geographic differences generally are more dramatic between major regions of the country, differences also exist even within as small a geographic area as a city. In Washington, D.C., for example, Woodward & Lothrop, one of the city's old-line retailers, has evolved from a conservative, traditional department store into one whose appearance and merchandise are directed toward young and affluent shoppers. Yet, while Washington affluence exists in all corners of the city, consumer tastes vary by area of the city. For this reason, Woodward & Lothrop adopted store-by-store marketing strategies for each of its fourteen outlets. Computerized tracking was used to identify potential customers and classify them by income, age, location, education, and style of living. Then each store was to some extent individually merchandized. In the downtown outlet, for instance, the basement merchandising was geared specifically to government workers and teenagers; subsequently, sales shot up 21 percent over previous periods. (See Application 5-3.)

Application 5-3
Geographic Segmentation—
Marketing a Cause as a Product

Political candidates have long dreamed of being able to pinpoint *potential* supporters geographically and then to concentrate on gaining their support and their dollars. With the use of attitude polling, computer technology, and sophisticated use of census data, this dream is nearing reality. In Missouri, just such an approach helped to defeat a proposed right-to-work amendment to the Missouri constitution that would have barred union-shop contracts.

The system began with a poll identifying the kind of Missouri residents whose attitudes on the issue seemed to make them reachable. That information was used to determine which of forty descriptors of citizens—ethnic, educational, economic, and geographic characteristics—appeared relatively favorable to the cause of defeating the amendment.

Those classifications were fed into a computer, together with census data on the same characteristics for all 6000 block groups in Missouri and their members' names, addresses, and telephone numbers.

Out of the computer came, in order of political potential, a list of those blocks that seemed worth exploring. That information was used accordingly in get-out-the-vote campaigns. In many cases, nonactivists were converted to activists.

"You can't run a big television campaign and tell all red-headed men in the audience to tune out," one of the originators of the technique said. "But you can find the people you want to reach this way, without disturbing the people you don't want to." Geographic segmentation can help do the job and pave the way to political success.

Source of data: "Campaigning by Computer Targets U.S. Voting Blocks," *International Herald Tribune,* Feb. 8, 1979, p. 3.

Analyzing Consumers' Behavior

This approach to market segmentation analyzes consumers' behavior in the marketplace and traces it backward to determine which common bonds and attributes result in that segment's behavior. This approach uses the remaining three bases for market segmentation: product usage, perceived product benefits, and lifestyles.

Product usage segmentation analyzes the "heavy users" of a product or brand and then develops marketing mixes aimed specifically at those segments. Marketers who examine product usage rates frequently find the "80–20 principle" at work—20 percent of the market accounts for 80 percent of the sales. This rule of thumb cannot be applied to every product, but it does point to the importance that a rather small group of buyers has for the health of many firms. For instance, in marketing Gablinger beer, Rheingold marketers did not fully recognize that 80 percent of the beer is consumed by 20 percent of the market. In billing its new product as being "low in calories," Rheingold ran into opposition from heavy beer drinkers who were not concerned with weight control—many, in fact, were proud of their bellies. In short, Gablinger failed because it was marketed as a diet drink to consumers who were not concerned about their weight; and those who truly are diet conscious do not drink much beer in the first place. It took Miller Brewing Company, with its Lite beer, to prove that the concept of low-calorie beer was a good one. But Miller aimed its product at beer drinkers, not dieters. It promoted Lite not so much as a low-calorie beer but rather as a beer that could be drunk in abundance without that "full" feeling—a real beer drinker's dream come true.

To many marketers, nonusers represent as clear a marketing opportunity as heavy users. (See Figure 5-3.) Some of those most interested in reaching nonusers are marketers in the public sector and in nonprofit organizations. For instance, The American Cancer Society regularly implores women to have cancer checkups, while the Council on Physical Fitness constantly reminds Americans to exercise, and various cultural groups seek new subscribers for lectures, symphonies, and other events. While the temptation to convert such nonusers into users is strong, most past strategies to change consumers have been resisted.

The "heavy half" approach to market segmentation is most attractive to many marketers because it is often relatively easy to identify and measure heavy users by relying on data that already exist in the marketing information system (MIS). Department stores, for example, can analyze the buying behavior of charge account customers, banks can assess how their services are used, and many syndicated

Figure 5-3   Examples of product usage segmentation. [*Adapted from Dik Warren Twedt, "How Important to Marketing Strategy is the 'Heavy User'?" **Journal of Marketing,** vol. 28, no. 1 (January 1964), p. 72. Used with permission of the publisher, the American Marketing Association*]

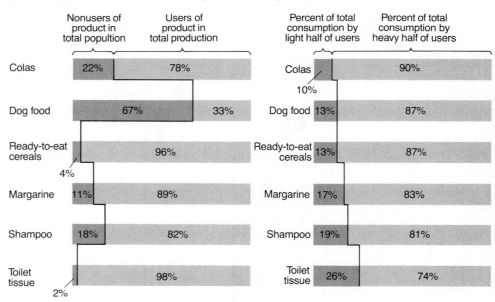

services provide information about heavy users of consumer products. But while the three bases for market segmentation that we have described so far are certainly helpful to marketers, they share a common fault: they are based on *descriptive* factors rather than *casual* ones. That is, they identify and describe the consumers within a market segment, but they do not provide an understanding of why those consumers behave as they do in the marketplace. The segmentation technique that is based on perceived product benefits goes a step further and looks at the core reasons for consumers' exchange behavior. This is a much more accurate way to pinpoint market segments.

Benefit segmentation analyzes information about consumers' wants and needs and translates this information into marketing programs that create and emphasize satisfaction of those desires. This approach assumes that the benefits being sought are the basic reasons why the market segments exist. Certainly, most consumers seek as many benefits as possible from the products they buy. But the *relative importance* they attach to various benefits can differ significantly. That is, consumers do not often expect a product to provide many benefits all at once; rather, they are looking for one overriding benefit—or satisfaction of a major, high-priority want or need. For instance, buyers of Levi's jeans seek "durability"; buyers of Elmer's Glue-All want "adhesion"; and buyers of Lego building blocks are purchasing "possibilities."

In practicing benefit segmentation, marketers must identify the basic need that consumers seek to satisfy—and reflect this in their marketing mix. On the basis of the research finding that 67 percent of the population considers itself as weight-conscious, late in the 1970s, H. J. Heinz began buying its way into the diet-food industry. It acquired Weight Watchers International and other companies that manufacture dietetic foods. Heinz identified two distinct benefit segments within this weight-conscious market—the *serious* dieters seeking substantial weight loss and the *cosmetic* dieters searching for figure improvement.

To reach the 38 percent of the population considered serious dieters, in 1980 Heinz used an advertising campaign stressing "guilt." An ad appearing in women's magazines showed a double-chinned woman staring from behind bars at a plate of lasagne. "Eat without feeling guilty," the copy explained. To reach cosmetic dieters, a segment composed mostly of female, college-educated, 24- to 44-year-olds with previous figure-improvement experience, the company believed an ad showing a chubby model would *not* do. As an executive told *The Wall Street Journal,* a campaign to attract costmetic dieters must appeal to "basic instincts" such as sex appeal and sensuality and use models he described as "something between Bo Derek and Shelly Winters."[2]

The last approach to market segmentation is one of the most promising ways to identify market segments. Called *lifestyle,* or *psychographic, segmentation,* it divides the market into segments according to how consumers live, as reflected by their

---

[2]"Heinz Tries to Reshape Demand for Weight Watchers' Products," *The Wall Street Journal,* July 17, 1980, p. 23.

values, attitudes, and interests. In researching the lifestyle patterns of consumers, marketers measure three things—activities, interests, and opinions:[3]

Activities are manifest actions which are usually observable, such as viewing an ad medium, patronizing a certain store, or buying a specific brand. The major categories of activities are leisure, work, and reverie. An *interest* in some object, event, or topic refers to the degree of excitement that accompanies both special and continuing attention to it. Interests may be of two types: instrumental, in which the topic of interest is seen as a means to an end; and terminal interests, which are viewed as ends rather than means. An *opinion* is a verbal or written response a person gives to a stimulus situation in which some question is raised. Opinions may be further categorized as beliefs, attitudes, or values.

Lifestyle segmentation, then, measures how consumers spend their time pursuing activities—the things in their surroundings that are of greatest interest and importance to them—as well as how they feel about themselves and the world around them. In addition, psychographic research gathers information about consumers' characteristics to help flesh out the picture of the market segments. Such demographic characteristics as sex, age, income, and education are often useful to marketers in completing the psychographic picture. In most cases, marketers concentrate on heavy users of a product. While such consumers are often viewed demographically, marketers can get a much more insightful view by adding the lifestyle dimension. This fuller view enables marketers better to satisfy major consumers' needs.

One of the most successful uses of lifestyle segmentation was developed by marketers of Schlitz beer. Before 1969, the company's advertising campaign centered on the appeal "When you're out of Schlitz, you're out of beer." But management decided that the impact of this theme was lessening, and so a new approach was sought. Informal research was conducted by means of visiting neighborhood taverns around Chicago and observing and talking to members of the target market, heavy beer drinkers. The portrait that emerged showed the target market to consist of males who drank a case of beer on the weekend, or even every day. While their achievements were few, their wishes and dreams were many, and they tended to admire those who had "made it"—especially in the world of sports. Solid demographic studies then added details to this informal picture of heavy beer drinkers. They were found to be young males with a high school education that usually led to a blue-collar job. More than nondrinkers, they sought pleasure and release from the responsibilities of family life and work. Most important to the marketers, these drinkers found release from their frustrations through male-oriented activities that included drinking beer.

As a result of this research, Schlitz formalized a new advertising campaign with the theme "You only go around once—Grab for all the Gusto you can." This approach appealed to heavy beer drinkers' sense of masculinity and satisfied their lifestyle fantasies. The campaign was very effective; when Schlitz's sales rose to

---

[3]Fred D. Reynolds and William R. Darden, "An Operational Construction of Life Style," in M. Venkatesen (ed.), *Proceedings of the 3rd Annual Conference of the Association for Consumer Research,* 1972, pp. 482–484.

second place in the early 1970s, many observers attributed it to this effective use of lifestyle segmentation. Thus, the many bases for segmentation can be combined to create the most effective marketing strategy.

The Market Segmentation Process

As you have noted from the examples given here, marketers generally do not rely upon only one basis for segmenting markets. The use of a single basis for segmentation for all marketing decisions would likely result in incorrect marketing decisions as well as a waste of resources. Marketers look for appropriate bases for segmentation. Then they flesh out the segment with various demographic descriptor variables to create a deep segment profile. Basing their research plan on the marketer's specific needs and knowledge of the market, researchers generally consider a number of alternative segmentation approaches. For instance, if a new-product decision is needed, then *benefit segmentation* may be appropriate; if an advertising theme is the decision focus, then *lifestyle segmentation* may be the right approach. To obtain the market segments most useful in making these decisions, marketers focus on bases related to buyers' responses to marketing activities, that is, on the bases that emphasize some form of consumer behavior in the marketplace.

Once the usable segmentation bases have been determined, marketers select from the vast number of possible demographic variables a set of appropriate descriptors to fill in the portrait of the segment. But the enormous quantity of such variables makes this selection a difficult task. To lead to marketing action, such descriptors should show some relationship to the actual buying behavior exhibited within the segment.

Once the various segments meriting distinct and separate marketing mixes have been defined and described, marketers then select one or more of these segments and develop an appropriate marketing strategy. This step, referred to as *target marketing,* formalizes the specific group or groups the marketer intends to serve by various bundles of utility. Such target selection would rest upon analyses such as forecasting the total market potential for each segment, assessing the competitive situation, estimating expected market share within each segment, determining the marketing mix and its costs to serve each segment, and reviewing the organization's own resources.

A study of the toothpaste market shows how a number of segmentation bases and descriptor variables can be used in combination with benefit segmentation to divide consumers into groups according to benefits sought. As Table 5-1 shows, each segment shares additional characteristics besides an interest in specific product benefits. For instance, the "sociables" segment tends to include younger people who smoke and who are highly social and active. Some brands of toothpaste are aimed specifically at that segment, and the lower part of the table makes some recommendations for effecting a good match between the marketing mix and that segment's needs. A close study of Table 5-1 will clarify why benefit segmentation is such an important marketing technique. On the basis of this picture of the market, target markets that the marketer wants to enter would be chosen and specific strategies developed to capture the desired sales. (See Application 5-4.)

TABLE 5-1 Segmentation of Toothpaste Market

	Segment name			
	Sensory segment	Sociables	Worriers	Independent segment
CHARACTERISTICS				
Principal benefit sought	Flavor, product appearance	Brightness of teeth	Decay prevention	Price
Demographic strengths	Children	Teens, young people	Large families	Men
Special behavioral characteristics	Users of spearmint-flavored toothpaste	Smokers	Heavy users	Heavy users
Brands disproportionately favored	Colgate, Stripe	Macleans, Plus White, Ultra Brite, Close Up	Crest	Brands on sale
Personality characteristics	High self-involvement	High sociability	High hypochondriasis	High autonomy
Lifestyle characteristics	Hedonistic	Active	Conservative	Value oriented
RECOMMENDATIONS				
Advertising copy tone	Light	Light	Serious	Rational two-sided arguments; stress price, product superiority
Depth of sell	Superficial and mood-oriented; shorter commercial, higher frequency	Superficial and mood-oriented; shorter commercial, higher frequency	Intensives, longer commercials (60-second ads)	Intensive, longer commercials (60-second ads)
Advertising copy setting	Focus on product	Socially oriented situations		Demonstration and competitive comparison
Media environment	Youthful, modern, active; heavy use of TV	Youthful, modern, active; heavy use of TV	Serious; heavy use of print	Serious; heavy use of print
Packaging	Colorful	Gleaming white (to indicate white teeth)	Aqua (to indicate fluoride)	

Source: Adapted from Russell I. Haley, "Benefit Segmentation: A Decision Oriented Research Tool," *Journal of Marketing,* vol. 32 (July 1968). p. 33.

Application 5-4
Effective Use of Market Segmentation—
Not "Lite" on Marketing Expertise

In 1970, Miller Brewing Company occupied the number seven spot in the number of barrels of beer brewed in the United States, trailing Anheuser-Busch, the "King of Beers," Schlitz, the brewer with "Gusto" in its sales and market share, and Pabst Blue Ribbon. But by 1977, Miller had catapulted to the number two spot. Miller was the fastest growing brewery in the country and it wasn't until 1980 that Anheuser-Busch finally began to hold its own against the high-flying Miller. Miller owes its meteoric growth to the effective use of market segmentation.

In 1970, Philip Morris acquired control of Miller and introduced to the company the concept of market segmentation, the technique that had brought such success to PM in the cigarette industry. The approach called for dividing the American beer market into demand segments, producing new products and packages specifically for each segment, and spending huge amounts on promotion.

With small exception, before Miller, most brewers ignored segmentation and relied on market aggregation. "Until Miller came along, the brewers operated as if there was a homogeneous market

for beer that could be served by one product in one package," observed a consultant to the beer industry. Miller turned that around with the following:

—By advertising its High Life brand as appropriate for motorcycle racers, rodeo cowboys, and oil drillers squelching an oil blowout. This strategy attracted the blue-collar, heavy beer drinker instead of the previous

upper-income, disproportionately female "Champagne of Bottled Beer" market.

—Women and older people were served by offering a 7-ounce pony bottle. These people felt the traditional 12-ounce size was just too much beer for them. Additionally, the 7-ounce size appealed to heavier beer drinkers who found larger bottles and cans getting warm on hot summer days.

—Miller Lite was aimed initially not so much at the low-calorie market as at the heavy beer drinker who was looking for a less filling beer that would allow consumption of even more beer than normal. Clever advertising featuring popular sports personalities helped target this market and make Miller Lite the most successful new beer introduction in this century.

—Under agreement with the German brewery, Miller offered Lowenbrau for those who wanted the status, the high-quality, the super-premium beer.

Source of data: "How Miller Won a Market Slot for Lite Beer," *Business Week,* Nov. 8, 1976, pp. 60–61; and "The Battle of the Beers," *Newsweek,* March 9, 1981, pp. 68–71.

Describing the Market

To segment markets effectively and make other marketing decisions, it is essential that marketers learn about consumers. This learning progresses through three stages: description, understanding, and prediction. Before marketers can do anything about understanding and predicting consumers' behavior, they need to be able to *describe* their market demographically. But this gives only a sketch of what the consumer is like. By seeking an *understanding* of consumers' exchange behavior, marketers get a much more complete picture of the people whose needs they must satisfy. And with this accurate description and firm understanding of consumers, marketers can better *predict* reactions in the marketplace.

This three-step process of learning about consumers leads to efficient, effective marketing. Toward that end, we next will examine some demographic variables that help marketers describe consumers in general. Then, in the following two chapters, we will explore the influences on consumers' exchange behavior in order to understand and predict reactions in the marketplace.

Population Factors

A market can be characterized as consisting of people who have purchasing power and the willingness to exchange. In equation form,

Market = people × purchasing power × willingness to exchange

Describing the market is the first step toward effective marketing. While each product places different demands on marketers in this regard, the market has some general characteristics that can be described by answering the questions "Who will buy?" and "How will they buy?" Thus, marketers delve into population trends and income projections in order to identify important changes and draft plans to meet them. The rest of this chapter focuses on the first two elements of our equation—people ("Who will buy?") and purchasing power ("How will they buy?").

Size and Growth

In 1981 the population of the United States stood at 230.5 million, and it continues to grow. Since the turn of the century, two distinct birthrate changes have had substantial impact on the makeup of our present and future population. During the years from 1930 to 1945, because of the Depression and World War II, the birthrate was unusually low; then, from 1945 to 1960, it increased by an extremely high rate that has been described as a "baby boom." Recently however, the birthrate has fallen off dramatically. In 1980, in the United States, women bore only a statistical average of 1.9 children each, compared with an average of 3.8 children per woman in 1957. A number of explanations have been offered for this lower rate. As society became increasingly modern, industrial, educated, and urban, it also experienced lower birthrates and death rates. Abortion and contraception were made available to more people. The traditional female roles of motherhood and homemaking were changed

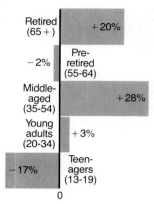

Figure 5-4 The changing age structure of the United States population, 1980–1990. (*The Wall Street Journal*, June 26, 1980, p. 29; U.S. Bureau of the Census data)

radically by the women's changing self-images. At the same time, concern has been growing that larger populations will deplete the world's limited resources. And, of course, the inflated costs of raising children have also limited procreation. (That cost has more than doubled in the last decade, now amounting to about $70,000 per child to age 17.)

While the basic birthrate in the United States is low, the downward spiral abated toward the end of the 1970s. From 1976 to 1980, the rate of births per 1000 American women of childbearing age actually climbed 5 percent. Apparently, more young women in their thirties are changing their minds about not having children. And more in their twenties are opting for a family and a career. As a result, Kimberly-Clark found the disposable-diaper market in the United States was growing at about 10 percent annually. And in 1981, Childcraft Education Corporation increased its infant products by 25 percent.

But if the basic low birthrate continues, it will not be sufficient to replace our present population. Even so, zero population growth is not in the immediate future. More births than deaths occur in any given year, and even if the current low birthrate continues, not until the middle of the twenty-first century will it result in zero population growth. With that will come a "stabilized age structure" in which all generations and age groups will be about equal in size; that is, the number of 55-year-olds will be about the same as the number of 5-year-olds and 35-year-olds. But that proportion certainly does not exist today. And, while the size and growth of our population are important to marketers, the projected age structure is of far greater consequence, for different age groups have different wants and needs that require unique marketing mixes.

Age Structure

Figure 5-4 shows United States census projections of how the age structure will change between 1980 and 1990. Basically, there will be more young children, fewer teenagers, and more young adults, many more early middle-aged adults, fewer later middle-aged persons, and more elderly people. The greatest growth will occur among the biggest-spending age group, adults aged 35 to 54.

Many companies are beginning to feel the effects of these trends and are planning how to cope with the changes. For example, companies that once catered to babies are finding that it pays to diversify. Gerber Products Company, the largest producer of baby foods, has dropped the word *only* from its long-used slogan "Babies are our *only* business" and has diversified into life insurance, printing, and prepackaged meals for single diners. And Johnson & Johnson is working both sides of the street. While it advertises its shampoo as being appropriate for older people as well as babies, it also owns Ortho Pharmaceutical Corporation, one of the largest producers of contraceptives—products for those who want to avoid buying the company's baby products.

Teenagers have long been a profitable market for records, clothing, and soft drinks. But changes in this age segment have also led to marketing changes. Levi Strauss, the company that put a generation of teenagers into denim, is feeling the crunch and is marketing a line of "Levi's for Men" (clothing that is cut more fully to accommodate men who are watching football rather than playing it). And even the Pepsi generation is growing up. Older faces are appearing in advertisements, including those for Pepsi Light, a diet soda with a slightly drier taste that is aimed at adults aged 18 to 49.

Marketers are already responding to the fastest-growing and largest-spending age segments—young and middle-aged adults. Skin-moisturizing lotions like Oil of Olay and Raintree are aimed at maturing women, and there are similar products for men who are growing older. Hair dyes, hairpieces, and wigs are also in great demand. Young and middle-aged adults often have good incomes, and their lifestyles reflect their economic success. They are a ready market for all kinds of consumer products, both familiar and new. Cars, electronic equipment, appliances, and especially housing

Application 5-5
Changing Age Mix—Cereals for Consenting Adults

Cereal marketers have long faced a fickle market, with consumers switching brands as frequently as ten times a year. A new brand, as a rule, is given only six months to establish itself before being edged out by another competitor. Only one-third of new cereal brands survive. Add to that a decline in the number of children 13 and under—America's breakfast-food eaters—and the problem is apparent. To counter this declining children's market, the cereal makers have further segmented the market.

The trend of cereals for the adult market started with the introduction of so-called natural breakfast foods with no nutrition-boosting additives. But the back-to-nature trend faded when it became known that natural cereals were high in fat and sugar and low in nutrition.

The naturals' market shrank from 10 percent in 1974 to 3 percent in 1980. Studies indicating the health benefits of high-fiber diets have made fortified, bran-based cereals the current trend. Quaker Oats' Corn Bran, Ralston's Honey Bran, and Kellogg's Most are among the new high-fiber cereals. To reach even smaller segments of this market, Kellogg is test-marketing "high-in-iron Smart Start" for women between 20 and 40 and is also considering developing a special product for the adult market 65 and over.

Promoting new adult cereals differs sharply from appeals to other groups. Television advertising is placed on early evening news shows or afternoon soap operas rather than on the traditional Saturday morning cartoon slot. Packages, of course,

skip the pictures of gremlins or pixies to grab attention. A box of Total, for example, shows charts and statistics which allegedly make a case for the product's nutritional benefits.

Says General Mills Group Vice President Arthur Schulze: "People are interested in a low-fat, low-cholesterol diet. That helped these products a lot."

Even some of the older statespersons of breakfast products are adopting to the new adult trend. Grape Nuts, around since 1897, is now being promoted as a yogurt topping. And Quaker oatmeal, the most popular cereal with 8 percent of the market, has started television advertising for the first time in a decade.

Source of data: "Food in the A.M.," *Time,* March 30, 1980, p. 53.

Application 5-6
Marketing to the Elderly—"Don't Add Insult to Injury"

"We're not all beautiful, but we're not all decrepit and toothless. We drink Pepsi, too."

So stated an elderly citizen to *The Wall Street Journal,* who went on to lambast companies that attempt to market to the elderly by portraying them as "half-deaf codgers."

Advertising agencies are beginning to recognize that you don't market successfully to the 55-plus population with tactics that are insulting.

A consultant gave the following advice on how to appeal to the elderly market:

Avoid cluttering ads or packages with too much visual information. Use action in commercials if it's relevant and isn't distracting. Avoid "talking heads," fast-speaking characters, or those who don't enunciate clearly. Present a clear, bright, and sharp picture. Keep the language and message simple, with the focus on one or two selling points. Relate new information to something with which the audience is familiar.

Most of all, don't insult older people. Try to present them as having a useful social function and not as being useless or incompetent. Make them active and attractive, but not so much that they'll make older viewers "jealous."

Source of data: "Advertisers Start Recognizing Cost of Insulting the Elderly," *The Wall Street Journal,* March 5, 1981, p. 27.

are among the major purchases that these people make in setting up a home and raising a family. And, for those in the "over-49" bracket, free spending is even more a reality. These middle-aged persons spend more than others on travel (perhaps symbolizing their freedom from children), eating out, and recreational vehicles. In fact, Coachmen Industries, Inc., has taken part of its recreational vehicle advertising away from *Trailer Life* and allocated it to *Good Housekeeping, Popular Mechanics, "50 Plus,"* and other magazines popular among older subscribers. (See Application 5-5.)

The elderly age segment is another growing market that presents many opportunities for marketers, and it will continue to grow as longevity increases. Demand will rise for health care and services, books, nursing homes, travel, retirement housing, and many leisuretime activities. But people in this age group do not like to be stereotyped, and marketers must be sensitive in communicating with them. Several years ago, the H.J. Heinz Company test-marketed a line of "Senior Foods"—lamb, beef, and chicken dishes in 8-ounce containers. After six months, the products were dropped because older people did not like to see their age reflected in the product's name. On the other hand, the marketing focus of Gerber Products Company does not inhibit older consumers from purchasing and consuming (for dietary reasons) an estimated 6 percent of its baby food. And a study conducted by Dannon Yogurt found that 25 percent of the company's sales were made to people over age 55. Like other age groups, the elderly have unique needs that marketers must try to satisfy. (See Application 5-6.)

Working Women

In 1981, among all women 16 years of age and older, 52 percent were holding jobs, compared with 32 percent in 1960 and 37 percent in 1970. This growth is particularly significant, since it involves many women who have small children. Besides their increased demand for child-care services, working women need briefcases, cars, credit cards, insurance, maid service, additional education, air travel, hotel room reservations, and clothes. In 1980, purchases of women's suits grew by almost 70 percent, while men's suits were down 12 percent. (See Figure 5-5.) And as more families eat out, the demand for restaurant services rises, while supermarket sales fall. Again, marketers must adjust to meet these challenges. (For further details on the impact of women on marketing, see Table 5-2.)

Number of Households

As more and more people live alone, the number of households also increases. Compared with the median age a decade ago, the median (middle) age for first marriage is up one whole year, and now fewer than 10 of every 1000 people get married each year—a rate that is expected to remain low. Also, the divorce rate is higher, with 40 percent of all marriages now ending in divorce. And widows account for a third of all one-person households. Demographers estimate that 45 percent of infants born in 1978 will live in one-parent families for part of their childhood.

How people live is important to marketers because it determines spending patterns. The greater number of households obviously increases the demand for housing. But automobile sales are also affected; single people buy 6 percent of all

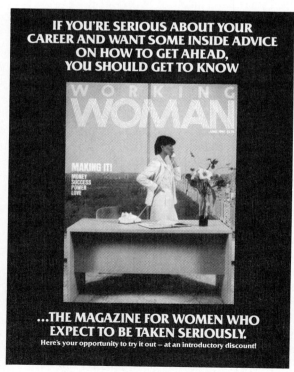

Figure 5-5 Women working outside the home are a steadily growing market, and marketers increasingly recognize its potential by offering new products, such as *Working Woman* magazine, aimed at aspiring career women. (Courtesy Working Woman)

TABLE 5-2 All about Women

FACTS ON FILE

1 Women annually spend an estimated $30 billion for new cars.
2 They buy or have a major influence on at least half of all car purchases.
3 Women account for 39% of new car purchases annually.
4 In 1980, 55% of the buyers of Buick Regal were women.
5 Driving to and from work is the principal use for cars bought by 67% of female car buyers.
6 A *Women's Day* survey showed 85% of new car purchases involve women, either shopping alone or with men, according to purchasers.
7 More than half of all women—52%—work outside the home.
8 Three-fifths of husband-wife households have two paychecks. In 1950, the figure was 36%.

9 Between 1960 and 1980, the number of working women increased from 23,000,000 to 40,000,000.
10 Warranty and service-related benefits, operating cost, ride, handling and safety are of greater concern to women than to men.
11 Women tend to be more concerned with the functional, practical aspects, while many men look more for a swinging image and self-expression in a car, according to a Ford official.
12 About 75% of all women car buyers work, and the typical career female is surprisingly young.
13 Young, single and working women have a much stronger preference than men for smaller cars. This trend, according to Ford, may be related to economics rather than preference.

Sources: Ford Motor Co., *Women's Day,* Buick division, U.S. Census Bureau. Reprinted with permission from *Advertising Age,* June 22, 1981, pp. S–24.

passenger cars but up to half of the small specialty cars. Appliance marketers have responded to single people's needs, providing a grill for one sandwich, a slow cooker for one serving of stew, and a fryer to whip up one plate of french fries. Campbell's Soup-for-One, Green Giant's single-serving casseroles, and Schenley's Cocktails-for-Two are all targeted toward this segment of the population.

Geographic Shifts

With some products, different geographic locations result in variations in consumers' preferences and product usage (see Table 5-3). As a result, marketers need to be attuned to geographic population shifts. Figure 5-6 indicates that certain areas of the United States are expected to gain population rapidly by 1990. The biggest increases will occur in the South and in the West as Americans move to the Sun Belt—the lower arc of warm lands from Southern California to the Carolinas. This shift reflects a restructing of American values, a shedding of the work ethic based on increased material rewards in favor of an improved quality of life as enjoyed through year-round outdoor activities, a more relaxed lifestyle, a lower cost of living, and reductions in crime, congestion, and pollution.

This movement to the Sun Belt has provided both opportunities and problems for marketers. For instance, supermarkets have limited their geographical expansion to the Sun Belt region where population growth is seen; on the other hand, interstate moving companies find the exodus of people from the Northeast a definite problem, since moving vans frequently return empty.

Within the nation there has been steady movement away from cities and toward suburbs. This trend, however, is less pronounced than it was in the two decades after World War II. Greater congestion, higher costs of energy, increased crime, pollution,

TABLE 5-3 Geographic Differences in Consumers' Behavior—The Best and the Worst Markets for Selected Products*

	The best	The worst
Beer and ale:	Milwaukee	Dallas/Fort Worth
Drinkers who consume	(67.9%)	(44.2%)
Bicycles:	Minneapolis/St. Paul	Atlanta
Adults who ever bought	(30%)	(18.5%)
Deodorants and antiperspirants:	Baltimore	Minneapolis/St. Paul
Adults who use once a day	(88.1%)	(78.3%)
Foreign travel:	Seattle/Tacoma (38)	Cincinnati
Adults who traveled in past 3 years	(38%)	(10.8%)
Fur coats:	Detroit (11)	Cincinnati
Adults who ever bought	(11%)	(6.4%)
Lipstick:	Seattle/Tacoma	Cincinnati
Women using at least twice a day	(58.2%)	(35.6%)
Motor oil:	Dallas/Fort Worth	New York
Adults who buy	(64.8 %)	(40.8%)
Panty hose:	Houston	Miami
Women who bought in past month	(61.1%)	(39.7%)
Paperback books:	Seattle/Tacoma	Dallas/Fort Worth
Adults who bought in last 30 days	(53.2%)	(31.3%)
Restaurants:	Seattle/Tacoma	Washington, D.C.
Adults who visited in past month	(72.6%)	(54.9%)
Scotch whisky:	New York	Cincinnati
Drinkers who consume	(35.9%)	(9.6%)
Tennis racquets:	Los Angeles	Cincinnati
Adults who ever bought	(17.5%)	(9.8%)

*Based on a survey of twenty cities.
Source: Niles Howard, "More Bang for the Ad Dollar," *Dun's Review,* October 1978, p. 107.

and racial tensions, as well as housing shortages, are expected to hold down growth in the suburbs. Such citylike problems in the suburbs are also expected to sharply increase population movement to rural areas. Between 1975 and 1980, about 1.4 million more people moved to rural areas than left them. Obviously, marketers must keep track of such trends in order to know where their markets are located. S. S. Kresge, for example, has opened "mini" K marts in towns of 8,000 to 15,000 population to meet this trend.

Despite this movement away from central cities, Boston, Washington, and Philadelphia are among the cities that have experienced new growth. Younger and older married couples with no children at home seem to be particularly interested in moving back. In many cities, the once-decaying areas—often referred to as the "Old Town"—are the fashionable places to live. But few experts predict an urban renaissance in the 1980s.

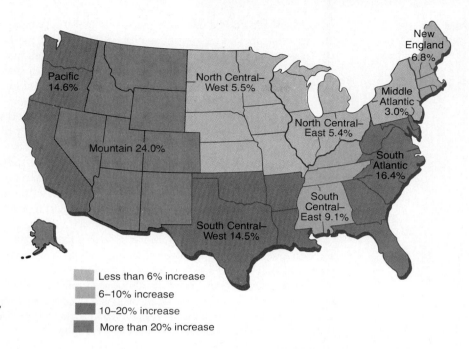

Figure 5-6 Shifts in the United States population, 1980–1990. (U.S. Bureau of the Census)

Purchasing Power: The Ability to Buy

While people are one element in our market equation, we also must look at individuals' ability to buy. Without the money to exchange for products, consumers have little importance to marketers. And since the ability to buy is based on income, we first must look at two factors that affect income: education and occupation.

Education

The level of education continues to rise in the United States and this has major implications for marketers. With 19 percent of the population attending or graduating from college, marketers must prepare not only for more sophisticated, wiser consumers but for consumers who have different needs and wants in the marketplace. Marketers of high-priced goods—television sets, quality furniture, automobiles—will likely benefit from this trend. Better-educated consumers generally demand higher quality in both goods and services.

Occupation

Closely related to education is occupation. In the 1940s the United States was primarily a blue-collar society; today the white-collar segment is almost as large, a reflection of education and the rise in service-related industries. In addition, the increased automation of production has diminished the need for production workers. For example, in the newspaper industry not many years ago, there was one operator for every typesetting machine; now that operator can supervise twelve computerized machines.

Income

Consumers' income takes many forms—wages and salaries, dividends, social security checks, interest, fees, and appreciation in assets. But marketers are most concerned with *disposable income,* the amount available for personal consumption after taxes are deducted. This is what the consumers have left to exchange in satisfying their needs and wants. But marketers are also very interested in *discretionary income,* the amount left after essentials (that is, *needs*) are provided for—such fixed items as food, clothing, transportation, shelter, and utilities. Because discretionary income goes toward satisfying wants rather than needs, the spending of this income is far more elusive to predict. Discretionary income purchases such luxuries as boats, second homes, and other top-of-the-line products. Table 5-4 shows how gross household income in 1990 is expected to compare with 1980 income.

Americans have always lived with the promise of "more." Yet, in the 1980s they face a shrinking standard of living—due in great part to the high rate of inflation. (See Figure 5-7.)

Between 1967 and 1973, real disposable income per person increased by 17.5 percent; over the next six years the gain fell to a meager 5.5 percent. And in the beginning of 1979, the rate of change turned negative.

The picture is even more dismal when looking at what is left over from income after taking into account spending on basic necessities, such as food and shelter. In recent years, the prices of essentials have skyrocketed. So the nation's real discretionary income in 1979 actually fell 4.6 percent below the 1973 level. Those families in the lower (less than $10,000) and middle ($10,000 to $30,000) income brackets have

TABLE 5-4 Distribution of Gross Household Income: 1980–1990 Projections*

	1980	1990
$ 0–$ 4,999	15.7%	12.8%
$ 5,000–$ 9,999	19.5%	17.2%
$10,000–$14,999	17.4%	15.0%
$15,000–$19,999	15.2%	13.6%
$20,000–$24,999	11.7%	11.6%
$25,000–$29,999	8.0%	9.2%
$30,000–$34,999	4.7%	6.8%
$35,000 +	7.8%	13.8%
	100.0%	100.0%
Median income	$14,208	$16,856

*Based on 1977 dollars and assuming a 2 percent growth in income each year.

Source: U.S. Bureau of the Census, *Current Population Reports,* Series P-60, No. 122, "Illustrative Projections of Money Income Size Distributions, for Households: 1980 to 1995." U.S. Government Printing Office, Washington, D.C., 1980.

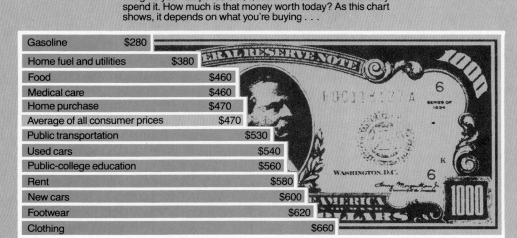

Imagine you had put aside $1,000 in 1970 and now are ready to spend it. How much is that money worth today? As this chart shows, it depends on what you're buying . . .

Gasoline	$280
Home fuel and utilities	$380
Food	$460
Medical care	$460
Home purchase	$470
Average of all consumer prices	$470
Public transportation	$530
Used cars	$540
Public-college education	$560
Rent	$580
New cars	$600
Footwear	$620
Clothing	$660

24 Prices and How They've Changed

	1970	1980	Increase		1970	1980	Increase
Eggs (dozen)	$ .62	$ .81	31%	Man's haircut	$ 2.61	$ 4.82	85%
Man's dress shirt	$ 6.97	10.41	49%	Milk (half gal.)	$ .58	$ 1.09	88%
Refrigerator	$288.62	$446.30	55%	Permanent wave	$14.61	$ 27.85	91%
Auto tire	$ 33.84	$52.59	56%	White bread (lb.)	$ .25	$ .49	96%
Bacon (lb.)	$ .97	$ 1.56	61%	Potatoes (lb.)	$ .09	$ .18	100%
Pork chops (lb.)	$ 1.19	$ 1.91	61%	Hamburger (lb.)	$ .67	$ 1.41	110%
Washing machine	$228.20	$378.49	66%	Round steak (lb.)	$ 1.32	$ 2.83	114%
Cigarettes	$ .43	$ .73	70%	Butter (lb.)	$ .87	$ 1.89	117%
Chicken (lb.)	$ .39	$ .67	72%	Bus fare	$ .35	$ .87	149%
Movie ticket	$ 2.02	$ 3.49	73%	Hospital room (semiprivate)	$54.42	$156.52	188%
Tomatoes (lb.)	$ .30	$ .52	73%	Gasoline (premium, gal.)	$ .38	$ 1.33	250%
Eyeglasses (with exam)	$ 41.44	$ 74.85	81%	Coffee (lb.)	$ .95	$ 3.48	266%

Note: Above numbers are national averages.

Figure 5-7   The impact of inflation. (*Reprinted from* U.S. News & World Report. *Copyright 1980, U.S. News & World Report, Inc.*)

felt the pinch the most. They have become the nation's "have-nots." Such families feel frustrated and cautious—and tend to downgrade their purchasing. Lower-priced, unbranded goods are more appealing. Big-ticket items are avoided. Less-expensive town houses are bought in place of houses. Vacations are taken closer to home. (See Application 5-7.)

Application 5-7
Inflation—Coping with the Shriveling Dollar

Cutting costs has become a permanent pastime for millions of consumers after a decade of soaring prices. Their challenge lies in finding ways to cope with rising costs. The do-it-yourself trend, clipping food coupons, moonlighting, shopping in bargain basements, buying easy-care clothing fabrics, and washing clothes in cold water are only a few of the tricks many consumers have used to offset the bite of inflation. Consider the following behavior:

—For the Wollenburgs of Cleveland, satisfaction comes from being able to turn other people's castoffs into treasures. "We don't see any reason to buy something new when you can find something better at less than a third of the price. Most of what we have is recycled from someone else's trash."

—The Williamses of Pittsburgh enjoy some of the luxuries they like (racket-club membership and vacations) because they economize in other spots. The children share clothes (Mrs. Williams says she never buys pink) and she makes most of her own clothes. Unused symphony, zoo, and theater subscriptions were dropped.

—In Englewood, Colorado, the Hipps purchased a new television set with change dropped in a jug every day for six months. This was supplemented with change obtained from regular trips to a recycling center that pays for aluminum cans.

—A single Denver woman, Joan McCarthy, has been dubbed the "champion of cheap" by her students. She teaches classes on "cheap living, cheap dating, and cheap Christmas" at Denver Free University. Living on $300 a month, she says, "I live way below the poverty level, but you wouldn't know it. "She does it by shopping at wholesale food stores, sharing housing costs with a roommate, shopping at thrift stores for clothes, and having dental work done at a local dental school. She also takes advantage of the many Denver establishments that offer free hors d'oeuvres, noting that "for a lot of people, that's dinner."

Sources of data: "How Your Neighbors Are Beating Inflation," *U.S. News & World Report,* May 18, 1981, pp. 61–62; and "What People Do to Adjust to Inflation," *U.S. News & World Report,* Dec. 14, 1981, pp. 52–53.

At the same time, the United States is seeing the emergence of another income class, the "haves." The richest 20 percent of American families (with incomes above $31,000) accounted for 41.6 percent of total U.S. income in 1979. These people have gained their wealth by choosing the right profession, realizing the income of a spouse, or having bought a home years ago. These households spend freely—especially in the luxury market. Albert Nipon, a New York company specializing in dresses retailing for $200 to $450, doubled its sales volume in 1980. Ethan Allen, Inc., reports sales of fine-quality furniture in its stores are up 12 to 20 percent. Purchases of gold and silver jewelry, yachts, imported autos such as BMW and Mercedes Benz, expensive Broadway theater tickets, and luxury apartments are all up—a result of their being bought by the "haves."

Chapter 1 noted that the United States has moved from a production economy to a sales economy to a marketing economy. Now, it is moving toward a *quality society,* one that demands better goods and more efficiencies in service. Such an era will require an even more sophisticated marketing effort, since discretionary income will likely exert a stronger influence in the marketplace.

Looking Back

This chapter emphasized *market description,* which provides a basis for segmentation. Before turning to Chapters 6 and 7, which focus on understanding consumers, review the following important points:

1 With a strategy of market aggregation, the market is not divided into segments; the main advantage of this approach is lower costs.

2 Market segmentation is the process of dividing the heterogeneous market into segments made up of elements that are similar.

3 In *concentrated marketing,* a firm serves only a single market segment.

4 The segmentation strategy that treats each consumer uniquely is called *market atomization.*

5 When choosing to serve several market segments, the marketer is practicing *differentiated marketing.*

6 The advantage of market segmentation is that the marketing mix can better match the needs and wants of the market segment, but it does so at higher costs to the firm.

7 For a strategy of market segmentation to be effective, the market must be identifiable and measurable, accessible, substantial, and responsible.

8 Markets can be segmented on the basis of consumers' characteristics (demographics and geographic location) or on the basis of consumers' behavior (product usage, benefits sought, and lifestyles).

9 The segmentation process focuses on buyer behavior as the basis for segmentation and uses demographic variables to profile the segments.

10 A market consists of people with purchasing power and the willingness to exchange.

11 The following population trends will affect marketing in the future: the most important age segment in the 1980s will be the post-World War II babies who are moving toward middle age; households with dual incomes will have a sustained impact on buying behavior; fewer children per family can be expected in the

future; the number of households will increase; the most pronounced population shift is the movement to the South and Western regions of the United States; suburbs and small towns will see the greatest increase in population.

12   The future generation of adults will be more highly educated than the present generation, which will make the United States an increasingly white-collar society.

Key Terms

If you aren't sure what each of the following words means, look back at the text. Numbers refer to pages on which the words are defined. Additional information can be found by checking the index and the glossary at the end of the book.

segment 134
aggregation 134
undifferentiated marketing 134
segmentation 136
concentrated marketing 138
market atomization 138
differentiated marketing 138
demographic segmentation 142

geographic segmentation 142
product usage segmentation 143
benefit segmentation 145
lifestyle segmentation 145
target marketing 147
disposable ,income 158
discretionary income 158

Questions for Review

1   What is the difference between *market aggregation* and *concentrated marketing*?

2   What are the four criteria for effective use of market segmentation?

3   Identify the *descriptive* bases for market segmentation.

4   What are some of the factors that have led to the lowering of the United States birthrate?

5   What are some of the changes that have taken place in the makeup of American households?

6   What is the Sun Belt, and what has been its significance to marketers?

Questions for Thought and Discussion

1   Describe how lifestyle changes could contribute to gains and losses in the pet food industry.

2   Do you think there is enough demand for companies to develop products specifically for left-handed people? What are some products that might satisfy the unique needs of such a market segment?

3   In 1981, General Motors' Cadillac Division brought out the Cimarron, 4 feet shorter than the typical Cadillac automobile, with stick shift on the floor, fat black tires, 4-cylinder engine, and drum-tight suspension. Priced at about $13,000, this Cadillac bore little resemblance to

traditional, luxurious Cadillacs. Why would GM market such a car?

4   An increasing number of beauty products are being marketed for older, more mature women. What current population trends would lead skin-care companies to make such a move?

Suggested Project

Research a number of magazine or newspaper articles that provide information concerning current trends in the United States population. Use this information to forecast a trend for the year 2000, and explain what implications it will have on maketing strategy of a particular company (such as Gillette, Revlon, or Chrysler).

Suggested Readings

Bartos, Rena: "Over 49: The Invisible Market," *Harvard Business Review,* vol. 58, no. 1 (January–February 1980), pp. 140–149. The market of consumers past 49 years of age must be segmented to understand the untapped opportunities for expanded sales.

Haley, Russell I.: "Benefit Segmentation: A Decision-Oriented Research Tool," *Journal of Marketing,* vol. 31, no. 3 (July 1968), pp. 30–35. This article shows the usefulness of segmenting markets on a causal basis rather than a descriptive basis.

Plummer, Joseph T.: "The Concept and Application of Life-Style Segmentation," *Journal of Marketing,* vol. 38, no. 1 (January 1974), pp. 33–37. The two concepts of lifestyle and market segmentation are combined to provide a better understanding of consumers and allow more effective communication.

Resnik, Alan J., Peter B. B. Turney, and J. Barry Mason: "Marketers Turn to 'Counter Segmentation'," *Harvard Business Review,* vol. 57, no. 5 (September–October 1979), pp. 100–106. With careful analysis, marketers can analyze the profitability of a strategy of offering simpler products with lower price tags.

Smith, Wendell R.: "Product Differentiation and Market Segmentation as Alternative Marketing Strategies," *Journal of Marketing,* vol. 20 no. 3 (July 1956), pp. 3–8. This classic article initiated the use of the market segmentation approach.

Statistical Abstract of the United States. This annual publication provides a wealth of data on many facets of American life; all marketing students should be familiar with it and its implications for marketing.

Wells, William P.: "Psychographics: A Critical Review," *Journal of Marketing Research,* vol. 12, no. 2 (May 1975), pp. 196–213. This article provides a thorough survey of psychographic studies and some case histories on the uses of psychographic research.

Wind, Yoram: "Issues and Advances in Segmentation Research," *Journal of Marketing Research,* vol. 15, no. 3 (August 1978), pp. 317–337. The author reviews the current status and recent advances in segmentation research.

Chapter
6

Social Influences on Exchange Behavior

Looking Ahead

Chapter 5 established an equation for defining the market.

Market = people × purchasing power × willingness to exchange

In trying to understand what leads to marketing success, we have already discussed *people,* as described by marketers, and their *purchasing power,* or their ability to make an exchange. Now we will begin to focus on the third part of our equation—the *willingness to exchange.*

In itself, the process of describing the market (Chapter 5) will not lead to effective marketing. Marketers also must understand *why* people in the market behave as they do. This chapter and the next explore some influences that affect people's willingness to exchange. First we will look at the social and situational influences on buying behavior—outside, environmental factors that influence consumers. Then, in Chapter 7, we will study the internal factors that influence an individual consumer's willingness to exchange.

Key Topics

Parties to the exchange process: initiators, influencers, deciders, buyers, consumers, and evaluators

The nature of culture, and some trends affecting American values

The effects of cultural influences on exchange behavior

The social class structure in the United States and its implications for marketing

How exchange behavior is influenced by reference groups, roles, and self-image

Family structure and decision making

How family roles influence exchange behavior

How various situations influence exchange behavior

Chapter Outline

A primary goal of marketing is to provide satisfaction to buyers within the economic system. To meet that objective, the marketing concept requires that organizational and individual buyers be the focus of all marketing efforts. That's why marketers are so deeply involved in gathering and analyzing information about the market. Their basic question is: *What does the market want?* Through the process of marketing research, the buying groups within a market are defined and described in terms of their general characteristics and their ability to buy. But that's not enough. Buying decisions are made by people—whether they relate to the purchase of major equipment for industrial use or a new pair of socks. And individuals have reasons for the buying decisions they make. To provide satisfaction, marketers must understand *why* people behave as they do.

Industrial and other organizational buying tends to be more rational, based on such considerations as quality, reliability, and price—and less subject to the vagaries of human nature. It is in marketing to the consumer market that the many complex reasons *why* people buy become so important. For this reason, our discussion will focus on the consumer-buyer. We will discuss the nature of organizational (including industrial) exchange behavior at the end of Chapter 7.

Human beings are complex, of course, and there's no reason to expect that marketers can be any more successful at explaining their behavior than the various social sciences have been. In fact, marketing has been called an interdisciplinary study because it relies so heavily on the behavioral sciences in order to understand individual buyers. The various branches of such disciplines as anthropology, economics, sociology, and psychology all provide marketers with valuable information and insights concerning people's behavior. But probably the most useful behavioral science for marketers is *social psychology,* the study of how human behavior is influenced by other people.

Human beings do not live in isolation. We have been called "social animals" because our entire lives are spent surrounded by other people. Modern society demands that we interact with others. And the people with whom we deal have a tremendous influence on our lives, including our buying behavior.

Perhaps we can never understand ourselves as well as we might wish. Certainly, behavioral scientists—and marketers—have a long way to go. But they have made a substantial start, and it is our purpose in this chapter and the next to see what they have learned. Marketers *need* to understand people, however complex. We will begin by studying how our social environment affects exchange behavior. Such things as culture, social classes, reference groups, and the family all play a part in how we behave in the marketplace. But first we need to look again at the exchange process in order to see how other people enter into it.

Parties to the Exchange Process

Early in our study of marketing we defined the *exchange process* as involving two parties, each with something to exchange, and some means for the parties to communicate their willingness to exchange (review Figure 1-2). However, like most

Figure 6-1 Six parties to the exchange process. (*Adapted from Philip Kotler*, Marketing Management: Analysis, Planning, and Control, *4th ed., Prentice-Hall, Englewood Cliffs, N.J., 1980, p. 134*)

definitions, this one is too simple. It passes over some important distinctions that marketers must recognize. A more accurate picture of the people involved at the receiving end of the exchange process is given in Figure 6-1. Instead of only one receiving party, it shows six: *initiators, influencers, deciders, buyers, consumers,* and *evaluators.* Some of these terms—especially *buyer* and *consumer*—are used interchangeably. But each term has a distinct meaning of its own, and each represents a separate stage in the exchange process. The participants (one or more, in each case) can be defined as follows:

Initiator: the person who first recognizes an unsatisfied want or need

Influencer: the individual who provides information about how to satisfy the want or need

Decider: the person who finally chooses an alternative that will satisfy the unmet want or need

Buyer: the purchaser of the product

Consumer: the person who uses the product

Evaluator: the individual who provides feedback on the chosen product's ability to satisfy

At all times, all six stages of the exchange process are acted out by a single person. For instance, suppose a student (the initiator) is studying late one night, alone (no influencer), and begins to think about food, which is available in a vending machine down the hall. The student walks to the machine, looks over the selections, and makes a choice (the decider), finally dropping a coin in the slot and pulling a leaver (the buyer). Then the student quickly eats the purchase (the consumer), feeling at least some satisfaction (the evaluator). In this case, only one person is involved in all six stages of the exchange process.

But exchange is not always so simple. Consider this example. A little girl and her friend are watching cartoons on television one morning when a commercial boasts about the delicious fried chicken available at Kentucky Fried Chicken (the initiators).

The girl remarks to her friend, "Gee, it sure sounds good!" Her friend (the influencer) replies, "It *is*. I was at Kentucky Fried Chicken yesterday, and I really liked their chicken." The girl then runs upstairs and asks her mother whether she can have some chicken from KFC. Her mother (the decider) says she can, and they tell the girl's father (the buyer) to bring some KFC chicken home for dinner. When the little girl gobbles up the chicken (the consumer), she announces, "Mmm, those chicken legs are really yummy!" (the evaluator). Later, however, her grandmother (another evaluator) expresses concern because her grandchild is eating so much fried food. In this example, the six stages of exchange are performed by six different people, each of whom play an important part in the purchase.

Astute marketers must recognize and understand the contributions made by all parties to an exchange. Nike Inc., the top-selling athletic shoe manufacturer, knows the importance of initiators, influencers, and evaluators. Nike, like many other concerns, has numerous athletes under contract. Some are paid in terms of a few pairs of shoes; others, such as tennis star John McEnroe and baseball pitcher Nolan Ryan, are paid handsome sums to wear Nike products. Consistent with the company's strategy, professional athletes are seen wearing Nike, and many amateur athletes follow as they try to imitate their heroes. Then follows the mass market of teenagers, children, and even unathletic suburbanites who wish to symbolize the health-and-exercise fashion of today. But athletes are not the only ones emulated. As the company's cofounder and chairman told *Forbes,* "A few years ago we had one shoe which was slipping. Then one night Farrah Fawcett appeared on *Charlie's Angels* wearing this particular shoe in close-ups, as she skateboarded during an escape scene. Within a few weeks, sales of that shoe doubled."[1]

In this chapter we'll look at four social groups whose members sometimes influence our willingness to exchange. These social influences on exchange behavior are culture, social class, reference groups, and the family (see Figure 6-2). Each can act as an *initiator* (we see material goods that others have, and we want them for ourselves), or an *influencer* (we talk with others in our social system to get information about meeting our needs), or an *evaluator* (we look to others for approval of our buying behavior). Now let's see how these groups help to shape our wants and needs, and thus our willingness to exchange.

Culture

As implied in Figure 6-2, culture is the largest of the many groups in which we hold membership. It has been defined as "a complex of values, ideas, attitudes, and other meaningful symbols created by [human beings] to shape human behavior and the

---

[1]"Nike's Fast Track," *Forbes,* Nov. 23, 1981, pp. 59–62.

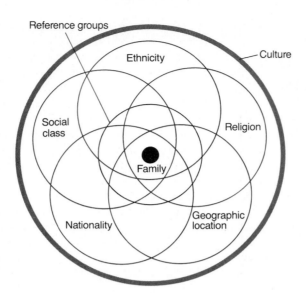

Figure 6-2 The individual decision maker (shown as a dot) within the social environment.

artifacts of that behavior as they are transmitted from one generation to the next."[2] As such, culture is the underlying determinant of much of our decision-making and buying behavior. It greatly affects why some products are preferred over others. Consequently, a realistic and useful analysis of exchange behavior must include an understanding of the cultural context that shapes consumers' needs and wants and is reflected in their decision making.

Actually, each of us belongs to several cultural groups. The largest one is *national heritage,* our identification with all the people in our nation. But we are also members of smaller groups (subcultures) within this larger society, which can be subdivided to reflect geographic, religious, or ethnic differences. For example, *geographic subcultures* influence people who live in different parts of the country to express different values and behavior patterns. As a result, their buying behavior also differs. Some of these regional differences are pronounced, and marketers must be aware of them. There are regional beer-taste differences, for instance; New Yorkers seem to prefer a more bitter beer, like Rheingold, while Californians like lighter beer, such as Coors. And in Texas, beer is served at a chilling 32 degrees—which tends to cloud flavor differences.

Many consumers also belong to *religious subcultures* that result in behavioral differences. Christians celebrate Christmas, while Jews observe Chanukah, the Festival of Lights. Both holidays trigger a flurry of activity in the marketplace, since gift giving is part of their traditions. Still, many consumers play down this aspect of holiday

---

[2]Alfred L. Kroeber and Talcott Parsons, "The Concepts of Culture and of Social System," *American Sociological Review,* vol. 23 (October 1958), p. 583.

observance, and others do not celebrate these events at all. Marketers must recognize and respect such differences.

The United States has been described both as a "melting pot" and as a "salad bowl," reflecting the many *ethnic subcultures* that coexist and mix within its boundaries. Our ties to ancestral backgrounds are still strong, and modern life provides more opportunities than ever to learn about other people's customs. A glance at the frozen food section of any supermarket offers proof enough: from blintzes to tamales to pizza, ethnic dishes of every variety compete for our attention.

From these few examples it's clear that subcultural groups greatly influence buying behavior. Whatever shared trait they are based on—religion, ethnic background, race—such groups present unique demands in the marketplace. To illustrate this point, we'll take a brief look at two of the largest subcultural groups in the United States: black Americans and Hispanic Americans.

There are more than 26.5 million black people in the United States, representing $140 billion in buying power. This group constitutes 11.7 percent of the population, showing a 17 percent increase since 1970. Blacks tend to live in the central city and to earn about one-third less than do whites. While the educational level of blacks is improving, only about one-half as many blacks go to college as do whites.

Within a given group, individual behavior is never uniform, and blacks are no more identical than whites. But some general observations can be made about the buying behavior of the groups:[3]

1 Compared with white Americans, blacks spend proportionately more income on clothing, home furnishings, transportation other than automobiles, and savings; they spend proportionately less income on food, housing, medical care, automobile transportation, and insurance.

2 Especially at the lowest income levels, black consumers tend to be more localized in terms of food-shopping behavior.

3 At all income levels, black women are at least as fashion-conscious as white women, and this trait increases with income.

4 Advertisements that use integrated models seem to have no adverse effects on either blacks or whites.

5 In terms of television viewing, blacks show a greater preference than whites for family entertainment and variety shows.

The second largest subcultural group in the United States is the Hispanic minority. This group, numbering 15 million in 1980, is composed mainly of Mexican-Americans, Puerto Ricans, and Cubans, and spends $50 billion annually.

---

[3]Charles D. Schewe, "Marketing to Blacks: Research Implications for Managers." *Atlanta Economic Review,* vol. 36, no. 5 (September–October 1976), pp. 34–40.

This segment of the population is growing much faster than the black minority—it increased 61 percent between 1970 and 1980. States with the largest Hispanic populations are California (4,500,000), Texas (3,000,000), New York (1,700,000), and Florida (858,000). Like the black American market, the Hispanic market exhibits some distinct buying behavior characteristics:

1 The Hispanic market spends more on food than other groups—mainly because of larger family size.

2 The Hispanic shopper feels lost in giant supermarkets and inhibited about asking questions there (probably because of language barriers). Yet, Hispanics still do most of their shopping in large stores rather than bodegas (small shops).

3 Hispanic households visit fast-food restaurants more frequently than do non-Spanish consumers.

4 Hispanics are highly brand-loyal, trusting well-known or familiar brands and making new brand introduction difficult.

5 Inhibited by language, Hispanics are often confused by multiple pricing and cents-off labels.[4]

To the degree that such traits can be measured for subcultural groups, marketers must attempt to satisfy the unique demands made by each group in the marketplace. To do that effectively, they must understand the foundations of cultural groups.

The Nature of Culture

In discussing society and its needs in Chapter 1, we noted that the members of a society work together to meet its needs. Working together is the foundation of cultural groups. When prehistoric hunters found that hunting alone was impractical, they banded together with other individuals, and their game bags were less often empty. Thus, the desire to survive spurred the beginnings of group life. A group's main purpose was to ensure its own survival. To meet this overriding need, group members developed rules of conduct. Today, we call such rules *norms;* they establish the boundaries of acceptable behavior within a cultural group. Whether the group is a family, a tribe, or a nation, its members must learn the norms and follow them. Members learn early in life that certain behavior will be approved or rewarded, other behavior will only be tolerated, and some behavior will be condemned and punished. Thus, a major characteristic of cultural groups is that they have norms which individual members are expected to learn and follow.

The process by which an individual learns cultural norms is called *socialization* or *enculturation.* We absorb cultural values, ideas, and attitudes through a number of

---

[4]Henry Assael, *Consumer Behavior and Marketing Action,* Kent Publishing, Boston, 1981, p. 274; David L. Loudon and Albert J. Della Bitta, *Consumer Behavior: Concepts and Applications,* McGraw-Hill, New York, 1979, pp. 155–161.

sources, primarily the family. But we also learn how to behave through religious training and through the educational process. Later, our behavior is refined by friends, peers, and the culture at large—everything from art to television. In short, we are indoctrinated. We are taught the values of society from earliest childhood on. And we tend to accept society's values and norms rather than risk social disapproval or punishment. (See Figure 6-3.)

Fortunately, this restrictive view of culture is offset by another characteristic: Culture is *adaptive*. As the needs of society change, its values change to meet those needs. Until recently, for example, the most important product of society was people. Population growth brought increased productivity and, with it, a better standard of living. Large families were encouraged. Lately, however, smaller families have come to be sanctioned as society faces the challenges of scarcity that have resulted from population growth. This adaptive characteristic of culture—its ability to change to meet its needs—is usually a very slow process. Since cultural values are handed down from generation to generation, change comes about slowly. But today's highly technological society makes more rapid change possible and often encourages it. In addition, the values and norms of smaller groups to which we belong may change faster than the overall cultural values do.

Since culture defines the values of a society and cultural norms influence how people live and behave, it's obvious that culture has important implications for marketers. That is, cultural values also determine wants and needs and set the boundaries for acceptable marketing behavior. Effective marketers must be aware of the cultural environment within which they operate. In Chapter 19 we'll see that international marketing is greatly affected by the cross-cultural differences that exist among the world's societies. Here, however, our interest is with the American value system. What cultural values and trends do we observe in the United States, and how do they set the boundaries for acceptable marketing behavior?

Figure 6-3 The process of socialization begins early in childhood and is reinforced by family, friends, and institutions. (*Bruce Roberts, Myron Wood/Photo Researchers*)

The American Value System

Cultural values have changed throughout the history of the United States, but the last decade has seen especially rapid change. Values still are passed from one generation to another, of course, but advanced technology and communication systems produce faster changes that have far-reaching effects on marketing. Let's examine some trends within the American value system and see how they influence exchange behavior.

Trends

The cultural institutions that shape American values have not been rigid enough, or powerful enough, to resist change. While the ability to adapt may have been the guiding force behind our democracy for more than 200 years, the changes in our cultural institutions have deeply affected how we think and live today. Consider, for example, the ongoing changes in family life, religious values, and our educational system.

In terms of *family life,* since the 1960s there has been less interaction between parents and their children. Today, it is not unusual for both parents to work, while children are left in the care of others. The idea that "woman's place is in the home" no longer has our unquestioning support. Women have joined the work force in ever-increasing numbers. Additionally, families engage in more social interaction than ever before (see Figure 6-4). As a result, children today are increasingly exposed to values outside the family.

Besides these new patterns in the parent-child relationship, American attitudes toward marriage and fidelity have changed family life enormously. Divorce no longer brings the social disapproval it once did. In 1981, divorces exceeded 1 million, a figure that is expected to double by the year 2000. As a result, the traditional roles of father and mother are often undertaken by a single parent. With the increase in white-collar managerial positions, working parents travel more, work longer, and interact less with their children. Then, too family members today are often separated from each other geographically, as one or another parent pursues a career. Also, family units are separated from extended families and community roots, as they move in pursuit of career improvements. All these changes may weaken the ability of family life to transmit cultural values. However, peers and community groups may substitute.

Our *religious values* have also changed drastically. In the past, churches and synagogues were the focal point of family life and social interaction. Today, however, participation in formal religious institutions has fallen off. Rejection of organized religions is particularly evident among young people—an attitude that will have even greater effects on future generations. In the future, marketers may find that personal values exert a greater influence on behavior than family or religious values do.

The changes in our *educational system* are also evident and substantial. While the general level of education has risen, it is of a different kind than in the past. Teachers and university professors once came mostly from the upper classes, and they tended to teach traditional values to their students. But now the teaching profession includes representatives from every part of our diverse population. Thus, in the classroom, too, young people are exposed to a greater array of values than in past generations. Students no longer are expected only to memorize facts and descriptions of traditional subjects; now they are encouraged to analyze, to question traditional approaches, and to find new solutions for problems. Today's teaching methods reflect our technological advances, and even the goals of education are shifting. While earlier generations

Figure 6-4 This ad, directed to marketers, stresses the new marketing opportunities that are being created by the changing nature of family life. (*Reprinted with permission of Triangle Publications, Inc.*)

valued education for its own sake, young people today emphasize its practical applications.

This brief survey of trends affecting just three of our social institutions provides a background against which we can view shifts in buying behavior. How are cultural value changes reflected in the marketplace?

Effects on Exchange Behavior

Table 6-1 lists some examples of how changing American values affect exchange behavior. In studying the table, it is useful to view many of these effects as evidence of an emerging value system. Like everyone else in our society, marketers must adjust to such changes.

For example, most Americans have traditionally subscribed to what is loosely called the Puritan work ethic, with its emphasis on hard work, general frugality, regular savings, and thrifty purchasing behavior. In the 1970s, such values came under siege by a value system which stressed the individual and encouraged play and pleasure. This evolution from the Puritan work ethic to an ethic of personal pleasure had a major impact on marketing. America, in the 1970s, became the "Me Decade," where self-gratification replaced denial of "frivolous pleasures." This orientation can be seen in many aspects of human behavior. The 1980s trend is toward a modified value system where both work and pleasure have a place. But the effects of the Me Decade are still evident.

TABLE 6-1
Some Trends in American Values and Examples of Marketplace Effects

LEISURE TIME

Increasing emphasis on enjoying leisure time is replacing the values of long, hard work; free time accrues from longer vacations, shorter work weeks, and more paid holidays—all evidence of our increasingly affluent society.

Winnebago: Deluxe recreational vehicle used for vacationing, camping, "roughing it"; may include all the luxuries of home and can cost as much as a stationary mobile home.

Bicycling equipment: Consumers' desires and abilities to spend time and money on this leisure activity have resulted in a proliferation of bicycle styles, colors, and special features.

Time-sharing resorts: As a hedge against inflation and as a guaranteed getaway, many Americans are buying vacation homes by buying the right to use a resort for a specific time each year. Owners within the system can swap their time and location with others.

Club Méditerranée: Designed as a "packaged experience," this tropical vacation system offers an escape to a place that's not merely a place but a whole world, a controlled, safe, carefully designed environment built for one's pleasure.

HEALTH

Affluence, more leisure time, and the focus on youthfulness all contribute to concern for feeling and looking healthy.

Jogging apparel, warm-up suits, athletic shoes: Apparel styled specifically for exercising not only is functional but also helps people to look and feel as though they are taking a serious approach to improving their physical well-being.

Weight-loss helps: Seventy million Americans perceive themselves as overweight. Diet foods, Weight Watchers International clinics, aerobic dancing classes, elegant spas such as California's Golden Door ($2340 a week), and diet books have become big business.

ORIENTATION FROM "ME" TO "WE"

The Me Decade of the 1970s, with its orientation toward self-satisfaction, has softened to a more balanced focus between self-gratification and responsibility. The "We Decade" of the 1980s emphasizes a longing for connectedness, for creative expression and a sense of commitment—but still with a sense of self-fulfillment.

Baby boomlet: A sharp rise in the birthrate in the early eighties is causing sales increases for Johnson & Johnson, Gerber, and Lady Madonna (the clothing store chain catering to pregnant women).

Tourism: Family vacations that focus on education and entertainment for the entire family (museums, Disney World, visiting the nation's capital) are on the rise.

Pepsi-Cola: The "Pepsi Generation" advertisements now depict close-knit families and other forms of togetherness.

Need for social support: Individuals, looking for enhancers of direct communication among human beings, embrace health clubs, vacations, games, and telecommunications. They also need "social surrogates," things such as video games and computers, that allow a person who is alone to feel that he or she isn't.

YOUTH

Increasing importance of education and learning are replacing the usefulness of longevity and experience. Because a large portion of the population is represented by children and young adults, the awareness of youthfulness has had great influence on our society; youthful traits are rewarded, and so older people want to be perceived as youthful.

Grecian Formula 16: Hair products for males restore color of graying hair, thus helping mature ("prematuraly gray") men to appear younger.

Cosmetic surgery: Lifting and smoothing layers of skin by surgery is most commonly performed on the face and eyes. Requests for "lifts" elsewhere on the body—arms, breasts, thighs, abdomen, even buttocks—are increasing; the object is to rejuvenate physical appearance.

Skin-care products: Many cosmetic marketers are offering "wrinkle protection" with such products as Maybelline's Moisture Whip Moisturizer and Jovan's Wrinkles Away.

WOMEN'S MOVEMENT

Women today enjoy greater independence and equality, as expressed through careers, changing roles within the home, and lifestyles other than marriage.

Clothing: Women's executive suits have been the growth product for clothing manufacturers.

Accessories: Briefcases have been designed specifically for women while magazines for working women have grown to reflect the contemporary roles played in today's society.

Insurance: Advertisements for life insurance, directly targeted toward working women, indicate the working wife's financial impact on the household's income.

ECOLOGY AND CONSERVATION

Increased education, affluence, and more leisure time have led prople to be concerned about environmental problems and diminishing natural resources.

Returnable bottles: Public concern in some states has forced bottlers to recycle beverage bottles and reduce the pollution caused by disposable bottles; in other states, some bottlers do this voluntarily.

Recycled products: Some manufacturers use recycled materials to produce new products—notably, paper; this is a result of concern for diminishing natural resources and an attempt to reduce waste by using and reusing materials as often as possible.

Biodegradable products: To curb pollution resulting from waste materials, some manufacturers use ingredients that will break down into harmless organic materials after products are used or discarded; laundry detergents are an example.

Shower regulators: To reduce waste of energy-eating hot water for showers, consumers have purchased gadgets to reduce the flow of water from shower heads.

Energy-efficient products: Consumers are focusing on the "total use cost" when buying energy-efficient housing, appliances, and cars. Emphasis is on durability, serviceability, and energy conservation.

For instance, society definitely views sex differently today in comparison with even a decade ago. No longer is the subject taboo. Sex once was valued primarily for its reproductive purposes, to ensure that society's needs for labor were met. Large families were the most efficient method of acquiring this labor supply. But, as society became industrialized, the need for labor diminished, along with repressive attitudes toward sexuality. Sexual values were changed further as a result of another technological innovation—birth control. With that, sex moved out of the closet and became a topic that is discussed freely and openly. In the marketplace, these changes are reflected both in the goods and services offered and in the promotional activities related to them. Few would argue that marketers have not kept pace with these changes in society's values. But at the same time they must not go beyond the limits that society's members will allow (see Application 6-1). Marketers have generously employed subtle sexual overtones as playful, slightly disguised appeals in marketing.

Another value that reflects the importance of personal pleasure is the rising interest in leisure activities. Americans who have been forced to compromise in many areas of life refuse to skimp on recreation. This shift can be seen in the marketplace in terms of increased camping equipment and services, tourism, sporting activities, and

Application 6-1
Cultural Values: How Far Can They Go?

Although television stringently regulates bra advertising, it's not uncommon today to see erotic and suggestive scenes on commercials that rival some of the rawest programs on the air.

The early 1980s saw a rash of sexually suggestive commercials. Two examples stand out and, depending on one's view, they are among either the most distasteful or the most creative.

First, there was the limited showing of a commercial which pictures a young man in bed with the bedsheets in disarray. The phone rings, the man answers it, and a woman's voiceover says, "You snore." To which he replies,

"And you always steal the covers." Following a few more seconds of bantering, a macho voice announces: "Paco Rabanne—a cologne for men. What is remembered is up to you."

Second was the series of commercials cut by the teenaged movie star Brooke Shields for Calvin Klein jeans. Her provocative pose with the jeans and her comment, "You know what comes between me and my Calvins—nothing," caused an uproar not only among the viewing public but also among the advertising community.

Madison Avenue advertising agencies debate whether this type

of sex advertising sells, or whether it distracts from the product since many feel commercials of this type are overstepping the boundaries of good taste.

Commented one advertising agency executive to *Time* magazine: "Numbers of viewers are going to conclude that only a flaky segment of society would respond to that kind of advertising. I don't want to be like those people, so I'm not going to wear that kind of brand."

Sources of data: "The Bum's Rush in Advertising," *Time,* Dec. 1, 1980, p. 95; and "Sexual Pitches in Ad Become More Explicit and More Pervasive," *The Wall Street Journal,* Nov. 18, 1980, p. 1.

amusement parks. About $1 out of every $8 spent by consumers goes to leisure. Consumers now look for conveniences and time-saving products, such as the self-cleaning oven and the automatic icemaker. Multimillion-dollar corporations have been created to satisfy the needs resulting from this change in values. One corporation that promotes itself as a leisure company is AMF; its marketing efforts for motorcycles, yachts, and sporting equipment are based on society's emphasis on personal pleasure and the pursuit of happiness.

We have seen, then, how cultural values influence our exchange behavior and are reflected in the marketplace. But other groups within the culture also mold our behavior. Next, we'll examine how social classes influence exchange behavior.

Social Classes

Social classes are relatively permanent and homogeneous divisions within a society in which individuals share similar values, lifestyles, interests, and behavior. Unlike cultural values—which may take years, if not generations, to change—social class values can change more rapidly.

With which social class do you identify? That's a leading question for two reasons. It assumes, first, that the different social classes can be enumerated and, second, that we can evaluate where we fit into these classes. The actual number of social classes in the United States is open to debate. The most popular classification scheme is the six-class structure shown in Figure 6-5. This classification shows two

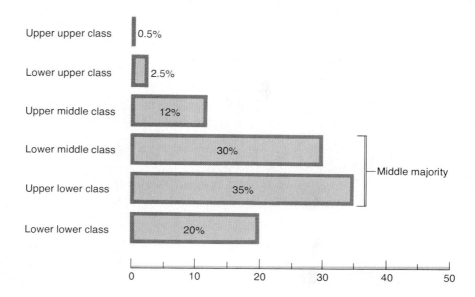

Figure 6-5   Social classes in the United States.

levels for each of three classes—upper, middle, and lower. Clearly, the greatest number of people are in what is called the "middle majority" (the lower middle and upper lower classes).

The social class system reflects some of the points we made earlier about how society takes care of its needs. Of the vast number of tasks that must be performed to keep society functioning, certain tasks are valued more highly than others. To ensure that its most important needs are met, society provides a reward structure that encourages the completion of these tasks. That is the basic idea underlying the social class structure. Society differentiates its many roles and ranks them according to what is most important. Various amounts of "the good things in life" are allocated to those who perform these roles. In short, those who perform the most important tasks get the greatest share of the rewards.

There also are different classes of rewards to be distributed for the accomplishment of society's tasks. These rewards usually take the form of property, power, and prestige. People who perform important or highly visible social tasks are paid more, and, logically, they can afford more material possessions, or property. But they also gain more influence, or power, over other people. And they often command more respect, or prestige. It is this prestige, this social approval, that seems to dominate the differences among social classes. People tend to look up to those in higher classes, wanting many of their privileges and advantages.

Social Class Determinants

In the United States, a person's social class is determined by many factors. Generally, a person's *occupation* is the most accurate single indicator of social class. The highest ratings go to the tasks considered most important by society. That is, occupations reflect their productivity to society. People in positions that have great positive influence on others (Supreme Court Justice, doctor, scientist, and even college professor) are accorded higher status than others who do not have such an impact (dock worker, cab driver, and bartender). But social class is also determined—at least in part—by *job performance,* or how well a person accomplishes his or her occupational task. And performance is usually closely allied to income, since better performers are generally better paid. In this way, income indicates social class, but it does not determine it.

Patterns of association can also indicate an individual's rank in society. Having frequent and close associations with other members of a particular social class is an essential aspect of defining one's own social standing.

A person is also ranked in society according to *possessions*. The type of material goods we own tells others what we think of ourselves. Possessions are symbols of class membership.

Values and *beliefs* are important too. The members of a particular social class tend to share common convictions, and they support similar values.

Finally, social class is reflected in the degree of *class consciousness* perceived by groups within society and by individuals within those groups. People who don't perceive class differences tend to see fewer differences between their position and that of others; as a result, they are less driven to acquire possessions that symbolize class membership.

Social Class and Exchange Behavior

Social classes and their makeup are of vital importance to marketers. People's behavior—especially their exchange behavior—is influenced greatly by social class. Like cultural values, social classes often set boundaries for acceptable behavior.

Table 6-2 gives some examples of how social class is reflected in exchange behavior. Marketers understand that they must use different methods to communicate with the members of different social classes. Such luxury goods as high-priced cars, diamonds, furs, and yachts are not marketed in the same way that work pants and hair

TABLE 6-2   The Influence of Social Class on Buying Behavior

Social class	Behavioral characteristics	Purchase behavior
Upper upper	Socially prominent, with inherited wealth Elite club membership Children attend private schools and top colleges Social position in society is secure Can deviate from social norms more than other classes—owing to security of social position	Spend money as if it were unimportant—but not ostentatiously Conservative clothing Elegance in social parties Possessions reflect British aristocracy— English Tudor homes, large lawns, servants
Lower upper	People who have "earned" their social position rather than inherited it (nouveaux riches): —corporate presidents —successful entrepreneurs —well-to-do lawyers —beginning physicians Socially mobile College educated, but not from top school Active people Highly seeking social esteem and prestigious social interactions Children showered with possessions	"Conspicuous consumption" is the rule Products symbolize their success and wealth: —swimming pools —yachts —furs —large homes —designer-name clothing
Upper middle	Motivation centered on career Moderately successful professionals: —owners of medium-sized companies —young junior executives on the rise	Purchases reflect quality Want to be seen as fashionable, having a nice home in a nice neighborhood Purchases are conspicuous but not showy

(continued)

Social class	Behavioral characteristics	Purchase behavior
	Highly educated class, but usually from state college as opposed to prestige university "Gracious living" is lifestyle pattern followed Demanding of children Cultivate broad range of interests, from civic to cultural	Automobile, home, and clothing are symbols of success
Lower middle	The "typical" American: —law-abiding —hard-working —church-going Occupations focus on nonmanagerial office workers and blue-collar jobs Continually striving to do a good job Respectability is the key motivation Conformity rather than innovativeness is the rule	Home is central possession —well-painted —respectable area Do-it-yourselfers Buy rather standard home furnishings Rely on magazines and retail literature for home furnishings information Work hard at their shopping; quite price-sensitive
Upper lower	"The working class" Routine day-to-day existence Jobs center on manual skills Reluctant to change Children are highly prized Little social contact outside the home Vacations center on visiting relatives Have little expectation of social movement	Live in declining areas of city, in small houses Purchase behavior is impulsive with new products and brand-loyal with repeat purchases Like national brands
Lower lower	Unskilled workers and unemployed Characterized as apathetic, fatalistic, and bent on "getting one's kicks" while one can Poorly educated	Impulsive purchasing Often pay too much for products and buy inferior products Do not evaluate quality or search out valuable information

curlers are. Through readership studies, marketers know, for instance, that workers who earn $5 per hour do not usually read *The New Yorker,* just as corporate executives are not avid readers of *True Confessions.*

The tendency for members of one social class to identify with and associate with other members of the same class has marketing implications that can be illustrated by a situation in New York City. So many Italian boutiques are crowded into an eleven-block stretch along Fifth Avenue in midtown Manhattan that the street is sometimes referred to as *La Quinta Strada.* Each shop strives to be the most exclusive on its block. Mario of Florence, for example, sells some women's shoes for over $400 a pair. At Richard Ginori, customers may select chinaware for prices ranging to $700 for one place setting. Obviously, such shops want to cater to the conspicuous consumers among the upper class. (See Applications 6-2 and 6-3.)

Application 6-2
Conspicuous Consumption among the Lower Uppers—
"The Only Proper Customer Is One Who Earns
$100,000 a Month"

Beverly Hills, California, may well be the capital of conspicuous consumption, and its Rodeo Drive has become one of the world's most exclusive shopping streets. Rodeo Drive has sixty stores stretching along a two-and-a-half block area; they include Courreges, Gucci, Hermès, Giorgio, Bally, Cèline, Ted Lapidus, Lothars of Paris, and other names familiar to the financially overprivileged.

Fred Hayman, owner of Giorgio, has a British club atmosphere in his shop. Espresso and cocktails are complimentary, while a pool table, a reading area with leather chairs, and a crackling fire entertain bored husbands while their wives look over the designer creations. Giorgio has no trouble paying for its exclusive overhead. Most United States retailers would be pleased to sell $100 worth of merchandise for every square foot of floor space, and Giorgio's shop averages

(Vic Cox/Peter Arnold)

$1000 per square foot. In 1980 its revenues were $4.5 million.

Gucci's Rodeo Drive shop records about 2000 shoppers a day in search of the $145 loafers and $200,000 diamond-and-pearl necklaces. One customer buys Gucci presents for friends from an attachè case stuffed with hundred-dollar bills. He enjoys drinking champagne out of new

Gucci loafers and then wearing them home.

Comedian Red Skelton calls Rodeo Drive a "nice, friendly street—but too expensive." But many Rodeo customers never even ask about prices. Recently, a young Japanese dashed into Hermès and selected a $1000 lambskin jacket, an $850 suede coat, three silk robes at $700 each, five blouses at $350 apiece, and many other items in rapid succession. While the salespeople added up his charges ($8000), he ran out, returning with new luggage to hold his clothing. He then rushed off to catch a plane. At Lina Lee, a customer spent less than five minutes—and more than $1900—buying three daytime dresses. When asked if she wanted to try them on, she replied, "No, no, I love them. I just know I want them."

Source of data: "Street of Big Spenders," *Time*, Feb. 13, 1978, pp. 76–77.

Application 6-3
Upper Lower Social Class—"Money Ain't Everything"

Does money determine one's social class? Not by any means, as Michigan's first $1 million lottery winner shows.

In 1973, Hermus Millsaps, 53 years old, jumped up on the stage of the Lansing Civic Center, the proud holder of a $1 million lottery ticket entitling him to twenty annual installments of $50,000. That lucky ticket allowed him to quit his $4.68-per-hour job sawing wood for shipping crates.

What did Hermus do with his windfall? He happily described the improvements to his one-bedroom bungalow that helped whittle his first $50,000 installment to only a little over $10,000 in four short months. (Hermus completely forgot about paying taxes before plunging into heavy spending.) Among his new acquisitions: extensive aluminum siding along the lower half of the house, new storm windows, a twin-oven gas range, a sun porch, a new outdoor grill, and dark green paneling and indirect lighting in the basement. There was also the $100,000 life insurance policy that called for annual premiums of $5000. And there was the new $1000 electric guitar and amplifier that allowed Hermus and his 47-year-old wife to enjoy their new-found free time singing away.

"I got to take it easy now," he told a reporter. "In fact, I spent a little too much to start with, but I put it to good cause . . . fixing up my house. That money really goes fast."

To escape the barrage of people seeking his financial assistance, Hermus took a vacation. He went back home to Emory Gap, Tennessee, to visit his mother. Wanting to share his new wealth, he brought her some new clothes, a stereo tape deck, and some flowers.

When asked about the possibility of moving, Hermus replied: "I could have gone out and bought a brick home in Bloomfield Hills . . . or a ranch home in Grosse Pointe, but we got our happiness in this place and there's no use moving out of the neighborhood." As content as he is with his household improvements, he does not regard them as an indication of happiness. "Money ain't everything," he says. "You can't take it and buy love. You can have all the money in the whole world, but if you ain't got love you ain't accomplished nothing."

Source of data: "First Lottery Millionaire Settles into Easy Living," *Detroit Free Press,* July 8, 1973, p. A-3.

Reference Groups

 A *reference group* is any aggregation of people that influences an individual's attitudes or behavior. The group serves as a reference point in evaluating individual behavior.

There are many types of reference groups. Some, called *primary groups,* are small enough and intimate enough so that all members can communicate with one another face to face. Examples include the family, an individual's social circle, and one's coworkers. Larger, less intimate *secondary groups* also influence behavior. Trade unions, religious organizations, and professional associations are examples.

From another point of view, people may belong to many kinds of *membership groups,* and they may hope to join other *aspirational groups.* A college student is a member of the student body (a membership group); yet, that student may wish to be out of school and be working, say, as a banker (aspirational group). As a member of the student body, the student may want to dress as others do—in jeans, sweater, and running shoes. But as someone who aspires to become a banker, the student also may want to dress in dark, conservative "banker's" clothes.

Norms are an integral part of the functioning of a reference group, just as they are with culture and social classes. To be accepted into a reference group, an individual must comply with the norms of the group. In short, norms promote conformity within a reference group.

In addition to the types of reference groups already named, there are *disassociative reference groups*—groups that a person wants to avoid. For some, Hell's Angels might be such a group, while others might object to being affiliated with a particular religious or political group. By not complying with the norms of such groups, a person avoids membership. Compliance with the norms is seen as an acceptance of membership.

Reference Groups and Exchange Behavior

It should be no surprise that reference groups also affect our buying behavior. Some research has examined the influence of reference groups on various product categories as well as on brands purchased within those categories.[5] Because the study was conducted quite some years ago, Figure 6-6 adapts some new examples to fit the research findings. The study assumed four possibilities:

1 A strong reference group influence on purchasing a product category and on buying a brand within a product category

2 A strong reference group influence on buying a product category but little or no influence on brand selection

---

[5]Foundation for Research on Human Behavior, *Group Influence in Marketing and Public Relations,* Ann Arbor, Mich., 1956.

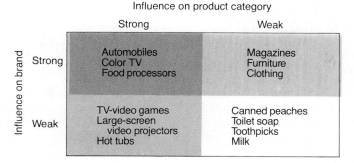

Figure 6-6 The influence of reference groups on buying behavior.

3 A strong influence on brand purchase but little or no influence on buying a category of products

4 No influence on product category or on brand selection

This figure suggests that our reference groups strongly influence whether or not we buy such products as cars, color TVs, and food processors; and if we *do* buy these products, reference groups influence which brands we select. As a teenager, having a car of your own raises your status among your peers. It doesn't really matter what kind of car it is—any car is a badge of freedom and independence. But note too that having a Porsche sports car is accorded more social approval than having a 1970 Dodge Dart. Thus, both product class and brand are influenced by reference groups. In addition, reference groups influence whether or not we purchase such products as TV-video games, large-screen video projectors, and "hot tubs" (as shown in Figure 6-6). But in these cases, reference groups do *not* influence which brands we select. If we own a hot tub, nobody really looks at the brand to confer approval—just having that health-oriented luxury is enough to be socially rewarded.

When it comes to whether we purchase such products as clothing, furniture, and magazines—things everyone has and needs—reference groups have little or no influence. But when we go to buy such products, we do tend to select brands that will meet with the approval of our reference groups.

Finally, some products are so ordinary and unimportant to us and to others (toothpicks and canned peaches, for example) that reference groups have no influence on whether or not we buy them, or on which brands we buy.

From this analysis, one general observation stands: When products are socially visible and conspicuously consumed, our buying habits reflect the influences of our reference groups. No one has to know whether or not we buy canned peaches, or which brand we buy. But a car is another matter—people *notice*.

Although marketers know a great deal about the influence of reference groups on buying behavior, it is difficult to use that knowledge in developing a marketing mix. The problem is the large number of different reference groups that may influence a buyer's behavior in varying amounts and at various times. Any one of these groups may influence a purchase. For example, when a college student shops for a new jacket, her final choice may reflect the values of her sorority, her family, her church group, her friends, or many other groups. It is difficult for marketers to know which reference group has the strongest influence. To compensate for this problem, marketers can turn to another aspect of reference group influence—role theory.

Role Theory

When Shakespeare wrote, "All the world's a stage/And all the men and women merely players," he summed up the fact that people go through life playing out parts. It is as though we were all actors on a stage. Clothing is our costume, and possessions are our props.

Essentially, *role theory* recognizes that people conduct their lives by playing many roles. We look to other people in our reference groups (our audience) for cues about which role to play and how to play it. Role theory holds that for *every* position in society there is a certain range of acceptable behavior. An individual is expected to behave in a certain way in order to carry out the requirements of a given position.

Behavior that is acceptable in one role may be unacceptable in another. For instance, a female member of society might occupy such positions as wife, mother, bridge club member, company executive, president of a neighborhood association, and tennis partner. Each position requires different behavior, different skills, and different talents. And the individual must change roles constantly in the course of a week. Her position as a mediocre bridge player contrasts with her authoritative position as a mother and an executive and with her prestige as head of the neighborhood association. Even so, a person usually experiences little difficulty in changing from one role to another.

How well one performs in a given role is determined by *role expectations:* the rights and privileges—and the duties and responsibilities that go with a role. Most people look to their reference groups for cues about how they are expected to behave. Thus, role expectations can be viewed as norms. Those who perform a role poorly may meet with the disapproval of the reference group involved.

Marketers both shape roles and use them as a basis for marketing. They help individuals to play their roles by providing the right costumes and props. For example, when students first go off to college, they want to be accepted by other students. They look to other students for cues. They study the college newspaper and visit stores to see which products are being offered. They want to know what is being worn by fraternity and sorority members and by the campus leaders, and what is acceptable or unacceptable in the reference groups with which they identify. Products help us perform our roles. We want to wear the right clothes, have the appropriate stereo, and hang out at the "in" spot. Table 6-3 lists some regional differences along these lines. (See Application 6-4.)

Self-Image and Exchange Behavior

Chapter 1 made the point that a product can provide both functional and psychological satisfaction to consumers. Thus, to provide items that satisfy people's wants and needs, marketers must be concerned with the symbolic aspects of products. In other words, they must develop goods that help people to fulfill their role expectations, goods that present the "right" image.

We all have some idea of what we are really like and of how we believe others see us. This view, called our *real self-image,* directs our behavior. But it often happens that a person's real self-image is at odds with how others actually see that person. For instance, someone who was an overweight boy but who later lost the extra pounds may still feel too heavy as an adult, even though other people do not see him as being overweight. Similarly, a business executive whose hair is turning gray may see that as a sign of diminishing youthfulness and vitality, whereas other people are amazed by

TABLE 6-3 Props and Costumes for American Role Playing: *Across the Nation— Thumbnail Guide to Americans' Tastes*

In a nation as big as the United States, the earmarks of status are likely to vary from one city to another. Some people take them seriously. Others don't.

For an idea of the variation in status symbols. *U.S. News & World Report* told staff members in key cities to ask people to list some popular status symbols and some that had fallen out of favor. Their findings:

In	*Out*
NEW YORK	
Mustaches	Long hair, beards
Wine spritzers	Tap water
Western bars	Singles bars
Wind surfing	Courses in education
Jungle motif in clothes	Skintight clothes
Jogging to work	Heavy drinking
Lightweight earphone radio-tape units	Electronic calculators
Fish and fowl	Red meat, frozen products
Cosmetic surgery for men	Bright colors in home decor
Living alone and liking it	Primal-scream therapy
CHICAGO	
Croissants, tacos	Bagels, pizza
1950s music	Country-and-western music
Levi's jeans	Designer jeans
Telephones in cars	Vanity license plates, CB radios
Antiques	High-tech decor
Calligraphy	Jogging
Wine bars	Salad bars
Cards, electronic games	Backgammon, Scrabble
Exotic plants	Pets
Buying through catalogs	Shopping
LOS ANGELES	
Owning property	Buying records
Cowboy bars, music, clothes	Golf, tennis
Pay TV, home computers	Gas-guzzling cars
Traditional weddings	Discos
Nancy Reagan red	Self-realization seminars
College business courses	Philosophy courses
Fad-diet books	Expensive vacations
Escapist movies	Raucous rock music
Anti smoking clinics	Jogging
Wash-and-wear hairstyles	Skateboards

Source: "Flaunting Wealth, It's Back in Style," *U.S. News & World Report,* Sept. 21, 1981, p. 62.

Application 6-4
Reference Group Influence—Shedding New Light on Lingerie

(Courtesy Cameo Coutures, Inc.)

It was not too many years ago that suggestive lingerie was a taboo subject, and most certainly it was not something for "wholesome" suburban housewives to discuss. But typical American views of "naughty" lingerie have radically changed.

For more than forty years, manufacturers have used home parties to market such household goods as copperware, cutlery, and plastic storage containers. But the selling method has spread. There

are now lingerie parties where groups of women gather to look at the latest in sexy undergarments. So in demand are items of this sort that one salesperson reports selling $300 worth per party. The salesperson says that some women buy such lingerie in groups, but they still will not venture into a store and ask for the same items.

"We took away the negatives," says Tiffany James, who runs Undercover Wear, "People don't have to pretend they are buying for a friend."

"At these parties, I am selling to the average suburban woman, the woman who has lingerie at the bottom of her shopping list, or is embarrassed to go into a department store to buy sexy lingerie because she feels apprehensive about what the

salespeople will think of her," says Tiffany James. "So I bring these items to them. They can try it on in the privacy of their own homes with their girlfriends. . . .Most of this is geared toward feeling good about yourself."

Begun in 1977, Undercover Wear had more than 1300 representatives organizing selling parties in over forty states in 1981. A competitor, Just for Play, begun in 1979, has 800 sales representatives working in ten states.

Source of data: "Tupperware, Step Aside," *Newsweek,* March 2, 1981, p. 56; and "Peddling Naughty Lingerie in Suburban Living Rooms," *Boston Globe,* March 8, 1977, p. 9.

the executive's energy and competence. As a result of their *real* self-images, these two people may seek out such products as dietetic foods, exercise equipment, and hair coloring. Whether or not they actually need the functional satisfaction which those products can provide, these people seek the psychological satisfaction demanded by their real self-images. From a behavioral standpoint, then, the real self-image can be most influential on a person's behavior.

This matter is complicated by the fact that we actually have two self-images. Besides the picture of ourselves as we think we "really are," we have a view of how we would *like* to be—our *ideal self-image.* In comparing ourselves with others, we may wish to be better-looking, more intelligent, wealthier, or happier, for example. And this ideal image also affects buying behavior. Consumers who see themselves ideally as having a high social position are likely to buy items that reflect status. They shop at exclusive stores and purchase expensive items. In short, their buying behavior reflects how they would like to be viewed. It doesn't matter whether we really look like the models who appear in a clothing advertisement; the important thing is that we would *like* to resemble them and feel that the symbols in the products will bring us closer to our ideal self.

The concept of self-image has important and far-reaching implications for marketing. Part of a product's bundle of utility is its psychological satisfaction, the image it helps to create. Marketers must attempt to match a product's image with the self-images of consumers in that market. The selection of one product or brand over another is often based on how closely each choice matches the consumer's real and ideal self-images.

Revlon's Charlie perfume provides a good example. While the advertising appeal for the aroma dominated by jasmine was "Sexy-clean . . . a different fragrance that thinks your way," the appeal was more than functional and olfactory. Charlie seemed to capture the modern women's purposeful new self-image. As Revlon's president told *Fortune:* "Charlie strides without being strident. She's twenty-seven, single, has a job, and supports the women's movement, though she's no bra-burning libber. Most of all, she's happy as hell in an era of dissatisfaction."[6] Introduced in 1973, Charlie was propelled to become the world's largest selling fragrance in 1980. (See Application 6-5).

The Family

The cliché "last but not least" certainly applies to this discussion of social influences on exchange behavior. Of all our reference groups, the family is most influential. It serves, in fact, as a filter for the values and norms of our overall social environment—culture, social class, and other reference groups. As our primary reference group, the family provides the ultimate experience in face-to-face interaction. And from the marketing point of view, the family differs from larger reference groups in that its members must satisfy their individual and shared needs by drawing on a common and relatively fixed supply of resources.

Family life is such an everyday, commonplace situation that it may seem unnecessary to discuss it. Yet some features of family living are very important to marketers—and they are not all obvious. One extremely interesting aspect of family structure is that, typically, we are all members of *two* families. First, the family we are born into is called a *family of orientation;* but later, most of us also establish a *family of procreation,* through marriage. This pattern results in a *nuclear family,* consisting of parents and children living together, and also an *extended family,* which includes the

---

[6]"Revlon's Smell of Success," *Fortune,* Dec. 31, 1979, p. 31

Application 6-5
Role Playing—Props at a "Prep Rally"

"It's all part of a growing trend to conservatism in the country. It also repudiates the ugliness and extreme looks of the sixties." So commented a Brooks Brothers executive to *Newsweek* about the "in" fashion—the "preppy look"—as the 1980s began. The fashion trend was inspired by a 334-page manual, *"The Official Preppy Handbook,"* in which the reader is told how to acquire the preppy look.

While clothes alone do not make a preppy, clearly the focus of the fad was on the "outfit." Listed as standard were the following:
—Shetland sweaters for men and Fair Isle pullovers for women
—Lacoste shirts complete with alligator insignia above the heart
—Kilt skirts, madras shorts, and khaki slacks—the bigger the better
—Foul-wearther moccasins from L. L. Bean—worn sockless in all but the most bitter weather

To be truly preppy, one's attire must come from an "in" source, such as Brooks Brothers in New York, J. Press in Cambridge, Massachusetts, G. H. Bass in Wilton, Maine, and L. L. Bean, a mail-order store in Freeport, Maine. G. H. Bass has tripled its production of Weejun loafers to 6000 per day. Another beneficiary of the movement is Stride-Ride Corporation of Boston, the owner of Sperry Top-siders. The shoe, with its teak-brown leather upper and white rubber sole, designed with a unique bottom to keep sailors from slipping on deck, sold about 600,000 pairs in 1979. In 1981, that volume jumped to 1.5 million pairs.

"It's the look everybody wants," a Steamboat Springs Colorado retailer told *The Wall Street Journal.* "Everybody wants to look like a WASP," said an executive of a company that imitates the original Sperry. "It's become the status shoe. You look like you're rubbing shoulders with wealthy people." And as *The Official Preppy Handbook* (Workman Publishing) advises: "When they're looking to see if you're prep, the first thing they look at is your shoes."

Sources of data: "There'll Always Be a Preppy," *Newsweek,* Dec. 8, 1980, pp. 88–91; and "A Shoe that Helps You Walk on Water Is a Big Hit on Shore," *The Wall Street Journal,* April 1, 1981, p. 1.

---

nuclear family as well as aunts, uncles, grandparents, and in-laws. All these people influence our lives and our buying behavior.

Our two-family system has some definite effects on marketing. Most young couples begin from ground zero in terms of housing, furnishings, cars, and hundreds of other products. Obviously, this situation creates a large market to be served. Then, too, more households have to be established because it's less common today for extended family members to live together. In the past, grandparents and other relatives often lived with the nuclear family, but today the size of households is more limited. Family life and structure are also affected by other trends we have discussed— fewer children, working wives and mothers, divorce, geographic mobility, single parents, dual incomes, and increased leisure time. Again, all these factors produce effects in the marketplace, from washing machines that handle smaller loads, to dinette sets that seat fewer people, to cars that carry four passengers instead of six.

Family Roles and Decision Making

The behavior of various family members at each stage of the decision-making process is of major importance to marketers. Family roles are the means by which a family meets its needs. When a single person decides to eat out, for example, the decision is based on only his or her own needs. But when that person gets married, the situation changes. A household forms, and its members are confronted with various decisions that reflect the needs of the family unit: Who will pay the bills? When will the grocery shopping be done? Who will wash the clothes? Who will cook dinner? These decisions can be made jointly, or they may be divided among the various family members. Early in the marriage, substantially more joint decision making may take place. At first the partners are still getting to know one another and each is concerned about learning the other's needs and wants. And there is more time available for discussing how decisions should be made. But, as children enter the family and as job and time pressures increase, there is greater need to allocate decisions and tasks to individual family members. The way roles are allocated in a family is of great importance to marketers, since it influences their decisions about a product's decision, packaging, distribution, and promotion.

Traditional Family Roles

A number of factors determines how roles are parceled out to family members. The way one is raised, cultural values, reference group values, the interest of each of the partners in the decision, and the personality of family members all have an effect on the process. Even so, relatively simple decision rules are usually employed in the allocation of roles. In addition, the various age segments of the population use different rules. Within American society, a large number of households have been socialized into what can be called *traditional roles,* which are allocated on the basis of where they are carried out and what kind of decision they require.

Usually, family tasks are apportioned in a way that ensures they will be handled effectively. In most traditional households, the husband leaves home to go to work, while the wife remains at home caring for the house and children. The result is that the husband takes on roles *external* to the home—arranging financing, buying insurance, and so on—while the wife performs tasks *internal* to the home—grocery shopping, decorating, cleaning. While this distinction between roles is certainly decreasing as modern yet traditional women become more active outside the home, the general distinction still holds for a large portion of the American population.

Additionally, family tasks are distributed on the basis of whether the decision reflects an instrumental or an expressive value. *Instrumental* values are mainly economic: they are means rather than ends. In traditional families, the male attends to instrumental tasks, those which involve functional matters such as the soundness of construction, the efficiency of a motor, or service and repair requirements. The female, on the other hand, takes care of tasks that reflect *expressive values*—arranging social engagements, picking out upholstery color and fabric, and choosing much of the family clothing. This distinction between instrumental and expressive values applies even when the main user of the product will be the other person.

Samsonite Corporation, the Denver-based luggage manufacturer, is well aware of the existence of such role allocation. After an expensive year-long study, the company found that 75 percent of all luggage was sold to women between 35 and 55 years of age. Moreover, women tend to buy matched luggage—whether one piece at a time or a whole set at once. They want fashionable, lightweight luggage, and they will sacrifice space to get those features. In contrast, male buyers are more interested in durability and capacity. To promote its luggage line to women, then, Samsonite earmarked $3 million for advertising. "What turns heads, makes friends easily, and often gets carried away?" asks one headline over a picture of a stylish, denim-jacketed woman with her Samsonite luggage. The punch line: "A bag named Sam."

Contemporary Family Roles

The following trends affecting women and their entrance into the working world have challenged traditional role assignments in American families:[7]

1 Birth-control techniques have allowed women to control the size and arrival time of their families—thus more easily allowing entry to the labor force.

2 Women are realizing greater longevity—there are more older women available for work.

3 The rising cost of living has fostered the need for additional income for low- and medium-income families.

4 Women have been offered many labor-saving devices that free their time for nonhousehold pursuits.

5 Most women enjoy working outside the house.

6 The role of working women has become accepted in our culture.

As a result of such trends, many Americans no longer agree that "a woman's place is in the home" or that "a man is lord of his castle." This increased role for women outside the home has had a sizable impact on the values, rights and responsibilities, and buying behavior of both women and men in modern families.

For many products, there is little difference in purchasing behavior between traditional and contemporary women, although the latter show greater concern for their physical appearance and condition. These values are reflected in a desire to project a youthful, fashionable image. The modern feminine orientation projects a cosmopolitan, self-confident, mobile attitude. Women's travel horizons have been broadened to include international frontiers, and they see leisure time as an opportunity for pleasure rather than for traditional activities like yard work, shopping, cooking, and talking with friends and relatives. Contemporary women participate more in activities outside the home. As a result of these new roles, contemporary women have a more powerful influence on the family's major purchasing decisions and on its social class orientation.

Women's changing self-images have forced a revision of male stereotypes as well, and contemporary men also exhibit changes. No longer are they limited to fulfilling a role as hunters and warriors or decision makers at the dining table. Many more men are now finding household duties and child-rearing responsibilities both acceptable and enjoyable. There is a happy release in learning that masculinity is not reduced by

---

[7]Suzanne H. McCall, "Meet the 'Workwife,'" *Journal of Marketing,* vol. 41, no. 3 (July 1977), p. 56.

showing emotion, or helping around the house, or sharing decisions. While such attitude changes have occurred mainly among younger, educated men, these trends and role changes are having an effect on exchange behavior. Contemporary men are striving for more balance in their lives rather than accepting the traditional work-oriented male roles. Thus, family, recreation, and community activities are showing a greater influence on spending patterns. Changes such as these are extremely important to marketers because they affect consumers' self-images, which, in turn, must be satisfied by the bundle of satisfaction offered. (See Application 6-6.)

Application 6-6
Changing Family Roles—A Moving Target for Marketers

As more women trod off to work and more men do chores at home, marketers are modifying their plans to reflect the changing market. Many products, formerly marketed largely to men, are now being geared to women. For instance, women have been found to make 60 percent of family vacation decisions, almost 50 percent of color-TV brand choices, and 39 percent of the new car purchases. Such findings are reflected in the sales pitches. Consider the following:

A General Motors advertisement shows a serious-looking woman in a tweed suit pondering the cost savings of a Pontiac.

A female store owner in a Tegrin shampoo commercial seeks counsel from a friendly pharmacist about her dandruff problem.

An elegantly dressed woman in a Drambuie Liqueur ad asks, "Isn't it time you knew an exciting drink to order—instead of taking a man's suggestion?"

The behavior profile of men also is changing rapidly. A recent

(Reprinted with permission of Triangle Publications, Inc.)

study found a substantial number of husbands doing household chores: 70 percent cook, 44 percent prepare a complete meal, and over half do major grocery shopping. Advertisers of grocery products have revamped their ads. Male joggers trot through margarine commercials, singing the praises of low cholesterol; blue-collar TV husbands hawk

baking soda, TV businessmen shout with glee while eating yogurt. Airwick Industries has renamed its "Chore Girl" scouring pads "Chore Boy."

Trying to hedge their bets, some household goods advertisers have employed sports celebrities who are popular with both sexes. Johnson & Johnson uses former Viking quarterback Fran Tarkenton to push its baby shampoo, "so men won't think it's a sissy kind of product," a spokesperson told *The Wall Street Journal*. Thomas J. Lipton, Inc., uses another former quarterback and TV commentator, Dallas's Don Meredith, to plug its tea. "Women dominate the hot-tea area, and we are trying to expand the male market by using him," said an advertising agency executive.

Sources of data: "More Food Advertisers Woo the Male Shopper as He Shares the Load," *The Wall Street Journal*, Aug. 26, 1980, p. 1; and "TV Ads Reflect Power of Working Women," *The Wall Street Journal*, Oct. 30, 1980, p. 33.

The Family Life Cycle

No discussion of the importance of family would be complete without noting the importance of age within the family. As one is born into a family, grows older, and establishes one's own family, many differences in values and general behavior occur. Quite naturally, these changes are reflected in purchasing behavior. Table 6-4 looks at some of the differences that arise as people journey through the family life style. While the stages reflect the traditional family, this summary also recognizes the contemporary trends toward divorce and remaining childless throughout one's life.

TABLE 6-4 Characteristics of Various Stages in the Family Life Cycle

Age group	Age	Behavioral characteristics	Products of interest
Early childhood	Birth–5	Total dependency on parents; development of bones and muscles and use of locomotion; accident- and illness-prone; ego-centered; naps; accompanies guardian shopping; may attend nursery school.	Baby foods; cribs; clothes; toys; pediatric services; room vaporizers; breakfast cereals; candy; books; nursery schools.
Late childhood	6–12	Declining dependency on parents; slower and more uniform growth; vast development of thinking ability; peer competition; conscious of being evaluated by others; attends school.	Food; toys; clothes; lessons; medical and dental care; movies; candy, uniforms; comic books.
Early adolescence	13–15	Onset of puberty; shifting of reference group from family to peers; concern with personal appearance, desire for more independency, and transition to adulthood begin.	Junk food; comic books and magazines; movies; records; clothing; hobbies; grooming aids.
Late adolescence	16–18	Transition to adulthood continues; obtains working papers; obtains driver's license; concern with personal appearance increases; dating; active in organized sports; less reading for fun.	Gasoline; auto parts; typewriters; cameras; jewelry and trinkets; cigarettes; books and magazines; sporting goods.
Young singles	19–24	Entrance into labor market on a full-time basis; entrance to college; interest in personal appearance remains high; increased dating; varying degrees of independence; activity in organized sports decreases.	Auto; clothing; dances; travel; toiletries; quick and easy-to-prepare foods.
Young marrieds	25–34	First marriage; transition to pair-centered behavior; financially optimistic; interest in personal appearance still high; learning to be homemakers, working wives, and husbands.	Home renting; furniture; major appliances; second auto; food; entertainment; small household items.

(continued)

Age group	Age	Behavioral characteristics	Products of interest
Young divorced, without children	28–34	Life style may revert back to young single; both males and females financially worse off than when married; most men and women will remarry.	Discos; therapists; clothing; auto; household goods; apartments.
Young parents	25–34	Transition to family-centered behavior; decline in social activities; companionship with spouse drops; leisure activities centered more at home.	Houses; home repair goods; health and nutrition foods; family games; health-care services; early childhood products (see above).
Young divorced, with children	28–34	Wife usually retains custody of children; husband provides child support; woman must look for employment; low discretionary income.	Child-care centers; household goods; condominiums.
Middle-aged, married with children	35–44	Family size at its peak; children in school; security-conscious; career advancements; picnics; pleasure drives.	Replacement of durables; insurance; books; sporting equipment; yard furniture; gifts.
Middle-aged, married without children	35–44	Small segment, but increasing in size; lifestyle less hectic than when younger; emphasis on freedom and being "carefree."	Vacations; leisure-time services; athletic products; personal health-care services; party-related products.
Middle-aged, divorced without children	35–44	Small segment; major lifestyle adjustment for both spouses; financial condition dependent on occupation and socioeconomic status; very unlikely ever to have children.	Self-help books; therapy; cruises; vacations, condominiums; household goods.
Middle-aged, divorced with children	35–44	Lifestyle changes are significant; some children may have resumed some responsibility for family's livelihood; divorced father has financial constraints; mother seeks employment if not already employed.	Condominiums; sports equipment; financial planning services.
Later adulthood	45–54	Children have left home; physical appearance changes; increased interest in appearance; community service; decline in strenuous activity; pair-centered.	Clothing; vacations; leisure-time services; food; gifts; personal health-care services.
Soon-to-be retired	55–64	Physical appearance continues to decline; interests and activities generally continue to decline; pair-centered.	Gifts; slenderizing treatments; manicures and massages; luxuries; smaller homes.
Already retired	65 and older	Physical appearance continues its decline; mental abilities and health may decline; home-body and ego-centered behavior.	Drugs; dietetic canned foods; laxatives; retirement communities; nursing home care; denture products.

Adapted from Fred D. Reynolds and William D. Wells, *Consumer Behavior,* McGraw-Hill, New York, 1977; Patrick E. Murphy and William A. Staples, "A Modernized Family Life Cycle," *Journal of Consumer Research,* vol. 6 (June 1979), pp. 12–22.

Situational Influences

So far, this chapter has emphasized the influence of *other people* on the exchange decisions of individuals. But other people are not the only outside influence; marketers must also recognize that the selection of a product or brand to purchase also depends on *how, when, where,* and *why* the consumer is *going to use it.* These outside environmental factors are called situational variables. Let's consider some of the types of situations that impact on the purchase decision.

Consumers are influenced by the *circumstances* surrounding the *purchase* of a product. When a shopper, looking for a favorite cereal, is confronted with a change in price, an out-of-stock condition, an attractive coupon on another brand, or some other inducement, the favorite brand may not be so favorite any longer. Such situational possibilities have direct implications for a marketer's pricing, distribution, and sales promotion activities. Clearly, the cereal marketer would want to know the nature of such outside factors and their impact on the market.

Consumers also are influenced by the *consumption situation.* The anticipated usage situation also directs a consumer's product and brand choice. Consider the different types of snack foods for the following uses: to eat along with lunch; to offer when friends drop by; to serve when very close friends are entertained at home; to eat while watching evening television; to get a quick energy pickup; and to have on a long car trip. Quality and appearance would be important when entertaining close friends, much less important when going on an automobile trip. And products purchased for multiple uses versus single uses may be different. Single-use consumption situations usually result in the purchase of consumer package goods, while multiple-use purchases are more likely to be durable goods where the influence of situational factors is likely to be less.

The paper-plate industry understands the importance of consumption-situation influences. In 1981, 44 percent of industry sales went to the 1-cent, plain white paper plate used primarily as an inexpensive, disposable means for serving meals of little social consequence. Decorated paper plates constituted 23 percent of industry sales and met the usage need for social gatherings where attractiveness adds social approval. A 23 percent market share went to sturdier, molded pulp plates designed for heavier helpings of food, while 10 percent of sales were of plastic foam plates with high insulation qualities for usage situations when the time between heating and eating is substantial.

Also of interest to the marketer is the *communication situation.* Where was a newspaper ad read—at home, on the train heading to work, or at the newspaper stand? Was a TV commercial viewed alone or with friends? Was the commercial seen on a program that was important to the consumer or on one that had little relevance to the consumer? IRI, the marketing research firm with the Behaviorscan service measuring the sales impact of TV commercials (review Application 4-3), also has begun rating television programs. Data on viewers' programs preferences can then be linked directly to their sales behavior, helping to uncover the direct impact of the communication situation on buying behavior.

Situational factors, then, have definite implications for marketers. Market segmentation often is influenced by the usage situation. The paper towels market, for example, can be segmented on the basis of usage situations. There are heavy-duty uses (cleaning windows, washing automobiles, and cleaning ovens), light-duty uses (napkins, placemats for a meal). Market analysis by situational variables also can uncover unmet opportunities. And situational factors help direct promotional activities. With paper towels, advertising to the light-duty segment would stress absorbency over strength, while color and design appeals would be emphasized for the decorative segment.

Exchange behavior, then, is influenced by many outside sources. In some instances, one or some are prevalent; in other situations, different influences have their impact. Successful marketing comes from a firm understanding of the importance of such outside variables.

Looking Back

Marketers must recognize that our environment influences our exchange behavior. In this chapter, we looked at how culture, social classes, reference groups, the family, and situational variables influence behavior in the marketplace. Next, we will examine how an individual consumer makes exchange decisions. But, before going on, review the following main points:

1 Marketing borrows heavily from the behavioral sciences in order to understand why people behave as they do in the marketplace.

2 The exchange process involves six parties, who may or may not be one single person.

3 People other than the consumer may act as initiators, influencers, deciders, buyers, consumers, and evaluators in the exchange process.

4 Exchange behavior is influenced by a number of cultural groups, including those formed on national, regional, religious, and ethnic bases.

5 Norms are the means by which behavior is controlled to meet the objectives of a group.

6 Culture is learned, adaptive, and transmitted from generation to generation.

7 American cultural values have changed greatly within the past few decades; attitudes toward social interaction, work, leisure time, family life, sex, religion, and education have all brought changes in the marketplace.

8 The social class structure reflects society's assessment of individuals' social productivity.

9   Each social class maintains different values and exhibits different buying behavior.

10 Reference groups tend to influence the purchase of items that are socially visible and conspicuously consumed.

11 Role theory can help marketers to understand buying behavior because products aid in the performance of our roles.

12 One's real self-image and ideal self-image are reflected in exchange behavior.

13 The two-family system in the United States creates substantial needs and wants for marketers to satisfy.

14 Marketers must understand family roles because they influence how tasks and exchange decisions are allocated.

15 Family roles have been changing recently, and marketers now must satisfy different needs.

16 The family roles one plays from childhood through adulthood have many marketplace effects.

17 Purchase, consumption, and communication situations often play a role in influencing exchange behavior.

Key Terms

If you aren't sure what each of the following words means, look back at the text. Numbers refer to pages on which the words are defined. Additional information can be found by checking the index and the glossary at the end of the book.

culture 168
norms 170
socialization 170
social class 177
social class determinants 178
reference group 182
primary group 182
secondary group 182

role theory 185
real self-image 185
ideal self-image 187
family of orientation 188
family of procreation 188
nuclear family 188
extended family 188
situational factors 195

Questions for Review

1 Must all six stages of the exchange process be acted out by six different people?

2 What do we mean when we say that culture is adaptive?

3 What are some of the factors that determine social class in the United States? What is the most accurate single indicator?

4 How do marketers use role theory in developing products?

5 Why is it necessary for marketers to understand how family roles influence buyer behavior?

6 Why is the family the most influential of all our reference groups?

Questions for Thought and Discussion

1   Which of the four groups discussed in this chapter would you expect to have the greatest influence on buying behavior in the future and why?

2   The *Queen Elizabeth 2* recently added two split-level penthouse suites behind the bridge. The price for a 90-day cruise was set at $160,000. For this, tourists get designer linens, separate china service, carpeted bathrooms, private patios, and anonymity—the Cunard Line won't disclose guests' names if they request privacy. Which of the groups studied would have the greatest influence in the purchase of such a suite?

3   Recently, many indoor tanning spas, such as Tan-Trific and the Endless Summer Tanning Salon, have enjoyed substantial success. What concepts from this chapter help us to understand why these ultraviolet treatments have such acceptance?

4   Americans are becoming more and more quality-conscious in their purchases—more willing to spend more to get more. On the basis of your reading, what accounts for this trend?

Suggested Project

Find two products that directly reflect the values, needs, or both of the four groups discussed in this chapter. Peel or cut off the labels from these products and put them in a folder along with a brief explanation of why each is a direct result of that group's influence.

Suggested Readings

Bartos, Rena: "What Every Marketer Should Know about Women," *Harvard Business Review*, vol. 56, no. 3 (May–June 1978), pp. 73–85. This article discusses four groups of women on the basis of their occupational status and looks at their buying behavior differences.

Belk, Russell W.: "An Exploratory Assessment of Situational Effects in Buyer Behavior," *Journal of Marketing Research*, vol. 11, no. 2 (May 1974), pp. 156–163. The study reported in this article launched the concern for situational variables and their effect on buying behavior.

Davis, Harry L., and B. P. Rigaux: "Perceptions of Marital Roles in Decision Processes," *Journal of Consumer Research*, vol. 1 (June 1974), pp. 51–61. Study results show the relative influence of husbands and wives on various product-purchase decisions.

Hirish, Robert D., and Michael P. Peters: "Selecting the Superior Segmentation Correlate," *Journal of Marketing*, vol. 38, no. 3 (July 1974, pp. 60–63. The authors explore the issue of whether income or social class is a better predictor of buying behavior.

Levy, Sidney J.: "Social Class and Consumer Behavior," in Joseph W. Newman (ed.), *On Knowing the Consumer,* Wiley, New York, 1966. This article enlarges on the various behavioral and consumption differences among the various social classes.

Loudon, David L., and Albert J. Della Bitta: *Consumer Behavior: Concepts and Applications,* McGraw-Hill, New York, 1979. This excellent textbook examines the important topics of exchange behavior and extensively illustrates concepts with real-world applications.

Scanzoni, John: "Changing Sex Roles and Emerging Directions in Family Decision Making," *Journal of Consumer Research,* vol. 4, no. 3 (December 1977), pp. 185–188. This article contrasts contemporary with traditional wives and looks at how the change in role has affected family decisions.

Schewe, Charles D.: "Selected Social Psychological Models for Analyzing Buyers," *Journal of Marketing,* vol. 37 no. 3 (July 1973), pp. 31–39. Four contemporary social psychological theories are examined, and their implications for marketing are offered.

Zaltman, Gerald, and Melanie Wallendorf: *Consumer Behavior: Basic Findings and Management Implications,* Wiley, New York, 1979. This more advanced text takes a sociological look at consumer behavior.

Chapter 7

Individual Influences on Exchange Behavior

Looking Ahead

In Chapter 5 we looked at the demographic trends that help marketers describe markets. But description is not sufficient. We need to understand our consumers, so in Chapter 6 we examined how other people in our social environment influence exchange behavior. But social influences do not fully account for consumers' willingness to exchange. We also are influenced greatly by our own perceptions, inner feelings, and personal motivations. In this chapter, then, we will look at what goes on *inside* consumers and how that influences their willingness to exchange.

Key Topics

The consumer as a black box: internal influences on exchange behavior

How motivation begins exchange behavior by activating the buyer

Why marketers are interested in how consumers attach meaning to what they sense

How the learning process can be used to increase satisfaction in the marketplace

How consumers compare alternatives against a set of desired outcomes

The influence of attitudes on exchange behavior

Some approaches to understanding human personality

A comprehensive model of how individual and social factors influence consumers' exchange decisions

How industrial organizations make purchase decisions

The Consumer as a Black Box

One of the things that marketing has borrowed from the behavioral sciences is the concept of the *black box*. As shown in Figure 7-1, marketers see consumers as being bombarded by stimuli (information) that lead to certain responses—in this case, exchange behavior. A stimulus can be anything that causes a response. It is a piece of information that an individual processes and then acts on. In marketing terms, stimuli include the marketing mix (product, price, place, and promotion); competing marketing mixes; and social influences (culture, class, reference groups, and family). As Figure 7-1 indicates, not all marketing stimuli result in exchange behavior. After being exposed to stimuli, an individual consumer still may seek additional information or may respond to a competing marketer's stimulus, or may do nothing at all.

But what actually goes on within consumers' minds as they process stimuli to arrive at a final response? Marketers—like psychologists and other behavioral scientists—cannot be sure of exactly what takes place. While we can observe *behavior,* we cannot observe *mental activity.* In short, a consumer's mind is like a black box—dark and unfathomable. To understand consumers fully, marketers must explore what takes place inside their minds, inside the black box.

That is our purpose in this chapter. We have already examined some of the stimuli bombarding consumers. We have looked at the marketing mix and at social influences on exchange behavior. Now we will explore some of the processes that occur *inside* consumers' minds—their motivation, perception, learning, evaluative criteria, attitudes, and personality. These concepts will all be brought together in a comprehensive model of consumer behavior. By understanding both the social influences and the internal influences on exchange behavior, marketers can better provide satisfaction in the marketplace. Finally, the exchange process that occurs within organizations will be explored.

Figure 7-1   The consumer as a black box.

The marketing mix
Competing marketing mixes
Social influences
    (culture, social class,
    reference groups,
    and family)

Stimuli

The consumer

Responses

Exchange
No exchange
More information
    sought

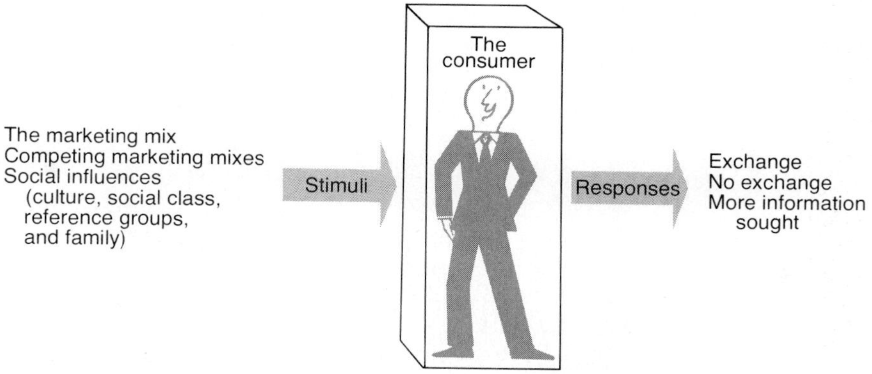

Motivation

Why do we behave as we do? Perhaps the simplest answer is to say, "Because we are motivated." Underlying motivation are unsatisfied needs and wants. These are the basic forces that activate our behavior. A *motive* is a stimulated need or want that consumers look to satisfy. We are filled with potential needs and wants; only when they are aroused do they lead to behavior.

Motives generally are classified into two broad groups. Some motives are *biogenic.* They arise from physiological states of deprivation such as when one needs food, drink, sex, or bodily comfort. Other motives are *psychogenic,* psychological states of tension arising from the need or want for prestige, belonging, pride, recognition, and the like. These underlie the problems consumers face in day-to-day living. Their solutions, then, represent the *benefits sought* by *markets.* (Remember benefit segmentation from Chapter 5?) Marketers must realize that products often solve problems and satisfy both types of needs and wants—often simultaneously.

Consider Neutrogena skin-care soap, the amber-colored, transparent bars that look attractive, smell nice, and don't irritate the face. At $1.75 a bar, Neutrogena fills a gap somewhere between a 47-cent bar of Ivory and an $8.50 bar of Clinique. It is billed as a mild soap product for people wanting healthy skin and willing to pay a premium for it. The successful company understands both the biogenic and psychogenic motives that activate the market. Neutrogena's president told *Forbes,* "What people think they're getting is what's important. With skin, half the problems are here," he said, touching his wrist, "and the other half are here," he added, pointing to his temple.[1]

Abraham Maslow has offered a well-known five-tier hierarchy of needs as a means for understanding motivation.[2] (See Figure 7-2). Basically, his theory states that a person has many needs. The five, in the order he keys on, are:

Physiological—the need for food, sex, drink, and shelter

Safety—the need for security, protection and order

Social—the need for affection, belonging to a group, and acceptance

Esteem—the need for self-respect, prestige, reputation, and status

Self-actualization—the need for self-fulfillment

A person will focus on satisfying the most important needs first. Those needs, according to Maslow's theory, are at the lower physiological level. The person will

---

[1]"If I Have the Doctor . . . ," *Forbes,* March 30, 1981, p. 64.
[2]Abraham H. Maslow, *Motivation and Personality,* Harper & Row, New York, 1954.

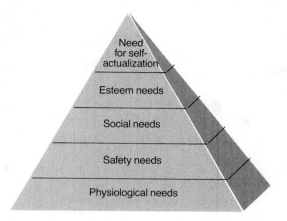

Figure 7-2 Maslow's heirarchy of needs.

then progress to higher levels on the hierarchy. Once an important need has been satisfied, its motivating power ceases and the person is activated to satisfy the next most important need. For example, people with a great hunger seek only food. But once McDonald's "Quarter-Pounder with Cheese" or Burger King's "Whopper" has come into their lives, their focus turns to higher-level safety needs. Of course, need satisfaction is not as rigid a process as Maslow suggests. Multiple needs can be met in the same act. People can satisfy many needs simultaneously. Eating a five-course dinner (physiological) at the Four Seasons restaurant in Manhattan (esteem) with one's closest friends (social) provides just such an example.

A motivated person is ready to take action. Arousal has started the process that will result in some behavior. But what shapes and influences that behavior? The answer lies in perception.

Perception

As consumers, we can easily make mistakes. We have not been provided with all the physical and mental abilities sometimes needed to be sensitive and discriminating agents in modern society. In a complex exchange situation, our senses can often betray us. Small wonder! There are many complexities associated with the concept of perception.

Most of what we know about the world around us comes to us through our senses—seeing, hearing, tasting, smelling, and touching. These sensate processes tend to be purely physiological in nature; that is, they involve our nervous system and do not take into account what we have learned from past experiences. Usually, there's little that we—or marketers—can do to influence how our bodies sense things. But perception is another matter, and it deserves marketers' full attention.

Perception is the process by which we attach meaning to what our bodies sense.

Besides sensory impressions, perception involves an individual's own "filling in" to complete the picture. Perception influences and adds to our sensory impressions by bringing our past experiences to bear on them. And it has been found that we very often perceive only what we want to perceive. That is, we interpret what we sense—and sometimes we distort it. This does not mean, of course, that when we look at a bar of soap we see an automobile. But it does mean that we bring subtle meanings to what we sense. In perceiving, we interpret what we see, hear, taste, smell, and touch—in a way that is meaningful to us.

Frito-Lay capitalized on understanding buyers' perceptions—or misperceptions. To fight consumers' image to snack chips as junk food, the company began adding detailed information on the nutritional contents to its packages. Additional text of bags of Lay's potato chips, for example, said a 1-ounce serving is equal to a cup of milk in calories and two slices of bread in salt. The company was not trying to make chips a nutritional food but, rather, was trying to change perceptual distortions. The company found that consumers thought they were one-twentieth as nutritional as they actually were. (See Application 7-1.)

So marketers must be interested in perception because it involves what consumers believe. Consider vodka. Most *objective* experts say that, except for price, all vodka is essentially the same. Yet consumers believe the various brands of vodka are different. Thus, vodka drinkers see Smirnoff as being vastly superior to brands that cost much less, even though the product is basically the same. But the Smirnoff brand and some imported vodkas, such as Stolichnaya, Finlandia, and Absolut, have been promoted as superior, and so consumers perceive them differently.

To provide satisfaction effectively in the marketplace, marketers must understand how all their marketing activities are perceived. The physical qualities of a product make up only part of consumers' total perceptions. Often, the psychological and symbolic characteristics of a product provide greater satisfaction than its tangible qualities do. Consider the deluxe-priced Smirnoff Silver and the 1980 entry, Smirnoff de Czar, which, at $12 a fifth, is the highest-priced vodka on the market. People gain gratification from feeling they are serving the best. Clearly, consumers' perceptions greatly influence exchange behavior.

To gain entry into a consumer's perceptual arena, marketers first must get their attention. But this is not easy. Think of the last time you watched television. How many commercials can you recall? You may have looked at them, but in all likelihood you can remember few. Probably, your mind wandered; you thought of other things instead of concentrating on the commercials. This is an example of *selective perception*. From the vast number of stimuli available in our complex, attention-grabbing world, we *choose* which ones will be given attention. This is called *selective exposure*. We sift and funnel stimuli, paying attention to considerably fewer than we are exposed to, and understanding only some of them. Finally, we remember still fewer of the many stimuli we receive. This is called *selective retention*. In short, what we learn about our environment—what we perceive—hinges on a very selective process. That's why marketers (whether in business, government, or education) go to great lengths to *get our attention*.

Application 7-1
Perception—Appealing to the Consumer's Senses

Looks, as we all know, can be deceiving. What looks like leather is often plastic, and even what looks like a full head of hair can very well be a hairpiece.

Now, we find we can't trust even our noses. Those irresistible odors—like that of freshly baked chocolate chip cookies—may be clever fakes. Retailers are finding odor is a persuasive stimulus, and one company is exploiting our sense of smell. International Flavors & Fragrances, Inc., is turning out chocolate chip cookie scents, as well as some that duplicate the smells of pizza, apple pie, baked ham, and others.

But the persuasive arts of retailers extend far beyond the use of these subtle odors. Consider color.

A consulting firm in Toronto has found a marketing tool in the use of the color yellow. The "philosophy of big yellow" was conceived a few years ago for Loblaws Ltd., a Canadian supermarket chain, to reenforce the company's image as a "bargain hunter's paradise." First, Loblaws put "feature-price" items under "Save" signs. It then put advertised items in one aisle and hung yellow "Save" signs overhead. Then the store began packaging all its generic foods in yellow. Two years earlier, Loblaws had introduced generic goods in black and white packages, and they were avoided by shoppers. But yellow packages were so successful that Loblaws began opening no-frills supermarkets in

Canada, painting the stores yellow—and again, success. The latest tactic is to put more and more ordinary merchandise in yellow packages.

A marketing consultant explains: "Yellow is striking and highly visible to the eye." Second, he holds that yellow has "negative associations," meaning that it connotes an image of cheapness—the very image the Loblaws chain wanted to convey.

Source of data: "Sight, Smell, Sound: They're All Arms in Retailers' Arsenal," *The Wall Street Journal,* April 17, 1979, p. 1.

Obtaining Attention

One requirement for perception to occur, then, is that attention must be given to the stimulus. The attention mechanism is a selecting device. It sorts through all the stimuli we are exposed to and chooses which ones will be noticed and, therefore, perceived. Whether or not attention will be paid depends both on the individual doing the perceiving and on the stimulus competing for attention. When the individual is attracted to or interested in the stimulus object, greater attention is given. Bright colors, loud sounds, large size, and movement all make a stimulus more noticeable than dull colors, soft sounds, small size, and immobility. In short, we perceive by exception; we notice mainly those stimuli which appear different to our senses. Hartz Mountain Corporation, the largest pet supply company, took this into account in marketing fish food. Consumers cannot tell differences between brands of fish food; fish food is fish food is fish food! And fish show little excitement over their food. So Hartz came up with a new fish food in pellet form. Fish will attack the pellets ravenously. Also, after about ten days, the fish's color brightens. Although the fish is not necessarily healthier—just brighter—the food fulfills the owner's psychological need to see his or her pet happy and healthy. And it goes a long way to bring attention to the Hartz brand.

The fact that we perceive by exception also has other implications for marketing. For instance, marketers must realize that an individual, over a period of time, adapts to changes in the environment. This is one reason why companies change their advertisements from time to time. What excites our senses and gets our attention today may have no effect tomorrow. People tend to adapt to stimuli. They become familiar with them. But when a stimulus is changed to depart sufficiently from prior experience, it can again arouse attention. "The Pause that Refreshes" and "The Real Thing" were slogans that the Coca-Cola Company discontinued when they were no longer gaining attention. Marketers must present stimuli that depart sufficiently from what is expected so that they will be noticed. Since we perceive by exception, doing things out of the ordinary is an important tool for obtaining attention.

The S. T. Dupont Company, a subsidiary of the Gillette Company that produces status products, has used this principle to bring attention to its pricy, handcrafted lighters. When the smoker snaps open a $150 to $400 Dupont lighter, it makes a recognizably different ring sound that immediately identifies it to the discerning as "a Dupont." One Japanese owner of a Dupont lighter reportedly attracts attention to *himself* by casually snapping the top.

Sensory Thresholds

Sensory thresholds, or limits, are another important aspect of perception that marketers must understand. Every human sensory process (touching, hearing, seeing, smelling, tasting) has an upper and a lower limit of responsiveness to stimulation. These boundaries set the limits above and below which stimuli cannot be sensed. For instance, human beings cannot hear the high pitch of a dog whistle. The pitch of the whistle is above what is called the *upper threshold,* the point at which further increases in intensity will not be noticed. Similarly, the *lower threshold* is the point at which further decreases in intensity will not be noticed. But what is of particular interest to marketers is the so-called *difference threshold:* the *smallest* increment of change in stimulus intensity that can be noticed by an individual.

There are times when marketers will *not* want to exceed the difference threshold. Consider the case of companies that produce chocolate candy bars in which the cocoa bean is a major ingredient. As cocoa costs increase, the companies can no longer make a profit on candy bars at current prices. What options are available? The companies can use less choclate or a chocolate substitute, but if this change is beyond the difference threshold and consumers do not like the resulting taste, satisfaction will not result and sales will decrease. Fear of exactly this led the well-known Kansas City–based Russell Stover Candies to reject the use of chocolate substitutes in its boxed candies at a time when cocoa bean prices nearly doubled.

Another option would be to decrease the size of the candy bar (see Figure 7-3); but if the smaller size is noticed, sales are also likely to fall. The third option, and the one most companies pursue, is to increase the price of the candy bar without proportionately increasing its size. Both the Nestlé Company and Hershey Foods Corporation followed this strategy in 1977. Prices of both companies' milk chocolate

Original size

Difference might
not be noticed

Difference would
be noticed

**Figure 7-3   The
difference threshold
applied to candy bars.
Consumers will notice
changes in size only if
those changes exceed the
difference threshold.**

bars went from 15 to 20 cents, while the Nestlé bar grew from 1 to 1.25 ounces and the Hershey bar from 1.2 to 1.35 ounces.

In some situations, the marketer may want to go beyond a particular difference threshold to gain attention and result in a certain perception. With 1982 models, the Big Three auto makers were faced with a problem. The market, they believed, desired an array of new and different offerings—yet the depressed industry had neither the time nor the money to fully redesign their cars. To help solve their problem, they added a few changes such as plush upholstery, paint stripes, new doors, and fenders to their basic models to give them the appearance of being sporty, luxurious models worthy of their higher sticker price. For example, Ford gave its subcompact Escort a sports-car effect by renaming it the EXP, removing the rear seat (leaving two bucket seats) in favor of a luggage area, and adding tachometer and dual exhaust pipes to give it "that sound." These rather inexpensive alterations provided the feeling of sportiness.

The concept of sensory thresholds is linked to the fact that we perceive by exception. In developing a stimulus that will get customers' attention, marketers must keep sensory thresholds in mind. By understanding the difference threshold especially, they can prepare stimuli that communicate effectively in the marketplace.

Sensory Discrimination

Sensory discrimination is the ability to distinguish between two or more similar stimuli presented to one sense mode. It occurs when stimuli are different enough to exceed the difference threshold. Marketers are interested in knowing whether their brands are noticeably different from competing brands. They want consumers to be able to distinguish among brands and to prefer theirs. And some marketers whose brands are not as well known as leading brands try to "piggyback" on the success of well-known brands by appearing similar to the market leader.

Many products, however, are not perceived as different, and cannot be. Brands of gasoline are an example. Consumers cannot tell the difference between the gasoline sold by, say, Exxon and Shell. Given many comparable gasolines, all of which make a car run, differences can be detected only by an expert. Other products that are viewed as being essentially the same are cigarettes, cola drinks, brands of beer, and aspirin.

When consumers cannot distinguish among brands, marketers turn to psychology to establish differences. Some gasoline buyers, for instance, may feel patriotic in buying the American brand, with its red, white, and blue color scheme. Gulf buyers, on the other hand, may expect friendly service because of the warm, friendly orange color that Gulf uses. Marlboro cigarettes present a macho image, while Virginia Slims appeal to feminist sentiments. In short, marketers rely on symbolic satisfactions to distinguish products so that consumers can perceive them to be different. (See Application 7-2.)

Gestalt Psychology

The German word *gestalt* translates roughly into "whole" or "total configuration." Gestalt psychologists believe that the perception of a stimulus involves a dynamic process which often results in something different from what could be expected if each element of the stimulus were considered separately. For example, in viewing the countryside we do not see hundreds of separate objects, even though they may be there. Instead, we see many things—trees, grass, fences, horses, perhaps—but we put the parts together in a way that makes sense. Each individual does this. We silently organize the separate stimuli to produce what we interpret to be a meaningful whole.

In doing their jobs, marketers can use gestalt psychology. That's what Kellogg's, the cereal manufacturer, did when it designed a billboard which positioned the company's name so far toward the right-hand side that the *g's* were cut off by the boundary of the billboard. This posed no problem for consumers, though, since they mentally inserted the final letters and perceived the word as *Kellogg's.* And since we perceive by exception, this advertisement caught people's attention.

Another example of the use of gestalt principles is seen in the television commercial for Budweiser beer, which includes the jingle "When you've said Budweiser, you've said it all." The jingle is repeated 1½ times in the commercial. After hearing the entire jingle, listeners hear for the second time, "When you've said Budweiser, you've . . . ' Their attention is enlisted immediately, and they mentally complete the jingle. Similarly, a recent lengthy advertising campaign for Datsun offered on radio the jingle "Datsun. . . . We are driven." Later, in a revised campaign, this was shortened to simply "Datsun . . . driven."

Basically, gestalt psychology sees human beings as *needing* to attach meanings to sensations, even when parts of them are incomplete or missing. Incompleteness creates anxiety in our minds, and so we silently provide what is missing to make sense out of what we see, hear, touch, taste, and smell.

Application 7-2
Testing Sensory Discrimination—
Risky? or Calculating?

In the late 1960s and early 1970s, the Joseph Schlitz Brewing Company was the pride of Milwaukee, the fastest-growing beer on the market, and clearly a challenger to Anheuser-Busch, the "King of Beers." But to cut costs, Schlitz began tampering with its formula in 1974, and Schlitz drinkers fled by the thousands. Growth slowed to a halt by 1976, and by 1980, production had plunged to a mere 15 million barrels a year, down from a high of 24 million in 1976. Despite the fact that Schlitz had reformulated its brew, its reputation continued to haunt the firm. In an effort to regain market share, Schlitz began conducting a series of live beer-tasting tests before vast audiences on network television; this tactic appeared to stake Schlitz's reputation in a series of 90-second commercials, telecast between the halves of football games broadcast by NBC.

In the beer tests, Schlitz was pitted against either Budweiser or Miller High Life, the two leading brands. Each tasting was performed by a panel of 100 beer-drinking citizens selected by an independent market-survey organization. None of the tasters was shown drinking the beer, in compliance with TV broadcasting regulations. The commercial began after the beer had been tasted but before the tasters had judged the brews.

The beer was served to the testers without labels and in identical opaque mugs so that it was virtually impossible to identify a brand by sight. Schlitz said it had made sure that each sample was fresh and chilled to just the right temperature—42°F. Schlitz never took on both competitors at one tasting. Alternate broadcasts features either Schlitz versus Budweiser or Schlitz versus Miller. Budweiser was not tested against Miller. "With two choices, it's simple," explained a Schlitz officer. "It's the simplest, cleanest type of taste comparison."

However, it would have been difficult for Schlitz to lose its taste test. The makeup of the testing panels was the most critical factors. When Schlitz was compared with Budweiser, the panel was made up of Budweiser drinkers—while with Miller comparisons, the panel consisted entirely of Miller drinkers. This gave Schlitz an advantage. If even a small number of Bud or Miller drinkers said that Schlitz was better, the company could claim a victory. And since there were no regular Schlitz drinkers on any of the panels, the TV viewer could not witness any defections from Schlitz.

The first test result was typical of all five—46 percent of Budweiser drinkers preferred the Schlitz brew. Yet, that was not as surprising as one might think. First, Schlitz was a better beer than in earlier times. Second, most American beers are subtly flavored and require a trained palate to distinguish among them. Finally, Schlitz knew in advance what kind of results to expect. In a series of preliminary tests, numbers ranging between 45 and 55 percent preferred Schlitz over competitors.

Source of data: "Schlitz's Crafty Taste Test," *Fortune*, Jan. 26, 1981, pp. 32–34.

Learning Theory

Closely tied to perception is *learning*, the behavioral changes that result from our experiences. Learning and perception are related because we can experience, and learn from, only what we perceive. Besides changes in physical behavior, learning includes changes in mental behavior, such as feelings, emotions, and personality.

What do we learn from our experiences? First, of course, we learn about the *objects* in our environment. We learn, for example, that motorcycles are different from bicycles, that houses are different from apartments, and that coffee is different from tea. But we also learn about the *functions* of objects—that motorcycles provide faster and easier transportation than bicycles, that houses offer more privacy than apartments, and that coffee has a stronger taste than tea. In addition, we learn *tastes*. We learn to like or dislike, say, spinach or cigarettes or Scotch, and we learn what is

Application 7-3
Learning and Unlearning—Rumors Spread like Wildfire

Did you know that:
McDonald's and Wendy's add red earthworms to hamburgers to boost their protein content?
Spider eggs are added to Life Savers' Bubble Yum?
R. J. Reynolds owns marijuana fields in Mexico?
General Foods' Pop Rocks Crackling Candy makes your stomach explode?
Profits from Entenmann's New York bakery are being funneled to Rev. Sun Myung Moon's Unification Church?
Wearing jockey shorts makes men sterile?

These rumors spread throughout the country duing the past few years and threatened profits. Businesses are struggling to find ways to head off rumors like these in the hope of minimizing the harm done to sales. The red worms rumor, for instance, reduced sales by 20 percent at McDonald's outlets.

Companies that have fought such rumors have tried a number of strategies. Among them:
Ignore the rumor in the hope that it will either pass with time or collapse from obvious absurdity. But don't count on it, experts caution.
Tackle the rumor head on by identifying it, ridiculing it, and dismissing it as often as possible to the largest audiences that can be reached. But watch out; you might make things worse.
Outflank the rumor by rebutting it without really repeating it and by limiting such responses to places where the rumor is known to be circulating. But be prepared for outbreaks elsewhere.

The cost of crushing a rumor is not cheap. General Foods ran full-page advertising in *The New York Times,* and about thirty other newspapers, mostly in the Northeast, to fight the Pop Rock rumor. The company declined to indicate the total cost of all the advertising, but just the full-page ad in the Sunday Times cost $18,240.

In another campaign, the Life Savers unit of Squibb Corporation spent "between $50,000 and $100,000, mostly on newspaper ads, "to counter the rumor about Bubble Yum.

The president of Life Savers believes that the company's attack on "these malicious and absurd rumors about harmful ingredients or foreign materials in Bubble Yum kept the rumors from spreading but never completely restored consumer confidence around New York. We haven't achieved the success in New York we had expected; our per capita sales here are below the rest of the country."

Sources of data: "Rumor-Plagued Firms Use Various Strategies to Keep Damage Low," *The Wall Street Journal,* Feb. 6, 1979, p. 1; and "Of Gingerbread Men with Pigtails, Rumor Problems at Entenmann's," *The Wall Street Journal,* Oct. 1, 1980, p. 35.

"tasteful" in clothes and behavior. *Wants* and *needs* are also learned. We learn to want little Izod-Lacoste alligators on our clothes, for instance, because "everyone else has them"; and we learn that we need certain nutrients in our diet to be healthy. In short, everything we learn about our environment and about how to function within it comes about by acquiring information through the perceptual process and thinking about what we have perceived. Application 7-3 shows how learning can work against the marketer.

Mental Associations

Figure 7-4 A lemon scent doesn't clean dishes more thoroughly, but it does satisfy a consumer want. (Randy Matusow)

The process of building mental associations, or connections, is one form of learning. We build associations between two or more stimuli or between stimulus and a response. Mental associations are a convenient way to understand the information that we receive. They are a kind of mental shorthand that allows us to process information more quickly than we otherwise could.

Consider, for example, the associations we have between certain colors and ideas. Black is often thought of as sophisticated while white usually conveys naivety. Red, orange, and yellow indicate heat, while blue and green are considered cool. Pastel shades are associated with feminity, youth, and softness, while dark colors are connected with maturity and respectability. The number of such associations that human beings make seems limitless, and they are not all obvious (as psychologists have proved again and again). But the important point for marketers is that people transfer their mental associations to objects which share the associated trait. Thus, in the United States, wedding gowns are white, not black; menthol cigarettes come in blue or green packages rather than red or orange; and baby clothes are seldom khaki or maroon.

Quaker State Oil Refining Corp., the country's largest refiner and marketer of motor oil, knows the importance of color associations. Quaker State has unusually strong brand loyalty. It stems largely from the company's strong association with the so-called Penn-grade variety of crude oil, a light, greenish crude that was used to refine the first motor oils ever used in the United States. The consumer's belief in the quality of Pennsylvania motor oil is so widespread that many major oil companies today add green dye to their Texas or Middle Eastern crude-based motor oils to simulate the Penn-grade oil.

Color is not the only trait for which we form associations. Size, shape, texture, taste, and smell—all sensory characteristics—can carry such hidden meanings. Marketers can use such associations to communicate quickly with consumers and tell them how a particular product will satisfy their needs. Thus, the smell of lemon, which is associated with freshness and cleanliness, is added to such products as furniture polish, shampoo, laundry soap, household cleaners, and cosmetics. While there is no *real* lemon juice in these products, the *smell* of lemon is used to communicate the idea of freshness to consumers. (See Figure 7-4).

In using such associations to communicate, however, marketers must be careful. Sometimes false associations are made in consumers' minds. For example, Goodrich

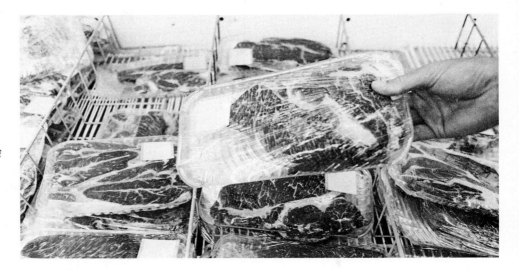

Figure 7-5 At least one supermarket chain promised that the side of meat you couldn't see was as good as or better than the side you could see. What are the advantages and disadvantages of such a promise? *(Randy Matusow)*

Tire Company found that consumers saw its advertisements as ads for the better-known Goodyear brand of tires. Consequently, the company mounted a major promotional campaign to dissociate itself in consumers' minds from Goodyear: "Goodrich does *not* have the blimp," its commercials announced.

Another problem that arises from mental associations is that sometimes undesired associations are built. Miller Brewing Company long touted its regular beer as the "Champagne of Bottled Beer" to associate it with the best. Yet heavy beer drinkers (and we saw what they are like in Chapter 5) saw the association as denoting high society, and so the brand was never popular with them. And a market study for After Six, the leading formal suit marketer, revealed that some men associate wearing a tuxedo with "putting on airs." In an attempt to reduce this association, the company developed advertisements showing formally clad men and women having drinks by a swimming pool: "Among this crowd of international celebrities are two truck drivers and a plumber," the ad begins. It finishes with "Who are they? Since our formal wear makes everyone famous, who cares?"

Besides using associations to communicate with consumers, marketers build into their marketing mix various *signs* that indicate what to expect in terms of quality, performance, or service. For instance, see-through wrappers indicate greater freshness because consumers can see the product and think, "If they'll let me see it, it must be fresh." (See Figure 7-5.) In the same way, a higher price is seen to indicate high quality. One large food-processing company in the Midwest offers two lines of heat-and-serve biscuits that are the same, except that one is priced several cents above the other. Although the dough that comes off the assembly line is exactly the same for both products, the company is using the sign of price to serve two distinct market segments: price-conscious consumers who buy only low-priced biscuits and quality-conscious buyers who want only high-priced biscuits. Neither group can be persuaded to buy the other segment's products, and so a higher price is used as a sign of assurance for the quality-conscious buyers.

The Learning Process and Marketing

For marketing purposes, it is useful to see learning as involving five major concepts:

1 A *cue* is an external stimulus that can come from any environmental source; it is perceived as a signal for action.

2 A *drive* is a strong motivating tendency that prompts action toward a particular end; it arouses an individual to a need state, such as hunger or thirst.

3 A *response* is whatever occurs as a reaction to a stimulated need.

4 *Reinforcement* is the extent to which satisfaction is derived from a response.

5 *Retention* is remembering what is learned.

In marketing terms, one most obvious cue is advertising, though any element of the marketing mix can function to stimulate action. Once marketers have identified some need among consumers, cues can be used to stimulate a marketing response (exchange, no exchange, or a need for more information, as shown in Figure 7-1). Reinforcement is offered to consumers by the extent to which an exchange matches their expectations; the greater the match, the greater the probability that consumers will make the same response under similar circumstances. Finally, marketers want consumers to remember what they have learned through the marketing effort.

Principles that Enhance Learning

While marketers cannot create drives within consumers, they can affect the amount of learning that takes place by how they handle the cues which stimulate learning. *The frequency with which cues are presented* is one important factor. When consumers are exposed to cues over a period of time, they are more likely to remember them than when they are exposed to many cues all at once. On the other hand, massive exposure to cues can lead to faster learning. Often, to introduce a new product, marketers will expose consumers to frequent cues in large doses. But after the product is understood and accepted, the cues presented will be strung out over a period of time to promote greater retention. Philip Morris followed this plan to introduce its highly successful Merit brand of cigarettes. In the first year, it spent more than $40 million on advertising (almost 50 cents for each dollar in revenue); in following years, the company reduced its advertising expenditures by Merit by reducing the brand's media schedule.

Getting consumers to participate also enhances learning. Thus, automobiles are often made available for a test drive; free samples of soap are sent to consumers' homes; and exercise equipment is offered for a free 10-day trial. Additionally, in general, *the greater the reinforcement, the greater the learning*. Yet some fine points must be recognized. Total reinforcement, where reward is given each time a certain behavior occurs, results in faster learning. Partial reinforcement, where reward is received only on some responses, leads to learning that is more difficult to extinguish. Thus, since new products or brands offered require fast learning by consumers, they should not experience any dissatisfactions. And once a brand has been used satisfactorily for a period of time, that is, once much learning has taken place, a failure on the part of the brand (partial reinforcement) may not change the convictions of the consumer.

Researchers find that *the first and last things in a series are learned best.* Advertisers know that the opening and closing of an advertising message must be worded carefully. Many messages end with a command: "Buy one today" or "See your dealer now."

Finally, *if consumers have learned to associate some stimulus* (Bayer aspirin) *with some response* (relief of headache), a *similar stimulus* (Datril or Tylenol) *will be associated more easily with the same result* (relief of headache). Thus, the second stimulus should be like the original stimulus that produced the association. The more similar stimuli are, the more likely that consumers will respond similarly to them. This explains why marketers can ride the coattails of those who have already introduced an innovation to the market. Schlitz Light and Anheuser-Busch's Budweiser Light purposely utilize the word light to promote a close association with the industry leader, Miller Lite. Companies that follow the leader can imitate the marketing program as well as the product of the leader.

Low-Involvement Learning

Recently, marketers have noted that the way consumers learn depends on how much they care about or are involved with a given product. Automobiles and home purchases are very important to their buyers, but consumers find most purchases of little importance to them. Bicycles, facial tissues, toothpaste,[3] and many more such products show low consumer involvement. To most of us consumers, the choice of which product to purchase is not one of the great burning concerns in our lives.

With low-involvement products, learning is done passively. Instead of actively seeking information to evaluate products before buying, consumers who passively learn are more information gatherers than seekers, picking up bits and pieces of information at random rather than processing information for a purpose. With low-involvement learning, reference groups have little influence on product choice because low-involvement products are not likely to be related to the values of groups. Television becomes a good medium to convey information to a passive audience since its animation has attention-getting value and high repetition fosters random information acquisition.

Coca-Cola Company took an aggressive advertising posture in 1982 when it switched its more relaxed, unassuming "Have a Coke and a Smile" campaign to a harder sell "Coke Is It!" campaign. Distressed by the success of Pepsi-Cola's very competitive "Pepsi Challenge" commercials where, in taste tests, consumers choose

---

[3]Nancy T. Hupfer and David M. Gardner, "Differential Involvement with Products and Issues: An Exploratory Study," in David M. Gardner (ed.), *Proceedings of the 2nd Annual Conference of the Association for Consumer Research,* Association for Consumer Research, College Park, Md., 1971, pp. 262–269.

Pepsi, Coke turned to a zippier, bolder, more competitive theme. "Coke is it! The biggest taste you've ever found, Coke is it! . . . The most refreshing taste around" was one commercial. And, realizing the low involvement consumers have with soft drinks, the company's media plan for 1982 stressed much greater frequency of broadcast advertising to emphasize repetition of the "message" and hence obtain greater brand awareness. Past programming of commercials had been spaced over longer periods of time.

Memory

After learning has occurred, that which has been learned usually is retained as a memory. But what happens to information that has been stored?

Information that has been acquired undergoes continuous mental operations called *cognitive* (thinking) *processes*. Three concepts are useful: leveling, sharpening, and assimilation. *Leveling* can be compared with forgetting. What we retain becomes shorter and more concise. We tend to remember only certain aspects of an experience. For instance, when thinking about a particular brand of after-shave lotion, we may recall *only* its sharp sting, and not its distinctive, pleasant scent. *Sharpening* is the opposite of leveling: much of what remains is more vivid and important than the actual event was. The sting of the after-shave lotion may have been sharp, but not as intense or painful as we recall. *Assimilation* is the process by which we choose what is to be leveled and what is to be sharpened. This selection depends on the habits, interests, and attitudes of each individual. Thus, some people may be particularly sensitive to pain and will remember the sting of the after-shave lotion above all else.

Evaluative Criteria

In Chapter 4, we said that marketing managers are essentially decision makers who choose among alternatives in order to solve a problem. Consumers also can be viewed as decision makers. Their cues and drives create a perceived problem, and their choice of a response is a solution to the problem. Like marketers, consumers also have objectives in their search for solutions. Consumers' objectives are reflected in their *evaluative criteria*: the features or performance characteristics that consumers expect in a particular product, brand, store, or organization with which they deal. Evaluative criteria apply to noncommercial marketing too. For instance, those who donate to charitable organizations expect their money to be put to a stated use. The choice of a political candidate to vote for depends upon what one expects that person to do once in office.

We use evaluative criteria in making all our daily decisions. Thus, the determination of evaluative criteria is a critical step in providing satisfaction in the marketplace. Marketers must provide what the market is looking for in order to provide satisfaction. But it is not enough to know only the criteria; marketers must know *specifically* what the underlying dimensions of evaluation are. They must know *how many* criteria are involved, the *importance* of each, and the *strength* of each.

Figure 7-6 The style of a telephone is very important to some consumers, not at all important to others. Which of these phones give more importance to style, or status, or dependability? (Courtesy of AT&T)

In a given exchange situation, for example, consumers may use only one criterion to make a decision. They may buy a pencil simply because it is available. Yet, in other exchange decisions, they may use many criteria. In buying a car, such features as style, safety, price, dependability, service, economy, color, accessories, and status may be involved. Usually, however, only five or six criteria come into play. And some of these may be far more important than others in the evaluation process. In buying a car, price, style, and economy may rank high on a consumer's list of priorities, while color may not be so important. Finally, a particular criterion may be stronger in one exchange situation than in another. For instance, style may exert a stronger influence when buying a car than when buying a clock for the kitchen. (See Figure 7-6.)

In applying evaluative criteria, consumers compare their alternatives against the criteria and then select the one that comes closest to matching what they want and need. This mental process as it might be applied to the selection of an automobile is shown in Table 7-1. Each potential car is rated according to the criteria listed at the left. The candidate which best meets the criteria (which gets the highest total score) provides the best match.

Another point about evaluative criteria is that marketers must know how their marketing mix compares with competing marketing efforts. For instance, it has been found that nonbusiness travelers who fly commercial airlines put great importance on

TABLE 7-1	Evaluative Criteria as Applied to Automobile Purchase						
		Rating (poor match . . . . good match)					
Criteria	Weight	1	2	3	4	5	Total
Style	10					X	50
Price	9				X		36
Economy	8				X		32
Dependability	6			X			18
Service	6				X		24
Accessories	4			X			12
Safety	3		X				6
Color	1	X					1
							179

the following criteria: duration of layovers, the airline's safety record, the cost of the flight, inflight time, and the number of stops. Since the most significant criterion is the length of time spent in layovers, the logical marketing strategy would be to reduce the amount of layover time. But this decision may be hasty. Further study may reveal that consumers believe layover time cannot be controlled by the airlines, and that all airlines are rated about the same in terms of layovers. If so, this criterion does not help consumers to differentiate among their choices. The marketers might do better to focus on their safety record in gaining consumers' attention and acceptance. Those criteria that are highest in importance and also perceived differently among competing products are called *determinant buying attributes.*

This element of competition raises the question of what marketers can do about evaluative criteria. Quite logically, if a marketer's brand matches (satisfies) an important evaluative criterion, this can be communicated to the market. For example, Life Savers, Inc., used a comparative campaign to pit its sugar-free Breath Savers against Warner-Lambert's Certs breath mints, which contain sugar. The Breath Savers commercial opened with a party scene and a guest's request for a breath mint. A Certs user is about to provide one when a woman interrupts and says, ''No, try my new Breath Savers. They really fight bad breath.'' When the Certs user counters, ''So do mine,'' the two begin comparing the relative merits of both products. The woman goes one up on the Certs user when she notes that Breath Savers are sugar-free. Her adversary is then moved to say, ''I'll try Breath Savers because I want fresh breath, but I don't want sugar.'' Here, the sugar-free factor is promoted as the determinant buying attribute.

If it is found that a product is perceived as being low on an important criterion, the marketers can improve performance in terms of this dimension. In 1981, international airlines found business travelers complaining about tight economy-class seating. Believing that more spacious seating was the most tangible benefit they could offer those full-fare business travelers who did not respond to free drinks and other perks, international carriers spent millions to replace rows of ten narrow seats with eight wider seats. (See Application 7-4.)

Another strategy is to *make consumers aware of criteria they have not considered*. Marketers of toothpaste did this by emphasizing fluoride; detergent marketers introduced biodegradable ingredients; and soft-drink marketers turned to formulas that are low in calories and caffeine. Still another strategy is to *change the importance placed on a particular criterion*. During the downturn in domestic car sales, automobile manufacturers tried to sell their inventories of large models by

---

Application 7-4
Evaluative Criteria and Determinant Buying Attributes—
Making the Best of the Worst Situation

As the 1980s began, it was clear that sales of foreign automobile had weakened the American economy. American auto executives all felt that imports were wrecking the domestic industry and were pushing for federal import quotas. The impact of foreign-made cars had been clearly substantial. In 1979, import sales increased 21 percent while domestic sales plunged 11 percent. More than one in every four auto buyers chose a foreign make.

Since the 1960s, United States auto makers have endeavored to regain the loyalty of the American consumer. Price inducements, new models, and multimillion-dollar advertising blitzes have all been tried. But a large number of Americans believe the overseas manufacturers are beating Detroit in creating useful, attractive, and fuel-efficient cars.

The important word is "believe." Many buyers obviously are convinced that the imports have the advantage in the major categories of quality and price.

"We have to keep telling buyers that Detroit does build small, fuel-efficient cars that fit their needs in *every way*," the marketing director for Chevrolet told *The Wall Street Journal*. A Ford executive added: "Sixty-five percent of the reasons people buy Japanese is that they have a certain perception."

But, as long as consumers "believe" in the imports, Detroit has its challenge cut out for the eighties.

Some in Detroit have muttered that importers are "waxing fat," largely on "mystique." Yet there's much more involved in this issue: The price of gasoline has skyrocketed, making fuel efficiency highly important.

Small cars are required to meet energy conservation values. Detroit did not react appropriately to the 1974 signs for the need for energy-efficient, small cars; domestic producers did not have the inventory.

"We got caught about 2 feet off base," said a Ford executive vice president. And that leaves Detroit with two choices. "You can create a new product, or you can take what you have and try to push it through with sales contests, prices, balloons, and whistles," said a former Big Three marketing specialist. Without much small-car product to market in 1980, American auto makers were forced to use the ballyhoo approach until the necessary retooling could be done.

Source of data: "More Americans Think Imported Autos Offer Better Quality, Prices," *The Wall Street Journal*, March 20, 1980, p. 1.

deemphasizing economy and stressing price; they offered sizable rebates to persuade people to buy large automobiles. But any attempt to change consumers' evaluative criteria is a difficult strategy to follow, since people are reluctant to change until their needs and wants also change. (See Figure 7-7.)

Attitudes

We often talk about attitudes in daily life, and most of us have at least an intuitive understanding of what they are. *Attitudes* are feelings that express whether we like or dislike objects in our environment. In marketing terms, consumers have attitudes about products, brands, retail outlets, salespeople, and advertisements. Marketers are obviously interested in developing the proper attitudes among consumers.

An important point for marketers to remember is that attitudes can develop only after consumers learn that an object exists and what its attributes are. Thus, attitudes are formed by perceiving information about an object and evaluating that information. In fact, consumers' attitudes toward a product come from their assessment of the product's ability to satisfy their requirements as expressed in evaluative criteria by affecting consumers' perception. That is, when we like a product, we tend to see only its good features; we selectively reject information about its weaker qualities.

Figure 7-7 The Seven-Up Company is trying to change consumers' wants by promoting a criterion not previously considered by soda-pop drinkers. *(Ray Pfortner)*

Research into the organization of attitudes indicates the most consumers can tolerate only limited inconsistency between their feelings toward an object and their beliefs about it. For instance, when a consumer has a positive attitude toward a particular brand of tennis racket and then hears a tennis pro say that another brand is superior in terms of power, the element of inconsistency has been introduced. The consumer will try (1) to regain consistency by rejecting the new information, (2) to modify the new information mentally, or (3) to change the original attitude.

Every consumer holds certain values very near and dear. These values provide anchor points for the individual. Attitudes that are closely related to the consumer's self-concept and basic values are said to have *centrality*. They are very difficult to change. For example, if young men hold the attitude that heavy beer drinking is part of being a "true man," their attitude toward beer will be much more difficult to change than the attitudes of young women. In short, the stronger an attitude is, the less likely can change be effected. Even so, attitudes do change constantly. Consider the automobile. In 1973, during the energy crisis, consumers disliked big cars and favored compact models. By 1976, big cars were again popular, and manufacturers instead had surplus inventories of compacts. But by 1979, the market had switched back to a desire for downsized models.

Besides the effect of centrality on attitudes, the strength of an attitude depends on the amount of information that has been stored to support it. As more information is received and stored, attitudes tend to polarize toward one or the other end of the scale (toward liking or disliking). People become less neutral. Thus, as brands are repeatedly purchased and used, attitudes become more crystallized, and thus more difficult to change.

Marketers must be concerned about consumers' attitudes because favorable attitudes lead to favorable exchange behavior. But there is more involved than this. Consumers' *intentions,* or what they plan to do, are also important. If favorable attitudes can be developed, consumers will intend to make an exchange, and this intention will lead to exchange. Yet, this still is not the full story. In many cases, *constraints* intervene between attitudes and behavior, and they may override the influence of attitudes. For example, a person may hold a favorable attitude toward a sports car and yet may not buy one. The reason may be simple: the car is too expensive. Or it may be very complicated: deep-rooted religious values foster a subconscious feeling of sinful waste when a great deal of money is spent on an automobile.

Many definitions of attitudes reflect the fact that attitudes do not lead to instant results in behavior. Attitudes are really an indication of a person's readiness to respond. Marketers want to develop favorable attitudes among consumers in their market because they want a positive orientation toward their product. Since they often cannot control constraints on exchange behavior, they develop a positive orientation so that exchange will occur when constraints are lifted.

Much of what marketers do is directed toward the development of favorable attitudes, which depends on the topics we have discussed so far. We have seen that evaluative criteria form the basis for attitudes, and that we establish our criteria through learning. This, of course, occurs only through the perceptual process

Figure 7-8 Steps consumers take in moving toward exchange. [*Adapted from Robert J. Lavidge and Gary A. Steiner, "A Model for Predictive Measurements of Advertising Effectiveness," Journal of Marketing, vol. 25, no. 4 (October 1961), p. 61*]

Application 7-5
Attitudes to Intention to Buy—Rebuilding a Positive Image

The number 13 is generally regarded as ominous, but for the Firestone Tire & Rubber Company, 500 is an anathema, and for good reason. In 1977, the Firestone "500" tire was recalled by the company following a congressional investigation sparked by reports of fatal accidents stemming from sudden blowouts. The effect of the recall was devastating—to both sales and profits, but perhaps more damaging was the effect on Firestone's image.

To rebuild its tarnished image, the company initiated a new $10-million-dollar advertising campaign in 1981 based on a humorous approach for its "721" radial tire. In the commercials. George Peabody, the fictitious designer of the 721, is given the seemingly impossible task of designing a better tire. "It's one tough tire to top" is the theme of the campaign.

In pursuing the George Peabody campaign for the 721, Firestone abandoned its corporate image campaign featuring Jimmy Stewart. That campaign began in 1978, soon after the 721's predecessor—the 500—was recalled. That campaign was considered "very successful" in softening the blow of the recall—the largest even in the tire industry.

Firestone's advertising director told *Advertising Age* that studies have shown the Firestone image to have steadily improved, although a "hard core"—less than 10 percent of the tire-buying public—remains hostile.

The new campaign's theme reflects the quality-goes-in-before-the-name-goes-on philosophy of Firestone's president, the former president of Zenith Radio Corporation. The president emphasizes a quality product because, to him, "image tends to come from people's own experiences with your product, not necessarily from what people read about you. The process of putting out products that perform well is the ultimate answer to improving that image."

Source of data: "Firestone in Rebuilding Bid," *Advertising Age*, March 2, 1981, pp. 1, 78.

described earlier. Figure 7-8 summarizes the chapter by outlining the steps consumers take in moving toward exchange. (See Application 7-5.)

Personality

While we use the term *personality* often, there is little agreement about its exact meaning or about what makes up a personality. In this discussion, we will use the common definition, which sees *personality* as a person's consistent pattern of responses. Because of this consistency in behavior, we can categorize people as being, for example, egotistical or stuffy or thoughtful or ambitious. Marketers are interested in personality because they believe it affects exchange behavior. Several approaches to studying personality have been advanced, and we will briefly explore some of the more important ones.

The Psychoanalytical Approach

The *psychoanalytical approach* to personality development is founded on the teachings of Sigmund Freud, who described three interacting components or personality: the id, the ego, and the superego. The *id* is the part of our psyche that seeks immediate gratification of all biological and instinctual needs. It is a strong drive that—unless it is controlled—will try to violate the norms of society. The *ego* is the mediator, the element that controls and directs the id so that gratification can be achieved in a socially acceptable manner. The ego controls behavior by selecting the instincts that will be satisfied as well as the manner in which they will be satisfied. This goal is accomplished by integrating the often conflicting demands of the id and the *superego,* the component of personality that reflects norms and inhibits impulses coming from the id.

This personality theory has many implications for marketing, in that it sees consumers as having conflicting desires which must be resolved in some socially acceptable way. Consumers are confronted with so many products that gratify wants—satin sheets, video games, popcorn poppers—but certainly don't satisfy needs. The superego imposes constraints—impractical, too expensive, wasteful of energy—that the ego must wrestle with in coming to purchase decisions. In many cases, marketing activities placate the superego—ads show advantages, prices are reduced, and so on.

The Trait-Factor Approach

The *trait-factor approach* to personality sees an individual as having a specific set of traits which make that person distinct and different from other consumers. This approach has received the most attention from marketers, who have attempted to relate the scores achieved on ready-made personality tests to exchange behavior. However, such attempts have met with little success. Studies relating certain personality traits to, say, automobile buying, magazine purchasing, or coffee consumption have not been especially helpful to marketers. But this outcome does not mean that personality traits do not relate to exchange behavior. Rather, some problems may arise from the tests used and from the types of traits studied.

The Lifestyle or Psychographic Approach

The study of consumers' activities, interests, and opinions, often termed *psychographics,* is an attempt to describe consumers within a market segment on the basis of their responses to statements about their values, concerns, and modes of living. (We saw this approach used to segment markets in Chapter 5.) Marketers who use this approach to studying personality have been more successful than those who use the trait-factor approach. They give the consumers a series of statements and ask them to indicate agreement or disagreement with each item. They then analyze the patterns of agreement and disagreement to get a picture of the "typical" consumers.

While psychographics has not solved the problem of describing consumers' exchange behavior, it has shed considerable light on the subject. For instance, one study of tourists visiting Massachusetts showed them to be independent, concerned with health, free from financial worries, careful buyers, interested in outdoor life, informal in their dress, and interested in taking pictures. Marketers can use such information to develop messages that emphasize informal outdoor life with plenty of fresh air and plenty of opportunities to take photographs.

A Model of Exchange Behavior

Behavioral scientists and theoreticians often conclude that their approach to explaining human behavior is the correct way and, therefore, superior to other theories. Chapters 6 and 7 have examined several ideas that add to our understanding of consumers and their exchange behavior. In many instances, we have looked at real applications of these concepts in the marketplace. But it is wrong to assume that perception alone, or social class alone, or *any* theory alone explains exchange behavior. In some cases, one or more of these concepts may dominate the exchange situation. But a more realistic view concludes that all these theories work and interact together to produce responses in the marketplace.

Figure 7-9 shows one attempt to integrate all the concepts and theories of exchange behavior in a single model. The focus of this model is on the *central control unit,* the consumer's "black box" described earlier. As we have noted, information and experience affect the evaluative criteria, which in turn lead to the formation of an attitude. (In turn, that attitude affects the evaluative criteria chosen, which then affect the information retained in memory.) And personality also influences the entire process. In short, the four components of the central control unit interact to form a filter through which all stimuli are processed.

Stimuli entering the *filter* are generally handled in four distinct, selective phases: (1) exposure, (2) attention, (3) comprehension, and (4) retention. These phases act to funnel the many stimuli that exist in our environment. As the arrows in Figure 7-5 indicate, it is the central control unit that determines which stimuli are included in each phase.

The outcome of this process is *problem recognition* (or want need arousal). It occurs when a consumer perceives a difference between an actual state and an ideal state. But problem recognition is not always resolved immediately. Constraints may intervene, and a holding condition may arise. For instance, a woman sees a new dress that she would like to have (a problem is created), but there is a shortage of money, (situational influence). To solve their problems, consumers typically search for additional information, first internally and then from outside sources. Even then, constraints may interfere with the exchange behavior. Only when constraints are gone will the consumer complete the exchange.

This process results in two outcomes: *postpurchase evaluation* and *further behavior.* First, the exchange is compared against the evaluative criteria that led to it.

The consumer determines whether the actual exchange lives up to expectations. This assessment may be immediate or it may take quite some time, depending on whether all results of the exchange can be evaluated at once or can be judged only over time. This evaluation—which is the level of satisfaction produced by the exchange—finally is stored in the central control unit, where it can influence further exchange behavior.

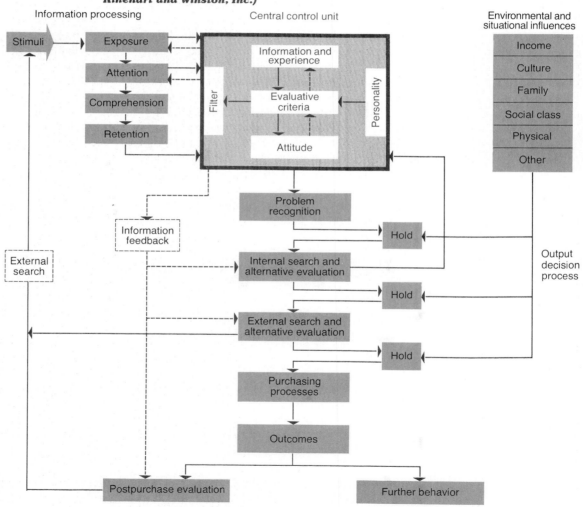

Figure 7-9   A model of consumers' exchange behavior. (Adapted from James F. Engel, David T. Kollat, and Roger D. Blackwell, Consumer Behavior, 2d ed., Holt, Rinehart and Winston, Inc., New York, 1973. Reprinted by permission of Holt, Rinehart and Winston, Inc.)

Organizational Exchange Behavior

Our look at exchange behavior would not be complete without viewing how organizations make such decisions. Organizations include intermediaries (retailers, wholesalers, and agents), governmental and other institutional buyers (hospitals, museums, associations, and the like), and industrial buyers (or manufacturers). Here, since the exchange process with organizations almost always involves purchase, the term *buying behavior* is more appropriate than exchange behavior and will be adopted for our discussion.

Intermediaries include more than 2.5 million diverse organizations with annual purchases totaling $1 trillion. Governmental buying is also sizable, reaching 20 percent of the gross national product (GNP) at the federal level and another 10 percent of GNP at the state and local levels. But by far the largest group of organizational buyers is the set of 12 million industrial manufacturers who buy between $2.5 and $3.0 trillion worth of goods and services a year. About one-half of all goods manufactured are sold to other manufacturers. So the size and scope of the industrial market are huge. Because of its magnitude, industrial buying has received most of the attention in understanding organizational buying behavior. Our remaining discussion will therefore focus on industrial buying behavior. Characteristics of industrial markets and products other than buying behavior will be addressed in Chapter 8.

Who Does the Industrial Buying?

Industrial buyers face three types of buying situations: new task, modified rebuy, and straight rebuy. The *new task* purchase is a first-time purchase; the *modified rebuy* is a routine purchase involving some changes, such as new prices, terms, varied product specifications, or new suppliers; the *straight rebuy* is the simple reorder of products already purchased. The new task purchase, like a consumer's first purchase of a new product, involves substantial information gathering by the buyer. Modified rebuy and then the straight rebuy require successively less information for making the decision. With industrial products, often many individuals or groups within the organization, referred to as the *buying center,* participate in the buying decision. Generally, greater joint decision making is found with new task buys, where information needs are greatest.

We noted in Chapter 6 that there are numerous parties to the exchange. Within the buying center, five major roles in the organizational decision-making process have been identified:

Users: These persons directly employ the product purchased. Since their job performance depends on the product, they often initiate the buying process.

Influencers: These people shape the criteria used in the ultimate buying decision. Technical and legal advisers often play this role.

Buyers: This diverse set of people can range from corporate executive officers to secretaries, depending on the product of interest. These people have the formal authority for selecting a supplier and negotiating the terms of sale. Buyers, quite naturally, also shape the specifications used in the purchase decision.

Deciders: These persons have the final say in the purchase process. They have the power to select or approve the final suppliers. With simple purchases, buyers are often deciders. With complex purchases, deciders are often high-level executives.

Gate Keepers: The flow of information in the organization is controlled by this group. Purchasing agents, salespeople, secretaries—even switchboard operators—can act in this capacity. These people wield a great deal of power, since control of information can control the outcome of a purchase decision. (See Application 7-6.)

Industrial buying centers contain humans. Consequently, purchase decisions are influenced by such factors as we discussed in Chapters 6 and 7—motivation, reference groups, family, beliefs, attitudes, and the like. Buying centers are also heavily influenced by environmental and organizational factors. Changes in the economy, the interest rate, competitive activities, regulatory changes, and technological developments as well as organizational objectives and policies, company systems, and organizational structure all play an important role in shaping a purchase decision.

Application 7-6
Understanding the Buying Center—Getting to the Top

Among "computerniks," the data processing experts running the machines in companies all over the United States, Data General is readily identified as a leader in the field of minicomputers. But that adds little to the coffers of the Massachusetts manufacturer— since data processing personnel rarely have the authority to make the purchase of a minicomputer for their company. What is worse, a company survey showed fewer than 10 percent of top corporate executives were familiar with Data General.

So Data General retained an advertising agency and fired a salvo of advertisements targeted at corporate bosses. Armed with an annual advertising budget of $4 million, the company bought television time on golf and tennis matches as well as news programs in fourteen major markets where top executives could be reached. Data General expected its commercials would be exposed to 45 percent of all top executives in the country.

One ad shows how a Data General minicomputer helps an Irish pub in its inventory control: A clerk exclaims, "Beer depletion emergency down at O'Leary's," and orders a new supply through her computer. Another commercial shows a ski resort operator preparing for the winter with the use of her computer.

Data General hopes to gain awareness of the company through this campaign and to be considered as an alternative. Said the corporate director of marketing communications, "I want to be on the shopping list. If there's three bids, I want to be one of them."

Source of data: "Data General Turns to TV Ads to Reach Corporate Bosses," *The Wall Street Journal,* Oct. 8, 1981, p. 31.

The Industrial Buying Decision Process

The industrial buying decision may be described as consisting of the same stages as the comprehensive consumer-decision process model just discussed—problem recognition, information search—(internal, then external), purchase decision, and post-purchase behavior. But the industrial purchase process can better be understood as an eight-stage process: problem recognition, general need description, product specification, supplier search, proposal solicitation, supplier selection, order routine specification, and performance review.[4] (See Figure 7-10.)

The *problem recognition* stage, like consumer buying, begins when an unmet need or want arises. A machine breaks down, a new product is planned, a supplier goes out of business, or some other major change occurs. Quite logically, the job of the supplier's sales force is to initiate need recognition with customers by showing new products, indicating new usages for existing products, and the like.

Once the need is recognized, the buyer progresses to the *general need description* whereby the general characteristics and quantity necessary are determined. This process may be simple for straight rebuys, but with newer and more complex purchases, other members of the organization—R&D people, engineers, users, for instance—would work with the buyer. The goal here is to identify and rank such features as durability, price, weight, energy, consumption, and similar factors.

Next, in *product specification,* the buying organization develops the specific technical characteristics that the product must meet. In many firms, an engineering unit will compare alternative product configurations to determine the best combination to meet the objectives of the buying firm. In the end, the team clearly defines in writing and in the most technical terms the specifications for the product to be purchased.

In *supplier search,* the most appropriate sellers, or *vendors,* as they are called, are identified. Referrals, trade directories, and trade magazine advertisements are some sources used. An initial list of vendor possibilities is whittled down to a smaller set; many are eliminated because of poor credit rating, geographical location, past pricing policies, and inappropriate size.

At the *proposal solicitation* stage, various qualified vendors are requested to submit proposals for satisfying the buyer's need. These proposals are reviewed and weak vendors dropped. Obviously, the proposal becomes a key tool for industrial marketers. As such, they should be marketing-oriented, not only technical. They should clearly show the buyer that the vendor knows the buyer's needs well and can satisfy them.

Next, the buying organization moves toward *supplier selection*. Here, members of the buying team often will draw up a list of desired supplier attributes and rate the suppliers being considered. Such attributes might include delivery promptness, supplier's financial status, quality of sales force, proposal quality, product price, technical support services, and credit arrangement. Often, buyers select a few suppliers from whom to purchase, so that they will not become totally dependent on

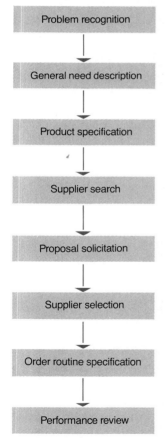

Figure 7-10 The industrial buying decision process.

---

[4]Patrick J. Robinson, Charles W. Faris, and Yoram Wind, *Industrial Buying and Creative Marketing,* Allyn & Bacon, Boston, 1967.

one supplier in case a problem should arise (should one vendor's prices skyrocket, the vendor go out of business, etc.).

In the *order routine specification* stage, the final order is written with a vendor. This order states the quantity purchased, terms of delivery and credit, the technical specifications of the product, guarantees, service policies, and so on. With routinely purchased products, the buyer often establishes a long-term relationship with a vendor to supply the buyer over a specified period of time at a given price. This *blanket contract* reduces the need to write up new purchase contracts each time stock is needed.

Finally, in the *performance review,* the buyer evaluates the results of buying from a particular source of supply. Often the buyer, rather than wait to hear from users, will request an evaluation. Clearly, aggressive sellers need to monitor their performance to ensure the delivery of satisfaction.

Looking Back

The past three chapters looked at the types of information marketers like to have about their markets. From this base of general and specific information about consumers, an appropriate marketing mix can be fashioned. In the next chapter we will begin to look at product, the first of the four major components of the marketing mix. But, before we move into that area, review these important points about individual influences on exchange behavior:

1   By looking inside a consumer's "black box," marketers can try to understand internal influences on exchange behavior.

2   Biogenic and psychogenic motives activate the exchange process.

3   Because of selective perception and selective distortion, consumers do not always perceive everything that they sense.

4   Attention must be paid to a stimulus before it can be perceived.

5   We perceive by exception, but we adapt to changes in the environment. To get our attention, the difference threshold must be exceeded.

6   Many products cannot be distinguished by sensory discrimination. So marketers rely on subjective stimuli to differentiate products and brands.

7   Gestalt psychology sees human beings as needing to attach meanings to sensations, even when parts of them are incomplete or missing.

8   Everything we learn about our environment and about how to function within it comes about by acquiring information through the perceptual process and thinking about what we have perceived.

9 Mental associations are a convenient way to understand the information that we receive.

10 There are certain principles that marketers can follow to affect the amount of learning that consumers do.

11 Consumers make exchange decisions on the basis of evaluative criteria; they choose the bundle of utility that best matches their criteria.

12 Marketers must know the specific criteria by which consumers evaluate their products and competing products.

13 Marketers believe that favorable attitudes must precede exchange behavior, and so much marketing activity is directed toward the development of favorable attitudes among consumers.

14 Constraints may intervene between attitudes and behavior that expresses those attitudes.

15 The psychographic, or lifestyle, approach to understanding human personality seems to be the most useful approach for marketers to follow.

16 All the concepts and theories of exchange behavior can be integrated into a single model of consumer behavior.

17 Industrial buyers are the largest buyers among the organizational buyers.

18 Industrial buying is performed by the buying center.

19 The industrial buying process generally involves eight steps.

Key Terms

If you aren't sure what each of the following words means, look back at the text. Numbers refer to pages on which the words are defined. Additional information can be found by checking the index and the glossary at the end of the book.

biogenic motives 202
psychogenic motives 202
motive 202

selective perception 204
selective exposure 204
selective retention 204
upper and lower thresholds 206
difference threshold 206
gestalt 208
learning 209
mental associations 211
cue 213
drive 213
response 213
reinforcement 213

retention 213
leveling 215
sharpening 215
assimilation 215
determinant buying attributes 217
id, ego, superego 222
psychographics 222
new task purchase 225
modified rebuy 225
straight rebuy 225
buying center 225
gate keepers 226

Questions for Review

1 Distinguish between the following terms: *upper threshold, lower threshold,* and *difference threshold.*
2 Use the concept of mental associations to explain why most menthol cigarettes are marketed in blue or green packages.
3 For marketing purposes, it is useful to see learning as involving five major concepts. What are these five concepts?
4 What are four strategies that marketers can use when focusing on evaluative criteria?
5 What alternatives face the consumer when discrepancy arises between new information received by the consumer and his or her original attitude?
6 Why does the psychographic approach to understanding human personality seem to be the most useful approach for marketers to follow?

Questions for Thought and Discussion

1 For many years, Hanes Corporation has used the promotional slogan "Gentlemen prefer Hanes" to market its line of hosiery. Use the information gained from this chapter to answer the following question, "Do gentlemen really prefer Hanes?"
2 Use the concept of mental associations to explain why Tidy Bowl toilet disinfectant is colored blue.
3 Do attitudes form from perceptions or do they influence perceptions?
4 Industrial purchases involve less emotion and fewer subjective inputs by the buyer. Why do you think this is so?

Suggested Project

Go to a local supermarket and make a list of those products in a particular section which best catch your attention. Note the reasons for their doing so (package size, package design, point-of-purchase display, etc.). Compare your results with those of other members of the class.

Suggested Readings

Bettman, James R.: "Memory Factors in Consumer Choice: A Review," *Journal of Marketing,* vol. 43, no. 2 (Spring 1979), pp. 37–53. The author reviews research and theory on human memory, emphasizing key findings and concepts of importance to marketing and consumer choice.

Britt, Steuart Henderson: "How Weber's Law Can Be Applied to Marketing," *Business Horizons,* vol. 23 (February 1975), pp. 21–29. This article extends the usefulness of difference thresholds to many areas of marketing management.

Engel, James F., Roger D. Blackwell, and David T. Kollat: *Consumer Behavior,* 3d ed., Dryden Press, Hinsdale, Ill., 1982. This text discusses in depth all topics covered in Chapters 6 and

7—and provides a comprehensive model that advances the authors' previous, less complex model, presented in this chapter.

Horowitz, Irwin A., and Russell S. Kaye: "Perception and Advertising," *Journal of Advertising Research,* vol. 15 (June 1975), pp. 15–20. These authors indicate that how the consumer sees the product depends on his or her state of mind.

Kassarjian, Harold H.: "Personality and Consumer Behavior: A Review," *Journal of Marketing Research,* vol. 8, no. 4 (November 1971), pp. 409–419. This article catalogs the research done on personality and emphasizes the trait-factor approach.

Lutz, Richard J. (ed.): *Contemporary Perspectives in Consumer Research,* Kent Publishing, Boston, 1981. This collection of articles emphasizes the psychological influences in marketing but also covers some interpersonal influences.

Meyers, James H., and Mark I. Alpert: "Determinant Buying Attitudes: Meaning and Measurement," *Journal of Marketing,* vol. 32, no. 3 (October 1968), pp. 13–20. This article looks at evaluative criteria and measures their importance in the buying decision.

————, and William H. Reynolds: *Consumer Behavior and Marketing Management,* Houghton Mifflin, Boston, 1967. This very interesting and readable treatment of all buyer behavior topics places heavy emphasis on marketing management applications.

Webster, Frederick E., Jr., and Yoram Wind: *Organizational Buying Behavior,* Prentice-Hall, Englewood Cliffs, N.J., 1972. This short book distinguishes the differences between household and organizational buying behavior.

Wells, William D.: "Psychographics: A Critical Review," *Journal of Marketing Research,* vol. 12, no. 2 (May 1975), pp. 196–213. This article reviews the research on and issues surrounding psychographics as an approach to personality.

Cases for Part Two

Case 1 National Life and Accident Insurance Company

The National Life and Accident Insurance Company (NLT) was founded in 1902, and for more than 70 years it exclusively sold industrial insurance policies—a type of insurance product sold door to door in small face values. Collection of premiums—often as little as 10 cents a week—was handled by agents who dutifully called on policyowners weekly.

As a result of this system, National Life had to process hundreds of thousands of applications and claims. Industrial policies were dropped from the company's product line in 1975, but the company has continued to prosper, growing from this solid base of industrial policyowners. Net income increased from $88 million in 1975 to $140 million in 1981.

To handle the flood of paperwork spawned by the small industrial policies, National Life was one of the first insurance companies to employ the computer. Although at first the computer was utilized simply to process applications and claims, it soon became obvious that the machine had the capacity and capability to extract valuable data that could readily be applied in other areas of the company. The first by-product could be used by the company for prospecting purposes. When applications for insurance are made, applicants are usually asked for the names and addresses of relatives and friends as references. The company found that this information could be pulled out of the computer and turned over to its agents. If the application was made in Georgia and listed a reference in Indiana, for example, the name could be forwarded to an agent in Indiana. In addition, since applicants also indicated whether they owned a home, these data were readily available and prompted National Life to found a property and casualty company. Today, National Life sells automobile and homeowners insurance in many of the Sun Belt states and is looking to expand throughout the country.

Recently the company again put its computers to good use when it opened its first "insurance centers" in shopping centers. For each opening of a center, NLT's marketers devised sweepstakes where a person had only to fill out and return a coupon to become eligible for the prizes. The coupons, distributed personally and also appearing in newspapers, did not require a person to talk with an agent. Included on the coupons were optional questions asking the sweepstake entrant to list the type of automobile owned, the name of his or her current insurance company, and the expiration date of the insurance contract. These entries were sent daily to NLT's data processing division. By the next morning, agents had a ready prospecting list for automobile insurance.

The computer is also utilized by National Life for cash management. Daily, the company's 4300 agents make collections from policyowners, and nightly, from the company's 250 branch offices, the computer transmits to the company's headquarters in Nashville the amount of funds collected and deposited.

1 For what other purposes might National Life and Accident Insurance Company utilize its computer system?

2 What other data would be helpful to National Life?

Source of data: Personal communication, July 1982.

Case 2   Milton Bradley

In 1982, James Shea, Jr., chairman of Milton Bradley, the Springfield, Massachusetts, toymaker, was striving to overcome a poor decision made four years previously. In 1978, the company failed to market an innovative TV video-connected game because its executives believed that the device was too expensive and that it was a fad that would soon pass. Company executives thought the game machine would be overtaken by the home computer. When the price of that computer dropped to only a few hundred dollars and people lost their fear of using terminals, they fully expected a drastic drop in consumer interest in machines that could do nothing but play games. For a period, it appeared that the right decision had been made. With successful tabletop, hand-held games such as Simon, however, sales boomed. The yearly gain in company sales between 1977 and 1980 was at a compound rate of 29 percent. Yet the situation of the 1980s proved the 1978 decision incorrect.

For the last twenty to thirty years, consumers have instantly recognized the 122-year-old Milton Bradley brand name, and the company savored a fine industry reputation. Milton Bradley became known as a solid, steady producer of board games such as Candy Land, Yahtzee, Hangman, and Battleship. Decades ago, the company began marketing seven board games, each of which still

sells over 1 million units a year. Such a record is difficult to find in the fad-conscious toy industry. But Chairman Shea was confronted with more difficult times in the 1980s.

While the well-known board games helped hold up earnings in 1981, profits decreased 37 percent to $20 million. Sales in 1981 slipped 9 percent to $381.4 million. At the same time, sales of video games enjoyed unprecedented growth. In 1981, these games registered a sales volume of $1.2 billion, triple that in 1980. And forecasters were telling Shea that 1982 sales should reach $2 billion. Shea and his senior vice president, George Ditomassi, Jr., were considering alternatives that would help them catch up to industry leader Warner Communications Inc.'s Atari and Mattel Inc.'s Intellivision, which had together captured a large portion of the market. In 1981, Atari's sales of game machines and plug-in cartridges were $740 million, while Mattel's $330 Intellivision brought in about $250 million.

Shea and Ditomassi were looking for an innovative product that differed from Atari-like consoles and from home computers. The company's objective was to develop a product superior to existing competitive games.

Shea believed the company's strategy should be to stay with toys of the entertainment type.

Some of the alternatives he and Ditomassi were considering included a product which incorporates cartridges that synthesize human speech and respond to spoken words. Another possibility was educational software for the mature-in-age market. Such a system would be designed to challenge the mind and not the hand-eye coordination of the player, as the current video games do. Milton Bradley was planning to introduce an electronic chess set in late 1982 or early 1983 which would sell for $200 to $300. Ditomassi was also taking 1982 to research the kinds of entertainment the over-55 market would prefer. Still another possibility under consideration was a machine which gives the player sensations of speed and danger.

Yet, in mid-1982, the pair of executives were unsure about which avenue they should pursue.

1 How might the electronics toy market be segmented?

2 Who are the parties to the exchange to whom Shea and Ditomassi must address their marketing?

3 What advice would you give Shea and Ditomassi?

Sources of data: "Milton Bradley: Playing Catch-Up in the Video-Game Market," *Business Week*, May 24, 1982, pp. 110–111; "Video Games Are Suddenly a $2 Billion Industry," ibid., pp. 78–83.

Case 3   Kellogg Company

Although Kellogg has a 40 percent share of the $8.3 billion cereal market, almost double that of its nearest competitor, General Mills, the company faces a number of problems. In early 1982, Arnold Langbo, Kellogg's executive vice president, was reviewing some of them with the company's chairman, William LaMothe. Foremost of these problems, in their eyes, is a gradual shifting of the core market for cereal consumption. Children are the country's biggest cereal consumers—eating 11 pounds per capita annually. But there are fewer people in this young population category. The largest population segment is between 20 and 50 years old, and, unfortunately for Kellogg, this group consumes little breakfast cereal.

While Kellogg's share of market clearly dominates the industry, it has decreased 3 share points since its 1978 high of 43.5 percent. Corn Flakes, Kellogg's industry leader, was introduced in 1906 and held a 5 percent market share in 1982. Four of Kellogg's older brands—Corn Flakes, Rice Krispies, Frosted Flakes, and Raisin Bran—account for 50 percent of Kellogg's annual sales. At the same time, General Mills has been much better at introducing successful new brands. Langbo and LaMothe agreed that more new products were needed to keep Kellogg's competitive edge.

In 1980, LaMothe was inspired to develop a new, sugarless product, eventually called Nutri-Grain. While traveling in Switzerland, he tasted a certain cereal, and he ordered Kellogg's researchers to develop a similar cereal that was tasty, felt good in the consumer's mouth, and had what the industry calls "bowl life," a resistance to becoming soggy quickly. This research resulted in four variations of a whole grain cereal—corn, wheat, barley, and rye. All four Nutri-Grain types were introduced simultaneously to avoid competitive counterattacks. Usually only one variety is brought out at a time in order to assess consumer response and reduce risk.

To reach the older market, Kellogg allotted $15 million to advertising, plus additional dollars to promote the brand directly to the supermarket chains. Under Langbo's direction, the company, departing from its usual media selections of women's books, television, and supplements, ran ads in such publications as *The Wall Street Journal*, *Self*, *Runner's World*, *Sports Illustrated*, *Vogue*, and *National Geographic*. This media schedule was targeted to reach the health-conscious 20- to 50-year-olds. Initial reaction from the retailers was extremely positive. Many stores made additional shelf space available for the new product. However, the consumer response to Nutri-Grain was slow to develop. By the spring of 1982, the new brand had captured just 1 percent of the total cereal market—enough to be considered successful, but far below Kellogg's expectations.

Langbo conceded to LaMothe that perhaps some mistakes had been made in the initial efforts. First-time purchases came rapidly, but the essential repeat purchases were laggardly. As a result, Kellogg discontinued the rye and barley versions of Nutri-Grain and introduced a new variety with wheat and raisins. Another promotional push was planned. While Nutri-Grain obviously had problems of its own, Langbo argued that people, as a group, tend to skip breakfast in order to sleep, thus causing a universal problem for the cereal industry. "Our biggest challenge," Langbo told LaMothe, "is to get people out of bed 10 minutes earlier in the morning to eat breakfast. If they do, there's a chance they'll eat one of our cereals."

1 What demographic and behavioral concepts are operating that both help and hinder Langbo's efforts?

2 What could Langbo do to promote people's making time available to eat breakfast?

Sources of data: "For Kellogg, the Hardest Part is Getting People Out of Bed," *The Wall Street Journal*, May 27, 1982, p. 31; "Beyond the Breakfast Table," *Forbes*, May 20, 1981, p. 65; "Outlook Brightens for Profitable Kellogg," *The New York Times*, March 25, 1982, pp. D1, 6; personal communication, Andrew Baer, Kekst & Co., New York, July 8, 1982.

Case 4 **The Seven-Up Company**

When Philip Morris bought The Seven-Up Company in 1976, speculation was that the giant cigarette maker—known for its aggressive marketing—would work wonders at the St. Louis soft-drink company which, throughout the years, had earned the reputation of being the most conservative member of the soft-drink industry. In effect, Seven-Up had been content to make one product and to count on steady earnings year after year.

Philip Morris, under the direction of its chairman, George Weissman, through skillful marketing had just made a star out of Miller Brewing Company, then the brewing industry's most lackluster firm. Weissman had also been very aggressive in the cigarette market. He had successfully introduced Merit, one of the hottest brands of the 1970s, and had propelled Marlboro to the No. 1 best-seller in the world.

In 1976, when Philip Morris took control of the Seven-Up Company, it had earnings of $42 million. In 1980, under the guidance of Philip Morris, the soft-drink producer reported a loss from operations of $7.1 million and in 1981 a loss of $1.7 million. Its market share decreased by almost 20 percent to 6.3 percent in five years. In 1981, Coca-Cola held 34.5 percent share; Pepsi had 25.1 percent; Dr Pepper had 8.2 percent; and Royal Crown claimed 4.1 percent of the $17 billion soft-drink industry. Such was the situation confronting Seven-Up's chief executive, Edward Frankel, as he attempted to improve 7Up's competitive position in 1982.

In one move, the company began advertising that 7Up was caffeine-free. The theme was: "No caffeine. Never had it. Never will." Marketing research had determined that 50 percent of soft-drink consumers were not aware that 7Up was caffeine-free and that 66 percent of the adults and 47 percent of the teenagers in the United States would be interested in caffeine-free soda. But only 12 percent of soft-drink sales come from lemon-lime drinks, while colas account for nearly two-thirds of industry sales. So, while a noncaffeine campaign may be beneficial, Frankel knew that it would not satisfy the company's aggressive parent, Philip Morris.

In the spring of 1982, Frankel introduced a 99 percent caffeine-free cola called LIKE. To differentiate its cola from others, 7Up pushed hard at the caffeine-free feature. The decision to position LIKE as noncaffeine was made by Philip Morris's Weissman, who grew increasingly convinced that consumer concern with caffeine is a growing issue.

LIKE was test marketed in eight areas, and it had an advertising and promotional budget of $2.5 million. Coke and Pepsi became disturbed at 7Up's positioning theme. Seven-Up, in an effort to gain at least a 10 percent share of the cola market in test cities, pushed hard at the 99 percent caffeine-free line, and sought to capitalize on many people's apprehension about caffeine in Coke and Pepsi. LIKE's advertising theme was: "You don't need caffeine and neither does your cola." Each introductory commercial focused on parent-child activity. In the beginning, the commercial centered on what a child needs (lots of love, encouragement, a dream, etc.). Then the action halted abruptly but focused on the child for a few moments as the announcer noted: "But there's something they [children] don't need. They don't need caffeine. That's why we created a cola with no added caffeine."

Frankel firmly believed there was room for LIKE in the marketplace but wondered whether his advertising approach was correct.

1 Evaluate the cola advertising campaign of 7Up in terms of the concepts of Chapters 6 and 7.

2 What advice would you give Frankel?

Sources of data: "Seven-Up Chief Believes Time Right for LIKE Cola," *Advertising Age*, March 29, 1982, pp. 2, 92; "Seven-Up's Sudden Taste for Cola," *Fortune*, May 17, 1982; personal communication, June 1982; "Philip Morris Battles Beer and Smoke Rivals as It Enters Cola War," *The Wall Street Journal*, June 30, 1982, pp. 1, 19.

PART THREE

Programming the Marketing Mix

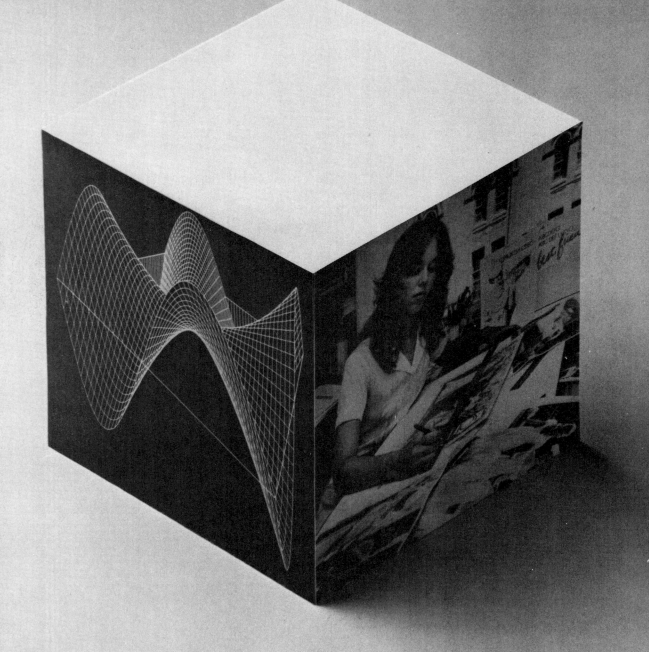

The perfect product at the right price with the proper promotion and distribution is a marketer's dream. Some marketers believe that dream has come true: they have a product that's "light," all-natural, affordable, and (best of all) used by everyone. What is it? Water!

Water is the country's hottest cold beverage. Sales of water nearly doubled between 1978 and 1982, and they are expected to reach at least $700 million by the end of 1983. Promotion and pricing are important considerations in marketing a product that has been "free" for ages. Perrier, which shrewdly positioned its bottled water as a chic drink and then heavily promoted it, increased sales from 3 million bottles in 1976 to about 200 million in 1982. About half of the water market is for bulk still water, the kind that is generally delivered in 5-gallon jugs. Still water is marketed by industrial giant Foremost-McKesson and consumer giant Coca-Cola Bottling Company of Los Angeles, which purchased Great Bear Spring Company in May 1981.

Promotional appeals for water have focused on being "in" and being healthy. According to the Environmental Protection Agency (EPA), industrial wastes threaten tap water in over 3600 locations in the United States. Pending EPA regulations to improve water quality could triple the cost of water treatment at a time when many cities are having trouble funding the current, less stringent regulations. Even with adequate treatment, tap water must be transported through decrepit iron and lead pipes. A marketing executive for a water supplier seems to be on the mark in stating, "There are plenty of signs that what's coming out of the tap isn't going to get any better." He feels that bottled water is becoming "not a luxury, but a necessity."

In the United States alone, there are 300 to 400 water bottlers, and the larger ones have been busy in the area of acquisitions. In the imported water market, Perrier now has about a 75 percent market share even with pricing up to $2.54 per quart. The success of Perrier's promotion of its sparkling water as a "status" drink took some of the pressure off the pricing issue. Evian Waters of France will distribute its nonsparkling mineral water at $1.99 per half gallon. Pricing was successfully test marketed in the Miami market, accompanied by a $500,000 advertising campaign. Expanded distribution will be bolstered by lots of promotion money—$1.5 million just in the Southeast. Canada Dry Corporation, which is being acquired by Dr Pepper Company, is repositioning its traditional club soda as a stand-alone carbonated water beverage. This trendy promotion will take the form of an $8 million media blitz.

Hot items as alternatives to bottled water are under-the-sink treatment systems that purify tap water. The industry leader, Culligan, experienced a 200 percent growth in its drinking water business in 1981. And Foremost-McKesson has created another alternative to costly bottled water. It has installed over 2000 Aqua Vend machines nationwide in supermarkets. The Aqua Vend dispenses filtered water for only 25 cents a gallon to consumers who bring their own containers. Foremost, too, finds water the fastest-growing segment in its food group. Plans have been made to install another 4000 vending machines by the end of 1984.

One of the biggest water markets is California, where about half of all domestic water is sold. In the Los Angeles area, about a third of all households consistently buy water. This remarkable penetration is due to promotion by Foremost and Coke. Together, the two companies funneled about $5 million in advertising and promotion to the LA market during 1981.

Convincing people to purchase water requires heavy promotion, and promotion cost is a factor in the high price of bottled water. But the major cost, which accounts for two-thirds of the total expenses, relates to place satisfaction—distribution and delivery. As a natural product, water is available only in specific locations and must be distributed nationwide. To ease distribution problems, entrepreneurs and companies are purchasing rights to natural springs around the country whenever opportunities present themselves. While many sources are still cheap, they are becoming increasingly more valuable. A wine merchant who invested $500,000 in water rights on both coasts commented, "Water today looks like the oil business in the mid-1950s."

Source of data: "Water's Rise: A Sales Torrent," *Business Week*, January 11, 1982, pp. 97 and 99.

Product

Promote laundry soap and luggage? Of course. Advertise beer and automobiles? Certainly. But market an accounting firm? You bet. The "Big Eight," as the top accounting firms are known, once considered marketing unnecessary, inappropriate, and beneath their dignity. No more. "Accounting firms are becoming twentieth-century marketers and, as such, are doing a lot of the things that Procter & Gamble does—segmenting and studying markets, developing new products for them, and marketing them," A New York public relations consultant who represents Ernst & Whinney told *The Wall Street Journal.*

Competition within the auditing industry got sharper in 1978 when the accountants' professional organization ruled that accounting firms were free to advertise. The lifting of a ban on direct solicitation of other firms' clients soon followed. "There is a snowball that is getting larger and will continue to grow, especially as larger firms get their act together in doing marketing," said a Coopers & Lybrand executive.

But accountants have a problem—one that manufacturers don't face. Accountants have only themselves and their expertise to offer. "You have to have ways to differentiate yourself," said an Ernst & Whinney director of client services.

Deloitte, Haskins & Sells advertises its expertise in such publications as *The Wall Street Journal* and *Inc.*, a magazine for small businesses. Peat, Marwick, Mitchell, & Co., Ernst & Whinney, and Coopers & Lybrand promote specific services in a variety of publications, including *Business Week, Forbes,* and trade journals. Price Waterhouse & Co., meanwhile, is advertising its computer-based program to help oil and gas companies do windfall-profits tax returns.

For planning a new software package, Ernst & Whinney cautiously entered market research, determining the needs and wants of the insurance industry. Questionnaires were mailed to top property and casualty companies. Then on-site interviews were conducted with insurance company managers in an effort to find out what they did and what they saw as necessary improvements. The result, a program called "Rescomp," was modified to accept both quarterly and annual data. "That's not earthshaking, but it really helps the people who want to use it," said an Ernst & Whinney partner.

Source of data: "Fierce Competition Forces Auditing Firms to Enter the Alien World of Marketing," *The Wall Street Journal,* March 18, 1981, p. 31.

Chapter

8

The Nature of the Product: Goods, Services, and Industrial Products

Looking Ahead

Having examined market descriptors and the main social and individual influences on exchange behavior, we are now ready to start exploring the marketing mix. The first task is to design the product. This chapter, the first of three dealing with the product, will examine the nature of the product.

Key Topics

The traditional approach to understanding the product

An expanded approach that sees the product as much more than simply goods and services

The classification of products

Differences between consumer products and industrial products

Brands, trademarks, labeling, packaging, and warranties

Chapter Outline

What is a Product?
The Traditional Approach
An Expanded Approach
The Boom in Services
The Broadened View of the Product

Product Classifications
Consumer Products
Industrial Products

Other Ingredients in the Product's Bundle of Satisfaction
Brands and Trademarks
Labels
Packaging
Warranties

Looking Back

What Is a Product?

If asked "What is a product?" few people would be unable to give an answer. One common response is that a product is "something we buy." But it must be clear by now that such an answer is far from complete. Chapter 1 made the point that marketers provide much more than just a stark-naked product. Their primary objective is to provide satisfaction—and that can take many forms.

Then, too, many people think of a product as being a tangible good—something physical, like a loaf of bread, an automobile, or a comb. But services are also products. When we hire a doctor or a lawyer, we are buying a product in the form of knowledge and expertise. In the same way, students buy a product when they enroll in school. They expect to receive benefits (satisfaction) in terms of knowledge that can be exchanged later for a job and a standard of living.

A product is the basic ingredient in the exchange process. The expectation that satisfaction will be realized through exchange is what a product represents. Thus, a product is the focus bringing buyers and sellers together to make an exchange. Let's investigate what this involves.

The Traditional Approach

A product can be seen as the entire bundle of satisfaction that is offered by a marketer to the marketplace. This bundle contains a potential for satisfaction that comes in part from the *tangible, objective* features of the product. For instance, the thirteen herbs and spices combined in Kentucky Fried Chicken provide a distinct and pleasing taste. Likewise, Mercedes Benz provides a bundle of satisfaction that includes fine performance features and a classic design. Thus, the physical features of a product provide some of the satisfaction that buyers expect to realize through exchange. The physical features cause buyers to expect that their functional needs and wants can be satisfied by the product.

Throughout this book, however, and especially in Chapters 6 and 7, we have made the point that satisfaction is also expected from the *intangible, subjective* features of a product. Thus, Oxxford Clothes can offer suits that sell for over $600 each. Besides the functional needs that such a suit satisfies, Oxxford is providing its customers with an ego boost, a feeling of "having arrived." To take another example, those electronic devices called "beepers," which physicians and other people carry to summon them when an emergency arises, can now be rented by the general public as well. Many people satisfy functional needs by wearing the device (some dog owners even attach beepers to their animals to get them to return home on cue). But other people emphasize that the beeper, being associated with the medical profession, makes them feel important. These two products, then, promise their buyers certain psychological satisfactions that may be even more important than the functional satisfaction they provide.

We also can view products in terms of *benefits*. Chapter 5 explained that markets are divided into segments on the basis of benefits which reflect the needs and wants of

Figure 8-1 By marketing one of its products as "so advanced, it's simple," Canon encourages nonprofessional photographers to buy a high-quality 35-millimeter camera. (Frank Siteman/Stock, Boston)

each market segment. A product's benefits must match, or satisfy, the market's desires. Often, there is a core need or want—some primary, overriding desire for satisfaction. Such primary needs and wants provide individual buyers with their most important criteria for making an exchange decision. For instance, in purchasing a tennis racket, an individual buyer may seek high tension in the strings, a metal frame, and a heavy weight. The desire for such product features indicates that this buyer is seeking the benefit of power above all else. Whatever other benefits a tennis racket may offer, this buyer wants one that satisfies the core need of power.

By identifying the core need that a product satisfies, and stressing that benefit, marketers can meet demand for their product. Marketers of the high-quality 35-millimeter cameras have found this out. Long considered too complicated for most people, electronic technology has been responsible for allowing them to meet the core need of the mass market—simplicity. Dubbed by many hard-core photography buffs as "Ph.D." cameras (for "Push here, Dummy"), such cameras now automatically focus, automatically set the size of the lens opening and shutter speed, and even automatically determine the need for a flash. Since their introduction in 1973, unit sales of 35-millimeter cameras had more than tripled by the end of the decade. (See Figure 8-1.)

Stressing the product's benefits has been found to work also in the marketing of eyeglasses, which, until a few years ago, were considered mundane products. Studies of the National Eye Research Foundation show that 80 percent of females and 52 percent of males who buy contact lenses choose them because of vanity. They have a core need to look better. For the same reason, expensive eyeglass frames have experienced a boom as people seek to satisfy their need to be attractive. Today, the ego-satisfying frames often cost more than the sight-providing lenses in them.

An Expanded Approach

Focusing exclusively on a product's core benefit, however successful, is a shortsighted marketing approach. As a bundle of satisfaction, a product must be seen to include every activity that a marketer performs to convey satisfaction—from the first recognition of a market's need to the ultimate evaluation of the product by consumers. That is, marketers must recognize and service *all* steps in the exchange process. A homemaker, for example, may choose to shop in a particular grocery store because of some dominant need or evaluative criterion, such as the lower prices promoted by A&P, Price Chopper, and others. But there are many more facets to a product than its ability to satisfy core needs, and effective marketers put them all together. In this instance, the homemaker will also be influenced by other ingredients in the bundle of satisfaction—the cleanliness of the store, its layout, how prices are displayed, the availability of certain products and brands, the courtesy of the staff, the length of the checkout lines, whether or not delivery service is provided, check-cashing privileges, opportunities to make special purchases. All these factors of the shopping experience combine to make up the total bundle of satisfaction, the total product exchanged.

Another, more limited, perspective sees a product simply as a set of tangible and chemical attributes that are assembled into an identifiable form. In this view, each separate product category is defined by a commonly understood descriptive name—such as pillows, needles, shirts, or gum. Thus, skin-care cream is skin-care cream whether it's Procter & Gamble's Wondra or Chesebrough-Pond's Cream & Cocoa Butter.

Yet perceptive marketers know better. In addition to this basic view of the product, consumers also buy an *expected* product. This additional perspective recognizes that there are certain minimal purchase conditions that must be met over and above the basic unsatisfied need or want. With skin-care products, price, scent, and greaselessness would be expected of Wondra, Vaseline Intensive Care, Oil of Olay, and the like; these qualities are over and above the ability to make the skin feel smooth and moist.

But really insightful marketers go a step further to realize they are not limited to offering the consumer *only* what they expect. Aggressive, successful marketers provide the base product and expected product with features never thought about by potential buyers, voluntary and unprompted aspects that exceed the consumer's expectations. This is called the *augmented* product. Clinique, an Estée Lauder company, has become the walkaway leader in the higher-priced department store cosmetic market by following such a tactic. The company gains counter space in the cosmetic department by offering its computerized beauty analysis that matches products to the specific needs of the customer. Customers are asked a set of questions and the answers offered aid the beauty consultant behind the counter to prescribe the correct blend of cosmetics.

Still another expanded view of a product recognizes *each brand* as being separate. It sees Anacin as a different product from Bufferin, and General Mills Wheaties as distinct from Kellogg's Corn Flakes. From this perspective, the only difference among products often is the difference in their brand names. And the true difference may exist only within consumers' minds. Therefore, the psychological satisfaction of products is the only real basis for comparison—and for marketing. With this expanded view of the product, any change— in packaging, brand name, color, design, and such—creates a new product. When Old Spice introduced a lime-scented product to its deodorant line, it created a new product. And since Procter & Gamble's Pert shampoo comes in two types—one for normal or dry hair and one for oily hair—marketers consider each a separate product with a distinct market.

The Boom in Services

Throughout this discussion we have stressed that products are bundles of satisfactions which provide both objective and subjective utilities and benefits. By this definition, services clearly are one category of products. In fact, the growth of services has been so great since World War II that some marketers see the United States as having the world's first service economy. Today, consumers spend close to 50 cents of every dollar on services. And the government projects further increases throughout the 1980s. America's labor force is decidedly service-oriented, with over 70 percent of the private labor force (excluding farm workers) working to supply services. (See Figure 8-2.) In the eighties, ten service industries are projected to show the greatest growth:

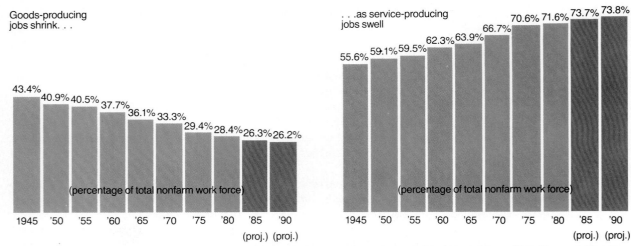

Figure 8-2   Moving toward a service society. *(Reprinted from* U.S. News & World Report. *Copyright 1981, U.S. News & World Report, Inc.)*

water and sanitary services, automobile repair, medicine and dentistry, hotels, nonprofit organizations, hospitals, credit and finance agencies, advertising, retail trade, and amusements and recreation.[1] Seventy percent of new jobs in our economy will be in these industries. So, clearly, services deserve the special attention of marketers—especially since there are distinct differences in developing marketing strategies for services rather than goods.

Describing Services   Even though goods and services both attempt to satisfy consumers' wants and needs, there are some important differences between these two classes of products. Two writers have suggested that products form a continuum which ranges from pure goods (say, automobiles) to combinations of goods and services (ski rentals) to pure services (legal counsel).[2] (See Figure 8-3.) As a product moves closer to a pure service, the greater will be the differences in marketing it. While defining a *service* is difficult, we can define it as an *intangible bundle of satisfaction exchanged in the marketplace to satisfy consumers' wants and needs.* Intangibility is an important differentiating feature of services. Let's look at it and some others.

Four characteristics are useful in distinguishing between goods and services:

---

[1]"Service Industries: Growth Field of '80s," *U.S. News & World Report,* March 17, 1980, pp. 80–81.

[2]John M. Rathmell, "What Is Meant by Services?" *Journal of Marketing,* vol. 30 (October 1966), pp. 32–36; and G. Lynn Shostack, "Breaking Free from Product Marketing," *Journal of Marketing,* vol. 41 (April 1977), pp. 73–80.

1 Tangibility

2 Perishability

3 Standardization

4 Buyer participation in terms of product formulation and distribution

Regarding these four characteristics, goods tend to be tangible, nonperishable, standardized, and low in buyer participation. Services tend to be just the opposite: intangible, perishable, nonstandardized, and high in buyer participation. Moreover, in providing satisfaction for consumers, services in general rely on *direct action* to be performed by the marketers, whereas goods rely more on *material objects* created by the marketer. Each of the above four characteristics that distinguish goods and services can be related to this idea of services as actions and goods as objects. Let's see how.

A product's *tangibility* refers to the degree to which it provides satisfaction from features which can be perceived physically through sight, sound, touch, taste, or smell. Thus, a bottle of Gatorade, a tube of Crest, a bar of Dial soap, and a Chevrolet are all highly tangible goods. They can be perceived easily through the senses. On the other hand, the services of a doctor, plumber, driving school, or tax accountant cannot be perceived by examining the same kind of physical cues. By definition, then, such actions (services) are intangible, whereas material objects (goods) are tangible. Intangibility creates problems for marketers. For instance, sampling of the product obviously cannot be used. Advertising has less to illustrate, and thus personal selling generally must be relied upon to promote services.

A second feature that often distinguishes goods from services is *perishability,* the degree to which a product can be stored. The satisfaction derived from a service like a

Figure 8-3 The goods-service continuum.

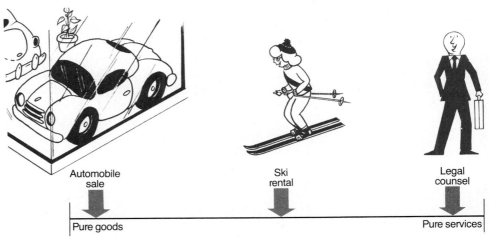

| Automobile sale | Ski rental | Legal counsel |

| Pure goods | | Pure services |

Cincinnati Reds baseball game, a seat on an American Airlines plane, or a room at a Holiday Inn relies on a time-related action between the buyer and seller. The satisfaction provided by the service cannot be stored. When a room stands vacant for a night, or when a jet takes off with empty seats, the satisfaction that each product could have provided is lost forever. The satisfaction derived from a good, however, tends to be less time-dependent. Del Monte's canned foods, Procter & Gamble's soaps and deodorants, and Van Heusen's shirts can be stored. Even goods that have relatively short shelf lives, such as flowers and milk, are not highly perishable when compared with most services.

As an official of a Brooklyn cultural center that presents ballet and theater productions told *The Wall Street Journal,* "We're in the business of selling a perishable product. In supermarkets, the lettuce wilts. In our case, the curtain goes up."[3]

Standardization is another product feature that distinguishes goods from services. A good, such as a razor blade or this textbook, can be produced with highly uniform quality on an assembly line. But services often depend on an action by the marketer to create utility, and so they tend to be nonstandardized. Most services are not produced in assembly-line fashion as goods are. Thus, on a given day the quality of service from a lawyer, or a mechanic, or a sports team can vary. Much of this effect is due to the inseparability of the service from the marketer. The service, most often, must be created and marketed simultaneously. Thus, time and place utilities are major concerns in the marketing of services. And many services then are tailored or customized to the specific needs of the customer.

In terms of *buyer participation* there tends to be a gap between the production, marketing, and consumption of goods, while services tend to occur within a single time frame. Thus, the buyer of a service is often involved in the formulation and execution of the service. But a good is produced in a factory and then distributed to buyers for consumption in a different time and place. In contrast, services tend to be produced, distributed, and consumed with less separation in terms of time and place. And the buyers of services such as medical care, automobile repair, or insurance policies often play a part in formulating a satisfying solution to the problem at hand.

The idea that services rely on actions to provide satisfaction, whereas goods depend on material objects, leads to important distinctions between these two categories of products. But we must emphasize again that these distinctions are not always clear-cut. A restaurant, a grocery store, and an automobile rental agency, say, may rely on a combination of both goods and services to provide satisfaction. The important point is that when a product has more characteristics of services than of goods, the ways in which consumers perceive and judge that product may be affected. Marketers must be prepared to deal with these characteristics and use them in creating a unique bundle of utility that satisfies the market's needs.

---

[3]"A Cultural Institution Succeeds by Marketing Its Wares Aggressively," *The Wall Street Journal,* Jan. 23, 1979, p. 1.

Some Marketing Implications

The adoption of marketing as a major business activity has come slowly to the service industry. A survey[4] of manufacturing and service firms found marketing to be less structured in service firms and less likely to have its own marketing executive. What marketing that is performed is not done in a formalized marketing department. Service firms are less likely to use outside marketing research firms, consultants, and advertising agencies. And, generally, marketing expenditures are less for service firms than for manufacturing firms. In short, service firms appear to have failed to adopt the marketing concept—and this key driving force cannot be ignored any longer.

Virtually all products possess some degree of intangibility—since psychological satisfaction is intangible. But services, as noted, move more toward intangibility and many are purely intangible—teaching, counsuling, lobbying, performing surgery, etc. With intangibles, consumers are buying promises. Promises, being intangible, should be "tangibilized" in the marketing process. Consumers can be given some anchor to hold on to. Insurance companies pictorially associate their services with something tangible—they offer "a piece of the rock," a "blanket or protection," or place you in "good hands." Lawyers work in somber Edwardian downtown offices; consultants speak confidently and wear conservative clothes; engineering proposals come in elegant leather-bound folders. Thus, symbols bring a sense of tangibility to an intangible in the customer's mind. (See Application 8-1.)

In terms of other traditional marketing activities, pricing practices are not much different for services than for goods—the price and value perceived must be in line. But, assuming a quality service, the marketer must stress its availability. For many services—banking, dry cleaning, travel planning, for instance—convenience is a prime concern. Many banks and even the U.S. Postal Service have turned to vending machines to satisfy their customers' needs around the clock.

Many service markefers tend to overemphasize the role of advertising in the marketing mix. Clearly, promotion is important, but it must fit the overall marketing plan for the service—rather than stand by itself. Personal selling, because it keeps the customer and marketer directly together, has the greatest impact on sales. Advertising should create a favorable image for the service. That's why with United Air Lines you fly "the Friendly Skies," and that is why Equitable is the "Nobody Else Like You" insurance company.

Once customers have bought, service marketers have the additional problem of holding them. Consider a stockbroker, a dry cleaner, an insurance salesperson. If the marketing goes well, the customers really never know what they are getting. Only when something goes wrong—your stock goes down, spots remain on your suit, an insurance claim is disputed—do you become aware of what has been, or has *not* been, received. Consequently, to keep consumers aware of the bundle of satisfaction they are receiving, marketers can remind them of what they are getting—and, again, should use the most tangible means of doing so. Periodic letters, newsletters, regular

---

[4]William R. George and Hiram C. Barksdale, "Marketing Activities in the Service Industries," *Journal of Marketing,* vol. 38, no. 4 (October 1974), pp. 69–75.

Application 8-1
Adding Some Tangibles to Intangibles—
Through Marketing, Physicians Competitively Heal Themselves

The supply of doctors is beginning to outstrip the demand. By 1990, the Department of Health and Human Services forecasts an oversupply of 70,000 physicians. In such cities as San Francisco and Chicago, the glut has already arrived. To become more competitive as businesspeople, many doctors are turning to marketing concepts. "Ten years ago, it really had a negative connotation if you were going off to a marketing seminar," said the chairman of the Academy for Health Services Marketing, an American Marketing Association affiliate. "Now, it's a very competitive market, and the environment has changed."

At seminars, doctors are given numerous pieces of marketing advice—some of which may seem very simple. But to most, these tidbits are all new ideas. About his service, one doctor said: "It's not something that's thought of as a business." But, he adds, "You do have to make a living out there." Some of the suggestions offered for tangible and intangible activities include:
Before opening a practice in a locale, check such data as unemployment rates, number of dual-income households, number of existing physicians, and birthrates.
Provide free clinics for joggers.
Meet patients on time.

Offer early morning, late evening, and weekend hours.
Conduct surveys of patient likes and dislikes.
Send flowers to patients who refer others to you.
Design progress-report booklets for each patient.
At the suggestion of a consultant, one physician invested $1400 in sending a newsletter to all his patients. Articles included such topics as "Traveler's Diarrhea: How to Make Fewer Trips on Your Trip" and "Intestinal Gas: The Inside Story."

Source of data: "Doctors Turn to Marketing to Get Patients," *The Wall Street Journal,* Sept. 1, 1981, p. 33.

---

visits, even nonbusiness socializing can help reinstate the presence and performance of the service. That's why advertising reminds you that Merrill Lynch is "bullish on America" and that when "E. F. Hutton talks, everybody listens."

Advertising should also stress the tangibles by helping the customer to visualize the benefits that are so hard to see. That's why Hertz, which promotes prompt service, has O. J. Simpson flying through the air and into his awaiting automobile. The marketing of services employs the same activities as the marketing of goods, yet the orientation toward the intangibility characteristic is different. (See Application 8-2.)

The Broadened View of the Product

As we have noted throughout our discussion, the product has been viewed traditionally as the good or service that is exchanged. This definition includes many things—food processors, razor blades, plastic trash-can liners, food items, hair styling, medical care, landscape services, babysitters, and dry cleaning. And though such a list would seem endless, the marketer's viewpoint of what constitutes a product has been broadened since the 1960s to include many things besides goods and services.

For example, marketers also market *people*. Actors, athletes, politicians, teachers —even students—can be marketed. Howard Cosell's colorful commentary and Barbara Walters's penetrating interviews have done much to market them. Former President Carter is another example. Just a few years before his presidential campaign, he appeared on the television program "What's My Line?" and no one could guess his identity as the Governor of Georgia. Yet, in 1976, he was elected president—and not through luck. Like goods and services, Jimmy Carter was marketed. As a result of a political survey commissioned in July 1972, the Carter team drew up a detailed marketing plan for the candidate to follow over the next four years. By 1976, the Carter name was a household word—most notably, in the White House itself.

Application 8-2
Marketing a Service—Blockbusters and Ballyhoo in Brooklyn

Marketing, shunned by the arts a decade ago, is proving to be the ingredient that may save many opera companies, symphonies, and ballets. The Minneapolis Guthrie Theater effectively employs billboards with pictures of Hamlet to promote subscriptions. The Milwaukee Repertory Theater Company, meanwhile, successfully distributed 350,000 flyers a year in malls, resulting in 10 times the sales of a decade ago. "It's a hard-sell approach," says an official. "We bombard people with this stuff and they finally break down and buy a subscription."

Few performing arts organizations have been as aggressive as the Brooklyn Academy of Music (Bam, as it calls itself). In 1969, BAM developed a management group charged with building attendance. Since its formation, BAM annual attendance soared from 90,000 to 320,000. Ambitious programming in theater, ballet, modern dance, symphony, and chamber music quickly put BAM back on the map—but more was needed. To increase subscription sales, BAM computerized its mailing list according to past consumer preferences. BAM's sales brochures are specifically designed to appeal to market segments, sometimes relying on gimmicks. BAM theater fans, for instance, received a leaflet claiming that drama subscribers were "among the most adventuresome people in town" and therefore were snapping up BAM *dance* subscriptions. Targeted pitches sell far more tickets than a general mailing, officials said.

BAM simplifies the portal-to-portal theater-going experience. Although more than half its audience live in Brooklyn, it operates an express bus service from Manhattan as well as parking lots near the theater.

Besides selling aggressively, the Brooklyn Academy has applied a marketing approach to pricing, an area not often considered by the performing arts. BAM commonly tests pricing by offering the same series at different prices. Then responses are compared. If the lower price is more successful, those who responded at the higher price receive refund checks—which are often returned to BAM as contributions, another handy source of income.

Source of data: "A Cultural Institution Succeeds by Marketing Its Wares Aggressively," *The Wall Street Journal,* Jan. 23, 1980, p. 1.

Marketers also market *places.* A glance at the travel section of a newspaper will provide numerous examples of advertising that promotes places to visit. Tourism officials in many states—New York, Florida, and Texas among them—are aggressively promoting their states to international markets. Texas has conducted annual travel missions to Britain, Germany, and Japan to personally promote the state. Florida has opened a London sales office to bolster its marketing efforts, which accounted for a whopping 40 percent increase in international tourists in 1980. (See Application 8-3.)

Marketers also market *ideas,* both pro and con. Physical fitness, energy conservation, and regular medical checkups have been encouraged, while smoking, litter, and child abuse have been discouraged. The Advertising Council of America has conducted campaigns around many social themes, including "Keep America Beautiful," "Join the Peace Corps," "Buy Bonds," and "Go to College." The Family Planning Foundation has marketed the idea of birth control, and the National Safety Council has emphasized safe driving in its messages to drivers. In 1981, Moral Majority, an organization whose members are "deeply concerned about the moral decline of our nation," ran full-page ads in *The New York Times, The Wall Street Journal,* and *The Washington Post* to explain its stand. "They have labeled Moral Majority the Extreme Right because we speak out against Extreme Wrong" read the ad's headline. The ad went on to present the group's stand on issues such as abortion, drugs and pornography, and equal rights for women.

In addition to all these applications, marketing can be used to promote both *companies* and *nonprofit organizations* as products. Many companies attempt to create favorable attitudes through public relations and advertising. Weyerhaeuser Company stresses its ecological concerns by advertising itself as "The Tree-Growing Company." And corporations like Mobil and Texaco emphasize the care they take in offshore drilling operations to show their concern for the environment. Even public television stations mount campaigns to increase viewers and get public support.

Stores, too, are marketed as products. The customers of a store receive not only merchandise but also the image conveyed by that store. In this sense, the entire store is an organization that is marketed. New York's prestigious Bergdorf Goodman, among others, realizes the importance of marketing its image as a product. In Christmas advertising, it has stressed the psychological value of a gift from its store: "Everything means more in a Bergdorf box." And customers pay for this added benefit because they value it.

Perhaps the most significant contemporary uses of marketing are its *nonbusiness applications.* Marketers give advice to churches about how to increase membership, to charities about how to raise money, and to art museums and symphony orchestras about how to attract patrons. The Republican party has invested considerable thought and resources in trying to develop a modern look. Likewise, the American Medical Association has launched a campaign to improve the image of doctors. And, with reduced enrollments, even colleges and universities have recognized the need to market their services, offering weekend masters' programs to business people and in-house programs to corporations. One college even provides classes on railroad cars, hoping to lure commuters into its fold.

Application 8-3
Broadened Marketing—
"New York, New York—It's a Wonderful Town"

(Courtesy of the New York State Department of Commerce)

Faced with such gargantuan problems as high taxes, dirt, crime, and fiscal crises as well as a sordid image, the state of New York initiated a true marketing strategy to improve its situation. Instead of using its 1976 advertising budget of $200,000 on advertising, State Commerce Commissioner John Dyson funneled the money into a marketing research effort. The results of the study showed that tourism was New York State's largest employer and New York City's second biggest business. As a consequence, New York State appropriated $4.3 million for advertising in 1977.

Market research also showed

that Broadway was still very highly regarded. Consequently, the Commerce Department coaxed advertising agencies, musicians, and such stars as Andrea McArdle of *Annie,* Yul Brynner of *The King and I,* and Frank Langella of *Dracula* to work for minimum wages, or free, to lure the tourist back to New York. Little Orphan Annie swears her undying affection, the King of Siam swoons with joy, and even Count Dracula purrs that he, too, just *loves* New York, "especially in the e-e-e-vening." They all became stars of one-minute commercials that were aired in Boston, Philadelphia, and fourteen other cities. In conjunction with this big

push, there were many other promotional efforts—an "I love New York" disco record sale, inexpensive show tours of the city, a shower of star-studded galas on Valentine's Day, and even a coordination of skyscraper lights to spell out "I love New York."

The Broadway theme continued throughout the 1970s with cast members of *Annie, Peter Pan,* and *Sugar Babies.* In 1980, the tourism budget was nearly $9 million. Was it money well spent? Apparently. In 1980, tourism revenues in New York were up 19 percent, compared with a 2 percent decrease across the United States. So pervasive is the "I love New York" jingle that it became a best-selling record in Japan in 1981, and an "I Love New York" bumper sticker was reported to be adhering nicely to the China Wall.

Source of data: "Wonderful Town," *Newsweek,* Feb. 20, 1978, p. 74. Copyright 1978 by Newsweek, Inc. All rights reserved. Reprinted by permission. Also, "The States Agree: They Love Tourists," *Advertising Age,* June 15, 1981, pp. S-21–22.

In an effort to market cultural appreciation, the Whitney Museum of American Art established a branch near Wall Street in New York City. The goal was to attract businesspeople by providing a refreshing haven from the rows of metal desks in nearby sterile offices. Seeking the lunch-hour crowd, the Whitney branch is open weekdays only, from 11 A.M. to 3 P.M. Weekly dance, "performance arts," and musical performances begin at noon. Exhibits change frequently and are limited enough to be viewed in a fraction of the lunch hour. The approach has been so successful that two other branches have been opened—one in Stamford, Connecticut, the other in midtown Manhattan.

The marketing of *nations* and their political ideologies is yet another contemporary application of marketing. Nations and political factions within them mount international campaigns to communicate important points about themselves to citizens of other countries. For example, when a group of leftist guerrillas in El Salvador kidnapped two of its employees, Beckman Instruments, Inc., agreed to pay for the publication of a long political statement in newspapers in the United States, Central America, and Europe. The political advertisement, covering two full pages in *The New York Times* and *The Los Angeles Times,* called for a halt to "the repression of the Salvadorian dictatorship." And when the Americans were taken hostage in Iran, the Iranian embassy in Washington ran a Christmas advertisement in *The New York Times* in which the Ayatollah exhorted Americans to "rise up against oppression."

From this brief survey, we see that the broadened view of the product is not confined to traditional goods and services. Marketing is also involved with such products as people, places, ideas, organizations, stores, and nations.

Product Classifications

One result of taking this broad view of products is that there are literally millions of products to be marketed. And new products are identified, developed, discovered, invented, or born *every* day. While each of these products demands a unique marketing mix, there also are useful ways for marketers to classify products into groups that share common characteristics and can be marketed similarly. One way to classify products is to divide them into *durable* and *nondurable* categories. This classification system reflects the life expectancy of a product. Bread, clothing, and magazines all have a short life expectancy and thus are nondurable. But refrigerators, television sets, and cars are classified as durable products because they are expected to last a long time.

Another way to classify products is according to whether they are *perishable* or *nonperishable.* Strawberries and flowers are perishable, while shovels and lawnmowers are nonperishable. This factor of perishability can be psychological as well as physical. Some products—especially fads and fashions—lose their value in the marketplace rapidly. (Citizen-band radios and the "cowboy" look in clothing are examples.) In marketing such perishable items, the provision of time and place utilities is of utmost importance.

Products can also be classified as *necessities* or *luxuries.* Necessities are items that are essential, while luxuries are products that match wants more than needs. Obviously, what is a necessity for one person may not be a necessity for another. While a car may be essential for a sales representative, a bank clerk may consider it a luxury.

Marketers also classify products on the basis of their *sensitivity to price.* For some items, demand is *price elastic* (demand for them is very sensitive to changes in price), while for others, demand is *price inelastic* (demand does not vary much with changes in price). Demand for automobiles is price elastic. This price sensitivity has led dealers to use rebates as a means of encouraging exchange. On the other hand, demand for such products as bread and milk is price inelastic. These products tend to sell at the same rate no matter what the price.

These classification systems of durable-nondurable, perishable-nonperishable, necessity-luxury, and elastic-inelastic are all useful ways for marketers to view products. Yet another common classification system focuses—as should all marketing —on the product's buyer. According to this system, *consumer products* are destined for use by ultimate consumers, while *industrial products* are used in the production of still other goods and services. Let's examine this classification system more closely.

Consumer Products

Not all consumer products are of the same type. Rather, they can be subdivided on the basis of how people buy them. Since the purpose of marketing is to satisfy wants and needs, it is logical to classify products on the basis of consumer behavior. Thus, consumer products can be divided into four subgroups: (1) convenience products, (2) shopping products, (3) specialty products, and (4) unsought products.

Convenience Products

Convenience products are items that consumers want to buy with the least possible shopping effort. Their selection is characterized by routine buying behavior. Though these products are bought often, consumers do not seek information about them. Examples include chewing gum, candy, milk, eggs, cigarettes, gasoline, and banking services. There are three types of convenience products: staples, impulse items, and emergency goods.

Staple items are convenience products for which consumers usually do some planning. Food items are good examples. Although consumers don't seek much information about milk, they do buy it often; and they *plan* to buy it when preparing to go to the grocery store. Banking is an example of a service that is a staple. Although some planning is involved, using a bank's services is really rather routine. With staple items, the brand or trademark can be very important in buyers' minds. And buyers want staple items to be located conveniently.

Impulse items are not purchased because of planning, but because of a strongly felt immediate need. Thus, distribution is an important factor in marketing impulse products. If they are not located conveniently, exchange will not take place. That's why items like candy, novelties, and inexpensive pens are placed near the cash register in many stores. Shoppers tend to react by impulse in deciding to buy, say, *People* magazine. Few consumers are likely to go out and shop for such an item, but they will buy it if it is easily available within their normal routine. (See Figure 8-4.) Telephone calls are an example of a service that is often purchased on impulse. The sudden thought of a friend can cause us to reach for the telephone.

Figure 8-4   A convenient location within a store is essential to the purchase of impulse items. *(Wil Blanche/Design Photographers International)*

Emergency products are items that are needed to solve an immediate crisis. Again, time and place utilities are the major ingredients of satisfaction. Price and quality are less important, although the product obviously has to be of sufficient quality to meet the emergency. That is, while the price of an adhesive bandage is of little consequence when one is needed, it *does* have to stick. Sales promotion devices such as posters and displays are critical in the marketing of emergency products, since consumers do not plan to purchase these things and thus must be made aware of them. For that matter, a final push at the point of purchase is a critical aspect of marketing convenience products.

Shopping Products

Consumers visit several stores to compare prices and quality before buying *shopping products.* Even before going into the store to examine such products, consumers may study magazines like *Consumer Reports,* or ask friends for their opinions about certain products, or study advertisements. In other words, before buying shopping products, consumers seek information that will allow them to compare two or more brands or substitute products.

As we noted earlier, even when two products serve the same function and are essentially similar, they can be considered as different products from the marketing viewpoint. Shopping products can thus be divided into two groups, depending on how consumers perceive them. *Homogeneous products* are perceived as being essentially similar (canned food items and home insurance policies are examples), whereas *heterogeneous products* are perceived as being essentially different (furniture, draperies, automobiles, and repair services are examples). With heterogeneous products, the different styles and aesthetic features are important, while price is less important. But homogeneous products pose problems for marketers because they are similar and must be differentiated in consumers' minds.

For instance, there are many smoke detectors on the market, and they all serve the same essential function: all are warning devices. From the marketing viewpoint, however, the similarity ends there. Each brand of smoke detector is technically different, performs somewhat differently, and sells for a different price. It is up to the marketers of each smoke detector to differentiate that particular product in the marketplace. Generally, they will try through advertising to show how their product is different from competing brands, and sometimes price will be used to distinguish one product from another. Homogeneous shopping products put demands on consumers because information is needed in order to sort the similar products and make a buying decision. For the same reason, such products require much attention from marketers.

Specialty Products

Specialty products are items for which there are no acceptable substitutes in the consumer's mind. Consumers are willing to search long and hard until they find them. Usually, the buyers of specialty products have investigated the products available and have decided which one they want to buy. And they are willing to search for an outlet for that particular product.

With specialty products, the brand name is extremely important. In fact, that may be most of what consumers are buying. Designers' fashions are a good example. People go out of their way to find a store that carries clothes designed by Halston, or Calvin Klein, or Bill Blass. Such designers attempt to generate demand for their clothing so that people will search for their products and buy nothing else. A similar situation exists with specialty services like dental and medical care. People do not want to accept substitute goods and services.

With specialty products, the willingness to shop is the critical variable, since substitute products are not acceptable. But specialty goods need not be expensive. Coors beer is a relatively inexpensive specialty good. Some beer drinkers will accept no other brand, and they have gone to great lengths to get their favorite. A Brooks Brothers shirt is another example. Because some men will wear nothing else, this New York store enjoys a sizable mail-order business.

Unsought Products

Unsought products are items that consumers do not readily realize they want or need. Most new products fall into this category until marketers promote their benefits and the needs they satisfy. Not so long ago, the trash compacter was an unsought product because people didn't know they had a need for one. But as the compacter was developed and promoted, the need for it came to be recognized.

Hospitals, convalescent homes, and cemetery plots are other examples of unsought products. Consumers do not shop for such things until a need arises. But when the need is recognized, the products are sought.

Cem-A-Care, a cemetery management organization in Fort Lauderdale, has taken a lead in selling an unsought good—caskets. In a casket service-center display room, consumers can choose their own casket and pay for them at today's prices, even though they will not be used for five, ten, twenty, or even fifty years. In Los Angeles, a fast-growing cremation chain aggressively advertises on television its low-cost services of cremation and the casting of ashes into the sea. Two rather blunt appeals are used: "Save the land for the living" and "Don't give your money to the undertaker. Save it for the living."

Industrial Products

We've noted that industrial products are goods or services used in the production of other products. Industrial goods encompass supplies, accessories, services, and even plant and equipment. The many raw materials and subassemblies that go into a finished car are all industrial products; they are marketed to automobile manufacturers, not to ultimate consumers. And the buyers of industrial products are different from the buyers of consumer products. It follows that the marketing of industrial products is also different. Let's see how.

Derived Demand

Figure 8-5 Michelin publishes travel guides so that consumers will drive more, thus increasing tire sales.

One of the outstanding characteristics of industrial products is that the demand for them is derived from consumer behavior. That is, since industry has no purpose except to satisfy the wants and needs of ultimate consumers, the amount of goods that can be marketed to industrial users depends on the ultimate consumer's demand for finished products. For example, a good deal of the demand for lumber depends on the demand for new houses, and much of the demand for steel is based on the demand for new automobiles. In the United States, 70 percent of total tire sales are to replace original equipment tires (those placed on new cars). This characteristic makes industrial buyers dependent on those who buy the finished product—consumers with whom an industrial marketer rarely has direct contact. The United States Steel Corporation, for example, sells a large part of its output to the automobile industry, which, in turn, converts that raw product into cars; only then is the original steel sold, through yet another dealer, to consumers.

As a result of being removed from the market that ultimately determines their success, marketers of industrial products often advertise directly to consumers. Very simply, this is an effort to promote more business. Thus, advertisements point out the advantages of steel products—cars, appliances, and so on. This promotion is paid for by the steel companies (either individually or in association). The industry wants to persuade people to buy new steel products. Obviously, the more steel products sold, the greater the derived demand for raw steel. This kind of reasoning led Michelin to produce its famous travel guides. (See Figure 8-5.) Initially, the tire company published ratings of restaurants in France to stimulate greater driving by French drivers. In so doing, greater tire wear would result.

Industrial marketers need to be every sensitive to consumers' moods and needs. Not only do they want to encourage demand for their product, but they also must be able to make accurate long-range forecasts in order to gauge production requirements. Thus, consumers' buying behavior is very important to industrial marketers, even though they don't sell products directly to consumers.

Price Sensitivity

Pricing of products is always a critical activity of marketing. But an important characteristic of industrial products is that *industry demand is not as price sensitive as ultimate consumer demand.* An industrywide price increase does not necessarily have an adverse effect on demand. If tire makers, for example, raise the prices for original equipment, the automobile industry will not stop putting tires on new cars. Given an industrywide price increase for tires, automobile manufacturers have three choices: (1) absorb the increase, (2) pass the increase along to ultimate consumers, or (3) put lower-priced tires on new cars. On the other hand, if the tire industry reduces prices, demand may rise slightly, since automobile companies may stockpile tires for future use.

An industry's demand for the industrial products it requires is less sensitive to price because the industry must have the products in order to manufacture its own products and stay in business. That is, when a price increase is compared with the ultimate value of the industrial product to its buyer, the cost is insignificant. An industrial buyer cannot stop purchasing industrial products and still stay in business.

While demand for an industry at large is not particularly sensitive to prices, it is a different situation for individual companies within that industry—especially when there are many makers of a specific good. *Individual demand may be very price sensitive.* Let's assume that Goodyear raises its prices for original-equipment tires, but Firestone does not. As a result, the demand for Goodyear tires is likely to decrease, while demand for Firestone tires will probably increase. In the real world, however, such a situation is unlikely. Instead, if one company raises prices but its competitors do not, that company is likely to roll back its prices rather than risk losing business to the other companies.

Fluctuating Demand

Demand for most industrial products fluctuates more widely than demand for consumer goods. This often happens because industrial demand, as we have noted, is far removed from ultimate consumers. In addition, the many intermediaries who handle the product as it moves toward buyers can wield a great influence on demand. The demand for industrial products reflects an anticipation of the buying action of consumers and intermediaries.

Even the most careful projections of demand by the manufacturers of industrial products may be inadequate because their customers may change course suddenly or alter their own projections. For example, if there is a sudden surge in consumer demand for new cars, automobile manufacturers may suddenly order a lot more steel to meet this sales surge. This, of course, will affect demand for the steel industry. And then the reverse may also occur: for any number of economic reasons, potential car buyers might put off buying a new car. Automobile manufacturers therefore would slow down production, and demand for the steel industry would fall. And, again, demand for industrial products may fluctuate if a major industrial buyer decides to stockpile materials, either to take advantage of bulk discounts or to hedge against price increases. Such changes result in large ups and downs in the demand for industrial products.

Knowledgeable Buyers

As a general rule, industrial buyers know their needs better than the consuming public does. And, besides knowing what they need, industrial buyers are aware of the many companies that can satisfy their needs. Thus, at first glance, it might seem that the job of an industrial purchasing manager is rather simple. On the contrary, however, purchasing managers must sort through many different goods and suppliers that can serve their needs.

Take, for example, the search for a spectrometer, a device used to analyze chemicals. There are at least a dozen different types of spectrometers on the market. A purchasing manager must decide which one is most efficient, of the best quality, and available for the best price. Industrial buyers, in short, are looking for value. Meanwhile, manufacturers of spectrometers must make their presence known to many companies—even those that only occasionally buy their products. Like most industrial suppliers, to do this they must rely on personal selling. Their sales personnel must be well acquainted with their company's product and must be able to discuss it convincingly with other experts who represent the customers. For many industrial products, postsale servicing is crucial. Also, since buyers of industrial products make heavy use of catalogs, industrial marketers must see that their line of products is listed in hundreds of source books and indexes.

Limited Market

While nearly everyone is a potential customer for consumer products, the number of industrial buyers is limited. There are only about 12 million customers for industrial products, compared with perhaps 230.5 million buyers of consumer products. Thus, the market for industrial products is more limited. For example, the number of apparel manufacturers who require computer-driven laser cutters is very small. First of all, not all apparel companies can afford such a device; second, only the companies that require precision cutting will want it. In such a situation, it is critical that the marketers identify their customers precisely. While they can't afford to overlook potential buyers, they also want to avoid wasting time and effort in making unproductive sales calls. Thus, the limited size of the market for industrial products makes it even more necessary that marketing activities be effective.

Geographic Concentration of Markets

Unlike the consumer market, industrial markets tend to be concentrated in specific geographic regions. Textiles, for instance, are produced throughout the South; oil production is most intense in the Southwest; steelmaking is concentrated in the Northeast and in Alabama; the coal mining is heaviest in Kentucky, Tennessee, and West Virginia. Given this situation, it is logical for industrial suppliers to set up distribution centers and sales offices within the regions they serve. Thus, manufacturers of textile machinery would be wise to locate in Columbia, South Carolina—within a stone's throw of textile giants like J. P. Stevens, Milliken, Burlington, and Cannon.

Although industries tend to concentrate geographically, they are not all restricted to one region. Some textiles, for instance, are also produced in New England. These companies also must be served by the supplier's distribution channels and sales personnel. When industrial buyers are not concentrated geographically, sellers may hire part-time sales representatives to serve accounts in outlying areas. Such agents may handle several products and may represent more than one supplier. These people act like members of a sales force, but they actually work for themselves. We will learn more about them in Chapter 13.

Rational Buying Behavior

The primary aim of industrial marketers—like that of their counterparts dealing with consumer products—is to satisfy their market's needs. These needs are also triggered by some stimuli, but industrial customers tend to have more rational reasons for buying than consumers do; they seek products that can be bought at the best price and are of the appropriate quality. Mostly, however, industrial products must perform a certain function and must meet the precise specifications of the buyer. And so many industrial purchases are made by groups—committees comprising R&D engineers, production managers, and cost-conscious accountants as well as the purchasing agent.

Thus, industrial marketers must do everything possible to satisfy the rational needs of their customers. They must help a company's purchasing manager to make good buying decisions in order to keep that customer's future business. Deliveries must be made on schedule, pricing must be competitive, and the quality of products and service must be high. Given the extremely limited market for industrial products, the success of each purchasing manager has a direct bearing on the success of the supplier. An unsatisfied industrial customer represents a loss of sales that is far greater than in the consumer market.

Long Negotiating Period

A consumer product may be purchased in a matter of seconds, but years may elapse before a final sale is made for some types of industrial products. Although the time frame may be long for industrial sales, a single purchase may involve many thousands of dollars. Industrial buyers, therefore, must weigh decisions carefully, and marketers may have to deal with several executives before a purchase is approved by the final authority. The time frame is also likely to be extended in the sale of industrial products that are made to order, such as an airplane engine. Before a final sale is made, specifications have to be developed, and perhaps a working model must be manufactured. Years can pass before such a sale is completed. Then, too, some buyers—particularly the government—may require that bids be submitted. This is always a time-consuming process.

Infrequent Sales

Besides the longer period it takes to close an industrial sale, marketers of industrial products make fewer sales. Industrial products are purchased less frequently than consumer products. Some companies buy certain products only once a year. But, since they buy in large quantities, the loss of an industrial sale can be a disaster.

Industrial Advertising and Personal Selling

Because industrial sales are infrequent and may take a long time to negotiate, marketers need to establish effective and direct contact with their customers. They do this through industrial advertising and personal selling.

The most effective media for industrial advertising are the industry trade magazines—specialized publications like *Textile World, Electronics,* and *Coal Age.*

There is very little waste circulation with such magazines, since they are read by the people within a specific industry. *Textile World,* for example, has a circulation of about 30,000—but only among textile companies or textile-related businesses. It would be inefficient for manufacturers of textile machinery or synthetic fibers to advertise in *Time* or *Newsweek,* since they want to reach only the key people within their industry. In addition, a four-color full-page advertisement in one of the weekly national magazines costs as much as $70,000, while a page in *Textile World* costs less than $3,400.

An industrial supplier must also use its sales force to keep buyers aware of its products, even though sales may not be completed for a long time. Again, the long negotiating period and infrequency of sales make each industrial customer extremely important. The sales force must maintain contact with all potential customers, because most industrial products are sold directly to the customers. In contrast, many consumer products, such as candy, are sold through an intermediary (a wholesaler). But there are few intermediaries in the industrial market. Industrial sales personnel must be a cut above the average salesperson because they often have to provide technical assistance along with the product. The training and management of the sales force are especially important in industrial marketing. While personal selling is key in marketing industrial products, it is also very costly. A study reports that in 1981, it took 4.3 calls on a customer to produce a sale.[5] At $136.02 per call, each sale cost an average of $589.18.

Personal service is another critical area of industrial marketing, and the sales force is often responsible for coordinating the activities that provide it. Suppliers' representatives work with the customer to develop specifications and schedules, and they work with the supplier to see that standards and deadlines are met. Many marketing tasks are accomplished through the sales force, including product development, promotion, sales, and service. When the time finally comes to complete an industrial sale, this kind of marketing effort yields handsome rewards. (See Application 8-4.)

Other Ingredients in the Product's Bundle of Satisfaction

We have discussed the main ingredient in the bundle of satisfaction—the product—and have seen that the core of the product is goods and services, but that this core has been broadened to include people, places, ideas, organizations, stores, and even nations. Then we examined how marketers classify all these products. But our view of the nature of the product is still not complete. We need to look at some additional features that provide the total bundle of satisfaction coming from the product.

While consumers buy a product in order to satisfy their wants and needs, satisfaction does not come only from that basic product. There also are increments of

---

[5]*Laboratory of Advertising Performance Report,* No. 8051, McGraw-Hill, New York, 1981.

Application 8-4
Industrial Marketing—
Applying Consumer-Product Techniques to Selling Industry

Typically, industrial companies develop a product in the laboratory and then ponder: "Now how are we going to sell it?" Loctite Corp. of Newington, Connecticut, has taken a different approach. There, the marketing of Quick Metal, a puttylike metal adhesive for repairing worn machine parts, preceded development. While providing products to satisfy the wants and needs of the consumer may be routine in other segments of the marketplace, many industrial marketers of noncustom products have ignored this concept.

Quick Metal got its start in early 1979 when Loctite executives began looking for ways to revive RC601, an unsuccessful, runny, green liquid that provided an adhesive function but was difficult to use. After interviewing equipment designers, production engineers, and maintenance workers, Loctite arrived at a strategy.

The target market: maintenance workers, who are more agreeable than their bosses about trying an unfamiliar product. "When the production line is down, the maintenance worker can buy anything anywhere that he feels will put the line back into production," noted a May 1979 company memo.

Part of the strategy involved writing advertising copy which deleted the traditional dull approach of industrial ads. Instead of describing Quick Metal in chemical terms, the tag line read: "keeps machinery running until the new parts arrive." The company also ran contests with distributors. Probably the most effective aspect of the undertaking was changing the name of the product from RC601 to Quick Metal.

The result: In addition to selling more than 100,000 tubes of Quick Metal in one week, Loctite developed detailed information about its sales force, improved morale, and boosted the sale of the company's other products. Between October 1980 and April 1981, Loctite retailers sold $2.2 million worth of the product. Traditional marketing methods, Loctite estimates, would have produced only $320,000 in sales.

Source of data: "Consumer-Product Techniques Help Loctite Sell to Industry," *The Wall Street Journal,* April 2, 1981, p. 29.

---

satisfaction that result from attendant features of what is bought—most notably from brands, trademarks, labels, packaging, and warranties. These product features strongly influence consumers' choices. And when a product is standardized, they can be the deciding factor in promoting exchange.

Brands and Trademarks

The American Marketing Association defines a *brand* as "a name, term, symbol, or design, or a combination, which is intended to identify the goods or services of one seller or group of sellers and to differentiate them from those of competitors."[6] A *brand name* consists of words, letters, or numbers that can be vocalized. Thus, Lady

---

[6]Committee on Definitions, *Marketing Definitions: A Glossary of Marketing Terms,* American Marketing Association, Chicago, 1960.

Figure 8-6 This trademark includes the brand name, but not all trademarks do. (Ray Pfortner)

Clairol, Bayer, and 3M are brand names. A *brand mark* is that part of a brand which is in the form of a symbol, design, or distinctive coloring or lettering. Examples include Charlie, the Star-Kist tuna; Tony the Tiger, on Kellogg's Frosted Flakes; Planter's Mr. Peanut; Morris, the Nine Lives cat; Pillsbury's Poppin' Fresh Doughboy; and the LaCoste alligator.

Trademark is essentially a legal term; it refers to a brand that is given legal protection because it has been appropriated exclusively to one marketer. All trademarks are brands, but not all brands are trademarks. A trademark can include both the brand name and the pictorial design. (Some people erroneously believe that a trademark is *only* the pictorial part of a brand.) The word *Ford* is a brand name; but when it's printed in a certain kind of script, it becomes a trademark. (See Figure 8-6.) A trademark does not have to be attached to the product, nor does it have to be a name. Some examples of trademarks that cannot be imitated are the shape of the Haig & Haig Pinch Scotch bottle, the Playboy Bunny costume, and the CBS eye. Even sounds can be trademarks. Although NBC has greatly cut back on its use of three musical notes with its call letters, those notes announced the beginning and end of each NBC program for years and were protected by law.

Sometimes a brand name becomes so well known and is so much associated with a particular use that it becomes a *generic name,* a term associated with the product class, not with a particular brand. Many generic names were once trademarks but by neglect fell into general use and became common property. Kleenex, for instance, is the brand name for facial tissues produced by Kimberly-Clark. Over time, however, people have used that name to refer to all facial tissues, and now many people believe that Puffs and Scotties are brands of Kleenex. While Kleenex is still a legally protected trademark, consumers often use the term generically. In the same way, Band-Aid and Xerox are often misused to describe classes of products when they are actually brand names. And many children no longer play dolls, they play "Barbies."

Ideally, a firm wants its brand to be preferred to the exclusion of others, making it a specialty product. Thus a company does not want its brand name to be used generically, because then promotion of the brand may lead to sales of similar but competing brands. Worse, the company may lose its exclusive right to use the name, as King-Seely did when surveys showed that 68 percent of the population thought that the word *Thermos* simply meant any vacuum-insulated bottle. Other examples of brand names that have fallen into generic use are the words *aspirin, nylon, linoleum,* and *shredded wheat.*

Companies go to great lengths to protect their trademarks and brands from falling into generic use. Coca-Cola Company has an entire department that monitors the unauthorized use of the words *Coke* and *Coca-Cola.* If a newspaper or magazine uses either word in lowercase type, its publisher will receive a letter from the company pointing out that the words must be capitalized when they refer to the specific soft drink made by Coca-Cola Company. Coca-Cola also obtained an injunction against a company that was selling posters with the words "Enjoy Cocaine" written in the familiar Coca-Cola script. Other companies have complained about Topps Chewing Gum Company, which markets "Wacky Packs," a series of satirical picture cards showing products with slightly distorted names such as "Killette Fright Guard" deodorant, "Ditch Masters Cheap Cigars," and "Ultra Blight" toothpaste. And Campbell Soup went to court to stop two novelty versions of its products. The gimmic cans looked like the genuine items, but titles included "Rat & Noodle" and "Cockroach Gumbo."

Classifying Brands

Brands are classified according to whether they are (1) family or individual brands or (2) national or private brands.

Marketers who handle more than one item often use the same brand name for all their products. This is a *family brand.* Examples include the General Electric brand for all that company's appliances, Sears's use of the Kenmore brand for its appliances, and A&P's Ann Page brand of food products. When products are of varying quality or type, marketers often use an *individual brand* for each item; each brand name is applied to only one product or brand. Thus, among its many products, Procter & Gamble markets Tide detergent, Sure deodorant, and Crest toothpaste. General Foods markets Maxwell House instant coffee, Maxim freeze-dried coffee, and Cycle dog food. Colgate markets Fab detergent, Baggies food and trash bags, Wilkinson razors and baldes, Reveal roasting wrap, Handiwipes, Pritt Glue Stick, and even a line of hospital products including surgical gowns and sheets. Some companies use both types of brands. Pillsbury, for instance, emphasizes its family brand on Pillsbury's Best flour, biscuits, and cake mixes; but it also uses the Hungry Jack brand for other biscuits and for pancake and waffle mixes.

Another basis for classifying brands depends on whether they are owned by producers or by dealers. Manufacturer brands are sometimes called national brands since manufacturers often promote them throughout the country. Thus, General Mills, General Foods, and General Electric are manufacturer brands. Dealer brands are sometimes called private brands. A&P's Ann Page, Montgomery Ward's Signature, and Sears's Kenmore are examples. This private designation does not seem appropriate, since each of those dealer brands is distributed and promoted more widely than many national brands.

Advantages and Disadvantages of Branding

From the *consumer's standpoint,* branding is helpful in at least five ways:

1 Well-organized brands are *easily identified,* which makes shopping easier. (Imagine a shopper in a department store trying to evaluate thousands of items without having the information a brand provides.)

2 The brand protects consumers by assuring them of *consistent quality.* (A favorable experience with a brand will likely lead to repeat purchases; a bad experience cues consumers to avoid that brand.) Therefore, marketers of branded products insist on good quality control.

3 A brand also assures consumers of *comparable quality,* no matter where a product is purchased. (Sony television sets should all have the same quality, whether bought in a discount store or in an appliance store.)

4 Brands may provide that increment of *psychological satisfaction* not otherwise available. (Often, status is associated with a brand name. The Bigelow Carpet Company stresses this side of its brand with the slogan "A title on the door rates a Bigelow on the floor," while Hallmark greeting cards have long been promoted by "When you care enough to send the very best.")

5 With branded products, there tend to be *improvements in quality* over the years. (Competition forces this improvement, since brand owners constantly modify products to ensure a stronger market standing for their brand.)

From the *marketer's standpoint,* branding also has many advantages:

1 A brand helps marketers in terms of *product differentiation* by giving them something different to advertise and promote. (A company's image is often built around its brand name, which can presell products to consumers and stimulate sales even more effectively than individual advertising can.)

2 Promotion of a particular brand allows marketers to *control the market* or increase their *share of the market.* (The promotion of unbranded products leads to sales increases for all products in that category.)

3 A brand helps its owner to stimulate *repeat sales* and build *brand loyalty*— consumers' insistence on having that particular brand. (Thus, branding reduces the number of buyers who will accept a substitute product from another company.)

4 Brand loyalty results in *less price competition,* since the brand itself creates a difference between two products. (When brand loyalty has been developed, consumers are often willing to pay extra for the particular brand they want; thus, a brand can return more in sales than its cost to develop.)

5 A brand can help marketers to *expand the product line.* (The quality associated with an established brand name will be attributed to new products that are marketed under that brand. Thus, Church & Dwight, the marketers of Arm & Hammer baking soda, was able to promote detergents, carpet deodorizers, and cat litter deodorizers under its famous brand name.) (See Application 8-5.)

While branding offers many advantages to consumers and marketers, we must also examine the other side of the coin. For marketers especially, there are several disadvantages. First, the development of an *effective brand name* is costly; it involves extensive testing and promotion. Then, too, some products are difficult to brand because they do not have many differentiating qualities. Nails, clothespins, paper clips, spray starch, fruits and vegetables, and matches are examples. Chiquita and Sunkist have been able to develop their brand of bananas and oranges respectively, and Hallmark has done the same thing with greeting cards—but only through costly promotion.

Application 8-5
Branding—Getting the Most for Your Money

As the cost of introducing new products has soared, many marketers are banking on new products which travel under the banner of existing, successful bound names.

"Names like Armour, Maxwell House, and Del Monte represent a huge investment over the years," the president of a San Francisco design concern told *The Wall Street Journal.* "The incredible cost of introducing new brands points out the need to hitchhike on what already exists."

Examples of this tactic are evident: Sunkist orange soda, Minolta copiers, Levi shirts and shoes, Del Monte Mexican food, Woolite rug shampoo, Easy-Off window cleaner, Gerber insurance, and Vaseline Intensive Care skin lotion, bath oil, and baby powder.

One company which has specialized in this strategy is Bic. Ten years ago, Bic Pen's only United States business was making ball-point pens. Today, you'll find the Bic name on shavers, lighters, and two other types of pens. Bic's

(Randy Matusow)

reputation for inexpensive, disposable products "is a very big plus for us, especially with new products," Bruno Bich, vice president for sales and marketing told the *Journal.*

However, this piggyback strategy is not always successful, as a string of companies have discovered. Failures include Arm & Hammer antiperspirant, Certs gum, Life Savers gum, Sara Lee Chicken & Noodles Au Gratin, and Listerol, a household cleaner from the maker of Listerine. Many of these failures were "me too" products and did not have any significant benefits different from those offered by established competitors. A familiar brand name alone doesn't guarantee success. The product is important too.

"If you're going to have your name on all your products," said Bic's Mr. Bich, "you should never produce a bad product. If you make a mistake, you'll hurt your whole company."

Source of data: "Exploiting Proven Brand Names Can Cut Risk of New Products," *The Wall Street Journal,* Jan. 22, 1981, p. 27.

Another disadvantage to marketers in branding is that it requires products to be consistent in quality. While this is an advantage for consumers, it is often technically difficult for marketers to ensure consistent quality. Finally, branding reduces the control that nonowners have over the marketing of a specific brand. For instance, in selling a manufacturer's brand, a retailer is often subject to decisions made by the producer affecting such matters as advertising, shelf positions, store displays, and even profits.

Generics—an Alternative to Branding

Since 1977, there has been a rush to provide consumers with no-name brands, called generics. With inflation cutting deeply into consumers' disposable income, generics rode into supermarkets heralded as a threat to brand marketers of all types. Marketed on the basis of acceptable quality products at lower prices, products seen as commodities by consumers—paper towels, frozen peas, coffee creamers, and chlorine bleach, to name a few—tend to be offered unbranded. For a generic to be successful, product quality must not be perceived as different from that of its branded counterparts. Its price must be significantly below the price of branded competing items. Many generic products are priced between 40 and 50 percent of the price of equivalent branded products. In terms of sales, the impact of generics in supermarkets has been slight—less than 5 percent overall. Yet, they are appearing in more categories. Supermarkets are not the only place where generics are found; other retail shops are selling unbranded drugs, liquor, even cigarettes. (See Figure 8-7.)

Figure 8-7 No-name brands offer satisfaction to price-conscious consumers. (Barbara Alper/Stock, Boston)

Selecting a Brand Name

The development of a good brand name is more of an art than a science, and it is no easy task. Some well-known brand names have come about rather quickly and through a random process; others have been developed only through extensive research and testing.

The generic term *crayon*, for example, had been used for years to describe a product originally derived from chalk. At about the turn of the century, however, Edwin Binney set out to make a crayon for children by adding oil and other pigments to the black marking devices his concern already sold to businesses. When he told his wife about the plan, she began musing: "Crayons and oil, crayons and oil. Crayolas!" Crayola has been the brand name since 1903. A similar random process led to the brand name After Six for tuxedos. In 1938, the company's president and an artist were working late on an advertisement. Noticing that twilight had fallen and the city's lights were on, the artist said, "Let's get out of here; it's after six." In a flash of intuition, a new brand name was created.

While these brand names for certain crayons and formal attire were developed rather easily and inexpensively, companies often spend great amounts of effort and money in developing new names. Chicago's A. M. International, née Addressograph-Multigraph Corporation, waded through 80,000 computer-generated name candidates and parted with more than $3 million to rid itself of a name that research showed to have a valuable public image. In return, it got two letters—*A* and *M*—and an *International*. The reason for the change: management felt the old name did not reflect the new technologies of the company.

Some brand names—like Frigidaire, Nine Lives, and Crest—are particularly good and can lead to success. The company's sales faltered in 1974, when the ski industry's sales dropped because of a recession and three winters of relatively little snow in the East. To meet this crisis, K2 marketed a line of small skis called Cheeseburgers, Cheeseburgers Deluxe, and K2 Briefs. The company's president summed up the effort: "What a dud. We dropped that crazy 'food and underwear' line like a hot potato. Professional people like doctors and lawyers weren't about to pay $185 for skis called Cheeseburgers."

Some brand names are successful even though they violate principles of good branding—mostly because they are promoted often enough and long enough for consumers to build associations. But this is a risky and expensive approach to branding. Instead, marketers can follow certain principles:

1 A brand name should suggest something about the product's benefits or use—its characteristics, quality, function, or action. *Hefty, Beautyrest,* and *Gleem* suggest benefits; *Nytol, Fluff, Whisk, Water-Pik,* and *Grippit* connote action.

2 A brand name should be easy to pronounce, spell, and remember. In this regard, *Tylenol* and *Datril* are weak, while short, one-syllable names like *Mum, Sure,* and *Lite,* are good.

3 A brand name should be distinctive. *Standard, Acme, National,* and *Smith* are poor by this measure, while the second *x* in *Oxxford* and *Exxon* helps to add a distinctive quality.

4 A brand name should be versatile enough to be applied to new products that are added to the line. Names like *General Motors* and *General Electric* serve this purpose better than a distinctive one like *Radio Corporation of America*. In fact, the *Radio Corporation of America* has become known as *RCA,* a much more appropriate name as radios lost their market growth.

5 A brand name should be adaptable to any advertising medium, especially billboards and television. Cities Service built adaptability into its new *Citgo* name by changing its green and white colors to the more distinctive red and blue.

6 A brand name should be pleasing when pronounced out loud. *Puffs* and *Scotties* are soft-sounding names for soft products, whereas the harsh *k* sound in *Kotex* lacks this appeal.

7 A brand name should be pronounceable in only one way. Smyth Furniture in Chicago has long ended broadcast advertisements with, "Do you say Smith or Smyth?" to play on the variations in sound.

8 No competitor should have the same brand name. After NBC reportedly spent $750,000 to develop its *N* logo, it found that the Nebraska Education Television Network (NETV) had been using a similar design for identification, and a settlement of $55,000 in cash and more than $500,000 in equipment to NETV had to be arranged. (Then, in 1979, as ratings did not improve, NBC brought back the peacock to remind viewers of "its long, honorable tradition.") To avoid such problems, Exxon Corporation (formerly Standard Oil of New Jersey) sent an army of researchers to check 15,000 telephone directories to make sure that the name *Exxon* was not already in use before spending an estimated $100 million to change its name.

9 A brand name should be such that it can be registered and protected legally. While not all brand names and marks may need legal protection, at some point in the life of the brand the marketer may want to add it.

Branding is such an important aspect of marketing that some companies do nothing but search for brand names. TCR Service, in New Jersey, has more than 4 million trademark applications on its computer. A company that wants to check whether its new brand name is already in use can retain TCR to do the job in less than 24 hours, compared with the weeks or months needed to search by hand.

Companies—particularly those which introduce many new products—will often register names with the U.S. Patent and Trademark Office even though they do not produce specific products under those names. After Six protected its trademark by also registering the phrases "After Five," "After Seven," and "After Eight." An executive for After Six indicated that they stopped at "After Eight" because, they figured, after 9 o'clock people were getting ready for bed, not dressing for an evening out.

Brands and the Law   Trademarks and brand names are protected by both federal and state laws. The Lanham Act (1946) spells out the procedures a company must follow in order to obtain a trademark. However, the simple act of registering a name does not grant ownership. To claim possession, a company must offer the trademarked product on a continuing basis and in interstate commerce. Failure to offer a trademarked product in interstate commerce can result in the loss of legal rights to the name. The trademark *Crosley* was owned by Ford-Philco for years. But when the company discontinued that line of appliances and did not ship products in interstate commerce, another company was able to claim the name.

Labels

Labeling is another product feature that adds to the bundle of utility. A *label* supplies information about the product or its seller. It may be printed as part of the packaging, or it may be on a tag attached to the product. There are three basic kinds of labels:

1 *Grade labels* identify the quality of the product by a letter ("grade A"), number ("No. 1") or word ("prime" or "choice").

2 *Informative labels* (such as "Keep away from heat or direct sunlight") advise consumers about the care, use, or preparation of products.

3 *Descriptive labels* explain the important characteristics or benefits of products.

Purposes of Labels   Although some products can be identified adequately by brand name alone, many require more complete identification of their nature and use. In short, the main purpose of labeling is to provide information. Processed foods, patent drugs, some cosmetics, textiles, and numerous other products are required by law to carry a fairly complete list of their ingredients. In addition, many companies provide information on labels because of pressures from consumer groups and competitors. Recently, labeling has come to include unit pricing, open dating, and nutrition labeling. *Unit pricing* shows the price per unit of standard measure (weight or volume), allowing consumers to compare values among competing products. Unit pricing is most often found on the shelf rather than on the product itself. *Open dating* tells consumers about the expected life of the product so that they can avoid products which may be spoiled. *Nutritional labeling* discloses the amounts of protein, fat, carbohydrates, and calories in processed foods.

Labels also give instructions about how to use products, such as washing instructions for garments, and storage and dosage requirements for drugs. Additionally, labels point out any safety hazards that a product may have. They specify the presence of poisons and tell what to do if the products are swallowed or used improperly.

Besides giving information about the product, labels also can provide promotional assistance. In general, they are an important opportunity for point-of-purchase promotion. Such promotion can add an ingredient of satisfaction to the bundle of utility offered. McDonald's, long criticized for the high caloric and low nutritional content of its menu, met the issue head on with an advertising campaign. Using a nutritional labeling format in a series of newspaper and TV ads, each ad stressed the nutritional content and stated that the figures were quoted from an independent testing service. The ad offered a pamphlet entitled "Good Food, Good Nutrition, and McDonald's." The campaign tied in with some in-store promotional displays.

Legal Aspects of Labeling

The importance and problems of labeling can be seen in the long history of legal concerns surrounding labels. Not only are there a large number of federal laws, but several states have statutes, too. Most prominent among these laws is the Fair Packaging and Labeling Act of 1966, which sets out labeling requirements and gives the Food and Drug Administration (FDA) and the Federal Trade Commission (FTC) discretionary power to set packaging regulations as required.

In 1973, the FDA released guidelines for nutrition labeling. Though most of these standards are voluntary, the pressures of consumer groups and competition tend to make them mandatory. Anticipating these standards, Del Monte gained a competitive edge over Kroger, Safeway, and several other major food retailers. In 1972, Del Monte added nutrition labels to its brands. Others waited until the FDA set the guidelines a year later to put such labels on their private brands. Consumer response to Del Monte's move was positive. By anticipating the legal requirements and being the first in the food industry to add nutrition labels, Del Monte added an increment of satisfaction and got a jump on its competitors.

Packaging

Packaging includes all the activities in product planning that are related to designing and producing the container or wrapper for a product. As still another part of the bundle of satisfaction, packaging is also an important part of the marketing mix. In fact, packaging often spells the difference between marketing success and failure.

Figure 8-8   Do the consumers of Animal Crackers receive any satisfaction from the package? *(Randy Matusow)*

Obviously, a package has functional purposes as a container to hold the product and as a shield to protect it. But the package is also the main way to identify the product, giving its brand name and information about how the product performs. In addition, the package is a major part of the overall promotional campaign. It gives consumers a final push toward exchange. Companies have come to realize that packaging is an art form, not just a necessary container that is thrown around the product at the last minute. (See Figure 8-8.) Indeed, packaging is often considered in the early stages of product development. Many marketers see advantages in including packaging experts in even the first brainstorming sessions.

Packaging can be used as a major component in the total bundle of satisfaction. Chicago-based fragrance producer Jovan, Inc. has used novel merchandising techniques that have turned the industry on its ear. Using what the company calls "mass-packaging"—packaging that substituted for billboards—Jovan has utilized

Figure 8-9 Jovan uses a distinctive packaging strategy to position its products. (*Courtesy of Jovan, Inc.*)

mass advertising and aggressive merchandising together with its distinctive packaging, to differentiate itself from the competition. For instance, to market its Musk Oil for Men, a direct assault was launched, with the package's large type proclaiming:

The provocative scent that instinctively calms and yet arouses your basic animal desires. And hers. . . . To take you a long way to where it's at. To the most pleasurable of conclusions. Because it is powerful. Stimulating. Unbelievable. And yet, legal.

(See Figure 8-9 and Application 8-6.)

Application 8-6
Packaging—
Camel Smokers and Their Love Affair with "Ol' Joe"

All too often, companies change their packaging and, in doing so, damage their bundle of satisfaction. One of the most successful packages has been the Camel cigarette pack, which depicts a camel (lovingly named Ol' Joe), two pyramids, and three palm trees. In the 1950s, R. J. Reynolds decided that the package would be more striking if the pyramids and trees were removed. The surgery was performed, but the public howled. Camel sales reflected the change instantly, falling sharply. Not surprisingly, Reynolds quickly returned the camel's props.

Reynolds, in the 1980s, again learned of the popularity of the original Camel pack. For a decade or more, the company's Camel brand of filters was as lackluster as its brown and white package. Then, to add a little spark to the brand, Reynolds decided to present both the filter and "light" version in the same package of its old, established nonfilter.

The consumer reaction, as in the 1950s, was immediate. Sales increased with the introduction of the "new" package. However, the change caused Reynolds some problems—the old packages piled up on supermarket shelves as the public demanded the new packages.

"If the old pack is still on the shelf, consumers will search through and find the new pack," said a brand manager to Reynolds. "You have a situation where you either pick up a product or it sits there until it grows old." (Cigarettes have a shelf life of about nine months.)

The Reynolds' executive won't say how many old Camel packs the company has taken back, except that the volume is greater than what's normally picked up to prevent sales of deteriorated goods. A vice president of Head Tobacco company, a distributor in Atlanta, said he recently shipped back "a couple of hundred" old Camel cartons, a return that is above normal for any brand.

Source of data: "Camel Maker's Problem: Smokers Who Just Can't Get Over the Hump," *The Wall Street Journal*, May 4, 1981, p. 27.

Social and Legal Aspects of Packaging

As the public at large has become interested in protecting the environment, marketers have had to find ways to dispose of packaging. After a package has served its marketing purposes, it becomes trash. Too often, that means litter. While most consumers would claim to be concerned about the environment, at the same time they demand convenience. This requirement translates into disposable packaging that is tossed away when a product is used. As a result, marketers find themselves walking a tightrope.

Many states now have laws requiring consumers to pay a deposit for containers of beer, soft drinks, milk, and other beverages. This legislation forces packagers and consumers to do a better job of recycling. (See Figure 8-10.) Biodegradable products and packaging have also resulted from public pressure to improve markets. When laws required beverages to be packaged in returnable containers, the manufacturers of plastic bottles saw their market shrink. But plastic packaging has also come under fire because it is derived from petroleum, an increasingly precious commodity. Legal and social pressures have also affected the metal industry, since metal cans ultimately become litter, too. Many aluminum manufacturers now encourage consumers to take their used cans to recycling centers. The use of biodegradable packages and recyclable materials has even been employed as a promotional appeal.

Figure 8-10   Returnable bottles affect the package as well as the exchange process. (Daniel S. Brody/Stock, Boston)

Warranties

A *warranty* is a manufacturer's promise that a product will perform its intended purposes. It also adds an increment of psychological satisfaction to the bundle of utility. Consumers are assured that defective products will be fixed or replaced. Actually, consumers have always had certain rights because of *implied warranties,* legal promises that are in effect even if not stated. In addition, both buyers and sellers are protected by *express warranties,* which are usually written. They specify the exact conditions under which a manufacturer is responsible for the product's performance.

Warranties are usually offered for higher-priced or complex products, such as household appliances, electronic items, and automobiles. Such products are bought infrequently, and people tend to shop for the best deal. Price is not the only factor in this decision-making process; often, a warranty is the factor that closes a sale.

Warranties are often offered for products that are sold through the mail or through catalogs. Since consumers usually must pay for products before receiving them, and the manufacturers are often unknown, a money-back offer reduces the risk that the buyer will be stuck.

Legal Aspects of Warranties

Unfortunately, warranties are sometimes misused and may even turn out to be worthless. In 1974, the Magnuson-Moss Act became law, and it went a long way toward setting standards for warranties. Known as the truth-in-warranty act, this law requires warranties to be expressed clearly, without excessive legal jargon. The intent is to assure consumers that products will perform as promoted. However, the law has had some unexpected repercussions, particularly the part that requires a company to state whether its warranty is full or limited. Many companies feel that the word *limited* is negative and may lead consumers to think it is being used to dodge responsibility. As a result, some companies have withdrawn warranties for their products rather than state specific limitations.

Looking Back

This chapter began to explore the product element in the marketing mix by describing its nature. The next chapter will focus on how new products are developed. First, though, review the following main points about the nature of products and their importance to marketing:

1 The product is the bundle of satisfaction that is transferred in the exchange process, and it includes every activity that provides satisfaction to consumers.

2 Different brands within a product category can be considered separate products.

3 Besides goods and services, marketers also market people, places, ideas, organizations, stores, and nations.

4 The most useful way to classify products is according to whether they are consumer products or industrial products.

5 Classifying consumer products is best done on the basis of buyers' perceptions and exchange behavior.

6 Industrial products and buyers differ in many ways from consumer products.

7 The bundle of utility includes—besides the major good and/or service—such ingredients as brand name, trademark, label, packaging, and warranties.

8 Marketers should follow certain principles in developing brand names.

9 A label carries verbal information about the product or its seller.

10 Packaging serves purposes in addition to protecting the product.

11 Warranties provide possible increments of utility by assuring consumers that the product will perform as expected.

12 Branding, labeling, packaging, and warranties are all subject to legal restrictions.

Key Terms

If you aren't sure what each of the following words means, look back at the text. Numbers refer to pages on which the words are defined. Additional information can be found by checking the index and the glossary at the end of the book.

expected product 243
augmented product 243
good 244
service 244
price elastic 253
convenience products 253
staples 253
impulse items 253
shopping products 254
specialty products 255

brand 261
brand name 261
brand mark 262
trademark 262
individual and family brands 263
national and private brands 263
generics 266
warranty 273

Questions for Review

1 How does the expanded approach of looking at a product differ from the traditional approach?

2 What are four characteristics which are useful in distinguishing between goods and services?

3 The most useful way to classify products is according to whether they are consumer products or industrial products. What are some other ways to classify products into groups?

4 In what ways do marketers of industrial goods establish effective and direct contact with their customers? Explain.

5 From the marketer's standpoint, branding has many advantages. What are some of these advantages?

6 What are the three basic kinds of labels? What is the main purpose of labeling?

Questions for Thought and Discussion

1 Wham-O Manufacturing Company, the principal manufacturer and marketer of Frisbees, wanted to keep the sales of its flying discs growing. Basing your answer on this chapter's discussion of the nature of the product, what advice would you offer?

2 You may choose to frequent a particular bar or club because of some dominant need or evaluative criterion, some benefit such as the relaxation offered by one spot or the lower prices promoted by another. What are some other ingredients in the bundle of utility offered by the bar or club you frequent that influence you to go there?

3 What type of consumer product do cigarettes represent? The marketers of Camel cigarettes have long used the slogan "I'd walk a mile for a Camel" in their advertising. What type of consumer product are they attempting to make the Camel brand of cigarettes?

4 The package on a product performs many functions. What do you believe the major purpose of the package, i.e., the album cover, would be when used in the marketing of record albums?

Suggested Project

Product was discussed from many perspectives in this chapter. Find advertisements or articles from periodicals which focus on each of the approaches to defining the product. Where appropriate, describe each approach in terms of brands, trademarks, labels, packaging, and warranties.

Suggested Readings

Bloom, Paul N., and William D. Novelli: "Problems and Challenges in Social Marketing," *Journal of Marketing,* vol. 45, no. 2 (Spring 1981), pp. 79–88. The authors review the problems that can arise when using conventional textbook approaches to marketing ideas and causes as products.

Bucklin, Louis P.: "Retail Strategy and the Classification of Consumer Goods," *Journal of Marketing,* vol. 27, no. 1 (January 1963), pp. 50–55. This often-quoted article extends the classification scheme of convenience, shopping, and specialty goods to retail stores.

Darden, Donna K., William R. Darden, and G. E. Kiser: "The Marketing of Legal Services," *Journal of Marketing,* vol. 45, no. 2 (Spring 1981), pp. 123–134. This article keys on the buyer characteristics and distribution of legal services.

Kendall, C. L., and Frederick A. Russ: "Warranty and Complaint Policies: An Opportunity for Marketing Management," *Journal of Marketing,* vol. 39, no. 2 (April 1975), pp. 36–43. This article shows how the effective handling of consumer complaints related to warranties can be a significant addition to the bundle of utility.

Kotler, Philip: *Marketing for Nonprofit Organizations,* Prentice-Hall, Englewood Cliffs, N.J., 1975. This book brings the basic marketing principles to the managing of five specific institutional areas: social action, health services, public services, educational services, and political marketing.

———, and Sidney J. Levy: "Broadening the Concept of Marketing," *Journal of*

Marketing, vol. 33, no. 1 (January 1969), pp. 10–15. This article steered marketing toward the untraditional products noted in this chapter.

Levitt, Theodore: "Marketing Intangible Products and Product Intangibles," *Harvard Business Review,* vol. 59, no. 3 (May–June 1981), pp. 94–102. Giving tangibility to imperceptible product features can aid both sales and postsales efforts.

Schutte, Thomas F., and Victor J. Cook: "Branding Policies and Practices," in Raymond M. Haas (ed.), *Science, Technology and Marketing,* American Marketing Association, Chicago, 1966, pp. 197–213. The highlights of a study of 200 manufacturing and distributing companies catalog the various factors giving rise to the growth and development of private branding.

Webster, Frederick E., Jr., and Yoram Wind: *Organizational Buying Behavior,* Prentice-Hall, Englewood Cliffs, N.J., 1972. This short book distinguishes the differences between household and organizational buying behavior.

Chapter

9

New-Product Development

Looking Ahead

In the previous chapter we considered what the product is. We saw that the product is much more than the tangible form that we get when we pay some money. We get a whole bundle of features that provide satisfaction. Yet the product has a basic core, a benefit that is the major feature offered. But how do some products come into being? This is the subject of this chapter.

Key Topics

How some products failed

What makes a new product a new product

Four patterns of diversification that marketers can choose from

The importance of sound logic in choosing new products to develop

How some product successes were created

The seven stages of new-product development

Chapter Outline

Marketing New Products
Patterns of Product Diversification
Rationales for Diversification

Stages of Product Development
Bringing New Products to Life
Organizing for New Products
New-Product Strategy and Idea
 Generation
Screening
Concept Development and Testing
Business Analysis
Product Development
Test Marketing
Commercialization

Looking Back

All the qualities of a product—its benefits, its packaging, its distribution, its name—contribute to the bundle of satisfaction through exchange, a process that often improves the consumer's standard of living. Indeed, our standard of living is improved constantly by the introduction of new products in the marketplace. New products result from innovation, the force that can propel a company to the forefront of its industry. Dow Chemical, IBM, Texas Instruments, Eastman Kodak, Intel., Polaroid, and Xerox are just a few companies that have developed products which significantly improved or even revolutionized our quality of life. The twenty-five years following World War II saw the introduction of some of the most dramatic commercial innovations in history, including television, computers, the transistor, the integrated circuit, containerized shipping, microwave ovens, office copiers, and instant cameras. (See Figure 9-1.) All these products, and countless others, have come into everyday use and have changed the way we live.

While the development of new products is fundamental to improving our standard of living, some people believe that the rate and the quality of product innovation have peaked in the United States. Recent product developments and innovations have tended to build on the existing state of the art—video recorders and video games, microcomputers, pocket calculators, and digital watches are but a few examples. Reasons for this present lag in innovation include mushrooming government regulations and the soaring costs of research and development. Various studies indicate that the failure rate for new consumer products ranges from a low of 33 percent to a high of 80 percent, although new industrial products fare somewhat better. This means that only two to six or seven of every ten products marketed are accepted by consumers. The incentive to develop new products is hardly favorable, given the costliness of marketing misfires. Polaroid, for example, lost an estimated $250 million with its recent introduction of Polavision, the instant-movie camera system. Even modest failures cost millions of dollars. The graveyards of marketing are filled with products that died prematurely. They failed for many reasons, but mostly because there was no need for them; their marketers had failed to perceive correctly the needs and wants of consumers.

Take Green Giant's Oven Crock Baked Beans, which came already sweetened in the can. Green Giant executives thought they had a real winner. They conducted taste tests that showed they had a significant edge over bland pork and beans by a 3-to-1 or 4-to-1 preference margin. But Oven Crock was a disaster when it hit the market. Surveys later showed that people who ate baked beans typically added their own fixings to the bland variety and didn't want someone to do it for them. Green Giant found that, while consumers liked its beans, the product solved no real consumer problem.

The 1970s were particularly hard on new-product introductions; a combination of inflation and the recession left many consumers in the mood to avoid purchase of some old products and, in particular, to ignore some unproven new products. Polavision, mentioned earlier, represents a good example of a victim of these economic uncontrollables. When the instant-movie system hit the market in 1978, the

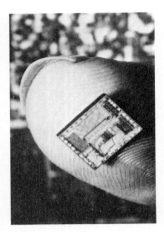

Figure 9-1   The tiny silicon chip stands as a symbol of the revolution in microelectronics, one of the most powerful product innovations of the past few years. (Courtesy Intel Corporation)

handheld camera was equipped with a bright light that tended to annoy small children. The images produced by the 8-mm film were exceedingly grainy and could be viewed on the 12-inch diagonal screen only if the viewer stood directly in front of it. And the show only lasted a mere 2½ minutes. Compounding its deficiencies was lack of sound. Those quality flaws, combined with a hardware cost of about $700, overwhelmed the cost-concerned consumer. By 1980, the marketing of Polavision was redirected to the much smaller industrial and business market, where it might be used in sales and medical applications, motion analysis for mechanical engineering, and sports training. (See Applications 9-1 and 9-2.)

Not only traditional, tangible products fail. The marketers of any new product may misread consumers and flop in the marketplace. Two examples are particularly striking, given their potential to satisfy demonstrated needs: the marketing of the World Football League and of the swine flu inoculation program. In the first case, marketers accurately determined that there was a demand for more professional football in such cities as Memphis and Birmingham—towns that turned out thousands for college football games. But what the league organizers overlooked was quality. In effect, the World Football League did not provide the level of satisfaction that consumers expected and demanded.

The swine flu program, however, fell flat because of an uncontrollable factor. In 1977, an epidemic of swine flu was expected to envelop the United States and take its toll on the citizenry. To counter this social problem, the federal government developed a marketing campaign to persuade Americans to be inoculated against this disease. Despite the demonstrated need for flu shots—along with all-out efforts in advertising, promotion, and distribution—people rejected the government's inoculation program. The product failed not because people did not fear swine flu, but because news reports raised doubts in their minds that the shots themselves were safe. The government marketers were unable to control consumers' perceptions of the new product, and it failed.

Marketing New Products

This matter of consumers' perceptions raises a question: Just what *is* a new product? Is a household cleaner with "ammonia added" a new product? What about the addition of a remote-control feature to a line of television sets? Is pay cable TV a new service or just plain old television? The marketing concept would lead us to define a new product as anything that consumers perceive as new. But that approach skirts the issue and loses sight of the fact that products can have varying degrees of newness. That is, new

Application 9-1
New-Product Success at Pillsbury—
"Sometimes You Win . . . "

A. C. Nielsen Company, an independent market research firm, found that more than 60 percent of all new grocery products test-marketed failed. If the products that bombed in the test kitchens are included, the failure figure rises to eight out of ten (80 percent).

One big winner, though, can compensate for all the losers, and Pillsbury came up with one of its biggest winners with Totino's Crisp Crust Frozen Pizza. Like almost all successful new products, Crisp Crust Pizza satisfied a specific want in consumers. "Crisp Crust is a textbook story of how you ought to do things," the vice president of frozen foods at Pillsbury told *The Wall Street Journal.*

In early 1976, Pillsbury conducted a series of focus group discussions around the United States. It handed out 2000 questionnaires designed to find out what consumers didn't like about frozen pizza. The response was outstanding: about 60 percent hated the crust, which was often compared to cardboard in taste. "We knew we could be head and shoulders above everybody else with a good crust," the executive said. So the crusty problem was

sent to the test kitchen, where Pillsbury chefs set out to develop an appealing crust.

Pillsbury decided to copy the fried pizza crust of Rose Totino, a Pillsbury vice president. But what worked in Totino's home kitchen couldn't be duplicated in Pillsbury's test kitchen. "The sudden heat from frying caused the dough to grow in *every* direction," said the vice president of R&D. "They came out contorted and all puffed up. When you're running a commercial frozen pizza operation, there's a carton at the end of the production line and the pizza has to fit into it."

Pillsbury spent months attempting to control the size, taking special precautions to keep the project a secret from competitors. For instance, when trial production runs were completed, frozen crust was shredded into tiny pieces and buried in a landfill.

Finally, the crust was perfect, and subsequent consumer taste tests confirmed that Pillsbury had a winner. "People liked it so much that they said, 'I don't believe it's frozen,' " said the R&D vice

president. In choosing an advertising strategy, Pillsbury decided to avoid the common mistake of promising the consumer too much. "Many advertising campaigns for frozen pizza said, 'We're as good as pizzeria,' " said the vice president of frozen foods. "That promise is totally unbelievable to the consumer." Pillsbury's ad campaign adopted a direct, realistic approach promising consumers that Totino's crust didn't taste like cardboard.

Crisp Crust pizza was introduced in August 1978, and keeping up with demand has become a problem. Crisp Crust has made Totino's the best-selling frozen pizza, garnering a 30 percent market share in 1980, up from 18 percent with the old Totino's pizza. With about $700 million of frozen pizzas sold each year, the success of Crisp Crust means additional sales of about $60 million a year for Pillsbury.

Source of data: "There's No Way to Tell If a New Food Product Will Please the Public," *The Wall Street Journal,* Feb. 26, 1980, p. 1.

Application 9-2
New-Product Failure at Pillsbury—
"... And Sometimes You Lose"

Painstakingly developed in Pillsbury Company's test kitchen, Appleasy was earmarked for market success, the result of three years of exhaustive research. It was cheap, easy to fix, and fast. It was also a "magnificent flop."

Pillsbury's search for an easy-to-prepare dessert began in June 1975. Ideas ranged from instant yogurt to Boston cream pie to a brownie with a fudge sauce topping. But the idea of a fruit dessert kept being repeated in focus group discussions with consumers.

The apple was chosen because "the majority of consumers eat and perceive apples to be good; you know, 'An apple a day keeps the doctor away,'" explained a marketing executive who joined Pillsbury after Appleasy had been

developed. Pillsbury's test kitchen, which is both a laboratory and a kitchen, developed a recipe using freeze-dried apples. All you had to do was add boiling water, stir, wait five minutes, and eat.

Consumer panels were mobilized to help pick a name. Hot Apple 'n Crunch was dropped in favor of Appleasy because Pillsbury marketers felt Appleasy better conveyed the convenience image. Following favorable consumer taste tests, Pillsbury in effect invalidated its testing by beginning to skimp on apples because their price had more than doubled. Appleasy was introduced in April 1978.

The market reaction? Not very many people liked it. There weren't enough apples, the cinnamon was overpowering, and the topping was too sweet. In an

effort to make the product both convenient and inexpensive, too much quality was sacrificed, and Appleasy went to the marketing graveyard.

"The product became less Appleasy and more starch and sugar," a Pillsbury marketer explained. He added, "A lot of people tried it but didn't come back for seconds. There was no problem with convenience, but lots of problem with quality." Exactly how much was lost on Appleasy, Pillsbury won't tell. The figure, however, was estimated to be well over $1 million.

Source of data: "There's No Way to Tell If a New Food Product Will Please the Public," *The Wall Street Journal*, Feb. 26, 1980. p. 1.

products can be classified on the basis of *how much* they differ from what is already on the market. Using that approach, new products can be categorized into three groups: real innovations, adaptive replacements, and imitative products. (See Figure 9-2.)

Real innovations are unique products for which there are true needs but no existing satisfactory substitutes. Such innovations include products that are quite different replacements for existing products serving existing markets. The handheld calculator is an example of a real innovation, since no substitute product can provide equivalent benefits. There are substitutes, of course, but only cumbersome ones that are often inaccurate—the human mind, which is often boggled by higher mathemat-

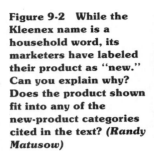

Figure 9-2   While the Kleenex name is a household word, its marketers have labeled their product as "new." Can you explain why? Does the product shown fit into any of the new-product categories cited in the text? (*Randy Matusow*)

ics; slide rules, which are difficult to operate, much less to find; and mechanical calculators, which are bulky and relatively slow. In this field, the calculator is an amazing innovation. And since its manufacturing cost is low, it is within the means of most consumers, from students to scientists to homemakers. The advent of this innovation in the marketplace spelled doom for mechanical devices like the slide rule.

Real innovations are not restricted to tangible goods or technical breakthroughs. They also come in the form of services. To cite one such service, one graduate student of marketing conceived of a clearinghouse for industrial products. Upon graduation, he formed Industrial Marketing Services (IMAS), a company that focuses on bringing buyers and manufacturers together. If a buyer is searching, say, for a special type of electrical component, IMAS uses a computer to locate manufacturers of that product and then relays the information to the interested parties. For this service, of course, IMAS charges a fee. The student saw there was a need, and he developed an innovative system to satisfy it.

Adaptive replacements also fall into the new-product category. These products introduce significant changes that allow them to replace existing products. One of the best examples is the ball-point pen, which has almost completely replaced the fountain pen, which many years earlier replaced the quill and inkwell. Similarly, more and more people are tossing aside their traditional ball-points for felt-tipped pens and erasable-ink ball-point pens, and a further replacement is sure to come eventually. Another instance of this process can be seen in the introduction of disposable lighters, which have made fluid-filled lighters all but obsolete, except as fine jewelry. Adaptive replacements abound in modern life. We wear synthetic clothing, dine on protein substitutes, and live in glass houses. Even ash baseball bats have been replaced by glass-and-nylon substitutes, and football is thriving on Astro-Turf.

Finally, there are *imitative products*, which are new to the marketer but not to the market. Thus, when Coca-Cola Company introduced Tab to the market, it followed the lead of Royal Crown Cola's Diet Rite. Later, Pepsi Cola (PepsiCo) added its own low-calorie entry, Diet Pepsi. And Perrier's market success as a pure bottled mineral water spawned competition by Poland Spring, Saratoga, Evian, and Ramlosa, to name but a few. The IBM computer is also an imitative product, since the first computer was developed by Univac. Similar examples can be found in the fields of processed and frozen foods, instant photography, office coppiers, disposable diapers, and countless household products. Generally, the more innovative a new product is, the greater the risk of failure and, simultaneously, the greater the expected profits. Imitative products are the least risky type of new product, but being "me too" items, the expected rewards are less as well.

From these examples, it may seem that the development of successful new products is a simple matter. But, even with careful planning, new products can easily end in failure. And products that are developed and marketed to satisfy some executive's whim or fancy have a high probability of failure. Again, the marketing concept tells us to focus on consumers, and new products are no exception. The desirable approach, of course, is to develop new products on the basis of sound, logical reasoning. The benefits that accrue from the successful introduction of a new product are far more likely to be realized if the marketer controls the product development process, rather than allowing it to happen haphazardly. The addition of a new product—called *diversification*—is not a simple matter, and it must be evaluated carefully by the company introducing it.

Patterns of Product Diversification

In Chapter 1, we listed a number of different activities performed by a firm: marketing, finance, personnel, research and development, purchasing, production, and accounting. While no one activity is more important than the others, production and marketing unquestionably have the greatest impact on a firm's costs and, ultimately, profits. Marketing is the function that determines which products a company ought to make; consequently, because of its veto power, marketing has enormous impact on the other managerial activities. The production function is also of great importance, because it usually represents a heavy financial investment by the firm. Unless a company develops the right plant and equipment, production quality cannot result, and consumers cannot be satisfied. Thus, most manufacturing companies revolve around production and marketing.

The introduction of a new product, or product diversification, thus centers on the business activities of production and marketing. Within these areas, there are four patterns of diversification, depending on whether the production and marketing activities *converge* (come together) or *diverge* (part). We will now look at four combinations of production and marketing and at their patterns of similarity (convergence) or difference (divergence).[1] The four patterns are:

---

[1]After Thomas A. Staudt, Donald A. Taylor, and Donald J. Bowersox. *A Managerial Introduction to Marketing,* 3d ed., Prentice-Hall, Englewood Cliffs, N.J., 1976, p. 208.

Convergent production and convergent marketing

Convergent production and divergent marketing

Divergent production and convergent marketing

Divergent production and divergent marketing

Convergent Production and Convergent Marketing

In this pattern of diversification, a firm adds new products by focusing on existing production facilities and the firm's existing marketing structure. As illustrated in Figure 9-3, products A, B, and C essentially use the same production facilities. Bic Pen Corporation offers a case in point. In the company's plant at Milford, Connecticut, common production facilities are used to make its lines of both pens and disposable lighters. Of course, certain machinery and processes differ, but both lines of products share the same raw material—plastic—and the packing equipment is the same for both. Finally, Bic's marketing program is essentially the same for both product lines. Thus, the production and marketing activities are convergent. Raw materials and purchased parts "converge" on the same production facilities, and finished products "converge" on common marketing facilities. With this pattern of diversification, a company builds on its existing assets—management talent, engineering abilities, production skills, plant and equipment, knowledge of the market and its behavior, brand image, and distribution channels. Thus, with a convergent pattern of production and marketing, a company introduces new products by exploiting its existing production facilities and existing marketing mix.

Toolkraft, a manufacturer and marketer of power tools located in the Northeast, is another example of this pattern. The company produces a full line of table saws, wood lathes, drill routers, band saws, drill presses, sanders, and radial saws. By using this convergent diversification strategy, Toolkraft plays on its existing engineering and production skills, its current raw material inventories, and its understanding of the market's needs, wants, and responsiveness.

The pattern of convergent production and convergent marketing is the most common diversification approach, for it carries fewer risks than other patterns. After all, with this pattern, marketers already know how to produce their products and how to market them. In addition, the pattern's economies of scale spread a company's

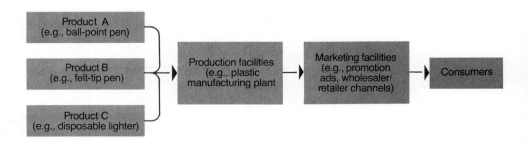

Figure 9-3 Convergent production and convergent marketing.

fixed costs over a large number of products. That is, by adding products which share existing production and marketing facilities, a company spreads its fixed costs of plant, machinery, sales expenses, and some advertising expenses over a larger number of products. The result is that the fixed cost per unit decreases. For example, if production machinery costs $10,000 and a company uses it to make 10 units of a product, the fixed cost per unit is $1000 ($10,000 ÷ 10). But if the company adds a product that uses the same machinery and produces 90 units of this new item, the fixed cost per unit drops to $100 ($10,000 ÷ 100).

Economies of scale in production are not the only savings realized from this diversification pattern. There are also economies in marketing. For example, when Campbell Soup Company advertises its Manhandlers brand of soup, it is also promoting its Chunky brand. Every time the Campbell name flashes before the eyes of the consumers, all products sold under that well-known name are promoted. This kind of brand name is called an ''umbrella'' because it embraces all products promoted under that name. The result is economies of scale in marketing; the fixed cost of advertising is spread over all products in the line. In the same way, whenever consumers see a display of Kellogg's Corn Flakes, they are likely to be reminded as well of Kellogg's Frosted Flakes or Kellogg's Rice Krispies.

The additional benefits of convergent production and marketing should not be overlooked. For example, materials may often be purchased more economically in large quantities. Thus, since Bic's pens and lighters are both made of plastic, the company can buy plastic crystals in bulk and take advantage of a quantity discount. Another benefit is that employment may become more stable, eliminating the costs and problems of hiring, training, laying off, and rehiring personnel. Convergent diversification also can help a company to avoid waste circulation in advertising, which occurs when an advertisement is seen by someone who is not a potential buyer of the product. With this diversification pattern, an advertisement for, say, a Toolkraft drill may be seen by people who are not interested in drills; but because the advertisement stresses ''high-quality power tools,'' someone with a need for a band saw may be attracted to the Toolkraft brand.

Convergent Production and Divergent Marketing

The second most common diversification pattern involves convergent production and divergent marketing (see Figure 9-4). This pattern is often found in industries that demand heavy capital investment for production—for manufacturing facilities and machinery. From the risk viewpoint, however, this pattern is considered less safe than a pattern of convergent production and convergent marketing. With this pattern, products A, B, and C all use the same production facilities, but they are marketed through different marketing mixes. Thus, marketing facilities are more flexible than production facilities, and they can be changed more easily and more quickly. After all, once a plant is built, it must serve for quite some time.

Weyerhaeuser Company provides a good illustration of convergent production and divergent marketing. Its product lines include wood products (doors, windows, house frames, clapboard shingling); paper products (cardboard boxes, milk cartons, fireproof insulation, Presto Logs); and garden mulch. All these wood-based products

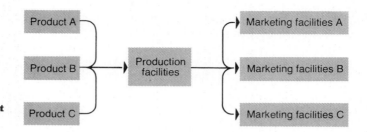

Figure 9-4 Convergent production and divergent marketing.

are produced with the same basic machinery in processes that reduce trees to various component parts. But the marketing requirements for each product are clearly different. One certainly does not advertise, price, and distribute 2 x 4's in the same way that artificial logs for the fireplace are marketed.

The diversification pattern of convergent production and divergent marketing tends to be found in capital-intense industries, since such firms want to maintain a high level of plant utilization in order to spread fixed costs. Thus, even though products may be marketed differently, they are added to keep the production processes rolling. This pattern is also found in industries that have seasonal or cyclical sales fluctuations. In this situation, a company will try to offset seasonal dips in sales by adding products that can be sold during slow periods. Toro provides an example of a company that has successfully expanded its line from seasonal to year-round products. Once essentially a marketer of lawn-care equipment, the company gradually added such new items as snow throwers and chain saws to its line, eventually increasing it to more than fifty products.

It must be recognized that the concepts of convergence and divergence are relative; that is, they occur in various degrees. Thus, the addition of a line of golf shoes to an existing line of street shoes is divergent in terms of marketing, but it is not so divergent as the addition of a line of industrial work shoes would be. This is because golf shoes, like street shoes, are purchased for style, whereas work shoes are purchased more for durability and protection. In other words, the marketing strategy for golf shoes is more like the strategy for street shoes than that for work shoes. Convergence and divergence, then, are relative, and the selection of a diversification pattern is less risky when the proposed product addition more closely matches existing product lines in terms of production and marketing requirements.

Divergent Production and Convergent Marketing

The third pattern, divergent production and convergent marketing, is shown in Figure 9-5. In this case, a firm uses different production facilities but similar marketing efforts. Spalding has this pattern; it produces golf clubs, golf balls, and golf clothes in separate production processes, but it markets all the products in roughly the same way—through sporting goods stores and pro shops. Because of the divergence in production, this pattern carries a higher degree of risk than patterns discussed earlier. But it allows a company like Spalding to trade on its marketing expertise. This pattern is useful for companies that have a strong family brand, such as General Electric,

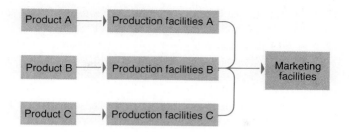

Figure 9-5 Divergent production and convergent marketing.

Westinghouse, and RCA. While the production requirements for toasters, clocks, television sets, blenders, mixers, radios, and other appliances differ greatly, all these products can be marketed through essentially similar efforts. In 1980, Frito-Lay, the PepsiCo subsidiary, diversified by purchasing Grandma's Cakes, a manufacturer of packaged cookies and cakes. The reasoning: Like salted snacks, baked goods are perishable impulse items that are best sold through the truck-to-store distribution system used by Frito-Lay. And Nabisco, the cookies and crackers company, is moving into salted snacks because of its strength in marketing. It is one of the few national food producers that deliver directly to supermarkets rather than using food brokers.

Colgate-Palmolive Company is another firm that relies on its marketing abilities in using this diversification pattern. As we have noted, the company manufacturers such diverse products as Pritt Glue Stick, Baggies plastic bags, Colgate shaving cream, Palmolive soap, Ajax cleanser, Fab detergent, and Colgate toothpaste, among many other products. While each of these products obviously requires a different or divergent production process, Colgate relies on its basic knowledge of consumers and on its established distribution system to market the various products effectively. Thus, Colgate converges on its marketing talents.

Divergent Production and Divergent Marketing

Figure 9-6 represents the final pattern, divergent production and divergent marketing. It involves different production facilities as well as different marketing facilities, and the pattern is used least frequently because it carries the highest risk and demands the greatest investment. In effect, each product addition is treated like a new and separate business. The pattern is used often by companies that are scientifically based and have a large research and development department. In such cases, laboratory discoveries can lead to opportunities to broaden the product line into totally new areas.

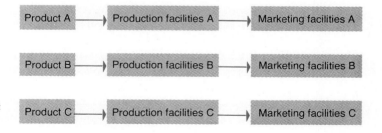

Figure 9-6 Divergent production and divergent marketing.

This pattern of divergent production and divergent marketing was quite popular during the late 1960s and early 1970s, as companies sought to expand their activities. One result was the development of *conglomerates,* vast corporate organizations with the resources needed to practice divergent production and marketing. For a time, when money was easy to borrow, the conglomerates were highly successful. But, as credit dried up and the economy slumped into a recession, many conglomerates crumbled. Essentially, they lacked the expertise required for the many businesses they were engaged in, and they did not have economies of scale to fall back on. The conglomerates that survive today—such as Litton, Textron, ITT, and Gulf & Western—have settled into various business areas which they now know how to manage. Litton, for example, makes typewriters as well as ships and microwave ovens; Textron manufactures watchbands and chainsaws; and ITT is involved with communications, bakeries, and hardware distribution, among other things. However, the pell-mell expansion of such conglomerates has apparently ended.

Although the concept of divergent production and divergent marketing was discredited somewhat by the conglomerate craze, prudent adaptation of this pattern makes sense in some cases. Sometimes, a divergent diversification becomes the jumping-off point for later convergence. For instance, as a hedge against fluctuations in car sales or any long-term decline in its automotive fortunes, Volkswagenwerke (VW) has begun an aggressive diversification program outside its traditional areas of product expertise. In 1979, the company began buying companies well entrenched in the office equipment and small computer market. Following its acquisitions, VW now markets typewriters, small business computers, copiers, calculators, and office supplies. The objective: to become a major force in the "electronic office of the future." "We have the basic ingredients for the office of the future, and we will be adding to them," said the president of a major VW subsidiary.[2]

Rationales for Diversification

None of the four diversification patterns explained here can be called "wrong," nor can any of them ensure automatic success. But a company's chances for success improve when it has a clear rationale for diversification—some logical reason for adding new products. In other words, products should not be added in a random, haphazard way. Basically, there are two sources of logic for diversification: the market rationale and the supply rationale.

The Market Rationale

The *market rationale* focuses on knowledge of the market as a basis for convergence in adding products. The idea is for marketers to broaden their conceptualization of what it is they are satisfying. Here, what may initially seem a divergent addition may in the end be rather convergent. By returning to the benefit concept and asking what benefit the product provides, marketers can get a broadened base from which to add all sorts of products. In short, they must look at their market and determine what they

---

[2]"VW's Latest Model: The Office of the Future," *Business Week,* March 3, 1980, p. 61.

are really selling. For example, American Telephone & Telegraph is not selling telephones but telecommunications. Its advertising slogan is "The Knowledge Business." And IBM's slogan "IBM: Helping to put information to work for people," reflects that it is an information company, not merely a seller of commercial equipment. Its product lines range from computers to software (programs) to typewriters to office copiers—all products that provide the benefit of information.

Colgate-Palmolive Company, as we have noted, uses divergent production but convergent marketing. This, too, is based on a market rationale, on knowledge of the market. The company is as comfortable marketing glue sticks as it is marketing plastic bags or toothpaste. Production facilities are different, but marketing activities are common.

The market rationale was also used by Levi Strauss & Co. in deciding to add a complete line of casual shoes with the slogan "Levi's for Feet." The company was confident that the nation's teenagers, young adults, and even older customers would want shoes to match their Levi's jeans, jackets, and shirts. Levi Strauss feels that the markets for both its jeans and the new line of shoes are essentially the same, having similar wants and needs, and open to the same marketing approach. Thus, Levi's successful entry into divergent production was based on a sound market rationale. As a further convergent addition, Levi Strauss added a line of men's sport and casual socks.

The Supply Rationale

Rather than use the market rationale as a basis for adding products, some companies —having a heavy investment in their source of supplies—use a *supply rationale*. Thus, they focus on their material supplies rather than consumers. Weyerhaeuser Company again provides a good example. In fact, Weyerhaeuser calls itself "The Tree Growing Company." Its sole corporate objective is to utilize fully every ounce of its source of supply—the tree. Consequently, it uses the lumber for door frames, windows, and the like—but it also uses the bark for garden mulch, the cellulose of the tree for insulation, the wood chips for particleboard and paper products, and the sawdust for making fireplace logs. Nothing is left unused, and this policy has led the company to serve many divergent markets.

Wolverine Worldwide, the producer of the famous Hush Puppies brand of casual shoes, sees itself as a marketer of brushed pigskin. Such a supply rationale has led the firm to add lines of handbags, western-style hats, and boats, work shoes, leather gloves—even an upholstery fabric made out of pigskin suede.

The idea, then, is that product diversification should be based on sound reasoning and should rely on some asset that a company already has. This may be knowledge about the market (market rationale). In adding products to the line, there is no right or wrong pattern, but a company should base its decision on a solid rationale and then exploit its strengths.

In some cases, both the market rationale and the supply rationale can be used in product additions. In 1977, the world's number-one maker of skis, Skis Rossignol, turned its attention toward tennis rackets as a diversification move. "According to a survey in the United States," reported Mr. Laurent Boix Vives, president, "80 percent of those who ski also play tennis. . . . The tennis rackets, which will use technology that we have developed in producing skis, are a logical expansion of our activities."[3] That technology, an injection method, uses pressure to mold glass fiber, polyethylenes, and various compounds into the final product. By 1981, Rossignol was marketing a broad line of rackets using all suitable materials—wood, metal, and graphite—and aimed to hit everyone from the middle of the market (at about $40 a racket) to the top (at $200 each). (See Application 9-3.)

Stages of Product Development

In the past few pages, we have examined the ways that product additions can be categorized. We have learned that new products have the best chance for success if they are developed to play on a company's existing strengths. In other words, sound logic is perhaps the most important ingredient for successful product diversification. While a market rationale or a supply rationale can provide a semiscientific method of determining what types of products should be developed by a company, the actual creation of new products is an entirely different matter.

Bringing New Products to Life

New products are conceived in many different ways. In the past, lone inventors like Alexander Graham Bell or Eli Whitney were often responsible for discoveries that led to new products. But such individual efforts are becoming less and less common. While independent inventors can still be credited with many breakthroughs, product development today rests more and more with large corporations than have the resources to devote to investigation and development. In fact, the United States Patent Office reports that 78 percent of new patents now go to corporations and to the government. Contrast this with the situation in the 1950s, when nearly half of all new patents were issued to individuals.

While companies and the government have "out-patented" individuals, foreign innovation outpaces that of the United States. In the 1950s, 82 percent of the major inventions brought to market were developed in this country. By the late 1960s, that figure had plummeted to 55 percent. Japan and West Germany, in particular, lead the world in pumping money into R&D seriously threatening America's dominance of world technology. From 1973 to 1979, foreign citizens obtained more than one-third of all patents issued by the United States government. America's competitive edge rests on a resurgence of innovation throughout its ranks. (See Figure 9-7 for a look at the decline in R&D spending in this country.)

---

[3]"France: A Ski Champ Tries Its Hand at Tennis (Rossignol)," *Business Week,* Nov. 15, 1976, p. 58.

Application 9-3
Using the Supply Rationale—Products Carved out of Soap

Procter & Gamble, the king of packaged consumer goods, has begun an attack on new markets. Many of them are institutional and commercial arenas, a far cry from its usual stomping grounds in the nation's supermarkets. It's quite a move for a company whose name is linked solidly with household products, consumer marketing magic, and advertising thunder. New products from P&G are now in such fields as prescription drugs, synthetic foods and food ingredients, and supplies for nursing homes.

New-product sales are expected to hit 20 percent of the company's revenues by the mid-1980s. These products broaden dramatically the focused market orientation of the company whose superior consumer marketing strategies are held in awe by competitors. This new orientation has stemmed from slow sales growth in its three consumer product groups: laundry and cleaning items (Tide, Joy, and Comet, for example); personal care products (Ivory soap, Crest

toothpaste, Scope mouthwash, and Pert shampoo); and traditional foods (Crisco oil, Duncan Hines cake mixes, and Folger's coffee). But its diversification strategy is not without a sound basis—P&G is utilizing its expertise in oils, fats, and pulps to diversify into faster-growing industries.

The company claims that all its new products have been spawned in some fashion from soap-making technology. Since the early 1900s, when P&G combined cottenseed oil with animal fats in its soap, the company's expertise has converged on two bases: oil and fats, and high-quality pulps. "This company has never left its base. We seek to be anything but a conglomerate," said P&G's chief executive.

P&G's long-standing products are the result of an ongoing evolution. The development of detergents and cleaners came logically from what the company knew about soaps. And soaps and detergents led to the development

of Prell and Head and Shoulders shampoos and Crest and Gleem toothpastes. Oil technology provided Jif peanut butter. The roasting and processing techniques learned in Jif led logically to P&G's 1963 acquisition of Folger's coffee. And pulps provided the convergences for Charmin and White Cloud toilet papers, Bounty paper towels, Puffs facial tissues, and Pampers diapers.

The same basis for convergence is there for the new nonsupermarket products. P&G's birth-control product relies on an ingredient in detergent that loosens dirt from clothes. And research on detergent "builders," chemicals halting calcium among other impurities in wash water from adhering to clothes, resulted in P&G's prescription drug Didronel, which prevents abnormal bone growth by tying up calcium in the body.

Source of data: "P&G's New New-Product Onslaught," *Business Week,* Oct. 1, 1979, pp. 76–82.

Some companies realize the importance of innovation and use it to their competitive advantage. Large technology-based firms sink huge sums into research. Bell Labs spent $1 billion on research in 1979—mostly to develop fiber optics—whereby information is moved in rays of light traveling through slender glass fibers rather than through electric currents moving through bulky cables. IBM spent $1.25

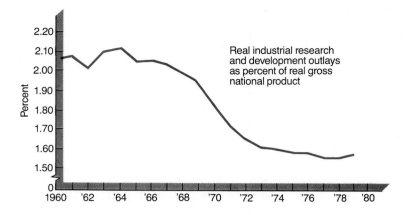

Figure 9-7   The decline in industrial R&D investment, shown here as a percentage of real GNP. *(Adapted from "A Diminished Thrust from Innovation,"* **Business Week,** *June 30, 1980, p. 61)*

billion in the same year and has become the first company to perfect the mass production of a silicon memory chip small enough to pass through the eye of a needle—yet able to store 64,000 bits of information. Such large-scale R&D investment is rare, however. But such innovation provides the basis for a marketer to offer a better bundle of utility to its marketplace. Competition is a major force in America to push back the frontiers of innovation. Unfortunately, this competitive push is countered by social and governmental constraints (regulations for ecological and consumer safety, for instance, reduce entrepreneurial incentive), the high costs of research (small enterprises cannot afford large-scale R&D), business emphasis on short-term, rather than long-term return on investment (managers often resist investing in research when they will not be instantly rewarded for it), and capital shortage (the high cost of borrowing funds).

Still, the facts remain: The key of America's future as a world trader lies in innovation, and the door to marketing competitive superiority rests with improved technology. Let's see how new products come to be.

Occasionally, a company's best research efforts are topped by sheer luck. In 1878, White Soap was one of twenty-four varieties produced by Procter & Gamble. One day a worker on his way to lunch forgot to turn off the steam power in a blending machine and an unintended amount of air was put into the mixture. Customers who received the accidental batch began to call for more of "that soap that floats," and Ivory Soap came into being. Buoyancy was a real advantage, for in 1878 wash water piped in from rivers was often murky and a sunken cake hard to find. Harley Procter, incidentally, felt he needed a dramatic slogan for advertising as well as an interesting brand name. The slogan emerged when chemical laboratory analysis found the product to be "99$\frac{44}{100}$ percent pure"; the name came from a favorite Bible passage of Procter's: "Out of ivory palaces whereby they have made me glad." (See Figure 9-8.)

But most new products today emerge from within the corporate structure, and their development is extremely costly. Polaroid, for instance, spent $600 million to

Figure 9-8   Ivory Soap has been going strong for over one hundred years, and it only began to float by accident! *(Randy Matusow)*

bring its SX-70 camera to market. By 1981, RCA had sunk $200 million into developmental costs for its video disc SelectaVision. And CBS spent $40 million over five years to develop a video disc, only to drop the entire project because of difficulties in development.

Organizing for New Products

The responsibility for new-product introduction has been handled in four organizational ways. Many companies operate with a *product* or *brand manager* framework. P&G, Kimberly-Clark, and Johnson & Johnson are examples. Each manager has complete responsibility for one product or brand—determining objectives, developing strategies, setting prices and advertising budgets, and working with the sales force. In many such organizational structures, the product or brand manager is responsible for creating new-product concepts and working them through the new-product development process. Other companies form *new-product committees,* generally composed of top management in many functional areas of the firm. These committees come together for the sole purpose of developing new ideas; once the task is complete, their members return to their regular company positions. New-product committees tend to be slow in making their recommendations. Other organizations set a *permanent, full-time new-product department* to bring new products on line. This department usually is a staff function with sizable power. A newer organizational concept is the *venture team.* At larger companies like Dow Chemical, Monsanto, and Westinghouse, groups of managers, each with a specialty needed in new-product development, are formed on a more permanent basis than new-product committees and charged with the responsibility of bringing a specific product to market. The team combines needed resources and expertise, such as product design, engineering, capital management, market analysis expertise, accounting representatives steeped in cost analyses and capable of determining return-on-investment estimates, and marketing specialists. Such a group usually is separated from regular duties and reports directly to top management.

Successful and even unsuccessful new products do not come about easily or cheaply. Their development involves a process that can be divided into the following seven stages, which we will examine next:

1 New-product strategy and idea generation

2 Screening

3 Concept development and testing

4 Business analysis

5 Product development

6 Test marketing

7 Commercialization

New-Product Strategy and Idea Generation

The first step in product development is new-product strategy and idea generation, the stage in which efforts are made to develop a large pool of possible product ideas. This is not always a formal exercise. As we have said, it often is a continuing process that involves many different groups. On the other hand, some companies do formalize idea generation by maintaining departments or committees to develop new products. R. J. Reynolds, for instance, has established a management group that is charged with the single task of dreaming up new cigarette brands. Once a brand proves itself in test marketing, it is assigned to another group within the company.

The sources for new-product ideas are many and varied. Even customers may write letters to companies suggesting new products, and the sales force also feeds new ideas to management. One study of technological innovation in two industries found that in 74 percent of the 137 innivations studied, the source of the innovation was the customer.[4] Many companies also encourage employees—particularly those on the production line—to come forth with ideas, often offering cash awards for good suggestions. Such incentives led a Sears employee a number of years ago to develop a new type of socket wrench that has proved very successful, and a General Motors production-line employee invented a machine that automatically seals a car's windshield to its body. In a case at Procter & Gamble, a loving grandfather, also a P&G engineer, was changing the diapers of his first grandchild. Deciding there had to be a better way, he brought the idea to his associates, and the concept of Pampers disposable diapers was spawned. And, of course, the research and development laboratories are a fertile field of innovation; scientists and technicians often make discoveries that lead to new products. Then, too, top management—the people closest to a company's overall situation—often come up with new-product ideas. Finally, one relatively new source of product ideas is the consulting firm which specializes in idea generation.

Basically, though, new products result from inspiration, perspiration, and a specific effort to develop ideas. One widely used method for generating ideas is called *brainstorming,* an approach which recognizes that new ideas are often a mixture of several ideas, some of them old. Brainstorming facilitates the development of new ideas through group discussion sessions in which a specific problem or goal is set forth and group members are encouraged to generate as many ideas about it as possible. Practicality is not important in a brainstorming session. Often, the wilder the idea, the better. As ideas start to flow, one will spark another, and within a short time hundreds of new ideas may be brought to the surface. Only then will they be analyzed in terms of practicality—which is the second step in product development. (See Application 9-4.)

A 1981 survey[5] of over 700 companies and more than 13,000 new-product introductions has found that companies recently have begun combining the idea generation step with an up-front analysis of the company's entire corporate business strategy and new-product strategy. Here, new-product ideas better reflect the

---

[4]Eric von Hippel, "Has a Customer Already Developed Your Next Product?" *Sloan Management Review,* vol. 18 (Winter 1977), p. 63.

[5]*New Products: Best Practices—Today and Tomorrow,* Booz-Allen & Hamilton, New York, 1982.

Application 9-4
Innovation—Spawning New Products as a Way of Life

In 1976, when a Texas Instruments employee, Paul Breedlove, suggested a talking calculator, his colleagues enjoyed a good laugh. But, unlike most companies, TI did not shelve Breedlove's idea. Instead, research began, and two years later "Speak and Spell," a learning aid for children, was introduced. Without the original idea and TI's willingness to take risks, a profitable product line would not have evolved.

To study ideas, TI has developed a program called IDEA. This acronym stands for identify, develop, expose, action. There are forty IDEA representatives at TI, and their task is to search out ideas and fund them. "We also have more structured innovation at TI. But you don't know when

(Courtesy Texas Instruments)

you might be missing a trick, where there might be a guy with an idea that has the trappings of a genius," a TI executive told *The Wall Street Journal*.

While TI has a reputation for innovation, the Gillette Company, staid and conservative in many ways, relies on innovation to dominate the razor and pen markets. The latest new pen product to emerge from Gillette is the brainchild of Henry Peper. His invention is the erasable ink pen. Like Breedlove of the talking calculator, Peper had to overcome a few belly laughs, but by 1980 the Peper erasable pen had captured 23 percent of the $190 million ball-point pen market.

Sources of data: "How Four Companies Spawn New Products by Encouraging Risks," *The Wall Street Journal*, Sept. 18, 1980, pp. 1, 24; and "Mr. Peper Ignores Experts to Make an Indelible Mark on Penmanship," *The Wall Street Journal*, Sept. 29, 1980, p. 25.

company's overall goals. This firmer understanding of the purpose of new products has greatly reduced the mortality rate for product ideas. In 1968, an earlier study[6] found fifty-eight new-product ideas were required to result in one successful new product. In 1982, the mortality rate was reduced to an average of seven ideas per successful new product.[7]

Screening

The second stage in new-product development is screening. Once a large pool of ideas has been generated—by whatever means—their numbers have to be pruned to a manageable level. Typically, developers must establish a method for choosing which

[6]*Management of New Products*, 4th ed., Booz-Allen & Hamilton, New York, 1968.
[7]*New Products: Best Practices—Today and Tomorrow.*

TABLE 9-1 Product Screening Checklist

Product addition criteria	Relative weight, A	1	2	3	4	5	6	7	8	9	10	Rating, A × B
Production criteria												
1 Must utilize existing machinery	.8				X							3.2
2 Must utilize existing labor force	.7					X						3.5
Marketing criteria												
1 Must complement existing product lines	.5									X		4.5
2 Must be promotable through television advertising	.5									X		4.5
3 Must be few direct competitors in existence	.4							X				2.8
4 Must be distributed through existing retailers	.2								X			1.6
											Total:	20.10

Product idea rating, B

Rating scale: 3.1–13.1 = poor; 13.2–22.1 = fair; 22.2–31.0 = good.

Minimum rating for further consideration = 8.7.

Adapted from Barry M. Richman, "A Rating Scale for Product Innovation," *Business Horizons,* Summer 1962, pp. 37–44.

ideas they want to examine more closely. There are obvious problems in the screening stage: Good ideas may be dropped, or bad ones may be adopted. One formal way to minimize such problems is to establish a checklist, as shown in Table 9-1. The first column lists various criteria that must be satisfied before an idea for a new product will be considered for development. Then, in the second column, each of these criteria is assigned a weight to indicate its importance. Thus, the marketers in this instance believe that utilization of production facilities (weighted at .8 and .7) is more important than the convergence of marketing facilities. (.5, .5, .4, and .2). The next step is for management to rate each product idea on a scale of 1 to 10, depending on how well it meets the various requirements. For example, these managers feel that some additional machinery (a rating of 4) and some additional labor (a rating of 5) will be needed to put this product into production. Yet, this product alternative appears to converge more on the marketing requirements, with ratings of 9, 9, 7, and 8 on the final four requirements. The last step is to multiply the ratings by the weight and sum up all the requirements to get a total score for the product idea. This score can be compared against a benchmark to see whether it meets the company's requirements. In this example, the product idea is fair (20.10); while it may remain under consideration throughout later stages of product development, its low overall score makes it subject to careful examination.

Of course, not all companies use such a formal process to screen ideas for new products. (See Application 9-5.) But even the mental steps that one goes through to evaluate ideas are similar to this approach. That is, the ideas are measured against some kind of evaluative criteria, and only ideas that meet these standards are considered for further development. As we saw in Chapter 3, the L'eggs division of

Application 9-5
The New-Product Development Process— Making Ideas Come Alive

A rich market has evolved in recent years. Companies have begun to contract with outside consultants to come up with new products. New-product consultants paved the way for such products as latex paint, frozen pizza, a dog shampoo, and the Wear-Ever popcorn popper.

At the Southwest Foundation for Research and Education, such oddities as tearing down and immediately rebuilding brand new General Motors engines, setting fire to stark white rooms, and training pekinese dogs to smell guns are commonplace—in the interests of research.

Typical of new-product consultants is Foster D. Snell Research, a part of Booz-Allen & Hamilton Inc. When Snell receives an assignment, it first agrees with the client company on objective criteria that the product must meet. Established in the beginning are relevance to existing product lines and the amount of money the company is willing to invest in manufacturing equipment. Setting

clear criteria focuses the project and presents the consultant from running off wildly on tangents.

As might be expected, product ideas often come from analysis of products already manufactured by the client company or from technology possessed by the company. To get the product ideas rolling, Snell gathers together staff members with backgrounds relevant to the assignment. After two hours of free-flowing discussions, it is not unusual for a hundred ideas for products to emerge. From these, the number is pared to six or eight. These ideas are then transferred to the actual development stages, ranging from models to consumer testing. In the end, perhaps only one will be marketed.

From start to finish, as much as eighteen months (a relatively short period in product development) will pass and Snell will charge between $20,000 and $50,000 for developing an extension to an existing product

line. For a major new product, the fee often tops $1 million.

"It is expensive—no doubt about it," said the president of Church & Dwight Co., New York manufacturer of Arm & Hammer products. "To enjoy direct control, a company often would be better off doing the research work itself. But if the work is outside your expertise, you can get faster results with an outside consultant," he contends.

Snell developed Arm & Hammer's nonpolluting detergent from start to finish in only nine months, which was "just fantastic," the official adds. The project sharply boosted Church & Dwight's sales, and the company later commissioned Snell to develop its successful noncaustic oven cleaner.

Sources of data: "Success Comes Hard in the Tricky Business of Creating Products," *The Wall Street Journal,* Aug. 23, 1978, p. 1; and "Industry, Government Are Farming Out More of Their Research," *The Wall Street Journal,* April 28, 1981, p. 1.

Hanes Corporation, for example, has established five criteria for determining whether a new product should be developed for a national market. Thus, the company will add a product if it (1) can be sold through food and drugstore outlets, (2) is purchased primarily by women, (3) can sell for less than $3, (4) can be packaged and displayed distinctively, and (5) will constitute at least a $500 million retail market not already dominated by one or two major producers. Having established this system for evaluating new-product ideas, L'eggs develops only products that meet these criteria. And at P&G, marketers evaluate new-product ideas by answering three questions:

1 Is there a *real consumer need* for the product idea?

2 Does P&G have the scientific and technological ability to develop the product?

3 Is the potential market for the product sufficiently large to promise making a profit?

Concept Development and Testing

The third stage in product development is concept development and testing. Throughout the stages of idea generation and screening, developers are working only with a product idea, a general concept of what the product might be. Now, through development and testing, they try to make that general concept more specific. For example, if they have determined that they will produce a new candy bar, three questions might be asked to make that general idea more specific:

1 *Who will buy the new product?* (A candy bar can appeal to children, adults, the elderly, or all three groups.)

2 *What is the primary benefit of the new product?* (A candy bar may appeal as a sweet; as a high-energy snack; or as an emergency food for diabetics.)

3 *Under what circumstances will the new product be used?* (A candy bar may be offered to children as a rewarding treat; or may be seen as a meal substitute; or it may be used by diabetics suffering from too much insulin.)

On the other hand, the developers might decide to produce a sugar-free candy bar, which would also cover many markets—the youngster who considers it a candy, the adult who is seeking low-calorie energy, and the individual concerned about cavities and tooth decay.

One of the outcomes of concept development is to provide the research and development team with some specific direction for developing the actual product. At Bristol-Myers's Clairol appliance division, for instance, a new-product team was working with the concept that ultimately produced Foot Fixer, a foot-bath massager that relaxes tired feet. In the concept development stage the team produced a complete consumer-product description—look, feel, size, price, features, etc., which minimized trial and error by R&D. The new-product team provided design sketches of the shape and size of the unit and specified the temperature requirements for the water heater, the intensity and type of massaging action, the specific product claims to be sustantiated, and the safety requirements.

After a specific concept has been developed for the new product, the next step is concept testing. Now the market comes into play, since the purpose of this stage is to test consumers' reactions to the specific product idea. This can be accomplished by using a verbal description or a picture of the product and asking for consumers' candid reactions. At this point, the developers want to know how they can improve the product idea even further. Most important, they want to know who will buy it.

Business Analysis

The next step in product development is the business analysis stage. The marketers must project costs, profits, and the return on investment for the new product if it were placed on the market. In short, they must determine whether the product will meet their objectives, which are often purely financial. This exercise will indicate whether it is feasible to market the product.

Business analysis is not a haphazard process; it is a detailed, realistic projection of both maximum and minimum sales and their impact on the company. For some products, such as another candy bar, marketers can use existing sales data to guide them. But with a new product for which sales data do not exist—as was the case for the marketers of the first trash compacter—only an estimate can be made. For instance, P&G, in developing Pampers, estimated that there were more than 15 billion diaper changes a year in the United States. In either case, sales projections alone are not enough. Marketers also must have some estimate of what it will cost to manufacture and distribute the new product. Until these costs are determined, it is impossible to forecast profits.

Thus, in the first four stages of product development—from idea generation through business analysis—the marketers are involved with information gathering. If doubt arises anywhere along the line, the product idea could well be shelved, before a great amount of time and money are invested in the product.

Product Development

If the first four stages of product development have not raised serious doubts about the feasibility of marketing the product, the specific concept finally enters the research and development stage, in which the idea is given a concrete, tangible form. Now the product is developed into something more real than just a picture or a drawing, and a prototype or model will be constructed. (See Figure 9-9.) During this stage, the marketers also seek a brand name to match the idea or concept; they develop different packages that suit the product; and they begin to identify the major elements of the marketing mix.

Gillette Company uses a unique approach to test shaving products during this developmental stage. Some thousand subjects in a dozen countries, including women, are asked to use the company's products in Gillette facilities or at home and to rate them in terms of comfort and closeness of shave. In addition, numerous testing devices are used, including high-speed cameras and electronic gadgets that measure

Figure 9-9 General Mills evaluates its products in the Betty Crocker test kitchens in Minneapolis, Minnesota. *(Michelle Vignes/Photo Researchers)*

whisker length to within millionths of an inch. Plastic casts of shaved faces are used to compare the closeness of shaves, and technicians measure and weigh the amount of stubble removed. All these data—along with reports from physicists, statisticians, and metallurgists—are fed into computers that store some fifty years of accumulated knowledge about every aspect of shaving. Such is the effort that goes into the development of products—even of disposable razors. Of course, not all marketers are prepared or willing to undertake such an extensive approach to product development, but Gillette's testing procedures illustrate the importance the company attaches to this stage of product development.

Test Marketing

The sixth stage in product development is test marketing, the process by which marketers attempt to measure the reactions of potential consumers of the real product. In a test market, efforts are made to isolate a particular group of buyers that will represent the market at large. The reactions of this test market will indicate how the product will be accepted by the overall market. In the last step, product development, research focuses on the more technical question of whether the product does what it is supposed to do. In this step, research tests the reaction of the marketplace.

After nine months of research at P&G, the product development team's first tangible product to meet the disposable diaper concept was a comfortable, reasonably inexpensive paper pad that was inserted in plastic pants. The then unnamed product was given to mothers in Dallas, Texas, to try. The result was an overwhelming "thumbs down." The product was sufficiently comfortable and absorbent, but P&G's

marketers forgot that in the heat of Dallas, mothers ignored plastic pants, not wanting to subject their babies to sauna bath treatment. Thus, it was "back to the drawing board"—but with almost certain product failure averted.

Most companies realize that it is preferable to spend $750,000 in a test market than to spend $20 million for failure in a national market. Even so, there are valid reasons for skipping the test-market stage. For example, Gillette Company introduced its Good News disposable razor without benefit of test marketing, simply because it knew that Bic was planning to introduce a similar product. The decision was a good one, in that the early introduction of Good News allowed Gillette to get a jump on its French competitor.

Usually, however, test marketing is critical. It allows marketers to obtain information that represents consumers' reactions to the product. In addition, a test market often provides guides for improving the marketing strategy, such as which type of advertising to use, or how to devise point-of-purchase displays. Occasionally, a test will also reveal distribution problems. The point is that marketers are actually advertising and distributing the product in a test market as they would when they go national. If they find, for example, that retailers won't give the product the necessary point-of-purchase space, they can correct the problem for a minimal expense before encountering it on a national basis.

Before entering the test-market stage, marketers must answer five main questions:

1 *How many cities or areas should be used in the test?* Studies have found that most marketers test new products in four cities or fewer.

2 *Which cities should be used for the test?* The idea, of course, is to find a test market that represents the total market. In this respect, test marketing is like sampling. Marketers seek cities that resemble the entire nation in terms of such demographics as age, income, and education. Some cities that are often used in test marketing are Columbus, Ohio; Grand Rapids, Michigan; Des Moines, Iowa; Savannah, Georgia; and Syracuse, New York.

3 *How long should the test market be conducted?* Testing ranges from a few months to years. A lot depends on the repurchase period, since an accurate reading of the product's acceptance cannot be attained until buyers make repeat purchases. The duration of a test also depends on the competition. If competitors introduce a similar product, the marketers might be forced to rush their own product to market. And, of course, cost is another consideration affecting the duration of a test market.

4 *What type of information should be gained from the test market?* Besides learning whether the product will be accepted by consumers, marketers also are testing their advertising, point-of-purchase materials, distribution plans, and so on. The test should provide information about consumer response to all these marketing-mix variables.

5 *What will be done with the information gathered from test marketing?* If results are excellent, the product may move directly into national distribution. If the test results are good but flaws are discovered, the marketers may want to correct their problems and run another test in another city. Finally—and this is not rare—if the product fails in a test, it will probably be dropped. This is what Gillette decided to do when it introduced a digital watch into thirteen cities. Although the venture cost the company millions of dollars, test results convinced Gillette that the watch would have a poor showing in the national market.

Occasionally, marketers will run into hostility among customers when test marketing ends. After Green Giant test-marketed frozen vegetables in pouches with butter sauce in San Francisco, the product was taken off the market until it could be prepared for national distribution. But people liked the product so well that they berated supermarket managers, demanding that they order it. Green Giant was forced to take out newspaper ads to explain the situation.

Marketers must always remember that the test market is intended to represent the entire market. Thus advertising, public relations, sales activities, and other items of the marketing mix must also represent the national marketing program. If any marketing activities cannot be reproduced in the national market, they would not be used in the test market.

Instead of test marketing in cities, some companies prefer to use panel tests. In this case they bring together groups of buyers—who again represent the target market—and have them test a product. Philip Morris, for instance, shuns test markets in favor of "taste test" panels, where large numbers of small groups of smokers use brands in the development stage and offer their reactions. Generally, panel tests offer two advantages: They shield new products from competitors, and they cost less than test marketing. Usually, however, they are not so reliable as test marketing, because they involve fewer people, and only certain kinds of people are willing to sit on panels. Panel testing provided Philip Morris with both a gigantic success and a gigantic failure. Its Merit brand of cigarettes was an instant winner, but later the company introduced Cambridge, an ultra low-tar brand, and it flopped in the marketplace. (See Application 9-6.)

Commercialization

The final stage of product development is *commercialization*. Now the marketers put the product into full production. Commercialization represents a major investment, since production facilities must be prepared to manufacture the product. Miller Brewing Company, for instance, invested $247 million to build a highly automated plant in Albany, Georgia, to begin brewing Miller Lite.

Usually, companies do not enter national distribution all at once. Rather, they roll out the new product, going from one geographic area to another. For example, U.S. Pioneer Electronics Corp. brought its video disc to market in 1980. It began by test

Application 9-6
Product Development— "Testing, 1, 2, 3 . . . "

If you think some of the television programs you see are terrible, imagine the ones that the networks scrapped. Programs offered by the networks are carefully tested in front of audiences, and generally, if they don't receive approval, they, aren't offered to the TV public.

The networks periodically gather live audiences to watch TV pilots. CBS does most of its own testing, while NBC and ABC use the services of Preview House, a controversial testing theater that many believe can make or break a show.

At Preview House, detailed demographic data are gathered from the audience prior to seating. Each member of the audience is allowed to vote via a small dial beside the seat which records either "very dull" or "very good." Each scene is judged by the audience. The theater seats are wired to a central computer and the computer matches each demographic profile with the participant's response producing "instant" cross-matched data. From these data, the networks are able to determine program appeal to different demographic groups.

Network executives maintain that this system provides them with insights. "It gives us valuable audience reaction to story lines, pacing, characters, and general likes and dislikes of a new show," said one network vice president of research.

Source of data: "Testing of TV Shows and Movies Is Gaining Adherents and Critics," *The Wall Street Journal,* Jan. 12, 1981, p. 1.

marketing its disc unit in four cities: Syracuse, Dallas–Ft. Worth, Minneapolis–St. Paul, and Madison, Wisconsin. Every 60 to 90 days thereafter, Pioneer added four additional cities. National distribution was not accomplished until 1981.

The addition of each distribution area requires heavy doses of introductory advertising. Surveys show that the food processing industry spends more than 4 times as much to advertise the introduction of a product as it does to advertise an established brand. It's not unusual for marketers to mount a multimillion-dollar advertising campaign to introduce a product. Thus, the Kellogg Company spent $20 million to introduce its adult-targeted cereals—Most, Honey & Nut Corn Flakes, Smart Start, and Raisins, Rice & Rye.

Clearly, new-product development represents a tremendous investment to a company, and most of the responsibility rests with the marketers. Throughout all seven stages of product development, they must make every effort to converge on existing strengths. A solid understanding of consumers' wants and needs is the key to successful product introduction.

Looking Back

In this chapter, we have reviewed some of the essentials necessary for the development of successful new products. To be successful means to pay close attention to the steps in the product development process. Before we move on to managing the product over its life, be sure you have firmly grasped the following main points.:

1   Innovation is the key to improving society's standard of living.

2   Product failure rate is very high.

3   There are varying degrees of product newness.

4   Benefits accrue to the marketer from controlling diversification rather than from letting it happen in a random fashion.

5   The reasoning behind diversification strategies can be applied to initial product development as well as to the addition of products to existing product lines.

6   The more convergent the pattern of diversity, the less risk will there be.

7   Each of the four patterns of diversification may be appropriate—success depends on the soundness of the reasoning behind the choice of a pattern.

8   The market rationale and the supply rationale provide reasonable bases for convergences in adding products.

9   Most new products are the result of extensive hard work and the expenditure of large amounts of time and money.

10   Many companies go through a seven-step process in new-product development.

11   There are many sources for new-product ideas for a company.

12   The business analysis step can be undertaken throughout the first three steps.

13   Product development is when the costs begin to get heavy.

14   Test marketing is a critical step in the product development process, but one that circumstances may force a firm to skip.

Key Terms

If you aren't sure what each of the following words means, look back at the text. Numbers refer to pages on which the words are defined. Additional information can be found by checking the index and the glossary at the end of the book.

real innovation 281
adaptive replacement 282
imitative product 282
diversification 283

Questions for Review

1 Identify the three types of new products and define each briefly.

2 What type of company does best under the pattern of divergent production and convergent marketing?

3 How does the market rationale differ from the supply rationale for adding new products?

4 Who are some important sources of idea generation? What is a specific method for producing ideas?

5 At what stage in the new-product development process do costs really begin to play a significant part?

6 What are the five major decisions in the test-marketing stage?

Questions for Thought and Discussion

1 Faced with such a high rate of new-product failures, why do you believe marketers work relentlessly at creating new products for the marketplace?

2 When we talk of the four patterns of diversification, we use the words *convergence* and *divergence*. Explain why you think it is important to speak to these words in relative terms.

3 To reduce its reliance on the costly cocoa bean, Hershey Foods Corporation has diversified into the macaroni and coffee business. What pattern of diversification has the company followed?

4 How might Gaines, the pet food marketer, test a new-product concept for a dog food?

Suggested Project

Generate at least three ideas for each type of new product noted in the chapter, and present these ideas to a class pool which has similar contributions from other members of the class. Then, as a group, try to prune your pool down to a total of three ideas for each type of new product. It will then be each student's task to take these nine product ideas through the concept development and testing stages and present his or her findings in written form to the instructor.

Suggested Readings

Berg, Thomas L.: *Mismarketing: Case Histories of Marketing Misfires,* Doubleday, Garden City, N.Y., 1970. An enticing sampling of some major well-known product failures, this book looks at why they were failures and how marketers can learn from their mistakes.

Crawford, C. Merle: "Strategies for New Product Development," *Business Horizons,* vol. 15 (December 1972), pp. 49–58. The author discredits the notion that a defined strategy for new-product development may discourage innovation and defines guidelines for developing new-product development strategies.

————: "Marketing Research and the New Product Failure Rate," *Journal of Marketing,* vol. 41 (April 1977), pp. 51–61. Nine possible explanations are offered as to why product failure is so high given marketers' sophistication in marketing research.

Hill, Richard M., and James D. Hlavacek: "Learning from Failure: Ten Guidelines for Venture Management," *California Management Review,* vol. 20 (Summer 1977), pp. 5–15. The authors recommend that organizations employing the venture-team approach to new-product development use a venture charter to define the group's functions, operating procedures, and boundaries.

Hisrich, Robert D., and Michael P. Peters: *Marketing a New Product: Its Planning, Development, and Control,* Benjamin/Cummings Publishing Co., Menlo Park, Calif., 1978. This comprehensive textbook focuses on all the activities involved in the process of bringing a new product into the market.

Riescz, Peter: "Revenge of the Marketing Concept," *Business Horizons,* vol. 23 (June 1980) pp. 49–53. The author examines the impact on innovation of the modern-day shift away from creativity of the R&D staff.

Rothberg, Robert R. (ed.): *Corporate Strategy and Product Innovation,* Free Press, New York, 1976. Thirty-six articles and the editor's essays examine the relationship between corporate strategy and product innovation in both consumer and industrial firms and focus on providing a clear and comprehensive guide to the execution of these vital corporate activities.

Spitz, A. Edward (ed.): *Product Planning,* 2d ed., Petrocelli/Charter, New York, 1977. This collection of readings provides great insight into the planning for new products as well as the stages in the new product development.

Chapter 10

Product Management

Looking Ahead

The past two chapters have looked at the nature of the product and at how new products are developed. But once a product is commercialized, marketers face the critical job of ensuring that it really does provide satisfaction to the market it is intended for. Again, a product's benefits must match the wants and needs of its consumers. In this chapter, we will examine how that matching process—called *product management*—is accomplished throughout the life of a product.

Key Topics

The major goal of product management: matching consumers' wants and needs

The importance of continuously adjusting a product to meet changes in the market

Some common terminology used in product management

The nature and stages of a product's life cycle

Some problems and issues that marketers face in managing a product throughout its life cycle

Chapter Outline

Product Management: A Matching Process
Needs and Wants Shift
Changing the Product
The Terminology of Product Management

The Product Life Cycle
Stages in the Product Life Cycle and Marketing Strategies Used
Additional Aspects of the Product Life Cycle

Some Product Strategy Problems
Too Much Variety, Not Enough Assortment
Reduced Economies of Scale
The Dangers of Full-Line Competition
Trading-Up and Trading-Down Problems
Blurring the Product Image
Brand Overextension and Cannibalism
Ineffective Product Positioning
Undesired Planned Obsolescence
Product Pruning Problems

Looking Back

In the last chapter we explored the steps that a new product takes to reach its market. Once on the market, however, a product is not left alone. It demands constant attention and management from the time it is conceived until it is finally withdrawn from the market. Thus, marketers must adjust the product throughout its life to match the ever-changing demands of the marketplace. The task is called *product management,* and we will now examine its goals, challenges, and strategies.

Product Management: A Matching Process

The basic goal of product management is to ensure that a product *matches* the wants and needs of consumers in its market. Too many marketers make the mistake of thinking that consumers feel and act as they themselves do and share the same wants. In fact, many marketing failures can be traced to such invalid assumptions on the part of marketers. In the excitement of introducing a new product, it's natural to hope that others will be equally excited by it. But professional marketers must not be carried away by their own enthusiasm. They must rely on the tools of their trade—on marketing research, especially—to match the product to consumers' wants and needs. The job of managing a product, then, is one of constantly monitoring the market and adjusting the product to meet the market's needs and wants. The better the product matches these needs, the more successful it is likely to be. Let's see what is involved.

Needs and Wants Shift

Although matching may sound like a simple exercise, it is, in fact, a complex objective to achieve. Even when matching is successful, marketers do not develop just one product and then throw it on the market for eager consumers to buy. The hitch, as we have seen in Chapters 6 and 7, is that the buying public is fickle—its wants and needs change constantly, and marketers have to recognize these shifts and adjust the product to match them.

Consider marketers in the automobile industry and their quest to match car buyers' needs and wants. Throughout the 1950s and 1960s, Americans thought of their huge, gleaming automobiles as status symbols, and marketers were confident that they had provided a good match between product and consumer needs. But then came 1973 and the oil crunch, which resulted in soaring gasoline prices. Since cars consume a large percentage of the nation's petroleum supply, car owners suddenly had to worry whether there would be a continuing shortage of gasoline. The price was getting too high to maintain their four-wheeled status symbols. Automobiles changed from symbols of prestige to means of transportation as car buyers said they wanted small, economical vehicles. Detroit's marketers responded to the market's needs and began to design energy-efficient but unexciting compact models.

But, in the automobile industry, such design and the subsequent retooling of production processes could not be accomplished until 1976. And before these

Figure 10-1 While the
auto-buying public kept
auto manufacturers
scrambling throughout
the 1970s, buying
patterns of the early
1980s have convinced
the public and the
marketers that small *is*
beautiful. *(Courtesy
General Motors
Corporation)*

compacts—Chevrolet Chevettes, Dodge Colts, and Mercury Bobcats—could be
rolled onto the showroom floor, car buyers once again shifted: they wanted their
bigger cars back. Consumers had forgotten the impact of the energy crisis and the
importance of gas conservation. They wanted fun and excitement to replace the
gloom and doom of inflationary times. Detroit again had to respond. This time only
minor changes were made to the smaller subcompact cars in an attempt to convey the
feeling of luxury, fun, and excitement. Chevrolet's Monza Spyder was given a jazzy
paint job and an optional V-8 engine, Ford's Mustang II Cobra was offered with what
Ford called a "very strong" optional V-8 engine that reportedly hit 60 miles an hour
about a second sooner than the Chevy Spyder, and Chrysler's boldly painted Road
Runner, a version of the normally sedate Plymouth Volare compact, was equipped
with the most powerful engine Chrysler was then making.

The love affair with "big" continued on into 1979. Rocketing demand for large
cars was so great that General Motors considered converting a compact-car plant to
build full-size Oldsmobiles. Ford Motor Company rationed V-8 engines because
demand was so insistent that it could hardly keep up. Detroit executives worried about
how they would sell the millions of small cars on which billions in new tooling had
been spent. Recalls Ford's president, "We all faced the specter of forcing the American
people to buy something they hadn't indicated they wanted to buy in large
quantities."[1] (See Figure 10-1.)

By 1980 that fear had disappeared. The revolution in Iran and the subsequent
upward surge in gasoline prices resulted in sudden death for big cars. In 1980, the
market share of big cars shot down from 42 percent to 33 percent. While Detroit's
small cars were on their way, the quantity was far below the demands of consumers.
And it would be 1985 before United States auto makers could expand their 4-cylinder
engine capacity to 40 percent of output. Meanwhile, smaller imported cars captured
record market shares as consumers swarmed to their showrooms.

---

[1]"U.S. Autos: Losing a Big Segment of the Market—Forever?" *Business Week,* March 24, 1980, p. 78.

In satisfying the fleeting passions of American car owners, marketers have had to change their product constantly—and in an industry that requires a long lead time to adjust production facilities. While the matching process is generally less complicated in other industries, all marketers must monitor their market's needs constantly and then adjust the product to satisfy consumers.

Changing the Product

Figure 10-2 Silly Putty competitors have identified children's fascination with a favorite superhero or cartoon character and have aimed their putty products at that want. The result is a drop in market share for the original Silly Putty. (Randy Matusow)

Matching the product to its changing market can be accomplished in a number of ways. One method is to change the *tangible features* of the product, as the automobile manufacturers do. Recreational vehicle makers also change their product to match shifting wants and needs. The increase in gasoline prices and the energy-conservation concern forced the recreation vehicle industry to turn out motor homes and travel trailers that were lighter and more fuel-efficient. In 1981, Winnebago Industries began producing a diesel model that is 30 percent lighter and 50 percent more fuel-efficient than earlier models. Coachman Industries reduced its 20-foot travel trailer to 1860 pounds from 3500 pounds, allowing it to be towed by the lighter, more popular cars of the early 1980s.

The manufacturers of men's underclothing have also changed the tangible features of their product to match consumers' desires. At one time, undershorts were available only in white. However, as marketing research indicated that men would purchase more exciting underclothes, the manufacturers adjusted their product to meet an expanding market; now men's shorts and undershirts are available in a variety of colors, fabrics, and designs. In a business that has grown less than 2 percent annually since World War II, this product change resulted in a 40 percent sales increase over five years. As an underwear buyer for J. C. Penney put it: "With everything new going on, men just got tired of plain white, just as people got tired of white sheets and pillow cases."

An improved match between the product and consumers' needs can also be accomplished by changing the *subjective features* of the product. With this adjustment approach, the tangible features of the product remain essentially the same, but the product's intangible features are altered. Take Binney & Smith Inc.'s Silly Putty, for example. Silly Putty's market share slipped to about 50 percent in 1981 from about 60 percent at its height. Competitors brought out equivalent putty products but called them Bugs Bunny putty, Spiderman putty, Hulk putty, and other names suggesting well-known figures. Said a Binney & Smith representative, "Kids don't really care about our putty, they care about their favorite characters." (See Figure 10-2 and Application 10-1.)

The Terminology of Product Management

Whether marketers change the tangible characteristics of a product or its subjective features, the goal is always to improve the product's ability to satisfy consumers' needs. To understand the matching process better, we will examine how it is conducted over the life of a product. But first we need to look at some important aspects of the product and its management.

Application 10-1
Finding a New Twist

Celebrities have long made good dollars by lending their faces and names to products—e.g., James Garner for Polaroid, Don Meredith for Lipton Tea. The celebrity often gives a product a measure of instant recognition which is difficult to obtain through conventional advertising.

Not only are real-life actors and sports figures capitalizing on the trend, but cartoon characters, too, are making their owners rich. The Pink Panther touts Safeco Insurance, and Bugs Bunny appears on behalf of a toothpaste.

Licensing is big business. Manufacturers across the nation are looking to cartoon characters and other licensable properties to give new or existing products that special competitive edge. And often, licensing proves to be a fantastically effective marketing tool, to the delight of those companies venturing into new markets. Meanwhile, other firms have seen licensed competitors gnaw away at their well-known name-brand products and market shares.

An example of what a cartoon character can do for a

(Courtesy American Greetings Corporation)

product is illustrated by the success of Strawberry Shortcake, a property of American Greeting Corporation, a part of General Mills.

Strawberry Shortcake is a little girl in a red dress and a pink bonnet. Her image appears on hundreds of American Greeting products—cards, party hats, pajamas, and gift wrap. Retailers have found Strawberry Shortcake a financial blessing. In her first

year, Strawberry Shortcake saw her products ring up sales of $100 million.

What makes her different from other cartoon creatures is that she was developed as one of scores of other characters whose images adorn American Greeting products. And she was a character without a past, with no storyline behind her. But her creation was not by accident. Research prior to her debut showed that consumers have great enthusiasm for strawberries.

"There's been nothing like it since *Star Wars* hit the toy industry," said a General Mills executive. "It's our Snoopy, it's our Raggedy Ann. We expect it to be around for years." By the end of her second birthday, Strawberry Shortcake had racked up a total of almost $2 billion in sales.

Sources of data: "Little Miss Was Born to Sell," *The New York Times,* Feb. 10, 1981, p. F-1; "Licensing Boom Envelops U.S. Industry as Makers Search for a Competitive Edge," *The Wall Street Journal,* June 1, 1981, p. 29; and "The Selling of the Smurfs," *Newsweek,* April 5, 1982, pp. 56–59.

Product Mix and Product Line

The various products that a company offers to consumers are called its *product mix.* For example, Coca-Cola Company's product mix includes coffee, citrus beverages, fruit drinks, plastics, and wine as well as carbonated soft drinks. Then, within the product mix, there are broad groups of products that are similar in terms of their use or their tangible characteristics. These are called *product lines*. In Coca-Cola's case, one product line, carbonated soft drinks, includes Coke, Tab, Diet Coke, Fresca, Sprite, Fanta, Mr. PiBB, Mello Yello, Ramblin' Root Beer, and "sugar-free" Ramblin' Root Beer.

Wide (Variety) and Depth (Assortment)

The product mix can be classified further in terms of how many different product lines it contains. If it includes a large number of product lines, it is called *wide* or *broad*. But if the product mix contains only a few product lines, it is considered *narrow* or *limited*. In addition, a product mix is called *deep* if a large quantity of variations are offered within a basic product line. Finally, the width of a product mix is also referred to as the *variety,* while the depth of the mix is also called the *assortment*. While Coca-Cola's soft-drink line is six product lines wide, it is nine products deep. Thus, the matching process can focus on changing an existing product line, on adding or deleting products from a product mix, or on changing the assortment offered. (See Figure 10-3.)

These important terms of product management can be clarified by considering the various products offered by watch manufacturers. The product line includes all kinds of time-keeping devices, from the traditional jeweled-lever movements of Swiss watch fame, to electric watches that are run by batteries, to quartz-crystal watches, to the digital watches powered by microchips. A given watch manufacturer may choose only a few of these alternatives for its product mix; these make up the width, or variety, of the product line—the variations on the basic product offered. In addition, within each of the product lines offered by a manufacturer are many variations of style, price, size, color, and so on; these variations make up the depth, or assortment,

Figure 10-3   The product mix at General Foods. (*Adapted from Carl McDaniel, Jr., Marketing: An Integrated Approach, Harper & Row Publishers, New York, 1979, p. 173*)

	Coffee	Desserts	Cereals	Household products	Pet foods	Other grocery products
	• Maxim freeze-dried coffee • Maxwell House coffee (regular) • Instant Maxwell House coffee • Instant Sanka coffee • Sanka coffee 97% caffein free	• Jell-O gelatin dessert • Jell-O pudding and pie filling • Jell-O instant pudding • Dream Whip whipped topping mix	• Grape-Nuts, 40% Bran Flakes • Raisin Bran, Sugar Crisp • Corn Flakes, Fruit Cereal • Honeycomb, Oat Flakes	• SOS soap pads • Satina ironing aid • Tuffy plastic mesh ball (dishwashing aid)	• Gaines Meal • Gaines Biscuits • Gaines Bits • Gaines Variety	• Kool-Aid soft drink mix • Log Cabin syrup • Tang instant breakfast drink • Baker's cocoa • Baker's instant chocolate flavor mix • Good Seasons salad dressing mixes • Good Seasons Open-Pit barbecue sauce • Good Seasons Shake 'n Bake seasoned coating mixes for chicken and fish

Width of product mix →

Depth of product mix ↓

of the product line. For instance, watch manufacturers may choose thousands of variations in terms of assortment: stainless steel cases, gold cases, or plastic cases; large, massive designs or tiny delicate ones; thick cases or super-thin ones; ornate, jeweled cases and bands, or simple, elegant designs; faces with arabic or roman numerals, or faces that display digital numbers. All these alternatives and more can be adjusted by watch manufacturers to match their market's needs and provide satisfaction to consumers. And since they can also change either the tangible or the subjective features of these product alternatives, the job of product management is truly staggering.

There are different types of markets, depending on the degree of match that exists between a product and its consumers' needs. A market that has a perfect match is called a *core market;* in other words, the product exactly matches its consumers' wants and needs. In a *fringe market,* however, the degree of match is not exact; consumers have to compromise somewhat in accepting the product. For example, a buyer is looking for a digital watch in the $10 to $25 range, with a reliable brand name, in a black casing—and one that also gives the seconds as they pass. In the store, all digital watches in the $10 to $25 range, with reliable brand names and indicating the seconds, can be found in silver casings only, not in black. The buyer may compromise because the product *almost* matches what is wanted. But if the watch is not available in the buyer's preferred price range—i.e., if it can be found only in the $50-and-up range—no match exists, and the watch will not be bought. When a product fails to match any of the consumer's wants or needs, the market is said to have a *zone of indifference;* no match exists, and the product will not be purchased.

Obviously, marketers try to design products that match the core market's needs. But when the core market is small, they attempt, instead, to provide as close a match as possible for a sufficiently large fringe market so that the product will be economically feasible to produce and market. Thus, product management is based on the marketing concept, for the matching process is aimed at satisfying consumers in either the core market or a substantial fringe market.

Given all the choices available to marketers, it's clearly important that they make decisions by focusing on consumers. While there is no substitute for imagination in the marketing process, even the best ideas must be filtered through sound principles and careful decision making. Our earlier chapters have explained what's involved in this ongoing process. Now it's time to examine results in the marketplace. What happens to a product during its life in the market, and how is it adjusted to match consumers' wants and needs?

The Product Life Cycle

Another concept that is critical to effective product management is called the *product life cycle.* As the term suggests, marketers see products, variations of products, and brands as going through a life cycle that begins with commercialization and ends with

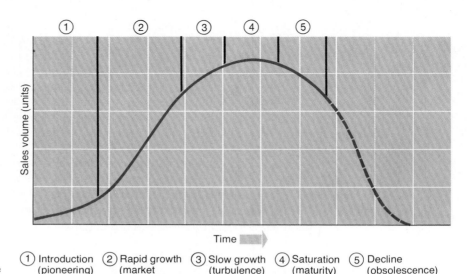

Figure 10-4 The five stages of the product life cycle.

① Introduction (pioneering) ② Rapid growth (market acceptance) ③ Slow growth (turbulence) ④ Saturation (maturity) ⑤ Decline (obsolescence)

removal from the marketplace. Note that this concept is not restricted to what traditionally is considered a product. For instance, brands—like Tide, Dr Pepper, and Right Guard—also go through a life cycle, as do such product classes as detergents, soft drinks, and deodorants.

The product life cycle is defined in terms of two dimensions, *sales volume* and *time.* As shown in Figure 10-4, the sales volume of a product changes over time. This change points to the basic importance of the product life cycle, for it provides marketers with indications of how they should fashion or adjust the marketing mix to best meet the wants and needs of consumers. We will now examine the stages in the product life cycle and various marketing strategies that are appropriate.

Stages in the Product Life Cycle and Marketing Strategies Used

As shown in Figure 10-4, there are five distinct stages in the product life cycle:

1 Introduction, or pioneering

2 Rapid growth, or market acceptance

3 Slow growth, or turbulence

4 Saturation, or maturity

5 Decline, or obsolescence

Introduction

The introduction or pioneering stage comes first in the product life cycle. It is marked by a very slow rise in sales (see Figure 10-4). Sales increase, but only very slowly—mainly because the product has not yet been accepted by its market. During this stage, there are very few competitors. Initial sales tend to be to high-income groups and to the core market—consumers who either have more discretionary income or find the product exactly what they want. Since the price of new products is often high (until the economies of mass production come into play), these are the consumers who can afford the new entry. The introduction is also a time for making frequent improvements in the product, since problems often arise that could not have been foreseen during development stages. In addition, an improper understanding of the market may make it necessary to adjust the product. Such adjustments can range from a major overhaul of the marketing mix to a minor change in style, color, or price.

The video disc product presents a good example. Introduced by Maganavox in late 1978, the TV attachment transmits movies and other fare to television set owners from a disc. The video disc was initially priced at $695. By 1981, only 35,000 units had been sold. Undoubtedly, sales were hurt by a string of technical problems: a speck of dust made the disc players stop and pause, or high humidity warped the record. The company would not realize lower costs and consequently lower prices until 1983, when an improved system would be ready. Yet, the potential of the market began to attract competitors. By late 1981, two others, an RCA model and a Japanese model marketed by General Electric, came on the market at $499.95 and $500 respectively.

Because of the uncertain response any new product meets when it is introduced, companies are reluctant to commit a major investment to production equipment. Instead during the product's introduction, only a limited quantity will be manufactured, using experimental production methods. In the food industry, a company will often contract with another firm to produce the product initially. Then, if sales in the introduction stage go well, the company will invest in its own machinery to produce the item in large quantity. In the video disc industry, the key to sales is the breadth and availability of disc programming. Yet, without knowing consumer acceptance, few in 1981 were willing to invest the $20 million required to build a disc-pressing plant.

The introduction of a new product is also marked by high advertising costs, since marketers strive to reach large audiences during the introductory stage. With many consumer goods, this advertising often involves buying time on high-rated television shows, which is extremely expensive. RCA accompanied its 1981 video disc entry, SelectaVision, with a $22 million advertising and promotion campaign. A month-long, prime-time network saturation television campaign was used with the theme "RCA brings the magic home."

In this stage, advertising and other communications are focused on building primary demand; that is, demand for the product class rather than for brands within the product class. Marketers must build acceptance of the concept of microcomputers in the home for maintaining Christmas card lists, family budgets, and favorite recipes; motorized bicycles as an alternative to cars; and the taping of TV shows for later viewing.

New products also present a distribution problem. Often, wholesalers and retailers are not willing to take a chance on new products, and marketers must be willing to assist them with advertising or promotional discounts. In a way, new products first must be marketed to those who will distribute them to consumers. Bic provides an interesting approach to solving this problem. When it first introduced its now-popular low-priced pen, Bic found that retailers didn't want the 19- to 29-cent pens cluttering up their shelves. They refused to carry the pens until they first saw some consumer demand. So the president of Bic had his friends, relatives, and employees bombard the stores with requests for Bic pens.

From a marketing strategy viewpoint, the major objective in this stage is to develop widespread product awareness and induce trial of the product by buyers. The product should be designed with a limited number of models to reduce confusion and allow easy learning about its nature and quality. Quality, with its requisite production-quality control, is critical to ensure repeat purchase. There are two pricing strategies open to marketers. One strategy is to price the product high to recover costs more quickly and allow for later price declines. Sony understood this approach with its Betamax video recording machine. It introduced a model at $2295, and sales were 2000 to 3000 units a month. Then, early the next year, it dropped the price to $1300, and sales quickly climbed to 5000 units a month. The other strategy is to price low to gain large buyer acceptance—as Bic has done with its pens. Price reductions in the form of discounts may also be necessary to obtain distribution outlets. Promotion activities should all create general awareness. Extensive personal selling to distributors, heavy distribution of free samples, large amounts of publicity, and rather substantial introductory advertising are all likely communication avenues to pursue in the introductory stage. With the Betamax product, Sony launched a $2 million advertising campaign, the largest ad campaign ever put behind a single Sony product.

Rapid Growth

During the growth stage of the product life cycle, sales rise at an increasing rate as consumers accept and demand the product (see Figure 10-4). Of course, not all products reach this stage; many die during their introduction. But if the product is successful at matching and meeting the needs of consumers, many competitors will soon enter the market with imitative products. As a result, the first major product adjustments tend to be made during this growth stage. Even functional aspects of the product may be changed. Additionally, prices may be decreased as production savings are realized and passed on to consumers.

In terms of distribution, more outlets are desired for the product during its growth stage, and additional retailers are sought. It is easier to obtain outlets during this stage, since the market's acceptance of the product has been secured. But the distribution front is also affected by intense competition during the rapid-growth phase. Obviously, most retailers cannot handle every line offered to them. In the case of panty hose, for instance, few retailers can afford to carry Hanes, L'eggs, and No Nonsense brands as well as the others available. Instead, the retailer settles on a few brands—generally the ones most often demanded by customers. Therefore, marketers must compete in order to have their product carried. Frequently, companies pay for retailers' space; this is common in the cigarette industry, where vending machines account for 20 percent of sales. Cigarette manufacturers pay the vending machine owner a monthly fee to carry their brands.

In the rapid-growth stage, the strategy objective is to build a strong market and distribution niche. The product line is expanded to appeal to more specialized segments, while at the same time any deficient product attributes are eliminated. With addition of product lines, price lines are also used to satisfy many segments' tastes—from low price to premium price. For example, after Polaroid moved into the rapid-growth stage with its SX-70 camera, the company introduced a stripped-down version, the SX-70 II; still later, the SX-70 III was introduced at an even lower price. While all three camera models provided the same major benefit, their price and appearance were different. This product strategy of Polaroid illustrates how the product line becomes flexible to match new market segments as they arise and are identified. With the intense competition for distributors, prompt credit for defective parts, as well as help for retailers in customer service, becomes very important. Promotional emphasis is to create brand preference (selective demand) rather than product acceptance (primary demand). It is also wise to promote the brand to middlemen (intermediaries) during this stage. Advertising is oriented heavily toward the mass media to get maximum exposure for the product. Meanwhile, the marketers must continue to gather information; they must look for new market segments and missed opportunities in the market, and they must keep an eye on all competitive activity. (See Application 10-2.)

Slow Growth

In this stage, sales continue to climb but now at a decreasing rate. Mass markets are reached, as just about everyone who wants the product has one. Marketers turn to annual models to secure replacement sales with existing owners. Product modifications tend toward style improvements. Profits are more difficult to obtain for both intermediaries and manufacturers as prices fall further in this stage. In fact, many competitors, eager to get into the market in the rapid-growth stage, find themselves unable to compete with lower prices and less demand. This stage is characterized by a great shakeout of the less capable competitors. The digital-watch market experienced just such a situation. The dizzying pace of price cutting, led by Texas Instruments (TI), forced a shakeout of competitors. Prices dropped in just five years from $2000 to $10. As a result, in 1977 there were virtually only three companies left in the business—TI, Fairchild, and Timex. And certainly, this stage finds few, if any, new competitors entering the digital-watch market. Gillette was discouraged in 1977 from doing so as TI continued its price reductions.

While marketers' attention is focused on establishing a market position during the rapid-growth stage, the emphasis of marketing strategy shifts during slow growth. Now the objective is to maintain and strengthen the marketing position and build loyalty among consumers and intermediaries. This is where the competition of the slow-growth stage pays off, for the number of competitors has been reduced, and weak, imitative products are driven from the market. Product lines are pruned by both producers and dealers to eliminate items that perform poorly, and the focus on product improvements is intensified to solidify the product's position in the market. Prices tend to drop further during slow growth, in an effort to attract consumers who found the product too expensive during earlier stages. Pricing also becomes a form of promotion during this stage, since the market grows less responsive to advertising, personal selling, and other sales promotion activities. Dealers become very important, too, because the product must be available at the retail level in order to gain new sales.

Application 10-2
Entering the Rapid-Growth Stage: Feeling the Flush of Success—But for How Long?

(Randy Matusow)

A new form of soap appeared nationally in 1980 and took the marketplace by storm. Minnetonka Inc.'s Softsoap, a liquid soap with a pump, was not taken seriously by the big soapers, and was considered little more than a fad. But by the end of its introductory year, Softsoap had run up $35 million in sales, and it held nearly 6 percent of the soap market. Minnetonka was initially formed in 1964 as a uniquely packaged,

specialty soap company. Its sales had climbed slowly up to $16 million by 1978. Founder Robert Taylor, pleased with the market acceptance of a new specialty product, the Soap Machine, decided to use the pump concept to break into supermarkets instead of the company's outlets of specialty stores, gift shops, and department stores.

After market testing in a dozen cities in late 1978, Softsoap rolled out nationally in early 1980. To gain supermarket distribution, food brokers were lined up. Without any similar product around, shelf space was rather easily obtained. And, appealing to retailers was a higher profit margin on this product than on bar soap.

Competitively priced at $1.49 for its 10.5-ounce bottle, Softsoap displaces five to nine soap bars, depending on usage rate (the cost of five to nine bars would be $1.65 to $2.20). Minnetonka spent $6 million on promotion in 1980, but increased that to an astounding $30 million in 1981 (spending equal parts for advertising and promotion through 200 million coupons). And in 1981, Minnetonka introduced a heavy-duty liquid soap called Worksoap.

By mid-1981, the established

soapers began to enter the market. Andrew Jergens launched a lotion-enriched competitor; Jovan's Yardley of London assaulted Softsoap with a $5 million campaign for its English Lavender; and Go-Jo Industries kicked off a $13 million-plus promotion campaign to support its LeSoap Liquid soap (packaged in 16-ounce pump bottles priced at $1.79 to $1.89), Tuffsoap, its heavy-duty alternative, and Showerup, a liquid shower and bath soap. About fifty small companies jumped into the fray in this low-technology field.

At the start of 1982, sales began leveling off as liquid soaps hit just under 8 percent of the total soap market. Some retailers began to take some slow movers off their shelves. Big guns, such as Procter & Gamble and Armour-Dial, had not yet entered the contest, perhaps expecting the market soon to have had its day in the sun.

Sources of data: "Is the Bar of Soap Washed Up?" *Business Week*, Jan. 12, 1981, pp. 109–116; "New Brands Start Attacks on Softsoap," *Advertising Age*, June 1, 1981, p. 91; and "Liquid Soap's Bubble May Be Bursting," *Business Week*, March 1, 1982, pp. 24–25.

During turbulence, or slow growth, the promotional emphasis shifts away from consumers, and advertising is aimed at dealers. Efforts to satisfy parts and service requirements increase. Sales promotion displays to assist dealers are also important. Now marketing intelligence focuses on product improvements, on new market opportunities, and on revising or refreshing the promotional themes used.

By 1981, the running-shoe industry was facing a slow- or no-growth year. The number of runners had leveled off at 20 million and the running shoe had lost some of its fashion magic. Competitive pressures forced Brooks Shoe Manufacturing Company to trim its work force. Etonic, a Colgate-Palmolive subsidiary, furloughed workers at its three plants. A shakeout of smaller running-shoe manufacturers seemed imminent, leaving the field to four or five strong competitors—Adidas, Brooks, New Balance, and the industry leader, Nike, with its 50 percent market share.

Saturation

During the saturation stage of the product life cycle, sales level off (see Figure 10-4). Trade-ins dominate the market, and everybody seems to have the product. Now sales are very sensitive to changes in the economy; they rise and fall according to basic economic forces. The number of competitors has tended to become stable by this point. The market is known, and it has grown as much as is likely. As the less effective competitors disappear from the scene, the market becomes highly segmented, and promotional distinctions must be designed for each segment. Because the market is so well defined, competition is intense during this stage, and firms must be more conscious of costs if they are to stay in business. That is, their opportunities for profits from new sales are severely limited, and they must rely on cost savings to increase profits.

Physical distribution is also very expensive and complex during saturation. The product is available in numerous and varied outlets throughout the market, and it is expensive and time-consuming to ensure that each outlet has the correct annual model, has sufficient repair parts to service existing products, and can deal with traded-in older models. By this point, too, the promotional emphasis has shifted away from advertising toward personal selling and sales promotion at the dealer level. And, since the market is saturated, it's unlikely that new competitors will undertake the expense and difficulty of introducing a new entry.

During the saturation stage, there are two main strategies for marketers to consider—the defensive and the offensive. With a *defensive strategy,* the goal is to hold the product's market share against competing products and to keep the product category from being eroded by substitute products. This strategy recognizes that the best defense is a good offense. By making some modifications in the marketing mix, marketers can gain additional sales, rather than lose ground to competitors.

With a defensive strategy, however, the focus is on cutting production costs and on eliminating weakness in the product or services. Dealers are extremely important during the saturation stage, and their selling effort is obtained through dealer-oriented promotional activities. Since the responsiveness to promotion is generally weakened at this point, pricing becomes more important. While promotion is still used to maintain consumers' and dealers' loyalty to the product, it is oriented more toward dealers than consumers. Coca-Cola, facing a diminished demand for its soft drinks induced by a baby boom, in 1981 began shifting dollars from national media into point-of-sale displays and price promotions designed to increase the loyalty of its 550 bottlers that produce, warehouse, distribute, sell, merchandise, and market the product. Packaging changes are emphasized to attract interest among consumers who have grown familiar with the product. Finally, when a defensive strategy is used during the saturation stage, marketing intelligence focuses on product improvements and on keeping alert for a permanent sales decline.

The other saturation strategy, the offensive approach, focuses on change for the better. Marketing intelligence efforts aim at finding (1) new markets and untapped market segments and (2) new ways to stimulate increased use of the product among existing customers. This attempt to break out of a stagnant market is called *product relaunching*. Attention is given to improving the quality of the product, at least as far as subjective features are concerned; appeals such as "New and Improved Tide," "Ajax with Ammonia-D," and "Lemon-Scented Mr. Clean" are examples. But tangible features can be added to the product, too. For example, while sales of tennis rackets were in a slump, sporting goods marketers saw tennis players turning to the oversized, jumbo rackets, such as the Big Bubba, Big Bow, Black Max, and the Prince.

Finally, style changes may also be initiated during the saturation stage. New or annual models can make existing models obsolete, a fact well understood by marketers of automobiles, television sets, and even ski boots. Style changes often are accompanied by changes in packaging or other product features. Sales of bubble gum, a saturated market, were blown up by the advent of Bubble Yum—a bubble gum in a chunk-style form. In its first year, sales of bubble gum soared 60 percent over previous years and encouraged competitors to enter the market.

The goal of revitalizing a mature product can also be achieved by changing its distribution channels—by going, say, from low-volume specialty stores to high-volume discount stores—or by using a new advertising appeal. Jell-O, the General Foods dessert, was showing its age with slowly declining sales throughout the 1970s. Hundreds of consumer interviews, however, found that Jell-O reminded consumers of pleasant family gatherings; there seemed to be an emotion about the product. To reinforce this emotional attachment, General Foods undertook a new campaign showing Jell-O fans of all ages shaking and eating their dessert as a chorus sings a snappy jingle: "Watch that wobble, see that wiggle, taste that jiggle . . . " By 1980, the Jell-O market share in the flavored gelatin market increased to 71.4 percent from 70 percent. As the company's general manager said, "To build volume, even if it's a half-percent, is a tremendous accomplishment."[2]

As products approach the saturation stage of the life cycle, it is important for marketers to look for new-product additions to offset the forthcoming decline and

---

[2]"Jell-O's Revival Shows Sales Can Grow with Older Products," *The Wall Street Journal,* Sept. 11, 1980, p. 29.

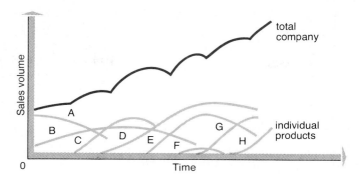

Figure 10-5 Product mix sales volume as result of each product line's life cycle. (Adapted from David J. Luck, Product Policy and Strategy, Prentice-Hall, Englewood Cliffs, N.J., 1972, p. 14. Reprinted by permission of Prentice-Hall, Inc.)

death of the existing product. Without a new product, the old one will die, perhaps taking the company with it. To avoid this catastrophe, most companies try to make additions regularly so that products exist in all stages of the life cycle, with new products constantly replacing old ones. Seeing the levelling sales of running shoes, Nike, for instance, added lines of hiking boots and deck shoes to maintain future growth. The overall objective is to ensure that the company's total sales for all products in the product mix continue to climb. (See Figure 10-5.)

Decline

As product sales turn downward, profits usually decrease, and competitors leave the scene. During this declining stage, the strategy for an individual company is to exploit the product to attain all possible profits before making the final decision to eliminate it. Because similar, competing products have been introduced, the original product has lost its distinctiveness. At this point, marketers do little to change its style, design, or other features. Prices tend to hold, though they may even go up if costs increase, and there is still a loyal core market. Prices may also decrease, however, if the marketer wants to reduce existing inventory and eliminate the product. Distribution outlets are phased out as they become unprofitable, but those serving core markets are maintained. Promotional expenditures are reduced to the minimum, and market information is gathered only to identify the point at which the product should be phased out.

The fact that the product is in the final stage of its life cycle does not mean that it is unprofitable. To the contrary, the decline stage can be very profitable for those marketers that stay in the field. By this time, many competitors have dropped out of the market, and the product itself has been cut back in terms of available colors, sizes, models, and so on. Thus, the product matches only the needs of its core market, and the buyers tend to be specialists. At this point, displays and promotion are not so important, since consumers who want the product are familiar with it and will ask for it.

A product can remain in this stage of the life cycle for years. The gasoline-driven electric generator is an example. At one time, there was fierce competition in this market, since electricity had not reached the rural areas of the country. Today, only a few manufacturers are left. They rarely, if ever, advertise their product, yet such generators sell for a premium price. With the elimination of convertibles from the Cadillac new-car lineup in 1976, Convertibles, Inc., of Lima, Ohio, began to modify Cadillac Eldorado hardtops for a hefty fee of $6500 each. So there can be a few bright spots in the decline stage—at least for some. (See Application 10-3.)

Application 10-3
Decline Stage—Barber Poles and Profits

(Courtesy William Marvy Company)

In days of old, when a man's hair stylist was known as a barber, the shop was open for business when the proprietor stepped outside his shop and started the spring-driven barber-pole motor which sent the twisted red, white, and blue stripes spinning.

Today, only one company remains which builds barber poles—the William Marvy Company. In 1950, there were five other barber-pole makers in the country. Sales grew steadily until 1967 when Marvy produced its 50,000th pole. In that year, there were 112,000 barbershops in the United States, compared with less than 70,000 now. In 1967, Marvy, working two shifts a day, produced 4,900 poles. Annual production has now slipped to under 1,000. Is the William Marvy Company near an end? To the contrary. "We just had our first million-dollar year,"

said William Marvy, the company's originator. The barber-pole business seems secure.

The market today is the replacement pole and modification. Clockwork poles that come in for repair return electrified, and the boom in poodle-grooming salons has helped Marvy's sales. His poodle pole has a row of poodles on one of its stripes. In addition, unisex hair cutting has not been a deterrent. His poles simply state "Hair Stylist" on the stripes.

But Bill Marvy realizes that he is a specialist. Seeing himself as a true businessman, he proudly proclaims, "We are barber-pole people. That's what we think about when we wake up in the morning, and that's what we think about when we go home at night."

Source of data: "In Minnesota: Poles and Profits," *Time,* April 21, 1980, p. 12.

Additional Aspects of the Product Life Cycle

The broadened conceptualization of the product (see Chapter 8) also fits into the product life cycle. Thus, celebrities go through a life cycle as products, and so do ideas and trends. Rock stars come and go, with some staying longer than others; the Beatles, for instance, enjoyed popularity as recording artists for a much longer time than did the Monkees or the Four Tops. And places have their life cycles, too. Jamaica and Nassau lost their long-held attraction for American sun worshipers because of political unrest and resentment toward tourists. To rekindle interest, a 1981–1982 advertising campaign suggested that Americans "come back to Jamaica . . ." And even ideas or causes have life cycles. The social concerns of the 1960s, which centered on civil rights, expanded in the 1970s and on into the 1980s to include concern for ecology and energy conservation.

The product life cycle, then, applies to all kinds of products, and the speed with which a product goes through its life cycle varies, depending on its classification. Durable goods, like trash compacters and microwave ovens, tend to creep through their introductory stage. Such products represent a sizable investment for consumers, and most buyers do not purchase them on impulse. By comparison, packaged consumer goods—like brands of detergents, toothpaste, and cigarettes—usually have a relatively short introductory period. They may pass through it in a matter of months, compared with years for a durable product. Fastest yet are novelty and fad products, such as citizens band radios, skate boarding, and knickers; for such fads, the introductory stage often meshes directly into rapid growth. These products tend to pass quickly through their remaining stages and to decline as rapidly as they arose.

Of course, exceptions are to be found among all classifications of products. While fashions tend to come and go quickly, some "classic looks" have been around for years. Such longevity is a measure both of the quality of the products and of the success of their marketing campaigns. By understanding the product life cycle and the various strategies involved, marketers can relaunch or refresh a product that is in the mature or decline stage. Products often begin a new life cycle. When a box of soap powder is emblazoned with the word *improved,* it's a sign that a new life cycle may be starting. And, although cigarettes are noted for having long life cycles, they are revamped periodically to meet consumers' desires. Thus, the addition of a filter, or menthol, or low-tar formula can lead to a new life cycle. When a product is refreshed, however, it is likely to have a relatively short introductory period because consumers are already familiar with the concept behind the product.

Along with automobiles and appliances, television sets have long been tied to twists and turns in the economic cycle. But advances in technology are making it economically possible to bring a vast variety of entertainment and information services into the home. Now video disc and videocassette recorders, video games, home computers, hi-fi sounds, cable TV, and even two-way communications (space phones) hook directly up with the home television set. All these innovations are prompting early replacement of aging sets and making a growth industry for a mature market. While 1980 appliance sales sagged 9 percent and autos fell 14 percent, television sales climbed 3.2 percent, close to a record surge. (See Figure 10-6.)

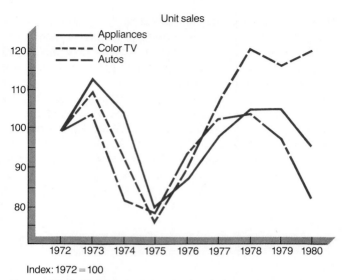

Index: 1972 = 100

Figure 10-6 Television's break from the economic cycle. *(Adapted from* **Business Week,** *Feb. 23, 1981, p. 881)*

Some Product Strategy Problems

In trying to match products with markets, marketers must decide which of the basic product strategies to use. In addition, they often face one or more of the following problems:

Too much variety, not enough assortment

Reduced economies of scale

The dangers of full-line competition

Trading-up and trading-down problems

Blurring the product image

Brand overextension and cannibalism

Ineffective product positioning

Undesired planned obsolescence

Product pruning problems

Too Much Variety, Not Enough Assortment

Marketers attempt to avoid developing product lines that have too much variety (width) and not enough assortment (depth). In such a situation, the problem is that marketing resources are spread too thinly over too many product lines. Marketers cannot properly match, on the assortment level, all the markets that may be interested in the broad product lines. The marketer cannot give each line the appropriate attention to ensure that dealers and consumers get the assortments they desire. When this happens, a marketer must prune, as Charles D. Tandy did with Radio Shack when he purchased it in 1964. At the time, Radio Shack was a small, Boston-based chain that was $1.5 million in debt. Tandy recognized the problem instantly: Radio Shack was attempting to market 25,000 different products, ranging from sporting goods to pots and pans. Tandy cut 90 percent of the line and focused on marketing electronic equipment to amateurs. At the same time, he ordered heavy advertising for the remaining products in the line. The formula worked—the company has continuously grown. By 1979, Radio Shack's gross profit hit an all-time high of 55.9 percent.

Reduced Economies of Scale

Marketers must keep in mind that as product lines are added, the economies of scale associated with mass production can be reduced or destroyed. This problem of manufacturing costs often occurs when consumer-oriented marketers attempt more and more to meet the individual needs of each consumer. Often, companies will add new lines without dropping older ones. Yet, marketers cannot expect to match every want and need of every buyer. They must recognize that a balance must be maintained between the desires of the market and the costs of producing to meet the market.

The automboile industry provides a good example of this problem. It is estimated that Chevrolet could produce a full capacity for over a year and never make the same car twice. The seemingly infinite variation of component parts and options—tires, shocks, clocks, radios—could create great inefficiencies if each buyer's car were custom-built. One way that manufacturers gain economies of scale as they produce various products is through the use of fewer parts as well as standardized components. Ford Motor Company, for instance, in its "complexity reduction" program, reduced the number of engine parts an average of 56 percent in one year. International Harvester's 1976 line of trucks had 50 percent fewer parts than its 1975 models. And NCR Corporation developed a "family" of standardized parts to be used interchangeably on such different products as medical computers and automatic bank tellers.

The Dangers of Full-Line Competition

Many marketers believe that they must offer a full complement of products in order to be successful. The broad offerings, they believe, give a competitive advantage owing to better matching of wants, customer recognition, dealer demand, and high promotional effectiveness. Yet, when this strategy is relied on in place of managerial judgement, being a full-line competitor becomes a trap, thanks to the addition of inefficient and unneeded products.

American Biltrite's Boston-based Industrial Products Division provides an example. Over the years, the maker of hoses, belting, and shoe soling had tried to be too many things to too many customers. The company had too many unprofitable items and accounts. In one operation, 48 percent of Biltrite's customers provided only 2 percent of its sales. As a result, Bilrite management reduced the number of items from 25,000 to 12,000 and eliminated 7,700 of its 15,500 customers. As a regional manager put it, "The problem with diverse lines is giving each product line the attention it deserves."[3] (See Application 10-4.)

Trading-Up and Trading-Down Problems

Marketers often segment markets on the basis of price and quality and attempt to market successfully to both the high- and low-quality markets. When marketers known for selling low-priced merchandise introduce products of higher price (and presumably higher quality), their action is called *trading up*. E. J. Korvettes, long known as an aggressive discounter, conducted some marketing research and found that its customers were not nearly as price conscious as they had been in the past. The result was that Korvettes tried to add a little chic by redefining itself as "a promotional department store" and aiming at a higher-income clientele ($12,000 to $15,000) by upgrading its merchandise and increasing its prices.

Trading down occurs when marketers produce and market cheaper lines than their original lines. As an example, Winnebago Industries, hit very hard by the energy crisis, manufactured and sold a motor home priced lower than its successful Winnebago model. And to serve the more price-conscious segment, Nike introduced a lower-priced running shoe. This is trading down.

This strategy of trading up or down is particularly difficult to carry out effectively. With trading up, the problem is that a stigma from the lower-priced line may well become attached to the new, higher-priced product. Can you imagine paying $500 for a watch with the Timex name on it? Successful trading up seems to come through gradual evolution; large leaps in price and quality that exceed the "difference threshold" are not well received by the market. Korvettes apparently did go beyond the difference threshold; in 1980, it closed its doors for the last time.

With trading down, the problem stems from the fact that the higher-priced line may be jeopardized by the new, lower-quality product. The quality image of the new line may detract from the higher-priced items. Five conditions are helpful in successful trading down: (1) The new product should be in a distinctly different form from the original product; (2) the buyer should easily be able to see value differences between the two; (3) different channels should be used to distribute the product; (4) a different brand name should be used; and (5) a different promotional orientation for the new product should be used. In short, the objective is to dissociate the old and the new product. Winnebago has followed at least some of these rules by naming its lower-priced model "Itasca," giving it a different chassis, and distributing it through 130 entirely different dealers. And Nike calls its lower-priced line of running shoes "One." All other Nike products appear under the Nike label.

---

[3]*Sales and Marketing Management,* Nov. 12, 1979, pp. 35–38.

Application 10-4
Trap of the Full-Line Competitor—Fattening Lean Menus

It wasn't too long ago that the nation's restaurant chains rested securely, assuming that they were in for a long spell of uninterrupted growth. Demographics showed that frequent restaurant goers, young single adults, were the fastest-growing segment of the population; increasing numbers of two-income families abounded; and dining out appeared to be a necessity. Experts predicted that dining out would soon push the restaurant industry's 37 percent share of the food dollar beyond 50 percent.

But the crystal balls proved to be cloudy. For two consecutive years (1979–80), the restaurant industry suffered real annual declines of about 2 percent. Consumers first shunned going out because of high gasoline prices. Then, reduced disposable income, cut by inflation, forced many to eat at home.

Many chains are finding that their narrow menus no longer work in a no-growth market. "We used to have one segment for this type of chain and another for that," said the president of Wendy's, "but now everyone is trying to be more things to more people." In a no-growth market, each chain is hoping to increase its market share by broadening its appeal. Even fast-food chains, which specialize in the fastest service possible with limited choices, are adding to their menus. Wendy's, which for years offered only chili and three kinds of burgers, in 1981 added salads, a chicken sandwich, and a children's hamburger. Victoria Station, Ponderosa, Steak & Ale, and other chains have added chicken and fish items to offset the declining demand for higher-priced beef items. "We just weren't going to accept a no-growth profile," said the chairman of Pillsbury Company's Steak & Ale chain. "We have to broaden our palate and price appeal."

Yet this strategy is not applauded by all experts. "They are developing an ambivalent image by trying to sell too many different products to too many different groups," said one industry observer. And not all chains are getting on the bandwagon. Jack-in-the-Box is withdrawing from regions where the company did not have enough stores to achieve marketing economies. Other chains are cutting back on ambitious expansion plans. And McDonald's has resisted the urge to add different products and has stuck to its original formula: "being the lowest priced, always looking for new markets, and putting efficiency above all else."

Sources of data: "Restaurant Chains: Surviving a Stagnant Market, *Business Week,* May 4, 1981, pp. 106–109; and "McDonald's: The Original Recipe Helps It Defy a Downturn," *Business Week,* May 4, 1981, pp. 161–162.

Blurring the Product Image

As noted earlier, products have images which stem from the symbolism that consumers read into the perceived features of the product. Sometimes marketers like to change the product during its life to "freshen" its image—and sometimes this attempt disturbs a strong niche in a market by trying to fit the product to another segment. In short, the product image may be blurred in the process to the point that its once firm foundation of customer preference is lost. Consider the following example.

For eighty-five years, Abercrombie & Fitch was the fabled emporium of the rich, catering to princes, presidents, and millionaire sports enthusiasts and offering $6000

Figure 10-7 Lines formed for the going-out-of-business sale at Abercrombie & Fitch in New York City. (*Jim Anderson/Woodfin Camp & Associates*)

custom-made buffalo rifles, $1188 Yukon dog sleds, portable stone furnaces for heating cabins on yachts, and even cashmere hunting underwear. But in 1977, having lost money for eight straight years, the company closed the doors of its Madison Avenue headquarters as well as its nine branch stores. (See Figure 10-7.) The problem was mostly an identity crisis. Its merchandising policies were changed several times in its final years, as management could not decide whether to continuing appealing to the carriage trade or to court the middle class with lower-priced items. So it carried silver, gold, and onyx chess sets for $18,000 as well as blue jeans for $8. The end result was that few customers knew just what kind of store Abercrombie had become.

In 1979, Oshman's Sporting Goods of Houston, Texas, bought the Abercrombie & Fitch name and mystique for $1.5 million and again opened the doors with new stores in Dallas and Beverly Hills. The new stores have some of the trappings of the old A&F—rugs bordered with Abercrombie's distinctive red, green, and black, plus high-backed Windsor chairs for tired shoppers. However, the new A&Fs are open at night and on Sundays. The reborn A&F will try to be a bit trendy and a bit traditional, but it will concentrate on sporting goods, sportswear, and glamorous gifts. Some of the old guard are skeptical. Said a buyer from the old A&F Chicago store, "They'll spoil the whole image. The people who shop at Abercrombie don't shop in the evenings or on Sunday."[4] (See Application 10-5).

Brand Overextension and Cannibalism

Often marketers, searching for increased sales, will modify a product in some way to gain new uses. One way, of course, is to change the product tangibly. For instance, cola marketers have offered caffeine-free colas for those concerned about the health

---

[4]"Abercombie Lives in Lotus Land," *Newsweek,* Sept. 24, 1979, p. 85.

Application 10-5
Maintaining an Image—
Keeping K mart on the Straight and Narrow—or Is It?

S. S. Kresge Company in 1962 began transforming itself from a sleepy variety-store chain into a national discounter—offering low prices, value, and service for a quick turnover of merchandise. This formula proved so successful that the Detroit-based company, now known as K mart Corporation, has 1900 stores across the country and has passed J. C. Penney Company to become the nation's second largest retailer. K mart's growth came as a result of never straying from the discount approach. When asked in 1976 why he thought Kresge had succeeded where others had failed, the company president responded, "We decided early what we wanted to be and we work hard keeping at it."

But by 1980, things changed. With stores in the top 300 metropolitan areas in the country, K mart's growth through expansion is limited. Hit additionally with a recession, fierce competition, and soaring operating costs, K mart saw it would be difficult to maintain its 20 percent annual growth rate. The strategic answer: Increase store volume from the cost-conscious customers attracted by K mart's low prices by offering higher-quality goods.

The tactical approach was to use more sophisticated merchandising. Merchandise is emphasized as much as the price. Clothing and other goods are being displayed in ways that are designed to stimulate impulse buying, and higher-quality goods, such as French perfumes, designer jeans, and Izod shirts, are being offered.

"I'll admit, we're reacting," said K mart's chief executive officer. "You'd be a fool in this business not to study your competition and react." He added, however, that with the cheapest prices in town, "a K mart will still be a K mart."

Sources of data: "At Kresge, Success Is Not Forgetting What You Are," *The New York Times*, Sept. 19, 1976, p. F–1; "Where K mart Goes Next, Now that It's No. 2," *Business Week*, June 2, 1980, pp. 109–114; "K mart Stores Try New Look to Invite More Spending," *The Wall Street Journal*, Nov. 26, 1980, p. 29; and "K mart's Plan to Be Born Again, Again," *Fortune*, Sept. 21, 1981, pp. 74–85.

implications of caffeine. Other product extensions do not involve actual changes in the product. The A. J. Canfield company has extended its bottled seltzer water by promoting its use as water for household plants, since carbon dioxide is essential for plant growth.

Marketers also use brand names as a means of launching product modifications or additional products. Brand modifications are common. For example, conditioners are added to Head & Shoulders to make a complementary "new conditioning formula" Head & Shoulders. Calories are removed to create a new Michelob Light beer. When this strategy is used, either the product line's width or depth is increased. In this way, marketers fill the gaps in their bundle of utility. But brand extension can be overdone, resulting in customer confusion or *cannibalism* (cutting into the sales of existing products).

To avoid market confusion, the product extension should be beyond the difference threshold, so it will be noticed and therefore not lost in the marketplace.

Cigarettes provide an example of consumer confusion. Basically, consumers cannot tell the taste differences among different brands—yet, between 1976 and 1979, 55 new brands were introduced to the market and crowded retail counters. Only brands fighting for sales at the point of purchase with expensive promotional displays and heavy couponing could survive.

Marketers must also be aware of the danger that new products or brands may very well cut into the sales of existing products. In 1976, Gillette marketed a disposable Trac II razor entitled Good News at 25 cents per razor. Consumers found they could buy the disposable razors more cheaply than their regular Trac II replacement blades. The new product therefore ate into Gillette's existing product's sales. However, the company was forced by competitive pressures to offer its disposable product. Bic and Schick both were readying disposable razors, and Gillette's thinking, unquestionably, was that it was better to cannibalize your own product than to have someone else cannibalize it.

New Extra-Strength Excedrin takes some sales away from regular Excedrin; Sheer Energy takes some sales away from the original L'eggs panty hose; and Bud Light takes some sales from Michelob Light and Natural Light beers. If marketers do decide to offer items that compete with their own products, they are gambling on capturing more sales from competitors than from their own line. They do not always succeed. In the cigarette industry, one-half of a brand extension's initial volume comes straight from the parent. For this reason, Philip Morris intentionally waits until competitors have forged a large enough following in a cigarette category before bringing out what it feels is a superior product. Virginia Slims Lights presents an example. "We could have brought out that version two years ago," said a Philip Morris executive. "But the brand still had growth in it, and the market was not ready for it. Now there is a reservoir of smokers interested in the Lights."[5]

General Foods and Nestlé provide failure and success stories in dealing with cannibalism. Also, there's a moral to their stories.

After ten years of development and the largest capital investment in product development in its history, General Foods introduced Maxim freeze-dried coffee as a new product that tasted more like brewed coffee than spray-dried instants. Its name, packaging, and promotion clearly traded on General Foods' coffee reputation by linking the higher-priced Maxim to Maxwell House. After introduction, General Foods' total market share in coffee sales slipped from 42 percent in 1968 to 39 percent in 1972.

In the fall of 1966, Nestlé introduced its freeze-dried coffee, Taster's Choice. Taking the opposite strategy, the consumer was never reminded of Nestlé's basic product, Nescafé spray-dried instant coffee, and was only slightly aware of the manufacturer. Nescafé dropped only slightly from 12 percent in 1968 to 11 percent in 1972—while the new Taster's Choice went from 1 percent to 13 percent of the market share in the same period. Nestlé's total market share rose from 13 to 29.6 percent

---

[5]"Cigarettes Sales Up—Maybe for the Last Time," *Business Week,* Dec. 17, 1979, p. 54.

between 1968 and 1980. The lesson to be learned: Avoid close identification between existing products and new competing products to minimize cannibalism.

Ineffective Product Positioning

The various features and benefits of a product give it an image among consumers, and marketers attempt to position that image in relation to (1) competing products and (2) other products in the line. In some cases, products can be marketed very successfully when they are positioned directly against similar products—by challenging the competition head on. Thus, General Motors' Cadillac and Ford's Lincoln are pitted directly against each other, and Bic's disposable lighter competes well against Gillette's Cricket. But other products do not fare well in this kind of situation, and so marketers, instead, try to differentiate their product by positioning it within the range of available products. For example, Avis grew into a highly successful agency for rental cars by positioning itself as number two in relation to Hertz. And Procter & Gamble has positioned its Charmin brand of bathroom tissue on the basis of softness—"Please don't squeeze the Charmin," said Mr. Whipple—and this led it to become the best-selling brand on the market.

Because a product's position or image depends on how it is perceived by consumers, marketers cannot directly control what will happen in the marketplace. Even large, successful marketers sometimes fail to position their product as they might like. Procter & Gamble has had some product-positioning problems with its Gleem brand of toothpaste, which was introduced in 1954. As the brand name suggests, Gleem was marketed as a whitener and was a huge success. In recent years, P&G emphasized the cavity-fighting qualities of Gleem by the addition of flouride in 1968 and the introduction of Gleem II. Yet, recent research showed P&G that Gleem II was still considered a whitener in spite of cavity-fighting ad copy. When asked by researchers what else they would like in a dentifrice, consumers answered "fresh taste." So, in 1977, P&G reformulated Gleem II with a "new cool burst of flavor" and played down the flouride in its advertising. Yet, consumers were still confused about its position; in 1980, market share had slipped to 3.3 percent from 5 percent in 1977.

Procter & Gamble has been more successful with its Crest. Introduced in 1955 when most toothpastes were sold for their whitening ability, Crest, with its stannous flouride ingredient, was advertised as a cavity preventer. Crest quickly grabbed a third of the market and has been a market leader ever since. But, in 1980, its share had slipped to 36.2 percent from 40 percent two years earlier. The cause: Aqua-Fresh, a brand introduced nationally in 1979 as a combination of taste and decay prevention, had gained 13.5 percent and a third place behind Crest and Colgate in the market share standings. So, in 1981, Crest changed its age-old formula to replace stannous flouride with sodium flouride and allow a better taste. Yet, rather than promote the taste side, P&G trumpeted the "Advanced Formula" as "clinically proven to fight cavities even better than before." P&G did not want to change Crest's position in the consumer's mind as it had done to the detriment of Gleem. (See Application 10-6.)

Application 10-6
Positioning—Carving Out a Niche

General Mills has shown its marketing ability in many related and unrelated industries. Among its businesses are restaurants, the Red Lobster and other chains; Kenner Products and Parker Brothers; specialty retailing, including the Talbots, a "preppy" mail-order house; and fashion—Ship 'n Shore blouses, Monet jewelry, and the unstoppable alligator brand, Izod/Lacoste. Now General Mills is into yogurt as well.

One of the whiz-bang product managers, Steven Rothschild, was promoted to marketing director in 1975 and got General Mills to buy a small Michigan company with a license from SODIMA, a French diary cooperative, to manufacture a distinctively tasty yogurt called Yoplait. (It's pronounced yo-play. *Plaît* is French for "please.") Rothschild was made president.

Research showed him that while only a third of the population regularly buys yogurt, they eat enough to make it a $500 million business. And another third of the population has never tried the product. Most of the yogurts are regional brands, with only Dannon yogurt, a unit of Beatrice Foods, being sold nationally. National distribution is Rothschild's goal. In 1981, Yoplait covered two-thirds of the country and built sales to about $60 million.

A marketing strategy designed to give Yoplait a "personality" lies behind these feats. The product is billed as the "yogurt of France."

Explains Rothschild: "The French are known for good foods." Its advertising is aimed at "early adopters"—in English, people most likely to try new products. ("We're on prime-time and late-night, but not daytime television.") Yoplait also sponsors bicycle races ("It's European"), at which one of its hot-air balloons can be seen hovering overhead (hot-air ballons were introduced in 1783 by a pair of Frenchmen).

"While people can copy our product, or try to," says Rothschild, "they can't copy our positioning."

Source of data: "The General Mills Brand of Managers," *Fortune*, Jan. 12, 1981, pp. 98–107.

Undesired Planned Obsolescence	Marketers sometimes use the strategy of forcing a product in their line to become out of date and then increasing the replacement market. This strategy, called *planned obsolescence,* exists in four forms:

Undesired Planned Obsolescence

Marketers sometimes use the strategy of forcing a product in their line to become out of date and then increasing the replacement market. This strategy, called *planned obsolescence,* exists in four forms:

1 *Technological obsolescence* results when technical improvements are achieved in a product. For instance, when it became possible for office copiers to print on both sides of a sheet of paper at once, the earlier, slower models of copiers were technogically obsolete. In the same way, jet airplanes eventually replaced propeller models, and electric can openers reduced the market for manual types.

2 *Postponed obsolescence* is a situation in which technological improvements are available but are not introduced until the demand for existing products declines

and inventories can be depleted. Then a new product is needed to stimulate the market. Gillette follows this strategy in introducing new shaving products; thus, the company held back on the introduction of Teflon-coated razor blades until consumers' interest in chromium blades had peaked.

3 *Physical obsolescence* results when products are built to last for only a limited time, as are car batteries, nylon stockings, and light blubs. For example, users of the *Directory of Executive Recruiters* are encouraged to purchase a new issue annually by having the book's paper turn yellow with age—it lasts just about one year.

4 *Style Obsolescence* occurs when the physical appearance of a product is changed to make existing products seem out of date. This strategy is most obvious in the garment and automobile industries, though it can be applied to all kinds of products.

The basis for use of this strategy lies in the marketer's belief in people's strong desire for something new. Variety and change seem to be almost instinctual in most people. Planned obsolescence has been heavily criticized as a strategy—particularly style obsolescence. It appears to foster the purchase of products that are not really needed by the market. It seems as if marketers have the upper hand and are dictating the purchases of consumers—with people following like sheep to buy whatever the marketers want them to buy.

American Telephone & Telegraph Company has recently come under fire for its "migration" policy. Migration, in AT&T jargon, means encouraging business customers to "migrate," or move up, to the latest generation of equipment. Following rate increases on their existing phone equipment, large corporate customers are urged to replace the old with new Bell equipment which, to Bell's advantage, is less costly to maintain and which, as critics have pointed out, also prematurely retires equipment that may be vulnerable to competition. This kind of strategy clearly draws sharp criticism.

But criticisms of this strategy have been met with some opposing arguments. Supporters of planned obsolescence indicate that the buyer is a person with a free will who has freedom to make his or her own decisions about purchase behavior—people are not forced to buy goods. Witness the refusal to buy the large (1973), then the small (1976), then the large (1980) cars coming out of Detroit. Furthermore, variety and change often provide additional increments of satisfaction. Having new products makes many people happier. Additionally, improvements in technological features lead to increases in the standard of living—a worthy goal in an economy. And this goal of improving the standard of living by its own nature must result in "obsoleting" existing products as improvements are made. So it appears that planned obsolescence is not all bad—unless abused by marketers. Where false or inconsequential changes are made and purchases induced under misrepresentation, of course, the marketing concept is not being adhered to and marketers are justly criticized. That is not the philosophy of this book.

Product Pruning Problems

As products age and decline or become obsolescent, marketers must recognize when to eliminate them from the line. Not all marketers, however, have a well-defined approach to this situation, and they are reluctant to phase out products. Since the company must bear the costs of carrying weak products, it is important that marketers have good reasons for retaining products when they have passed their point of profitability.

The first task in identifying when to prune products is to set up an information system that focuses on sales changes, trends in market shares, the return on investment, and profits. By monitoring these aspects of a product's performance and establishing criteria for evaluating them, marketers can terminate products intelligently. Sometimes the decision to delete is an easy one, but at other times it is quite difficult.

Before eliminating a product completely, one of three strategies may be appropriate. First, the marketers may adopt a *continuation strategy* simply by following their past strategy until the product is dropped. Or they may decide to follow a *milking strategy* by cutting back the marketing expenses sharply in order to reduce costs and secure profits in the product's concluding stages. Finally, they may follow a *concentrated strategy* by aiming all marketing efforts at the strongest market segment and phasing out the other segments. Profits can be reasonable at this time. For example, Standard Brands' Curtiss Division was breaking even in late 1977. The product mix had a few highly profitable candy products such as Butterfinger and Baby Ruth—but a raft of unknown losers. In a year, the division eliminated a score of jelly bean, marshmallow, and hard candy products. The product pruning cut sales 30 percent, but the division stepped up marketing for the few remaining products. As a result, profits increased 45 percent in 1979 on a 30 percent sales increase—all in a market of declining candy consumption.

Once marketers have decided to drop a product, they must still ask three questions: (1) Can the product be sold to another marketer, or should it be allowed to die? (2) If the product will be terminated, when should the end take place? (3) In what quantity are replacement parts available? This last matter is especially important because marketers do not want to damage their image by selling a product that cannot be repaired.

Looking Back

This chapter has focused on the product life cycle as a means of aiding marketers in managing the product as it serves the needs of its market. Effective adjustment of the product offering is the key if the demands of the market are to be met. The next chapter will look at how marketers put a price on that product—but before we venture into this new area of study, let's be sure we have grasped the following major points presented in this chapter.

1 The goal of product management is matching the product with the wants and needs of the market.

2 A sound understanding of the market is a prerequisite for effective product management.

3 The market changes, and the product must be continually adjusted to meet these changes.

4 Product adjustment can be carried out by changing objective and subjective features of the product.

5 Product mixes made up of product lines have width and depth, which are also called variety and assortment.

6 The degree of match between the product offered and market demands determines whether the market is core, fringe, or a zone of indifference.

7 The product life cycle has two dimensions—product sales and time.

8 Each stage of the product life cycle has its own set of characteristics.

9 Locating the stage in the product life cycle that your product is in aids in determining appropriate strategies.

10 Traditional products are not the only "products" to go through the product life cycle.

11 The length of the product life cycle varies for different products and brands.

12 Products can jump from later stages back to earlier growth stages through product refreshing.

13 Two different overall strategies can be employed in the saturation stage.

14 Some product lines can have too much variety and not enough assortment.

15 Adding standardized components can help reduce economy-of-scale problems as the product mix widens.

16 A marketer need not be a full-line competitor to be successful.

17 In trading up or down, the key is to dissociate the new from the old product.

18 The product's image can be blurred when marketers attempt to refreshen the image of the product.

19 Some cannibalism can be avoided by dissociating the new and the old product.

20 Marketers should seek a product position in the marketplace that is not being held by other products or brands.

21 Product-deletion strategy can be profitable—if properly carried out.

Key Terms

If you aren't sure what each of the following words means, look back at the text. Numbers refer to pages on which the words are defined. Additional information can be found by checking the index and the glossary at the end of the book.

product mix 311
product line 312
width 312
depth 312
core market 313
fringe market 313
zone of indifference 313
product life cycle 313

defensive strategy 319
product relaunching 320
trading up 326
trading down 326
cannibalism 329
planned obsolescence 332
milking strategy 334
concentrated strategy 334

Questions for Review

1 Briefly describe how the six terms *mix, line, width, depth, variety,* and *assortment* relate to one another.

2 During which two stages in the product life cycle would you find a managerial emphasis on cultivating primary demand and serving core markets?

3 Identify some of the promotional strategies found in the *growth stage* of the product life cycle.

4 What is meant by the term *product relaunching?*

5 What are the five conditions that seem to be helpful in using a trading-down strategy?

6 What are four types of planned obsolescence?

Questions for Thought and Discussion

1 Perhaps the most famous doll ever, Mattel's Barbie, is over 20 years old. How might Mattel adjust this product to meet the wants of the marketplace?

2 In what stage of the product life cycle do you believe waterbeds to be? Why?

3 Union Underwear Company acquired the BVD Company, maker of low-priced underwear for men and boys. With little growth expected at the low-quality end, Union wanted to upgrade the line from about $4 at retail to $7. What would you suggest to Union as it undertakes this product strategy?

4 Consider the marketer of thermos bottles. How might one use the product-positioning strategy to open up new market segments?

Suggested Project

Carefully analyze the characteristics identifying each of the five stages in the product life cycle. Find examples of existing products you believe to be in each of the stages. Back up each one with a picture of the product and a discussion of why you believe the product is in that stage. Be sure to include some nontraditional products.

Suggested Readings

Buell, Victor P.: "The Changing Role of the Product Manager in Consumer Goods Companies," *Journal of Marketing,* vol. 39 (July 1975), pp. 3–11. This award-winning article looks at the current status and changes in the responsibilities of product managers within domestic companies.

Dietz, Stephen: "Get More out of Your Brand Management," *Harvard Business Review,* vol. 51 (July–August 1973), pp. 127–136. The strategic role of the brand manager in determining the product strategy is dependent upon the brand's stage in its life cycle.

Enis, Ben M., Raymond LaGarce, and Arthur E. Prell: "Expanding the Product Life Cycle," *Business,* vol. 20 (June 1977), pp. 46–56. The life cycle of a given *brand* can be influenced by strategies set by the marketer; the life cycle for *products* is less easily managed.

Hise, Richard T.: *Product/Service Strategy,* Petrocelli/Charter, New York, 1977. This book, treating new-product development, life cycle management, and product elimination, provides a framework for decision making about all kinds of products and services.

Sachs, William S., and George Benson: *Product Planning and Management,* Penn Well Publishing, Tulsa, Okla., 1981. A management-oriented treatment of all aspects of product planning and development is presented in this text.

Journal of Marketing, vol. 45, no. 4 (Fall 1981), pp. 60–96. This special section of the *Journal of Marketing* makes a distinctive contribution to the long-standing controversy over the managerial value of the product life cycle.

Smallwood, John E.: "The Product Life Cycle: A Key to Strategic Marketing Planning," *MSU Business Topics,* vol. 21 (Winter 1973), pp. 29–35. This frequently referenced article looks at products in the various stages of the life cycle and the implications of these stages for marketing mix activities.

Wasson, Chester R.: *Dynamic Competitive Strategy and Product Life Cycles.* Challenge Books, St. Charles, Ill., 1974. This text focuses on the product life cycle and the various marketing mix decisions appropriate in building an *effective* marketing strategy for the entire life of the product.

Worthing, Parker M.: "Improving Product Deletion Decision Making," *MSU Business Topics,* vol. 23 (Summer 1975), pp. 29–38. This article reviews existing approaches to dropping products from the product mix and views some important criteria that indicate when product deletion is appropriate.

Cases for Part Three begin on page 600.

Pricing

Cutting prices may at first blush seem like an excellent marketing tactic, but marketers have learned, and often painfully, that it's often better to adjust other elements in what they offer.

The sluggish economy of the early 1980s forced many pricing experiments. During the doldrums of the period, a number of marketing strategies were toyed with, but few companies resorted to outright price cuts. General Motors, for instance, offered financing terms that were well below the bank rates for persons who bought new cars in 1981–82 and then financed their purchases through General Motors Acceptance Corporation. Chrysler and Ford relied on the cash rebate for new cars. Both tactics worked, but none of the three actually cut the list prices of their vehicles.

Meanwhile, M&M/Mars found another way to increase value without taking the unheard-of step of actually lowering prices. Faced with lower demand—perhaps the result of the economy—the company increased the weight of several candy bars by an average of 10 percent without changing the price of the product. Mars claims that this increased value for the same price increased sales by 50 percent.

Wilson Harrell thinks cutting prices permanently is good strategy. He will test his strategy by introducing a new spray cleaner, 4+1, which he claims is as good as Windex, Glass Plus, Fantastik, and Formula 409. It will sell for less than half the price of its competitors. The 4+1 brand will consist of concentrated cleaning liquids to which consumers will add water (4 parts water to 1 part of the cleaner) and will supply their own spray bottle (probably a recycled one from a competitor). Savings on water, weight, and packaging volume will help Harrell offer his product at a reduced price. If the technique is successful, Harrell's Products Four Inc. will join a growing list of marketers that are trying unconventional approaches to product value.

Helene Curtis emphasized low prices for its Suave hair-care products and increased its market share. Gold Seal doubled the market share of its Snowy dry bleach with a low price and the slogan "A little Snowy bleaches like a lot of Clorex 2."

Church & Dwight is experimenting with a price-plus-value strategy. After changing the formula for its Arm & Hammer laundry detergent to one the company says is more effective but less costly to make, it cut its price to about 50 percent of the price per ounce of other major brands.

Source of data: "Spray Cleaner to Test Notion that with Price, Less is More," *The Wall Street Journal,* May 21, 1981, p. 29.

Chapter 11

Price Determination

Looking Ahead

Having examined the essential activities that marketers undertake in making product decisions, we now can truthfully say that we have a product. But there is much more to learn, and the next two chapters explore pricing. First we will examine the nature of a product's price and how marketers determine what it will be. Then, in the next chapter, we will study various pricing policies and see how prices can be varied to meet certain conditions.

Key Topics

The nature of a product's price

The importance of price on the effective operation of the economy as well as on a firm's prosperity

The various factors that influence the determination of price

The importance of various types of costs to those setting the price

How wholesalers and retailers price products

The relation of demand to the upper limits for a price

The impact of competition on price determination

Chapter Outline

The Nature of Price
The Importance of Price to the Economy
The Importance of Price to an Individual Firm

Strategic Price Determination
Objectives
Costs
Approaches to Pricing
Demand
Competition

Looking Back

As one of the 4 P's identified in Chapter 2, price is a critical part of the marketing mix. In fact, the price charged for a product—whether a house or a tube of toothpaste—may be the most visible part of the marketing mix, and it is closely compared with the prices of competing products. Thus, price is an extremely important consideration for marketers in satisfying the needs and wants of consumers.

It is not simple to arrive at a price that both satisfies consumers and provides the company with a profit. Marketers walk a thin line in determining how much to charge for a product. If they sell it at an artificially low price, no profits will be realized, and ultimately the product will fail. But if the price is too high, sales will be difficult to attain, and again the product—and the company—will fail. Obviously, then, the determination of price is a key function of marketing. Let's examine what this involves.

The Nature of Price

Figure 11-1   The word "Sale" seems to have magic powers to stimulate consumers. (Randy Matusow)

Price goes by many other names—rent, tuition, fare, rate, interest, toll, premium, honorarium, and even bribe. But all these names add up to one thing: what consumers pay for a product or service. In short, any transaction can be seen as an exchange of something of value, usually money (price), for a bundle of satisfaction (product). The key to determining a product's price lies in understanding the *value* that consumers perceive in the product. And that value results from their perceptions of the total satisfaction provided by the product.

A product's bundle of satisfaction includes not only its tangible features but also its intangible characteristics, such as store image, guarantees, and brand name. Even so, the product's price is often the overriding ingredient that leads to an exchange. The price itself can be a major increment of satisfaction. Some consumers, for instance, gain satisfaction from buying and owning an expensive product. There is a definite status appeal at work when Rolex can sell its President model for men at $7950. Surely more is involved than the simple need for a timekeeper. At the other end of the scale, many consumers derive satisfaction from getting a product at a "good price." They like to get, say, five double-edge razor blades for only $1.49 when the regular price is $2.49. The word *sale* alone often stimulates exchange. (See Figure 11-1.)

This "consumer's love of low price" was put to work by McDonald's. With television advertising, Ray Kroc, McDonald's founder and senior chairman, announced a 5-cent reduction in the prices of the chain's hamburger and cheeseburger. McDonald's ads proclaimed, "Some good news for you. We are cutting prices 10 percent on our most basic items. . . . We are doing this to give our customers some relief from inflation. It's a nice saving for the family budget—and how many prices do you see going down these days?" Then the ad ends with Kroc's reminding the consumer that "Nobody can do it like McDonald's can."

These high- and low-price examples stress some important points: Price is a substantial part of the bundle of utility, and a product's value is often what consumers perceive it to be. Thus, buyers help set the value for products. Furthermore, price often makes no difference to a buyer. This is particularly true with products bought on impulse or to meet an emergency. It is rare for a consumer to think about the price of potato chips when a snack is wanted, or about the price of aspirin when a headache strikes.

From an expanded view, then, price is what is exchanged in order to acquire something else of value. Of course, not all exchanges involve money. For example, in the barter system, goods of one kind are exchanged for something else of value, and the two parties to the exchange determine the value of the goods traded. Thus, a baby's crib that is no longer needed may be traded for a set of theater tickets, or two children may swap baseball cards, perhaps deciding that one Reggie Jackson or one Pete Rose is worth three obscure players.

In still other instances, the price may be a combination of money and goods. This is the case when a car buyer trades in an old model to obtain a new one. The value of a used car, or a pair of worn-out tires, or a nonworking refrigerator is subtracted from the price of the new item, and the money finally exchanged is reduced by that amount. (See Application 11-1.)

Application 11-1
Barter—"Let's Make a Deal"

When a farmer in the 1800s needed some goods he couldn't raise, grow, or make, he often traded goods for it. Life without cash, lines of credit, and credit cards was the order of the day.

Today, as people are squeezed by inflation, the barter system is making a comeback, and it represents big dollars from coast to coast.

In fact, so popular is bartering that many companies have emerged that specialize in bringing people together so they can barter goods. For example, Barter Systems, Inc., based in Oklahoma City, anticipates that it will arrange bartering throughout the country which will carry a price tag of $100 million in 1981. Some of the barters being arranged appear to have no limits. The company, for instance, recently arranged the swap of a jet airplane belonging to a tire company for $1.3 million worth of coal.

"There was a guy in Pittsburgh who had an inventory of 700 skateboards. He was about to go bankrupt. He joined Barter Systems and within six months he no longer has those skateboards," said Jean Joyner of Barter Systems.

High unemployment also boosts bartering among people who have plenty of time and can't sell their services for cash. Several hundred *Detroit Free Press* readers accepted the paper's offer to run free three-line advertisements offering barter deals. One reader wanted to swap dog grooming for plumbing. Another offered "instruction in Christianity" in exchange for food.

Sources of data: "Bartering Grows," *The Wall Street Journal,* Sept. 18, 1980, p. 1; "Using Barter as a Way of Doing Business," *Business Week,* Aug. 4, 1980, p. 57; "Bartering for Almost Anything," *The Nashville Tennessean,* Sept. 27, 1981, pp. 2E–18E; and "As Barter Boom Keeps on Growing," *U.S. News & World Report,* Sept. 21, 1981, pp. 55–58.

The Importance of Price to the Economy

Many economists consider pricing to be the major factor that keeps the economy in balance. One function of prices is to retain and allocate resources to their most efficient use. That is, prices help us to distribute our limited resources, for when demand for a good or service is greater than the available supply, prices rise. For example, in the mid-1970s the price of coffee suddenly jumped from a little more than $1 per pound to almost $5 per pound. Because there was a shortage of coffee beans, demand outpaced the supply. But when coffee growers began to charge large food-processing companies a premium for this limited supply of raw materials, demand was brought back into line by the final prices charged to consumers. By 1978, wholesale prices of coffee fell back to about $2.75 per pound. And a glut of coffee in 1981 produced even greater price reductions—coffee dropped to a price as low as $1.59 per pound.

Another important function of prices is helping to determine a company's profits. It is profits that enable companies to spend money for research and development. Thus, profits can ultimately lead to new technology and to better products that provide more satisfaction and an improved standard of living. In addition, of course, a company that has higher profits can afford to pay its employees and stockholders more. This results in higher wage rates and dividends, which allow individuals to collect greater amounts of personal income. In this way, prices influence the spending and saving habits of consumers. When the price of a product rises, an individual may decide to buy less of that product and more of something else that is less expensive; or the individual may decide to put more money into savings and wait until prices come down.

The prices of products in the marketplace thus have many effects on the overall economy and on the standard of living for individual consumers within the economy. In setting prices, marketers must consider these long-run effects as well as their own desire for profits. After all, they, too, must operate within the economy, and their decisions affect their general well-being along with profits.

The Importance of Price to an Individual Firm

For any business firm, profits are determined by the difference between its revenues and its costs. But revenue depends both on the prices charged by the firm and on the quantity of product sold. Suppose a manufacturer produces 100 typewriters and prices them at $200 each. When all the typewriters are sold, the company will have taken in revenues of $20,000. And if the cost of producing the typewriters is $16,000, the manufacturer will realize a profit of $4,000. The profit equation is, therefore:

$$\text{Profit} = \text{total revenue (price} \times \text{quantity)} - \text{total cost}$$

A product's price has a strong effect on its sales. For some products, an increase in price may result in an increase in sales revenues; for other products, a price reduction will lead to a greater number of sales. Thus, the price attached to a product has considerable impact on a company's revenues and, ultimately, on its profits. In addition, the price of a product often determines where it will be sold. When retailers can realize higher profits by carrying higher-priced items, they are more likely to handle such products. Minnetonka, for example, gained national distribution for Softsoap by increasing retailers' profit margins to 26 percent from the 21 percent normally received on bar soap.

Marketers strive for *nonprice competition*. If the bundle of utility offered has sufficient allure for reasons other than price, marketers are than free to adjust prices upward and thereby create greater profits. The most obvious route to this end is by producing a superior product, but other tangible and intangible features can enhance the desired demand effect. Calvin Klein jeans, Bill Blass neckties, and Louis Vuitton luggage all command higher than usual prices because of their designer "status" labels. Consumers usually do not dwell on the price. Such product pull (status) reduces competitive comparison by shoppers. Advertising is a major means by which nonprice competition is conducted. Thus, nonprice competition is much more difficult to use with undifferentiable commodities, such as baking soda, thread, and spray starch.

It should be clear, then, that price is enormously important to marketers, both because of the profit equation and because of the symbolic aspects of the product's price. Marketers must give attention to the price as an important strategic decision. Pricing strategy involves the determination of an initial price for the product and the adjustment of the price over its life cycle. Pricing in the later stages of the product's life cycle is easier than at the beginning, since marketers usually have more information by that time.

In selecting a strategy, marketers must look to the environment and anticipate changes in those factors that influence successful pricing. Considerations of social responsibility, legal restrictions, economic conditions, suppliers' prices, and supply levels, as well as cost fluctuations, demand adjustments, and competitive activities, all influence pricing strategy. Pricing strategy affects the firm's entire marketing program, which, in turn, determines the firm's success as well as the total satisfaction provided to consumers and society in general. Given that the price variable has such impact on the economy, on individual firms, on consumers, and on society as a whole, we need to understand how prices are determined.

Strategic Price Determination

When we walk into a store, we are surrounded by a sea of products, each with a different price: $49.95 for a tennis racket, 99 cents for a pair of panty hose, $1.50 for a magazine, $8.95 for a special breed of tropical fish. We now want to examine how organizations put a monetary value on products. We want to see how all those widely varying prices are determined.

Average price per lb. of choice
beef; estimates for March 1979

$2.23

Retailer
adds 57¢

$1.66

Wholesaler
adds 9¢

$1.57

Intercity transportation
adds 2¢

$1.55

Slaughterhouse
adds 6¢

$1.49

Farm to slaughterhouse
adds 2¢

$1.47

Farmer's share
per net lb. (average 1,000 lb.
steer yields 420 net lbs. for
retail sale)

In setting prices, marketers can choose between a one-price policy and a flexible-price policy. With a *one-price policy,* the marketer assigns one price to the product and offers that same price to all customers who purchase the same quantity of the product under the same conditions. Supermarkets, department stores, discounters —in fact, most mass merchandisers—use a one-price policy. Unless consumers are willing to pay the price displayed, there is no exchange.

With a *flexible-price policy,* the marketer offers the same products and quantities to different customers at different prices—depending on their bargaining power, friendship, good looks, and other factors. The negotiated prices paid at a tag sale or a flea market are an example of flexible pricing, as have been the prices paid for American automobiles and real estate. However, few products are actually sold in this manner. In these exchange situations, sellers do not really expect buyers to pay the sticker price, or the asking price. Rather, they intend to achieve the exchange only after some haggling to determine the product's value. A flexible-price policy is very helpful in meeting the prices of one's competition as well as in appeasing marketers' appetites when they are hungry to make a sale. (Application 11-2 reviews some of the marketing conditions that are leading American auto makers away from full-scale flexible pricing.)

Most exchanges today result from a one-price policy, but that doesn't mean that everyone pays the same price. While this may sound like contradiction, note that under a one-price policy, the same price is asked from all customers who buy the *same quantities* of the product *under the same conditions.* Thus, while a product may be assigned a particular price, in some situations that price may not be the actual price paid for each unit purchased. In Chapter 12, we will examine how prices may be adjusted, but first we must understand how the initial price is set.

The initial price of a product is called the *list price,* or *base price,* and most prices are determined from that starting point. In other words, the list price is the price that buyers are normally asked to pay for the product.

By the time consumers enter a store to buy a product—whether a magazine, a candy bar, or a television set—a whole series of price determinations has occurred. First, the raw materials have been sold to producers at a given price. Then the manufacturer has put a price on the finished product that is sold to wholesalers, namely, the intermediaries who buy products in large quantities and then distribute them to retailers. For the various services they provide, wholesalers add a *markup,* or *mark-on,* to the manufacturer's price before selling the product to retailers. And since retailers also must be paid for their services, they add another markup before offering the product to consumers. Thus, it is the price set by retailers that consumers finally see. (See Figure 11-2.) To understand how that price is determined, we need to look at how manufacturers establish their prices. Four factors are especially important: objectives, costs, demand, and competition.

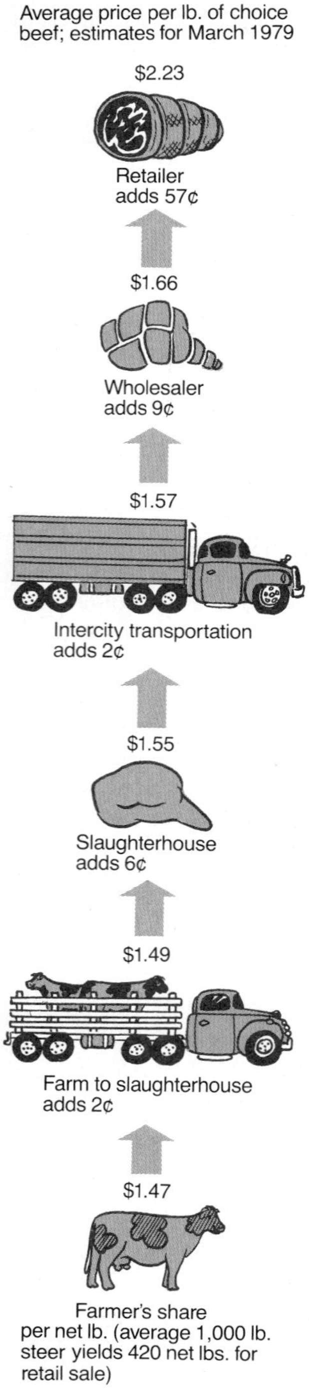

Figure 11-2 How prices climb to the consumers. (Adapted from "Meat Bites Back," Time, April 23, 1979, p. 62)

Application 11-2
From Flexible- to One-Price Pricing

When General Motors introduced the J subcompacts to the marketplace in 1981, it abandoned its tradition of the spartan, bargain-basement model that generations of auto dealers have counted on to bring economy-minded buyers into the showroom. Instead, the J-line cars came equipped with weighty options. The Chevrolet Cavalier features power brakes, a rear-window defogger, plush reclining seats, a radio, and digital clock as standard items—and a sticker price of about $6800. Other Js were even more fully equipped.

This marketing tactic went against the grain of twenty-five years of Chevrolet tradition. GM is apparently learning a Japanese lesson in selling cars, a skill once thought to have been exclusive to Detroit. In 1980, imports took one-quarter of the American market, and the Japanese imports led with 20 percent. The Japanese imports routinely come with a long list of standard features—and one fixed price. The implication is: "American cars come as basic cars, we come fully equipped. Therefore our cars are higher quality."

The old Detroit game was to price the base model as low as possible—to the point of hairline profit margins—and then to urge buyers to purchase options at extra costs. As a result, Detroit grew fat. The stripped versions were seen more frequently in ads than on the road, seldom accounting for more than 5 percent of sales.

Market researchers also say the new marketing is fitted to a new breed of auto buyers. The younger buyers who have turned to the imports do not like haggling, a practice that has become so much a part of buying an American car.

"What we term 'new generation' car buyers, those under 44, don't like to hassle with salesmen," the manager of marketing planning for Chevrolet said. "These people want to see a car that's equipped the way they want and only deal with one price."

Source of data: "GM Loads Up on a Japanese Strategy," *The New York Times*, May 3, 1981, p. F1.

Objectives

We observed in Chapters 2 and 3 the importance of goals for marketing programming and for decision making in general. Before an effective marketing job can be accomplished, managers need to determine their objectives. Pricing is no exception. Unfortunately, however, few firms consciously determine their pricing objectives, and fewer still have explicit written statements of such goals. Objectives can be categorized into three areas that we will examine: Sales objectives, profit objectives, and competitive objectives.

Sales Objectives

Pricing objectives should be tied to the overall objectives of the company. Since a fundamental goal of most organizations is to grow, it follows that *sales growth* would be a reasonable goal of pricing. Even so, growing sales do not automatically ensure growing profits. In fact, many companies have been caught in a profit squeeze over the past two decades. While their sales have grown in general, their costs have disproportionately grown even more; the end result has been smaller profit.

On the other hand, some companies want to avoid sales growth, aiming instead at *maintaining sales*. Such organizations realize that sales growth and expansion bring increased complexity, greater responsibility, and more problems. Therefore, their pricing objective is to maintain sales.

A pricing objective that is similar to the growth or maintenance of sales is the *growth and maintenance of market share*. For example, growth of 1 percent of market share in the automobile industry results in about $700 million in additional sales revenues—no paltry sum. But while market-share growth may be the pricing objective of Ford and Chrysler, General Motors in the 1960s and most of the 1970s sought to maintain its market share, which was in the area of 60 percent of the total automobile industry. It is well known that the government keeps a watchful eye on GM's market share. If it becomes too large, the government may view the company as dominating the marketplace and force GM to sell off one or more of its divisions to reduce its dominance of the market.

Compagnie Générale des Establissements Michelin, the French radial-tire maker, took an aggressive road in its bid to become the world's industry leader. For thirty years, Michelin emphasized the quality of its radial tires and set premium prices. But, in 1980, Michelin established an objective of increasing its American auto tire market share by 6 percent and its truck tire market share by 10 percent. To achieve these goals, it radically slashed replacement tire prices. Tires that once sold at 30 percent premium were set at prices comparable with those of Goodyear, the industry leader, and Firestone.

Finally, the pricing objective of some companies is simple *survival*. Organizations that find it difficult to compete may well drop their prices—sometimes drastically—in order to generate the cash needed to pay bills and remain in business, hoping that conditions will change and allow them to regain a firm position in the marketplace. Mazda Motors of America, the sales organization of the Japanese automobile manufacturer, provides an example. The company enjoyed four good sales years until 1974, when gasoline prices and low mileage ratings sent sales plummeting. Mazda's organization of dealers was in danger of disbanding—disaster for any automobile manufacturer. In order to survive and reverse the decline, the company plunged into a major rebate program, offering $500 to the dealer and $500 to the customer. This was an expensive way to ensure sales, but it worked. The dealer network stayed intact, and Mazda was able to survive and produce more economical models by 1976.

Profit Objectives

Cost pressures have led more and more companies to seek financial goals through pricing; that is, they have become increasingly profit-oriented. One common pricing objective is *profit maximization,* obtaining the highest profits possible. However, in practice this goal is operationally unrealistic, since a firm can never know when it has reached this objective. Data about costs and demand are difficult if not impossible to estimate with the needed accuracy. In addition, profit maximization is tinged with the idea of "profit gouging," and neither consumers nor people in government take kindly to companies that seek excessive profits. Finally, if a firm's profits are excessive, competitors will be attracted to that industry.

Sometimes a firm can come close to profit maximization by tying customers to its products for long periods of time. For example, some cameras for amateur photographers are sold almost at cost. The company's goal, of course, is to sell film, which is impossible if people don't have cameras. But once the camera is in hand, the buyer will purchase the company's film repeatedly. A similar situation exists for the sale of razors and razor blades.

Another pricing objective, a more frequent one, is *target return on investment;* that is, the firm seeks to regain a certain percentage of its investment as income. This *return on investment* (ROI) is the ratio of profits to invested capital (buildings, machinery, offices, and so on). Thus, the ROI equals profits divided by capital. With this pricing objective, a firm seeks a predetermined average return for its entire set of operations. This return is equated with the compensation that the firm expects for the use of its capital. Such a pricing objective is traditionally found in firms that are monopolies or leaders in their industries—such as General Motors, Du Pont, International Harvester, and Union Carbide. General Motors, for instance, sets its objective at a 20 percent return on investment (after taxes), while International Harvester reportedly sets its goal at 10 percent.

More recently, the pricing objective of many companies has emphasized *cash flow.* This objective centers on generating cash as fast as possible and maintaining a steady flow of cash into the business. Emphasis on cash flow resulted from the recessionary trend of the 1970s that stretched into the 1980s and, particularly, from the high cost of borrowing money. With goods not selling, a cash squeeze resulted; cash reserves dwindled and lowered the ability of companies to finance future expansion. To generate cash, many companies pruned mediocre products and reduced prices to eliminate costly inventory. This was the pricing objective sought by Chrysler Corporation when it took the lead in offering large rebates to help move new cars off the dealers' lots.

General Motors chose another solution. In 1981, the company newly retooled its plants to produce its 1982 intermediates and J-car subcompacts. Since new plants take a while to reach maxiumum capacity, the result was a limited ability to supply GM's most popular automobiles. GM decided to boost prices abnormally high on these limited lines to bolster its cash flow and squeeze out the greatest amount of profits on these models.

Competitive Objectives

Many firms consciously price their products to *meet* or *prevent competition.* In a number of industries, there is a definite price leader, and the other companies simply follow the leader in setting prices. For instance, R. J. Reynolds traditionally sets cigarette prices, which other companies quickly imitate. In other situations, a company may enter a market with extremely low prices in order to discourage competitors. In still other situations, a marketer may price to reduce threats from aggressive competitors. But such competitive objectives can be costly. Zenith, for instance, watched its market share erode as RCA aggressively priced its color television sets. To stop such competition, Zenith countered with three successive price reductions—the last one at a time when seasonal demand was on the rise. The result was a sizable $4.7 million loss for Zenith in that year.

Costs

The costs associated with bringing a product to the market are a crucial ingredient in determining its price. Such costs represent the "floor" for the price—the minimum level at which it can be set—for prices that are less than costs provide no profit and soon banish the firm from the market. Some firms do set prices below total costs for some products, but only for a short time. In the long run, the prices charged must cover all the costs incurred in marketing the product.

But to say that "costs" are the basis for the price is too simplistic, for there are many components to the cost. We will look at these various cost components and then examine some ways that marketers use them to determine the list price for a product. Table 11-1 lists seven types of costs that influence pricing. We will examine them now.

Fixed Costs

Total fixed costs (TFC) are costs that do not change, no matter what the quantity of output (see columns 1 and 2 of Table 11-1). Such costs normally include executives' salaries, plant and equipment depreciation, property taxes, employees' health insurance premiums, and the like. These costs exist whether the firm produces a million units of the product or chooses to produce no units at all. While fixed costs can change in the long run (when a new plant is built, for instance), they remain constant in the short run.

Variable Costs

Total variable costs (TVC) are costs that fluctuate, depending on the quantity of output (see columns 1 and 3 in Table 11-1). Variable costs typically include raw materials, fuel, workers' wages, packaging, sales commissions, freight, and other such charges. If no products are produced, no variable costs are incurred. And we know that, in practice, variable costs can change as the level of output increases, since discounts often are given for large quantities of raw materials and workers tend to become more efficient at making the product. Over time, however, these cost efficiencies are lost, and average variable costs rise (see column 6).

Total and Average Costs

As shown in column 4 of Table 11-1, *total costs (TC)* are the sum of total fixed costs (column 2) and total variable costs (column 3). That is,

$$TC = TFC + TVC$$

Any change in total costs can be attributed to changes in variable costs, since fixed costs by definition do not change.

TABLE 11-1 Types of Costs for an Individual Firm

(1) Quantity of output, Q	(2) Total fixed cost, TFC	(3) Total variable cost, TVC	(4) Total cost, TC	(5) Average fixed cost, AFC	(6) Average variable cost, AVC	(7) Average total cost, ATC*	(8) Marginal cost, MC
0	$50	$ 0	$ 50	$ —	$ —	$ —	
1	50	20	70	50.00	20.00	70.00	$20
2	50	32	82	25.00	16.00	41.00	12
3	50	40	90	16.67	13.33	30.00	8
4	50	44	94	12.50	11.00	23.50	4
5	50	48	98	10.00	9.60	19.60	4
6	50	54	104	8.33	9.00	17.33	6
7	50	64	114	7.14	9.14	16.28	10
8	50	80	130	6.25	10.00	16.25	16
9	50	108	158	5.56	12.00	17.56	28
10	50	150	200	5.00	15.00	20.00	42

*Note: Average total costs (col. 7) decrease but then increase for the last two items. Here, average variable costs (col. 6) have been increasing faster than average fixed costs (col. 5) have been decreasing. The increased rate of change in average variable costs is due to such factors as using a less efficient work force, paying higher prices for raw materials, and paying overtime and other costs associated with a reduction in efficiency.

There are three types of average costs: average fixed costs (column 5), average variable costs (column 6), and average total costs (column 7). The *average fixed cost (AFC)* results when the total fixed cost (column 2) is divided by the quantity of output (column 1). From Table 11-1 we see that for a quantity of eight items produced,

$$AFC = \frac{TFC}{Q} = \frac{50}{8} = 6.25$$

In a similar fashion, by dividing total variable cost (column 3) and total cost by the quantity of output, the *average variable cost (AVC)* and the *average cost (AC)* respectively are determined.

Marginal Cost

Finally, the *marginal cost (MC)* is the cost of producing one more unit than the most recent unit produced (see column 8 in Table 11-1). This is the "extra" cost of making just one more unit of the product. It is the difference between the total cost of producing the last unit of product and the total cost associated with producing one more unit. And, again, since the part of the total cost that is fixed remains constant, the only change that takes place is in the total costs, or the change in total variable costs.

Let's look at the marginal cost of producing unit 9 of the product. Since the marginal cost is the *change* in total costs,

$$MC \text{ of unit } 9 = TC \text{ of unit } 9 - TC \text{ of unit } 8$$
$$= 158 - 130$$
$$= 28$$

or

$$MC \text{ of unit } 9 = TVC \text{ of unit } 9 - TVC \text{ of unit } 8$$
$$= 108 - 80$$
$$= 28$$

In the real world, marketers perhaps rely on costs more than on any other component in the determination of the list price. While costs cannot always be determined exactly, the estimates are usually accurate enough to suggest the reasonable limits for profitable pricing. With that disclaimer in mind, let's examine some approaches to pricing that are often used in the business world.

Approaches to Pricing

Formula Pricing

Many producers resort to a simple formula to arrive at their selling price. Formulas are often used because they are easy to apply and they eliminate judgment on the part of the price setter. Such formulas emphasize either the cost components just described or the elements that make up the most components—such as direct labor or materials or administrative overhead.

A large management consulting firm, for example, uses a very simple formula in pricing its services. It determines the daily fees paid to its consultants who work on a project (a variable-cost component) and then multiplies these amounts by 3. This pricing approach allows one-third to cover the salaries of the consultants, one-third for overhead expenses (office space, secretaries, phones, and so on), and one-third for profits. But formulas can also be more complex. For instance, in the electronics industry, the pricing formula has been found to be: Price = material cost + direct labor cost + 100 percent of direct labor for overhead + 120 to 180 percent of direct labor for all other costs.[1] Table 11-2 shows how these two formulas can be applied in pricing three different products.

Such formulas are used in the hope that the final price will be sufficient to cover all costs (even though they are not all used in the computation) and still leave some profit. The main problem with this simple and quick approach, as with all cost-oriented approaches, is that it does not consider whether the market will pay the price that is determined. In short, demand considerations are ignored. Also, this approach totally

---

[1]"Management Problems in the Electronics Industry," *Management Research Summary,* Small Business Administration (November 1962), p. 3.

TABLE 11-2   Examples of Formula Pricing

MANAGEMENT CONSULTING FIRM

	Projects			
	1	2	3	Total
Variable cost (consultant's fees due)	$200	$100	$150	$ 450
Overhead cost	$200	$100	$150	$ 450
Salaries (consultant's fees paid)	200	100	150	450
Profit	200	100	150	450
Daily consulting fees charged	$600	$300	$450	$1350

ELECTRONICS INDUSTRY

	Products		
	1	2	3
Material cost	$1.50	$0.50	$1.80
Direct labor cost	0.30	0.10	1.00
Overhead (100% of direct labor cost)	0.30	0.10	1.00
Other cost (150% of direct labor cost)	0.45	0.15	1.50
Selling price	$2.55	$0.85	$5.30

neglects competitive actions to underprice. Often competitors can do it for lower costs or less profit and thus steal sales from the formula pricer.

Cost-Plus Pricing

While many firms have their own unique formulas for pricing, others often use the *cost-plus approach*. This determines the list price by adding a reasonable profit to the cost per unit, or average total cost. The price setter simply uses the table of costs, taking the appropriate average cost for the desired quantity of output and then adding an amount for profit. For instance, using Table 11-1, if the firm were to produce 8 units of the product, the average cost would be $16.25; the marketer then might add $5 per unit for profit, bringing the unit selling price to $21.25.

This cost-plus approach ensures that all costs will be covered and that the desired profit level will be achieved. However, it relies on forecasted costs, which can be dangerous because costs often change rapidly. Moreover, this approach also fails to ensure that the quantity of output will actually be sold, since the marketer cannot know whether the price of $21.25 is in line with consumers' perceptions of the value of the bundle of utility. And if fewer than 8 units are sold, the firm's profit picture may be bleak at best. For instance, let's assume that only 5 units are sold, bringing total sales to $106.25 (5 units × $21.25). From Table 11-1, we see that the total cost of making all 8 units (3 of which are still in inventory) is $130.00, resulting in a loss of

$23.75. Once again, this illustrates the importance of knowing the demand for the product when determining its price. Even so, many industries rely heavily on cost approaches to set the prices for products.

Of course, there *are* some situations in which the cost-plus approach to pricing is perfectly suitable, but in those cases the level and nature of demand are established and known. The level of consumption for some products is stable from year to year, and not very sensitive to price changes. Examples include milk, bread, paper clips, and bobby pins. For these and other staple items, consumption does not vary much, and minor price changes have little effect on demand.

Competitive bidding situations also lend themselves to the cost-plus approach. In many buying situations—especially those involving the government—a known quantity of the product is needed, and a number of firms are asked to submit bids (prices). For instance, McDonnell-Douglas, Boeing, and other airplane manufacturers may be invited to bid on a government contract to provide ten jet airplanes for the Air Force. Since the quantity (demand) is known, the associated costs can be estimated and the price can be computed by the cost-plus approach.

Cost-Plus Pricing by Intermediaries

Earlier, we noted that the price which final consumers pay is the result of several markups, added as the product makes intermediate stops along the way from producers to consumers. In setting their prices, wholesalers and retailers basically use a cost-plus approach. Let's see how this works.

If a wholesaler pays $20 for a product from the manufacturer, the wholesaler must charge customers more than $20 in order to make a profit. If the wholesaler adds $5 to the price and then sells the product to a retailer for $25, the markup is $5. This includes an amount to cover all wholesaling costs beyond the manufacturer's price for the product, plus something to ensure a profit. Since markups are usually expressed as a *percentage of the selling price,* in this example the wholesaler's markup is 20 percent, which is rather typical. In turn, the retailer would add a markup to $25, the cost of the product from the wholesaler. This retailer's markup is usually between 40 and 60 percent, depending on the type of product handled. Assuming a 50 percent markup on selling price, the retailer would charge final consumers $50 for the product. Thus, at each intermediate step, the price is determined on the basis of some rather simple calculations. First, the *selling price (SP)* of an intermediary is the sum of the cost *(C),* or the price of the good, plus the markup *(M):*

$$SP = C + M$$

If the markup is expressed as a percentage of the selling price, the formula can be reduced to two variables—the cost of the product *(C)* and the selling price *(SP):*

$$SP = C + \% \, SP$$

And, since each intermediary knows the cost of the product and also knows what percentage of markup is desired, the determination of the intermediate selling price is quite simple. Some intermediaries use the same markup for all products, while others use different markups for different items. Grocery stores, for instance, use a markup of 6 to 8 percent for soap and sugar, 15 to 18 percent for canned goods, and 25 to 35 percent for meats and produce.

Pricing by Target Return on Investment

Using this popular approach, the price setter seeks to obtain a predetermined *percentage return* on the capital used to produce and distribute the product, or a specific total dollar return. This method is similar to the average-cost approach, and an example will show how it works.

Assume that a company with the costs shown in Table 11-1 has invested $200 in the development of the product and expects a 10 percent return on that $200 capital investment. The expected profit is 10 percent of $200, or $20. The $20 is simply added to the fixed cost, as shown in Table 11-3; in short, the percentage return is treated as a fixed cost of doing business. Then the average costs are computed again to arrive at the price charged, which now includes the desired profit (percent return). In this case, the price for eight items is $18.75.

This approach, as with other cost approaches, gets an "A" rating for simplicity. And if the company sells all the items planned, it will achieve its target return. However, the approach ignores the demand side—as well as competitive price strategies—and the targeted return is not guaranteed. Look at Table 11-4 and see what happens to return on investment if the firm sells five items rather than the eight items planned. They still have three items in inventory and are realizing a loss—and consequently a negative ROI.

TABLE 11-3   Target Return on Investment for an Individual Firm

(1)	(2)	(3)	(4)	(5)	(6)	(7)	(8)
	Total fixed cost		Total cost	Average fixed cost		Average total	
Quantity of output, Q	plus target return, TFC	Total variable cost, TVC	plus target return, TC	plus target return, AFC	Average variable cost, AVC	cost plus target return, ATC	Marginal cost, MC
0	$70	$ 0	$ 70	$ —	$ —	$ —	
1	70	20	90	70.00	20.00	90.00	$20
2	70	32	102	35.00	16.00	51.00	12
3	70	40	110	23.33	13.33	36.67	8
4	70	44	114	17.50	11.00	28.50	4
5	70	48	118	14.00	9.60	23.60	4
6	70	54	124	11.67	9.00	20.67	6
7	70	64	134	10.00	9.14	19.14	10
8	70	80	150	8.75	10.00	18.75	16
9	70	108	178	7.78	12.00	19.78	28
10	70	150	220	7.00	15.00	22.00	42

TABLE 11-4   Target Return with Less than Estimated Sales

Estimated sales: 8 items		*Actual sales: 5 items*	
Total revenue (estimated)		Total revenue (actual)	
(8 × $18.75) =	$150.00	(5 × $18.75) =	$ 93.75
Total fixed cost		Total fixed cost	
(excluding target return)	$ 50.00	(excluding target return)	$ 50.00
Total variable cost	80.00	Total variable cost	80.00
Total cost	$130.00	Total cost	$130.00
Profit (loss)	$ 20.00	Profit (loss)	($36.25)
Return on investment = $\frac{20}{200}$ = 10%		Return on investment = $\frac{(36.25)}{200.00}$ = − 18.12%	

Pricing by Marginal Costs

Using this approach to pricing, a firm sells an additional unit of product for the extra cost of producing that unit. Referring to Table 11-1 again, we see that the marketer would sell unit 7 for $10, rather than for $16.28, which would recover cost fully. Of course, full recovery would follow if the average total cost of the product were charged. But in this case the seller recovers only part of the costs—perhaps the variable costs or the out-of-pocket costs of making that next unit. In practice, the seller will not get precisely the marginal cost, the $10, but, instead, will realize something greater, though still less than the average cost.

Obviously, pricing on the basis of marginal or near-marginal costs is not the best solution, since profits cannot be realized unless all costs are recovered. But there are times when such a pricing strategy may be advantageous to a marketer. For example, if a firm is threatened with a plant shutdown but wants to keep its labor force employed, this "survival" approach to pricing may be useful. In addition, marketers who are engaging in a price war may resort to this tactic to drive competitors away. And when consumers' acceptance of a new product is sought, the "special introductory offer" may approximate this approach. Finally, when marketers want to build traffic for their store, they may price a few items at below full cost; attractive prices, it is reasoned, will bring more than the usual number of shoppers to the store, and they may also purchase more of the regularly priced items. Such low-priced items are called *loss leaders.* (See Application 11-3.)

The Importance of Costs in Contemporary Pricing

Throughout recent history, firms faced an inflationary economy that raised costs to unprecedented levels. Consequently, the rising costs squeezed profits, since sales did not increase much and companies chose the defensive tactic of increasing prices to maintain their profit margins. For instance, in 1976 Du Pont explained its 6 to 10 percent price increase for synthetic fibers as being necessary to recover costs. The company was squeezed by a major increase in the cost of petroleum-based products used as raw materials; and, of course, the costs of labor and transportation also rose. Such cost problems plagued nearly every industry, and their impact can be

Application 11-3
Marginal Cost Pricing—
Freezing Out? . . . Warm Up Empty Rooms

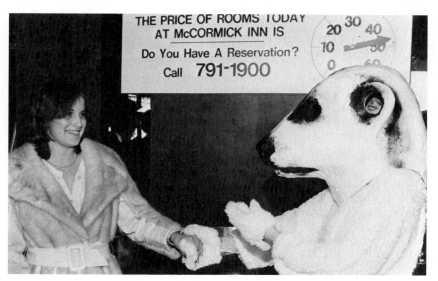

THE PRICE OF ROOMS TODAY
AT McCORMICK INN IS

Do You Have A Reservation?

Call **791-1900**

(Photo Idea, Inc.)

Hotels around the country live by their occupancy rate, the percentage of rooms that are rented on a given date. Occupancy rates are somewhat seasonal; for instance, the Thanksgiving and Christmas holiday season tends to be a slower time since most frequent travelers are home with their families.

Hotels and motels operate on a basis of high fixed costs (the costs of the building, heating, and maintenance) and rather low variable costs (the costs of maid service and laundry, mainly). As a result, the rental of a room at even a low rate often covers variable costs and adds something to cover the fixed costs. Such reasoning led Chicago's McCormick Inn to offer an extraordinary consumer opportunity—"Rooms by Degree."

Chicago is known for its blustery winters, but for some travelers the weather was a bonanza. The McCormick Inn offered a variable room rate linked to the temperature outside. As the temperature dropped, so did the cost of staying at the McCormick Inn. If the temperature outdoors was 20 degrees, for example, the cost of a room was $20. If the thermometer dipped to zero or below, the room was free. Guests making reservations for three or more days in advance could enjoy room rates based on the check-in temperature. Prior to registering, guests were allowed to wait outside the building and choose a time and temperature at which to check in. This special was offered to guests between November 16 and December 30, 1979.

How successful was it? Very! The temperature throughout the period rarely dropped below 40 degrees!!

Source of data: Based on press releases, McCormick Inn, Chicago, Nov. 1979.

dramatized by an example from the fruit and vegetable canning industry in 1975. At that time, the only cost which had not risen was the cost of farm crops, which actually dropped. But agricultural products made up only about 36 percent of the cost of producing a can of food. Tin cans, for example, had more than doubled in price since

1967, and the container accounted for about 25 percent of manufacturing costs. Labor, which made up about 16 percent of the total cost, was 35 percent higher than in 1972. And the cost of waste removal, water treatment, and energy all rose dramatically and contributed to the problem. As a result, prices moved upward but still did not match the cost increases. Such increases have persisted in many industries since the energy crisis of 1973 and 1974. In 1981, Detroit auto makers recouped their higher manufacturing and transportation costs by boosting the once minor "destination charge." Once an incidental item in a new-car purchase, fees became uniform for each model (instead of being based on distance between assembly plant and dealer) and often amounted to less than half the actual destination fee. General Motors Corp. justified the charges by saying they reflect transportation costs in the broadest sense—including shipment of all parts and materials used in building the vehicle. These examples make it clear that the cost component is a major factor in contemporary price determination. This pass-on charge is tacked on the sticker price, so the total price is not inflated in advertising and other promotional materials.

Demand

While the costs for the product set the lower end, or "floor," for the price, the level of demand establishes its upper limits—the "ceiling." As noted earlier, if the expected satisfaction that will come from the product is less than the price of the product, no exchange will take place. In short, *demand* reflects the upper limits of what consumers are willing to give up in order to obtain the product.

To clarify this point, consider the following. In 1976, Polaroid introduced its revolutionary instant-movie system at a list price of about $650. The system had some problems: There was no sound option, movies were short, the screen was small, and the picture was dark. As a result, consumers were not buying. Despite some product adjustments such as slow motion and stop-action, potential buyers continued to resist, and prices slid to as low as $270 in 1979—a saving of 60 percent and $80 below the retailers' own cost. By the end of 1979, only 50,000 to 75,000 units had been sold—and Polaroid took an inventory tax loss of $68 million. The price and perceived value were out of line.

Demand is difficult for price setters to estimate; it is elusive and changes often. Consumers are fickle, and their attitudes, values, needs, and wants change—often rapidly. Keeping on top of their moods and whims regarding what they will pay for products is extremely difficult. As we noted in Chapters 6 and 7, it is tricky at best to read consumers' minds and thus understand demand. Certainly, marketing surveys can and do help to identify the level of demand, but there is still a great deal of difference between what consumers say they will do and what they in fact do, especially when the exchange of money is involved. The true test is in the marketplace, where prices can actually be tested.

As further proof of the difficulty in estimating demand, we note that some high prices are not only accepted but accepted enthusiastically. General Electric, for instance, introduced its Touch 'n Curl mist hair curler for $27, and it outsold a similar hair curler priced at only $15 by as much as 45 percent. Litton Industries reported that its $499 counter-top microwave oven accounted for more than 70 percent of its sales of counter-top models. And Litton's best-selling microwave oven-range combination with a list price of $1099 outsold models that were $400 cheaper. Even at discount stores, where blouses and shirts are priced at $2.99 to $11, the $11 items typically sell best. Such buying behavior indicates a concentration on quality in today's market-place. Many people are buying fewer goods but insisting on higher quality. Such situations show that estimating demand is not only difficult but challenging. Estimating what price level is high enough to meet demand without going too high makes pricing decisions more of an art than a science—contrary to the implications of pricing through cost formulas. It's essential, then, that marketers understand and consider demand when setting prices. (See Application 11-4.) Now, let's examine the demand factor.

Application 11-4
Demand Pricing—Hitting the Ceiling?

It might not seem to be the brightest idea that the General Electric Company ever came up with: a clunky, squared-off light blub that is priced at $10. GE spent $20 million and four to five years developing a long-life bulb and brought it to market in 1981. And GE was not alone— Westinghouse Electric Corp. and North American Philips Lighting Corp. joined them. But why the flurry of competition?

The new lamp, which uses miniature flourescent tubes or tiny arc lights, lasts five years and can save about $20 in electric bills over its life. The GE bulb's shape resembles a double-scoop ice cream cone while the Westinghouse version looks like a 7½-inch-long fireplug. Because of

(Courtesy General Electric Company)

technical similarities, consumers will find it difficult to decide which brand to buy.

From a manufacturer's standpoint, the marketing will be very competitive. GE holds the edge in that it controls about one-half the market for incandescent bulbs. And its dominance is clearly evident in many stores where GE bulbs are

either stocked exclusively or occupy most of the display space. Hardest hit in the bulb race is the handful of small lamp makers that have spent years to develop lights that conserve energy. As a Westinghouse executive said, "Nobody is predicting that utility rates are going anywhere but up."

Even so, persuading the consumer to spend 10 times as much as usual on a light bulb will require intensive promotion. "We face an enormous education process," said the manager of product planning at Westinghouse's Lamp Division.

Source of data: "The Race to the $10 Light Bulb," *Business Week,* May 19, 1980, p. 124.

TABLE 11-5	Revenue for an Individual Firm		
(1) Quantity demanded, Q	*(2)* Price, P	*(3)* Total revenue, TR	*(4)* Marginal revenue, MR
0	$32	$ 0	
1	30	30	30
2	28	56	26
3	26	78	22
4	24	96	18
5	22	110	14
6	20	120	10
7	18	126	6
8	16	128	2
9	14	126	− 2
10	12	120	− 6

Types of Demand

Table 11-5 shows the typical demand situation facing most firms today. We see from columns 1 and 2 that as the price for a product decreases, the quantity purchased goes up. Conversely, as the price goes up, the quantity purchased goes down. Because of this situation, we say that there is an *inverse relationship between price and quantity.*

Also illustrated by Table 11-5 are the *total revenue (TR),* which is the result of the price times the quantity sold, and the *marginal revenue (MR),* which is the increase in total revenue that results from the sale of one additional unit of product. That is, the marginal revenue is the "extra" revenue that results when the next unit of product is sold. It is derived from the *change* in total revenue that is acquired by selling the product at a given price.

The inverse relationship between price and demand is exemplified by sales for digital watches. When they were first introduced to the market in 1974, they were priced at over $200, and total sales were 650,000 watches. But prices began to drop until, by late 1975, they hovered at around $50; 1975 sales climbed to 3.5 million units. Then, in 1976, as prices fell to below $20, sales rose to 15 million watches.

Not all products, however, have this traditional price-quantity relationship. The demand for some products is such that, up to a point, higher prices bring a higher volume of sales (see Figure 11-3). The prestige wristwatches mentioned at the beginning of the chapter fall in this category; no additional sales are likely to be generated for Rolex's President watch by lowering the price from $7950 to $7500. But products do not have to be unusually expensive to have this kind of relationship. In examining exchange behavior, we noted that Pillsbury has marketed two lines of "heat and serve" biscuits that are identical except in terms of packaging, brand name, and price. Two price segments exist—the price shopper and the quality shopper. Many homemakers apparently are willing to spend extra money to be assured of quality. That higher price gives them security. The same applies to baby foods,

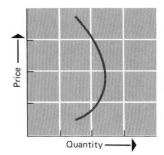

Figure 11-3 The demand curve for prestige and high-quality products.

dietetic foods, and smoke detectors. Consumers tend to believe that higher price indicates higher quality, especially with products that could have undesirable consequences or with those that have large brand-to-brand differences in quality and social status. Price is also used as a clue to quality when no other information about the product is known.

Price Elasticity

It is interesting to note that consumers are more sensitive to price changes in some cases than in others. This sensitivity is termed the *price elasticity of demand,* which reflects changes in the quantity purchased relative to changes in price. In practice, the elasticity of demand can be classified into three types (see Figure 11-4):

1 With *elastic demand,* a percentage change in price brings about a *greater* percentage change in the quantity sold (generally in the opposite direction).

2 With *inelastic demand,* a percentage change in price brings about a *lesser* percentage change in the quantity sold (generally in the opposite direction).

3 With *unitary demand,* a percentage change in price brings about an *equal* percentage change in the quantity sold (generally in the opposite direction).

In situations of *elastic demand,* the market is quite sensitive to changes in price. For example, the automobile industry has found that in most situations, its market is quite elastic; that is, a given percentage of price reduction will result in a greater percentage of sales increase. This fact led the industry to offer rebates as a means of stimulating sales during the days of sluggish demand. It also led the industry to oppose legislation that would add to the manufacturing costs of forcing auto makers to provide antipollution devices and improved safety features. Those higher costs would translate into higher price increases, which in turn would lead to an even higher percentage drop in sales.

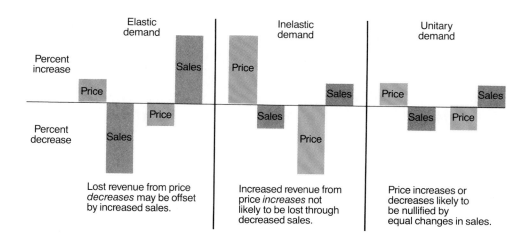

Figure 11-4 Elastic, inelastic, and unitary demand.

In situations of *inelastic demand,* the market is rather insensitive to changes in price. Thus, the total revenue for a product decreases as the price per unit falls. This is so because consumers do not purchase enough additional units of the product at a lower price to make up for the revenue lost through the price reduction. Even though greater sales volume results from the lower price (as in the usual relationship between price and quantity), the increase in sales is not enough to raise or even maintain total revenue. An inelastic demand is typical for such products as salt, milk, and even gasoline. Economists estimate that the elasticity of gasoline is 0.15—a 10 percent rise in gasoline prices causes a 1.5 percent decline in demand. But gasoline consumption is becoming increasingly sensitive to price—several years ago, this elasticity figure was well under 0.10.

Situations of *unitary elasticity* are usually found where there are many sellers whose products may easily be substituted for one another. No one seller, then, can influence the price to an appreciable extent. The demand for many agricultural products reflects unitary elasticity, since a single farmer cannot control the prices at which products will be sold. Thus, prices rise and fall in accordance with supply and demand, rather than as desired by producers.

Price Ranges

Consumers rarely seek products with a single, firm price in mind. Instead, they typically identify a need or want and then seek satisfaction within a range of prices. In fact, it seems that people may refrain from buying a product both when its price appears too high and when the price appears too low. This lower limit is tied to the price-quality relationship. Apparently, consumers feel that a price that is too low signifies low quality ("You get what you pay for"). So, while we usually talk of demand in terms of the ceiling price, the demand concept may well provide an idea of the floor, or lower limit, too. Traditionally, the level of demand indicates the upper limit, beyond which exchange will not happen. But demand is not tied to just one price figure; it really comprises a range of prices. The marketer's job is to set the price appropriately within the limits set by the market.

Determining the Level of Demand

As we have noted, price setters have a great deal of difficulty determining exactly what the level of demand for a product really is. However, there are some techniques that marketers use to get a handle on the price that the market will accept. Marketers sometimes rely on rough judgment, but intuition is not the best method, since it is a hodge-podge of hunches and guesses. Still, hidden within those "guesstimates" may be some correct judgments, and a marketer's experience is certainly better than picking a price out of a hat. Marketing experience makes judgment much more appropriate as a basis for pricing decisions—particularly when the marketer has dealt with the product or the market in the past.

In some cases, historical sales and price information may be available and can be subjected to sophisticated statistical methods to arrive at a quantitative estimate of demand. But the value of this approach is restricted by two important factors: the data used and future conditions. In many cases, available data do not exactly fit the present needs of the price setter. While the government publishes vast quantities of data about all sorts of products, they may not apply to the marketer's situation. Knowing, for example, the relationship between pear prices charged by farmers and the resulting pear sales may have little value in determining price levels for canned pears in a supermarket. Additionally, we have already seen that consumers' demand can be expected to change. Data that reflect past levels of demand may not indicate future levels. Therefore, statistical methods of estimating demand may be more acceptable for staple products like milk and bread than for new products or for fashion or fad items.

Marketers also turn to surveys and market experiments to test the level of appropriate prices. Market researchers often attempt to get at what consumers will pay simply by asking them. But a question like "Would you pay X dollars for Y item?" must be interpreted cautiously, for there is a big difference between the willingness to pay, say, $9000 for a Chevrolet Impala and the behavior of really plunking down that amount of money. Surveys might be more useful in determining price levels for industrial goods, since industrial buyers are more aware of the impact of prices on the firm's operations, and their approach to prices is more rational than that of most consumers.

Market tests may also be useful. When different prices are tested in two or more markets, consumers' reactions to each price can be gauged. The product is then priced at whichever level produces the desired objective.

Finally, marketers look at the levels of prices for substitute products, especially those of competitors. This aspect of price determination is examined a bit later in the chapter.

Breakeven Analysis

Often price setters are confronted with a number of possible prices that seem reasonable and are close to the prices of similar products or brands. As an aid in setting the price, they may turn to breakeven analysis, which brings costs into the picture.

Breakeven analysis focuses on the volume of sales at that point where total revenue equals total costs, i.e., where no profit or loss is incurred. This approach assumes a given price and a knowledge of costs; and once the breakeven volume is determined, price setters can ask whether it is a feasible volume of sales. To cover costs, this sales volume must be reached. If the marketers are not relatively sure that the given price will generate at least that breakeven volume of sales, then the product should not be priced at that level—or maybe the product should not be put on the market at all. Let's look at how breakeven analysis works.

The basic idea of breakeven analysis is that the price of a product sold goes to cover its own variable costs as well as to leave something to cover the fixed costs of producing the product. As shown in Figure 11-5, the *breakeven point* is reached when enough products have been sold to cover their own variable costs along with the *total* fixed costs. At sales volumes less than the breakeven point, total fixed costs will not be

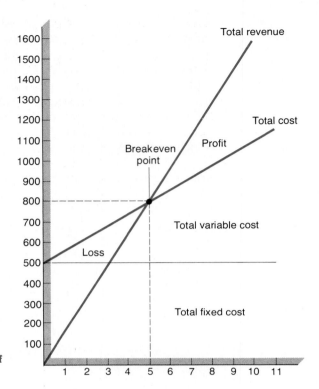

Figure 11-5 Breakeven point with selling price of $160 per unit.

covered, and a loss will result. At sales volumes greater than breakeven, anything over the variable costs becomes profit.

The breakeven point can be determined by the following equation:[2] Of course,

$$BE \text{ volume (units)} = \frac{TFC}{\text{fixed-cost contribution}}$$

or

$$BE \text{ volume (units)} = \frac{TFC}{\text{selling price} - \text{variable cost per unit}}$$

price setters still must decide whether the necessary volume of sales can be achieved. They do this by examining a number of different prices, as shown in Table 11-6, and then comparing the needed volumes for each price. The price is determined on the

---

[2]The term *fixed-cost contribution* refers to that amount of the selling price which is left over after variable costs have been accounted for.

TABLE 11-6 Computation of the Breakeven Point

(1) Unit price	(2) Unit variable cost, AVC	(3) Contribution to fixed cost	(4) Total fixed cost	(5) Breakeven point (units)
$120	$60	$ 60	$500	8.3
160	60	100	500	5.0
200	60	140	500	3.6
300	60	240	500	2.1

basis of which combination of price and volume seems most appropriate and most likely.

Breakeven analysis makes two simplifying assumptions. First, it assumes that the variable cost per unit is constant—but we learned earlier and saw in Table 11-1 that variable costs depend on the volume produced. Second, breakeven analysis assumes that any quantity can be sold at a given price. In reality, however, we know that for a given price, there is a maximum quantity which will be sold, and that this reflects the top limit of demand. (This relationship is shown in Table 11-7.) Price setters, then, must compare the breakeven volumes of various prices with what they believe are the maximum volumes which can be sold at that price. If the estimated maximum volume is below the breakeven quantity, then that price is rejected. The price finally selected is that one which gives the greatest amount of profit. In Table 11-7, the sale of five items at a price of $200 results in the greatest profit ($200).

TABLE 11-7 Relationship of Breakeven Analysis, Total Revenue from Market Demand, and Profits

(1) Unit price	(2) Market demand at given price (units)	(3) Total revenue TR = (1) × (2)	(4) Breakeven point (units)	(5) Total cost of units sold*	(6) Total profits (spread between TR and TC at number of units sold) (3) − (5)
$120	7	$ 840	8.3	$920	$ −80
160	6	960	5.0	860	100
200	5	1000	3.6	800	200
300	2	600	2.1	620	−20

*Fixed cost ($500) plus variable cost ($60 per unit) times quantity demanded.

Breakeven analysis is a useful tool for price determination. But it is most appropriate when the product line is small and variable costs can be computed easily—as is the case with fast-food chains and motels.

Competition

While costs set the floor for the price and are used most often to determine the list price, and while demand sets the upper level, or ceiling, for the price, price setters also have to consider the prices of alternative bundles of satisfaction that buyers might choose. Most often, those alternatives are the products offered by competitors, but this need not always be the case. New products, for example, satisfy needs that were never taken care of *in the same manner.* Thus, warmup suits replaced sweat suits for joggers and other sports enthusiasts; leather athletic shoes replaced canvas tennis shoes and sneakers; and steel tennis rackets replaced wooden ones. In each case, the price of the traditional products presents potential buyers with a reference point for judging the value of the new products. And this reference price will be compared with the price of the new product, as will the differences in expected satisfaction. For instance, if $39.95 for a warmup suit does not give at least $25 more in perceived satisfaction than a $14.95 sweat suit does, the exchange will probably not take place.

Most often, though, buyers can compare the prices of directly competing products—of Colgate versus Crest toothpastes, Nestlé's Souptime versus Lipton's Cup-a-Soup, or Wilson versus Spalding golf clubs. In many such cases, competitors' prices become the key to price determination. For example, when Eastman Kodak entered the instant-camera market—a segment of the photographic business dominated by Polaroid—Kodak followed its usual strategy: it priced the camera cheaply in order to maximize the profits on film sales. Kodak priced its first two cameras at $53.50 and $69.50, in direct competition with Polaroid's Pronto versions priced at $66.00 and $83.00. But Kodak's film price was $7.45 for ten prints, while Polaroid's was $6.99.

Similarly, in the nonaspirin analgesic market, two competitors—Bristol-Myers and Johnson & Johnson's McNeil Laboratories—brought Datril and Tylenol to the marketplace amid heavy price competition. McNeil Laboratories was first on the market, pricing Tylenol at about $3 for 100 tablets. In introducing Datril, Bristol-Myers advertised it as a nonaspirin equivalent to Tylenol but lower in price. In many cities the difference was as much as $1 on 100 tablets. Of course, a price-cutting campaign followed, with the result that the price for 100 tablets of the nonaspirin product settled at about $1.29. (See Application 11-5.)

Obviously, then, competitive pressures are extremely influential in setting prices for products. In fact, competitive pricing is the key ingredient of discount department stores, cut-rate drugstores, and generic supermarkets. Their appeal is in offering products for prices below those of direct competitors. But, for most price setters, price determination requires a solid understanding of the complete costs of the product and an indication of what consumers are willing to pay for the product. Marketers then must temper these two inputs with information about competitors' prices.

Application 11-5
Competitive Pricing—Putting the Squeeze on Retailers

(Courtesy Canon U.S.A., Inc.)

For years the competitive struggle to market copiers has resulted in both handsome promotions and discounting. Now, it appears that the higher-priced market is also in for a round of price competition as Japanese companies like Cannon, Sharp, and Minolta *eye* the big copier market dominated by Xerox. The result, *Business Week* says, could be a brutal price war and a classic market struggle.

Caught in the middle are 15,000 independent office-equipment dealers. Price cutting already has reduced dealer margins by 25 percent and more. Meanwhile, the manufacturers, working with lower margins themselves, have cut back on the volume discounts for smaller dealers and on the amount of time allowed for payment after delivery.

"The price cutting is ferocious; it's ridiculous; it's like wild dogs in the street," Michael Haber, president of Atlantic Photocopy, a New York City dealer, told *Business Week*. He says that office-equipment stores in Manhattan are slashing up to 35 percent off the list prices of many popular models. Haber knows firsthand the damage this kind of price war can bring. His company is still operating in a Chapter II reorganization after eighteen months. He attributes this business condition partly to excessive discounting by competitors.

Source of data: "The Squeeze on Copier Dealers," *Business Week,* July 6, 1981, pp. 78–79.

Looking Back

This chapter explored the nature and importance of price determination in an organization's marketing mix. We began by examining four factors that contribute to the decision about what the list price should be: objectives, costs, demand, and competition. The next chapter concludes our discussion of price determination by looking at pricing policies and the ways that marketers adjust initial prices. But before doing that, review the following important points:

1 The perceived value of the product is the key to price determination.

2 Price is a major ingredient in the bundle of satisfaction offered to consumers.

3 Price acts to ration and allocate scarce resources in the economy, bringing profits to the firm and, ultimately, satisfaction to society.

4 Most consumers' purchases today are made under a one-price policy.

5 Price determination is more an art than a science, and it begins with a pricing objective.

6 Cost-oriented pricing is simple to use, but it neglects market demand.

7 Cost-oriented pricing is useful in situations where the quantity demanded is known and where the market is rather insensitive to price.

8 Intermediaries use a form of cost-plus pricing that centers on a markup.

9 Marginal-cost pricing cannot be used over a long period of time.

10 Contemporary pricing decisions, given recent inflationary trends, have relied on costs as a determinant.

11 It is extremely difficult to know how high a price consumers will accept.

12 Some products do not exhibit an inverse relationship between price and quantity (demand).

13 Consumers usually seek satisfaction within a range of prices.

14 Breakeven analysis helps marketers to estimate the feasibility of various price alternatives.

15 Competitive pricing compares the prices for alternative means of satisfying wants.

Key Terms

If you aren't sure what each of the following words means, look back at the text. Numbers refer to pages on which the words are defined. Additional information can be found by checking the index and the glossary at the end of the book.

Questions for Review

1 Briefly describe the major difference between a *one-price policy* and a *flexible-price policy.*

2 Why is it difficult for firms in large industries to meet the pricing objective of *growth and maintenance of market share?*

3 What is the major problem with using a formula approach to pricing?

4 What are the three classifications of *price elasticity of demand?* Which would marketers rather face if they wished to raise prices indiscriminately?

5 What are the two misleading assumptions behind breakeven analysis?

6 What are the major factors of consideration essential to price determination?

Questions for Thought and Discussion

1 At the height of its success, Perrier, France's bottled natural mineral water, retailed for 69 cents or more for a 23-ounce bottle. What made this an appropriate price?

2 What makes pricing an innovative new product more difficult than pricing adaptive replacements or imitative products?

3 Suppose a firm is operating at a level where its total revenue covers all the variable costs but only part of the fixed costs. In the short run, if it cannot raise prices or lower variable costs to compensate for this loss, should the firm then continue to operate?

4 Electronic games that beep, light up, and talk have been carrying "pricy" price tags—yet have been so eagerly sought by consumers that shortages have existed. How should Mattel or Milton Bradley determine the price for such a toy?

Suggested Project

Do a price-comparison study of several brands of products sold through different outlets in your area. When recording these data, try to note what additions to the product's bundle of utility may account for any price discrepancies. See what conclusions you can draw from this experiment.

Suggested Readings

Brooks, Douglas G.: "Cost-Oriented Pricing: A Realistic Solution to a Complicated Problem," *Journal of Marketing,* vol. 39 no. 2 (April 1975), pp. 72–74. A relatively simple, yet effective, model for cost-oriented pricing that achieves the profit goal is presented.

Dean, Joel: "The Role of Price in the American Business System," in *Pricing: The Critical Decision,* The American Management Association, New York, 1961, Report No. 66, pp. 5–11.

This work discusses the effects of environmental changes on the pricing decision, with particular emphasis on profitability and the marketing concept.

Jackson, Barbara Bond: "Manage Risk in Industrial Pricing," *Harvard Business Review,* vol. 58 (July–August 1980), pp. 121–133. This article provides a framework for analyzing and evaluating prices in the face of cost uncertainties.

Jones, D. Frank: "A Survey Technique to Measure Demand under Various Pricing Strategies," *Journal of Marketing,* vol. 39, no. 3 (July 1975), pp. 75–77. A case study is used to discuss a simple but flexible survey technique to measure demand with various pricing approaches.

Oxenfeldt, Alfred: "A Decision-Making Structure for Price Decisions," *Journal of Marketing,* vol. 37, no. 1 (January 1973), pp. 48–53. A comprehensive and systematic guide to integrating and managing the pricing decision within a firm is presented in this article.

Riesz, Peter C.: "Price versus Quality in the Marketplace, 1961–1975," *Journal of Retailing,* vol. 54 (Winter 1978), pp. 15–28. This study of 1062 brands affirms the positive relationship between price and sales due to quality perceptions by consumers.

Shapiro, Benson P., and Barbara B. Jackson: "Industrial Pricing to Meet Customer Needs," *Harvard Business Review,* vol. 56 (November–December 1978), pp. 119–127. This article explains why industrial marketers should set prices according to their customers' perceptions of product benefits and costs, not their own.

Tucker, Spencer A.: *Pricing for Higher Profit,* McGraw-Hill, New York, 1966. This quantitative text treats the economics of the pricing decision.

Chapter 12

Price Administration

Looking Ahead

The last chapter explored the nature of the price ingredient in the marketing mix. We looked closely at four major factors that shape the list price offered to consumers: objectives, costs, demand, and competition. This chapter examines a fifth influence: pricing policies. After looking at pricing policies, we will explore various ways to adjust the base price to meet certain conditions in the marketplace.

Key Topics

The nature of the two major pricing policies: skimming and penetration

How retailers adjust the list price to match consumers' demand

How marketers adjust the bundle of satisfaction to be in line with forced prices

The major approaches to pricing throughout a product's life cycle

How price is administered and adjusted to meet special market conditions

The important legal considerations that affect pricing

In Chapter 11 we looked at four forces that influence the determination of a list price for a product: The *costs* set the floor for the price; the level of *demand* sets the ceiling; the level of *competitive prices* provides a benchmark against which to compare price alternatives; and, of course, all these factors must be considered in light of the pricing *objectives*. But even after all this, the final list price cannot yet be determined. Often, a firm's specific policies temper the price even after costs, demand, and the competitive situation have been accounted for. A company's approach to pricing may range from intensely aggressive to passive, depending on its pricing objectives. The first section of this chapter will focus on various pricing policies and will provide the final input to determining what the list price will be. Then we will examine how companies for various reasons adjust the list price to meet certain needs and demands of the marketplace. Finally, the chapter will conclude with a discussion of some legal aspects of pricing.

Pricing Policies

The pricing strategy of a marketing organization can be set to work through use of pricing policies. *Policies* are general rules intended to keep an organization's decisions in line with its objectives. In other words, policies are guidelines that assist the members of an organization who make daily decisions. Without policies, decision makers run the risk of selecting a course of action that neither fits the strategy nor furthers the organization's goals. *Pricing policies,* then, should result in consciously set prices that help the firm to reach its objectives. There are two main pricing policies for marketers to follow—skimming and penetration—as well as some variations of these approaches. One of these two approaches is primarily selected as the best way to price new products. We will examine them now.

The Skimming Policy

When marketers first introduce a product, they often will follow a skimming policy to set its price. With this approach, the price is set at a high level, and the objective is to sell the product initially to the core market. Later, when the core segment has been reached, the price will be adjusted downward to appeal to consumers who are more price-sensitive. In this manner, total revenue is maximized. Let's look at some numbers to show how this is accomplished.

The demand schedule shown in Table 12-1 indicates that if the initial price is set at $26, the marketers will realize three sales, for a total revenue of $78 (3 × $26). But consider the following alternative. If the initial price is set at $30, there will be only one sale; but if the price is then dropped to $28, a second sale will be made. Thus, under this approach the two sales include one buyer who would have bought the product at the higher price—that is, only one *additional* sale will be made at the lower price. Then, if the price is lowered again—to $26—a third sale will result, and the total revenue for all three sales will be $84 ($30 + $28 + $26). The point is that this is $6

TABLE 12-1 Demand Schedule and Total Revenue for an Individual Firm

(1) Quantity demanded, Q	(2) Price, P	(3) Total revenue, TR	(4) Marginal revenue, MR
0	$32	$ 0	
1	30	30	$30
2	28	56	26
3	26	78	22
4	24	96	18
5	22	110	14
6	20	120	10
7	18	126	6
8	16	128	2
9	14	126	−2
10	12	120	−6

more than if the price were set initially at the lower level of $26 ($84 − $78 = $6). (See Figure 12-1.)

There are a number of conditions that make a skimming policy effective. The approach is most appropriate when demand for the product is likely to be rather insensitive to price. If this were not the case, the initial high price could not attract enough buyers to make the product profitable. Skimming is also effective when there are price segments within the market. It works well, too, when consumers know little about the costs of producing and marketing the product and are unlikely to realize that they are paying a premium for being among the first to acquire it. Finally, skimming works best when there is little likelihood that competitors will enter the market rapidly. Competition often leads to price cutting, which puts a quick end to the attractive profits that accompany a skimming approach.

From the price setter's standpoint, skimming offers several advantages. Developmental costs are often substantial for new products, and the attractive revenue-

Figure 12-1 A skimming policy to set new-product price.

Three sales, initial price of $26

Consumers 1, 2, and 3 buy product for $26 = 3 × $26 = $78

Three sales, skimming to $26

Consumer 1 buys product in January for $30 = 1 × $30 = $30

Consumer 2 buys product in March for $28 = 1 × $28 = $28

Consumer 3 buys product in August for $26 = 1 × $26 = $26

$84

generating feature of skimming is helpful in recovering costs rapidly. Furthermore, if the firm initially produces the product on an experimental basis but plans to develop its own manufacturing facilities later, a skimming policy can be used to limit demand until mass-production capabilities are established. And, of course, since a high price is often equated with high quality, a skimming policy can develop a prestige image for the product. Finally, marketers know that it is easier to lower the initial skimming price than it is to risk consumers' resistance to a later price increase. Thus, as the initial price falls, new markets may be tapped that were not anticipated. This is what happened in the calculator industry. As prices broke through the $100 barrier, sales suddenly began moving from the industrial market into the far larger consumer market. Then, in 1981, Texas Instruments knocked $50 off its $300 top-of-the-line TI-59, a calculator that was already widely discounted to $199. It also threw in a $20 cash rebate. That pricing approach brought the model within reach of the student market.

For all its advantages, however, skimming also has certain disadvantages. First, it attracts competitors. The initial high prices yield high profits for the marketer, and usually there is a rush among competitors to introduce similar products. And the higher the initial price, the more likely that competitors will be attracted to the market. Price setters realize that consumers will use the price of an existing alternative product as a reference point, and so they aim for a price that is in line with that of substitute products. An inappropriate price level may well damage sales throughout a product's life, or even lead to its early end. For instance, Du Pont priced its Corfam imitation shoe leather at too high a level relative to existing alternatives, and the product was unable to find a solid market. Another consideration with skimming policies is that they often make it necessary to revise the marketing mix in order to serve the new target markets that are identified as prices drop. For example, as the lower price attracts mass markets, advertising is likely to replace personal selling in importance, and the distribution pattern is likely to shift from specialty stores to high-volume mass merchandise outlets. Thus, changes in marketing skills and resources are needed by management in order to make a skimming policy work well.

With some skimming policies, prices drop very rapidly, while in other situations, the price reductions come about slowly. Thus, in three years the price of pocket calculators fell from $240 to under $20. Digital watch prices also dropped fairly rapidly over a 3-year period—from over $200 in 1974 to about $50 in 1975, and then to less than $20 in 1976. On the other hand, since Polaroid Corporation held the patent on instant photography until the end of 1975, it was allowed the luxury of not having to worry about competition. As a result, initial high prices could be reduced in increments over the life span of the patent, a policy that yielded substantial profit.

The Penetration Policy

In contrast to the skimming approach, a penetration policy calls for low prices and high volume. In following this approach, price setters believe that the attraction of a low price will lead to such a high sales volume that the total profit will be greater than could be realized by a higher price. The idea is to reach the entire market with a low price, thus generating the greatest demand.

Penetration policies are often used when the market is not divided into price segments—when there is no "élite" market willing to pay a high price. Such a policy is appropriate for new products that are not socially visible and do not symbolize social status. The penetration approach is generally useful when the market is price-sensitive, and when a lower price will really attract a larger volume of sales. It is also used frequently in cases where competitors can enter the market rapidly, since the lower prices may make it less attractive to market similar products. In addition, a low price may offer a competitive advantage in entering an established market. Thus, when Bic entered the disposable pen market dominated by Write Brothers and Lindy, the company priced its pen at a lower penetration price of 19 cents. Finally, penetration pricing is useful when a firm can establish large-scale production plans and reap the benefits of economies of scale.

Like the skimming approach, however, penetration pricing also has disadvantages. Although the retardation of competition is a major benefit of this approach, marketers should never feel secure with their market position—even when they are offering an attractive low price. In fact, a low price often results in losses during the product's introduction, while it is gaining consumers' acceptance. With a low-price strategy, the breakeven point is not reached until a larger quantity is sold. Consequently, a penetration policy carries a greater risk than does a skimming policy, with its higher price. But, on the positive side, penetration pricing can open up new markets never before served.

In 1980, Eastern Airlines became the sixth airline to enter the transcontinental traffic. Eastern previously served the Eastern seaboard and the Mid-Atlantic area, but went coast to coast mainly because its new jumbo jets were flying far below capacity. In an effort to penetrate the transcontinental market, it offered a one-way coach fare of $99, good only for a month. The gimmick forced competitors to respond with a $129 no-strings fare. As a representative of United Airlines said, "At current fares, we'd need 150 percent capacity to turn a profit."[1] By late fall, Eastern took the lead to raise prices to $414 on New York–Los Angeles flights and $432 on New York–San Francisco flights. Competitors followed promptly. (See Application 12-1.)

These two pricing policies of skimming and penetration need not be considered mutually exclusive. That is, they are not either/or alternatives, and sometimes a skimming policy is followed by a penetration policy. For example, Texas Instruments was once a price leader in the digital watch industry, setting both the upper and lower price levels. But once the low-price barrier of $50 was broken by competitive pressures and price cutting, Texas Instruments quickly adopted a penetration approach. In 1977, it was the first company to introduce a $10 watch line by producing cases made of high-performance plastic.

But even though they can be used in combination, skimming and penetration policies do represent the extremes of pricing. Skimming is a high-price approach, while penetration is a low-price strategy. Some companies follow one of these policies

---

[1]"The Rate War in the Skies," *Newsweek,* Aug. 11, 1980, p. 62.

Application 12-1
Penetration Pricing—
"Up Up and Away at Prices Down to Earth!"

In 1980, Texas Air Corporation started a new subsidiary, New York Air (NYA), and entered the East Coast New York–Washington run. It charged $49 on weekdays, $29 after 7 P.M. and on weekends, and still made money, while the major competitor on that route, Eastern Airlines, was only marginally profitable at its $60 shuttle price. This 18 to 52 percent price reduction was offered on nine daily, regularly scheduled flights. Before New York Air's first flight, Eastern countered with a $77 go-Saturday-return-Sunday excursion—still higher than NYA's bargain. How can Texas Air make money?

New York Air differs from Eastern in its marketing strategy. First, it will sell only reserved seats. Eastern, meanwhile, guarantees to carry any passenger who shows up in either city to take its shuttle. NYA thus cuts out backup planes, crews, and flight attendants, which are major overhead costs for Eastern. "They'll be utilizing two aircraft (N.Y.–Washington). We have seventeen (Washington–N.Y.–

(Courtesy New York Air)

Boston)," noted an Eastern spokesperson.

Also in NYA's favor is cheaper labor. Most of its start-up pilots were experienced fliers who had been furloughed from other airlines. Such nonunion pilots, with no seniority, command only $30,000 a year; a senior Eastern

DC-9 captain earns $42,000 to $70,000 a year.

New York Air's support personnel are also nonunion. Flight attendants and ticket and reservation agents are interchangeable, giving management greater flexibility and lower costs. New York Air's twin-engine DC-9s are also more fuel- and labor-efficient than Eastern's three-engine 727s. "Our facility at LaGuardia (N.Y.) is an inexpensive portion of American Airlines' hanger," said a NYA executive. In Washington, New York Air shares convenient space in the main terminal.

Who makes up New York Air's passenger market? "New York Air will bring 3 million new passengers into the market—all the train, bus, and car travelers. Half their traffic won't come out of Eastern's hide, it will come from Amtrak and Trailways," says an airline industry expert.

Source of data: "East Coast Dogfight," *Forbes*, Nov. 24, 1980, p. 40.

exclusively. In the chemical industry, for instance, Du Pont tends to focus on high-margin specialty products, at first pricing them high, then gradually lowering the price as the market builds and competition grows. A different approach is taken by

Dow Chemical Company, which stresses low-margin commodity products and prices them low in order to secure a dominant market share and build profits in the long run. Being manufacturers, Dow and Du Pont operate in a pricing situation which is unlike that facing wholesalers and retailers. But each type of business takes whichever pricing approach best suits its markets, cost structures, and other variables.

Other Pricing Policies

While skimming and penetration are by far the most common approaches to pricing, they do not cover the full range of policies available to price setters. Let's now look at some other pricing strategies used by marketers.

Prestige Pricing

We have already noted that some consumers see the intangible features of a product as being of distinct importance in choosing among available product offerings. We have seen, too, that price can be an important element in conveying a product's image. In fact, some marketers make it a point to present an image of quality by means of the price tag. Thus, certain beers, automobiles, cosmetics, and liquors are given a prestige image through this pricing policy.

Curtis Mathes, which manufactures and markets a line of television sets, explicitly states in its advertising copy that its sets are the most expensive on the market. In taking this approach to pricing, the company recognizes that there is a segment of the market which wants high quality and believes that price is a good indicator of it. Such consumers care more about quality than about price, and marketers can satisfy that need through prestige pricing.

In 1981, Polaroid introduced a new Polaroid 600 instant camera, called the Sun Camera, and an accompanying film line. Based primarily on the benefit of ridding minor shadows in photographs, Polaroid priced its luxury model at $95, a big jump over the $25 Polaroid Onestep. Film was priced at $9.95 for a 10-shot pack. Said a company marketing executive, "People are willing to pay for quality nowadays."[2]

Price Leading

In some industries, there are distinct and identifiable companies that set the prices for all other competitors. These companies tend to be the dominant and most powerful firms in their industries, and their prices set the structure for other companies. For example, Gillette holds about 60 percent of the market in the razor-blade industry, making it the price leader. Other companies that lead their respective industries include U.S. Steel, IBM, Kodak, and Du Pont. (See Application 12-2.)

Customary Pricing

With customary pricing, the basis for price determination is traditional. In other words, marketers try to avoid changing the price from its accepted level, and they will adjust the product in terms of size and content in order to hold the price. Candy bars are an example. The traditional 5-cent bar has given way to the 25-cent and 30-cent and even 35-cent bars—but not easily. Hershey, for instance, changed the price of its bar

---

[2]"Selling New Polaroid 600 Line May Require Teaching Camera Users Why They Need It," *The Wall Street Journal*, June 25, 1981, p. 29.

Application 12-2
Price Labor—Setting the Pace at IBM

"When IBM sneezes, the rest of the computer industry catches double pneumonia. That's an axiom among the computer giant's competitors—and this year, IBM's maneuvers have left them in intensive care," observed *Newsweek* in a story outlining IBM's new small and medium-size computers, called the 4300 series. IBM sent the industry into a tailspin not only with its new product line, but with its departure from industry tradition by pricing its powerful new models slightly below their predecessors.

"It's as if Ford introduced a car that got 40 miles a gallon, never needed an oil change and sold for $3,000," said E. Drake Lundell, Jr., editor of *Computerworld,* the industry's weekly trade journal. "The competition wouldn't be too

happy, but a consumer would say hallelujah."

And consumers did respond forcefully. Within a month of the announcement in January 1979, IBM received a whopping 100,000 orders for its 4300 line. So heavy was demand, IBM resorted to a lottery system to determine which customers would get the first deliveries. Some buyers were told that their orders could not be filled before 1982.

The pricing strategy had a devasting impact on IBM's competition. Computer users, afraid of investing in obsolete equipment and hopeful that IBM's new pricing standard would be extended to its big computers, canceled orders with IBM competitors and long-term contracts with computer-leasing firms. Many manufacturers slashed

prices on their own models in response.

IBM's strategy, however, temporarily flattened IBM's own revenues. Many customers stopped buying older models in order to wait for the new computers. So, late in 1979, the giant raised prices 5 to 7 percent on most of its data processing and word processing products—a clear admission that its original pricing for the 4300 series was too low. Some experts believe that the 4300 pricing boomerang was largely responsible for an 18 percent decline in earnings during the third quarter of 1979.

Sources of data: "IBM's Latest Blitz," *Newsweek,* Aug. 13, 1979, pp. 62–65; and "Why IBM Reversed Itself on Computer Pricing," *Business Week,* Jan. 28, 1980, p. 84.

only four times between 1949 and 1981, but the weight (quantity) of the bar changed many times. (See Figure 12-2.) As a result, consumers in 1981 paid 5 times as much for a Hershey bar as they did in 1949, but they got only 5 percent more product.

Survival Pricing   While some companies are strong enough to attempt to price competitors out of business, others use a pricing policy that is aimed simply at staying in business. Faced with declining profits—whether brought about by competitive pressures, rising costs, or slackening demand—some firms use survival pricing to keep afloat until the crisis is over. This approach is also useful for organizations that are engaged in a price war. Earlier in this chapter, we saw this approach taken by Eastern's transcontinental competitors when Eastern entered the New York–Los Angeles and New York–San Francisco markets with its below-cost price of $99.

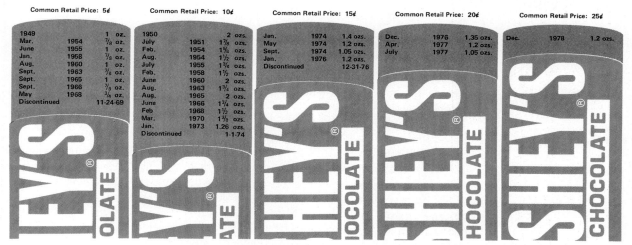

Figure 12-2   The roller-coaster ride for Hershey's milk chocolate bar. (Adapted from "Misadventures of Cocoa Trade," The New York Times, Feb. 25, 1979, pp. F1 and 4)

Strategic Price Adjustments

We now have looked at the major factors that influence price determination. Costs, demand, and competition are the main influences, and they are guided by the organization's objectives and by the pricing policies designed to achieve those objectives.

In some cases, however, certain other considerations about consumers must also be taken into account before the final price can be established. Such considerations usually affect transactions at the retail level, rather than manufacturing or wholesaling. We treat them separately here because they *do not always* influence final prices; even so, they often are appropriate and useful guidelines for price setters to consider. That is, certain adjustments can make the final price more attractive to consumers and can lead to increased sales. The following price adjustments, then, reflect the way consumers view a product and its price. Such price changes must also fit into the overall strategic plan for the organization.

Demand-Related Adjustments— Psychological Pricing

Some prices have more appeal than others, either because they are traditional or because they match some inner logic of consumers. Thus, prices like $8.31 for a necktie or $28.72 for a toaster may not be psychologically "comfortable." For other products, however, such unrounded prices may be totally acceptable—53 cents for a package of slivered almonds or $2.69 for Skippy's peanut butter. While psychological pricing is often used to make a price seem lower, it also can be used to emphasize the relationship between price and quality. For instance, consumers may not be particularly attracted to a skin lotion that is priced too low. That is, an 8-ounce jar of lotion priced at 49 cents may not be as appealing as the very same cream at $2.98. At 49 cents, the quality association is not there. Let's look at some psychological pricing approaches.

Odd-Even Pricing

The odd-price form of psychological pricing is achieved by making the end of the price an odd number (1, 3, 5, 7, 9) or some number just below a round number (99, 98). Many marketers believe that consumers react to such price distinctions, and, indeed, retailers do use certain prices more often than others. Odd pricing is based on the feeling among marketers that a price of $9.99, for instance, appears lower to consumers than $10.00 does. This difference of only 1 cent gives the illusion that the price is in the lower range of $0.01 to $9.99, rather than in the range of $10.00 to $19.99. While it is customary for marketers to price in this manner, studies of consumers' sensitivity to such price distinctions do not conclusively support the approach.

While less frequently used, some marketers price products at even numbers such as "3 for $1" for candy bars or $1650 for a prestige watch. Some even go so far as to work backward so that the even dollar price includes the tax. They feel that consumers feel more comfortable with paying even amounts.

Price Lining

Price lining is a technique most often practiced by retailers, but some manufacturers and wholesalers also use the approach. It is based on the fact that most retailers have more than one product to price, and a number of substitute products or brands within each product category. For instance, a women's clothing store may offer a variety of silk scarves. But consumers will not respond to a series of minor price differences, such as scarves at $9.50, $9.60, $9.70, $9.90, $10.00, and so on. Instead, buyers prefer a *few* prices that seem to differentiate the product into "lines" based on some attribute like quality or prestige. The retailer may price scarves at $7, $10, $12, and $20. These prices clearly indicate that there are scarves for the economy-minded at $7, medium-quality scarves at $10 and $12, and top-of-the-line scarves at $20. With price lining, then, a limited number of prices are established for the products or brands within a product class.

Price lining makes it less confusing for consumers to distinguish among an array of available products. Buyers can decide which level of quality or price they want, and then they can shop for products within that line. And from the retailers' standpoint, price lining simplifies their own buying and pricing.

The theory underlying price lining is that different market segments. or target markets, can be served best through different prices. But the practice raises some important issues for retailers, since it's difficult to determine how many segments there are, or which ones it is profitable to serve. In addition, retailers must be careful in setting the initial price lines so that they match the prices sought by various market segments. The price differentials must be substantial enough that they do not blur the price lines; that is, consumers must be able to distinguish the various lines easily. At the same time, however, the lines must not be priced so far apart that no market segment is being served.

Promotional Pricing

Many marketers, especially retailers, recognize that consumers love bargains. They know that a price lower than normal has considerable appeal. As a result, many marketers use the price variable not only to promote sales for low-priced products but also to draw customers into the store and generate sales for other products. In this situation, the lower-priced products are referred to as "traffic builders"; more technically, they are *loss leaders,* or *price leaders.* Such products are priced below the usual full markup, and they are chosen for their promotional appeal. Most likely, the retailer has large stocks of such items to sell, and wants to attract customers into the store in the hope that, once there, they will also buy other products that are priced at the usual markup. Price leaders are usually well-known, highly desired, somewhat expensive branded goods. Thus, customers readily recognize that their prices have been slashed.

In 1980, after a year of flat sales, fur coats were a big loss-leader item at many stores. A full barrage of marketing techniques were employed—rebates, hard-sell television advertising, deferred payment programs, and markdowns of as much as 80 percent. Such posh department stores as Neiman-Marcus and Magnin joined hands with smaller retail stores in the push to clear out inventories. Said one retailer, "The idea is to create traffic. If we create traffic, we do a lot of business. It helps create mob psychology."[3]

Unit Pricing

Confronted with a sizable sea of prices, consumers often become confused when trying to compare alternative product offerings. Is a 7-ounce bag of Frito-Lay potato chips priced at $1.09 a better buy than a 5-ounce bag priced at 89 cents? Marketers have responded with *unit pricing.* Here, each separate package size of a product carries a price for the package and a price expressed in terms of price per ounce, pound, pint, or some other standard measure of quantity. First used in the early 1970s, unit pricing has been employed mostly by supermarket chains and with grocery products.

The purpose of unit pricing is to help consumers make more economical purchases. Yet, there are costs associated with its use—special labels (see Figure 12-3) and labor costs for the retailer as well as reduced brand loyalty as price competition increases. Research has found consumers shifting to store brands and realizing savings as a result of unit pricing. Yet those with the most to gain—the lower-income shoppers—were found to use it less than better-educated, higher-income shoppers.[4]

---

[3]"Sale of Mink Coats Strays a Fur Piece from the Expected," *The Wall Street Journal,* March 21, 1980, p. 30.

[4]Kent B. Monroe and Peter J. LaPlaca, "What Are the Benefits of Unit Pricing?" *Journal of Marketing,* vol. 36, no. 3 (July 1972), pp. 16–22; and Michael J. Houston, "The Effect of Unit Pricing on Choices of Brand and Size in Economic Shopping," *Journal of Marketing,* vol. 36, no. 3 (July 1972), pp. 51–54.

Figure 12-3   Do you use the information listed on unit pricing labels as you shop? Why do retailers use the system, considering the extra costs involved with it? *(Randy Matusow)*

Other Forms of Price-Product Adjustment

In Chapter 11 we noted that price is equated with the value consumers expect to receive from an exchange. Often, price increases are avoided because it is thought—usually correctly—that they will result in fewer sales. In other cases, price increases have been instituted, but in an amount less than cost increases, thus lowering the desired profit level. To compensate for cost increases and forced price rises, marketers have devised some ways to maintain the balance of the equation "Price equals or is less than expected value." Let's examine how they do this.

Changing the Product's Quantity or Quality

When a marketer finds that costs are increasing but a related price increase would hurt sales, the quantity or the quality of the product can be changed. Ideally, of course, consumers will not perceive these changes, or, if they do, they will not be annoyed by them.

In some cases, marketers meet cost increases by changing only the *quantity* of the product—as we've already noted in the case of candy bars. Similarly, one vending-machine company faced this problem when coffee prices leaped suddenly. Since the company already had raised its price from 15 to 20 cents during a period of two months, it decided instead to reduce the quantity of coffee delivered by the machine into each cup. Few consumers noticed the difference. In the same way, Procter & Gamble reduced the size of its rolls of Charmin toilet paper to 500 sheets from 650 sheets and of its Bounty paper towels to 100 sheets from 125 sheets—yet maintained prices at the same level; the Brewery Restaurant in Chicago held the price of $1 for a piece of cake by reducing the size of a portion; and numerous products have suddenly become available in "economy" sizes.

In other cases, the actual *quality* of the product is changed to meet rising costs. Thus, Wilbur Chocolate Company of Lititz, Pennsylvania, joined the many manufacturers of commercial chocolate that switched from cocoa butter to a vegetable-fat substitute. Although the change is noted clearly on the product's label, few consumers can distinguish a flavor difference, and the nutritional value and caloric content are the same as for cocoa butter.

In 1979, M&M/Mars acted similarly. The Standard Brands subsidiary used artificial chocolate based on inexpensive palm oil rather than cocoa butter, the standard ingredient for the rest of the industry. And in 1980, M&M/Mars boosted the weight of its major brands (Snickers, Milky Way, and Three Musketeers) an average of 10 percent but did not increase the price. Thus M&M/Mars increased the value side of the "price equals value" equation in an attempt to gain market share.

In the ideal situation, of course, marketers strive to achieve a reduction in quantity without lowering consumers' level of satisfaction. This has been done successfully by many newspapers and magazines that have reduced the size of their pages without changing their overall content. For instance, *The Wall Street Journal* shrank its width by 2 inches—but without changing its content. *House & Garden* cut its page size to hold newsstand and subscription prices, as did *Better Homes and Gardens.* "There are smaller photographs and fewer words," a *Better Homes and Gardens* representative told *The Wall Street Journal,* "but you can convey the same idea and information in less space. A magazine isn't like a candy bar, where there's only a certain amount to consume."[5] (See Application 12-3.)

Changing the Basic Product	Sometimes rising costs and rising price levels force an individual product's price up to the upper limits of demand. In that situation, marketers can change or adjust the basic makeup of the product in order to keep it in line with what the market will pay. The industry has done this as consumers resisted rising prices for canned beverages. To counter this reaction, manufacturers began to produce their beverages in powdered-mix form. Price-conscious consumers can thus add their own water to prepare their favorite beverages at a cost they are willing to pay. Pioneered in 1928 by Kool-Aid, a General Foods product, the mix-it-yourself beverage market recorded a 50 percent sales gain in 1974 and added another 50 percent increase in 1975—while sales of canned varieties dropped 20 percent in each of those years.
Changing the Bundle of Satisfaction	Marketers are aware—intuitively, at least—that what consumers buy is made up of many ingredients, i.e., product accessories, packaging, delivery services, guarantees, and so on. In order to meet rising costs, some marketers have "unbundled" their product, offering only those ingredients which are requested explicitly. In this way, consumers are charged only for those parts they desire.

---

[5]"Consumers Find Firms Are Paring Quantities to Avoid Price Rises," *The Wall Street Journal,* Feb. 15, 1977, p. 1.

Application 12-3
New Packages—New Prices

(Ray Pfortner)

Ocean Spray Cranberries, without tampering with quality, plans to increase its 11 percent share of the $2.1 billion juice market. This feat involves reducing prices by 10 to 25 percent and holding profit margins steady. How? Ocean Spray hopes to achieve its objectives by introducing a new kind of package—a foil-lined paperboard container that promises to be just as effective as glass bottles or metal cans, but less expensive.

Savings from the new container are being passed on to the consumer. "This is the most significant new product launch in 15 years," says Harold Thorkilsen, president of Ocean Spray. The company plans to spend $30 million over five years to install new packaging equipment, and will hike its ad budget at least 60 percent to acquaint consumers with the container.

Ocean Spray's marketing plans specify introducing the package nationally in single-portion sizes which feature built-in straws. Later, a one-liter package will be added. But the company's "best opportunity" to increase sales, says Mr. Thorkilsen, is a line of unfrozen juice concentrates. Consumers will save 20 to 25 percent on the cost of juice by adding their own water.

Ocean Spray's new packages compete with its existing containers, which remain on the market. But Mr. Thorkilsen says he's confident that, with lower prices, "on balance we'll improve our share of the total juice market."

Source of data: "Ocean Spray's New Package and Prices," *The Wall Street Journal,* June 4, 1981, p. 29.

Many department stores, for example, now charge extra for home delivery, gift wrapping, and shopping bags. Similarly, many gasoline stations let drivers pump their own gas, thus saving a few cents per gallon. Meanwhile, other marketers have added features to products in an effort to increase their appeal. Just as Crackerjacks have been valued because of the "free" prize in each box, premiums and other giveaways have become a common addition to products ranging from bank services to laundry detergents. For example, as fuel costs doubled and recession and inflation increased, many national airlines resorted to gimmicks to lure air travelers. Eastern gave senior citizens a 50 percent price break on summer Florida flights, and on midweek flights, children under 18 flew free when accompanied by an adult. Western Air Lines tried to build a steady customer base by offering a 50 percent discount on any future Western flight once the passenger had made five full-fare flights between San Francisco and Los Angeles. The Big Three airlines, United, American, and TWA, brought lottery games to the sky, offering everything from free drinks and headsets to free flights. (See Application 12-4.)

Changing the Exchange Transaction

Marketers also can make a product's bundle of satisfaction more attractive by changing the activities performed at the point of exchange. For example, many retailers offer credit to their customers without charging interest on the unpaid

---

Application 12-4
Changing the Bundle of Satisfaction Utility—
Bare-Bones Grocery Shopping

(Courtesy NCR Corporation)

In response to consumers' tight-fisted mood, grocery retailers are experimenting with all sorts of alternatives to the traditional supermarket. The Pick 'n Save warehouse food store operated in Gurnee, Illinois, is an example. There's no butcher, no baggers, no deluxe delis, no individual pricing.

In common with other Pick 'n Save warehouse stores, the Gurnee store requires customers to bag their own groceries. One retailer estimates that bagging groceries for shoppers raises a store's labor costs anywhere from 35 to 50 percent.

The warehouse store also saves by displaying products right in the cases, stacked on pallets or shelves. Some products are bought only when they carry a sizable manufacturer's discount. When big discounts are available to the store, it buys "by the semi-truckload," whether the product be soda pop or disposable diapers. The resulting high sales volume makes up for narrow margins.

Another cost-saver is the scanning system that eliminates the need to mark prices on each item. The retailer programs prices into a computer in the back room, and that price is picked up by the checkout scanner, as shown in the photo. Product prices are given on the shelves and bins.

Variations on the warehouse store abound. Some have fresh meat; others sell less produce. Some of the stores refuse checks, and some charge for grocery bags. Several have cut back on nonfood items, and many have only half the variety of Pick 'n Save, which offers about 12,000 items, close to the 15,000 a full-service supermarket generally stocks.

Source of data: "Food Stores with Few Services Spring Up to Lure Increasingly Frugal Consumers," *The Wall Street Journal,* Jan. 23, 1981, p. 42.

balance—which is certainly a form of price reduction. In fact, offering customers the opportunity to use credit cards, such as MasterCard and Visa, makes it possible for buyers to have the merchandise immediately without having to pay cash. Since the customer possesses the merchandise for a period of time without having to pay for it, this is also a price reduction. Even some churches permit the use of credit cards for making donations, and many people find it an appealing way to contribute.

Many forms of sales promotion, such as trading stamps and coupons redeemed, represent a form of price reduction as well. Inflation-weary consumers show increased enthusiasm for such forms of savings. Finally, by altering the form of payment, marketers may increase exchanges. One Evanston, Illinois, furrier accepted stock certificates instead of cash in exchange for fur coats during a recent recession. The stocks were valued at 25 percent higher than their depressed market value.

Pricing Products over the Life Cycle

The market changes rapidly. What consumers want today is different from what they wanted yesterday and what they will want tomorrow. In Chapter 10, we noted that products go through a life cycle and that marketers must adjust their strategies throughout a product's life. The price, for example, must be adjusted to conform with what the market wants, just as the product itself has to be adjusted. Let's examine how pricing differs throughout a product's life cycle. We'll look at new products, mature products, and declining products.

Pricing New Products

The pricing of new products presents a major challenge to marketers. They know little about the costs associated with making the new product, or about the level of price that the market will bear, or about competitive reactions to the new product. Considering the rate of product failures, the importance of the pricing decision is clearly critical.

The difficulty of pricing depends in large part on the product's degree of newness. In Chapter 9, we noted three classes of new products: innovative, imitative, and adaptive replacements. *Innovative products*—those functionally unlike any other products—are most difficult to price. Consider, for example, the motorbike on skis that the Chrysler Corporation began to market in the winter of 1980. Called Sno Runner, this recreational vehicle consists of a moped frame mounted entirely on skis and propelled by cleats on a roller chain connected to a two-cycle engine. The Sno Runner can travel up to 25 miles per hour at a range of 91 miles. How could its marketers begin to know what people would pay for such a product, or how potential competitors might react? In this case, the market demand was unknown. There were no comparable marketing experiences to evaluate, and the product might have many unknown uses. The company priced the snow bike at $645, while bulkier snowmobiles, perhaps the closest substitute product, sold between $1200 and $2500. But much of this pricing decision had to be based on the marketers' intuition.

With products that are unique, then, the major pricing decision is whether to follow a skimming or a penetration policy. The marketers must determine the level of price sensitivity among potential consumers, and they must consider how quickly competitors will enter the market.

New products that have identifiable substitutes or that replace existing products are classified as *imitative products* and *adaptive products*. In these cases, price setters have more to go on. Thus, although Gillette's Eraser Mate was the first erasable ink pen on the market, it still had to compete with regular ball-point and felt-tip pens. The critical and key issue for marketers was how much consumers would pay for the product's perceived differences in function, symbolism, or appearance. When there are no such differences perceived, the price cannot vary much from the levels that exist for alternative products or brands.

Pricing Mature Products

As products move from the growth stage into the saturation stage, price adjustments are usually necessary. Flexibility is the key to establishing a pricing strategy. With mature products, most sales are replacement sales. Price increases during this stage usually result from upward surges in costs, not from increased demand. To stimulate exchange, then, price hikes are usually not the correct strategy. Most often, a stable pricing strategy is the best approach.

While a price reduction may seem the logical way to stimulate sales for mature products, this tactic depends on the price sensitivity of consumers and on the competitive situation that exists in the market. With some products—such as hairpins and clothespins—a price reduction is not likely to increase sales and, in fact, would probably lead to lower profits, since the quantity sold is likely to go unchanged. Additionally, with mature products a substantial number of competitors are likely to react by also lowering their prices, thus diminishing or destroying the ability of the price reduction to stimulate sales. At the same time, market share can be gained at the expense of competitors by pursuing an aggressive pricing strategy. Purex Industries, Inc., made its first moves into low pricing in the early 1970s by reducing the prices of its branded Purex bleaches and detergents to 20 percent the leading brands. The strategy enabled Purex to capture about a 25 percent market share of the total liquid bleach market by 1981.

Pricing Declining Products

Once sales for a product begin to dip, marketers have two pricing alternatives, depending on their long-run plans. If they want to prune the declining product from the line, their pricing strategy would be to continue to lower prices, preferably in stages, until all inventory has been sold. Alternatively, they can maintain prices but cut expenses to make profits. Here, promotional expenditures are often curtailed to hold profitability.

As competitors leave the market, the sources of supply for the product dwindle, and often there is a certain market segment that still needs the product. Since this need can be quite strong, the firms that remain in the market during the later stages of the product's life cycle may actually be able to increase their prices.

Price Administration

Our discussion so far has been oriented toward determining a product's base price (list price). This is the price that normally confronts buyers when they consider a purchase or an exchange. Now we will examine how the base price is adjusted to meet certain market conditions. Such adjustments are termed *price administration,* and the conditions that warrant them include:

1 Sales made in different quantities

2 Sales made under different policies of credit and collection

3 Sales made to different types of intermediaries, who perform different functions

4 Sales made to buyers in different geographical locations

Under conditions like these, it is not feasible to charge the base price, and so certain adjustments must be made. But, again, such adjustments must be in line with the pricing strategy. We will now look at how the list price is adjusted through discounts, leasing, and geographical pricing.

Discounts

Discounting is a pricing strategy whereby sellers give deductions from the list price in the form of cash or something else of value—even free merchandise. In return, buyers perform some marketing service that is equivalent to, or more than, the value of the discount. There are five forms of discounts: quantity, cash, trade, promotional, and seasonal.

Quantity Discounts

This form of price reduction encourages buyers to purchase larger than normal quantities of the product or to buy all from a single seller rather than to buy smaller quantities from several sources. The discount may be based on the dollar amount or on the quantity of units purchased. It may be applied to sales of a single product, a limited number of products, or a mixture of products in a line. There are two types of quantity discounts: noncumulative and cumulative.

Noncumulative quantity discounts are offered on each individual sale made to a buyer. For example, manufacturers or wholesalers may set up discount structures such as the following, which was developed by a manufacturer of deep-fat fryers and food disposers:

Number of units purchased	Discount of total net dollar purchases
1–9	No discount
10–19	2 percent
20–24	3 percent
25 or more	5 percent

In this example, buyers are encouraged to purchase a greater number of units with each order and to make fewer orders over a period of time. This procedure helps the seller because it minimizes billing, order handling, and shipping costs. Additionally, of course, once the sale is made, the seller is assured that the entire quantity sold will disappear from inventory. This decrease reduces the seller's insurance and storage costs. Thus, noncumulative quantity discounts help a seller to hold down costs in several ways.

Cumulative quantity discounts are price reductions that are applied to a buyer's total purchases over a set period of time. Although they lack some of the cost-saving features of noncumulative discounts, they do tend to tie a buyer to the seller for as long as they buyer wants to take advantage of the discount. Cumulative quantity discounts are thus a reward, or bonus, to regular customers. They are used especially in the purchase of perishable items and high-priced consumer products, as well as of heavy industrial machinery or equipment that is seldom bought in quantity.

Besides the direct cost savings we have noted, quantity discounts offer other advantages to sellers. For instance they promote longer production runs and thus lead to economies of scale. They also help in stimulating sales of slow-moving items.

In the minicomputer industry, quantity discounts have been a long-established tradition. Minicomputer makers offer discounts of up to 40 percent to original-equipment manufacturers. However, IBM, the price leader, had not offered such discounts until 1979 when sales of its Series/1 minicomputer did not live up to company expectations. In an unprecedented move, the company offered discounts of up to 15 percent on Series/1 hardware and licensed programs in order to move more minicomputers.

Cash Discounts

These price reductions are given to buyers who pay their bills within a stated period. Two aspects of the sale are specified: the amount of the reduction and the period of time covered. For instance, a discount of 5/10, n/30 indicates that if the bill is paid within 10 days of the invoice date, a 5 percent discount will be given. But if the bill is not paid within the 10-day period, the entire amount, the net, is due within 30 days of the invoice date.

Most buyers in large organizations are quick to take advantage of such discounts for fast payment. While the reductions may seem small at the time, they add up over a large number of purchases. From a seller's standpoint, cash discounts reduce the risks associated with bad debts by encouraging buyers to pay bills quickly. The longer a seller waits for money, the greater the risk that the bill will not be paid. Additionally, of course, the money that is owed represents capital that can be reinvested in the seller's business; it increases cash flow.

Trade Discounts

Trade discounts (also called *functional discounts*) constitute payment to intermediaries for the performance of various marketing activities, depending on their sequence in the distribution system. Such intermediaries perform the vital overall activity of providing time and place utilities for a product. More specifically, however, they provide services that manufacturers would otherwise have to perform. These services are discussed fully in the next chapter. Basically, intermediaries sell and move products for other marketers who are at earlier stages in the exchange process. The trade discount compensates the intermediaries for those activities.

Trade discounts are based on the retail list price, and they specify the amount of price reduction that an intermediary can take. While they vary tremendously from industry to industry, their rationale remains the same: they compensate the intermediaries for their services. But besides being a form of payment, trade discounts offer some advantages to the manufacturer. They provide some control over the retail price that is finally put on a product. Some products—such as prestige and high-quality items—must be given an appropriate price when they reach the retail level. By varying the amount of the discounts offered, manufacturers can force wholesalers and retailers to sell the product at the desired price while still meeting their own profit needs. In addition, some manufacturers may want to gain the support and services of high-cost intermediaries, and high trade discounts are a means to that end.

Promotional Discounts

These reductions from the list price are offered by sellers as payment to intermediaries for carrying out promotional activities. Manufacturers need local promotional efforts in the form of advertising or special in-store displays. Often, for nationally distributed products, it is a formidable task to accomplish this promotion within the numerous local markets a manufacturer wants to reach. Instead, the responsibility for this activity is passed along the distribution channel to local intermediaries, who are compensated through promotional discounts. A grocery store, say, will run an advertisement in the local paper for a "special" on Del Monte canned pears. The store receives a promotional discount to cover all or part of the cost. Such discounts can take the form of a percentage reduction in the price paid, or they can be cash payment to the intermediary. Sometimes the allowances are made in the form of promotional materials that the manufacturer supplies to the intermediaries.

Seasonal Discounts

The demand for many products is highly seasonal—swimsuits, air conditioners, and home insulation are examples. To counteract the slack periods of demand for such products, manufacturers give discounts to customers who place orders in the off season. Since this smoothes out the sales pattern for the product, the manufacturer can use production facilities more efficiently. In addition, this type of discount shifts the cost of storing the product to those further along in the distribution channel. (See Figure 12-4 and Application 12-5.)

Leasing

While leasing arrangements are also considered a form of price administration, they are actually a completely different form of payment. With leasing, the user of the product does not own it outright but, instead, rents the function it provides. This arrangement offers some advantages to both sellers and buyers. The approach was once used mostly by manufacturers of highly technical, high-cost industrial equipment, such as computers, photocopying devices, and other business machines. But now the price adjustment approach has spread to include so many product areas that leasing has become a major pricing strategy. This surge in leasing has been fueled by recent high interest rates that make borrowing for purchase too expensive.

Application 12-5
Rebates—A New Form of Discounts

Auto executives in Detroit feel as though they were waging World War III. Japanese imports and extraordinarily high interest rates are causing heavy casualties in the auto industry. Ford Motor Company reported a staggering $1.5 billion loss for 1980. Chrysler Corporation subsequently announced even heavier 1980 losses, and earlier, General Motors reported 1980 as its first profitless year since the Great Depression. Even the much smaller American Motors had a $197 million loss. Desperate for sales, the auto makers turned to a costly weapon—rebates to customers who buy slow-selling models.

Selling cars with rebates is

Let's get America Rolling!

That's what General Motors and GM dealers are out to do. By offering genuine old-fashioned, All-American good deals now through March 19.

That's right. GM and GM dealers from one end of America to the other are going all out to get the economy moving again. How? By offering hefty cash incentives on some of GM's most popular new 1981 cars. Just take delivery now through March 19, 1981, and get your bonus check from General Motors. Or, if you prefer, apply it to the down payment on your new GM car. Either way, you'll be getting a genuine old-fashioned, All-American good deal. While getting a great GM car in the bargain.

$700 BONUS	**$500 BONUS**
• CHEVROLET CAMARO	• CHEVROLET CHEVETTE
• CHEVROLET MONTE CARLO	• CHEVROLET CITATION
• PONTIAC FIREBIRD	• PONTIAC PHOENIX
• PONTIAC GRAND PRIX	• OLDSMOBILE OMEGA
• OLDSMOBILE CUTLASS SUPREME	• BUICK SKYLARK
• BUICK REGAL	

NOTE TO FLEET BUYERS: See your participating GM dealer for details on fleet bonus.

NOTE TO FLEET BUYERS: See your participating GM dealer for details on fleet bonus.

Get yours while the getting's good.

See your participating General Motors Dealer

(Courtesy General Motors Corp.)

risky business. "It will have a positive but temporary effect," says Maryann Keller, auto industry analyst at Paine Webber Mitchell Hutchins. Rebates don't boost sales by increasing demand, but, rather, by borrowing from future sales by stimulating customers who were planning to buy cars eventually to buy now. What's more, the cash-rebate programs are not only risky, but expensive. Auto analyst David Healy, of Drexel Burnham Lambert, estimates that GM's "Let's Get Rolling Again" campaign, which began in March 1981, would have cost the company well over $25 million the prior month.

Source of data: "The Reluctant Rebaters," *Newsweek*, March 2, 1981, p. 59.

When consumers buy a product outright, they are paying for satisfaction that it will provide over its entire life. But in a leasing arrangement, the buyer does not own the product; its function is only rented for a specified time or for a specified amount of output. For the *lessor,* the one who leases out the product, this arrangement offers advantages over selling the product outright. In the first place, it may not be feasible to sell some products outright, since their research and development and production costs may be so high that the selling price would be beyond the limits acceptable to the market. In such cases, buyers just cannot afford to purchase the product. Yet, in the long run, this situation can be profitable to the lessor, since rental fees are usually substantial, and the total revenue that may be gained over the life of the product is often far higher than would be realized if the product were sold rather than leased.

Figure 12-4   Summer clearance sales often involve special off-season purchases by retailers. (Randy Matusow)

Additionally, the rental of a piece of equipment tends to bind its renter to the service and supplies of the lessor. Those who rent an IBM computer are likely to purchase that company's special computer programs, cards, and paper for printouts. However, the main disadvantage for the lessor is that the capital required to produce the equipment may not be recovered as quickly as would be possible if the product were sold. Thus, a leasing arrangement can be implemented only by companies that have large financial resources.

From the perspective of the renter (the *lessee*), there are also special advantages to leasing rather than buying. The major one is that the lessee can gain use of the product without investing capital which can be used for other purposes. This may lead to tax advantages, too, since rental payments are deductible as operating expenses. Such payments are often more substantial than the depreciation allowance that could be deducted if the product were purchased. And without the need for large capital investment, firms can enter markets much more easily than if they had to purchase all the equipment needed to operate.

Also of great value is the ease with which lessees can take advantage of new technology and equipment. When a technological breakthrough occurs and present equipment becomes obsolete, the newest equipment can be leased to replace the outdated product. And the problems associated with maintenance service are eliminated for the lessee, since those tasks are most often handled by the lessor, and the rental fee is often tied to the operation of the machine. If it cannot operate, the meter is not running—which usually leads to quick and excellent service. Finally, leasing is especially advantageous for industries that have sporadic or seasonal production schedules (like home construction and farming) since the equipment is leased only for the period it is needed for production.

Geographical Pricing

Often, companies find that the location of buyers presents some problems in terms of freight charges. In some cases, buyers are closer to competitors; and if each seller's list price is the same, a buyer will purchase from the seller who can offer the lower "extra" freight charge. Additionally, some buyers may see the delivery of the product as an important service in the total bundle of utility, and they expect that such a service will simply be part of the base price. Marketers have devised ways to handle such problems, and we will look now at the more common solutions.

F.O.B. Pricing

Many marketers let buyers take on the burden of transportation costs—especially when a market is located near the seller and when transportation charges are slight. In such cases, the seller quotes an "f.o.b. factory" or "f.o.b. point of production" price for the product. The *f.o.b.* stands for *free on board,* which means that title to the product is transferred to the buyer at the point designated. Thus, the responsibility for and costs of moving the product fall on the buyer. The problem with this approach is that it can severely limit the size of the market, since buyers who are far away will not want to bear the higher shipping charges.

The opposite geographical pricing strategy is to charge *f.o.b. destination,* in which case the seller pays all transportation charges and also retains title to the product until it is in the hands of the buyer. Of course, this can be a costly arrangement, but such a pricing strategy may be needed to gain sales among distant buyers.

Uniform Delivered Pricing

To enlarge the geographic size of a market, sellers often offer the same, or uniform, delivered price to all buyers, regardless of their location and the actual freight expense involved. In this situation, the seller quotes a base price for the product plus some standardized freight charge, which tends to be the average rate for shipping to all locations served by the seller. Thus, some buyers (those far away) are charged less for freight than the seller actually pays. In short, the seller absorbs some of the freight charges out of profits. Meanwhile, buyers who are near the seller are charged more than the true freight cost—an amount referred to as "phantom freight."

Freight Absorption

This variation of uniform delivered pricing seeks to offset the advantage of close competitors by charging the same freight rate that the nearest competitor charges. Consider a buyer located in Los Angeles who may buy an equivalent product to yours from a seller in San Francisco and pay only $10 freight (see Figure 12-5). If that Los Angeles buyer purchased from you (you're located in Chicago), the freight charge would be $29. In this situation, you would charge the Los Angeles buyer $10 freight, thus absorbing the $19 difference out of your profits.

Figure 12-5 Freight absorption.

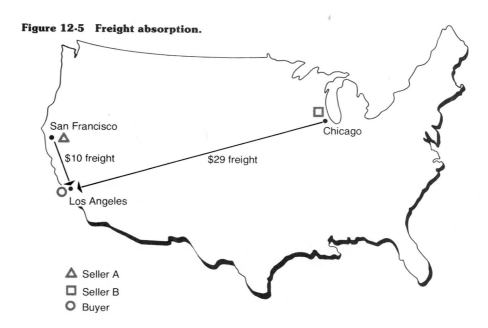

Basing-Point Pricing

Basing-point pricing is another variation of uniform delivered pricing and another way of expanding the market's size. It occurs in two variations: single basing-point pricing and multiple basing-point pricing.

Under *single basing-point pricing,* the seller chooses a specific geographic location (called the *basing point*) and charges all buyers the list price for the product plus the freight rate computed from that basing point. Since the place of origin is usually not the basing point, the actual freight cost does not necessarily enter into the charge at all. For example, a seller located in Chicago who wants to expand the market eastward but whose biggest competitor is located in Pittsburgh may set Pittsburgh as the basing point. Thus, in selling to a Boston buyer, freight is charged from the basing point—that is, from Pittsburgh. This eliminates competitive differences that result from freight charges. The seller absorbs that part of the freight charges which is not recovered from the buyer.

Our choice of Chicago and Pittsburgh as competitive examples was deliberate. The most widely known single basing-point system was developed in the early years of steel manufacturing in and around Pittsburgh. Under what was called the "Pittsburgh plus" approach, buyers were quoted the mill price plus freight charges from Pittsburgh. But as steel production expanded to other locations—like Gary (Indiana), Detroit, and Cleveland—the "Pittsburgh plus" approach penalized buyers in the newer production areas, since they paid freight costs all the way from Pittsburgh. In short, they were paying phantom freight. To counter this, the multiple basing-point approach was devised.

With *multiple basing-point pricing,* two or more geographic locations are designated as basing points, and buyers pay the base price plus freight charges from the nearest basing point. Thus, if Chicago and Pittsburgh were designated as basing points by a Pittsburgh seller, a buyer in, say, Denver would pay the base price plus freight charges from Chicago (the closer of the two basing points). Since the product is still shipped from the production point, Pittsburgh, the seller again absorbs some part of the real freight costs.

Zone Pricing

With *zone pricing,* a seller—again trying to expand the geographic size of the market—breaks the geographic area served into two or more zones. This approach is like that of the United States Postal Service, which charges zone prices for parcel post shipments. Each buyer in a given zone is charged the base price plus the standard freight rate for that zone, which is based on some average cost of shipping to all buyers in the zone. Again, the buyers who are located at points in the most distant zone are subsidized by buyers in the nearest zone, who are paying phantom freight.

The Legal Environment of Pricing

In Chapter 2, we noted the importance of external, uncontrollable forces that exert considerable influence over marketers' decisions. Pricing is one area affected by the uncontrollable variables. Such things as the environment, demand, competition, and social responsibility are all outside the marketers' control and yet strongly affect pricing decisions.

Within the pricing area, perhaps, no uncontrollable variable is more imposing than the legal environment. Of course, laws also affect the product, distribution, and promotion decisions; but pricing has received special attention from legislative bodies, whose main concern has centered on preserving competition. We have already noted the competitive importance of the pricing variable. Not only does it regulate competitive activity, but it also can be used effectively to destroy competition. As society's watchful protector, the government has gone to great lengths to preserve the competitive environment on which our economy depends.

The most important federal law affecting pricing is the *Robinson-Patman Act* of 1936. Since it is a federal law, it applies only to interstate commerce, the definition of which has been expanded by the courts over the years. Originally, the law was enacted to enhance the competitive situation among small retailers, who, after World War I, faced strong challenges from large chain and mail-order retailers. Large size brought some definite competitive advantages in terms of quantity discounts, economies of scale, and greater financial power—all of which weakened the competitive position of smaller retailers. Thus, the Robinson-Patman Act was enacted to protect independent smaller retailers who were damaged further by the Depression of the early 1930s. The act was written in general enough terms so that it is applied to manufacturers as well as to retailers, and its major provisions have far-reaching effects on price determination and administration. A discussion follows of the aspects of this law which affect pricing.

Price Discrimination

The major thrust of the Robinson-Patman Act is to prohibit price discrimination among different purchasers of products of like grade and quality when the effect of such discrimination lessens or injures competition. The act also provides that, to be guilty, the seller must knowingly practice such discrimination, and that buyers who encourage the practice are equally guilty.

We have just examined various situations in which the list price may be adjusted to serve some marketing purpose. As long as there is a difference between the prices offered to two or more buyers of the identical product, price discrimination results. But not all price differences are illegal, since the law states that the differences must damage competition and that buyers must purchase products of "like grade and quality." This latter provision makes the law extremely difficult to interpret, for intangible features (such as brand name, labeling, and price) can lead to different perceptions of the product and thus may justify price differentials. Thus, price differentials are allowed when they are made in response to changes in the marketplace or the marketability of the product. For instance, if the demand for the product shifts, or if the product is damaged, price differences are allowed.

Another situation in which different prices are not discriminatory occurs when they are offered to meet an equally low price of a competitor. In this case, the seller can show that the price difference followed on the heels of a price adjustment by a competitor. Thus, the price differential does not injure competition but, rather, encourages it. It would be suicidal for the firm not to adjust its price, especially when the competitor's price is lower. Finally, the price setter can claim that the product did not cross state lines and thus was not interstate commerce. While these defenses seem straightforward, their interpretation through the years has been quite complex. Marketers engaged in pricing decisions that reflect price differentials must be well aware of the finer points of the law.

The Robinson-Patman Act also says some specific things about the adjustments involved in price administration. While many of these matters are not completely resolved and are still subject to legal interpretation, we will look now at their implications regarding discounts and geographical pricing.

Discounts

While discounts per se are legal under the Robinson-Patman Act, as noted above there must be some cost savings that justify their existence. For example, with *noncumulative quantity discounts,* there are definite cost savings in billing, order handling, and storage that can be passed on to buyers, but the amount of the discount cannot be greater than those cost savings. It is not required that all cost savings be shared with buyers, but rather, that some can be held back for the buyers' use. *Cumulative quantity discounts,* as we have noted, do not produce the same cost savings and are harder to justify under this defense. They are further under fire because they tend to tie buyers to a seller for a period of time, thus actually lessening competition. Additionally, the size of most quantity discounts (of both varieties) is determined intuitively, and useful cost data are often not available to support their legality.

Trade discounts are not mentioned specifically by the Robinson-Patman Act, and so their legality is not completely resolved. However, it has generally been accepted that they are legal as long as they are offered equally to all competing buyers. *Cash, seasonal,* and *promotional discounts* are all legal—as long as they, like all other forms of discounts, are offered to all buyers and accurately reflect cost savings.

Geographical Pricing

When marketers offer a product *f.o.b. factory,* there is no price differential resulting from location. Consequently, such a pricing approach is quite legal. However, when price differences do arise, the issue of legality becomes equally complex. In general, the legality of *freight absorption* is quite clear. It is legal as long as the competing firms do not get together and devise some mutually advantageous set of prices. Such collusion is illegal under the Robinson-Patman Act.

The legality of basing-point pricing is still in question. Court cases have been decided both ways, and so the issue tends to depend on the situation. The major questions revolve around such matters as collusion and phantom freight. Some instances of basing-point pricing do involve collusion; when multiple basing points are used, firms sometimes agree to set up basing points that are mutually advantageous. This, of course, has been deemed illegal. For example, if two or more companies in the two steel centers of Pittsburgh and Gary, Indiana, decided to designate each other as basing points, the competitive advantage of location would be removed. Additionally, when two buyers of a product are in competition and one pays phantom freight while the other does not (due to the basing-point system), this is discriminatory pricing and is illegal.

Zone pricing is considered legal per se, but the delineation of zones must not show evidence of collusion. Additionally, the zones must not be set up so that buyers in different zones are in competition; otherwise, again, discriminatory pricing exists. Thus, a zone that splits Minneapolis and St. Paul would be suspect, since buyers in each zone would be likely to be competitors, yet would pay different prices because of varying zone rates.

Looking Back

With this chapter, our description of how marketers determine prices concludes. We have examined how the list price is determined and how it is adjusted to meet certain market conditions. We have also seen the importance of the uncontrollable variables —particularly legal constraints—on price setting and administration. Before proceeding to the next chapter, review the following important points:

1 Pricing policies are vital to the achievement of pricing objectives.

2 Certain market conditions foster reliance on a skimming policy, while other conditions lead to a penetration policy; alternatively, the two policies can be used together.

3 Some products are priced simply on the basis of psychological appeal.

4 There is no evidence that consumers are more sensitive to odd-even pricing than to other types of prices.

5 Price leaders are used to build traffic.

6 Many ingredients in the bundle of satisfaction can be altered to maintain the balance between price and expected satisfaction.

7 Innovative products are the most difficult to price.

8 Pricing approaches should be most flexible during a product's mature state.

9 There are more cost savings to be realized with noncumulative quantity discounts than with cumulative quantity discounts.

10 Discounts are price reductions given for the performance of marketing activities.

11 Leasing is an alternative to selling a product outright.

12 Geographical pricing is the practice of adjusting prices according to the locations of buyers.

13 Sellers would like the freight costs they absorb to be offset by an equal amount of phantom freight.

14 The goal of government action regarding pricing is to preserve competition.

15 The Robinson-Patman Act of 1935 focuses on price discrimination.

16 The key to the legality of discounts is whether or not cost savings exist.

17 Discounts must be offered equally to all buyers; else, they are discriminatory.

18 The legality of basing-point pricing and zone pricing is subject to the interpretation of courts.

Key Terms

If you aren't sure what each of the following words means, look back at the text. Numbers refer to pages on which the words are defined. Additional information can be found by checking the index and the glossary at the end of the book.

skimming 370
penetration 372
odd-even pricing 378
price lining 378
loss leaders 379
noncumulative quantity discount 386
cumulative quantity discount 387

cash discount 387
trade discount 387
promotional discount 388
seasonal discount 388
f.o.b. 390
uniform delivered pricing 391
basing-point pricing 392
zone pricing 392

Questions for Review

1 Under what conditions would the use of a skimming policy be most effective in setting prices?

2 Which category of intermediaries is most likely to use a price-lining approach to price adjustment?

3 What are some ways that marketers can effectively pass on cost increases to the consumer without actually raising the price?

4 Name the five types of discounts most commonly granted by marketers in exchange for specified activities by intermediaries and consumers.

5 List some of the advantages of leasing rather than purchasing for both the lessor and the lessee.

6 Which consumers would tend to benefit and lose most from a *uniform delivered pricing* approach to geographical pricing?

Questions for Thought and Discussion

1 Bic Pen Corporation and Gillette Company have been involved in an intense pricing battle over disposable cigarette lighters. The result has meant lower profit margins for manufacturers and retailers as well. What options do you see open for either company?

2 Monroe Auto Equipment, the auto parts maker, wants to gain market share by lowering its prices on replacement shock absorbers. From your understanding of this chapter, what alternatives could the company use to reduce prices?

3 To sell goods to purchasers with bank credit cards, marketers pay a service charge

to the credit card companies—generally 1 ¾ percent of card sales to MasterCard, 3 percent for combined MasterCard and Visa. Should marketers offer a discount to shoppers who pay cash?

4 You have learned in these two chapters that price is affected by many factors, including costs, competition, demand, and corporate policies.

Drawing on other material learned so far in this text, indicate some additional environmental factors which affect the prices that marketers ask for their products.

Suggested Project

Contact a local concern that rents products to the public. Ask those in charge what they believe the advantages are to consumers of renting their products rather than buying them. Then ask a few customers as they enter the store. Compare their answers with those offered in this chapter.

Suggested Readings

Gabor, Andre, and Clive J. W. Granger: "Price Sensitivity of the Consumer," *Journal of Advertising Research,* vol. 4 (December 1964), pp. 40–44. Empirical evidence shows that the dominance of pricing below the round figure (99, 98) in some markets may not have any effect upon the consumer.

Monroe, Kent B.: "Buyers' Subject Perceptions of Price," *Journal of Marketing Research,* vol. 10 (February 1973), pp. 70–80. The author reviews behavioral science concepts affecting pricing decisions.

———: *Pricing: Making Profitable Decisions,* McGraw-Hill, New York, 1979. This comprehensive yet understandable text treats all facets of pricing.

———, and Albert J. Della Bitta: "Models for Pricing Decisions," *Journal of Marketing Research,* vol. 15 (August 1978), pp. 413–429. This literature review discusses the most common pricing models.

———, and Peter J. LaPlaca: "What Are the Benefits of Unit Pricing?" *Journal of Marketing,* vol. 36, no. 3 (July 1972), pp. 16–22. The results of a number of experiments are offered here to indicate the influence of unit pricing both on the consumer purchase decisions and on the costs of retailers.

Tarpey, Lawrence X., Sr.: "Buyer Liability under the Robinson-Patman Act: A Current Appraisal," *Journal of Marketing,* vol. 36, no. 1 (January 1972), pp. 38–42. This article reviews important court decisions in attempting to answer the question: What is the legal responsibility of buyers who bargain for preferential prices?

Taylor, Bernard, and Gordon Wills (eds.): *Pricing Strategy,* Brandon/Systems Press, Princeton, N.J., 1970. This collection of readings touches on all the aspects of this topic—psychological aspects of pricing, economic and managerial influences on prices, price as an index value, and variations from list price.

Warshaw, Martin R.: "Pricing to Gain Wholesalers' Selling Support," *Journal of Marketing,* vol. 26 (July 1962), pp. 50–54. The author suggests some principles for dealing with the problem of controlling the price through the channel by setting discount policies.

Cases for Part Three begin on page 600.

Distribution

For years the giants of the computer and office-equipment industries—IBM, Data General, and Xerox, to name but a few—have grown prosperous by selling their products to the large industrial companies. Over the years, these companies have developed sophisticated channels of distribution to reach the big business market.

Now a new market has been identified: the 4 million small businesses with fewer than 200 employees each, and 6 million home offices which are also showing a demand for the services provided by the computer and office-equipment industries.

Traditional distribution systems, consisting of the direct sales representatives and distributors who buy the bare-bones systems and add the software, are not practical for the small-business market. Small-business equipment does not yield the big profit margins of big business, and small business commands more service than the typical large customer.

"You can't afford to have a direct salesman selling these products," Deme M. Clainos, marketing manager of personal computer operations for the Hewlett-Packard Company, told *Business Week*.

To resolve this problem, computer and office products manufacturers have been experimenting with a number of new marketing channels. Included in the new bag of tricks are retail stores, mail order, and product sales through local office-supply dealers.

Xerox, for instance, has been testing the retail office-product store, which in many ways competes with the traditional local office-supply outlet. The Xerox outlet offers everything from typewriter ribbons and copiers to computers. In another tactic, Xerox is marketing its products through mail-order catalogs, independent sales representatives, and office machine dealers. IBM sells its small computers nationally through its Business Computer Centers.

Meanwhile, the giants are struggling not only with one another over this lucrative small-business market, but also with the smaller computer vendors like Tandy and Apple Computer, Inc.

Apple, in an effort to reach this market, has created a distribution network with regional sales and service centers, and Tandy has expanded its computer store concept.

Source of data: "Tapping the Mom and Pop Market," *Business Week,* Oct. 27, 1980, pp. 165–172.

Chapter 13

Describing the Marketing Channels

Looking Ahead

Now we have a product with a price on it, but that's certainly not the end of a marketer's job. The product still has to be moved physically into the hands of ultimate consumers—a task that is called *distribution*. This is the first of two chapters that examine the distribution activities of marketers.

Key Topics

How time and place utilities are added to a product

The expanded concept of distribution

Why intermediaries are useful in moving products

The specific activities that intermediaries perform

What retailing and wholesaling are all about

The various types of retailers and wholesalers

The Nature of Distribution

A key element of providing satisfaction in the marketplace is distribution, the marketing activity with perhaps the lowest profile. Distribution involves the physical movement of products to ultimate consumers. The methods of distribution are numerous, and in this chapter we will examine some of them.

The distribution activities of marketers are critical. The most innovative product at an attractive price is worth absolutely nothing if it is not available to buyers when they want it. A product's availability, then, is one requirement of an exchange. And it is distribution that provides time and place utilities.

Distribution is not simply a matter of moving products into the hands of consumers; it involves a product's movement throughout all stages of development—from resource procurement, through manufacturing, to final sales. Raw materials that are extracted from the earth offer little satisfaction until they reach the hands of a producer who turns them into a finished product of some kind. Thus, raw materials must be moved physically in order for potential satisfaction to be realized by consumers. Distribution is a key aspect of adding value to raw materials, of building an appropriate bundle of satisfaction, and of moving products to market.

Place Utility

Distribution activities provide place satisfaction to a product. If the product is located closer to its consumers, their total satisfaction with it is enhanced. In general, consumers do not like to travel far or expend much effort to obtain products. Many marketers have tried to bridge this barrier by making sure that products are located conveniently. Vending machines are a good example. They make products available to consumers in schools, offices, airports, and other public places. Mail-order houses like Sears and Montgomery Ward also make it easy for customers to obtain products without leaving their homes. And for some consumers, that's especially important. People who are too busy to shop or who are unable to because of health or other reasons can thus select from a broad range of products with little effort. The Horchow Collection, a mail-order marketer, even has had one customer who was in prison for life. Though he lost his case in court, he still wanted to show his appreciation to his lawyer; so he periodically sent Horchow $10 toward a layaway plan to buy the attorney a gift. Clearly, this consumer's exchange behavior was limited to his mailbox, but distribution activities made it possible for him to obtain satisfaction.

Hanes Corporation marketers also realized that products must be located conveniently, and so they make their L'eggs brand of panty hose available in supermarkets, rather than just in specialty and department stores. And when Mead Johnson first introduced Metrecal, its line of low-calorie food substitutes, it used drugstore outlets in order to assure consumers of the product's safety and nutritional value. But once the safety of the product was established, the marketers found that it had become a convenience good (like any other food product), and so the supermarket was the logical place to distribute it.

But there is another side to the distribution coin. With some products, easy availability detracts from the bundle of satisfaction. That is, part of the satisfaction for consumers may arise from the challenge of finding the item, or from making a great effort to obtain it. To be able to say, for example, that your candlestick was imported from Italy, or that you bought your designer outfit while on vacation in New York City, may actually increase the satisfaction you derive from the product. This is especially true of shopping goods and specialty items. Part of the satisfaction may well be that the product is unique—that it is not available locally. Then, too, some consumers like the status that is associated with the ability to travel great distances to obtain possessions. For some products, then, satisfaction is enhanced by easy availability, but for other products, satisfaction is derived from successfully obtaining them even when it's difficult. Astute marketers correctly identify the "place" needs of their market and then distribute the product accordingly.

The key to providing place satisfaction, then, is ensuring that the product is presented in the *appropriate* place. Having the right product in the right place can help to stimulate an exchange. Somehow, we just don't feel comfortable about buying an expensive suit in a run-down, dirty store; similarly, we might feel a bit strange shopping for a $14.95 watch in a store like Tiffany's. By selecting the appropriate place to make a product available, marketers can add to the bundle of satisfaction that is offered.

Ireland's Waterford Glass, Ltc., one of the finest makers of hand-crafted crystal, controls 25 percent of the United States crystal market as a result of having created an elitist image for its high-quality product. Ads in such magazines as *Gourmet* and *The New Yorker* and restricted distribution to only quality-image department and specialty stores have made Waterford the best-selling fine crystal in America. As demand has spread beyond the carriage trade, Waterford has resisted cashing in on mass markets. By maintaining the appropriate places for its product, the company has maintained its upper-class aura; there's no appeal to owning a product that almost anyone can buy.

To carry this idea of the "right place" a step further, we must note that consumers may prefer to obtain some products very privately. Many people feel a bit anxious about approaching a druggist to ask for a remedy for athlete's foot or constipation or even sleeplessness, and such products are often better located in inconspicuous places where they can be purchased privately. The professional services of a doctor, a lawyer, or a psychologist are conducted in confidence partly for this reason, and they are often made available in a discreet manner. So the marketer's distribution job is not simply to make a product easy to locate, but to make it available in the appropriate place and manner. (See Application 13-1.)

Neutrogena has parlayed this concept for its "medicinal" soap. The company built a credible image by marketing among two institutions that consumers already trusted—the medical profession and luxury hotels. Some sixteen Neutrogena sales-people, out of a total of sixty-six, visit only dermatologists and enlist them to recommend Neutrogena to their patients. Additionally, mini 1-ounce bars of Neutrogena sit on bathroom basins in some 300 luxury and resort hotels across the United States. Instead of hotel logos on the bars, the company has its own clinical label.

Application 13-1
Time and Place Utility—Trading on Time

(Courtesy Federal Express)

"When you absolutely, positively must have it there tomorrow," you can—thanks to Federal Express. Guaranteed nationwide delivery of small packages the morning after pickup is unquestionably an idea whose time has come. Federal Express, since its founding in 1971, has met this need. Evidence of fulfilling this need is reflected by the company's profits, which have multiplied at the astounding annual rate of 76 percent since 1976.

The Federal Express concept is built on the fact that the population has moved away from the central cities while still demanding downtown conveniences. Everything from TV-promoted gadgets to the latest technology is still expected to be available, no matter where anyone lives.

Miniaturization of scientific devices was another spark that propelled the company. Federal Express founder Frederick Smith recognized that the number of items that could be packaged in a 10-pound container was soaring, as were manufacturing costs. It would be impossible for manufacturers to keep inventory at every point in the distribution system. Also, as passenger airlines moved toward bigger jets, their ability and desire to carry small packages nationwide would diminish.

Not foreseeable but certainly advantageous were the effects of the fuel crises on other commercial airlines and the poor reliability of the U.S. Postal Service's regular mail.

Federal's success has become aviation history. Federal focuses on moving small packages fast. Over 2000 radio-equipped company-owned vans pick up the packages, which are loaded on company-owned planes to ensure complete control, and then flown to a "hub" in Memphis. All the packages are sorted through the night and reloaded onto outbound planes. Federal claims that it delivers 99 percent of its packages overnight and that the odds of a package being lost, damaged, or stolen in its closed system are 4500 to 1.

As the small package market slowed in 1981, Federal branched into competing directly with the U.S. Postal Service by offering overnight service on letters. Federal expects to handle 100,000 overnight letters a day and to boost its revenues to $2 billion by 1985.

Sources of data: "Federal Express Rides the Small Package Boom," *Business Week*, March 31, 1980, pp. 108–112; and "Federal Express Dives into Air Mail," *Fortune*, June 15, 1981, pp. 106–108.

Selecting the "right place" can be an important addition to marketing the bundle of satisfaction.

Time Utility

Geography (place) is not the only dimension of distribution that marketers must consider. There is also the time element. Time and place utilities intertwine in the sense that traveling does take time. The closer a product is to consumers, the less time they will have to spend transporting themselves to where the product is available, and some consumers put a premium on saving time. But time utility does not come only from bridging distance. Goods and services must be available at the *right* time.

Consumers' needs—and particularly wants—are often fleeting. What they want right now, they may not want next year, or next month, or even in a few minutes. This is particularly true in the case of impulse buying. You see a beautiful blue-and-white scarf in a display case but would really prefer the same design in maroon and white. You look around for what you want but are unable to find it. Then a clerk tells you that the maroon-and-white scarves are sold out, but the store will be getting a shipment in a week or so. What are the chances that you'll return to that clothing store after the allotted time to buy the maroon-and-white scarf? And even if you do wander back to the store later and find the scarf, in those two weeks your mood may have changed, or you may no longer have the discretionary income to spend, or other things may have altered your wants and needs. Thus, one more key to providing satisfaction in the marketplace is making products available when they are wanted.

As with place utility, however, marketers sometimes increase the satisfaction that a product provides by increasing the time needed to obtain it. Consumers' anticipation of the bundle of satisfaction can enhance its value. When you have devoted a lot of time to pursuing a product and then finally get it, it means that much more to you. Consider that scarf we just mentioned. Suppose you first had seen that particular kind of maroon-and-white scarf on someone you liked and admired, and you had been trying to find one exactly like it for a couple of years. You visited more clothing shops than you care to remember, but all to no avail. Under these circumstances, if you finally *are* able to locate the scarf, you probably will value it above all others. In short, the difficulty and time involved in finding the scarf have enhanced its value. Thus, the decision about what kind of time and place utilities to build into a marketing mix depends—like all marketing decisions—on a proper understanding of consumers' needs and wants. (See Application 13-2.)

A Broadened View of Distribution

So far, we have concentrated on the distribution of goods rather than services. But a service also has to have appropriate time and place utilities to enhance its bundle of satisfaction. Services, too, have to be located properly and be available when consumers want them. Look at what automatic teller machines (ATMs) have added to the convenience and availability of banking services.

Such nonprofit organizations as Goodwill Industries and the Salvation Army understand that a convenient location stimulates exchange. They make it easy for

Application 13-2
Place and Time Utility—
The Wrong Place Is the Right Place,
and the Wrong Time Is the Right Time

(Joan Menschenfreund)

In an eleven-block enclave on Manhattan's Fifth Avenue, a covey of hyperexclusive Italian shops caters to the very uppermost crust. Ferragamo, a shoe salon, is set back from Fifth Avenue (or, as it is known to some, Quinta Strada), all the harder for the uninitiated to find. And that's the way the exclusive retailers want it. Says Piero Nuti, Ferragamo's general manager, "Most of our customers are celebrities. We seldom see anyone else." Bulgari, the jeweler so exclusive that Cartier seems a volume discounter by comparison, is secreted in the Pierre Hotel, away from the window-shopping hoi polloi.

The appeal of these shops resides in their reserving themselves for their small band of conspicuous consumers. Some discourage even light customer traffic. Silversmith Ugo Buccellati breathes a sigh of relief when only two customers a day come to shop. Gucci, purveyor of leather goods, and perhaps the snobbiest of all, knows how to keep its goods scarce and desirable. Its sales staff learns all the tricks of inhospitality, and to discourage browsers, Gucci goes so far as to close for lunch. Manager Antonio Cagliarini prefers this Italian custom because "it's good for the employees and for our type of business. Our regular customers know we're closed, and that's it, finito."

Across the country, at Bijan men's clothing store on Beverly Hills' Rodeo Drive, the country's most exclusive street, another ploy is used: when the store is open for business, the door is locked. Would-be customers confront a sign "By Appointment Only" and are screened by a uniformed doorman to determine whether they have an appointment. The closed-door policy, says the proprietor, keeps the "untasty" away from the Persian silk rugs, Austrian crystal chandeliers, and antique armoires, not to mention the chic and expensive suits, suede jackets, and fur coats that are sold to the extremely wealthy. "To be my customer," the proprietor declares, "you must earn $100,000—a month."

Sources of data: "Quinta Strada," *Time,* May 31, 1976, pp. 85–87; and "Trendy Men's Store Finds Locking Door Is a Key to Its Success," *The Wall Street Journal,* Jan. 22, 1981, p. 1.

people to donate unwanted clothing, appliances, and other items by locating drop boxes at various points where individuals can pass conveniently and with little investment of time. If this provision of time and place utilities were not taken into account, far fewer items would be contributed.

Those who market people as products also must be concerned with distribution. Aspiring actors, actresses, singers, comedians, and so on know how important it is to be in the right place at the right time. Their big break, perhaps, has been to appear on the "Tonight Show," which provides exceptional national exposure. Politicians also recognize the importance of distribution. Ronald Reagan traveled across the nation before he became President, making speeches, shaking hands, and generally becoming visible to his market, the voting public. As his campaign rolled on, he spent more time in the critical states of Michigan, Illinois, Ohio, and Pennsylvania.

Health and social services are distributed throughout communities to make them accessible to the public. Hospitals, of course, have staff on duty around the clock. Counseling agencies also extend their hours beyond the working day, often providing a full range of services during evening hours and on Saturdays. The hesitation many people feel about using counseling services makes it imperative that the time and place distribution be as broad as possible, so that the service is available when it is needed. And in California, voter registration forms have been distributed through businesses—including fast-food chains. Attesting to the importance of place utility, a state official told *The Wall Street Journal:* "A lot of people don't know where their county courthouse is, but everyone knows where the nearest McDonald's is."[1]

Intermediaries

As we have seen, exchange cannot take place unless a product has time and place utilities. To give products this feature and thus make exchange possible, many marketers rely on intermediaries, who go by many names: middlemen, retailers, wholesalers, distributors, agents. The terms *intermediaries* and *middlemen* are used interchangeably to refer to independently owned and corporate-owned business concerns that help move products from producers to ultimate consumers. As we will see, intermediaries provide various services as products move through the distribution channel.

There are many types of intermediaries. One rather broad way of classifying them divides intermediaries into two groups, depending on whether or not they take title to the products (that is, depending on whether they actually purchase the products outright). *Merchant intermediaries* take title, while *agents* do not. Agents simply help buyers and sellers to get together; they facilitate the exchange without ever buying the products themselves.

There are two types of merchant intermediaries: retailers and wholesalers. *Retailers* are intermediaries who sell products primarily to ultimate consumers. Retailers also may buy from other intermediaries as products move through the distribution channel. *Wholesalers* are intermediaries who distribute products primarily to commercial, professional users—to retailers; to manufacturers (who use the goods to make other products); to the government; and to large institutions that purchase in quantity, like colleges and hospitals. Wholesalers also may function as links within a

---

[1]"California," *The Wall Street Journal,* Apr. 12, 1979, p. 1.

distribution chain, in which case they buy and sell products among themselves. Finally, the term *distributor* is used to refer to wholesalers of various types, whose services we will examine later in the chapter.

Distribution Problems and Solutions

Why do we need so many kinds of intermediaries? What do they do that justifies their existence? In Chapter 11, we saw that they seem to cost quite a bit of money. Wholesalers sell their goods at about 20 percent over their buying price in order to cover costs and still earn a profit, while retailers require an even greater markup to operate profitably. And it is we—the ultimate consumers—who support all these intermediaries. What do we get for our money? What benefits do intermediaries provide to consumers?

The various intermediaries exist because the marketing of products presents some real problems. First, there's the matter of *geographical distance* to be solved—the physical separation of buyers and sellers. Second, as we have noted, products must be in the appropriate place in order to *stimulate exchange*. In general, intermediaries solve these problems by distributing products in a way that gives them time and place utilities. But the process of matching product and market is complicated further by the distance variable, for consumers in different locations want different things. Thus, a Vermont furniture buyer is likely to want a colonial or Early American style, while a buyer in Arizona would probably prefer something more contemporary.

We discussed how regional differences affect buying behavior in Chapter 5, but how does a manufacturer know about all these differences and then orient production to meet the various needs? This is the crux of the *assortment problem*—assembling the correct assortment of products to match the unique and different wants and needs of the markets to be served. Let's look now at how intermediaries solve these problems of distance, exchange stimulation, and assortment.

Essentially, the distance and exchange stimulation problems are solved by a process called *sorting*, which involves the concentration and dispersion of products. That is, products are brought together at one geographical point *(concentration),* and then they are moved in large quantities down the distance scale, closer and closer to ultimate buyers *(dispersion).* Moving products in large quantities is much more economical than moving many small quantities. Through concentration, a large supply of products is moved closer to where it will be needed. At this less distant geographical point, the concentrated supply is broken down into smaller quantities that are then dispersed to buyers in the amounts desired.

For example, consider the wheat output of farmers in the Midwest. Many buyers in many locations have use for this wheat. In Minnesota, Pillsbury uses it for flour and muffin mixes; Dreikorn's bakery in Massachusetts needs it for bread; and Mrs. Paul's in Pennsylvania uses it in pie crusts. How do farmers in Nebraska, Iowa, and Illinois get their crops to these and other companies throughout the United States? Each could load up trucks and drive to all these places to sell the grain, but this distribution method would clearly be inefficient. Instead, farmers throughout the Midwest region combine all their crops at a centrally located grain elevator, and then the wheat is shipped in large quantities to various points throughout the country. Thus, sorting overcomes the distance problem by distributing products in a more economical manner. Let's examine the main benefits derived from the sorting process of intermediaries.

Fewer Transactions First of all, sorting is economical by its very nature. Since the intermediaries perform the tasks of concentration and dispersion, fewer transactions are required to distribute products. Figure 13-1 shows that with four producers and four consumers, the number of transactions is cut in half. Since each transaction costs money, a reduction in the number of transactions obviously increases the efficiency of distribution. The use of intermediaries allows each producer to transport a quantity of products sufficient to meet the needs of all four consumers; without an intermediary, however, each shipment would be smaller. And since the intermediaries make it possible to move larger quantities, an assortment of products from each of the four producers is available to meet the needs of each of the four consumers. Furthermore, it is less costly to ship large quantities than to move small amounts. And along with all these benefits comes the convenience of having products located closer to consumers when they need them.

Consider the magazine industry. Magazines are distributed through two channels —customer subscriptions and single-copy sales at drugstores, newsstands, convenience stores, supermarkets, and chain stores. With rising postal rates, the single-copy channel has become more important. Here, ten national wholesalers move more than

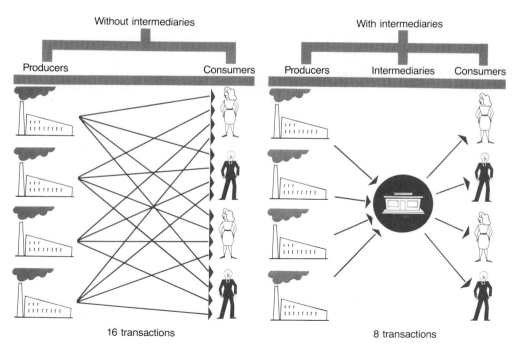

Figure 13-1 How intermediaries reduce transactions in the distribution system.

33,000 different magazines to about 500 regional wholesalers. The regional wholesalers then distribute the magazines to the retail outlets. Since magazines are perishable products, speed is very important. *TV Guide,* for instance, is stocked in more than 150,000 establishments within 36 hours of its printing. Thus, concentration and dispersion reduce the complexity of moving magazines into the hands of its reading market.

Closer to Market

The fact that intermediaries are located geographically closer to consumers than most producers results in major benefits. The nearness to consumers makes it possible to assess the needs and wants of a particular market much more accurately. Since the intermediaries actually talk and work with the buyers of the product, they learn firsthand about the demands of the market. This knowledge then can be communicated back to the producers so that the most appropriate assortment of products can be manufactured to match the market's desires. The communication between intermediaries and producers, then, helps to solve the assortment problem.

In the magazine industry each year, $200 million worth of magazines are returned unsold and must be shredded. Without this cost, the industry could more than double its profit. To reduce this loss, wholesalers provide detailed information on returns and sellouts by area and magazine type. This information helps publishers regulate the number of magazines shipped to an area and helps wholesalers and retailers select the proper combination of magazines for an area served.

Communication also helps to stimulate exchange. Since intermediaries will not buy products that they cannot sell, even potentially satisfactory products will not be repurchased if they do not move off the intermediaries' shelves. Communication between the intermediaries and producers results in a better match of products and consumers' needs, and so exchange is stimulated.

Reduced Total Inventory

Within a distribution system, products must be stored so that they will be available when the market wants them. Paradoxical as it may seem, when intermediaries are part of the overall distribution system there is actually less total inventory stored than when none are used. From Figure 13-1 we see that with one intermediary, there are five places to store inventory (four producers plus one intermediary); but without that intermediary, there are only four storage points (the four producers). Although it seems to follow that there must be more inventory in a system that has five storage places rather than four, that is not the case. Instead, because the intermediaries are closer to consumers and have a more accurate sense of their needs, they can better select which products the market will want. And when the assortment of products more accurately matches the market's needs, exchange is stimulated, and less inventory stays on the shelves. Without the intermediaries, producers would offer less appropriate assortments and exchanges would be fewer, leading to a backlog of products in producers' inventories. The use of intermediaries thus reduces the total inventory within the distribution system.

Again in the magazine industry, the flow of information is used to reduce inventories. *Cosmopolitan,* for instance, provides wholesalers with specific marketing information to aid them in their sales promotion. Cooperation between channel members is hoped to realize a goal of 95 percent sellout.

Services of Intermediaries

The use of intermediaries definitely helps products to flow through the distribution system more efficiently and more effectively than if the job were left to producers. Additionally, we noted in Chapter 1 how important the concept of specialization has become to modern economies. Intermediaries are specialists in distribution, and producers specialize in production. In today's complex world, it would be a tall order to be effective at both production and distribution. So intermediaries specialize in the very important task of moving products to consumers efficiently and effectively. In doing this, they perform various activities that we will examine now.

Buying

As we have noted, intermediaries monitor and anticipate the needs of the people they serve. The intermediaries purchase products (or, if they are agents, they determine sources for products) and then make them available when the market wants them. Intermediaries have a broad knowledge of the sources of supply for the markets they serve, and this is a prerequisite for assembling the proper assortment of products. A given lumber retailer, for example, is unlikely to have current, complete information regarding which lumber mills supply which products and where the best price can be found. Wholesalers and agents, however, must secure such information as part of their job. Since they often buy or arrange sales of lumber, they must learn everything they can about suppliers. Similarly, since consumers do not frequently purchase such products as lawn mowers, swing sets, and fishing rods, they do not know exactly which products are produced or where they are available. Since retailers often buy such products, however, they can ensure that the right ones are made available to consumers. And, of course, we have already noted that the intermediaries serve the vital function of communicating the market's concerns to manufacturers, thus helping to ensure that products match consumers' needs.

Selling

Many manufacturers are small companies with limited financial resources, and so they cannot make all the needed contacts with their market. Instead, intermediaries in many ways act as their sales force. The cost of selling is the cost of making a contact, and each contact is expensive. With intermediaries in the distribution system, the number of contacts needed to reach a set of ultimate consumers is reduced.

Additionally, the market served by an intermediary is the specialty of that intermediary, whereas a manufacturer entering the market would probably be a stranger. Moreover, intermediaries are closer to the market, which adds a personal touch to exchange. Sales are stimulated when buyers know the person with whom they are dealing.

Bulk Breaking

A basic principle of distribution is to ship products in large quantities, which is far more economical than sending small shipments. Freight rates per unit are reduced when wholesalers purchase products in carload or truckload quantities. But since retailers do not sell such large amounts themselves, the wholesalers divide the total shipment into quantities that retailers can use. In turn, the retailers receive products in cases or boxes. Again, however, ultimate consumers want smaller quantities of products, and so the retailers divide their shipments into appropriate amounts for consumers.

Transportation

Besides their other services, intermediaries often provide a means of moving products between geographical points. The delivery of products by wholesalers allows retailers to hold smaller inventories than would be possible otherwise. If the need for an item arises, it can be supplied quickly, since the transportation system is ready and available. Many retailers also provide delivery service, which stimulates exchange with final consumers. After all, few buyers of console television sets are willing or able to carry their puchases home.

Storage

In order to ensure time and place utilities, intermediaries must store products and be ready to provide them when they are wanted. This storage function is an important aspect of serving the market. But it also takes some of the burden off manufacturers, who pass the storage function along in the distribution system. Thus, consumers get the products they need when they want them, and total inventory in the distribution system is reduced.

Financing

Some intermediaries aid their customers by offering attractive credit policies. Retailers often are small firms with fewer financial resources than wholesalers. Therefore, to provide the products needed in the ultimate market, wholesalers offer liberal credit options to their customers. Few manufacturers would be able to offer comparable financial assistance. A lumber producer like Boise-Cascade, for example, could not possibly finance all, or even many, of the retail lumberyards across the United States, and financing them would require an incredible amount of paperwork, to say nothing of the risks involved. But an individual lumber wholesaler serves far fewer retailers and may be willing to offer financial assistance to stimulate sales.

Risk Bearing

Most intermediaries take title to the products they sell. Thus, they assume the risk of not selling the products, and the manufacturer bears no legal responsibility for them. If the product deteriorates, or goes out of style, or becomes obsolete for some other reason, the intermediary takes the loss. Additionally, wholesalers and retailers usually stand behind their products; thus, buyers who obtain faulty, damaged, or unwanted items can get satisfaction more quickly from the intermediary than from the producer. Similarly, consumers can go directly to the retailer who sold the product, rather than having to deal with the wholesaler or producer.

Management Services

Intermediaries also provide management assistance to their customers. Often, retailers are less skilled than wholesalers when it comes to accounting techniques, in-store promotional displays, advertising, sales training, and inventory control. Thus, whole-salers and agents can give appropriate advice and instruction that benefit the retailer. Manufacturers, usually located miles away from most of their retailers, cannot provide this service with any regularity—and they only specialize in their own products. The retailer benefits, then, in terms of sales, while the wholesaler or agent who gives assistance chalks up substantial goodwill with the retailer and paves the way for additional business.

These, then, are the main services that intermediaries perform, and the need for them would not disappear if intermediaries did not exist. Very likely, responsibility for these functions would fall on manufacturers, who would have to store and transport products, perform the buying, selling, and bulk breaking, and bear all the risks. As we have seen, however, the manufacturer is a production specialist. These important distribution functions can be carried out more efficiently and more effectively by the intermediaries who specialize in such tasks—retailers and wholesalers. We'll examine their operations more closely now.

Retailing

Retailing includes all activities associated with selling goods and services to ultimate consumers. Although we usually think of retailers as merchant intermediaries who own stores, it's also accurate to consider teachers, lawyers, doctors, and consultants as retailers. They, too, market products to ultimate consumers. Thus, hospitals can be seen as retail outlets, and patients are their customers. Colleges are retailers of education, and such organizations as charities, funeral homes, and churches also fall into the retail category. (See Application 13-3.)

The Scope of Retailing

In 1977, there were approximately 1.85 million retail establishments in the United States, not counting the organizations we just included in our broadened definition of retailing. This figure represents 50,000 fewer establishments than existed in 1972.[2] It has remained *relatively* stable since 1939, with new retail businesses replacing those that failed. But the consumer population has swelled, as have gross sales. In 1939, the sales volume for all retailers was about $48 billion; by 1980, this figure had grown to over $950 billion.[3] So, while the number of retailers is not growing, the amount of business they transact has increased enormously. Of the 1.9 million retail firms in 1972, 53 percent had annual sales of less than $100,000. This volume accounted for only 8.4 percent of total retail sales. However, 3.9 percent of the retail firms in 1972 had sales over $1 million, which accounted for 53 percent of total retail sales. Let's compare these statistics with those from 1977. In 1977, the proportion of total retailers with sales under $1 million had risen to 6.4 percent and accounted for 58 percent of total sales. Clearly, the trend is toward fewer small retailers and more giants, with the giants capturing an increasing percentage of the sales volume.[4]

---

[2]*Statistical Abstracts of the United States,* 1980.

[3]U.S. Bureau of the Census, *Monthly Retail Trade, January 1981.*

[4]*Statistical Abstracts of the United States,* 1980.

Retailers Classified

Retailers operating today come in a wide variety of forms. One way of classifying these organizations is shown in Figure 13-2, which divides them on the basis of:

1   The amount of shopping effort required of consumers

2   The ownership of the retail operation

3   The extent and types of product lines handled

4   The various functions performed

Application 13-3
Retailing—Filling a Gap in the Marketplace

(Gwendolyn Stewart for Business Week)

Now, when you visit a Sears store, you can have your teeth fixed while your car is getting a new muffler in the auto service department. During the past few years, the trend toward dental clinics has mushroomed across the country, and such dental shops are becoming common. They are found in retail outlets ranging from department stores to drugstores and as self-standing units in the suburbs.

Joining the movement toward offering health care services in retail settings are optometrists, podiatrists, chiropractors, and hearing aid specialists.

The floodgates for the new distribution approach by dentists were opened when the U.S. Supreme Court held that professional associations could advertise.

Advertising has radically changed the industry. With dentists and other professionals, advertising in earnest, price competition, evolving clinics, and even loss leaders came into vogue. Some dental services offered $20 specials which included the initial examination and x-rays. Such service in the traditional dental office would cost $40 to $45. Extended hours and walk-in services are alos featured in the dental shops.

American Dental Centers, Inc., of Cleveland, operates on a six-figure advertising budget and has annual sales of $2 million. Meanwhile, Universal Dental Center of New York offered discount coupons for consultation on dentures.

The impact of the dental clinics on conventional dentists is evident. Many have begun to open their offices several evenings a week and on Saturdays. "I think we're seeing a sign of the times," says Dr. Charles R. Mitchell of Downers Grove, Illinois, treasurer of the Academy of General Dentistry, the organization of conventional family dentists. "Professionals are having to become businessmen and to market to their target consumer group."

Source of data: "Moving the Dentist's Chair to Retail Stores," *Business Week,* Jan. 19, 1981, pp. 56–58.

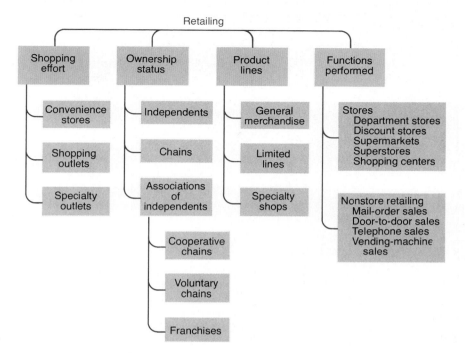

Figure 13-2
Classification of retailers.

Shopping Effort

We noted in Chapter 8 that products can be classified according to the shopping behavior of the market they serve. The same can be done for retailers, although the type of store is not tied to one type of product; that is, convenience stores do not handle only convenience products. Rather, retailers are classified according to how consumers perceive the store, the kind of image the store conveys, and the characteristics of the store.

Convenience stores, for example, are located centrally, near the residences or workplaces of their target customers. Such stores may carry wide assortments of products—shopping goods, convenience items, specialty products, and even unsought goods. Their owners emphasize location, parking, easy movement within the store, long hours, and quick checkout service. Convenience stores stock an average of 3000 fast-moving items, such as beer, cigarettes, candy, soft drinks, milk, bread, and, recently, gasoline. In the United States in 1960, there were 2500 convenience stores; by 1980, there were 34,000, not including gasoline stations. While attention is drawn here to merchandise stores, convenience stores would also include the likes of McDonald's and Holiday Inn, where patronage is based on the criteria cited above. (See Application 13-4.)

Shopping stores are retail outlets that seem to be favored by consumers shopping for certain types of products, such as clothing, appliances, or dry cleaning. The managers of such stores attempt to create a perceived difference between their stores

Application 13-4
Convenience Stores—
Needing More than Time and Place Utility

The small, jam-packed convenience store flourished during the past two decades on the strength of selling milk, ice cream, candy, coffee, and cigarettes. Premium prices were the rule, the result of staying open long after the supermarkets had closed.

But changes are coming and there are strong indications the past benefits are becoming liabilities. At least, that's the verdict of a study by SRI International Inc., a research firm in Menlo Park, California. Some of the problems cited by SRI are these:

Today's consumers feel their finances are stretched to the limit and are less likely to make costly late-night purchases.

Several products that formed the core of business are falling out of favor. Consumers are older and more health-conscious today. Candy consumption, for instance, has fallen off, and weight-conscious consumers are avoiding dairy fat.

Milk sales are also declining because the baby-boom generation has matured and there are fewer children.

Tobacco sales have been flattened in response to antismoking campaigns and to mounting evidence that cigarettes are detrimental.

Many convenience stores have developed a negative image. Consumers apparently see the outlets as dirty and understaffed and as hangouts for undesirables.

To boost declining sales, convenience stores have added new items, including gasoline and fast foods.

Over 15,000 stores now sell gasoline—while fewer than 1,300 did so in 1979. Oil companies are entering the market, either by purchasing stores or by developing their own at existing gas stations. Sun Co. acquired Stop N Go Foods, Inc., in 1976, then added Fast Fare, Inc., and Mr. Zip, Inc., three years later. Atlantic Richfield has started to add grocery shelves

at some gas stations, dubbing these stations "AM/PM minimarkets."

Convenience stores selling hot sandwiches, soups, and coffee jumped 86 percent in 1977 alone, and the trend continues. These fast-food items are aimed at blue-collar and office workers at lunchtime. One untapped market for convenience stores is in quick-to-fix dinner entrées.

If their food business is to grow, convenience stores also will have to change their image. One consumer says he feels he can enter a store "sweaty and dirty" after playing ball because the employees look the same way. A female customer says: "I don't want someone who's been dusting cans, handling money, and sweeping floors" to serve food.

Source of data: "Convenience Stores Battle Lagging Sales by Adding Items and Cleaning Up Image," *The Wall Street Journal,* March 28, 1980, p. 16.

and those of competitors. Advertising emphasizes these differences, and salespeople are trained to give knowledgeable service and advice.

Finally, *specialty stores* are retail outlets for which consumers develop a strong allegiance and preference. The commitment to shop in the store may be based on the selection of products offered, the service, the reputation, or something else. Saks Fifth

Avenue, Lord & Taylor, and Brooks Brothers are examples of specialty stores. While such stores seem to enjoy a prized competitive position, they must strive continuously to ensure their customers' loyalty.

Ownership Status

Another useful way of classifying retail operations is based on ownership. Thus, a retailer may operate independently or may be part of a chain, a cooperative, a voluntary chain, or a franchise operation.

An *independent retailer* owns a single outlet that has no affiliation with any other retail units offering similar lines of merchandise or similar services. The vast majority (about 90 percent) of retail operations fall into this category, and individual outlets can be large in size like a department store or small like a local print shop. Independent retailers are their own bosses. They are able to develop close personal relationships with customers and thus can make fast decisions in response to the market's desires. Many boutiques, flower shops, tobacco shops, bakeries, lawyers, and dentists fall in this category.

Chain stores are retail organizations consisting of two or more units under a single owner. Such operations usually handle the same or similar lines of merchandise or service, are designed and decorated similarly, and rely on centralized buyers to select their merchandise. Some chains are national operations, like Sears, A&P, Woolworth's, Holiday Inn, and H & R Block; others are regional retailers, like Ralph's supermarkets and Walgreen's drugstores. Additionally, some chains (like Kroger's) retain complete ownership of all their stores, while others (like Firestone tire stores) own only a few outlets, allowing individual operators to own the others. For the most part, chains are large organizations that have a great many outlets and produce large sales volumes.

Chain retailers enjoy the advantages of large-scale operations—such as quantity discounts, a strong financial position, mass-media advertising, brand loyalty, the high efficiency that leads to lower unit costs for customers, and better management expertise. Often, chains also do their own transporting, warehousing, financing, and other services usually delegated to intermediaries or producers. Such advantages make chain retailers competitively stronger than independents, but they do not dominate retailing in every merchandise area. For instance, while chains own over 90 percent of the department and variety stores operating today, they account for only about 54 percent of sales in the food industry.

Independent retailers as a group have become increasingly effective in competing against corporate chains. In some cases, retailers attempt to gain the advantages of large-scale operations but still retain the benefits enjoyed by independents. To do this, they establish one of the following forms of organization: a cooperative, a voluntary chain, or a franchise.

In a *cooperative organization,* independent retailers combine their resources to maintain their own wholesaling operation. This approach allows the individual retailers to take advantage of large-scale purchasing, since they pool their orders to wholesalers and other suppliers. Often, they also will engage as a group in mass advertising and branding. At the same time, though, these independent retailers still keep control over their own operations.

Voluntary chains are like cooperative organizations except that in this case a wholesaler initiates and runs the organization. Wholesalers sometimes find the number of their retail customers dwindling; to counter this erosion of their market, they may form a group of independent retailers, who again benefit from the advantages of large-scale operation. The wholesaler agrees to serve the member stores in return for the members' agreement to buy most of their merchandise through the wholesaler. Examples of voluntary chains include the Independent Grocers Alliance (IGA), Ben Franklin, Western Auto Supply, and Shopco, a voluntary chain of variety stores.

Another way to gain the advantages of large-scale operation is through franchising. A *franchise* is a legal contractual relationship between a supplier (either a manufacturer or a wholesaler) and several or many small independent retailers. Franchised outlets have become very popular, particularly in the retailing of travel, food, and other services. Holiday Inns, Dairy Queens, Midas Muffler shops, 7-Eleven stores, McDonald's, Hertz, and H & R Block are all examples. Under a franchise agreement, the franchisor exerts some controls on how the franchisee runs the business and, in return, provides the franchisee with an established brand name as well as operating assistance. The types of assistance vary widely. Some franchisors provide a complete operating plan that specifies hours, type and color of uniforms, and training programs. (McDonald's trains its franchisors at Hamburger University, and Midas Muffler has its M.I.T., Midas Institute of Technology.) Others provide only the merchandise that the franchisee will sell. The franchisees pay a royalty based on gross sales volume. For this fee, the franchisor buys national advertising and may supply packaging or other ingredients of the product.

The fast-food industry provides a good example of different franchise requirements. McDonald's owns or leases nearly all the land and buildings used by its 5747 stores. As the franchisee's landlord, the franchisor has power. McDonald's franchisees, for example, are not allowed to own any other fast-food restaurants, and they have no territorial rights or protection. At the other extreme is Wendy's, which encourages the growth of large franchisees. That policy has enabled it to balloon from 100 to 1881 stores in five years. Burger King does not allow franchisees to own any other fast-food business and also insists that owners live within an hour's drive of their Burger King store. Such restriction makes sure that the proprietor, and not simply a manager, is always nearby to give the store personal attention. (See Figure 13-3.)

Many franchises established in the late 1960s and early 1970s failed to yield all they promised. Some fields of retailing, such as fast-food franchises, were overdeveloped and oversold, and a number of franchise chains failed. As the franchising boom of the 1960s slowed down, some franchisors attempted to make quick profits by selling too many franchise agreements. Many of these agreements were based on limited marketing research and suffered from generally poor planning and management. Now the franchise approach to gaining the chain-store advantages of centralized management and coordinated marketing seems to have stabilized. Growth can still be expected, but it is likely to be slower and more controlled than in the past.

Figure 13-3   Franchises have become increasingly popular in businesses such as fast food, car rentals, and even tax-preparation services. Franchising agreements differ widely, even within the same type of business. Name some franchised businesses in your community. *(Ray Pfortner)*

Product Lines

The variety (width) of products offered, along with the assortment (depth) within product lines, provides another means of classifying retailers. Thus, *general merchandise retailers* carry a wide range of products for customers. The "general store" so common in western movies presents a good example. Such stores carried every type of goods needed by their customers—food, hardware, fabrics, seed, and farm implements. While these stores have all but disappeared, their modern-day counterpart has emerged through what has come to be called "scrambled merchandising" and "conglomerate merchandising." That is, in the search for additional profits, retailers have added product lines that traditionally have been carried by other retailers. For example, discount stores have added grocery products and automotive accessories, while grocery stores have added cosmetics, hardware, and even clothing. Such additions may make today's general merchandisers look like the old general store, but they operate on a much larger scale. In a broad sense, our shopping centers can be considered general merchandise retailers, since they cater to so many needs of the market they serve.

Today's largest general merchandiser is Sears, Roebuck and Company. With sales of $18 billion in 1981, Sears has almost 50 percent more sales volume than K mart, the second-largest nonfood retailer. Sears provides just about every nonfood line imaginable in its approximately 900 stores throughout the United States. It offers its own private brands (Craftsman power tools, Kenmore appliances, Cheryl Tiegs signature line of clothing, and Sears tires) as well as national brands. As the 1980s began, Sears found itself in serious profit and growth trouble. The company was top-heavy in management, which resulted in noncompetitive higher administrative expenses. This made Sears the highest-cost mass merchandiser in the business. To correct its off-center course, in 1981 Sears added a host of financial services—stock brokerage, real estate, and money market funds—to its already substantial services base, including All State property, casualty, and life insurance, mortgage life insurance, and savings and loan operations. Such a strategy has given Sears the appearance of a gigantic, consumer-oriented banking institution.

In contrast, *limited-line retailers* offer an inventory that is held to only one or several similar lines. Hardware stores, drugstores, and stationery and printing shops are examples. Rather than emphasize variety, limited-line stores build patronage by offering a deep assortment and expertise within that product line. In short, limited-line retailers do not attempt to satisfy a large range of needs and wants; instead, they aim to satisfy one or a few needs much more completely.

Specialty-line retailers go a step further, offering only one or two product lines but substantial depth within those lines and an even greater expertise. Examples of specialty stores include tobacco stores, ice-cream parlors, bakeries, card shops, and interior decorating services. Since these retailers offer such a limited product line, they can be counted on for an excellent assortment from which to choose. Successful specialty stores usually have knowledgeable buyers who know just what items to select for sale to consumers. And, because they purchase in such a limited merchandise area, they often can get good quantity discounts and pass their savings on to customers.

Functions Performed

While you may already be familiar with at least some of the classes of retailers we have looked at, you will no doubt be more familiar with the types of retailers we shall look at next. They are classified according to the major activities or functions they carry out. These types of retailers account for the bulk of retail sales; the first five are actual store types, while the remaining four represent nonstore retailing.

Department stores offer a wide variety of product lines, but the depth within those lines varies from store to store. These retailing operations are usually organized into departments to facilitate marketing and internal management. Typically, they include departments for cosmetics, clothing, appliances, and housewares, but recent trends have been toward adding service departments, such as travel assistance, insurance, and even tax preparation. In fact, most department stores emphasize "service" as one of their major benefits—delivery, credit, alterations, and atmosphere being among the services offered. Macy's, Sears, Penney's, Neiman-Marcus, and Marshall Field are prominent examples.

There are also department store chains, the most prominent of which is Federated Department Stores of Cincinnati. This chain has fifteen department store divisions and owns some of the country's best-known retailing operations: Bloomingdale's and Abraham & Straus on the East Coast, I. Magnin and Bullock's on the West Coast, Filene's in New England, Foley's and Sanger-Harris in Texas, Burdine's in

Florida, Shiloto's in the Midwest, and Rich's in the South. Most department stores originally were located in downtown areas, but now they have established branches in suburban shopping centers as well.

Department stores of late have lost customers to inflation. In contrast, low-priced stores have remained strong, as have those appealing to the carriage trade. To recover, many department stores have abandoned carrying a full line of goods because of cost pressures from discounters and from specialists in hard goods. Many, now referred to as "junior department stores," concentrate on selling high-markup, more fashionable, more exclusive items and eliminate high-priced goods, such as appliances, carpets, and furniture—all of which require heavy investment. As the big-growth years have faded for department stores in general, many are turning more aggressive in order to counter the trend. More marketing research is being utilized. To better target their market, many stores are remodeling entire floors into specialty shops. And bargain basements have become important to compete with the onslaught of the discounters.

Discount stores are self-service, general merchandise stores that combine low prices and high sales volume to achieve profits. This form of retailing began shortly after World War II, when there was a tremendous demand for all sorts of products that could not be purchased during wartime. The first discounters rented inexpensive large buildings, purchased large quantities of nationally branded durable goods, spread them all over the building, and then let customers browse without sales assistance, obtaining payment as they exited with goods in hand. Today's discounters, however, operate very differently. They offer credit, have plenty of sales clerks, are located in good sites, merchandise many different lines of products, and advertise in mass media. In short, many discounters have successfully upgraded their image by improving the quality of their facilities and services, and some limited-line discounters have come on the scene. Examples of modern discounters are K mart, Woolco, Target, and Zayre's.

Inflation has caused problems for some of the old-line discounters. Selling goods at low profit margins and selling to low-income customers, who suffer most during difficult economic times, double the difficulty for discounters. Today's successful discounters give value and quality to their customers. Upscale discounters such as Caldor's, the Target, and Wal-Mart Stores, Inc., thrive by selling quality goods at low prices. (See Application 13-5.)

Supermarkets are large self-service stores that carry a full line of food products and—more often than not—a number of nonfood products. These large grocery stores, which began in the 1930s, were the first mass merchandisers. Supermarkets emphasize convenience items, a minimum of service, price appeal, and large parking areas where appropriate. Since their profit margins are very low, they must maintain careful control over costs. (Table 13-1 lists the largest grocery chains.)

Within the supermarket designation, we have recently seen the entry of what has come to be known as the *superstore*. This is a combination of a general merchandise discount operation and a supermarket. The key difference between this new form of retailing and supermarkets lies in the range of consumer needs served. While supermarkets concentrate on food and housekeeping products, superstores attempt

Application 13-5
Cutting Costs at Retail—Less Service with a Smile

More and more retailers are abandoning the old notion of "service with a smile." Sears, J. C. Penney, and Montgomery Ward have taken the lead in drastically reducing services.

Retailing executives have ready explanations for the service cutbacks. First, there is a shortage of knowledgeable people who are willing to toil as clerks. Second, high costs are hitting stores just when customers have become more value-oriented. Increasingly, retail stores will be characterized by price and value promotions, with limited merchandise selections and store layouts aimed at increasing sales. The consumer will see signs and displays instead of salespeople.

"It's a fact of life we all have to live with: There's going to be less direct sales help, as well as less-qualified and -motivated sales help," Peter E. Monash, senior vice president of Doody Co., a Columbus, Ohio, retail consulting firm, told *The Wall Street Journal.*

Target, the large discounter, has cut service to near zero without losing customers. Bruce Allbright, Target's president, says, "We don't want to sell anything that won't fit into a shopping basket." The reason for this strategy is that larger goods require costly service people. Fewer departments are now staffed. In a typical store, only five departments are staffed, down from thirteen a year ago.

Mr. Allbright aims to rid his stores of such merchandise as swing sets and mixed paint, both of which require salesclerk's time. Already gone are mufflers, which involved difficult installations, locked shelves for stereo tapes, and window shades that needed cutting. Target also has redesigned checkout counters and trained cashiers to record prices by touch, improving productivity by more than 20 percent.

At Target, signs and displays abound as replacements for salespeople. They are used for anything from specifications for TV antennas to reminders to pull carts through the checkout areas.

Cost savings translate into lower prices—at least 5 percent lower on most items most of the time. For example, Calvin Klein jeans sell for $25 a pair at Target, $17 less than at a service-oriented competitor's store. Seiko gold quartz watches that normally retail for $295 are sold for $200 here.

"If a customer has to make the choice between waiting an extra five minutes in line and saving money, he'll put more value in prices," says Mr. Allbright. "The average customer realizes he's making a trade-off when he comes to Target."

Source of data: "Many Stores Abandon 'Service with a Smile,' Rely on Signs, Displays," *The Wall Street Journal,* March 16, 1981, p. 1.

---

to provide for just about every need and want that an "average" person might have. Their product lines include, for example, garden products, stationery, records, tires, apparel, gasoline, and even many household services, like laundry, banking, and shoe repair. In short, superstores are the ultimate in one-stop shopping. In comparison with regular supermarkets, these retailing operations generally have twice as much traffic, three times the sales, and four times as many products.[5]

---

[5]Walter J. Salmon, Robert D. Buzzell, and Stanton G. Cort, "Today the Shopping Center, Tomorrow the Superstore," *Harvard Business Review,* January–February 1974, pp. 89–98.

TABLE 13-1 The Ten Largest Grocery Chains in 1980	
	1979 sales (in billions)
1 Safeway	$13.7
2 Kroger	9.0
3 A&P	6.7
4 Lucky	5.8
5 Winn-Dixie	4.9
6 American Stores	4.9
7 Jewel	3.9
8 Grand Union	3.3
9 Albertson's	2.8
10 Supermarkets General	2.4

Source: U.S. News & World Report, July 7, 1980, p. 53.

Supermarkets have been plagued by a number of problems, such as soaring costs, brutal competition, and a changing market. Beginning in the late 1960s, sales volume suddenly began leveling off. This reflected a slowing of population growth, resistance from consumers (who had become inflation-weary, smarter, and harder to please), and the impact of the food service industry, which includes restaurants, fast-food chains, and all other eating places. To counteract these problems, many supermarket chains have taken to building superstores. Others, remaining smaller than superstores, have added a number of the services of superstores—dental and legal services, diet advice, and flower shops—to offer variety and lure shoppers.

A major move in supermarkets is the offering of store-label, or generic, products. Such goods retail for 30 to 60 percent below the price of national brands. There are also the even more extreme no-frills or "box" stores. These stores look less like grocery stores than warehouses. They provide limited selections of commonly used items. Customers take boxes and cans right out of the shipping crates and then put their purchases in bags themselves. The benefits of these measures are prices of about 25 to 40 percent less than regular supermarkets. But many box stores don't offer meat, produce, or frozen foods.

An outgrowth of the population movement from the cities to the suburbs, *shopping centers* are groups of retail stores that are planned, developed, and controlled by one organization. That developer may be a major department store or an individual investor. The center is built to be free of traffic congestion in a convenient location outside the inner city, and to have a wide variety of stores to meet all the needs of the market it serves. Usually, each shopping center has at least one major department store as its focus and many limited-line and specialty stores. Some recently developed shopping centers are designed to have enormous regional pull, including as many as five major department stores in addition to all the other smaller shops and stores.

Entering the 1980s, shopping center development has been slowing down. In 1980, only nine major regional centers opened, although twenty had opened in 1978.

The Northeast and Midwest have seen the greatest decline. Some specialty urban malls, such as Boston's Faneuil Hall and Baltimore's Harborplace, have become premier tourist attractions, but the traditional suburban shopping center is falling upon hard times. To counter, a new twist has been added: the discount mall, where off-price and factory-outlet retailers band together to sell brand-name goods at 20 to 50 percent off department store prices.

Not all retailing is done in stores, however. There are four important forms of nonstore retailing: mail-order, door-to-door, telephone, and vending-machine sales.

Mail-order retailing is accomplished by description. Buyers usually do not see the product until it arrives at their homes in the mail. Mail-order retailing may involve catalog sales, direct-mail promotion, or advertising through the mass media. Catalog sales are conducted by general merchandise retailers like Sears, Ward's, Penney's, and Spiegel. In addition, many marketers of such products as apparel, health improvement techniques and equipment, books, and records conduct mail-order sales by placing advertisements in the mass media. This approach has both advantages and disadvantages. Operating costs are certainly lower than in normal store retailing, for the marketers can use low-rent locations. Consumers can browse through a catalog or evaluate an ad's offer during their leisure, making purchases without having to invest time and effort in leaving home to shop. And the variety of products that can be offered in catalogs is wide. However, it is often difficult to get a buyer's attention through catalogs and advertising, and many consumers are reluctant to make purchases without actually seeing the product. In addition, postal rates have become expensive, and the cost of producing elaborate catalogs can be very high. Even so, mail-order selling is a growing form of retailing in the United States. In 1980, it accounted for fully 10 percent of all general merchandise sold.

Door-to-door retailing includes all types of exchanges in which the transaction occurs in the consumer's home. Door-to-door sales may be conducted by producers (Avon, Sarah Coventry, World Book Encyclopedia) or by retailers (bakers, dairies, fruit and vegetable peddlers). They may call directly on consumers (see Figure 13-4) or use the "party plan" method, in which one customer sponsors a party for many friends and acquaintances, and a salesperson plans activities that revolve around viewing the product line. As guests purchase products, the salesperson asks them to sponsor future parties. In this way, the number of sales contacts increases, and an attractive and sympathetic surrounding is provided for the marketer.

In-home retailing is attractive to some consumers both because of the convenience of not having to leave home and because the salesperson can provide highly personalized service. From the marketer's standpoint, door-to-door retailing permits the most aggressive sales techniques, and it is especially useful for selling unsought goods like insurance and reference books and for showing products that retailers are reluctant to handle. The main disadvantage, however, is that contacts with customers are very expensive, since the salesperson's commissions usually are high in order to motivate aggressive selling. Then, too, consumers are often resistant to salespeople who invade their privacy; this attitude can reduce the chances of sales. And now, with

**Figure 13-4
Door-to-door selling is a familiar form of retailing.
(Lizabeth Corlett/Design Photographers International)**

so many women working, it is more difficult to find customers at home. Most people seem to prefer shopping in stores, and so door-to-door selling does not make up a large segment of retailing.

Telephone retailing involves the sale of goods and services over the telephone, and it is a growing form of retailing. Telephone orders are solicited by advertisements in newspapers and magazines and on radio and television, as well as through the telephone directory's yellow pages. The use of toll-free telephone numbers also has increased the number of consumers who shop by telephone. In addition, marketers may themselves initiate contact with prospective buyers by telephone. Through WATS (Wide Area Telephone Service) lines, a marketer located in any part of the country can inexpensively use the phone to solicit sales. As a result, long-distance solicitation is now used for magazine subscriptions and books, among other products, and its use is likely to increase.

Vending-machine retailing is a nonpersonal form of selling in which customers buy products directly from conveniently located machines. Products range from chewing gum to complete meals, though most sales involve cigarettes, candy, and beverages. In addition, machines have been designed to handle sales of air-flight insurance, T-shirts, music (in juke boxes), shoe shines, and even worms for fishing. And banks are also making increasing use of machines to transact business during nonworking hours.

Vending machines can expand a marketer's distribution into places that could not otherwise be utilized—restrooms, libraries, and hospitals, for instance. And they are open twenty-four hours a day. Still, vending-machine sales are not without problems, and they are expensive. Products often must be priced higher than they otherwise would be in order to compensate for operating costs. In addition, perishable goods must be replaced often, and machines are especially vulnerable to vandalism and burglary.

The Future of Retailing

In order to be effective, retailers (like all marketers) must keep abreast of the changes around them and must adapt to this dynamic environment. In the past few pages, we have looked at several recent developments and trends in retailing. But what is likely to happen in the future? One theory, called the *wheel of retailing,* seems to be borne out by developments in retailing.[6] This theory states that an innovation in retailing begins a cycle. At first, the innovation is viewed skeptically, but over time it takes hold in the market, usually because of low prices made possible by the innovation. For instance, around the turn of this century, department stores were an innovation that replaced smaller retail stores. The first department stores were simple and spartan in

---

[6]Malcolm P. McNair, "Significant Trends and Developments in the Postwar Period," in A. B. Smith (ed.), *Competitive Distribution in a Free, High-Level Economy and Its Implications for the University,* University of Pittsburgh Press, 1958, pp. 1–25. For a refinement of this theory, see Stanley C. Hollander, "The Wheel of Retailing," *Journal of Marketing,* vol. 26, no. 3 (July 1960), pp. 37–42.

Figure 13-5   With computers in more and more homes, "shopping by computer" may become a logical extension of "shopping by phone." (Courtesy Apple Computer, Inc.)

their operations, and they could offer low prices. But, according to the theory of the wheel of retailing, efficient innovative retailers become much larger over time, offering many more lines, better facilities, and other costly features. Then, as they become mature institutions, other retailers find an innovative way to lower costs and compete through low prices. This is what happened with department stores. The discounters came on the scene during the 1950s; they, too, changed their operations over time, growing bigger throughout the 1960s and 1970s; and now they are the target of some yet-unknown new method of retailing. Today's trends may already spell the end of their era.

For example, the day may soon be upon us when we shop by a combination of telephone, television, and computer (called *servo-selling,* or *robot retailing*). In this system, routine convenience goods can be viewed on home television screens through cable television. Shoppers can select desired products by telephone, and a computer will control inventory and directly charge the buyer's bank account for items ordered. While such a method of shopping may sound incredible, it lies just around the corner and is part of the checkless, cashless society that many foresee. This innovation, many experts believe, will be the next revolution in the wheel of retailing. (See Figure 13-5.)

Other retailing trends include an increase in various types of nonstore selling. Some forecast that by the year 2000, as much as one-third of all general merchandise will be sold outside of stores. And, as we have noted, mail-order sales and telephone retailing are also expected to grow. In addition, there is a trend toward two extremes in the size of retail stores. At one end are the large mass merchandisers (superstores), and at the other are the small retailers (boutiques and shops). Already there seem to be fewer and fewer medium-sized retailers. In line with this trend, there is a growing concentration of retail business; smaller retailers are increasingly being purchased by large retail corporations. At the same time, many small retailers are attempting to enjoy the benefits of large size by forming cooperatives and voluntary chain associations.

The times have not been particularly good for retailing. Profits have dwindled for years, and not all discounters, supermarkets, department stores, and variety stores have fared well. While some—like Penney's and K mart—have suffered less than others, the trend in retailing is toward improved management. In the future, we can expect to see better uses of computer technology, particularly as it applies to information systems, inventory control, and accounting. Marketing efforts also will be reassessed, and greater reliance on marketing research can be expected. The use of automated materials-handling systems is likely to increase as emphasis shifts toward greater efficiency and increased productivity.

Cost reduction will be the key to success, and reliance on self-service in all forms of retailing will likely expand. And, given the low growth rate expected for the 1980s, greater internationalization by the larger retailers is expected. On the domestic front, more aggressive marketing techniques will be used as retailers fight for market share by taking business away from rivals.

Wholesaling

Wholesaling intermediaries make exchanges for the purpose of resale or business use. Broadly speaking, any transaction from one producer or intermediary directly to another producer is a wholesaling exchange. Thus, if a retailer sells napkins to a restaurant or paper and pencils to another retailer, the sale constitutes a wholesaling transaction. In short, *wholesaling* includes all sales made to any person or organization other than ultimate consumers, those who use the product for personal, nonbusiness purposes.

In this section we will examine intermediaries who engage *primarily* in wholesaling, and the term *wholesaling intermediaries* will include both wholesalers and agents. *Wholesalers* are merchant intermediaries who take title to (own) products and perform the activities needed to move them through the distribution channel. *Agents* are wholesaling intermediaries who do *not* take title to products, but they do perform many of the activities of wholesalers. In addition, some firms set up sales branches to conduct their own wholesaling activities.

The Scope of Wholesaling

In 1977, there were 382,837 wholesaling establishments in the United States, compared with 369,792 in 1972. Of these, 80 percent were merchant wholesalers and 9 percent were agents; the remaining 11 percent comprised manufacturers' sales branches. These figures have remained flat since 1972. However, the wholesale trade volume nearly doubled over the five-year period from 1972 to 1977, from $695 billion to $1.26 trillion. Merchant wholesalers account for a little more than half the sales volume, while agents account for 10 percent. Moreover, the total sales of wholesalers were greater than those of retailers, who in 1977 did $725 billion of business.[7] This reflects the fact that wholesale figures include multiple transactions as products move through the distribution channel. In many cases, a product will be sold several times to more than one wholesaling intermediary as it passes through the channel. All these sales are reflected in the total figure.

Wholesalers Classified

As is the case with retailers, a wide range of wholesalers exists to take care of the various needs of producers and retailers. Here we will look at three broad categories of wholesaling intermediaries: merchant wholesalers, agents and brokers, and manufacturers' sales branches. See Table 13-2.

Merchant Wholesalers

These are the firms we usually refer to when we speak of wholesaling. They are also sometimes called *jobbers* or *distributors*. Merchant wholesalers are usually independently owned operations, and they take title to the products they distribute. Earlier in

---

[7]*Statistical Abstracts of the United States,* 1980.

TABLE 13-2   Wholesaling by Type of Establishment

Type of operation and kind of business	Establishments (in thousands)		Sales (in thousands)	
	1972	1977	1972	1977
Wholesale trade	369.8	382.8	695,224	1,258,400
Merchant wholesalers	290.0	307.3	353,919	676,058
Manufacturers' sales branches, offices	47.2	40.5	255,679	451,855
Merchandise agents, brokers	32.6	35.1	85,626	130,488
Kind of business				
Motor vehicles, automotive equipment	36.5	38.9	83,016	147,112
Furniture, home furnishings	9.5	11.1	12,359	22,032
Lumber, construction materials	15.9	15.7	28,095	46,179
Sporting, recreational, photographic goods	6.7	6.6	11,146	16,521
Metals and minerals, except petroleum	8.0	9.4	43,488	80,298
Electrical goods	21.2	24.9	49,349	69,999
Hardware, plumbing, heating equipment	17.4	18.6	18,600	30,605
Machinery, equipment, supplies	73.8	84.0	80,692	165,057
Paper, paper products	10.7	11.7	17,280	32,509
Drugs, drug proprietaries	4.0	3.6	12,666	19,445
Apparel, piece goods, notions	12.4	13.0	27,933	39,895
Groceries and related products	38.5	38.0	106,457	182,905
Farm-product raw materials	14.8	14.8	52,401	110,332
Chemicals, allied products	6.4	8.5	24,621	51,661
Petroleum, petroleum products	31.3	22.6	46,284	116,780
Beer, wines, distilled alcoholic beverages	7.0	6.7	19,885	26,979
Miscellaneous	55.7	54.9	60,952	100,090

Source: Statistical Abstracts of the United States, 1980.

the chapter, we noted some specific activities that intermediaries perform—buying, selling, transporting, and so on. These activities provide the basis for classifying merchant intermediaries into two groups: full-service wholesalers and limited-service wholesalers.

Full-service wholesalers provide almost all the services that a wholesaler can supply, and they also are divided into two types: general merchandise service wholesalers and limited-line wholesalers. *General merchandise full-service wholesalers* handle a broad line of nonperishable items, such as drugs, cosmetics, hardware, automotive accessories, and plumbing supplies. From this wide variety of products—both convenience and shopping products—they supply many kinds of retailers, such as drugstores, hardware stores, appliance stores, and even small department stores. In contrast, a *limited-line full-service wholesaler* carries only a few product lines but offers a full range of services. This kind of wholesaler might carry only one line of such products as electrical supplies, grocery products, or paint. Such wholesalers tend to service single-line or limited-line retailers.

TABLE 13-3 Comparative Profits for Retailers versus Wholesalers

Type of product(s) sold	Percent net profit	
	Retailers	Wholesalers
Men's and boys' clothing	4.1	2.9
Footwear	5.2	3.0
Furniture	4.4	3.0
Hardware	4.5	3.0
Electrical appliances, radio, and television	4.0	2.2
Paint, wallpaper, and supplies	5.5	3.3
Lumber and supplies	3.46	2.3

Source: "The Ratios," *Dun's Review,* October 1979, pp. 143–146.

In general, full-service wholesalers have done well over the last thirty years. Their percentage of the wholesale trade has actually increased in the face of stiff competition from agents. At the same time, there are pockets of industries that have lost dominance. Thus, aggregate share of market may not be an accurate measure of their true success. Also, net operating profit for wholesalers is generally low—quite a bit lower than for retailers. (See Table 13-3). Full-service wholesalers, because they do perform so many services, have high operating expenses (14 to 20 percent of sales). Limited-line wholesalers are an outgrowth of the need to reduce costs. (See Application 13-6.)

A number of wholesaler types offer less than a full range of services and are appropriately called *limited-service,* or *limited-function, wholesalers.* In general, these wholesalers do not play a major role in the distribution of products, yet they are important within some trades. There are five major types of limited-service wholesalers, and their titles depend on the services that they do or do not render.

Cash-and-carry wholesalers are a boon to small retailers who cannot afford the higher costs of a full-service wholesaler. These retailers simply pay cash and transport products themselves, procedures that lead to cost savings. Cash-and-carry wholesalers operate the same way as a retail store, but they deal only with retailers. By holding back on financing and transportation, cash-and-carry wholesalers have held their operating expenses to about 9 percent of sales. These limited-service wholesalers do not fit the needs of larger supermarkets and other mass retailers—but rather, have found a niche with small retailers.

Drop shippers are best known for the fact that they do not take physical possession of the products they distribute, even though they technically own the products that pass between the seller and the buyer. Drop shippers deal primarily with full rail carloads or truckloads of items such as coal, lumber, and chemical products; they would be expensive to unload and reload. The basic purpose of drop shippers is

Application 13-6
Wholesaling—Becoming More than Just Meat and Potatoes

Joseph R. Hyde III of Malone & Hyde, Inc., a Memphis-based food wholesaler, has taken a radical move to find growth for his company. Looking to the future, Malone & Hyde has diversified into retailing—drugstores, sporting goods, and auto parts outlets. Although Malone & Hyde's new businesses are retail, Hyde maintains that food wholesaling and retailing share common ground. "All deal with the management of inventories—how to move goods through a warehouse." As of 1981, Hyde's nonfood operations contribute 9 percent of net sales and 18 percent of operating profits.

Hyde may be seeking new markets because of the changing nature of food wholesaling, a maturing industry. Most family-owned supermarkets, which form the core of Malone & Hyde's 2500 customers, long ago linked themselves to one or more wholesalers, instead of individually buying directly from farmers and manufacturers. Total food shipments have become static as the population has stabilized. Food wholesalers have grown in dollar volume mainly through inflation or acquisition, or by driving out smaller competitors.

Malone & Hyde has greatly expanded its offered services. In the sixteen states that it serves, the company sells a full line of groceries, trading stamps, and services for grocers—including property, life, and health insurance, along with accounting.

The industry's rapid consolidation is expected to continue, but at some point, the chances for additional acquisitions and larger market shares will decline. Hyde expects his growth in food wholesaling to average about 10 percent per year. But achieving this will require outstanding marketing. Among the so-called voluntaries in the business—companies like Malone & Hyde that sell without requiring contracts—growth rates have followed inflated food prices, reaching 18.9 percent in 1974 but dropping to only 10.8 percent by 1978. Diversification is seen as the key to substantial future growth at Malone & Hyde.

Sources of data: "Malone & Hyde: A Food Jobber Seeks Growth in Nonfood Retailing," *Business Week,* Jan. 28, 1980, pp. 117–118; and "Auto Shack Gears to Basic Market of Do-It-Yourself," *The Memphis Commercial Appeal,* Sept. 29, 1981, p. 17c.

to know appropriate suppliers and match the needs of their buyers. They are facilitators of exchange. Since they have no inventory, operating expenses are very low—4 to 5 percent of sales.

Wagon, or *truck, wholesalers* sell products right from their vehicles. Such wholesalers deal most often with perishable items like tobacco, potato chips, and candy; they perform most of the functions of a full-service wholesaler. These intermediaries make deliveries at the same time they make sales calls. Thus, retailers can keep low inventories of these risky items. Since fuel costs and truck maintenance are high, so are the operating expenses of about 15 percent.

Mail-order wholesalers resemble mail-order retailers, sometimes selling to ultimate consumers as well as to retailers. Mail-order wholesaling is used to distribute sporting goods, jewelry, and hardware, especially to retailers in remote areas.

Finally, *rack-jobbers,* a rather new form of wholesaler, focus on selling nonfood items that are sold in food stores through displays—housewares, toys, health and beauty aids, and drugs. They are like truck wholesalers, but they offer the additional service of displaying the products on racks in the store. These wholesalers often take unsold goods back, thus reducing the risk taken by retailers. Rack-jobbers, because they service the displays, distribute to many stores emphasizing self-service. They build the displays, fill them, and even price the goods. These intermediaries have branched out from supermarkets to hardware stores, drugstores, and variety stores.

Agents and Brokers   These intermediaries never own the products they help to exchange; their primary activity is bringing buyers and sellers together and facilitating the sale. They usually perform only a small number of services—even fewer than limited-service merchant wholesalers do. Agents work on a commission basis, ranging from 2 to 6 percent of the selling price. They perform a particularly useful function for small producers who cannot afford the high costs of hiring, training, and paying their own sales force. Typically, an agent already has a wide base of customers in a given geographical area, and this cultivated market is then presented with the producer's product. Thus, an agent functions as a sales representative for various producers. Agents and brokers usually specialize according to types of customers, products, or product lines. There are five types of agents.

Manufacturers' agents are independent salespeople working for a number of manufacturers of related but noncompeting lines. The major benefit of this form of agent is the spreading of the cost of a sales contact over many products. Often, manufacturers' agents are used in sparse sales areas, while a firm's own sales force covers major sales territories. Many marketers use manufacturers' agents to develop a new territory, since the agent already has a ready set of sources. Since commissions are paid only after the sale, the operating costs of a sales force are bypassed. This saving is countered by the manufacturers' loss of control over the agent's selling efforts. For this reason, the importance of manufacturers' agents has declined over the past forty years.

Selling agents act as the entire marketing arm of a manufacturer, handling the entire output and often controlling the entire marketing plan for the firm. Such agents have authority to set prices and determine promotional expenditures. They even often help finance the manufacturer. These intermediaries are found in small, undercapitalized, production-oriented manufacturing firms—especially apparel, coal, lumber, and metal products companies.

Brokers' main job is to bring together buyers and sellers, particularly where there are large numbers of small ones. They maintain a good market information base and use it to bring parties together for exchange. Brokers generally represent sellers and have little authority in negotiating the agreement. Because their services are limited, their costs are very low. Brokers operate mostly in the food industry—but also in used machinery and real estate.

Commission merchants are found in the distribution of agricultural products. They take possession of the goods, though never own them. They operate when the producer ships goods and oversees the sorting process. They have much authority to make pricing decisions for the sellers they represent.

Finally, *auction companies* help bring buyers and sellers together in markets such as used cars, tobacco, art objects, fruit, and furs. Their job is to provide for the display of goods and for the inspection of merchandise.

**Manufacturers'
Sales Branches**

Some manufacturers have bypassed wholesalers altogether and have set up their own sales branches. In 1977, such branches represented 11 percent of the total wholesaling trade and accounted for 36 percent of wholesaling sales. This disparity reflects the fact that most sales branches are placed in the best territories. They resemble merchant wholesalers in that they deliver, offer credit, give promotional assistance, and provide other services. They carry an inventory and process orders from that inventory. These intermediaries usually work with petroleum products, chemicals, and commercial machinery and equipment.

Looking Back

We have now looked at various aspects of marketers' distribution activities. Distribution adds time and place utilities to a product, and it sets the stage for possession utility. In the next chapter, we will see how marketers choose a channel of distribution for their products. But first, review the following important points:

1   Place utility comes from reducing the geographical distance between producers and consumers; it sometimes can be increased by making products *less* easy to obtain.

2   While making products available at the right time is usually the key to increasing satisfaction, sometimes *not* having them readily available can increase satisfaction.

3   The distribution activity is not limited to physical goods but also must be undertaken to market services, people, organizations, and stores.

4   Intermediaries exist to solve three major problems: distance, exchange stimulation, and assortment. Sorting solves these distribution problems.

5   Intermediaries reduce the number of transactions by providing a communication line between producers and consumers.

6   With intermediaries the total inventory in the distribution system is actually reduced.

7   Intermediaries perform many specific activities in distributing products; even if no intermediaries existed, these activities would have to be performed— probably by the manufacturer.

8 Convenience stores are the fastest-growing type of food retailer.

9 Independent retailers have used cooperatives, voluntary chains, and franchises to compete against large corporate chains.

10 The contemporary trend in department store retailing is to reduce the product lines to include more high-margin goods.

11 Modern-day discounters do not perform marketing activities as the original discounters did shortly after World War II.

12 Some supermarkets are evolving into superstores.

13 Not all retailing is performed in a store.

14 The "wheel of retailing" is a theory that explains the development of retailing innovations.

15 The total volume of sales for wholesaling merchants is greater than that for all retailers.

16 While there are many different types of wholesalers, merchant wholesalers conduct most wholesaling exchanges.

17 Agents do not take title to the merchandise.

Key Terms

If you aren't sure what each of the following words means, look back at the text. Numbers refer to pages on which the words are defined. Additional information can be found by checking the index and the glossary at the end of the book.

sorting 406
independent retailer 415
chain store 415
cooperative chain 415
voluntary chain 416
franchise 416
superstore 419
shopping center 421
wheel of retailing 423

servo-selling 424
merchant wholesaler 425
drop shippers 427
rack-jobbers 429
agent 429
manufacturers' agent 429
selling agent 429
broker 429

Questions for Review

1 Briefly describe how *not* making products readily available can also increase consumer satisfaction.

2 Briefly define *sorting*.

3 Why is it more efficient to have intermediaries perform specialized distribution activities, rather than the manufacturer?

4 What are some important advantages that independent retailers have over chain-store operators?

5 Briefly define the term "limited-line retailer." Give three examples.

6 What is the major difference between wholesalers and agents as intermediaries?

Questions for Thought and Discussion

1 It was noted in the chapter that goods must be in the appropriate place so that exchange is stimulated. Getting the right goods in the wrong store can do much to detract from their appeal. Why is it, then, that we can see some of the same brand-name items in small specialty stores as we can see in K mart or similar chains?

2 After some 75 years of being identified as a retailer to small-town America, the J. C. Penney Company has begun to transform itself into a chain of moderate-price department stores with the emphasis on higher-price fashion. Draw upon the chapter material to discuss how Penney's might carry out this transformation.

3 There has been an acceleration of buying back franchises from individuals in the fast-food business. Companies find that they can make more money by operating the units themselves. Give some possible explanations for this phenomenon.

4 Since World War II, merchant wholesalers' share of sales to retailers has declined from 47 to about 35 percent. How do you account for this decrease?

Suggested Project

Find an area where there are street vendors located in retail shopping areas. Talk with some of the shopkeepers to get their views on whether street vending is good or bad for the more traditional retail trade.

Suggested Readings

Alderson, Wroe: *Dynamic Marketing Behavior,* Richard D. Irwin, Homewood, Ill., 1965. This classic scholarly book develops the underlying justification for distribution channels.

Bates, Albert D.: "The Troubled Future of Retailing," *Business Horizons,* vol. 19 (August 1976), pp. 22–28. This article provides some guidelines that will maximize the retailer's chances of survival in a rapidly changing environment.

Buskirk, Richard, and Bruce Buskirk: *Retailing,* McGraw-Hill, New York, 1979. This interestingly written, example-filled text comprehensively assesses the decision areas of retailing—from legal issues through store design and promotion to controlling the operation.

Cox, Reavis: *Distribution in a High-Level Economy,* Prentice-Hall, Englewood Cliffs, N.J., 1965. This comprehensive and very readable text reviews and synthesizes empirical work in distribution channels.

Hollander, Stanley C.: "The Wheel of Retailing," *Journal of Marketing,* vol. 24 (July 1960), pp. 37–42. This landmark article details a theory for the rise and fall of specific retailers within the retailing institution.

Hunt, Shelby D.: "Franchising: Promises, Problems, Prospects," *Journal of Retailing,* vol. 53, no. 3 (Fall 1977), pp. 71–84. The author gives a good summary of franchising along with an excellent bibliography.

McNair, Malcolm P., and Eleanor G. May: "The Next Revolution in the Retailing

Wheel," *Harvard Business Review,* vol. 56, no. 5 (September–October 1978), pp. 81–91. This article analyzes the enormous consequences of telecommunication systems on shopping.

Rosenberg, Larry J., and Elizabeth C. Hirschman: "Retailing Without Stores," *Harvard Business Review,* vol. 58, no. 4 (July–August 1980), pp. 103–112. The authors argue that in many areas of retailing, stores will become obsolete as telecommunications replace shopping outside the home.

Chapter 14

Determining and Managing the Marketing Channels

Looking Ahead

We have now examined the various intermediaries in a distribution system and how their services give a product time and place utilities—two important ingredients in providing satisfaction to consumers. Next we will look at how marketers select which intermediaries to use to provide the ultimate satisfaction: possession utility. This chapter explores the decisions that marketers must make in developing a distribution strategy, the tactical decisions needed to actually move products to consumers.

Key Topics

The different channels of distribution available and how marketers determine which ones to use

Factors that influence the choice of intermediary

Sources of conflict in a distribution channel and how cooperation is obtained

The nature of physical distribution and how it supports the distribution strategy

The activities and goals of physical distribution

Chapter Outline

The Nature of the Channel of Distribution
Channels for Consumer Products
Channels for Industrial Products
Multiple Distribution Channels

Criteria for Determining Distribution Strategy
Market Coverage
Control
Costs

Determining the Quantity and Quality of Intermediaries

Channel Management: Gaining Cooperation and Avoiding Conflict
The Nature of Channel Conflict
Reducing Conflict to Increase Cooperation
The Legal Environment of Distribution

The Nature of Physical Distribution
Forecasting Demand
Order Processing
Inventory Management
Storage
Materials Handling
Protective Packaging
Transportation
The Goals of Physical Distribution
The Total Cost Approach to Physical Distribution

Looking Back

In Chapter 13, we saw that various intermediaries are responsible for moving products from producers to consumers. In doing this, they give a product time and place utilities. Having goods and services in the right place at the right time lays the groundwork for possession utility, which ultimately provides satisfaction to consumers.

This chapter looks closely at the total channel of distribution. We will see how marketers determine which intermediaries to use in moving products to the market. Our focus will be on the goals and strategies of distribution management, including the sources of conflict among channel members and how cooperation is obtained. Finally, we will examine physical distribution—how products are actually moved through the various channels.

The Nature of the Channel of Distribution

The *channel of distribution* is the route taken by a product and its title as it moves from the producer to ultimate consumers. Products do not simply fall into the hands of those who want or need them. Marketers must take deliberate steps in order to provide the appropriate time and place utilities by moving products from the processor to intermediaries and finally to ultimate consumers. Thus, a product takes a definite route, or channel, on its way to consumers, and it makes stops at several points along the way.

As products move from producers to consumers, various exchange transactions occur. First, of course, the product is exchanged for some kind of *payment,* which usually takes the form of money. But that is not all that is exchanged. In most cases, the *right to use* the product also changes hands throughout the distribution channel. And title to the product, or legal ownership, gives each owner along the way complete rights to use the product in any manner desired. In addition, as we noted in Chapter 13, *information* is exchanged as products pass from owner to owner. Communication among the various people in the distribution channel lets manufacturers know the needs and wants of the market they serve, allowing them to match their product to consumers' needs. Throughout the distribution channels, then, exchanges occur in the form of payment, passage of title, and information. And since these exchanges are the key to providing satisfaction in the marketplace, marketers want to choose the path for products that results in the most advantageous exchanges along the way.

Suppose, for example, you wanted to drive from Hartford, Connecticut, to Cleveland, Ohio. There are a number of routes you could take. You might go down I-84 to New York State, then pick up I-80 to travel through the rolling Pennsylvania Dutch countryside, and finally take the Ohio Turnpike into Cleveland. Or, instead, you could follow I-91 up to the Massachusetts Turnpike, there connecting with the New York State Thruway, which would take you through upstate New York past Syracuse, Rochester, Buffalo, and Erie; then you could go down to the Ohio Turnpike and continue into Cleveland. But there are still other routes that would take you to your destination. If you preferred, you could travel through the Berkshire Mountains and then loop down to Cooperstown to visit the Baseball Hall of Fame and wander through the Finger Lake region of New York before going on into Cleveland. Obviously, many other routes could be mapped, depending on your taste for scenery and the time you could afford to spend in traveling. In short, your objectives would determine which route you would take. If you were in a hurry, the shortest, most traveled roads would be most attractive.

Similarly, in marketing there are a number of routes or networks of intermediaries through which products can travel on their way to final users. And depending on the marketers' objectives, different routes offer different advantages. We'll look now at the various distribution channels that can be used for consumer products and for industrial products.

Channels for Consumer Products

While there are a number of alternative distribution channels involving various combinations of producers, intermediaries, and consumers, five are of major importance. The most frequently used channels for distributing consumer products are shown on the left side of Figure 14-1.

A—Manufacturers (or Originators) to Consumers

Channel A in Figure 14-1 is the shortest, simplest, and often quickest way to distribute consumer products. It is an approach well known to consumers in the form of door-to-door retailing. Companies that use sales representatives to sell such products as life insurance, encyclopedias, magazines, household goods, and vacuum cleaners are using this distribution channel. The door-to-door sales of milk, newspapers, and (in the past) ice are other examples of this approach to distributing consumer products. Today's most famous example is probably the "Avon Representative," who seems to have replaced the "Fuller Brush Man" as a neighborhood fixture. But companies that sell products by mail are also using this channel, as are farmers who sell fruits and vegetables directly to consumers at roadside stands. This channel employs no intermediaries; it is a "direct" or "short" channel, since products move directly from the hands of producers or originators into the hands of consumers. As channels employ more intermediaries and make more intermediate stops, they are referred to as being more "indirect" and "longer." Thus, directness and shortness in a distribution channel are matters of degree.

B—Manufacturers (or Originators) to Retailers to Consumers

Channel B in Figure 14-1 is the most visible distribution channel for us as consumers. A large number of our purchases—automobiles, clothing, gasoline, and paint, for example—are made through this channel. In this case, the manufacturer usually has a sales force that contacts the retailers, displays the products, and takes purchase orders. The retailers then sell to ultimate consumers. Certain originators may also sell to retailers in this channel. For example, fisheries bring their catch to the retail fish market, where consumers can then make their purchases. Additionally, many manufacturers also establish retail outlets at factories to sell directly to consumers. Sara Lee, the Chicago baked-goods company, does this. Finally, some manufacturers own

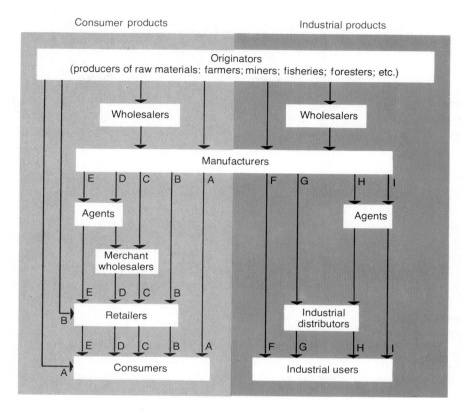

Figure 14-1 Typical channels of distribution for consumer products and industrial products.

retail stores throughout the country, which is the method Sherwin-Williams uses to distribute its paints.

C—Manufacturers to Merchant Wholesalers to Retailers to Consumers

Channel C in Figure 14-1 is most often used by small manufacturers and small retailers to distribute such products as drugs, lumber, hardware, and many food items. Products that have a large market need such a channel, since manufacturers often do not have a large enough sales force to reach the mass market effectively themselves. Thus, the wholesalers with their network of retail contacts and the retailers with their customers make up a large web of contacts that otherwise would be beyond the reach of most manufacturers.

D—Manufacturers to Agents to Merchant Wholesalers to Retailers to Consumers

Channel D in Figure 14-1 is the longest and most indirect of the frequently used distribution channels. This channel presents the benefits of a large network of contacts. In Chapter 13 we saw that most wholesalers perform a greater number of services for retailers than agent intermediaries do. Even so, agents can be especially useful for making contacts and bringing buyers and sellers together. For this reason, some manufacturers prefer to use agents. They are especially common in the food industry, where they are called *food brokers*. Ocean Spray, the marketer of cranberry products and juices, for instance, uses 75 food brokers selling to its retail stores, another 20 who sell to food-service buyers, and still another 25 who handle both outlets. Recently, it also added H. J. Heinz's 150-plus food-service sales force who call on other wholesalers and provide access to the restaurant market.

E—Manufacturers to Agents to Retailers to Consumers

Channel E in Figure 14-1 shows that some manufacturers bypass wholesalers entirely when getting their products into the hands of retailers. For example, food-processing companies often do business with large grocery chains that perform their own wholesaling functions, and so wholesalers are not needed. Sporting goods producers and paper manufacturers move their products to appropriate retailers by using a system of manufacturers' representatives.

Channels for Industrial Products

We noted in Chapter 8 that industrial products have some distinctly different characteristics from consumer products, and that their market is different as well. It follows that the distribution channels used for industrial products will also be different. The right side of Figure 14-1 shows the four major channels that industrial marketers utilize to move products to consumers.

F—Manufacturers to Industrial Users

We learned in Chapter 8 that industrial markets are usually concentrated in certain geographic areas. Thus, the distance between customer contacts is less than it is with a mass consumer market. In addition, many industrial products require the personal attention of the manufacturer in order to match the buyers' needs. Channel F in Figure 14-1 is the most frequently used industrial channel. It is the short, direct channel which links industrial users to producers through the use of producers' sales representatives. This channel is used by many metal manufacturers (U.S. Steel), conveyor-belt producers (Rapid Standard), and makers of construction equipment (John Deere). IBM has built its reputation in main frame computers by selling direct to industrial buyers.

G—Manufactuers to Industrial Distributors to Industrial Users

Industrial distributors are the counterparts of wholesalers. They take title to products and perform the same functions that wholesalers do for consumer products. As shown by channel G in Figure 14-1, industrial distributors act as the sales arm for many smaller manufacturers that serve industrial markets.

H—Manufacturers to Agents to Industrial Distributors to Industrial Users

Channel H in Figure 14-1 represents the fact that industrial manufacturers sometimes need the storage facilities provided by industrial distributors. In this channel the agent facilitates the sale of products, and the industrial distributor stores them until they are needed by users. The distributor thus provides quick service to meet the users' needs.

I—Manufacturers to Agents to Industrial Users

In channel I of Figure 14-1, industrial distributors are bypassed because their services are not needed. This kind of channel is used to distribute many forms of agricultural products.

While the channels illustrated in Figure 14-1 are the ones most often used to distribute industrial and consumer products, other combinations may also be employed. Wholesalers, for instance, are sometimes used to facilitate transactions between originators and manufacturers, and more than one wholesaler may be used in any channel. In addition, retailers of consumer products may sell to a manufacturer; for instance, a variety store may sell stationery or other office supplies to a manufacturing concern. Our point is that marketers have many options in moving products to final users. While the channels described above are the ones that are used most often, they are by no means the only choices available to marketers.

Multiple Distribution Channels

Not all marketers confine their distribution system to a single channel. Some marketers use two or even several channels of distribution. In fact, those who are employing a divergent marketing strategy are usually forced to use multiple channels. For instance, companies that sell both consumer products and industrial products would have to use more than one channel in order to serve the separate markets. Paint manufacturers thus may use their own retail outlets and franchised dealers to sell to consumers, and at the same time they may also sell products directly to painting contractors. Oil companies often use three channels to serve (1) ultimate consumers, through gasoline stations and discount stores; (2) garage mechanics, through automotive parts distributors; and (3) automobile manufacturers, through direct sales representation. And computer manufacturers now need more than one channel, as computers are sold to the growing market of household and commercial users as well as to industrial users.

Marketers may also choose to serve a single market through several different distribution channels. For example, STP Corporation sells oil and gasoline additives both in service stations and in supermarkets, while General Electric distributes many of its small electrical appliances through discount outlets as well as through catalog retailers. In this way, the marketers reach consumers whose needs are similar but whose buying patterns are different.

While technically not illegal, marketers using multiple outlets have come under fire because of possible antitrust violations. B. F. Goodrich Co., for instance, has recently faced legal suits in California, Colorado, and other western states for selling tires through both franchised dealers and its own stores. The plaintiffs claim that the rubber company used its double role to fix the price of its products and divide up markets between company-owned and independent stores.

Then, too, the marketers of similar products may want to distinguish their offerings by using a different channel. This is done especially when there are quality differences between the products. Winnebago Industries reacted to the energy crisis by producing two models of mobile homes—one priced lower than the other—and, as we noted in Chapter 10, distributing them through separate channels.

Criteria for Determining Distribution Strategy

Given all the channels of distribution available to marketers, how do they determine which channel or channels to use? This is not a matter to be taken lightly; distribution decisions must be made in terms of a company's overall marketing objectives and strategies. Most are made by the producers of products, who are guided by three overall criteria: market coverage, control, and costs.

Market Coverage

A key consideration in selecting a distribution channel is the *size of the potential market that needs to be served*. We saw in Chapter 13 that intermediaries decrease the number of transactions that are necessary in order to contact a market of a given size. But consider the repercussions of this fact. While a producer could make four direct contacts with ultimate consumers, if that same producer instead contacts four retailers who, in turn, make four contacts each with ultimate consumers, the total number of market contacts has increased to sixteen. It is in this fashion that the use of intermediaries increases the market coverage. And if that producer instead contacts four wholesalers who each contact four retailers, and they, in turn, each contact four ultimate consumers, the total number of market contacts increases to sixty-four. Figure 14-2 illustrates this point: The longer the distribution channel (that is, the more intermediaries used), the greater the market coverage.

Market coverage is an important dimension for many marketers. For instance, almost one-half the population over 15 years of age are potential buyers of Trac II razors. This is a lot of people, and it takes a long channel of distribution to ensure that the appropriate number of contacts are made. At the other extreme, only a few people are potential buyers of Mack trucks, and so the market coverage need not be so substantial. The market for heavy trucks is only about 300,000 customers, and 3000 of these buy 90 percent of all the big rigs used. It should be clear, then, that a major consideration in the choice of a distribution channel is the desired level of market

Figure 14-2   Length of distribution channel and market coverage attained.

coverage, which, of course, depends on the nature and size of the market to be served.

The business-machine industry provides a good example of the importance of market coverage. Stimulated by falling prices and the cost-cutting and space-saving benefits of microchip-based copiers, word processors, typewriters, and calculators, the market broadened to include 10 million smaller businesses—4 million small businesses with fewer than twenty employees plus 6 million other businesses operating out of the home. The broader market potential increased the need for market coverage. To cover this market, companies had to forgo distribution direct to buyers which could be too costly; instead, they created retail stores as a new distribution channel. Xerox Corp. had opened twenty-six stores by the end of 1981 and planned hundreds more by the mid-1980s. Direct selling continued as the distribution channel for the Fortune 1000 companies, which can place orders for hundreds of units.

Control

Another important criterion that marketers use in determining which distribution channel to select is *control* over the product. A short distribution channel gives the greatest control to producers. Each time the title passes from the hands of the producer, control is lost, since buyers can do just about anything they want with the product. They own it. They can let it sit in their warehouse, display it poorly on their shelves, or market it in any way, however unacceptable.

Some products have an image of high quality, and if they were to appear in discount stores and low-quality department stores, their ability to stimulate exchange would diminish. Thus, the marketers of exclusive designers' apparel or limited-edition art objects use shorter distribution channels, selling directly to the retail outlets in which they want their products displayed. Additionally, many products need aggressive selling activity and servicing by retailers in order for exchange to occur. Marketers want to use only those intermediaries who can and will provide the services needed to sell the product. They will carefully choose a shorter, more direct distribution channel.

When the home computer market began emerging, manufacturers who rushed to distribute to this market found no existing outlets. The initial retail outlets were the 7000-plus Radio Shack stores across the country. Computer manufacturers learned quickly that the technical ability needed to sell computers was often beyond the capabilities of the clerks who were accustomed to selling stereos and less complex electronic equipment. Customers were not getting the proper service. To resolve this distribution problem, computer companies opened their own stores while Radio Shack developed a set of 150 specialized computer centers.

Costs

Finally, in selecting a distribution channel, marketers also must consider *costs*. Many consumers believe that the shorter the channel, the lower the cost of distribution (and the lower the price to them). This probably arises from advertising that says, "Avoid the middleman—buy directly from the factory and save!" We have seen, however, that intermediaries are specialists and that they usually can perform the distribution

Application 14-1
Channel of Distribution Strategy—Testing the Waters

During the 1970s, IBM was faulted for concentrating on the traditional mainframe computer business and ignoring an attractive minicomputer and personal computer business. IBM's market share in 1970 was about 60 percent. By 1980, its share had fallen to about 32 percent. IBM no longer is putting all its eggs in one basket, but is targeting virtually every new growth area of the computer business. Its stated goal is to exceed its traditional 13.3 percent growth rate. To assist in meeting this objective, IBM is exploring distribution alternatives.

Because computer hardware costs have plummeted, it is virtually impossible to continue the industry practice of selling computers exclusively by direct sales. Profit margins demand low-cost avenues of distribution.

"When you are selling very high-volume, standard products, you don't need as much of a customized marketing operation," IBM's president says. "We now ship a lot of things to customers that they unpack and install themselves. That's a far cry from a few years ago, when the computer arrived in a padded van with a bunch of fellows to carry it to the third floor."

functions more efficiently than producers can. Thus, the costs of distribution to the producer are usually *lower* when intermediaries are used in the distribution channel. In addition, a short, direct channel usually requires a substantial investment on the part of the manufacturer, who must maintain a sizable sales force and clerical help in order to process orders and service customers.

Creative thinking can sometimes work to circumvent the high cost of personal contact. Oshkosh B'Gosh, the marketer of unstylish work clothing, opened up a needed distribution system to children's clothing stores by using the untraditional method of sending out direct mail solicitations to hundreds of potential buyers. Response was so great that the company has been unable to fill all the orders—its children's bib overalls now outsell all its adult clothing.

From this brief discussion it should be clear that a shorter distribution channel generally results in limited market coverage, greater control over the products, and higher costs for the manufacturer. Conversely, a longer channel leads to greater market coverage, less control over the product, and reduced costs for the producer. Marketers must decide which of these alternatives is more appropriate for meeting their own objectives as well as consumers' needs. Different products, markets, and manufacturers, of course, require different distribution arrangements. In deciding what kind of channel to use, marketers at the manufacturer's stage must consider such factors as the market's size and location, whether the product is intended for industrial use or consumers, the quantity of products exchanged, the perishability and service requirements of the product, the marketer's financial position and management abilities, and the types of intermediaries available. Only then does the real task of distributing products get under way. (See Application 14-1.)

	Texas Instruments	Tandy	Digital Equipment	Ohio Scientific	Wang	Hewlett-Packard	Apple	Xerox	IBM	Control Data	Data General
Systems houses	▪	▪	▪	▪	▪	▪	▪				
Manufacturers' sales forces		▪	▪		▪	▪	▪	▪	▪		
Manufacturers' retail stores		▪	▪					▪	▪	▪	
Manufacturers' business computer centers		▪					▪		▪		
Authorized dealers or distributors (wholesalers)			▪	▪		▪	▪	▪			
Office equipment and supply stores		▪		▪		▪	▪				▪
Independent computer stores				▪		▪	▪				▪
Franchised computer stores		▪					▪				
Department stores				▪							
Mail order				▪				▪*	▪*	*Noncomputer office equipment	

(Business Week, *Oct. 27, 1980, pp. 165–168*)

Unlike the small manufacturers such as Apple and Tandy, however, which can afford to gamble on only one or two alternative channels to traditional computer distribution, IBM is testing almost every conceivable sales channel. In addition to retail stores, IBM has opened Business Computer Centers to attract small business owners. The pitch is given at seminars and at hands-on demonstrations to selected groups of potential customers. IBM is also using such mass-merchandising techniques as toll-free 800 numbers and mass mailings. (Some alternative channels being explored by computer manufacturers are shown here.)

Source of data: "No. 1's Awesome Strategy," *Business Week,* June 8, 1981, pp. 84–90.

Determining the Quantity and Quality of Intermediaries

Once the appropriate channel(s) of distribution have been determined, the marketer must settle on the actual number of intermediaries to employ; this is referred to as the *intensity of distribution.* There are three alternatives: intensive, selective, and exclusive distribution.

With *intensive* distribution, wide market coverage is achieved. In the extreme, intensive distribution means that *every* available outlet where consumers might possibly look for the product carries the item. Intensive distribution is necessary for most convenience goods—bread, newspapers, and candy. While intensive distribution is highly desirable for some manufacturers, retailers don't find it always so desirable—it means outlets competing with one another for the same customer. Thus retailers shun intensively distributed goods, thereby limiting the degree of intensiveness.

Hanes Corporation recognized the importance of intensive distribution for its L'eggs brand of panty hose. In the early 1970s, it changed its distribution of panty hose from a limited number of shopping stores—department and apparel shops—to an intensive distribution system of drugstores, supermarkets, and other convenience outlets. The result was industry leadership. Hanes has capitalized on its success by piggybacking panty-hose distribution with the L'erin line of cosmetics and a line of children's books.

Selective distribution reflects the use of a limited set of outlets in a given territory rather than a very large number. Selective distribution is generally used with shopping and specialty goods—products with extreme brand awareness and loyalty. Here, the manufacturer actually may decline to sell to some distributors, preferring to rely on a smaller, more dedicated set of intermediaries. But this selective policy puts greater burden on the intermediaries to move goods. And often manufacturers put constraints on the "chosen" distributors to ensure aggressive selling. Retailers may be expected to advertise locally and maintain well-stocked displays.

Exclusive distribution limits the intermediaries to one per given territory. Here, producers obtain maximum control in a given market. Retailers are often directed with respect to advertising, pricing, and sales promotion policies. Often, too, they are expected not to carry competing lines. (This prohibition is risky, though. While not illegal per se, it can be interpreted as reducing competition and ruled in violation of the Clayton Antitrust Act of 1914.) From the intermediary's standpoint, exclusive distribution ensures all the sales in that territory and protects against price slashes by competitors (since there aren't any). This latter feature is of particular concern as retailers fight for their profitability.

After the number of intermediaries to be used has been determined, marketers must select the specific intermediaries that they will employ. In this decision they are guided by some specific criteria. The most important criterion is that an intermediary must be serving the market to which the manufacturer wants to have access. (See Application 14-2.) Some of the other considerations are indicated by the following set of questions:

1 Is the intermediary *located close* to the desired market?

2 Can the distributor provide the *needed services* to the buyer?

3 Does the intermediary have the *talents* and *skills* to advertise effectively locally and to arrange promotional displays?

4 Are the *product lines* presently carried by a distributor *complementary* to the new line that would be carried?

5 What *competitive product lines* are carried?

6 Does the intermediary have *sufficient financial stability?*

7 Does the intermediary have the necessary *managerial talent* to be successful in carrying the line?

Application 14-2
Serving the Market the Manufacturer Wants Access to— Weaving and Bobbing!

Adjusting to changing markets is one of the hardest jobs for a small business. Small-computer retail businesses are seeing their market change, and are having difficulty adapting. The first computer stores opened in the mid-1970s and generally regarded hobbyists and home users as their market. Consequently, a majority of them stocked computer kits and later such components as chips and computer boards.

In 1980, the small-business market opened up. Composing that market are businesses and professionals—such as doctors, lawyers, and the like. The change will bring problems to computer stores that don't respond with proper management and staffing, and that don't identify their market and provide satisfactory service. For many store owners, adjustment will be very difficult because they lack experience in running a business.

The early entrepreneurs were primarily interested in computers and often knew very little about financing, cash flow, inventory, or sales. Now computer stores must select their markets. Those who try to service everyone will face problems. In the same store, you find hobbyists playing computer games, business people looking for accounting software, and others trying to discuss hardware. "These are going to become separate markets. It's going to be necessary for stores to find a suitable market niche and then develop that particular area," said an industry consultant.

In many cases, it also calls for a different kind of salesperson, because business people are usually uncomfortable with technical language. "We try to get someone whom the businessman can talk to almost as a consultant," says a spokesperson of the Computer Store chain. "The salesman can suggest solutions to the problems without traumatizing the businessman with technical jargon."

Service will be increasingly important, says William D. Barton, president of Datel Systems Corp. of New York. "A lot of my business is repeat, and you earn it through service and support," he reports. "We are now in a world of professional use. The retail store has to grow up and be able to afford the type of service that businessmen get from other vendors."

Giving away service can create problems for stores, however. "We discount as long as the customer knows what he is getting at that price," says Edward J. Ramos, president of Super Business Machines in New York. "If he buys at discount he gets no support." Many computer retailers, Ramos says, "lost their shirts by discounting and then giving free service."

Source of data: "Computer Stores Must Adapt to Changing Customer Needs," *The Wall Street Journal,* July 6, 1981, p. 15.

Sometimes, even though intermediaries exist who meet a manufacturer's criteria, they are not always available. For instance, Philip Morris in 1978 acquired The Seven-Up Company. Known for its aggressive marketing, Philip Morris is entering the cola business, which accounts for two-thirds of soft-drink sales. Of 7Up's 464 bottlers, 149 are primarily Pepsi bottlers and 87 are Coke bottlers. Thus, it is highly unlikely that these bottlers will sacrifice their valuable franchises to take on an unproven cola from The Seven-Up Company. However, Seven-Up thinks it can overcome this hurdle, and it is now talking with Miller Beer distributors (another Philip Morris property) who could handle distribution chores. "Quite frankly, they're going to be reluctant to give up their Coke or Pepsi line in favor of a new 7Up cola," the president of 7Up's largest franchised bottlers told *Fortune.*[1] Another way around this problem, early watchers speculated, may be for 7Up to distribute directly to stores from a central warehouse, bypassing bottlers altogether.

Channel Management: Gaining Cooperation and Avoiding Conflict

Once the marketers have chosen the channel and have selected the intermediaries to distribute their product, the next step is to make certain that the product moves smoothly through the entire channel. This job is called *channel management.*

We noted earlier that a system is a set of related elements that have a common purpose. A distribution channel surely meets this definition, for each channel member—producer, intermediary, consumer—is one element in the overall system. They are linked together through their exchanges of products, payments, use rights, and information, and their common purpose is to satisfy consumers by providing time and place utilities for the product. To meet this goal, the distribution channel must be viewed as a *total system* that provides time and place utility. It is to the advantage of each channel member to work with the others toward this utlimate goal. A smooth-flowing, cooperative channel of distribution can provide a real competitive advantage to marketers.

In reality, however, instead of operating as a total system of distribution, most channel members operate somewhat independently. Each has individual objectives—profits, sales volume, the development of a particular image, and so forth—and the objectives of one channel member may not be consistent with those of another. Furthermore, each channel member may deal with many other members. A manufacturer sells to many different wholesalers or retailers, just as wholesalers buy

---

[1]"Philip Morris Undiversifies," *Fortune,* June 29, 1981, p. 64.

from various manufacturers and sell to many different retailers. Under these circumstances, it's difficult, sometimes impossible, for each individual channel member to satisfy all the suppliers and customers involved. In serving the diverse needs of retailers, for instance, a food wholesaler may well carry the canned peas of Del Monte, Green Giant, and Stokely Van Camps. Retailers want to carry a variety of brands. But the manufacturers, of course, would much rather have only their own brand carried by the wholesaler. As a result, the wholesaler cannot perfectly satisfy the interests of the retailers and the manufacturers, whose channel of distribution thus breaks down. In short, there is often conflict rather than cooperation among channel members, and marketers must anticipate and understand the sources of conflict.

The Nature of Channel Conflict

The goal of channel management is to reduce conflicts among members to a minimum and to induce as much cooperation as possible. There are two main types of conflict in a distribution channel: vertical conflict and horizontal conflict.

Vertical Conflict

Vertical conflict arises frequently. It occurs between channel members who are at different levels—between producer and wholesaler or retailer, for instance, or between wholesaler and retailer. Each member, as we noted, is expected to perform certain functions for the other members. For example, a manufacturer expects a wholesaler to display products aggressively to retailers. When this is not done, conflict is likely to arise. Table 14-1 summarizes the main expectations that each channel member has for the other two types of members. When expectations are not met, conflict is the probable result.

Let's look at a real case of vertical conflict in the soft-drink industry and how it was resolved. It's no secret that the key to Coca-Cola's hold on the soft-drink market lies with the 550 bottlers that produce, warehouse, distribute, and market the product. The interests of the independent bottler and those of Coke are not always aligned. Coca-Cola thrives on selling syrup. But sales volume is not always the bottler's top priority. A bottler can increase short-term profits by cutting back on capital improvements like new equipment and by raising prices.

For a long time, the bottler had a big advantage over the Coca-Cola Company: a fixed price for syrup—the basic price was fixed by contract at $1.125 per gallon. In 1978, as Coke faced rising costs of labor, transportation, and ingredients, it proposed amending its contract to tie syrup prices to sugar prices and to the consumer price index.

The bottlers were not anxious to renegotiate, so Coke had to sweeten its offer. The company offered to allot at least 8 cents a gallon to advertising and marketing programs, twice the level of the mid-1970s. Coke also agreed that if sugar were ever replaced as the sweetener, the bottlers would reap the savings. And in 1980, Coke authorized bottlers to use high-fructose corn sweetener to replace up to one-half the sugar in the beverage—saving bottlers about 6 cents a gallon. The result of this give-and-take was that more than 80 percent of the bottlers had signed the new agreement by 1981.

TABLE 14-1   Potential Sources of Channel Conflict

Manufacturer expects:

Wholesaler
To be familiar with manufacturer's products
Not to carry competitors' brands
To pass along customer ideas and
    complaints
To sell at low margins
To pass along discounts
To pay on time
To actively push manufacturer's products
To allow credit for retailers
To service many retailers
To meet shipping schedules
To keep adequate inventories

Retailer
To be familiar with manufacturer's products
To honor warranties
To provide adequate display space
To pass along customer ideas and complaints
Not to develop private brands
To offer such services as delivery and
    installation
To maintain low prices
To pass along discounts
To run advertisements on manufacturer's
    products
To keep a quality image
To service many customers
To keep adequate stock
To maintain convenient hours
To open branch stores, deliver, etc.

Wholesaler expects:

Manufacturer
To produce quality products
To provide packaging
To provide a wide, deep line
Not to sell to retailers
To sell at low prices and give price
    concessions
To provide monies for extensive consumer
    advertising
To offer liberal credit terms
To give exclusive distribution rights

Retailer
To accept wholesaler's assortment
To provide adequate display space
To maintain low prices
To pass along discounts
To pay promptly
To promote wholesaler's lines
To order on a regular basis
To place orders in bulk quantities

Retailer expects:

Manufacturer
To produce quality products
To produce a wide, deep line
To introduce new products
To honor manufacturer's warranties
To provide attractive packaging
To suggest retail prices which permit large
    margins
To provide in-store displays and give
    advice, etc.
To provide monies for extensive customer
    advertising
To supply adequate amounts of popular
    items
To deliver shipments on time

Wholesaler
To provide a wide assortment
To know product line
To provide low prices and allow price
    concessions
To have helpful, personable salespersons
To provide cooperative advertising
To allow liberal credit
To provide fast delivery in small quantities
To offer a liberal returns policy

Adapted from Ben M. Enis, *Marketing Principles: The Management Process,* 3d ed., Goodyear Publishing, Santa Monica, Calif., 1980, pp. 484–485.

Horizontal Conflict   Horizontal conflict occurs between channel members who are at the same level—between two or more wholesalers, say, or between two or more retailers. Such conflict can be found between intermediaries of the same type (such as two competing supermarkets), or it can occur between different types of intermediaries (such as a department store and a discount store). Generally, the second type of horizontal conflict is more common. So many retailers have turned to scrambled merchandising and have added product lines which formerly were carried by other types of retailers that there is intense competition among many more stores for the same customers. For instance, drugstores must now compete with discount stores, supermarkets, small grocery stores, and even department stores. Similarly, specialty paint stores now have to compete for buyers with lumberyards, hardware stores, discount stores, and department stores. Sherwin-Williams, as an example, recently opened 1500 home-decorating centers that sell wallpaper and floor coverings as well as paint. These stores compete with Sears, Roebuck & Co., which sells most of its paint at a discount to draw customers, and with hardware stores that are themselves Sherwin-Williams customers. (See Application 14-3.)

Application 14-3
Horizontal Conflict—
Assault on the Battery

Gould, Inc., one of the country's largest replacement battery companies, has long manufactured batteries under private labels.

Now, the company is shifting its distribution strategy and is attempting to sell batteries directly to the consumer. In doing so, Gould is offering competition to some of its biggest customers—J. C. Penney, K mart, and Montgomery Ward, all of which sell Gould batteries under their own labels.

Gould is testing in the Chicago area a direct sales approach to motorists. It has equipped twenty-four vans with battery inventories, and the vans are answering emergency calls in seven counties with a toll-free number. The van driver will either sell a stranded motorist a battery, or charge a fee of $15 simply to jump-start the stranded vehicle.

Gould is spending $7000 monthly to lease vans in the Chicago area. Even more is being spent to promote the service through ads run in the Chicago newspaper, as well as in radio and TV spots.

The company is taking a major risk with its new distribution strategy. Gould manufactured about 6.5 million batteries last year on a private label basis for several mass merchandisers. By competing directly with those private labels in the retail market, Gould will "certainly be putting its position with those customers in jeopardy," says Martin A. McDevitt, Jr., a vice president with Robert W. Baird & Co., a Milwaukee investment banking firm.

Source of data: "Gould Gets a Jump on Roadside Battery Service," *Business Week,* June 15, 1981, p. 132.

Reducing Conflict to Increase Cooperation

With all these potential conflicts within a distribution channel, how do some of the bumps get smoothed out? How is conflict avoided and cooperation encouraged? Two major approaches exist. One way is through exercising power in the channel, and the other way is through the development of vertical marketing systems. Let's see what is involved.

The Channel Captain

In many distribution channels, one member tends to exert the greatest influence over other channel members. This member is called the *channel captain*. Throughout our discussion of channel determination, we took the point of view that the channel is determined by the producer of the product. But this is not a complete picture. It's true, generally, that such manufacturers as Procter & Gamble, Gillette, General Electric, and General Motors are the dominant forces in the distribution of their products. They select the channel to use, its length, and its channel members. But in other instances, retailers are the strongest force in the channel. Thus, Sears, Penney's, and Federated Department Stores can pretty much dictate the design, price, and terms of sale from most manufacturers. Occasionally, even wholesalers may dominate the channel.

Such power accrues to the channel captain because that member possesses some competitive advantage—perhaps a brand name that ensures market demand or, more often, financial clout that can humble other channel members. In short, the channel captain is in a position to enforce cooperation by a show of power. This may not actually reduce the conflict that exists, but it does suppress it, since the conflicting goals of less powerful channel members are not achieved. And from the channel captain's standpoint, at least, the channel is once again running smoothly.

Coca-Cola again provides us with an example of channel captaincy power. During the ten years from 1965 to 1975, Dr Pepper propelled its cherry-flavored beverage out of small towns in the South and Midwest into major markets across the country. Again the key to success in the soft-drink industry lies in the distribution network of bottlers that buy syrup from the soft-drink company and then bottle and distribute it to the markets they serve. In 1975, Dr Pepper set out to secure the largest bottler in each of the markets it served, thus growing to the fifth-largest soft drink, with a 5 percent share of the market. (In 1975, Coca-Cola had 35 percent of the market; Pepsi Cola had 21 percent; 7Up controlled 7 percent; and Royal Crown had 6 percent.) To accomplish this sales gain, however, Dr Pepper had signed up 25 percent of Coca-Cola's then 739 franchisees. The selling of Dr Pepper by Coke bottlers, of course, was in direct conflict with the goals of Coca-Cola, which markets its own cherry-flavored drink, Mr. PiBB. Even Coca-Cola's hometown franchisee in Atlanta was one of the runaway bottlers that distributed Dr Pepper, an acute embarrassment for Coke. But Coca-Cola resolved this conflict by quietly pressuring many of the wayward bottlers to return to the fold. Coca-Cola, with its dominant market share, can be very persuasive in getting bottlers to live up to its expectations.

Vertical Marketing Systems

The second approach to resolving conflict in a distribution channel is to integrate the channel members. Thus, if the conflict arises because of different objectives among members, the channel—or the parts of it that are in conflict—is simply restructured into a new organization. And since the new organization has its own objectives to meet, the conflict seemingly disappears. We will now look at three types of vertical marketing systems that accomplish such integration: corporate, administered, and contractual marketing systems.

Under a *corporate vertical marketing system,* integration is achieved through single ownership of the production and the distribution operations of the channel. For instance, the producer may purchase the retail outlets, thus not only manufacturing the product but also controlling its retailing through ownership. Firestone is an example of such a manufacturer, since the corporation owns a substantial number of retail outlets that distribute its tires. In a similar arrangement, some retailers also own their own production facilities. Among others, Revco D. S., Inc., the nation's largest discount drugstore chain, has become a producer of drugs and related items.

In these relationships, the objectives of the channel member that is purchased become secondary to the goals of the corporate owner. Ideally, this should eliminate conflict and encourage cooperation throughout the distribution channel.

Under an *administered vertical marketing system,* cooperation is ensured primarily through the economic power of one channel member. Here, one channel member provides some means by which the other channel member can become more successful. The difference between an administered system and a channel with a captain is that the administered system *formally* establishes the power of one channel member. This dominant member then exerts power throughout the channel by developing overall marketing plans to promote and distribute the product. The plan itself formally identifies the power relationship that will exist. Coors beer, Samsonite luggage, and the products of Magnavox Corporation are distributed through administered systems. The reason why such systems are needed is that even powerful organizations cannot afford to own all the retail outlets required to distribute most products. Nor is ownership necessary, if the administered plans are sound and can be carried out effectively.

Under a *contractual vertical marketing system,* a number of independent organizations are banded together by contracts to form a unified distribution system. This kind of vertical marketing system is the fastest-growing. Such contractual arrangements include wholesaler-sponsored voluntary chains, retailer-owned cooperatives, and franchise systems. In Chapter 13, we described these distribution arrangements and noted their advantages in terms of economies of scale. Additionally, they lead to greater coordination throughout the distribution channel. (See Application 14-4.)

The Legal Environment of Distribution

Companies that attempt to control the distribution of their products face the possibility of violating the Sherman Antitrust Act, the Clayton Antitrust Act, or the Federal Trade Commission Act. Four methods of control are frequently employed—usually by manufacturers. While none is illegal as such, each can be deemed illegal if used to substantially lessen competition, tend to create a monopoly, or be in restraint of trade.

Application 14-4
Maintaining Cooperation in the Channel of Distribution—"Caterpillar's Backbone!"

Traditionally, Caterpillar Tractor Co. has dedicated itself to one mission—providing the best construction equipment available. Much of Caterpillar's secret in meeting this objective is the support it gives to its vast dealer network. It's virtually impossible for competitors of Caterpillar to get a dealer on their side. Here's why.

"We approach our dealers as partners in the enterprise, not as agents or middlemen," a Caterpillar executive told *Business Week*. And a dealer commented: "They have consistently supplied us with superior products and a high-quality program of parts and product information."

When the dealer is kept happy, this euphoria spreads easily to the businesses that actually use the product, in this case, Caterpillar products. One secret is to keep the dealer well supplied with parts.

One approach to inventory problems is a national distribution center. Any dealer can order a part for any Caterpillar product and have the part delivered the next day. To cap off its dedication to dealers, Caterpillar buys back excess parts, and runs dozens of training programs for dealer employees.

There's even a course in Peoria to encourage children of dealers to remain in the business. "We had a dealer's son who was studying for the ministry and had a secondary interest in music," an executive recalled. "By the time we sent him home, he had changed his career plan. He has become one of our most successful dealers."

Source of data: "Caterpillar's Backbone: A Long Dealer Network," *Business Week*, May 4, 1981, p. 77.

Basically, the government is attempting to ensure a freely competitive environment for business. Let's look at the four frequently used control approaches.

With *exclusive dealing,* the manufacturer does not allow dealers to carry competitive products. While not all exclusive dealing is illegal, it tends to be unlawful when the agreement is made between a very large manufacturer and a very small dealer. Here, the power of the manufacturer is looked upon as a restraint of trade. Exclusive dealing is also often deemed unlawful when the manufacturer has a dominant share of a given market. When the exclusive contract actually improves competition, such as when the manufacturer is small and/or just getting started, exclusive deals are even looked upon favorably by the courts.

With *dealer selection,* manufacturers try to select those dealers to whom they will sell—and prohibit selling to others. In 1919, the U.S. Supreme Court firmly established the right of the producer to choose to whom to sell—as long as no intent to create a monopoly exists. Dealers, however, cannot be dropped for handling competitors' lines.

With *tying agreements,* the producer forces the dealer to buy additional products to secure one highly desired product—or the dealer is at least restrained from buying the said product from some other source. Generally, such agreements are viewed as in violation of the antitrust laws. They are seen as legal when a new company is trying to enter a market, when the producer is trying to maintain a desired level of quality, or when an exclusive dealer is required to carry a manufacturer's full product line.

Manufacturers use *exclusive territories* to ensure that dealers sell only to customers within their territories. Where such closed sales territories lessen competition and restrain trade, they have been viewed as illegal in some recent court decisions. Such judicial bodies seek to foster competition among intermediaries handling the same brand.

Recently, the Federal Trade Commission investigated Hartz Mountain, the large pet supply company, and succeeded in stopping some of its trade practices. Hartz Mountain promised to cease such tactics as setting up exclusive dealer plans that bar distributors and retailers from trading in other brands, to stop making payments or giving discounts to persuade dealers to boycott Hartz Mountain rivals, and to avoid spreading false statements around the trade that a competitor was going out of business. Such hard-sell tactics reduce competition.

The Nature of Physical Distribution

Determining the distribution channel is a strategic decision; it establishes the overall plan for moving products into the hands of ultimate consumers. However, still missing are the tactical decisions that actually mobilize the movements of the products. The best distribution plans can easily falter if the distribution channel is not supported by the decisions needed to ensure that products are moved through the channel appropriately.

Physical distribution, or *logistics,* provides the support necessary to carry out the distribution plan. While decisions about the distribution channel are concerned with providing time and place utilities, it is the logistical system that is responsible for actually moving products in a way that accomplishes this goal. The objective of physical distribution decisions is summed up by the statement of Robert Woodruff, former president of Coca-Cola, who said: "Our policy is to put Coke within an arm's length of desire." Thus, an effective physical distribution system can make important additions to the bundle of utility that buyers consider as well as being an excellent means for an individual firm to create a competitive differential for its product. In fact, a survey of 216 industrial purchasing agents showed that physical distribution ranked second only behind quality (but ahead of price) as a factor in their buying decision.[2]

But ensuring that the objective of physical distribution is achieved is no simple task, for the development of the logistical system is complex and costly. To see why, consider the job Armour-Dial faces daily. The company must make certain that its Dial

---

[2]William D. Perreault, Jr., and Frederick A. Russ, "Physical Distribution Service in Industrial Purchase Decisions," *Journal of Marketing,* vol. 40, no. 2 (April 1976), pp. 3–10.

brand of soap, which comes in four colors and three sizes, is available throughout the world. More than 7 million bars of Dial are sold per week, and retailers carry whichever mix of sizes and colors moves best for them. It is up to Armour-Dial, through its logistical system, to ensure that what the consumers want is available.

In Chapter 2, we noted that physical distribution costs account for the largest part of each dollar consumers spend. In fact, about 19 to 22 cents of every dollar goes to pay the costs of distributing products. In terms of the overall economy, physical distribution makes up over 20 percent of our gross national product. Clearly, a lot of money is directed toward ensuring time and place utilities. Yet, without this investment, much satisfaction would be lost, for products must be available when we want them. Physical distribution adds to consumers' satisfaction and improves the standard of living by ensuring that the *right products* are available when consumers want them—in the *right place* and at the *right time*. Thus, the first objective of the physical distribution system can be summed up in one word: *service*. And this term applies to services as well as goods.

In the airlines industry, carriers have been wooing travel agencies by leasing them and installing automated reservations terminals at their sites. Travel agencies which booked about 65 percent of all air flights can use these computers for information on all flight schedules and air fares. The airline that does the leasing increases its chances of sale by ensuring that its flight information comes up first when route information is requested. As the United Airlines program director said, "It's a distribution system that's vital to our health and will become more important in the future."[3]

We have emphasized that a business is a system, that marketing is a system, and that the channel of distribution is a system. Likewise, physical distribution is a system, one that calls for the movement of products to bring about time and place utilities. Furthermore, this logistical system is not confined to the manufacturer-consumer distribution channel. It also includes the movement of raw materials (such as ore, oil, and farm products) from originators to processors at the manufacturing level. And, of course, physical distribution includes the movement of finished products from producers to consumers.

Consider, for example, the distribution system needed to move flour into the hands of consumers (see Figure 14-3). Flour begins as a simple seed that producers must distribute to wheat farmers. The wheat they reap must be transported to a grain elevator (assembler), where it is graded and combined with other farmers' crops (concentration). From there it moves to the miller (processor), who grinds the wheat into flour. This new finished product then starts its journey toward final consumers through a network of wholesalers and a retailer (grocery store).

Each time an exchange is made in this distribution network, supply and demand among the various channel members must be coordinated. The needs of ultimate consumers must be relayed throughout the entire network to each channel member so that proper amounts of the product can be made available when demanded. This is

---

[3]"Airlines Fight over Systems for Bookings," *The Wall Street Journal,* Jan. 18, 1982, p. 25.

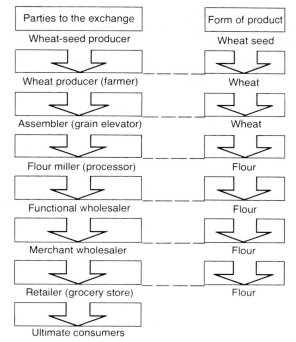

Figure 14-3   The physical distribution of flour. (Adapted from J. L. Heskett, Robert M. Ivie, and Nicholas A. Glaskowsky, Jr., Business Logistics: Management of Physical Supply and Distribution, Ronald Press, New York, 1964, p. 24)

a major task of the distribution system, since the length of time between the original planting of the seed and the consumer's final purchase of the flour may be three years or more. One growing season is needed to obtain the wheat seed; another is needed to grow the wheat; and then, most likely, another season—or a good portion of it—is taken up in grinding the wheat and transporting the flour to consumers. Along the way, the seed, the wheat, and the flour must all be stored, and various forms of the product must be transported seven times. This is why such a large proportion of the prices we pay for products goes toward their physical distribution costs.

But storage and transportation are not the only activities that must be accomplished during physical distribution. Various other activities are also elements of the total system, and many decisions have to be made to give a product its desired time and place utility. We will now examine the following elements of a total system of physical distribution:

1 Forecasting demand

2 Order processing

3 Inventory management

4 Storage

5 Materials handling

6 Protective packaging

7 Transportation

Forecasting Demand

The key to efficiency within a physical distribution system is correctly identifying the wants and needs of the market and, therefore, of those making intermediate exchanges. The amount of flour that consumers will want in three years has substantial impact on the growing patterns of wheat farmers and on the supply patterns of wheat-seed producers. A miscalculation of demand for the final product can result in overstocking or understocking at intermediate points and may lead to over- or underproduction of wheat and wheat seed. Correctly forecasting the level of demand, then, is the key to properly controlling the flow of products throughout the logistical system. Forecasting the need for products like bread, milk, and flour may be relatively simple, since their consumption tends to be rather stable; but the demand for such products as automobiles, housing, and certain types of clothing is much more difficult to forecast.

The distillers of Jack Daniel's whiskey, Brown-Forman, have experienced some of the problems involved in forecasting. Recently they found that the prestigious "sippin' whiskey" was in short supply in retail stores—but Brown-Forman could do nothing to rectify the situation. To enhance its taste, Jack Daniel's is aged for four years before it is offered for sale. Thus, each year's forecast and the resulting production have repercussions far beyond the immediate future.

Order Processing

At each intermediate exchange point within a distribution system, the needs of the next channel member are interpreted by placing an order for products. Thus, the retailer orders flour from the wholesaler, who, in turn, orders replacement flour from the distributor, and so on back through the entire channel. How well the products flow among channel members depends on how well and how quickly orders are processed at each step along the way. This involves many clerical procedures that, while routine, may take much time and may present many opportunities for mistakes. Throughout the system, an incorrect or inefficient flow of information can disrupt the flow of products to consumers.

Inventory Management

While forecasting demand is a vital part of determining the flow of products, actual demand may not be the same as the forecast. Thus, products must be stored in a way that will compensate for inaccuracies. The storage (inventory) of products is a way to safeguard against the inability to meet demand directly from the assembly line. It is an expensive activity, for it involves storage space costs, insurance, handling costs, and the costs associated with obsolescence. These costs can be decreased by reducing the size of the inventory, but then the marketers run the risk of losing sales because the product is unavailable. In the ideal situation, the demand for the product can be forecasted perfectly, and the inventory can be built up at an appropriate time to meet that demand. In reality, however, marketers must balance the higher cost of inventory against the costs of lost sales.

Inventory managers face two major decisions: They must determine what quantity of products to order and when to place the order so that products are constantly available. Both decisions are related to the level of service that each

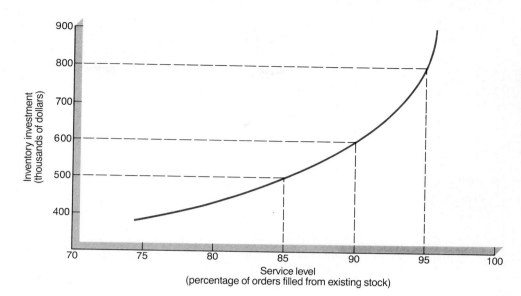

Figure 14-4 Inventory costs related to level of service.

channel member wants to provide for customers. But the relationship between the costs of holding inventory and the service level is not proportional. Figure 14-4 shows that to maintain a service level of 85 percent—that is, to ensure that 85 percent of incoming orders can be filled from existing stock—may cost $500,000. To increase this service level by 5 percent (to 90 percent) would require a 20 percent increase in inventory investment (an increase of $100,000); and to boost it another 5 percent would require an additional increase of $200,000 (33 ⅓ percent). Thus, inventory decisions must find a balance between the service available from existing inventory and the costs of that inventory. One manufacturer, Del Monte Foods, tried for years to maintain a 100 percent service level so that customers would never face a stockout. But the company later relaxed its service level to 98 percent so that it could take advantage of the large savings in inventory investment.

Storage

Products that are held in inventory must obviously be kept somewhere. Storage management is concerned with the size, number, and locations of facilities to house inventory. Most small retailers hold their inventory in the basement or in a storeroom within their stores. At the other extreme, many large channel members maintain a system of warehouses located throughout the country to make products quickly available to customers.

To store their inventory, channel members can choose from private or public warehouses. *Private warehouses* are owned and controlled exclusively by their users, while *public warehouses* are owned by independent contractors that rent space as needed to various channel members. Since public warehouses do not require a large investment, marketers can expand or contract as the need arises.

The size of the warehouse needed depends, of course, on the size of the inventory. But, when demand for the product is seasonal or widely fluctuating, public warehouses offer more flexible storage space. The number and location of warehouses depend on the marketers' goal in terms of service level. The more warehouses used, the greater the availability of the product. In some cases, large concentrations of customers (as would be likely in large cities) may make it economically feasible for a network of private warehouses, while less concentrated markets may necessitate good use of public warehouses. Warehouses can be located either close to customers or close to plants; the former location provides quicker availability.

Distribution Centers

Most people think of a warehouse as a large building in which products lie around unused. This contradicts the basic idea of physical distribution, which implies flow and movement. Thus, in the 1950s, storage facilities were updated and were renamed *distribution centers*. These are streamlined storage facilities that are geared to taking orders and delivering products within a fully integrated system. The buildings of a distribution center are modern and usually confined to one floor so that products are less likely to remain for long in some out-of-the-way place. Within the structure, products are moved efficiently through the use of automated equipment, and computerized inventory systems allow firms to meet customers' needs rapidly. All these improvements in the storage activity help to cut excessive inventory and reduce storage and delivery time.

Eastman Kodak maintains such a distribution center at O'Hare Airport in Chicago. From this center, the company can move parts and products to virtually any point in the country in a matter of hours. Such a new concept in storage underscores the fact that companies are in the business of moving products, not storing them.

Materials Handling

Within plants and warehouses, products must be moved about often, and they must be easy to extract when they are needed. The materials-handling system is responsible for carrying out these tasks efficiently and effectively. Conveyor systems, forklift trucks, special containers, and computer-driven robots are among the equipment used to increase efficiency. In order to meet the demands of the production and distribution systems, these components must be integrated in some way to allow for economical movement of products in response to customers' needs. Items in inventory must be readily available for assembly, packing, and shipping. Materials handling has been made more efficient by the development of large, standardized, easy-to-handle containers in which smaller packages are loaded for shipping. The increased use of this materials-handling method (called *containerization*) has greatly improved the efficiency of transportation while reducing losses from damage and theft in transit.

Protective Packaging

In Chapter 8, we noted that packaging has a number of purposes, one of which is protecting the product. This aspect of packaging is especially important when it comes to distribution, since products that are damaged at any point in the distribution channel will lose some or all of their ability to provide satisfaction. And if they make it to the end of the channel—to consumers—damaged products may have lost their utility entirely. Thus, great care must be taken to ensure that damage does not occur to products in transit.

The packages and containers used to ship products should be compatible with the materials-handling system and should fit compactly into transportation equipment to reduce freight costs. In addition, shippers should be aware that the various methods of transportation may have characteristics that make them unsuitable for particular products. For instance, railroad cars are usually very hot, while airplane storage areas get extremely cold; products shipped by either of these methods, then, must be suitable for or unaffected by temperature extremes or must be packaged protectively. We will review the various transportation methods next.

Transportation

A major decision area within logistics is that of determining which mode of transportation to use in shipping products from the manufacturer to various channel members and then to consumers. All transportation companies are classified by law into four types: common carriers, contract carriers, private carriers, and exempt carriers.

Common carriers serve the general public by transporting goods with standard practices set by regulatory bodies (although the emphasis has turned away from regulation for some types of common carriers, as we will see below) or by company rules. Most interstate carriers are common carriers, including buses, railroads, airlines, trucks, and water carriers.

Contract carriers ship goods on a contractual basis; that is, they agree to make a specified number of shipments to specific destinations for an estimated price. Many contract carriers specialize in certain types of goods; examples include household movers, automobile trucking companies, and chartered planes. Sometimes thousands of trucks are operated under contract by a single owner.

Private carriers are shippers that own the goods being shipped. The goods are related to the company's principal business, and the company employs the drivers and either owns or leases the equipment used. Large grocery chains, for example, usually have their own fleets of trucks.

Exempt carriers, as their name indicates, are shippers that are exempt from state and federal regulation. They are involved mostly with moving unprocessed agricultural products, and trucks are usually the method of transportation.

Having classified the four types of carriers for shipping products, let us now examine the five main transportation methods: railroads, trucks, pipelines, waterways, and airplanes.

Railroads

Railroads are still the most frequently used method of transporting products in the United States, although this dominant position has been challenged by the development of other modes of transportation. In 1980, for instance, railroads carried 37 percent of all intercity freight, a drop from 44 percent in 1960 and 61 percent in 1940. But, owing to high energy costs, many marketers are turning to the rails as a means of transportation. A slight increase was shown in 1980. This rise arrests a decline that has been going on since the Depression days of the 1930s.

Railroads are used especially for long-distance shipments of heavy cargoes like coal, lumber, and sand. (See Figure 14-5.) Rail is a low-cost form of transportation that is more convenient than water routes and that can offer greater capacity than trucks. Still, railroad transportation is not without problems. It is limited to where tracks are located, sometimes making rail transport less accessible than other shipping methods. However, this disadvantage has been offset somewhat by *piggyback service,* whereby preloaded trucks are taken directly onto railroad flatcars and thus can deliver products to their destination without intermediate loading and unloading. Additionally, railroads charge substantially less for carload lots than for shipments that are less-than-carload lots, because the goods are packed by the shipper and unloaded by the receiver. This practice reduces the paperwork and handling involved and induces shippers to transport large quantities at one time.

In 1980, the passage of the Harley O. Staggers Rail Act created a mild revolution in the marketing of railroads. Prior to this law, which applied to all railroads, freight rates were regulated and supervised by the Interstate Commerce Commission (ICC). But this new legislation gave railroads zones within which rates could be raised or lowered without ICC permission. This change has greatly increased the marketing flexibility of railroads and has substantially reduced regulation of the industry. Additionally, the increased demand for coal in the United States has given a lift to

Figure 14-5 Rail lines are still unbeatable as a means of transporting heavy cargoes, such as coal, long distances over land. *(Courtesy Illinois Central Gulf Railroad)*

railroad business. The years of 1980 and 1981 were far from dismal ones for the railroad industry.

Trucks

Trucks carry about 23 percent of all freight between cities and certainly are the most popular carrier within cities. Our network of interstate highways has been a boon to the trucking industry, and equipment improvements have brought greater flexibility to truck transportation. It's relatively easy to design a truck to match the needs of the product being shipped, and trucks have been most useful in transporting high-value products over short distances. Truck shipments require less handling than railroad shipments, and therefore packaging does not have to be so protective. Additionally, trucks can go directly from the seller's location to the buyer's destination. Thus, the extra handling that is needed with railroad transportation (the loading and unloading at each terminal) is avoided, and the total cost of truck transportation is often less than the cost of shipping by rail. However, truck rates are not lower than railroad rates, even though trucks generally provide low-cost, fast, dependable, and flexible transportation. On the other hand, because of their size trucks are not particularly suitable for shipping bulky items.

The Motor Carrier Act of 1980 substantially loosened the regulatory grip of the ICC on the trucking industry. Interpretation of the law is not yet complete, but truckers clearly have freedom to reduce rates that used to be set and to add new services. Thus the trucking industry has become much more competitive, causing greater emphasis on marketing. As a consultant told *Business Week:* "Before, the approach was, 'Here we are—ship with us.' Now marketing is becoming more important. Carriers are offering more services and are tailoring them to shippers' individual needs."[4]

Pipelines

There are about 200,000 miles of pipeline in the United States, not including the Alaska pipeline. Such products as crude oil, natural gas, and gasoline are transported by pipeline. This means of transportation accounts for 23 percent of all domestic intercity freight. The growth of pipelines during this century parallels the growth of automobile transportation, since the main products moved by pipeline—petroleum products—serve the needs of the automobile owners. Pipelines are our most dependable method of transportation. During the frigid winter of 1977, the pipelines could operate, while railroads, trucks, and barges were rendered useless by ice and snow. Pipelines are also an inexpensive means of transportation. They require little maintenance, and so few employees are needed to keep them operating. Still, pipelines are a slow means of transportation; most liquid products move through them at only 3 to 4 miles per hour. In addition, their routes are inflexible and are subject to much government regulation.

Waterways

Water transportation was the first important method of shipping products, which is one reason why most large commercial cities are located near a major source of water. (See Figure 14-6.) Today, our great rivers, lakes, and coastal waterways are still of

---

[4]"What Deregulation Has Done to the Truckers," *Business Week,* Nov. 9, 1981, p. 70.

Figure 14-6 Water transport led to the growth of large commercial ports, and water is still an important distribution method. *(Elizabeth Piers/The Port Authority of New York and New Jersey)*

prime importance in the transportation system. They are especially useful for shipping large, bulky items of low value, such as cement, sand, gravel, steel, grain, and lumber, because water transportation is the least expensive shipping method in that large quantities of products can be moved at one time. However, water transportation is very slow—only pipelines are slower—and some water routes are subject to freezing during the winter.

Airplanes

Movement of products by air is the fastest, though the most expensive, transportation method. As a result, air transportation accounts for less than 1 percent of total domestic tonnage. It is used primarily to ship products that have a high unit value and low bulk, as well as highly perishable and emergency items. Airplanes are limited both by size and structure in terms of the types of products they can accommodate. Furthermore, not all destinations have airports or the means to handle air shipments. Even so, improved airline technology will make air transport more important in the future.

Table 14-2 presents a comparison of the five major transportation methods in terms of ton-miles, and Table 14-3 compares them on four important criteria.

Additional Freight Services

Using the five principal modes of transportation, marketers can take advantage of a number of additional services to help them move products. One is the *United Parcel Service* (UPS), a privately owned shipping service that makes pickups and deliveries of goods and guarantees 3-day service. *Bus lines* also can be used for high-value, low-bulk items. In addition, there are transportation intermediaries called *freight forwarders* that serve small shippers by pooling many shipments to take advantage of lower rates, passing some of the savings on to the shippers. Finally, a group of

TABLE 14-2 Estimated Distribution of Intercity Freight Traffic in the United States (billions of ton-miles)

Transportation method	Billions of ton-miles, 1980	Percentage of total				
		1980	1979	1975	1960	1940
Railroads	932	37.3	35.7	37.0	44.1	61.3
Trucks	565	22.6	24.2	21.4	21.7	10.0
Waterways						
Great Lakes	113	4.6	4.9	5.2	7.6	15.5
Rivers and canals	307	12.3	11.7	11.4	9.2	3.6
Pipelines	575	23.0	23.3	24.8	17.4	9.6
Airplanes	5	0.2	0.2	0.2		
Total	2497	100.0	100.0	100.0	100.0	100.0

Source: *Yearbook of Railroad Facts,* Association of American Railroads, Washington, D.C., 1981, p. 36.

TABLE 14-3 Ranking of Transportation Modes by Cost and Time Criteria

Mode	Cost (1 = highest)	Average delivery time (1 = fastest)	Delivery time variation (1 = lowest)	Loss and damage (1 = lowest)
Rail	2	3	4	5
Truck	3	2	3	4
Water	5	5	5	2
Pipeline	4	4	2	1
Air	1	1	1	3

Source: Ronald H. Ballou, *Basic Business Logistics,* Prentice-Hall, Inc., Englewood Cliffs, N.J., 1978, p. 134.

shippers that transport similar items may band together to form a *shippers' cooperative,* thus also benefiting from lower freight rates. (See Application 14-5.)

The Goals of Physical Distribution

As we have noted, the first objective of physical distribution can be summed up in one word: *service.* That is, the purpose of the distribution system is to ensure that the *right products* are available when consumers want them—in the *right place* and at the *right time.* But this overall goal of service has several aspects that we should examine.

Availability of Products

The most basic aspect of the service goal is product availability. Suppliers at each point in the distribution system must anticipate demand and be able to furnish *all* items ordered by customers. This ability depends on the accuracy of forecasts. When any channel member is out of stock, customers are inconvenienced and must either search for another source or wait until the products are made available. In either case, customers have not received the service they expected and desired. Quaker Oats,

Application 14-5
Transportation Costs—Beating the System with a System

The soaring costs of distribution have prompted many manufacturers to look outside their firms for help, and a new type of computer service business is coming to their rescue. A few small service companies have built a data bank of freight rates based on a variety of combinations of weight, product, destination, origin, and type of carrier.

While some large shippers have developed their own systems, most companies are wading through rates and tariffs, trying desperately to control the rampant freight increases resulting

from fuel prices. In 1979, distribution costs increased 9 percent for United States manufacturers—to $209 billion, their largest single expense after labor and materials.

The services of the new data banks typically cost the manufacturer $20,000 to $30,000 per year, but the results can be worth many times the investment. Electrolux Corporation discovered it was paying $1.22 more per 100 pounds when it shipped in loads less than 500 pounds. As a result, the company has reduced its under-500-pound shipments from

35 percent of its total to about 4 percent of its total.

Pfizer uses the up-to-date data base to balance service needs with freight costs. A Pfizer vice president estimates that the service has saved the firm $1 million in recent years. "There's no way we could do this manually," he says. With the computer, "we can spend more time analyzing data rather than crunching numbers."

Source of data: "Saving Money when Freight Rates Are Computerized," *Business Week,* Feb. 25, 1980, pp. 111, 114.

through a company-sponsored study, found that poor availability of products had substantially dampened retailer enthusiasm for its product line.

Recent high interest rates for borrowing money have made inventory very costly since the cost ties up money that could be used elsewhere in the company. Many companies in the distribution channel have dropped their inventories to all-time lows and are counting on manufacturers to maintain their stocks and provide fast delivery.

Accuracy in Filling Orders

Another aspect of the service goal is the degree to which products received match the order sent. Few things are more maddening than to wait for an order and then receive the wrong shipment. The buyer then must place a new order and wait again, hoping the correct order will be sent. Mistakes can be made in this regard during order writing, order receiving, or order filling. Often, customers incorrectly indicate their needs, especially when the telephone is used. Errors are also common in transcribing orders from purchase orders to shipping orders, because different intermediaries may misunderstand each other's ordering systems and documents.

Safe Service

Products that are received in damaged condition cannot provide the expected level of satisfaction, so the service level is reduced. Therefore, the factors that may result in damaged products—materials handling, storage, and the transportation method—must be considered in order to build in the proper amount of protection. Usually, faster transportation results in less damage, even though it is more costly.

Speedy Service

The time lag between the need for a product and its receipt by the customer is a key aspect of service. It often happens that a channel member has an immediate need for products, and the quicker they can be received, the greater the satisfaction (since sales will not be lost). Additionally, being able to get products promptly may allow the customer to reduce inventory or not carry any at all—thus pushing the storage function back in the distribution channel. To show the importance of delivery time in the bundle of utility within actual companies, Pillsbury has the goal of "third morning rail delivery anywhere in the U.S.," while Xerox has a separate division of 12,000 service personnel "to put a disabled machine anywhere in the continental United States back into operation within three hours after receiving the service request."

Many physical distribution activities must be performed between the time when a need for products is recognized by a channel member and the receipt of those products. And these activities take time—order writing and transmitting, order processing, order filling, and final shipment of products. Unfortunately, however, reduction in time usually leads to increases in costs. For example, computerized order processing is faster than manual processing, and air transport is faster than truck transport; but each method is also more expensive than its alternative. Thus, channel members must be keenly aware of their customers' needs in terms of time. They strive to remain competitive in this regard, that is, they do not raise costs by providing speed that is not needed or wanted.

A computerized order-entry system for Kellogg's cereals has greatly increased order-filling accuracy and speed. In a recent year, the company completely filled 98 percent of its orders. Using a centralized teleprocessing system, sales representatives phone orders to Battle Creek, where operators feed them into computers. With the salesperson still on the line, the orders are logged, prices checked, and the date and location of the delivery confirmed. Salespeople can similarly check the status and location of rail cars on which the products are being shipped.

Dependable Service

Closely aligned with speed of service is the channel member's reliability in making deliveries when promised. Customers make plans that often depend on the receipt of products as scheduled. Other channel members should let customers know when they can expect delivery. Scheduled delivery dates must be reasonable, and all efforts must be made to meet them. But dependability also costs money, and channel members must strike a balance between reasonable service and costs.

The soft-drink industry has recently come closer to reaching these physical distribution goals. Bottlers of soft drinks are now increasing the use of "advance sale delivery systems" whereby they find out just how much of each brand their customers want *before* company trucks leave the plant. While this may seem logical, it is new to the soft-drink industry. "They used to just load up a truck not knowing how much of each brand to deliver," a Coca-Cola executive told *The Wall Street Journal*.[5] But now demand can be better forecasted, brands made more available, and service made more dependable. An added benefit is the increased likelihood of success for new

---

[5] "Soft Drink Companies Prime Their Weapons in Market-Share Battle," *The Wall Street Journal,* April 26, 1979, p. 1.

beverages. As trucks are loaded to meet advance orders, more space is available to carry innovative products which can gain initial shelf space. Much of the early success of such products as General Foods' Country Time lemonade and Sunkist orange soda, the joint venture of Sunkist Growers (the fruit-raising cooperative) and General Cinema Corporation (the soft-drink and movie theater company), has been attributed to this "advance sale delivery system."

The Total Cost Approach to Physical Distribution

By now it should be clear that there are two main objectives of physical distribution. The level of service is important, of course, because it ensures that channel members—including customers—will be satisfied. But as the service level is improved, the costs of distribution increase. Thus, the basic decision rule in physical distribution is to minimize total distribution costs while maintaining a satisfactory level of service.

Defining or identifying the satisfactory service level is difficult, but channel members must understand their customers' needs. Often, this ability comes through experience. But costs, on the other hand, are more easily known. They can be measured and estimated according to various guidelines and principles in addition to experience. Generally, the costs of shipping decrease when slower methods of transportation are used, while the costs of inventory rise (since more products must be stored to meet potential demand). Thus, the costs of storage are traded off against the costs of transportation. A "satisfactory" level of service, then, is the best combination of inventory and transportation costs, or the point at which total physical distribution costs are lowest.

This guideline is slightly misleading, however, since it reflects only two cost factors, inventory and transportation. There are many other sources of costs, and the goal of physical distribution is to minimize the *total* cost of all activities in the

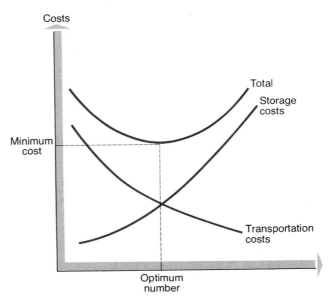

Figure 14-7 Physical distribution tradeoff.

system—packaging, order handling, order filling, and so on—while still maintaining a satisfactory service level. So the problem is much more complex than we have indicated. The lowering of one cost may increase other costs in the distribution system. Thus, a slower means of transportation may well lead to increased inventory costs and higher costs for protective packaging, along with increased expenses relating to order processing (see Figure 14-7). Therefore, the determination of the minimum total cost for the entire distribution system is best accomplished through statistical methods, and this can be achieved only if the proper information is made available. Chapter 3 discussed the concept of the marketing information system (MIS), and physical distribution is an area ripe for use of this concept. Thus, the MIS should include accurate and relevant data for use by the distribution manager. Inventory levels and costs must be monitored; transportation rates and alternative carriers' performance levels should be known; and warehouse reports should deal with space utilization, labor requirements, and the movement of inventory. Only through a detailed analysis of all these facets of the total distribution system can the goal of cost minimization be achieved. (See Application 14-6.)

Application 14-6
Minimizing Total Cost—A Trade-Off in Time Saves Nine

Management routinely relies on a bevy of consultants for advice. Now a new type of consultant is being employed, one that doesn't submit high fees and expense vouchers. The help is coming from computers, and even in these days of runaway inflation, the payoff can be considerable. For instance, at Florida Power & Light Co., the computer showed that centralizing the inventory distribution system would result in efficiencies. After centralizing, the utility saved $13.5 million in annual inventory carrying costs. And at National Airlines, Inc., the computer showed the carrier how to save as much as $500,000 a month in fuel costs.

These helpful computers are part of a decision support system. With such a system, executives can sift through the effects of a number of operating decisions and chances in a matter of minutes to find the best, or the least costly, solutions to manufacturing, distribution, and marketing dilemmas.

Shaklee Corp. used its computers to cut delivery time to its customers, and managed to save $850,000 in operating costs. It also has stored details on more than 500 line items, 360 customers, and its 100 distribution centers. The system's initial task was to find the best way to reduce delivery times without increasing the cost of production or distribution. The system quickly determined the impact that various delivery requirements would have on transportation costs, the cost of operating distribution centers, and the cost of carrying inventories.

"For the first time," Charles D. Fry, manager of materials analysis and planning, says, "management is able to understand the financial impact associated with various service-level decisions." Without the computer model, he says, "there is no quantifiable way to determine the cost. And decisions become political issues between the sales side of the company, which would like a warehouse in any town where there is a reasonable demand, and the distribution side, which wants to minimize costs."

Source of data: " 'What If' Help for Management," *Business Week*, Jan. 21, 1980, pp. 73–74.

Looking Back

We have now seen how the channels of distribution are selected and mobilized to move products from producers to ultimate consumers. This chapter has focused on the flow of the title to products as they move closer to their market and on the actual physical movement of products; a comparison of the five major methods of transportation was included. Before moving on to the next chapter, which looks at the promotion decisions that marketers must make, be sure you have understood the following important points:

1   The channel of distribution involves a series of exchanges in terms of products, payments, use rights, and information.

2   Some channels of distribution are used more frequently than others, and marketers sometimes use more than a single channel.

3   The channels of distribution for consumer products are different from those used for industrial products.

4   The selection of a distribution channel depends on such criteria as market coverage, control over the product, and costs; shorter channels result in less market coverage, more control over the product, and higher distribution costs.

5   Selecting a distribution channel for a new product is often a difficult decision, and established marketers have an advantage over new entrants to the market.

6   In choosing specific intermediaries for the distribution channel, the most important criterion for marketers is the degree of access to the desired market.

7   The channel of distribution should be viewed as a total system in which cooperation among channel members is encouraged and conflict is avoided.

8   Channel conflict results when channel members do not meet the expectations of other channel members; vertical conflict is more frequent than horizontal conflict.

9   The channel captain can exert power to overcome many of the conflicts that may exist in the channel; while manufacturers often serve as channel captain, other members may also fulfill this role.

10   Vertical marketing systems are a formal means of reducing channel conflict.

11   The physical distribution system supports the decisions made about which channel members and which distribution system to use.

12 Physical distribution is a total, interdependent system whose activities are expensive.

13 The five major modes of transportation are railroads, trucks, pipelines, waterways, and airplanes.

14 The goal of physical distribution is to provide a satisfactory level of service while minimizing costs; this may involve trade-offs between inventory costs and transportation costs.

15 The *total* cost of the entire distribution system must be minimized, and the MIS is essential to achieving this goal.

Key Terms

If you aren't sure what each of the following words means, look back at the text. Numbers refer to pages on which the words are defined. Additional information can be found by checking the index and the glossary at the end of the book.

channel of distribution 435
intensive distribution 444
selective distribution 444
exclusive distribution 444
channel management 446
vertical conflict 447
horizontal conflict 449
channel captain 450

corporate vertical marketing system 451
administered vertical marketing system 451
contractual vertical marketing system 451
physical distribution 453
inventory management 456

Questions for Review

1 What is the difference between a "short" and a "long" channel of distribution?

2 What are the three most important criteria for marketers to consider in choosing a channel of distribution?

3 Briefly describe the major difference between vertical channel conflict and horizontal channel conflict.

4 What are the three types of vertical marketing systems? Which type has had the greatest growth of all the systems in recent years?

5 What is the major difference between inventory management and storage management?

6 What is the most frequently used mode of transportation? What are some of its advantages relative to other modes?

Questions for Thought and Discussion

1 Snack-food producers are worried about the developing trend toward consumption of food away from home. Based on what you learned in this chapter, what must these producers do, then, to protect themselves?

2 Metamucil laxative is the best seller in drugstores, with a 13 percent share, followed by Phillips with 7 percent and Ex-Lax with 4 percent. But in food stores, Metamucil has only started to enter the field and is far behind its competitors. What will be necessary to ensure the success of its distribution into this new market?

3   Many distributors feel they are caught in the middle as pressure tightens from both manufacturers and buyers. Customers seem to be asking for more and more, while manufacturers are giving less and less. Do you see any ways to ease this pressure?

4   In the apparel industry, retailers are no longer booking orders in advance of specified shipment dates; instead, they are buying much closer to the actual selling season and then asking manufacturers to space out deliveries to suit the stores' sales forecasts. What is the impact of this change on apparel makers?

Suggested Project

Write a short research paper which discusses the future of railroads as a viable mode of transportation. Include factors such as (1) the recent impact of accidents on the railroads' reputation for safety and (2) appropriations now being allocated to make them safer and more efficient.

Suggested Readings

Ackerman, Kenneth B., and Bernard J. LaLonde: "Making Warehousing More Efficient," *Harvard Business Review,* vol. 58, no. 2 (March–April 1980), pp. 94–102. Carrying a high labor quotient and easily mechanized, the warehousing function invites the attention of efficiency-seeking management.

Aspinwall, Leo: "The Characteristics of Goods and Parallel Systems Theories," in Eugene J. Kelley and William Lazer (eds.), *Managerial Marketing,* Richard D. Irwin, Homewood, Ill., 1958, pp. 434–450. This classic and often quoted work focuses on channel development as a function of the type of goods marketed and explains a parallel relationship between distribution systems and promotion systems.

Ballou, Ronald H.: *Basic Business Logistics,* Prentice-Hall, Inc., Englewood Cliffs, N.J., 1978. This book presents an excellent discussion of the various aspects of physical distribution. Especially good is the discussion of physical distribution costs.

Lekashman, Raymond, and John F. Stolle: "The Total Cost Approach to Distribution," *Business Horizons,* vol. 6 (Winter 1965), pp. 33–46. The authors spell out the nature of real cost and discuss when and how to use a total cost approach.

Rosenbloom, Bert: *Marketing Channels: A Management View,* Dryden Press, Hinsdale, Ill., 1978. This text provides a comprehensive, integrated presentation of literature on marketing channels within a systematically developed managerial framework.

Stern, Louis W. (ed.): *Distribution Channels: Behavioral Dimensions,* Houghton Mifflin, Boston, 1969. This collection of readings focuses on issues related to minimizing conflict and maximizing cooperation in the distribution channel.

Trombetta, William L., and Albert L. Page: "The Channel Control Issue under Scrutiny," *Journal of Retailing,* vol. 54, no. 2 (Summer 1978), pp. 43–58. A review is offered of court decisions that affect a company's ability to control the distribution of its product through the channels.

Walker, Bruce J., and Joel D. Haynes (eds.): *Marketing Channels and Institutions: Readings on Distribution Concepts and Practices,* Grid, Columbus, Ohio, 1973. This collection of articles stresses the key areas of channel management.

Weigand, Robert E.: "Fit Products and Channels to Your Markets," *Harvard Business Review,* vol. 55, no. 1 (January–February 1977), pp. 95–105. The author gives examples of various combinations of markets, channels, and products and provides the conditions that give rise to what he calls multimarketing.

Cases for Part Three begin on page 600.

Promotion

When R. J. Reynolds introduced its Now brand into the highly competitive cigarette market in 1976, it had two messages to communicate. The first message focused on the tangible product. Ad copy would stress Now's low tar, easy draw, and good taste. Research had shown that the people especially interested in low-tar cigarettes were affluent, "citified," in their mid-thirties, and presently smoking higher-tar brands. RJR felt this group gave them "an opportunity to grow. We're below average there."

This market also set the tone for the pitch of the promotional campaign. RJR's second message was about the psychological reason for smoking the new cigarette. People would puff away at Nows not for their kookiness (à la Benson & Hedges), their ruggedness (Marlboro), or their countrified restfulness (Salem). Now would appeal to the snob, the arriviste, successful and proud of it.

Taking its cue from the beauty industry, RJR orchestrated a high-toned communication effort. Several hundred thousand "opinion makers," whose names were culled from prestige publications, executive associations, posh clubs, and Who's Whos, received a discreet solicitation from RJR chairman and president William D. Hobbs.

"Usually when you introduce a mass-marketed product you go to the A&Ps," said Allan H. Johnston, RJR's brand development manager. "In line with the image we wanted, we took a more select distribution approach. We anticipated—correctly, it turned out—that on the basis of our advertising and general image, we would get as much as a 10 percent volume for Now in stores in well-to-do neighborhoods such as those on the Upper East Side of Manhattan."

Said Johnston, "We made use of thought-leader publications—*Business Week, Fortune*—to a much greater extent than we normally do. We turned to publications that were heavily targeted to an upper-income group."

Point-of-purchase displays and even the Now package, a silver box with embossing, were carefully designed and produced to look elegant and rich. As Johnston reported: "Initial distribution levels of 50 to 90 percent were achieved in the first roll-out markets as retailers were wooed with buy-in discounts, free goods, and vending machine and display allowances." By 1980, 250 million packs were being sold annually.

Sources of data: "Can High-Fashion Sampling Sell Cigarettes?" *Product Management* (Oct. 1976), pp. 25–27; and "The $150-Million Cigarette," *Fortune*, Nov. 17, 1980, pp. 121–125.

Chapter 15

Communication and the Promotional Mix

Looking Ahead

Now we begin our exploration of the last of the 4 P's—promotion. So far, we have seen how products are developed, priced, and then moved to market. Now we will examine how people learn about these "bundles of utility." This chapter will illustrate that the communication which marketers perform does much to increase the satisfaction that consumers derive from a product.

Key Topics

How marketers communicate with the market in just about everything they do

The specific activities that make up the communication process

The major promotional activities that marketers engage in

What the promotional mix is designed to accomplish

The factors that shape the promotional mix

How marketers determine how much to spend on promotion

Chapter Outline

Communication in Marketing
Marketers and Communication
The Communication Process

The Nature of the Promotional Mix
Advertising
Personal Selling
Sales Promotion
Public Relations
Publicity
The Objectives of the Promotional Mix
The Importance of Promotion

Determining the Promotional Mix
Market Influences
Product Features
Stage in the Product's Life Cycle
Costs
Company Policies

Determining the Promotional Budget
Percent of Sales
Competitive Parity
All Available Funds (Total Allocation)
Task (Objective) Approach

Looking Back

Earlier chapters have examined how products are developed and managed, priced, and moved to market. Now we are ready to explore that aspect of marketing which may seem most familiar to consumers—communication and promotion. This is the last of the 4 P's that make up the marketing mix. Having seen how product, price, and place come together to satisfy consumers' needs and wants, we'll now examine how promotion is used to encourage exchange in the marketplace.

Communication in Marketing

Without communication, few exchanges would be made. Communication provides information. It tells consumers in the market that a product exists, and it attempts to show how the product matches that market's wants and needs. In short, the purposes of communication are to *inform* and *persuade*. (And, of course, communication is a two-way street. We have already seen how consumers communicate their wants and needs back to the marketer.)

The consumers who make up a market must know that a product exists; otherwise, they cannot recognize how the product can satisfy their needs and wants. Thus, the first purpose of communication in marketing is to provide information. But even then, consumers may hesitate to make an exchange. They need assurance that the product can provide what they want or need. Hence, some persuasion is necessary to encourage consumers to cross the threshold of exchange behavior and actually take steps toward owning the product. This persuasion aspect of marketing communication overcomes consumers' hesitancy by inducing or creating a favorable psychological disposition toward making an exchange.

Some categories of products require very little persuasion on the part of marketers. All that is needed is simply to inform the market that the product does, in fact, exist. This situation occurs when the match is nearly perfect between a market's wants and needs and the satisfaction offered by a product. Hand-held electronic toys provide perhaps a good example. Such games closely match the wants of many children who seek visual stimulation, a challenge, and, of course, entertainment. And parents in particular appreciate products with long "play-value" where their children do not get quickly bored with a toy after a sizable expenditure. Electronic toys satisfy parents' needs since they often require time to master. For consumers and buyers who have such wants, electronic toys provide an excellent match. Buyers needed little encouragement to make an exchange because they recognized that the product would provide satisfaction. Marketers thus could focus primarily on the informational aspect of communication.

With other products, however, a great deal of persuasion is needed before an exchange will be made. In such cases, the match between the product and the market's needs and wants is poor, or is not obvious. Therefore, consumers must be persuaded to make an exchange. They cannot recognize, for example, that *Fluoristat,* the fluoride ingredient in Advanced Formula Crest, has better cavity-preventing ingredients than *Fluoristan,* the ingredient in the old formula Crest, simply by looking at or tasting the two products. They must first be informed about this feature of the product and then be convinced that it will satisfy their needs. Apparently, consumers were. After heavy introduction and promotional campaigns, P&G's Crest toothpaste shot up to 41 percent market share from 35 percent the year before.

In still other cases, there may be a good match between the product and the market's needs, but consumers don't want to recognize it. Falling into this category are prearranged funeral services and cancer checkups. In these cases, the information that the product exists and can satisfy such needs is rarely sufficient to encourage exchange. Persuasion is needed to induce the exchange. Thus, communication actually increases the satisfaction that consumers can derive, for without it, they would not take the final step toward owning the product.

Marketers and Communication

But just how do marketers actually communicate with their market? The primary way is through the promotional activities of advertising, personal selling, and sales promotion. These are the major communication tools that marketers use to encourage exchange. But they are not the only means by which marketers communicate. In fact, as we have noted, the *entire* marketing mix is essentially concerned with communication. Seen from this viewpoint, practically everything that marketers do—every activity that is perceived by the market—communicates something about the bundle of satisfaction offered. Let's quickly review the communicative aspects of the marketing mix.

First of all, the *product* communicates form utility, partly by the function it serves but often also by the symbolic satisfaction it conveys. Thus, gold watches are given at graduation or retirement to communicate achievement; diamonds communicate lasting love; and metal tennis rackets communicate power. Services also communicate various things. Dry cleaning communicates protection from moths; massages communicate relaxation and special attention; automobile repair services communicate dependability. And even less traditional products—people, places, ideas, organizations, and so on—communicate something. Bob Hope communicates humor; a trip to Bermuda communicates romance; and banks communicate security for one's financial assets (see Figure 15-1).

A product's *brand name* also has communicative aspects. It assures consumers of consistent quality and tells them that the product will perform as expected. Thus, Colgate-Palmolive's Irish Spring soap communicates the feeling of freshness that is associated with the spring season. Even the colors of green and yellow are intended to suggest cleanliness and freshness.

The product's *packaging* also communicates, identifying the product, the brand, and its characteristics. Frozen vegetables packaged with a well-known national label like Green Giant immediately suggest quality, while unknown brands do not. Similarly, consumers have been found to believe that bread wrapped in cellophane is fresher than bread wrapped in waxed paper. And liquid detergents like Wisk, Ajax,

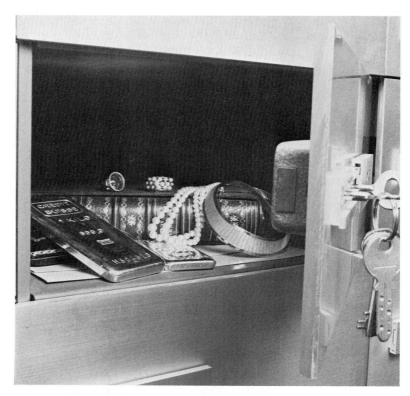

Figure 15-1 Strongboxes for deposit of customers' valuables communicate security in a very real sense. (Paolo Koch/Photo Researchers)

Lysol, and Mr. Clean are all packaged in "broad-shouldered" containers (see Figure 15-2) to communicate the idea of strength and power.

Warranties communicate, too; they guarantee satisfaction. When marketers provide a warranty, they are telling consumers that they expect the product to perform as claimed, and that they will stand by the claim—even after the exchange is made.

The *price* of a product also communicates. It tells consumers what the marketers believe the product is worth in an exchange. We noted in Chapter 11 that high prices often communicate high quality (even though in some cases it may not actually exist), while low prices are often perceived to indicate lower quality. High prices may also convey status, achievement, and, for some consumers, a feeling of exclusivity. On the other hand, price variations and discounts convey such meanings as "out-of-season," "damaged," or "bargain."

The *distribution system* serves a communicative function, too. In general, the selection of a distribution channel and the movement of products through it communicate time and place utility. More specifically, however, the selection of specific intermediaries communicates a great deal about the product. Expensive

Figure 15-2 Has the "broad-shouldered" bottle used to package many cleaning liquids consciously reinforced your image of their effectiveness? (Randy Matusow)

watches are not sold in low-quality discount stores, and low-priced jeans are not found at Brooks Brothers or Saks Fifth Avenue.

Finally, of course, the *promotional activities* of advertising, personal selling, and sales promotion have the single purpose of communicating. Along with the other elements of the marketing mix, marketers use promotional activities to communicate directly with the consumers, informing them that the bundle of utility exists and persuading them that it will satisfy their needs. In short, all marketing activities are designed to communicate the total amount of satisfaction that a product makes available to its consumers. And good marketers realize the importance of ensuring that all communicative activities work together to convey a positive message. Too often, however, companies rely exclusively on advertising or on personal selling to communicate their message. What is really needed is a total communication approach in which every marketing activity tells something about the bundle of utility offered. Thus, all activities should be coordinated and aimed toward the objective of presenting a uniform message to consumers, focusing on the product's ability to provide satisfaction.

Binney & Smith is best known for its ever-popular Crayola crayon. While it dominates that $55 million market, the crayon market dwindled throughout the 1970s, owing to the declining birth rate and soaring materials costs. To create sales and profit growth and present a new image (as opposed to its past image as a company that was somewhere between content and asleep), Binney & Smith took aggressive action. In the early 1980s, the company increased brand recognition and its deep involvement with children by the following:

Adding annually four or five new products such as high-priced Crayola coloring/activity books, Crayola "Color-Me Transfers," the "Crayola Caddy," and Crayola Children's Makeup.

Nationally distributing an in-store display called the Crayola Fun Center, which holds an array of 37 Crayola brand items.

Significantly increasing its advertising budget by 15 percent to $2.8 million. Changing the advertising focus away from print ads and toward TV.

Emphasizing the distinctive Crayola green and yellow colors on all Crayola products.

Changing some existing non-Crayola brand names, such as Artista watercolors, to the Crayola name.

Licensing the use of the Crayola name to companies selling "little people" products such as clothing, flashlights, book bags, hair clips, and jigsaw puzzles.

The results have been increased brand recognition and increased sales. Sales of watercolors, formerly Artista but now Crayola, spurted up 20 percent, for instance. (See Application 15-1.)

Application 15-1
Total Communications—Banking on Ed

(United Press International Photo)

"I'm a salesman," he says. "I started out as a salesman, and I've been a salesman all my life."

Speaking to *The Wall Street Journal* was Ed McMahon, a self-described huckster, who has become a household face as a result of the *Tonight Show.*

While most celebrities are more than willing to sell themselves on behalf of a product, Ed McMahon goes one step further. He actively solicits his advertising clients, particularly banks and other financial institutions.

McMahon places ads in trade journals and *Advertising Age* in which he outlines his endorsement services. His promotion company, McMahon Communications Inc., responds to inquiries with a four-color brochure touting Ed McMahon, and he frequently hosts cocktail parties at banking conventions.

It is quite apparent that McMahon's marketing plan works. In the past four years, he has become the commercial spokesperson for thirty-eight banks and savings and loan institutions. This work, of course, is in addition to his role for Budweiser, Alpo dog food, and Mannington Mills carpet.

Why would a financial institution want Ed McMahon as its spokesman? "You tend to think of him as selling beer or as America's greatest yes man, but the important thing to remember in marketing is that his image is on that tube every night," said Ira Nathanson, senior vice president at Unity Savings in Chicago. Unity did extensive marketing research before hiring Ed McMahon "to determine who would be the least offensive spokesman and who could carry our message the strongest." The research showed McMahon to be head and shoulders above anybody available in Chicago."

And William R. Drake likes his visibility. His agency handles the advertising for Provident Federal Savings in Boise, Idaho. "He is a walking, talking logo for Provident," says Drake about McMahon. "We can just put his face up somewhere and everyone identifies that with Provident."

Source of data: "Ed McMahon's Spokesmanship Has Become a Growth Business," *The Wall Street Journal*, July 9, 1981, p. 27.

The Communication Process

To develop total communication approaches effectively, marketers must understand the communication process. Communication is the process of exchanging meaning. It is a system comprising seven elements: source, receiver, message, message channel, encoding, decoding, and feedback (see Figure 15-3). The communication process begins with a *source* (a person, a group of people, or a formal organization like a

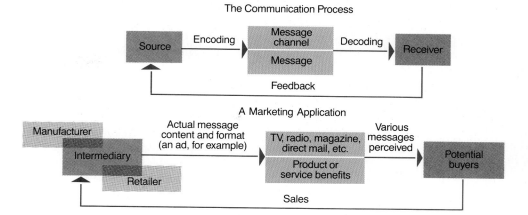

Figure 15-3 The communication process.

company) that wishes to communicate with someone else, a *receiver* (which likewise may be a person, a group of people, or an organization). The source, then, wishes to convey some idea or meaning to the receiver. The means for doing this is the *message channel,* and that which is communicated is the *message.* There are many kinds of message channels—spoken or written words, pictures, and gestures are examples. In marketing, for instance, the pictures in newspapers and magazines and spoken words on television and radio.

Effective communication depends on the key elements of encoding and decoding. *Encoding* is the process by which the source translates the meaning or idea into signs (the message), and *decoding* is the process by which the receiver interprets those signs. Obviously, how a message is encoded affects how it is decoded. Thus, encoding can greatly affect the quality of communication, and effective marketers understand this. They are acutely aware of the need to choose the proper signs to convey their meaning. The marketers of 7Up for example, chose the word *un-cola* to communicate that their beverage is a perfect substitute for cola drinks. (By playing on the word *cola,* they convey the idea that light-colored 7Up is a welcome change from all the darker beverages available.) Haagen-Dazs ice cream, although entirely American and manufactured in New Jersey, sold 40 million pints in 1980 and commanded superpremium prices. Part of its allure comes from its totally meaningless brand name which conveys the aura of "imported from Scandinavia." Bic marketers, however, ran into communication problems when they branded (encoded) their panty hose line with the name *Fannyhose,* for the market decoded the message as meaning the product was intended for heavy women. The brand was one of Bic's few failures— and the reason was faulty communication.

Many companies are turning to letters as a means of changing their image—and many obscure their identity by doing so. NLT Corp., the Nashville-based insurance holding company, clouded its identity when it changed its name from The National Life and Accident Insurance Co. The reasons for a change were many, since the corporation is much more than one insurance company. Included within the corporation are cable television production, the Grand Ole Opry, a theme park, a string of savings and loan institutions, and a computer company. But, NLT means little to those outside of Nashville. Subsequently, the company has spent heavily to recreate a public identity.

With other companies, however, the turn to letters has caused no problems. RCA (Radio Corporation of America) and PPG (Pittsburgh Plate Glass) have been successful name changes—mainly because the letters were already firmly established in the consumer's mind as abbreviations before they were officially adopted.

We can see, then, that the choice of signs used to convey a message is crucial to the successful transmission of meaning. And the key to the correct choice of signs is knowing the audience or receivers, for they will decode the message according to their own *experiences and knowledge*. Therefore, an understanding of the audience is a prerequisite for effective communication. Johnson & Johnson knew this when it introduced Tylenol, a substitute for aspirin and other pain relievers. Before becoming a brand name, the word *tylenol* had no meaning to most people, as it is a shortened form of one ingredient in the pain reliever. Its adoption by Johnson & Johnson as a brand name was based on the belief that the market would associate it with prescription drugs, which, of course, are thought to be stronger and more effective than over-the-counter products. In this case, the marketers were right; they understood the knowledge and experience of their audience, and in mid-1982 Tylenol held a 37 percent share of pain relievers. Their message was communicated effectively. But in the fall of 1982, deaths in Chicago and Philadelphia linked to cyanide-laced extra-strength capsules greatly altered consumers' associations with the word Tylenol. In other cases, sources often make the mistake of using unclear signs in their message. Words like *good, better, best,* and *improved* may have little meaning if they are not tied to some common reference point between the source and the receiver. What, for example, is meant by such phrases as "a dependable automobile," "longer-lasting taste," "more gentle to your hands," or "new and improved"?

This raises an important point. The word *communication* is based on the Latin word meaning "common." Thus, the objective of communication is to share something in common. In order for this to happen, the meaning to be conveyed must be encoded and decoded properly. That is, the source must understand the *field of experience* within which the receiver will decode a given message. Figure 15-4 depicts the fields of experience that surround the participants in the communication process. If the two fields of experience do not overlap, the participants have nothing in common, and communication will not be effective. The greater the overlap between

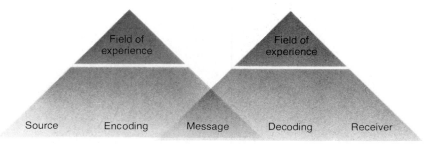

Figure 15-4 How communication works.

the experiences of the participants, the easier and more effective the communication will be.

Returning to Figure 15-3, we see that *feedback* is the means by which the source checks the degree to which the message was conveyed correctly. For example, teachers use class discussions, questions, and examinations to determine how well they have communicated with students. In similar fashion, marketers use sales results, letters of complaint, inquiries, marketing research, and advertising research to determine the effectiveness of their communication. Any problem or interference that reduces the effectiveness of communication is termed *noise*. For instance, Frost 8/80, a new liquor that *looked* like vodka but *tasted* like whiskey, failed because the marketers' visual cues (signals) did not match the consumers' field of experience in terms of sight and taste. Noise interfered with the signal, and the distortion was disastrous for the product. After less than two years on the market and an estimated loss of $2 million, Frost 8/80 was withdrawn. (See Application 15-2.)

The Nature of the Promotional Mix

Although we have seen that marketers communicate by every activity which can be detected by the market, they primarily rely on promotional activities that have the sole purpose of communicating with consumers. We will now review the five main promotional activities used by marketers: advertising, personal selling, sales promotion, public relations, and publicity.

Advertising

Perhaps because of its visibility to consumers and because of its glamour, advertising is probably the best known of all the methods of promotion. *Advertising* is an impersonal form of communication that is paid for by an identified sponsor and is relayed by the mass media—newspapers, magazines, television, radio, direct mail, transit vehicles, and billboards. Because the message channel of advertising is not personal, the message cannot be adapted to match the needs, wants, characteristics, and interests of each and every receiver or consumer. Consequently, advertising is not as targeted as some other promotional methods. Since it is aimed at mass groups rather than at individual consumers, it must make use of rather basic appeals—sex, prestige, esteem, hunger—to obtain the receivers' attention. In short, advertising messages cannot be aimed toward any one individual.

In addition, with advertising, the feedback from receivers to source is usually relatively slow. While salespersons can get immediate reactions from consumers in terms of sales (or no sales), advertisers may not get a response for quite some time. And it is often difficult to trace a sales response to any one advertisement. As a result, an advertising message is further limited in its ability to match the desires, experiences, and problems of receivers. Thus, communication through advertising is susceptible to a good deal of noise and distortion. In sum, it is no simple task to advertise effectively.

Application 15-2
Encoding and Decoding—The Not-So-Soft Drink

Anheuser-Busch, in the late 1970s, developed a new drink aimed at a special market—the adult soft-drink consumer—that would be "a socially acceptable substitute for alcohol." After considerable testing, Chelsea was introduced. This amber-colored lemon, lime, ginger, and apple blend soft drink was unique among the major brands. It contained no chemical preservatives, caffeine, or saccharin. It had a third less sugar and a third fewer calories than the traditional soft drink. It maintained a head of foam, just like beer. Expensive packaging, including foil wrapping on the bottle, distinguished the product, which was priced at a premium above all other soft drinks, including the market leader, Coca-Cola, in its five test markets.

The Food and Drug Administration, the Federal Bureau of Alcohol, Tobacco, and Firearms, and the alcohol-control boards with jurisdiction in the test markets agreed that Chelsea was a soft drink. But Chelsea's debut set off a blizzard of criticism. The "not-so-soft drink" advertising slogan implied to some that

(Courtesy Anheuser-Busch, Inc.)

Chelsea contained the "hard stuff." Its package made it look like a clone of Michelob, Anheuser-Busch's widely recognized premium beer. Even the color seemed very close to that of beer.

Chelsea's label clearly stated: "Less than ½ of 1 percent alcohol." But, neoprohibitionists used that very forthright statement to claim that Chelsea represented a "pernicious attempt to predispose children toward beer drinking." The objectors included the then Secretary of Health, Education, and Welfare, Joseph Califano, Senator Orrin Hatch of

Utah, the Seventh-Day Adventists, and the Virginia Nurses Association. None of these objectors seemed to realize that virtually all soft drinks contain traces of alcohol. Nor did they seem to understand that Anheuser-Busch was attempting to provide a *substitute* for alcohol.

Faced with boycotts and extremely negative publicity, Anheuser-Busch quickly halted advertising in its test markets, and Chelsea died a sudden death.

Source of data: "Felled by a Head of Foam," *Fortune,* Jan. 15, 1979, p. 96.

Furthermore, in absolute terms, advertising is expensive. The sponsor whose name or sign adorns the advertisement must pay for this form of communication—and pay dearly. The cost of a one-page advertisement in a major magazine easily mounts to tens of thousands of dollars, while a minute of time on the most popular

TABLE 15-1 Selected Advertising Expenditures, 1981

Rank in advertising expenditures	Company	Total expenditures, in millions	Advertising as percentage of sales
1	Procter & Gamble Co.	$671.8	5.6
2	Sears, Roebuck & Co.	544.1	2.0
3	General Foods Corp.	456.8	5.5
5	General Motors Corp.	461.0	0.6
15	McDonald's Corp.	230.2	3.2
26	U.S. Government	189.0	
54	Kellogg Co.	102.1	4.4
68	Clorox Co.	80.8	11.3
86	Hershey Foods	56.5	3.4

Source: *Advertising Age,* Sept. 9, 1982.

television shows may run as high as a quarter-million dollars. Table 15-1 gives some examples of the advertising expenditures of major companies.

In spite of these drawbacks, advertising has some distinct advantages over other promotional activities. While it is expensive in terms of absolute dollars, it is very efficient in terms of exposing the message to the market. Television, in particular, reaches a huge audience. Many marketers believe it reaches the most people for the lowest cost.

Another advantage of advertising is that the message can be conveyed to the audience many times and can be reinforced through many different media. A print from a successful TV ad can appear in selected magazines and newspapers, for example. This is in contrast with personal selling, in which the message can be delivered only when the consumer is in direct contact with a salesperson. Thus, advertising provides the opportunity for a marketer to convey the message often, in different forms, through different media.

On the negative side, however, advertising is not very flexible, since the message cannot be tailored to fit each member of the audience. And while mediocre advertising is easy to develop, good advertising is a much more difficult undertaking. Thus, not all advertising merits or gains the attention of consumers. While exposure to the message may be high, the number of receivers who actually respond to it may be quite low. Many times, the advertisement is remembered, but sales do not follow. Given the great expense of advertising, marketers may waste much effort and money if their messages are not received. Then, too, the effectiveness of advertising is difficult to measure. Finally, because of its impersonal nature, advertising is not generally as persuasive as personal selling, which we'll examine next.

Personal Selling

Personal selling is person-to-person communication in which the receiver provides immediate feedback to the source's message through words, gestures, expressions, and so forth. Such instant feedback allows the source to make instantaneous changes

Figure 15-5   While personal selling involves high costs, it's an unbeatable way to make contact with potential buyers. *(Sybil Shelton/Peter Arnold, Inc.)*

in encoding to adapt the message to the receiver. For example, if a salesperson detects that a prospective buyer dislikes the features or the price of a product, he or she can stress the advantages and benefits of the product's features, or justify the price, or even show the customer some other product. (See Figure 15-5.)

Unlike advertising, personal selling focuses on communicating with only one or a small number of receivers. This method obviously is limited to the number of personal contacts that can be made. Another disadvantage is that the cost of each contact is much higher than with advertising. Even so, because of its adaptability and its "personal" nature, personal selling has much greater persuasive impact on consumers than advertising does.

Avon Products and Fuller Brush Company are two marketers that have achieved national prominence through personal selling. In recent years, both companies have increased the number of representatives selling their products. Avon has taken the additional step of computerizing its lists of customers in order to provide better service while reducing the number of unprofitable contacts. Some 50 million households are reflected in this effort, and they are serviced by more than 300,000 representatives in the United States and Canada alone. Such figures make it clear that direct selling is a long way from becoming outmoded.

Sales Promotion

People often confuse sales promotion with the broader term *promotion,* but sales promotion is simply one special type of promotional activity. The American Marketing Association defines *sales promotion* as "those marketing activities, other than personal selling, advertising, and publicity, that stimulate consumer purchasing and dealer effectiveness, such as displays, shows and expositions, demonstrations, and various nonrecurrent selling efforts not in the ordinary routine."[1] This definition is very broad and includes a great many different activities. In fact, practically everything that we commonly think of as "advertising" but which does not use mass media falls into the category of sales promotion. Such activities include in-store displays, free samples, trading stamps, coupons, rebates, refund offers, premiums, sweepstakes, and trade shows.

Sales promotion activities are usually tied in with advertising or personal selling (or both), and they tend to support the theme of these other activities. But sales promotion is typically used to motivate consumers at the point of purchase, when they are about to make their decision to buy or not buy. Effective sales promotion can have an important impact in persuading the consumer to make an exchange. Often, sales promotion is used at infrequent intervals throughout a product's life cycle, while advertising and personal selling are used on a continuous basis. A sales promotion activity is usually intended to increase sales over a short period of time, while personal selling and advertising have long-term goals. Finally, not all sales promotion is geared toward ultimate consumers; it is used as well to spur sales to intermediaries and to industrial buyers. Intermediaries are frequently the intended audience for displays and various contests at industry trade shows and conventions.

Public Relations

Public relations (PR) is a promotional activity that aims to communicate a favorable image of the product or its marketer. Every organization deals with many important groups, called *publics,* such as stockholders, the government, intermediaries, the community at large, employees, suppliers, customers, and the news media. While public relations goes far beyond the basic needs of marketing, a favorable image certainly helps marketers to do the job of providing satisfaction. It is in this sense that public relations is considered a marketing activity, and it is often related to the marketing department or part of it.

Publicity

An activity usually included within the public relations function is *publicity,* which occurs when an organization has information disseminated about itself through the mass media but does not pay for this exposure. Publicity, then, refers to information that is communicated through newspapers, magazines, television, or radio. While an organization does not pay to have this information published, its marketers spare little effort or cost to see that the story reaches the media. Public relations personnel send press releases, feature stories, and photographs reflecting the favorable side of the organization to the media. However, this distribution does not ensure that the media will publish the information as received. They may throw it away, alter it, or completely rewrite a story before it is communicated. Marketers have little control over publicity, in comparison with advertising, personal selling, and sales promotion.

---

[1]Committee on Definitions, *Marketing Definitions: A Glossary of Marketing Terms,* American Marketing Association, Chicago, 1960, p. 20.

But when the information *is* transmitted, the audience tends to find it more believable than if it came from a sponsor, since the medium has little to gain by taking the position stated in the news item.

Publicity can result in negative images as well as positive ones. Various marketers have had to contend with adverse publicity such as that affecting artificial sweeteners (cyclamates and saccharin), asbestos in insulation and hair dryers (carcinogen), tampon usage resulting in toxic shock syndrome, and Tris in children's sleepwear. And much of such criticism is *alleged,* perhaps never to be substantiated. In any case, unfavorable publicity often leads to the banning of such products, or at least to resistance among consumers and the public at large. Ford's Pinto, accused of having an unsafe gas tank, went off the market even though Ford was vindicated in the courts. And P&G's Rely tampon was voluntarily withdrawn from the market with an after-tax loss of $75 million—even though no scientific proof was offered at the time that toxic shock syndrome was caused by Rely. (See Application 15-3.)

Application 15-3
Public Relations—Spreading the Word

Affectionately referred to as "government communicators," they are better known as "flacks." No one knows exactly how many of these public relations types are in Washington, but one estimate is 19,000. They easily cost the taxpayers $400 million a year.

These 19,000 or so PR people spin out much of the government news you read and see. While a simple press release sufficed in the past, government "communicators" have turned more and more to sophisticated tools—advertising campaigns, television commercials, videotape cassettes, full-color brochures, and glossy magazines.

Joan Claybrook, administrator of the National Highway Traffic Safety Administration, has responsibility for recalling cars for repair of defects, telling the auto industry how many miles its cars should get, telling motorcyclists to wear helmets, and warning young Americans about driving after drinking. She worries that her agency's message isn't getting across. To get her messages to the "people," Claybrook is in the TV commercial business.

"We have a very nice new public service spot about drunk driving," she says. "But we are competing with thousands of other people doing God's work, and our spot—like the rest—gets on so late at night, hardly anyone is watching."

The popular 30-second commercial is one of five produced by Masai enterprises, a black-owned advertising agency in Los Angeles. In it, actors dressed in actual costumes from *Star Wars* recreate the movie's rowdy cantina scene. The message conveyed is that even in space, you shouldn't let a drunk friend drive home. The object of the commercial, says Miss Claybrook, is a most difficult one to achieve—to change social custom.

Robert Marx, the department's audiovisual specialist, says 900 prints of this commercial were distributed to TV networks and individual stations that show the public service spot at their discretion. "We have no way of knowing how many times they are shown," Mr. Marx says. "It is a public service and we don't want to bother them with a lot of reporting requirements."

Source of data: "Washington PR Staffs Dream Up Ways to Get Agencies' Stories Out," *The Wall Street Journal,* May 23, 1979, p. 1.

The Objectives of the Promotional Mix

The basic objective of the promotional mix is the same as for all marketing activities—to bring about an exchange. Yet, the exchange may not be a sale in the usual sense. Marketers often attempt to get consumers to accept an idea ("Don't smoke") or to view a person favorably ("Ronald Reagan, man for the 80s"). And even in cases where a sale *is* the ultimate goal, promotional efforts may not be aimed toward achieving immediate results. In general, then, we can say that the objectives of promotion may be communication as well as sales.

Many marketing organizations use promotion to create, reposition, or improve a faulty identity. For instance, Allegeny Airlines merged and advertised extensively that it was now USAir. Visa changed its worldwide brand name from Bank Americard and Visa to simply Visa and accompanied the change with a massive promotional campaign. To standardize its identity, Nissan, the Japanese company that marketed Datsun cars, removed the Datsun brand and replaced it with its own Nissan name. And some marketers seek just to gain the confidence and goodwill of their market. Exxon, Texaco, and others employ advertising to communicate that they are companies conducting research on energy conservation and alternative energy sources—not just oil companies.

In Chapter 6 we noted that the exchange process begins with the recognition of a need; this is followed by an influencing period, a time of decision, the actual exchange, and consumption. And this entire sequence is followed by evaluation of the exchange. In short, any exchange is the result of various stages of experience. When marketers develop promotional activities, they know that consumers will go through these stages before the actual exchange of the product. More specifically, these stages are referred to by the acronym *AIDA: a*wareness, *i*nterest, *d*esire, and *a*ction. Marketers know that no exchange *(action)* will result unless consumers want *(desire)* the product. But desire cannot come about until consumers are first *interested* in the product. And, of course, no consumers can be interested in the product unless they are *aware* of its existence. Thus, these stages are sequential, and they represent viable goals for a promotional program. As represented in Figure 15-6, then, marketers first want to build awareness

Figure 15-6 The promotional goals of marketers (AIDA).

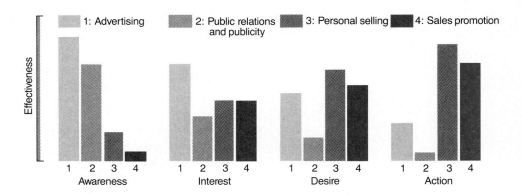

Figure 15-7 The promotional mix and AIDA.

for the product, which is consistent with their basic purpose in communicating—to inform. But once consumers *are* aware of the product, marketers turn to the persuasive aspects of communication to build interest in and desire for the product and, ultimately, to obtain action in the form of exchange.

Some promotion, however, *is* aimed at creating immediate action. Sales promotion activities come closest to this objective on a regular basis. Often, even in the cases of advertising and personal selling, the market has sufficient awareness, interest, and desire to bring about immediate exchanges. But in other situations, marketers intend only to inform about the product's characteristics, ingredients, and capabilities, and to create a favorable impression of the product so that—when a want or need arises—consumers will both *know* about the product and *want* to make the exchange. Thus, we can say that the promotional mix attempts to communicate a message as well as to secure an immediate exchange. Promotion, then, attempts to create *future* as well as *current* exchanges.

Figure 15-7 shows the relationship between the four stages of AIDA and the effectiveness of each of the five promotional methods. Advertising is seen to be highly effective in creating awareness, but its persuasive impact is less during later stages. Personal selling (with its fewer contacts) is less effective in creating awareness, but it is most effective in creating desire and action. Sales promotion has its greatest effect when pushing consumers over the threshold and into exchange; as noted earlier, its impact is greatest at the point of purchase (or exchange). Finally, public relations and publicity are helpful in creating awareness, but they have little sales impact.

The Importance of Promotion

In Chapter 1, we saw that all the functions in the "satisfaction system" are equally important. If any one function is missing, the system breaks down. The same can be said about the ingredients in the marketing mix, those activities that go together to form the bundle of satisfaction. And promotion is an especially important element of this mix for a number of reasons.

The industrial revolution provided the means to build our affluent society, and rarely today do we have to worry much about satisfying our basic needs for survival—food, water, clothing, and shelter. Instead, most of our purchasing revolves around satisfying wants. Needs, however, usually stimulate a greater drive within consumers, and so goods and services that satisfy needs tend to "sell themselves." But, with the huge number and variety of wants making up the marketplace, consumers need a great deal of information in order to understand how certain products can satisfy them. Thus, in an affluent society, there is a greater need to stimulate exchange, which is accomplished through promotional activities.

In addition, many products on the market are similar, and intense competition often exists among the marketers in an industry. Promotion can provide that extra ingredient in the bundle of utility which makes a given competitor's product just that much more satisfying. In other words, promotion itself can provide a degree of satisfaction. The emotion imparted by seeing "Mean Joe Greene" drink a Coke and then toss his sweaty football jersey to an adoring young fan; the elegance, simplicity, and beauty of the Miller High Life "Christmas Greetings" ad with the horse-drawn sleigh moving gracefully through the snow; the wittiness and entertainment of Bill Cosby's playful antics focusing on Jell-O® Brand gelatin dessert—they all lend a sizable increment of satisfaction to the bundle of satisfaction offered the market. (See Figure 15-8.)

Figure 15-8 For a wide variety of products, promotion in itself can provide satisfaction. Name three products, in addition to Miller Beer and Jell-O Brand Pudding, which appeal to you personally simply because of their promotional mix. (Courtesy Miller Brewing Company and General Foods Corporation)

Chapter 5 explained how marketers identify market segments and create specific products, prices, and distribution programs to match the needs of the segment they are striving to serve. But how can the people in a market segment know they are the goal of the marketers' efforts unless that fact is communicated? For instance, Armour Food Co. attempted to capture a large segment of the hot-dog market by appealing to children—the largest group of hot-dog consumers. Armour used the advertising slogan "Armour Hot Dogs, the dogs kids love to bite." The next year, the company attempted to broaden its market by appealing to mothers with a slightly revised slogan: "Armour Hot Dogs, the dogs moms love to bite." Eventually, the company went even further, changing the appeal to "dads" and finally to "everyone." Promotion, then, is the most effective way to tell the people in a market segment that a product is intended specifically for them.

And marketing has been referred to as "the battle for the consumer's mind." Marketers strive to find a position vis-à-vis competitive products and brands with the market's perceptions. Promotion is the key to staking a territory within the mind. Consider Colgate-Palmolive's $49 million expenditure for advertising and sales promotion for the national launch of Fresh Start laundery detergent. Commercials opened with a song, "Start the day fresh, America, get a fresh start every day." Morning scenes involving fabrics included a man donning a T-shirt and a woman getting out a tablecloth. An announcer noted, "Now you don't have to wake up to the same gray, dingy clothes. Fresh Start combines the best of powders and liquids to clean the gray even the leading detergent leaves behind." Clearly, promotion positions this brand as a heavy-duty whitener. No other of the 4 P's that create the marketing mix has as much power to position as promotional activities do.

Another reason that promotion is so important is that, in some cases, it makes up the largest part of marketing expenses. Most marketers regard promotional expenses as being top secret, and so information about such expenditures is difficult to obtain. But it has been estimated that promotional costs account for about 25 percent of total marketing costs. This makes the promotional effort an important part of any marketer's program, and doing a poor job can be very wasteful and costly.

Promotion is often the only component in the marketing mix that can be changed quickly in a time of declining sales. Other adjustments—in product, price, or place—often take more time to enact or are impossible to implement. For example, it took the automobile companies three years to adjust their cars (product) to smaller sizes when, in 1980, consumers again decided they wanted small cars. And price decreases to encourage sales may lead to lower profits, while distribution adjustments take too much time to effect. But changes in promotional appeals or the media used can be accomplished relatively quickly. Thus, changes in promotional activities can be used to stimulate purchases when sales start to falter.

Finally, promotion can be used to aid in the demarketing of certain products. It can do much to reduce the use of scarce resources. Thus, advertising asks consumers to buy smaller cars, to use less gas and electricity, and to avoid upsetting the natural balance and beauty of our forests, water resources, and air.

Determining the Promotional Mix

Chapter 13 explained that channels of distribution are determined by an analysis of various factors which dictate either a long or a short channel. Marketers must also consider many things when determining which communication activities to use—advertising, personal selling, or sales promotion—and indeed which, if any, of these activities are appropriate for the market. Because communication is a total system, marketers rarely rely on only one promotional tool. Rather, they use a combination of communication techniques, each of which supports and reinforces the others. In this way, they are more likely to communicate effectively and get their message across.

While this statement is true, marketers do tend to emphasize one promotional technique over others for specific products. In determining which promotional activity to emphasize, they must consider at least five factors: market influences, product features, the stage in the product's life cycle, costs, and company policies. We will examine these determinants of promotion now.

Market Influences

As is the case with all marketing activities, promotional decisions should be based on an understanding of the market. Its size and nature can dictate both the type of promotional tools needed and whether any methods should be limited or avoided completely. For instance, a market that is dispersed widely throughout the United States will require a large number of contacts in order to communicate a message effectively. Advertising that uses the mass media is the best way to achieve this goal, since the size of the market and the range of locations do not allow marketers to use a costly system of personal contacts. For this reason, Procter & Gamble—the company that has the largest advertising expenditures—devotes well over a half-billion dollars annually to advertising its consumer products. Other very large users of mass-media advertising include Sears, Roebuck and Company, General Foods, Warner-Lambert, General Motors, and American Home Products—all marketers with large, widely distributed markets.

The opposite situation requires a different solution. Small, geographically concentrated markets warrant emphasis on personal selling. In this case, a mass-media advertising approach would reach many people who are not really part of the market, or who are outside its geographical limits. And since the advertising must pay for each contact made, much money and effort would be wasted. Thus, it makes little sense for Mack Trucks, which wants to reach only about 300,000 potential customers, to use national television advertising to promote its trucks. Rather, Mack spends some $2 million yearly to communicate through trade organs like *Overdrive* and *Fleet Owner*.

Additionally, in concentrated markets the geographical distance between contacts is reduced, thus making it less expensive to reach all the market's members. This is why personal selling is used extensively to market industrial products, whose consumers are concentrated and relatively easy to reach. Furthermore, because industrial products are usually more costly than consumer products—and the effects of purchasing are more far-reaching—industrial buyers often need the encouragement and reinforcement that a personal contact can provide. A trucker who spends $60,000 for a rig needs the assurance of a sales representative, or even of a high-level company official.

The "personal touch" of a salesperson is not reserved to industrial products, however. Many consumers need the reassurance that a salesperson can give best. General Motors, the fifth-largest advertiser, spends about $400 million a year to promote its products nationally, even though the key to its consumer sales is still the personal contact provided by local dealers.

In determining the promotional mix, marketers also must consider their overall strategy for distributing products. In using a *push strategy,* the product is sold by the producer's salespeople to intermediaries, who in turn sell to other intermediaries or to ultimate consumers. Thus, the product is pushed as it moves through the channel. With a *pull strategy,* however, the manufacturer tries to create demand for the product so that consumers will ask retailers to supply it. Thus, the retailers have to order the product from their suppliers, and in this way the product is pulled through the channel. In terms of promotion, a push strategy needs personal selling, while a pull strategy must rely on advertising. Thus, promotional emphasis is determined by whether the marketer's receivers are intermediaries or ultimate customers.

Product Features

Analysis of the nature of the product also helps marketers to determine their promotional mix. Personal selling is emphasized when a product has a high unit value, since consumers often need persuasion to prod them into making the exchange. When a demonstration is needed to show the product's main feature—such as the suction power of a vacuum cleaner or the strength of an industrial glue—personal selling is far more effective than advertising. Personal selling is also important for goods and services that must be tailored to the needs of the market, as is the case with investment securities, insurance portfolios, industrial conveyor systems, or electrical or legal services. And goods and services that are purchased infrequently do not warrant extensive advertising. Finally, personal selling is usually needed when trade-ins are a major part of the exchange process, since the old item must be inspected and evaluated by a representative of the marketer.

Advertising is a more effective promotional tool for products that are purchased frequently, like convenience goods. Marketers of specialty and shopping products can also use advertising to create awareness, but usually some attentive personal selling is also needed to point out the advantages of the product over competing ones. Advertising is also most appropriate for products that have hidden qualities (such as the lack of phosphates in Tide detergent, the Teflon coating on certain razor blades, and the fluoride in Crest toothpaste). Advertising helps, too, in communicating highly emotional appeals (AT&T's "Reach out and touch someone"; Kodak's "Catch your memories on Kodak film"; and Virginia Slim's "You've come a long way, baby"), and when the product can be differentiated from its competitors ("Take the Pepsi challenge"; "Hertz . . . where winners rent"; and "Nothing beats a great pair of L'eggs").

Because advertising is aimed at groups, the message must appeal to all members of the group. Thus, emotional appeals and unknown aspects of the product are hooks on which to hang the message. Some products, of course, do not meet these criteria but still are rather heavily advertised. A case in point is Hallmark, which emphasizes that its greeting cards are to be used "When you care enough to send the very best."

Besides much advertising to consumers, there is substantial emphasis on sales promotion activities. Bic Pen Corporation, for example, advertises heavily to consumers but knows the value of point-of-purchase promotion as well. Numerous surveys have shown Bic that, while product advertising plays a major role in creating brand identity, seven out of ten small retail purchasing decisions are made on impulse, at the point of purchase. Thus, Bic emphasizes exciting retail displays for its 200,000 retailers in drug, food, variety, discount, stationery, and department stores.

Sales promotion is particularly effective for impulse items that have features which can be judged best at the point of purchase. The real satisfaction of toys, for instance, can be seen when consumers can pick up the toys and actually play with them. Likewise, many magazines need exposure at supermarket and drugstore checkout counters, where people can leaf through them while waiting to make their purchases.

Stage in the Product's Life Cycle

Chapter 10 observed that products go through a life cycle. After their introductory stage, they move through growth to maturity and eventually into decline. In each of these stages, the emphasis of promotional activities should vary. For instance, during the early stage of pioneering the product's entry into the market, the marketer must stimulate primary demand—demand for the product itself, rather than for a particular brand. Consumers must get used to the idea of having a trash compactor, or a video recording system or solar heating before specific brands can be differentiated. During this first stage, too, promotional attention should focus on informing and on creating awareness. The market must know that the product exists and must learn about its attributes. Exposure is the key, and advertising is the best way to get it. During the beginning stages of a product's life cycle, then, marketers must rely on advertising to build demand. (See Application 15-4.)

Also during the first stage, a product may need to be pushed through the distribution system. Getting intermediaries to accept the product may require a substantial investment in personal selling. Trade shows, fairs, and conventions are often a good way to sell the product to channel members, greatly reducing the number of contacts needed to make the product familiar and desirable.

Finally, publicity is often useful during the early stages of the life cycle. New products are often newsworthy, and communication in the form of publicity can help overcome resistance to a new idea.

As products move beyond their introductory stages, the promotional mix calls for increased advertising, but the message changes from information to persuasion. Marketers now face stiffer competition, and they must stress the benefits and advantages of their product as compared with competitors' offerings. Additionally, the aim of promotion changes from developing primary demand to creating selective

Application 15-4
Advertising in the Introductory Stage—"Priming the Pump"

Can you sell personal computers the way you sell cars, cornflakes, and antiperspirant preparations? The computer industry thinks so and is turning the marketing problem over to Madison Avenue. IBM, Tandy Corp., and Apple Computer Corp. are now relying on network television and other national media to push their wares.

Advertising for the computer makers promises personal fulfillment, warmth, and friendship. IBM's message appeals directly to a consumer's self-image, "built for a person, not for a special use." It "will help a person be more productive . . . more creative. And those are reasons for a person to feel good."

Obviously, IBM is attempting to humanize its machines. In a series of spots called "Flower," IBM features an actor who looks like Charlie Chaplin. Pantomiming, the character glances at a manual, whisks a computer keyboard onto his lap, and plays it as if he were composing a tune. Words zip across the video screen. Charlie is captivated just as he is by the fragrant deep red rose on the

How to balance the books.

To maintain a strong foothold in financial and accounting matters, a businessperson could use the IBM Personal Computer.
It helps with accounts payable by generating everything from vendor files to month-end credit records.
It saves time on accounts receivable by printing invoices and consolidating multiple transactions. The computer even writes checks.
And it uses general ledger packages that improve control and productivity today, so you won't be off balance tomorrow.
To get an in-depth account of programs from both Peachtree Software Inc. and BPI Systems, Inc., visit an authorized IBM Personal Computer dealer.
You'll find the quality of the IBM Personal Computer is what you'd expect. The price isn't. **IBM**

The IBM Personal Computer
A tool for modern times

For a store near you (or information from IBM about quantity purchases) call (800) 447-4700. In Illinois, (800) 322-4400. In Alaska or Hawaii, (800) 447-0890.

(Courtesy IBM)

table beside the machine. The rose is intended to exemplify nature's liaison with technology.

Apple Computer also advertises on network TV but takes a different approach,

sponsoring Walter Cronkite's CBS science series, "Universe." Apple's pitchman is Dick Cavett. "We picked a friendly, smart person to demystify computers and sell a friendly, smart machine," Frederick Hoar, an Apple executive told *The Wall Street Journal*.

Tandy Corp., the largest maker of personal computers, meanwhile, buys time on football broadcasts. Tandy's commercials follow the more straightforward demonstrative strategy. One shows the uses of a family computer working on a child's math problem, playing games, doing household budgets, and so on.

The manufacturer's major task is teaching and persuading potential customers to exploit personal computers. Securities analysts and IBM's competitors say that IBM's entry into the personal computer market will speed up the creation of an entire "system" to expand the applications of personal computers.

Source of data: "Makers Try the TV Sell for Computers," *The Wall Street Journal*, Sept. 4, 1981, p. 21.

demand—demand for a particular brand within a product class. Now marketers must usually invest greater sums of money in competitive promotional activities. The high cost of this often reduces further the declining profits associated with later stages of the life cycle.

During the decline stage, new products overtake old ones, which are finally abandoned. Unless sales can be revived by a change in the market or by repositioning the product, promotional expenditures are usually reduced substantially or eliminated during this stage. Advertising, in particular, is ineffective when a product's primary demand takes an unfavorable turn.

Costs

In many marketing situations, costs are the major consideration in choosing a promotional tool. But they often tend to act as a constraint, rather than as an indicator of which activity to pursue. Generally, advertising, in the aggregate, is the most expensive means of promotion. While data on advertising expenditures are difficult to obtain, the costs are high, and smaller companies usually cannot afford this expensive promotional tool. Sometimes, to make the best use of limited funds, marketers will invest their promotional budget in advertising within a small geographic area, even though the product has national appeal. Then, as the product gains market acceptance and more funds become available, the advertising audience is expanded.

The costs of personal selling vary, depending on the type of product and the personal service required. In general, though, the cost per contact is very high for this form of promotion. Salespeople require salaries, transportation expenses, lodging, and food, plus other expenses. Additional costs include those for recruiting, training, and supervising sales personnel and management. As a percentage of sales, the costs of personal selling can be rather high—say 5 to 15 percent. One way that many small manufacturing companies can avoid the high cost of maintaning a sales force is to use independent agents, thus eliminating the costs of recruiting and training. And since agents are paid on a commission basis and receive nothing until a sale is made, additional savings are possible. But agents have many other products to sell, too, and they often are not as aggressive as a company's own sales force would be.

Company Policies

Some companies develop a promotional effort that is consistent with tradition or with policies that have been built up over the years. They take pride in providing special promotional programs to preserve good relations with their customers, even though the return in terms of sales may not be as great as it perhaps could be if expenditures were allocated differently.

For instance, Brown-Forman Distillers of Louisville, Kentucky, now owns Jack Daniel's Tennessee Whiskey, but the company has not changed some of the sales promotion techniques that Jack Daniel's used to create a "homey" image for many years.

The company created the Tennessee Squires Association, whose membership is made up of faithful Jack Daniel's drinkers. Members receive a deed for a square foot of land in the hollow where the whiskey is produced, a certificate of membership suitable for framing, and a letter from the company president. Periodically, members get letters dunning them for taxes or asking permission to fish and hunt on their land.

And the distillery has long been a tourist attraction. Those who visit at noon are treated to lunch southern style at a Civil War-era boarding house. Upon their return home, luncheon attendees receive a personal thank-you from the president and a snapshot of their tour group.

Such techniques were developed when Jack Daniel's was a small regional distillery depending on word of mouth to spread its virtues, but Brown-Forman maintains that image to satisfy long-term customers and maintain good relations throughout the distribution channel.

Determining the Promotional Budget

The ultimate objective of promotion is to build sales. However, the effect of promotion on sales is almost impossible to determine. Each sale is the result of a complex interaction of all marketing activities—packaging, displays, brand name, pricing, and distribution outlets. If marketers knew the effect of a dollar spent on promotion, they would be able to determine how much is needed to generate a desired level of sales. But such is not the case. Furthermore, the relationship between sales and promotion is not always the same. Therefore, because it is difficult to know the sales effectiveness of promotional expenditures, marketers turn to other means of determining a promotional budget. The most widely used methods are percent of sales, competitive parity, all available funds (total allocation), and the task approach.

Percent of Sales

With this approach, the following year's promotional budget is determined by applying some percentage of the past year's sales, or by a percentage of anticipated sales, or by some combination of these two. The percentage figure is determined by using a traditional percentage, an industry percentage, or some formula, or simply by managerial judgment. See the percentage of sales figures in Table 15-1.

This approach is simple to use and provides a handy means of comparing competitors' expenditures. But it violates a basic marketing principle, which is that promotion is intended to stimulate sales. Instead, with this approach, as sales go down, so do promotional expenditures. Instead low sales should be stimulated by increasing the promotional budget.

Competitive Parity

Marketers often use the average ratio of promotion costs to sales for their industry in determining the amount to spend on promotion; in other words, they allocate an amount equal to that spent by competitors. This approach adds a measure of competitiveness to the strict percent-of-sales approach. However, it assumes that competitors know what they are doing and that their goals and objectives are similar to yours. That, of course, is not often the case.

The competitive-parity approach to determining promotional allocations can be seen among the marketers of medicated skin products. The top seven advertisers in

1979 spent between $6.799 million and $4.491 million, a very narrow range. Here's the breakdown:[2]

Top Advertisers	Promotional expenditures
Noxzema (Noxell)	$6,799,800
Johnson & Johnson Baby Powder	5,774,400
Porcelana (Jeffrey Martin)	5,594,500
Chapstick (Miller-Morton)	5,087,200
Johnson & Johnson Baby Oil	4,999,500
Ben-Gay (Pfizer)	4,910,900
Clearasil (Vick)	4,491,300

All Available Funds (Total Allocation)

With this approach, the marketer allocates all available funds to promotion. While this is an easy solution, it too has limitations. "All available funds" essentially means profits. But profits have little relation to promotion, since they are a function of the firm's total costs, including manufacturing, executives' salaries, administrative overhead, and so on. Thereoretically, then, this approach makes little sense. And investing all profits in promotion can easily lead to lower profits in the next period, since it may not be necessary to spend so much on promotion. Furthermore, this approach may result in lost opportunities if an upper limit is imposed but promotional expenditures still fall below the amount needed to generate a sizable change in sales. That is, the investment of just a bit more in promotion could change the sales picture dramatically, but this approach disallows the investment.

Brown-Forman Distillers Corp. used this approach to gain a foothold in the wine industry. As demand for wine surged and demand for bourbon was declining during the mid-1970s, the firm took cash thrown off by its old-line bourbons—Old Forester, its original product, and Early Times—to fund an aggressive promotional campaign for its then little-known Bolla and Cella brands of Italian wines. As a result, Bolla and Cella ranked fourth and seventh among imported wines in 1980.

Task (Objective) Approach

In determining the promotional budget, marketers should first establish what they would like to accomplish; then they can decide what promotional investment is needed to reach their goals. As we noted earlier, sales goals are difficult to relate to promotional expenditures, but that approach makes the most sense. And some firms *can* arrive at a reasonable estimate of what they will require to reach certain objectives. Marketing research and past experience are good guides. Test markets provide an experimental setting in which various levels of promotional expenditures

---

[2]*Product Marketing,* August 1980, p. 46.

Application 15-5
The Task Approach—Barclay Shoots for the Moon

For the past ten years, Brown and Williamson Tobacco Co., the United States subsidiary of British American Tobacco, has seen its market share gradually erode as companies like R. J. Reynolds and Philip Morris have flexed their marketing muscles with a host of low-tar brands.

B&W was slow to realize that smoking preferences were changing and, as a result, had no low-tar brand to offer its customer base.

In a move that will have substantial effects on the company, B&W startled the tobacco world with the most aggressive marketing campaign in cigarette history in an effort to carve out a niche in the lucrative low-tar category.

Its vehicle was Barclay. For its introduction, Barclay had an advertising and promotional budget of $150 million. This appropriation compares with $50 to $100 million traditionally spent on a brand introduction.

Hardly a magazine exists which doesn't carry a four-color Barclay ad; and many issues of some magazines will carry several ads, strategically placed throughout. Promotions have been elaborate too. For instance, instead of giving away free *packs*, B&W distributed coupons for *cartons* of Barclay and the company has paid 70,000 retailers to display the brand at their checkout counters.

Initial results show that the campaign is working. B&W claims that it now has 2 percent of the cigarette market—a marketing coup when one considers a 0.5 percent share is considered a winner in the cigarette industry.

John Alar, president of B&W, predicts that Barclay will become one of the top cigarettes "in the not-too-distant future." This status would require at least a 3 percent market share, and Barclay's share may well be 4 percent if it reaches its goal of one-fourth of the ultra-low tar (6 or fewer milligrams of tar) market.

Source of data: "Novel Barclay Pitch Fires Up Sales for Brown and Williamson," *The Wall Street Journal*, April 30, 1981, p. 29.

can be tested and observed to determine the point of diminishing returns on promotion expenditures. Results can then be applied to the total market, and an appropriate promotional budget can be determined. Finally, of course, some marketers' experience allows them to make a reasonable estimate of the costs involved in reaching certain promotional goals. (See Application 15-5.)

Looking Back

In this first chapter about promotion, we have explored how marketers communicate through the promotional mix they fashion and how they arrive at a promotional budget. Before going more deeply into the three major promotion activities— advertising, personal selling, and sales promotion—review the following important points made in this chapter:

1   Marketers communicate with their market in every activity they undertake that is perceived by the market.

2   All marketing activities should be coordinated into a "total communication" program.

3   Communication is the process of exchanging meaning.

4   Encoding and decoding are the keys to effective communication, and knowledge of the audience is a prerequisite.

5   There are five main promotional activities: advertising, personal selling, sales promotion, public relations, and publicity.

6   Personal selling is a more flexible means of communicating than advertising, but it costs more per contact.

7   Advertising focuses on groups rather than on individuals, as personal selling does.

8   Generally, sales promotion is used to support advertising and personal selling.

9   Marketers have little control over publicity.

10   Promotional objectives can be made up of communication goals as well as of sales goals.

11   Advertising is most effective during the earlier stages of AIDA, while sales promotion and personal selling are better during later stages.

12   The promotional mix is determined by the market, by the product and the stage in its life cycle, by costs, and by company policies.

13   A push strategy relies on personal selling, while a pull strategy makes it necessary to depend on advertising.

14   Of the various methods for determining the promotional budget, the task (objective) approach is most appropriate.

Key Terms

If you aren't sure what each of the following words means, look back at the text. Numbers refer to pages on which the words are defined. Additional information can be found by checking the index and the glossary at the end of the book.

communication 474
encoding 479
decoding 479
noise 481
advertising 481
personal selling 483
sales promotion 484
publicity 485

public relations 485
AIDA 487
promotional objective 487
promotional mix 491
push strategy 492
pull strategy 492

Questions for Review

1 Briefly describe the major difference between the terms *encoding* and *decoding.*

2 What is meant by *noise?*

3 Is the term *sales promotion* synonymous with *promotion?* Why or why not?

4 Briefly describe the relationship between advertising effectiveness and the stages of AIDA.

5 Indicate which type of promotional activity would be most appropriate in each of the stages of the product life cycle.

6 What is the major pitfall in using the percentage-of-sales approach to determine the promotional budget?

Questions for Thought and Discussion

1 Cigarette manufacturers have consistently spent more each succeeding year in promotional outlays, yet cigarette sales have been increasing at a smaller rate. What reasons can you give for this apparent "waste" of promotion?

2 Motion pictures are turning to promotional campaigns to increase their revenues. What types of promotional actions might be recommended for a movie such as *Raiders of the Lost Ark?*

3 What would you recommend for a promotional mix for waterbeds?

4 Do you think it pays to advertise during a recession? Why or why not?

Suggested Project

In this chapter, the logic for emphasizing advertising in the promotional mix was explained. Select five magazine advertisements which you believe defy these principles, and indicate why you chose each.

Suggested Readings

Cash, Harold C., and William J. E. Crissy: "Comparison of Advertising and Selling," in *The Psychology of Selling* (Personnel Development Associates, Box 36—Station A, Flushing, N.Y.), 1965. This often-quoted article defines the different roles of advertising and selling.

Engel, James F., Martin R. Warshaw, and Thomas C. Kinnear: *Promotional Strategy,* 4th ed., Richard D. Irwin, Homewood, Ill., 1979. This standard text treats all the decision areas of the promotional mix.

Kincaid, William M., Jr.: *Promotion: Products, Services, and Ideas,* Charles E. Merrill Publishing Co., Columbus, Ohio, 1981. This basic text describes the basics of promotion within the marketing program.

Kotler, Philip, and William Mindak: "Marketing and Public Relations," *Journal of Marketing,* vol. 42, no. 4 (October 1978), pp. 13–17. This article clarifies the roles of each activity within the firm.

Lilien, Gary L., Alvin J. Silk, Jean-Marie Chaffrag, and Murlidhar Rao: "Industrial Advertising Effects and Budgeting Practices," *Journal of Marketing,* vol. 40, no. 1 (January 1976), pp. 16–24. This article points out that research has not played an important role in determining advertising budgets.

Nickels, William G.: *Marketing Communication and Promotion,* 2d ed., Grid, Columbus, Ohio, 1980. The purpose of this book is to describe the concepts, principles, and procedures needed to create more open dialogues among society's institutions.

Nolte, Lawrence W.: *Fundamentals of Public Relations,* Pergamon Press, New York, 1974. The basic theories and principles of public relations are explained, and information is provided on implementing public relations activities.

Schramm, Wilbur (ed.): *The Process and Effects of Mass Communication,* University of Illinois Press, Urbana, 1954. This book of readings is the classic on concepts and methods of communication.

Stanley, Richard E.: *Promotions: Advertising, Publicity, Personal Selling, Sales Promotion,* 2d ed., Prentice-Hall, Inc., Englewood Cliffs, N.J., 1982. Promotion is treated as an integrated whole, since the reader is given the basic knowledge with which to understand, plan, execute, and evaluate promotional programs.

Strang, Roger A.: *The Promotional Planning Process,* Praeger Publishers, New York, 1980. This book presents a detailed description of the promotion planning process for established brands of consumer goods.

Chapter 16

Advertising

Looking Ahead

In the last chapter we saw that marketers communicate in nearly everything they do. Now we will examine the details of one of the major—and perhaps most glamorous—ingredients in the promotional mix: advertising. Advertising does much to inform and persuade consumers: by so doing, it adds another important ingredient to the bundle of satisfaction.

Key Topics

The magnitude of advertising expenditures

The different types of advertising

The advertising management process and the determination of objectives

Why the message is the heart of the advertising program

The various media that can carry the advertising message

Some social issues related to advertising

Chapter Outline

Communication, as we noted in the last chapter, is performed by marketers in many ways. For some companies—particularly those marketing packaged consumer products, like Procter & Gamble, General Foods, and General Mills—advertising serves as the major communications tool. The advantage of advertising, of course, is that the message reaches tens of thousands of people at one time. A single television commercial aired during the Super Bowl game may be seen by more than 100 million people. And advertising has given us such notions as:

"Coke is it"

"Your baby's comfort begins with Luv's"

"For all you do, this Bud's for you"

"Volkswagen does it again"

At Black Flag's Roach Motel, "Roaches check in . . . but they don't check out"

This chapter examines the different types of advertising that are available to marketers and then considers how an advertising plan is put together.

The Nature and Scope of Advertising

Advertising, which is impersonal communication paid for by a sponsoring company or organization and which uses mass media, is communication that both informs and persuades. It can change consumers' beliefs, attitudes, and images. Miller Brewing Co., for example, has continuously offered clever, entertaining television commercials with witty dialogue to push its Lite beer as "great tasting, less filling." The humor/sports personality formula featuring such celebrities as "Marvelous Marv" Throneberry, Bubba Smith, Dick Butkus, Billy Martin, Mickey Spillane, and the "spokesman for the spokesmen," Rodney Dangerfield, have greatly stimulated interest in Miller Lite Beer and have helped push Miller's overall market share from 12 percent in 1976 to 21 percent in 1980, while giving Miller Lite about 50 percent of the low-calorie beer market.

To do this job effectively, enormous expenditures are required. In fact, advertising is a giant industry in itself. In 1980, for example, companies and organizations spent $54 billion on this form of communication (see Table 16-1). This figure represents 2 percent of the country's gross national product—the total sum of all goods and services sold in the United States.

Before we explore how an advertising program is determined, we need to examine the variety of ways in which advertising can be classified. Three major elements of the communication model, the source, the message, and the receiver, provide a framework for categorizing the various types of advertising.

TABLE 16-1 Advertising Expenditures in the United States, 1980		
Advertising medium	*Expenditures (in billions)*	*Percentage*
Newspapers	$15.5	28
Television	11.3	21
Direct mail	7.5	14
Radio	3.7	7
Magazines	3.1	6
Business papers	1.6	3
Outdoor displays	.6	1
Miscellaneous	10.7	20
Total	$54.0	100

Source: Advertising Age, Sept. 14, 1981, p. 48.

The Source
The Sponsor

One way to classify advertising is on the basis of who sponsors the communication. (See Table 16-2.) Certainly much advertising comes from the producers of products. Of the 100 largest advertisers in 1981, all were manufacturers, with the exception of the U.S. government, Sears, K mart, and J. C. Penney. But intermediaries also do their share of advertising in order to communicate with their customers. The wholesalers advertise to retailers, other wholesalers, manufacturers, and service establishments. And retailers also advertise—to consumers. In fact, Table 16-1 shows that the largest advertising expenditures go toward newspaper advertising, which is sponsored mostly by retailers of goods and services, although television, with the maturing of cable systems, is expected to garner more of the retail business.

In line with a broadened concept of marketing, advertising is also used to promote nonprofit and nonbusiness exchanges. Hospitals, political candidates, environmental groups, educational institutions, the armed services, and government agencies all use advertising to communicate with their markets and stimulate changes.

TABLE 16-2
Advertising Sources

Sponsors
Manufacturers
Intermediaries
Nonbusiness organizations
Payment
Individual
Cooperative
   Horizontal
   Vertical

Figure 16-1 Public service ads, such as this one for the American Cancer Society's Anti-Smoking Program, show how nonprofit organizations use the marketing concept to promote ideas, such as good health. *(Courtesy American Cancer Society)*

(See Figure 16-1.) The Department of Defense is one of the top fifty national advertisers.

In 1980, as an example, television, radio, and print advertisements were targeted at the 4 million young American men eligible for registration for the draft. Singer Lou Rawls, United States Olympic hockey coach Herb Brooks, and actor Ken Michaelman served as spokespeople in the Selective Service System's messages. The copy message: that there is no active military draft, that registration now is merely a safeguard against an unforeseen national emergency.

Payment

While most advertising is sponsored by an individual or an organization acting alone, some is also performed under a cooperative arrangement. There are two types of cooperative advertising: horizontal and vertical.

With *horizontal cooperative advertising,* the costs are shared by a group of marketers at the same level in the distribution channel. Some of the largest advertising compaigns are of this type. Usually, they attempt to stimulate exchanges for all products, regardless of brand, or to promote an idea. For example, three companies—

Coca-Cola, Levi Strauss, and Ford—all have a deep interest in the millions of persons in this country between the ages of 18 and 29. To help market their products to this younger set, they combined their promotional efforts in a sweepstakes in which ten winners received "Denimachines"—Ford vans displaying Ford, Coke, and Levi ensignias and equipped with $10,000 in assorted accessories ranging from television sets and citizens band radios to denium upholstery. Coca-Cola claims that the fully equipped van was worth $18,000. To promote their sweepstakes, the companies spent $14 million and received 3.6 million entries, making the campaign one of the most successful contests on record.

With *vertical cooperative advertising,* costs are shared by marketers at different levels in the distribution channel. Thus, manufacturers and wholesalers may share the costs of advertising to retailers or manufacturers, and retailers may share in the cost of advertising to consumers. For example, Eastman Kodak periodically joins its dealers in advertising cameras, film, and print processing to ultimate consumers.

Of the two kinds of cooperative advertising, vertical is more prevalent than horizontal. Often, part of the agreement between the manufacturer and the retailer is that the retailer will sponsor local advertising of the manufacturer's product. This makes sense, since both will benefit as the product is pulled through the distribution channel. Additionally, the costs of the advertising are spread, and the communication is reinforced throughout the entire distribution channel.

The Message

The type and purpose of the message conveyed also provide a good means of categorizing advertising. (See Table 16-3.) *Primary demand advertising* attempts to build demand for an entire class of products. It stimulates acceptance of a revolutionary idea or concept. Thus, to promote new products in the introductory stage of the life cycle, marketers use primary demand advertising. When home computers were introduced into the American market, for example, consumers first had to be informed about the general benefits of the product. Often, too, industry trade associations or

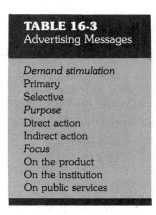

TABLE 16-3
Advertising Messages

Demand stimulation
Primary
Selective
Purpose
Direct action
Indirect action
Focus
On the product
On the institution
On public services

groups of many marketers promote primary demand for their products. The American Dairy Association urges consumers to drink three glasses of milk a day and to use butter rather than margarine. In one year the association spent $28 million convincing Americans that "Milk is a natural"—without promoting any particular brand. Similar primary demand campaigns have been sponsored by the Wool Growers, the Cotton Council, and the Florida Citrus Commission. Funding for such advertising comes from companies who are members of the industry group. For instance, the American Council of Life Insurance assesses some 1800 member insurance companies for advertising fees.

In contrast, *selective demand advertising,* is aimed at promoting a specific individual brand of product. Instead of stimulating exchanges for all competitors' brands, selective demand advertising attempts to obtain a larger share of the market for a given brand. Most advertising is of this type, even though all selective demand advertising, by its nature, stimulates exchanges for similar products. The basic difference between primary and selective demand advertising, then, is one of emphasis.

In addition, advertising messages can be classified as direct or indirect action advertising. With *direct action advertising,* the purpose is to stimulate immediate exchange behavior on the part of the receiver, or perhaps some other immediate behavior such as requesting information, sending in funds, asking for a free home trial, or soliciting a salesperson's call. For example, advertising by grocery stores in Thursday's newspapers attempts to stimulate weekend sales, and many appeals end with a command for action: "See your Ford dealer today." Sometimes television commercials give a toll-free number and encourage consumers to call immediately to get more information or to place an order. All these are illustrations of direct action advertising.

Amtrak's $11 million "Get into Training" campaign was aimed at persuading people to try traveling by train. Radio commercials supported by print advertisements emphasized passenger service, thus departing from the traditional railroad preoccupation with "hardware"—such as "Keep the trains running above everything else." As Amtrak's director of advertising and promotion told *Advertising Age:* "First-time trial is an important consideration in our advertising."[1]

Indirect action advertising is aimed instead at the attention, interest, and desire stages of consumers' awareness. While the advertiser would not mind getting immediate action, the focus is on building recognition for the brand and on gaining a favorable attitude among consumers so that when the need or want arises, they will make the exchange. Often, such advertising promotes a company's image by pointing out features and benefits of the product that are less important than the core need. Such appeals help consumers to perceive the total bundle of utility so that when the time comes, they are ready and willing to make an exchange. (See Application 16-1.)

Finally, an advertising message can be focused on the product, on the institution, or on some public service. Most often, though, advertising focuses on the product. But

---

[1]"Ads Get Amtrack 'Into Training,' " *Advertising Age,* Jan. 21, 1980, p. 4.

Application 16-1
Nonbusiness Advertising— Spreading the Word

Although business discovered the power of advertising eons ago, organized labor has just begun to use ads as a marketing tool. "The use of professional advertising by labor unions has doubled in the past couple of years," says a consultant to the AFL– CIO's building and construction trades department, "and the number of union leaders talking about it is probably up tenfold."

Much of labor advertising is designed to correct "misconceptions" about organization members. "Lots of people have the feeling that labor is just out for the next buck," Lee White, public affairs director of the Communications Workers of America, told *The Wall Street Journal.* Last year, the CWA started running nationwide TV commercials showing, for example, that a telephone switchperson may also be the neighborhood basketball team's volunteer coach.

The AFL–CIO's building trades department is experimenting with computerized direct mailings to 75,000 nonunion members in the winter of 1980. The purpose of the

mailings is to promote union views on right-to-work laws. Later mailings could reach as many as 3 million persons. Meanwhile, the American Federation of State, County and Municipal Employees is conducting research and asking potential union members for their views on labor. These data are analyzed and adopted to the union's marketing efforts.

Source of data: "More Unions Try Slick Advertising to Educate and Influence the Public," *The Wall Street Journal,* Sept. 30, 1980, p. 39.

it also can key in on building a good public relations image for the marketer, in which case it is called *institutional advertising.* Pharmaceutical companies thus often emphasize an image of competent research, integrity, and concern for consumers. And when the energy crisis drew attention to the oil industry in the mid-1970s, a rash of advertisements appeared to convince consumers of the oil companies' concern for energy conservation, for providing for future energy needs, and to the general state of the environment. During this period, Mobil Oil alone spent $10 million per year telling consumers about its policies regarding ecology and energy and about its involvement with community affairs and interests.

Another form of marketing communication is *public service advertising,* which aims to change attitudes or behavior for the good of the community or the public at large. Thus, in the 1970s, the Department of Health, Education, and Welfare sponsored advertising with the message "Be wise . . . Exercise." Similar campaigns have been mounted to get the public to stop smoking, to recycle waste products, to drive safely, and to seek help in fighting various addictions.

The Receiver

Advertising also can be classified on the basis of its target audience, its receivers. (See Table 16-4.) Most advertising that we are familiar with is consumer-oriented. Such advertising can be divided into two broad types: national and local. These terms do

TABLE 16-4
Advertising Receivers

Targets
Consumers
  National audience
  Local audience
Producers
Trade organizations

not—as is often thought—refer to geographic distinctions. Rather, *national advertising* is sponsored by manufacturers, whereas *local advertising* is directed toward consumers by retailers.

Two other important target audiences of advertising are industrial manufacturers and intermediaries. Advertising aimed at these markets is much less visible, often appearing only in trade publications like *Coal Age, Supermarket News,* and *Textile World.*

Advertising Management

Having looked at the various types of advertising, we are now ready to examine how advertisements are planned and executed, and how their results can be identified. This general process is called *advertising management.* Effective advertising does not usually result from blind luck. It demands a well-defined process that is based on the marketer's knowledge and understanding of consumers. Let's see what is involved.

Advertising Objectives

Like the marketing program itself, the advertising management process begins with the establishment of goals. Basically, the goal of advertising is to stimulate exchange. Marketers advertise in order to achieve action in the marketplace—in other words, to sell their goods and services. Often, they want immediate action. But many advertisers fail to recognize that there is an even more fundamental objective of advertising, which is to communicate effectively. And one prerequisite for obtaining exchange in the marketplace is that the desired meaning of the message actually be conveyed.

The general goal of advertising, then, is to stimulate exchange by pushing the demand curve for a product to the right (see Figure 16-2). If advertising does its job properly, for a given price a greater quantity of the product will be exchanged (quantity *B* rather than quantity *A*). Of course, this goal implies that price is not the main concern of consumers. In fact, advertising attempts to make consumers want the product so intensely that the price factor is greatly reduced or even eliminated from the exchange decision.

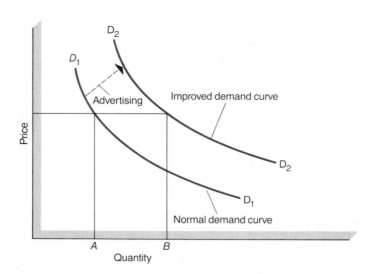

Figure 16-2 The expansion of demand through advertising.

Additionally, we have also seen that advertising often attempts to stimulate action over an extended period of time, first making consumers aware of the brand or product and then building an intention to exchange. Thus, another general goal of advertising is to create product recognition and to change consumers' attitudes to a more positive state. In general, as we noted in Chapter 15, advertising is more effective at creating awareness, interest, and desire among consumers than it is at precipitating the actual exchange.

While the broader goals of advertising are attractive, they are too general to be implemented effectively in an advertising program. Instead, marketers need specific goals that can guide them in developing their total advertising program. Usually, such objectives are stated in terms of sales, or sales assistance, or competition, or image building. We'll examine such goals now.

Sales Objective

Sales-oriented advertising objectives are consistent with the general advertising goal of stimulating exchange. When the introduction of a new product is the goal, advertising is the fastest way to inform a large market that a new product or an improved product exists. It is not uncommon for the introduction of a new product to require a tremendous advertising expenditure. When Brown & Williamson Tobacco Corp. introduced Barclay cigarettes, we noted in the last chapter, it spent more than $50 million in advertising alone during the first six months; similarly, General Foods invested more than $20 million to introduce Cycle dog food. Obviously, not every company can afford such large advertising expenditures, and neither Brown & Williamson nor General Foods expected sales results to justify their investments for a number of years. But, when the advertising goal is to achieve sales results for a new product, the cost of informing and persuading consumers is extremely high.

Advertisers also attempt to increase sales by informing and persuading the market about new uses for an existing product, thus increasing consumption of that product or brand. For this reason, Texize Chemicals Company advertises that its Glass Plus—which is labeled as a glass, appliance, and cabinet cleaner—is also useful for cleaning table tops, bathroom fixtures, and even vinyl upholstery. For the same reason, Campbell Soup Company features ads that promote recipes which include the company's soups as major ingredients. Jell-O even produces a recipe book called *The Joys of Jell-O* to demonstrate numerous additional uses for its product.

Advertising is also used to increase the sales of goods and services out of season. Thus, cleaning establishments promote the dry cleaning of woolens as a moth preventive during the summer months, and department stores offer air conditioners at pre-summer prices and skis at postseason savings.

Some marketers use advertising simply to maintain brand loyalty among consumers. Once a brand has attained a profitable market position, it usually is imitated quickly. To keep their present customers from changing to a competing brand, marketers rely on advertising. Thus, even though Coca-Cola and Pepsi Cola have maintained rather constant market shares for years (about 35 percent for Coke and 25 percent for Pepsi), both companies advertise extensively, primarily to maintain their share of the market. Coca-Cola's 1981 advertising budget, for example, was $197.9 million, while Pepsi Cola's was $260.0 million. The airline and automobile industries offer similar examples of advertising that is related to sales maintenance objectives.

Sales Force Assistance Objectives

Often advertising is used to support a salesperson's call or to uncover potential customers. Such advertising is directed toward "prospecting." It asks the receiver of the message to contact the marketer for additional information or to arrange a salesperson's visit. For instance, in an effort to obtain more corporate accounts American Express places print advertisements that include a coupon which interested parties can send to the company to obtain more information. On receipt of the coupon, American Express either mails additional information or arranges for a salesperson to visit and interview the potential customer. The coupon also provides a secondary service, since it allows the company to identify how well the campaign is going and how well the magazine or newspaper in which the ad appeared is received. In other instances, advertising reinforces the appeals offered by a salesperson or emphasizes the theme or directives of the overall advertising campaign. Such reinforcement does much to heighten the impact of a marketer's promotional mix.

Competition-Related Objectives

Some advertising is undertaken to combat the effects of competitors' advertising. While much advertising is performed in order to convince nonusers of a product to use it, a great deal more advertising aims to take sales away from competitors' brands. For years, Hershey was touted as a very successful marketer that achieved results without any consumer advertising, relying instead on word-of-mouth communication to attest to the quality of the company's products and to secure sales. But the company began losing its market share to other candy manufacturers, a situation that finally led it to begin consumer advertising in 1969. By 1980, Hershey vaulted into the top 100 national advertisers with an advertising budget of $42.7 million.

U-Haul International, Inc., also provides an example of setting competitive objectives. The company was shaken by competition from Jartran, Inc. Founded in 1978, Jartran became the first company in years to compete with U-Haul in renting one-way trailers for use between cities. In 1981, U-Haul suffered a $13 million loss compared with profits of $23.6 million the year earlier. U-Haul blamed that loss almost entirely on Jartran's aggressive $6 million advertising campaign in 1980. The ads claimed Jartran's vehicles were safer, more comfortable, and more fuel-efficient— for lower rental prices. To counter, U-Haul launched its own $6 million ad campaign in consumer and recreational magazines to help persuade potential dealers of its support. Prior to the Jartran challenge, almost any media advertising beyond the Yellow Pages was considered frivolous by the company founder.

Image-Building Objectives

Companies often initiate institutional advertising to improve their image within the overall market. Such advertising may be targeted toward consumers or toward intermediaries within the trade. Slogans like "We bring good things to life" (General Electric) and "When E. F. Hutton talks, people listen" help to create a positive image.

Sometimes a more defensive approach to image building is required. For instance, Life Savers brought out a new bubble gum called Bubble Yum that quickly became the hottest product to hit the billion-dollar chewing-gum industry since sugarless gum. But rumors somehow swept through the Greater New York area claiming that the gum was laced with spiders' eggs—a rumor that clearly took its toll on sales. To combat this situation, Life Savers placed full-page advertisements in thirty newspapers throughout northern New Jersey, southern Connecticut, and New York. "Someone's telling your kids very bad lies about a very good gum" proclaimed one ad that ran in the papers. Through such advertising, Life Savers managed to convince consumers that nothing was wrong with its product.

Developing the Message

At the core of effective advertising is the translation of the objectives into a specific message which the marketers must then encode. As noted in Chapter 15, this demands sound knowledge of the market. Like all marketing activities, then, effective advertising depends on the good performance of marketing research.

The development of the message produces the focal point for the entire advertising program. All other steps support the message and aid in its delivery. Among the early steps of message development are the tasks of writing copy, selecting illustrations, and preparing the layout. *Copy* includes all the written or spoken elements of the message, including headlines, the advertiser's name and address, coupons, and the message itself. The copy should directly reflect the objectives of the advertising, for these objectives are the reason why the message is being created. The language and urgings of the copy must also reflect the product's positioning. For instance, the decision about whether Granola bars and Space Sticks are to be sold as candy substitutes, as snack foods, or as desserts would greatly affect the content of the message. The theme provides a thread by which various advertisements are tied together to maintain an association between the marketer and the product. Advertising messages and their themes can be low key, with little pressure toward immediate action on the part of consumers, or they can be hard-hitting and aimed at direct, instant results in the marketplace. Recessionary times and intense competition seems to have resulted in a tendency for many of today's marketers to take the second (i.e., the "hard-sell") approach in developing their messages.

The *illustrations* used in advertising may consist of photographs, graphs, charts, painting reproductions, drawings, cartoons, or any other kind of visual devices that accompany the copy. Such devices can be used to gain attention, to arouse interest and desire, or even to lead to desired action. The illustration program should relate to the appeal and wording of the copy. Cartoons and animation have been used often and successfully to get an advertising message across. For example, in little more than ten years, Vlasic Pickle Company has clobbered Heinz, Del Monte, and other marketers with a campaign that used only cartoons. Vlasic's approach has also helped to boost per capita pickle consumption to 10 pounds per year—attesting clearly to the important potential that advertising illustrations can hold.

The *layout* of an advertisement is its overall structure—the positions assigned to the various elements of the copy and illustrations. The placement of headlines, copy, illustrations, and the marketer's name and logo—as well as the amount of free space in the ad—all contribute to its effect. The layout helps to tie the ad together and can add much to its final impact.

Common Advertising Approaches

Advertisers can take many approaches in developing their messages. Some of the more common approaches are the following:

1 Testimonials are advertising messages that are presented and endorsed by someone who is seen as an expert and is trustworthy and believable to consumers, rather than an unknown model or actor. James Garner and Mariette Hartley reportedly receive $3 million a year for their sincere and amusing conversation about Polaroid products. (See Figure 16-3.) So, ensuring believability does not come cheaply. (See Application 16-2.)

2 Humorous advertising falls into the soft-sell category, but there is a danger that the humor will overshadow the message and the product. Some cite Alka-Selzer's commercials ("I can't believe I ate the whole thing") as being a classic example of how a humorous message can attract wide attention but still fail to boost sales. Some even think the commercials contributed to the product's sales decline. On the other hand, we have noted the impact of humor for Miller Lite beer.

3 Sex is and has been an often-used appeal and illustrating device for advertising messages; however, research shows that generally it is not very effective in getting a message across. Consumers tend to focus on and give attention to the sex object while ignoring the sponsor's message. Brooke Shields's advertising for Calvin Klein designer jeans, however, proved extremely effective. Sales jumped by as much as 300 percent during parts of the campaign—although much of this increase may be attributed to publicity given the series. Researchers have also

Figure 16-3   Storyboard for one of the series of testimonial ads Polaroid uses to promote its products. (Courtesy Polaroid Corporation)

found that sexual appeals work differently for males and females. Men are more likely to give attention to advertising that includes nudity, while women are much more attracted by scenes that convey a romantic setting.

4   Comparative advertising now names the sponsor's competitors and in many instances undercuts their products. Until 1973, the television networks followed a policy of not directly naming competitors in ads, but in that year the Federal Trade Commission pressured them into allowing it. Examples include Remington Rand's claim that its electric razor Mark III "took off an average of 18 percent more beard than Schick"; TWA's challenge to American Airlines and United Airlines on terms of "on time" performance; and the so-called Pepsi Challenge, which claims that many Coke drinkers prefer Pepsi in blind taste tests.

5 "Slice-of-life" advertising portrays consumers in realistic or reasonably realistic situations. The people, settings, and comments depicted in such ads are easily identifiable and consistent with consumers' perceptions of their lives and lifestyles. Such advertising has introduced us to such lovable characters as Mr. Whipple (Charmin tissues), Madge the manicurist (Palmolive dishwashing liquid), Rosie (Bounty towels), and the lonely Maytag repairman.(See Figure 16-4.)

6 Musical themes stress association between the brand advertised and some jingle or song. Successful jingles can keep the brand in the top of the consumer's mind. Two examples: "Our L'eggs fit your legs" and Diet Pepsi's "Now you see it . . . now you don't."

7 Fantasy advertisements stress the ideal self-image of the potential buyer. Thus, many perfume and cosmetics commercials stress the impossible but desirable.

Application 16-2
Testimonials— Sometimes You Win, Sometimes You Lose

Fees for a full-blown celebrity to go on television and endorse your product can range anywhere from $100,000 to over $1 million annually. And while celebrities can provide a product with a major push, they can likewise result in embarrassment and a tremendous credibility loss, to say nothing of dollars.

Marketers know that any celebrity endorsement can backfire, and there are numerous examples of advertising campaigns which have come to crunching halts because the celebrity slipped.

When Roberto Duran surrendered to Sugar Ray Leonard in the much-heralded welterweight title bout of 1980, not only the gamblers who had

bet on Duran shed tears but executives of 7Up were a little more than dismayed—they had just cut a series of commercials featuring Duran.

"Even if you've got Saint Peter, you've got some kind of risks," an advertising executive told *The Wall Street Journal*.

Marketers can never be absolutely certain that their celebrity will not stumble; atheletes fall into slumps, celebrities show up in X-rated movies, and death intervenes occasionally to destroy even the most creative and expensive commercials.

The risk of using stars also holds the chance for great success. Lever Brothers decided on George

Brett, third baseman for the Kansas City Royals, to promote Lifebuoy soap. Lever's advertising executives began to worry when Brett was injured early in the season, but he soon returned to lead the American League in hitting. Lever Brothers was jubilant.

The risks, while intimidating, are worth the anxiety to many marketers. A credible spokesperson can create awareness for a product in rapid order.

Source of data: "When Ads Feature Celebrities, Advertisers Cross Their Fingers," *The Wall Street Journal*, Dec. 4, 1980, p. 33.

Figure 16-4 By portraying Mr. Whipple in Charmin's slice-of-life advertising campaign, actor Dick Wilson has become one of the most memorable advertising characters of all time. (Ira Berger)

8 Scientific evidence ads present the results of research to substantiate the claim made by the sponsor. Crest toothpaste has long used clinical tests to show its cavity-fighting ability. (See Application 16-3.)

Selecting the Media

While the message is the heart of an advertising communication, it cannot be successful if it is not presented to the market. Thus, the proper message channel must be selected to convey the message. The proper placement of an advertisement is as important to effective communication as the message itself is.

Early in the chapter, Table 16-1 listed the various mass-media and advertising expenditures for 1980. Each of these media has its own characteristics that result in advantageous or disadvantages. Marketers must understand these characteristics in order to select the proper medium for their message.

Newspapers

Newspapers claim the largest share of advertising expenditures (28 percent). This medium offers extensive market coverage on a local level, for almost every home receives a newspaper that is read by many members of the family. Newspapers are a

Application 16-3
Advertising Message—
Let an Ad Be Your Umbrella

While most marketers still hold to the tried-and-true method of advertising a single brand, more and more marketers are experimenting with what is called the umbrella strategy.

Best known for the umbrella type of advertising is General Electric's image ad with its theme of "We bring good things to life." Within a 60-second spot, GE gets its image message across, along with plugs for as many as thirteen different products.

Another company experimenting with the umbrella message is Scott Paper, which pushes four different types of paper products as "Value products

from Scott." Joining the list of umbrella converts are Nabisco, Procter & Gamble, Johnson & Johnson, Purex, and R. J. Reynolds Tobacco.

Often the umbrella message is used to give a lagging or minor brand a push in the national media when, if the product stood alone, the message could not be economically justified.

"Everybody has some doggie brands," a food marketer told *The Wall Street Journal.* "If you try to promote them alone, you've got a zero."

Umbrella tactics need a common theme, such as Scott's emphasis on value. A Johnson &

Johnson umbrella-strategy promotion used National Baby Week to promote twelve brands. But advertising messages can become blurred and, critics say, the messages sometimes overshadow the products. "General Electric's ads are nice," says the marketing vice president for a company that has used umbrella advertising, "but I keep waiting for them to sell me something."

Source of data: "Umbrella Tactics Can Help Sell Products and Cut Costs," *The Wall Street Journal,* July 16, 1981, p. 27.

flexible means of delivering advertising messages, since ads can be inserted with only a few days' notice, and their copy can be more complex than the broadcast media allow. Production quality is fair, and the cost per contact is relatively low. Finally, the message is as permanent as the newspaper itself.

However, newspapers have some disadvantages, too. With the exception of a few papers like *The Wall Street Journal* and *The New York Times,* most newspaper circulations are local; they do not reach national or large regional markets. The reproduction quality is poor, compared with that of magazines. This drawback keeps marketers from placing newspaper ads that require intricate detail or flawless reproduction.

Magazines

Magazine advertising can have strong visual impact because of good reproduction quality, and most nationally distributed magazines offer marketers regional advertising space as well. Magazines have well-defined, highly identifiable markets, so marketers can match the target audience to the magazine's audience. Furthermore, magazines are kept for a longer time than newspapers, and they are read by many people other than the individual who subscribes. For example, *Business Week* has a pass-on rate of

4.5 which means that an average of 4.5 people read *every* copy sold. In addition, magazines are read at a more leisurely pace than other print media, and so it is more likely that the advertising will be seen and understood. But magazine advertising is expensive when compared with newspaper advertising, and magazines are not published as often.

Television

Television is the fastest-growing mass medium. It reaches virtually all target consumers, since few homes are without a television set. Homemakers can be reached during the day; children are in the audience on Saturday mornings; and businesspeople are tuned in most evenings. Thus, by choosing an appropriate time, program, and station, an advertiser can reach the target audience fairly accurately. Television also provides marketers with geographic flexibility, for they can choose between national and local advertising. Most important, however, is the distinct advantage that television can convey a message to both the eyes and the ears. The impact is enormous. Some distinctive advertising aimed at potential television advertisers has billed the medium of television as "the sum of all the alternatives," attesting to its high impact.

The obvious disadvantage of television is its cost. In 1981, a 30-second commercial on *M*A*S*H* or *60 Minutes* was priced at $150,000. Super Bowl XVI in 1982 drew $345,000 for a 30-second advertisement. No wonder that only the larger marketers, such as Gillette, Miller Brewing, Exxon, and Coca-Cola, are placing commercials at Super Bowl time. Another disadvantage is that a television message is not permanent; it is lost forever if the market's members are not viewing precisely when the message is aired. And television does not lend itself well to long messages, such as those needed for specialized products like heavy equipment. (See Application 16-4.)

Cable TV Systems

Cable, although on the scene for decades, is coming of age as scores of companies rush to set up systems. Before very long, viewers may well have a selection of sixty or more channels, and the maturity of this medium will most definitely impact advertisers. In the future, advertisers attempting to reach a select segment of the market hope to be able to buy advertising time on a cable system that programs to a specific audience, like sports fans or classical music devotees. Already, a New York production company is putting together a financial news program and is making its advertising pitch to corporations that now advertise in magazines like *Business Week* and *Fortune*.

Radio

Radio serves local markets and offers extensive local coverage to advertisers. It is also very selective. For example, rock stations appeal to young members of the market, while classical stations tend to have more mature listeners. And many stations focus on special-interest groups, appealing to Hispanics, blacks, blue-collar workers, high-income groups, and so on. Radio is also a relatively inexpensive advertising medium. Finally, it is fairly flexible in that commercials can be placed at deadlines very close to airtime.

Like television messages, however, radio messages last only for a short time. Moreover, since they appeal only to our sense of hearing, messages that require visual impact cannot be easily conveyed by radio.

Application 16-4
Television Commercial Production—
A Million Saved Is A Million Earned

Over $5 billion was spent on network television advertising in 1981. That was a 10 percent surge over 1980. The filming of commercials alone cost nearly $500 million. Producing a 30-second commercial ran between $45,000 and $60,000. With these huge sums, corporate financial experts are now looking to reduce these expenses. Two large advertisers, the Gillette Company and General Foods, figure they save more than $1 million annually by such experts' service. "We are watching every buck. The more that is saved on production, the more money there is to buy air time," said the manager of marketing services at Eastern Air Lines, Inc.

Procter & Gamble, whose network TV budget is nearly $400 million, has cut $1500 per commercial by using 16-millimeter film rather than the better quality but more expensive 35-millimeter

film. P&G and some other large advertisers use in-house staffs to scrutinize the bids of competing producers. And at P&G and General Foods, a "cost plus fixed fee" system is used whereby the advertiser pays the costs of the producer plus an amount for the producer's profit and overhead. Since all costs are fully documented, this system allows greater control over production costs.

On other fronts, costs are checked by renting sets rather than building them. Commercials for Heublein's Harvey's Bristol Cream were shot in a New York City mansion rented for $2500 per day. "If you had to build what was in that home, it would cost you $9000," said a production director for D'Arcy-McManus & Masius, Inc., Heublein's ad agency. The agency also created four Golden Griddle syrup commercials at the same time.

The cost was $100,000. If not produced together, the cost of each commercial would have been $34,000. And with rising wages negotiated for actors by their union, the Screen Actors Guild, the number of people performing in commercials has been reduced. In filming a commercial for *Shibumi,* a best-selling book of Ballantine Books, Inc., showing the full face of a model was avoided. Thus the model could be paid as an extra rather than as a principal.

While there is a lot of concern over costs, some advertisers believe the selling impact may be lost. One producer declared that too great attention to financial considerations is "not conducive to good creative work."

Source of data: "Cutting the Cost of Commercials," *Business Week,* Feb. 15, 1982, pp. 118–121.

Direct Mail

Direct mail is the most personal and individualized of all the mass media. It is certainly the most selective, for each contact is selected individually (or in groups that share some common bond, like income). Direct-mail advertising has a minimal amount of waste circulation; that is, most of the people it reaches are members of the target market. The copy can be very flexible, and each letter can appear personalized. The quality of the reproduction of the letter can be geared to meet the specific needs of the market, and the time of the message is not restricted. On the other hand, many consumers consider direct-mail advertising to be "junk mail," and they dispose of it quickly without reading it. Also, since the costs of mailing are rising, the cost per contact can be quite high.

Outdoor Advertising

Outdoor advertising involves the use of billboards and other signs and displays as advertising media. Most billboards are owned privately and are rented to advertisers for a period of time. Generally, a number of sites are used in order to get wide exposure. Outdoor advertising is more effective when it includes motion; thus, some cigarette billboards blow smoke rings, and some beer billboards show the bottle tipping to pour. In general, billboards and signs offer flexibility and intensive market coverage.

Again, however, there are some negative features to this form of advertising. Unless the product is widely used, there is much waste circulation with outdoor advertising. While local campaigns may be economically feasible, national coverage through this medium is extremely expensive. And the message must be short so it can be large enough to be easily seen when placed on the billboard.

Transit Advertising

Transit advertising makes use of signs inside and outside buses, taxis, streetcars, and commuter trains. (See Figure 16-5.) Like other outdoor advertising, this medium exposes the message to a captive audience and can be targeted to specific markets—to commuters and travelers, for example. It also provides the opportunity to repeat the message, since consumers often use the same transportation method more than once. Finally, transit advertising is a relatively inexpensive medium for conveying the marketer's message. Again, however, the message must be fairly short, and it is delivered only to those within the vicinity of the ad. (See Application 16-5.)

Figure 16-5 Transit advertising: moving "billboards" provide high exposure at a relatively low cost. (Randy Matusow)

Application 16-5
Transit Ads—Putting Bugs into Advertising

Advertisers are constantly searching for visibility, and that they get from Beetleboards International. Breaking with traditional media in 1972, Charles E. Bird, a Los Angeles marketing consultant, put 100 brightly painted Volkswagens on the road splattered with pop-art decals advertising United Airlines, Sony, and *Time* magazine. By 1978, over 8800 Beetleboards were puttering through Canada and the Caribbean as well as the United States.

Advertisers pay $175 a month for each car (though quantity discounts are available). Privately owned Beetles are used, though the owner must meet strict requirements. Safety, insurance, and age legality conditions must

be met (cars advertising cigarettes must be driven by owners over the age of 21), and drivers must put on an average of 42 miles a day. Only well-coiffed owners can advertise Clairol hair products, and only ski club members advertise Stag ski wear, all in an attempt to make drivers and products compatible. VW owners get a paint job, decals, and $20 a month. (The company also pays as much as $175 to have the decals removed.)

Dr Pepper Company launched a unique campaign using twenty-seven vehicles in the Dallas–Fort Worth area. The Beetles were designed to look as though they had a see-through body. The design reveals a driver dressed in blue jeans and a back

seat loaded with Dr Pepper. The slogan "I'm a Pepper" and "Be a Pepper" cover the doors and the fenders.

Do Beetleboards work? Apparently so. Burke Research found recall for Beetleboards was 11 times greater than for billboards, and Pounders & Associates found brand recall for Bacardi imports grew from 9.5 to 34.7 percent.

Sources of data: "How Beetleboards Put the Bugs into Advertising," *The New York Times,* Jan. 8, 1978, p. F3; "Beetleboards Keep Growing: Enters Caribbean with Foreign Moves Ahead," *Marketing News,* April 7, 1978, p. 6; and "Beetle Boards Get New Vehicle," *Advertising Age,* June 16, 1980, p. 315.

Criteria for Selecting Advertising Media

With all the advertising media available to marketers, how do they select which ones to use? Table 16-5 compares the relative advantages and disadvantages of the various media in terms of the characteristics we have examined. The decision regarding media selection is clearly a crucial one. While it may seem that most attention is given to building the message, improper placement of advertising can destroy its overall effect. The message may involve more creative processes, but media selection is the crucial act of matching the advertiser's needs and objectives with the characteristics of the audience. Because some two-thirds of every marketer's advertising budget goes to place messages in the media, the following factors are extremely important in the selection:

1 The objectives of the advertising program

2 The characteristics of the medium under consideration

TABLE 16-5   Media Characteristics Compared (plus = relatively high, minus = relatively low)

Medium	Audience size	Selec- tivity	Exposure time	Quality of repro- duction	Complex- ity poten- tial	Wasted circu- lation	Flexi- bility in placing the ad	Avail- ability of medium	Prestige	Cost
Newspapers	+	+	+	−	+	+	+	+	−	−
Magazines	+	+	+	+	+	+	−	+	+	+
Television	+	+	−	+	−	+	−	−	+	+
Radio	+	+	−	−	−	+	+	+	−	−
Direct mail	−	+	−	+	+	−	+	+	−	−
Outdoor	+	−	+	−	−	−	−	−	−	−
Transit	−	−	−	−	−	−	−	−	−	+

3   The characteristics of the medium's audience

4   The requirements for properly conveying the message

5   The cost of the medium

Media selection is essentially a matching process. If the marketer wants to introduce a new product, for example, the medium chosen should offer wide coverage of the potential market. Thus, direct-mail and transit advertising would probably be poor choices. But perhaps the most widely used criterion for selecting an advertising medium is the profile of its audience. *Cosmopolitan,* for instance, reaches 13.5 million readers over 17 years of age. Compared with national averages, the 1981 *Cosmopolitan* reader had the following characteristics:

	Percentage of Cosmopolitan readers	Percentage in average United States population
She's young (18–34)	65.4	38.5
She's well educated (attended college)	44.3	28.0
She works	65.2	48.1
She makes money (individual income $10,000+)	30.8	20.7
She's big city (metro areas)	79.8	73.3
She's single	50.9	38.4
Median age	29.9	42.3

Thus, if a marketer wanted to convey a message to just such a market, *Cosmopolitan* might be an appropriate medium. Nearly all media have such audience profiles, and the selection of media is essentially a process of matching the target audience goals of the advertiser to the opportunities for reaching an audience by various media.

The medium chosen must also be able to convey the message intended by the marketer. Some media are not suited to demonstration, verbal explanations, or complex messages—an important consideration in selecting a medium. Another important factor is the relative cost of the medium, though this usually acts more as a constraint than as an indicator of the best medium. Overall, it is quality that counts, not quantity. It is far better to use the one medium that best matches the audience than to use a number of media that do not reach the target market.

To emphasize this point, some marketers use the *cost-per-thousand* (CPM) figure as a guide to making media buying decisions. CPM is the dollar cost per each 1000 readers or viewers. For example, if *Time* magazine charges $63,895 for a full-page, four-color ad and has a readership of 20,881,000, the cost per thousand readers will be $3.06. If the cost for a similar full-page, four-color ad in *Newsweek,* with a readership of 17,908,000, is $45,665, its cost-per-thousand will be $2.55. Thus, a surface examination will indicate that *Newsweek* will be a more efficient medium to reach consumers. Yet such cost comparisons hide important differences: Both magazines don't reach exactly the same consumers; one magazine may get greater attention to ads than the other does; an advertisement in one magazine may be seen as more believable than an ad in the other; and where many placements are used, using different magazines may have a greater impact than massing exposures in one magazine.

R. J. Reynolds, for example, in one year relied almost exclusively on the cost-per-thousand method for spending. The approach caused RJR to become too heavily represented in mass-circulation magazines. Six to eight different RJR brands could be found in a single issue. Not only did this abundance produce clutter, but ads for the Winston and Camel brands, smoked mostly by men, often appeared in women's magazines. Clearly, this method of media selection must be used with caution.

Measuring the Effectiveness of Advertising

Perhaps one of the most difficult problems facing marketers is that of assessing the effectiveness of their advertising. Individual advertisers spend millions of dollars on this activity, and yet they do not really know much about how well it is working. The difficulty arises because the effectiveness of advertising is most often tied to sales. Marketers want to see sales results for their advertising dollars, even though advertising is only one of the activities they undertake to achieve a sale. Many things go into a consumer's decision to exchange—the product, its package, its warranty, its price, and the ads that the consumer has seen or heard. But it is almost impossible to calculate precisely just which sales were produced by advertising. The major exception to this limitation occurs with direct-response advertising, when the consumer must immediately return a card or send in money. In that case, the effect of advertising is easily measured.

Regardless of the difficulties in measuring the effectiveness of advertising, marketers do use various methods to test results at two stages in the advertising process: (1) to see whether proposed advertising should be used and, if it will be, how it might be made better; and (2) to see whether existing advertising should be continued, modified, or stopped. To answer these questions, marketers use *pretests* (before the advertising is transmitted to the target market) and *posttests* (when the ads have been implemented). Posttests are especially useful in providing information for the development of future advertising.

Pretests provide marketers with information about the likelihood of an ad's success. Most pretests involve a panel, or "jury," of people who react to ideas, concepts, pictures, appeals, and layouts before these are communicated to the market at large. Early in the process of creating advertising, the marketer may use a *focus group interview,* in which a group of consumers who represent the market at large are questioned about various aspects of the ad. Discussion often leads to changes in wording, layout, appeals, and colors used. The consumers' opinions are considered more reliable than the judgment of the marketers.

As print ads approach their final form, groups of consumers are often asked in a pretest to choose which ad they prefer among pairs of ads in a series. Or they may be asked to rank the ads in a way that gives the marketers a better idea of which advertising options appear best. In addition, consumers may be asked to evaluate advertising in terms of their likes and dislikes.

In pretesting commercials for the broadcast media, marketers sometimes use projection rooms in trailers to show the ads to consumers, who then either discuss the ads, fill out a questionnaire about their effectiveness, or select the one commercial they like best. But such tests are questionable. The simulated "at home" viewing situation is still artificial, and marketers should be careful when drawing conclusions from such tests.

Recognizing the problems of measuring the direct effects of advertising on sales, marketers turn to posttests that indirectly measure consumers' abilities to recall ads and recognize brands. To test the effectiveness of print advertising, personal interviews are conducted to guide consumers through the magazine or newspaper page by page. Respondents are classified into groups (expressed in percentages), depending on whether they (1) remember seeing a particular ad, (2) associated the sponsor's name with the ad, and (3) read half or more of the copy. Starch Readership Reports, a research service, labels these three categories "Noted," "Seen-Associated," and "Read Most." These classifications can then be combined to provide an indication of recognition for an ad. With the Starch service, entire advertising campaigns can be compared over a long period of time, or an individual ad can be tested. The Starch service also provides in-depth interviews to get more information about consumers' reaction to advertising.

For posttesting television advertising, marketers can use the Total Prime Time (TPT) studios of Gallup & Robinson. In this case, sample television viewers are asked to trace their individual viewing patterns for the previous evening. Their ability to recall commercials is then tested in terms of sales points and persuasiveness. Two scores—"Commercial Recognition"(CR) and "Proved Commercial Registration" (PCR)—are reported for every commercial that is broadcast during prime-time viewing hours. Respondents are asked such questions as "Which ads for automobiles do you recall seeing?" "What did the ad look like?" and "What did the person in the commercial say?"

Although these pretest and posttest measures have been used with some degree of success, much improvement is still needed. Since the major goal of advertising is to precipitate exchange, it is necessary to develop positive attitudes toward the product or brand. Instead, most posttest research into advertising effectiveness deals only with the early stage of product awareness. A more appropriate measure of the effectiveness of advertising would focus on attitude changes and how they influence exchange behavior. (See Application 16-6.)

Application 16-6
Measuring Advertising Effectiveness—
"It's the Best We Can Do! Or Is It?"

One of the major problems facing marketers is how to weigh the effectiveness of advertising, and despite the many electronic marvels of this age, evaluation is still a sought-after art.

Lack of expertise is reflected in the number of TV commercials which are produced and never seen by the vast majority of viewers. It is estimated that more than 4000 commercials, valued at $75 million, are made annually but scrapped.

Why are they scrapped? Advertisers, for lack of any quantitative methods of evaluation, rely largely on a company, Burke Marketing Research, which evaluates commercials by the random telephone survey.

Commercials are run in several major cities, and interviewers then call viewers to see if they recall seeing the commercials. The ad is given a recall rating from 0 to 100. An average score is about 25. If very few respondents recall the ad, then, more times than not, it is declared a dud and is scrapped.

Many marketers feel that advertisers often rely too heavily on this system.

Details on the survey results, including comments from consumers and recall scores for specific elements of the commercials, are sent later, but the score figure is the center of the recall controversy. "People are looking for a magic number that'll free them from decision making," says Shirley Young, executive vice president of Grey Advertising. "Those who will defy the numbers are few and far between."

Many advertising research executives say young managers, eager to make scientific judgments, often rely too heavily on Burke flash scores. Young & Rubicam, the nation's largest advertising agency, has also criticized the reliability of the recall "flash" scores. The agency found scores varied when commercials were retested. One commercial scored only an 8 on its debut but a 21 on its second run. Scores may also be affected by the type of show in which the spot appears.

A spokesperson for Burke counters criticism by saying that many marketers overestimate the test's power. "We never said it does everything. The best place to measure the effectiveness of advertising is at the cash register, but that is very difficult to do."

Source of data: "Should 200 Viewers' Memories Decide Whether Ads Live or Die?" *The Wall Street Journal,* July 24, 1980, p. 19.

Advertising Agencies

Most large retail stores have their own in-house advertising departments to handle the entire advertising process—from planning and designing ads, to writing copy, to laying out the ads, to placing them in media. In small manufacturing companies, advertising management is usually undertaken by the sales division. In large marketing companies, there is usually a separate department that oversees all advertising activities. In general, as companies get larger in size, they tend to look for help from advertising agencies.

Advertising agencies are privately owned firms that specialize in performing the tasks of advertising. Such agencies began as brokers for the media; they located advertisers to buy newspaper space. But today's agencies are another matter. Now, they devote their efforts to providing important services for their clients, namely, the advertisers. Full-service agencies perform a complete range of activities, from planning a campaign through its execution and evaluation. Some agencies have gone a step further, offering many marketing activities that are not related to the media, such as marketing research and package design. Thus, some agencies today can be seen as marketing consultants.

What an Advertising Agency Does

As illustrated in Figure 16-6, most advertising agency personnel fall into five major categories: research, creative, production, and media people, and account executives. The research arm complies information about the clients' advertising campaigns,

Figure 16-6 The advertising agency.

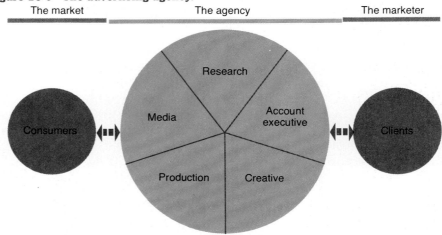

conducts surveys among consumers, and coordinates the evaluation of advertising effectiveness. The creative department comes up with new approaches to advertising and is responsible for designing the ads used. The production department must translate these ideas into actual messages. When television is involved, this department produces or coordinates the filmed commercials. The media department selects the media in which the advertising will be placed; it matches the characteristics of various media audiences with those of the target market. The account executive provides the link between the agency and its client-advertisers. This executive keeps the lines of communication open between the advertiser and the agency, as well as coordinating research, copy, production, and media activities within the agency. All activities performed by the agency are approved by the client, under the account executive's guidance.

Compensation of Advertising Agencies

Advertising agencies are compensated indirectly, not by the advertisers but by the media in which ads are placed. This practice reflects the origins of the agencies and their role as representatives of the media. An agency receives a commission, generally 15 percent, on all advertising placed with the media. Thus, sales are listed as "billings"—the amount of advertising money placed in various media. If an agency places a commercial on a television program for $100,000, it bills the client-advertiser $100,000 but pays the medium only $85,000. Advertisers who do not use an agency still pay $100,000 to the medium. Thus, the 15 percent commission is a form of discount with which the agency must pay its expenses.

However, in situations where extra-large costs are incurred—as when extravagant ads are produced or high-priced endorsers are used—the additional fees are paid by the advertiser. Some agencies today are moving away from the 15 percent commission toward a strict "fee" basis of compensation. In other cases, advertisers are experimenting with new compensation plans. They might guarantee an agency the costs of services plus a percentage of the income generated by the advertising.

Reasons for Using an Advertising Agency

Under what circumstances do marketers engage the services of an advertising agency? First of all, the advertiser may use an agency whenever it cannot afford to maintain a full-time department staffed by the talents an agency provides. Because an agency spreads its personnel costs (the major costs involved) over many clients, each advertiser can share in this pool of talent without making the complete investment. In addition, since an agency's primary activity is advertising, it brings to each client whatever experience, knowledge of markets and media, and expertise in advertising strategies it has developed for other clients. Yet the 15 percent commission must be worthwhile for the agency—it must cover costs and provide some profit.

Then, too, economics enter the picture. Since an advertiser pays the same amount to the medium whether or not an agency is involved, it makes little sense not to take advantage of an agency's expertise. (See Application 16-7.)

Application 16-7
The Ad Agency—"Not just a Lot of Hot 'Ayer' "

You don't have to be small to be creative in the advertising agency business. This has been proven time and again by N. W. Ayer, one of the oldest and one of the largest agencies in the country.

Founded in 1869 by Francis Wayland Ayer, a young school teacher, Ayer has prospered throughout the years by coming up with outstanding creative ads.

For years, the agency thrived on three major accounts, R. J. Reynolds, DeBeers Consolidated Mines, and *The Ladies Home Journal.* And for each of these clients, Ayer created slogans that remain with us today. For the Reynolds Camel brand, "I'd walk a mile for a Camel," for DeBeers, "A diamond is forever," and for the *Journal,* "Never underestimate the power of a woman."

For a period, many thought Ayer had lost its creative touch. The agency moved its operation to New York from Philadelphia, built up an overseas network of affiliates, and got a new chairperson, Louis Hagopian, in 1976. In three years, Ayer more than doubled its billings and bounded to new heights. H. W. Ayer is now again considered one of the premier agencies in the country.

Some of Ayer's latest campaigns include the successful "Reach out and touch someone," for AT&T; "Join the people who joined the Army," for the U.S. Army; and "America is turning 7Up," for, of course, 7Up. The resurgence of this agency has been so strong that one of its competitors has offered it the greatest compliment for the large firm; "Ayer is like a creative little agency."

Source of data: "A Breath of Fresh Ayer," *Time,* June 9, 1980, p. 53.

A Critical Look at Advertising

Now that we have looked at the steps by which advertising is developed, it seems appropriate to consider the value of all this effort.

Advertising is both praised and criticized. It has been acclaimed for helping to raise our standard of living by communicating about products that can and do satisfy our wants and needs. Advertising also encourages competition, which stimulates the economy. And it lowers the costs of products by simplifying or replacing expensive personal selling as a means of contacting the market, and by moving products through the distribution channel more quickly. This helps consumers to satisfy their day-to-day needs and desires. In addition, advertising helps to improve the quality of products since marketers who use advertising must constantly find better ways to differentiate their products, and usually accomplish this goal through product improvements.

To these positive comments about advertising as a means of communication we must add the voices of various critics. They claim that advertising is better at persuasion than at providing information. Thus, they believe that advertising has an unhealthy influence because it persuades consumers—including children—to buy products they do not really need or want. In this regard, advertising has been criticized for creating an excessively materialistic attitude that wastes our scarce resources. Some assert that advertising removes products from price competition by creating high levels of demand, which leads to higher prices and thus reduces competition. Finally, of course, advertising has been criticized for being false, boring, and irritating.

The debate about the merits and drawbacks of advertising continues. While defenders of advertising have made their points well known, the critics have also left their mark on the attitudes of both the business community and the public at large. Today, there is growing distrust of advertising and its function in society. But the practice is firmly established, and the best way to counter criticism is to retain the advantages that advertising offers while making every effort to alleviate its weaknesses and eliminate its flaws. Some of the means by which this objective is being accomplished will be discussed in Chapter 20.

Looking Back

This chapter has explored the nature of advertising and its role in the promotional mix. Before we examine the other major methods of promotion—personal selling and sales promotion—be sure you have understood the following important points about advertising:

1 An advertising message researches large masses of consumers at once.

2 Specific objectives should be established as the first step in advertising management.

3 The content of an advertising message should be tied to the objectives.

4 Copy is the heart of an advertisement, while illustrations and the layout add impact.

5 Each of the mass media has identifiable advantages and disadvantages.

6 The key to media selection is matching the characteristics of a medium's audience with the target market.

7 Measuring the effectiveness of advertising is one of the most difficult research problems.

8 Advertising research is performed at two stages in the advertising process: when advertising is developed (pretest) and after it has been conveyed (posttest).

9 Advertising agencies are specialists in advertising.

10 The media, not the advertisers, generally compensate the advertising agencies.

11 Advertising is both defended and criticized, and both sides have raised important points.

Key Terms

If you aren't sure what each of the following words means, look back at the text. Numbers refer to pages on which the words are defined. Additional information can be found by checking the index and the glossary at the end of the book.

horizontal cooperative advertising 505
vertical cooperative advertising 506
primary demand advertising 506
selective demand advertising 507
direct action advertising 507
indirect action advertising 507
institutional advertising 508

public service advertising 508
national advertising 509
local advertising 509
advertising management 509
copy 512
illustrations 513
layout 513
cost-per-thousand 523
focus group interview 524

Questions for Review

1 Who are the various "sponsors" in the communication process model?
2 Briefly describe the major difference between primary demand and selective demand advertising.

3 Name some of the sales-oriented goals that marketers tend to set up and reach in developing advertising programs.
4 What are the basic ingredients of an advertising message?
5 What are some of the more

important criteria used in media selection?
6 What are the cost and talent incentives for using an advertising agency rather than doing ads "in house"?

Questions for Thought and Discussion

1 Advertising can even be used to "sell" mental health—that is, to make people recognize problems and help people solve them. Surprisingly, it has been found that using ads which pose questions rather than ads which give answers is far more effective. What can account for this phenomenon?
2 United States companies pay millions of dollars a year for celebrity endorsements to sell

products. But do American consumers actually buy these products because they are recommended and/or approved by the celebrities?
3 Some marketers are using fear in their advertisements to jolt their consumers into awareness of their message. Do you think fear appeals (such as showing the devastating results of fire damage to a home as a means

of marketing household insurance) work?
4 Many advantages to using direct mail as an advertising medium were listed in the chapter. One point that must be reemphasized, however, is that it is the only medium in which effectiveness can be rather easily measured. Why isn't this so with other advertising media?

Suggested Project

Find a print ad for each of the types of advertising noted in Chapter 16. Clip out the ads and post them in a folder, labeling each type.

Suggested Readings

Aaker, David A. (ed.): *Advertising Management: Practical Perspectives,* Prentice Hall, Englewood Cliffs, N.J., 1975. This anthology focuses on practical implications for the management of advertising, promotion, or communication.

Anderson, Rolph E., and Marvin A. Jolson: "Technical Wording in Advertising: Implications for Market Segmentation," *Journal of Marketing,* vol. 44, no. 4 (Winter 1980), pp. 57–66. This article tells why advertisers may be ill-advised to avoid technical language in print media messages directed to household consumers.

LaBarbera, Pricilla, and James MacLachlan: "Time-Compressed Speech in Radio Advertising," *Journal of Marketing,* vol. 43, no. 1 (January 1979), pp. 30–36. The value of speeding up a radio commercial without a perceptible change in general voice quality to heighten impact is analyzed in this article.

Lavidge, Robert J., and Gary A. Steiner: "A Model for Predictive Measurements of Advertising Effectiveness," *Journal of Marketing,* vol. 25 (October 1961), pp. 59–62. The hierachy of effects of advertising is presented as a framework for measuring how successful advertising actually is.

McNiven, Malcolm A.: "Plan for More Productive Advertising," *Harvard Business Review,* vol. 58 (March–April 1980), pp. 130–136. The author describes a productivity program by which a company can allocate the various costs of advertising in line with company goals and marketing strategy.

Michman, Ronald D., and Donald W. Jugenheimer: *Strategic Advertising Decisions: Selected Readings,* Grid, Columbus, Ohio, 1976. This collection of readings provides depth in the area of advertising management.

Roman, Kenneth, and Jane Maas: *How to Advertise,* St. Martin's Press, New York, 1976. This book is a professional guide for the advertiser: what works, what doesn't, and why.

Smith, Robert E., and Tiffany S. Meyer: "Attorney Advertising: A Consumer Prospective," *Journal of Marketing,* vol. 44, no. 2 (Spring 1980), pp. 56–64. Some ways are proposed for reducing information gaps between professional advertising and consumer selection criteria.

Wright, John S., Willis L. Winter, Jr., and Sherilyn K. Ziegler: *Advertising,* 5th ed., McGraw-Hill, New York, 1982. A comprehensive treatment of all the decision areas of advertising is provided.

Zabriskie, Noel B., and William G. Nickels: "Reducing Promotional Costs through Management of the Media Buying Function," *Marquette Business Review,* vol. 15 (Winter 1971), pp. 185–191. This article discusses the cost aspects of shifting to in-house advertising.

Chapter

17

Personal Selling and Sales Promotion

Looking Ahead

Having taken a long look at the nature of advertising and how it is accomplished, we might be led to believe that it is the most important of the promotional tools. But this chapter will demonstrate a different view. Advertising is just one of the promotional activities marketers engage in—perhaps the most useful one in terms of making consumers aware of products and their brands. But now we are ready to examine other promotional tools that have their impact when awareness of, interest in, and desire for the product have been stimulated. Closer to the time of purchase, personal selling and sales promotion help move consumers into action. This chapter will show how personal selling and sales promotion help effect exchanges in the marketplace.

Key Topics

How a salesperson's job is different from what most people think it is

The various types of sales jobs

Why personal selling is so important—even to consumers

The steps in the personal selling process

The activities of sales managers

The nature of sales promotion

Some important and frequently used sales promotion techniques

In Chapter 16 we saw that advertising is the main promotional tool used by marketers to build an awareness of the product or its brand among consumers. Now we will look at personal selling and sales promotion, the two promotional activities that have the greatest impact as consumers move from awareness, interest, and desire toward the actual exchange. The first part of this chapter focuses on the personal selling process, while the second part examines the sales promotion activities of marketers.

Personal Selling

The activity called selling touches all of us throughout our lives. When we are young, we sell our parents on the idea of more candy, new bicycles, better baseball gloves, or fancier dolls. Later, by our words and our actions we sell ourselves to our peer groups. Eventually, as adults, we find that one secret to landing a job and securing a future is that we must get out and sell ourselves.

To many people, the idea of selling is equated instantly with the activities of marketing. This idea, of course, is misleading. It has its origins in the sales era that we discussed in Chapter 1. Historically, after the production processes were refined sufficiently so that an enormous supply of products rolled off the assembly lines, a critical need developed to move these products into the hands of consumers. At no other time in history has the significance of the salesperson in the exchange process been so prominent. In helping to complete the exchange transaction, salespeople became the key to a company's success. But we have seen throughout this book that selling activity is not always consistent with marketing philosophy, whose main tenet is ensuring the satisfaction of consumers. Marketing involves far more than moving products into consumers' hands, for the products must satisfy needs and desires. Still, many people do not understand that selling is but one of the many activities which make up marketing.

The American Marketing Association defines *selling* as "the personal or impersonal process of assisting and/or persuading a prospective customer to buy a commodity or service or to act favorably upon an idea that has commercial significance to the seller."[1] This definition is very broad; it includes many of the activities of marketing that we have studied. Yet, first and most important, marketing is the entire process of communication. In contrast, selling, or personal selling, is but one of the three main promotional activities and provides individual-to-individual, one-on-one communication between the marketer and the members of the market. As such, it involves people—salespeople—and that is where the personal selling process begins. Let's take a look.

---

[1]*Marketing Definitions: A Glossary of Marketing Terms,* American Marketing Association, Chicago, 1960, p. 21.

The Salesperson's Job

A salesperson today can be seen as the marketing manager for an entire territory. But rather than being a mere pusher of products, a salesperson wears many hats. The core job of a salesperson is to locate prospective customers and convert them into buyers, following up the transaction to ensure that complete satisfaction is provided. This simple view must be expanded, however, for in order to achieve the objective of an exchange, a salesperson must undertake a "total selling activity." Such a goal brings the salesperson into contact with many different people—purchasing agents, research and development scientists, corporate presidents, secretaries, warehouse receiving personnel, accountants, sales managers, and other marketing managers.

It's thus clear that a salesperson must engage in many activities. He or she must be an information gatherer, a problem solver for customers and for their companies, an influencer, an ego booster for the customer, an in-store display arranger, a coordinator of the company's marketing activities, and, sometimes, even a repairperson. Salespeople bridge the gap between marketers and their markets. Thus they promote the flow of communication and help to relay important information to the marketing organization. This puts them in the middle of the marketing endeavor. And in such a position, salespeople must serve the goals of both the marketing organization and the customer.

The effective performance of sales activities certainly demands many qualities. Those who go into sales must be personable, of substantial intelligence, attractive in appearance, and pleasing to other people. In addition, salespeople must be able to understand the product they are selling; they must be able to recognize a customer's true needs; and they must absorb their sales training and be able to think—especially on their feet. Effective salespeople can analyze the market's needs, noting the economic and competitive trends within the industry and relating them to the needs and wants of the market. Salespeople must be well versed in all aspects of their products, and this obligation sometimes requires that they seek information beyond that supplied by their employers. Finally, salespeople must know thoroughly how their firms operate, including credit and pricing policies, the length of time needed for delivery or adjustments for damaged goods, and many related matters.

To see how extensive all these activities are, consider the job of a salesperson for Eastman Kodak Company. Each salesperson should be familiar with the more than 6000 products that the company offers in its product line. The salespersons must see that photography dealers receive their orders on time, that proper credit is arranged, and that all merchandise is in good condition upon delivery. At the same time, Kodak salespeople must check constantly to see that retailers' displays are set up correctly, and they must keep track of competitors' activities and relay this information back to the company's decision makers at their headquarters in Rochester, New York.

Types of Sales Jobs

Clearly, the types of jobs that salespeople perform run a wide gamut. While some sales jobs are not very creative and, in fact, take little talent to perform, others involve a great deal of creativity. The job of a bakery salesperson who drives a truck and delivers loaves of bread to retail stores is far less demanding than the job of someone

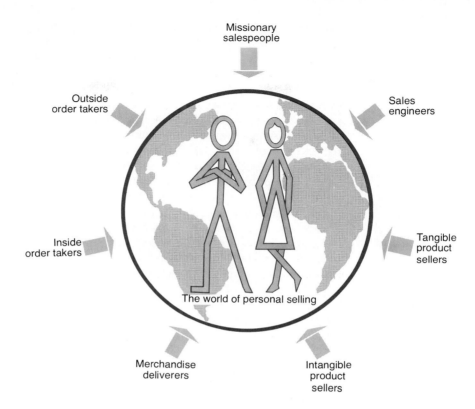

Figure 17-1 Types of sales jobs.

who sells conveyor-belt systems to industrial concerns. To underscore the differences, we'll look at seven types of sales jobs ranging from those which involve littler creativity on the salesperson's part to those which demand much creativity. (See Figure 17-1.)

Merchandise Deliverers

A wide variety of sales jobs emphasize the activity of delivering products over selling responsibilities. Examples include people who provide newspapers, milk, and heating oil to private homes or bread and potato chips to retail stores. In these cases, a pleasant personality and good service may lead to increased sales, but these selling responsibilities are less important than reliability and the actual delivery of the products.

Inside Order Takers

In many selling situations, buyers have made up their minds before they meet with the salesperson. This is the case especially in retail stores, where the salesperson does not leave the place of business. Such salesclerks can make suggestions and generally assist buyers, but usually their main function is to take orders.

Outside Order Takers

Many toiletry and household products are sold to retailers by means of the manufacturer's outside sales force. In this case, salespeople travel to and visit with regular customers for the purpose of taking orders. Such salespeople are discouraged from selling any additional products; instead, they simply service the retailer's needs in terms of products that are on their shelves already. The selling of additional products is handled by marketing managers at a higher level within the organization.

Missionary Salespeople

Missionary salespeople are not expected or permitted to solicit orders. Rather, they make calls to promote good will toward the marketing organization and to help customers arrange their own promotional activities. They are often more like teachers than salespeople. Distillers, brewers, manufacturers of rubber, and pharmaceutical companies use such missionary sales personnel. On receiving orders from customers, these salespeople relay them to the distributors.

Sales Engineers

When the products sold are to be used in a buyer's manufacturing or research department, much of the sale transaction depends on the salesperson's knowledge about how the products will perform the function for which they are purchased. In such instances, the services of highly trained engineers who are versed in technical knowledge are critical to the selling activity.

Tangible Product Sellers

The selling of such products as encyclopedias, vacuum cleaners, washing machines, computer equipment, and earth-moving equipment requires more creativity than the jobs we have discussed so far, because, in these cases, customers often are not aware of their needs or do not realize how a particular product can satisfy those needs. Thus, the salesperson may have to serve additional functions.

Intangible Product Sellers

Perhaps the ultimate in sales creativity is involved in selling intangible products like advertising, life insurance, legal services, and prearranged funerals. With such products, salespeople do not have something that can be seen, touched, or smelled by the buyer. Intangibility adds to the risks perceived by a potential buyer, thus increasing the difficulties of ensuring the buyer's confidence and gaining the sale. This category represents the most challenging type of personal selling.

The Broadened Concept of Personal Selling

It should be no surprise that personal selling is not restricted to business firms and other commercial ventures. For instance, college football coaches attempt to sell their university's athletic and educational programs to high school athletes, and their selling process is not unlike that involved in a typical business situation. Recruiters for the armed forces also use personal selling to encourage young people to enlist. Similarly, employees within any organization must "sell" their supervisors on any ideas they have for corporate action. It can be seen, then, that personal selling is related not only to the selling of goods and services but also to the selling of ideas, activities, and even feelings. The techniques of personal selling can be used by all people and in all sorts of situations. Everyone can benefit from studying the selling process and applying it to daily life. The entire process of selling is one of dealing with people—which is as much the key to effective day-to-day living as to effective marketing.

The Importance of Personal Selling

While thousands are engaged in the advertising industry, the number of people who are employed in personal selling is in the millions. A major portion of our population is engaged in this vocation in some way. And of all the promotional activities, personal selling takes up the greatest portion of the budget. While the advertising expenditures of all companies amounts to $54 billion, the money spent on personal selling has been estimated to be about 2½ times that of advertising.

The Impact on Society

Salespeople also perform important functions by helping society to solve certain problems. That is, by recognizing society's needs and providing information about products, salespeople bring about exchanges that reduce society's needs. By so doing, they encourage the consumption process, which usually improves a society's standard of living. But perhaps the most important contribution that personal selling makes is to spread information about innovations. By nature, people resist changes, even though many new products can improve their lives. Through its persuasive aspects, personal selling often can encourage consumers to cross the exchange threshold, thus leading them to accept innovations. (See Figure 17-2.) Other marketing activities do not have so much influence in terms of making innovations acceptable to people.

The Impact on Companies

From a company's standpoint, the cost of personal selling is not small. While typical corporate expenditures for advertising run from 1 to 3 percent of sales, the cost of employing a sales force ranges from 8 to 15 percent of sales. In many companies, then, personal selling makes up the largest single operating expense.

Even so, companies definitely profit from investments made in personal selling. Salespeople have an enormous impact at the point of sale, and many exchanges would not be made without the encouragement supplied by a salesperson. It is easy for the potential buyer of a product to ignore an advertisement, but it is far more difficult to disregard the face-to-face contact of a salesperson. In short, the persuasiveness of salespeople is an important factor in promoting exchange. Given the intensity of competition among marketers, persuasiveness is often the determining factor in convincing a consumer to make an exchange.

Figure 17-2   Selling is the personal side of marketing. (Grant Compton)

Besides encouraging exchange, however, salespeople perform a number of other important activities for a company. One of their most important functions is to provide "intelligence"; they relay important information to their organizations, which helps to make the entire planning and marketing effort effective. Information about competitors' product innovations or pricing policies or about customers' dissatisfaction is important input to effective marketing decision making. And salespeople also provide many services for customers. They arrange deliveries, help with bookkeeping practices, train the customers' salespeople, and offer promotional assistance. In addition, since many customers have contact with the marketer only through the salesperson, personal selling may form the basis for a company's image among its customers. All these services greatly expand the bundle of satisfaction that is offered. (See Application 17-1.)

Application 17-1
The Salesperson's Job—
More than an Order Taker

When Louis J. Manara began selling chemicals for Cyanamid in 1971, the job was relatively straightforward. He was told little about his division's goals, and practically nothing about the costs of his line. His assignment was relatively simple: Sell all you can, as fast as you can.

But in the past decade, the salesperson's job has become much more demanding. "'Salesman' is just too narrow a word," one marketing manager told *Fortune* magazine. A decade ago, it was sales, and more sales. Now a salesperson doesn't merely sell. Gathering information, determining customers' needs, following competition, and advising management on the type of financial package needed to get an order are all parts of the salesperson's expanded role.

This probing for market intelligence is not the only new duty a salesperson is expected to perform. Mediating credit disputes between the company and customers also falls to the salesperson. He or she has to sort out customer complaints concerning products and keep abreast of fast changes in both government regulations and world markets. "Ten years ago," Manara said, "we had backup people to handle all this. But most of them have been let go. We have to be far better informed than we were then."

Manara's experience is not unique. Out of economic necessity, management is pressing far greater duties on the sales forces. And Manara has met the challenge. He has won Cyanamid's top sales award three times in his nine years of selling for the firm.

Source of data: "The New Life of a Salesman," *Fortune,* Aug. 11, 1980, pp. 172–180.

The Impact on Consumers

While our attention so far has been focused on what salespeople can do for marketers, customers also benefit from the services provided in personal selling. It is still true that some people may be "sold a bill of goods" by a salesperson, but it is also true that *most* salespeople sincerely want to satisfy their market's needs. By easing the exchange of a bundle of satisfaction, salespeople help to reduce consumers' needs and increase their satisfaction, thus raising their standard of living.

Many activities that salespeople perform for their company also benefit the company's customers. Information about products, additional services, and the personal touch all go together to improve the satisfaction derived by consumers. And salespeople often provide another forgotten benefit: they help to reduce anxiety on the part of buyers. Both before and after an exchange, customers may be psychologically "uptight" about the product and anxious to know whether it will perform as expected. They may wonder whether some other product or brand might suit their needs better. But because of the personal relationship that is built up between a salesperson and a customer, such fear and anxiety can be reduced. This, too, adds to a buyer's total satisfaction.

The Impact on Salespeople

The job of personal selling has many rewards for those who perform it. Of all marketing jobs, sales provides one of the greatest opportunities for individual financial gain. It is not uncommon for some salespeople—particularly those in industrial markets—to make over $100,000 a year.

Jobs in sales have many attractive features. While salespeople must, of course, account for their time, they are not under constant supervision. Thus, they have much flexibility in allocating their time. Most salespeople can determine their own schedules, and few have to punch a clock. They also benefit from knowing that they have helped to satisfy the market's needs.

In terms of career opportunities, most firms have more job openings in sales than in other marketing areas. Sales positions provide a deep understanding of a market, and such experience can be invaluable for those who want to move up to top levels of management.

Having examined the nature and importance of personal selling, we are ready to take a close look at the selling process itself—and at how it is managed.

The Selling Process[2]

We have already noted that the core steps in the salesperson's job are locating prospective customers, converting them to buyers, and following up to ensure satisfaction. Yet this view is too simple. Let us now look at some more specific steps and some examples of how these steps can be carried out. The steps in the selling process are, as shown in Figure 17-3,

1 Locating prospects

2 Presale preparation

3 The sales presentation

4 Handling objections

5 The close

6 Postsale activities

Locating Prospects

One cannot sell a product unless one can find a buyer. Thus, *prospecting*—the process of locating and classifying potential buyers of the product—is the first step in the selling process. The first phase of prospecting is obtaining leads on potential customers. A *lead* is the name of any organization or individual who may be a potential customer. Next, those leads are qualified. If leads can both (1) benefit from the use of the product and (2) afford to buy it, they are classified as true prospects.

There are many ways that salespeople obtain leads: birth and wedding announcements in newspapers for photographers and insurance salespeople, for

---

[2]Parts of this section are adapted from Frederick A. Russell, Frank H. Beach, and Richard H. Buskirk, *Textbook of Salesmanship,* 11th ed., McGraw-Hill, New York, 1982.

Figure 17-3   The selling process.

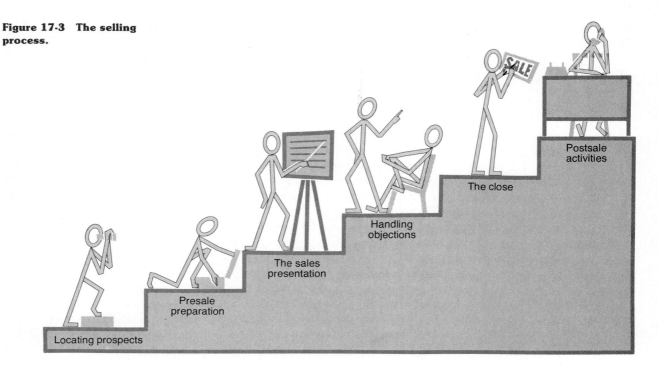

Postsale activities

The close

Handling objections

The sales presentation

Presale preparation

Locating prospects

example, and F. W. Dodge reports listing building permits issued to producers of building materials. Other sources include directories of membership in trade associations or civic organizations, friends, sales managers, and replies from company advertising.

Real estate sales personnel can be particularly creative in their search for prospects. The good ones often cruise the streets looking for clues such as "For Sale by Owner" and "For Lease" signs, vacant buildings, and signs of new construction. One particularly aggressive industrial property salesman in Los Angeles located manufacturing companies that might be interested in moving by looking for plants where the parking lots were overflowing. His usually correct reasoning was that if the firm has outgrown its parking, it's probably outgrown its plant as well.

Presale Preparation   Before contact with prospects is made, the salesperson must become properly prepared. This means he or she should be well versed in the techniques of selling and knowledgeable about the products being sold, and should have gained insights into the nature of the prospects. As we will see in the next section, it is the responsibility of the sales management to train salespeople in the methods of selling and to provide knowledge about the company's products. But information gathering depends on the salesperson. Successful salespeople are those motivated to accumulate facts helpful in approaching and appealing to prospects—and these facts vary with each type of prospect. But simple information that is often easily obtainable—the prospect's age, family situation, interests, occupation—can be the key to avoiding the danger of starting off on the wrong foot as well as the key to landing the sale. For example, a little research that uncovers a purchasing agent's pet peeve (for instance, not being contacted before the salesperson goes directly to the department where the product will be used) can be helpful in building rapport. A simple "I always believe in first contacting a firm's purchasing agent before seeing anyone else in the company" can be a most effective opener for the salesperson in greeting this purchasing agent.

In other organizations, presale preparation is more formal. At Orion Research Inc., Cambridge, Massachusetts, marketers of sophisticated analytical instrumentation equipment, for instance, a computerized inquiry-handling system combines sales leads with relevant information for effective follow-up. Called the Comprehensive Computerized Marketing System (CCMS), the system contains more than 150 pieces of company literature and selects the right ones for each customer or prospect inquiry. It also informs the salesperson on the kinds of action each inquiry should get, monitors the salesperson's follow-up until the order is won or lost, and builds a databank that provides analytical reports for management.

The Sales Presentation

Armed with information, the salesperson is ready to make contact with the customer. The first step is to gain the person's attention. The simplest and most often used way to do so is to walk in, shake hands, and introduce oneself—yet this has little impact or flair. Many salespeople gain attention by beginning with a question—"Are you big enough to profitably use an IBM 370?" or stating a definite benefit—"I can save you 40 cents a gallon on all the milk you sell." Others use still more unusual methods to start off. One enterprising cinder block salesperson used to enter the buyer's office, walking very slowly and gingerly carrying a concrete block laid carefully on a red velvet pillow as if the product were the Crown Jewels of England. He never had to worry about gaining attention for his rather standardized product.

After gaining attention, the salesperson must develop a two-way sales communication that will help the prospect to understand the product better, while at the same time instilling confidence in the product and making it appear better than that offered by the competition. (See Figure 17-4.) To achieve the desired learning on the part of the buyer and avoid any misunderstanding, good salespersons use the tools of effective communication. Dramatization and visualization have been shown to be effective. For instance, instead of saying "These tires are tough," a more imaginative salesperson might be more dramatic: "Picture yourself with your family speeding down a lonely country road at 60 miles per hour. All of a sudden, some lunatic coming the other way swerves to miss a cat in the road and you are forced onto the shoulder of the road. You smack over an enormous pothole, jarring every bone in your body. But you'd not have to worry about your tires—your steering would be stable. These tires can take it."

The use of slides, pictures, samples, models, and demonstrations can also be particularly helpful in clearly getting your point across. Some salespeople capitalize on

Figure 17-4   An effective sales presentation begins with gaining the customer's attention, then proceeds with effective communication between seller and buyer. (Hazel Hankin/Stock, Boston)

the knowledge that many grown-ups never lost their love of tinkering with mechanical ''toys.'' Consequently, their presentations are replete with miniature models.

Product tests also can be effective in getting one's point across. One typewriter salesperson was challenged on the sturdiness of his machine. So he drove one wheel of his car over the typewriter, gathered up the machine, and typed a letter on it. Strong evidence indeed—and the point was learned.

Handling Objections   Often during the sales presentation a prospect will raise objections. Such objections tell the salesperson how far he or she is from making the sale. Objections show where there's a mismatch between what is wanted and what is offered by the salesperson. But salespeople must be sure they are perceiving the *real* objection, which may be somewhat different from that stated by the prospect. Objections provide a chance for the salesperson to bring out additional benefits of the product or reemphasize the features important to the buyer. The most difficult type of prospect is the one who clams up and waits in stony silence while the salesperson strives to gain a clue as to how the sales talk is progressing.

There are many ways to handle objections, and the method to be used depends on the situation as perceived by the salesperson. People dislike being contradicted directly, so a straight denial of the objection is typically avoided. The most widely used method seems to be the "Yes . . . but . . ." or indirect-denial approach. For instance, a real estate salesperson, faced with the objection that "Your lots are too far out of town," countered with, "That's what a lot of people thought about every lot we put on the market two years ago. But now all those 'far out' lots are built up, and the property value has doubled. It pays to think ahead."

The Close

The focal point of the sales presentation is the close, the point when the order is actually secured. It's not easy to make the close—and many good salespeople run well in the selling race but just can't make it to the tape. Many alternative approaches to the close exist:

—*Closing on a minor point:* "Would you like the brush with the long bristles or the short bristles?"

—*Standing-room-only close:* "This is the last set of sheets we have at this price. Tomorrow we'll have to sell them at the regular price $4.00 higher."

—*Offering special incentives:* "If you buy today, we are authorized to give you an additional 25 gallons at no extra charge."

—*Asking for the order:* "I really want you to buy this now so we both can get a good night's rest."

Postsale Activities

As with all marketing, the job of the salesperson is not complete when the sale is made. Follow-up activities are needed to ensure that the customer is completely satisfied. Checking back with the buyer gains goodwill for both the salesperson and the organization represented. Often, purchases need to be adjusted to ensure a better match, such as when buyers improperly forecast their needs, and sometimes instruction in the installation or use of the product is necessary. Too, the follow-up can produce the names of prospects. Finally, many salespeople become fast friends of their customers—and the follow-up can be instrumental in creating long-lasting relationships that ultimately increase the likelihood of repeat sales.

The smart salesperson strives to make friends by sincere yet subtle means. Passing along tips on new business to clients, bringing fresh ideas for creating profit, and helping obtain capable personnel can all produce favorable feelings. In short, the salesperson should express a genuine interest in the customer or prospect.

One outstanding salesperson of office machines services only one customer—a large bank. This salesperson regards herself as an integral part of that bank, and even jumps in to help when there is a work overload in departments that utilize her machines. When she delivers a new machine, she makes sure that the employees operating it are sufficiently instructed in its use. She constantly studies the bank's record-keeping system and makes suggestions for improvement. In short, she views herself as "the bank's special vice president in charge of bookkeeping and accounting machines.'' She even recommends competitors' machines when she knows they are better than hers. And her employer is understanding about it, for goodwill and a solid relationship are the key to a long-lasting relationship with the customer.

Those, then, are the major steps in the personal selling process. It is not easy to undertake them effectively and to be successful at all times. But if the salesperson abides by the marketing concept and applies this philosophy while on the job, selling can be one of the most rewarding activities in marketing. Few other positions in marketing have such close personal contact with the market—and few others can actually furnish visible proof of the satisfaction that is being provided.

Sales Force Management

Salespeople are not just born, regardless of popular notions on the subject. Rather, they are recruited, selected, trained, motivated, compensated, supervised, and controlled. These are the major tasks of sales management. (See Figure 17-5.) And these tasks reflect the managing of the ''outside'' sales force, those salespeople who travel away from the home base and contact geographically distant customers. Let us now look more closely at these activities.

Recruiting and Selecting Sales Personnel

The first task of sales management, of course, is to obtain a sales force. Hundreds of candidates may be screened before a suitable person is selected. Thus, the recruiting activity is an attempt on the part of the marketing organization to ''sell'' itself as a job opportunity to the most desirable candidates. Companies use many means to recruit a sales force—newspaper advertisements (see Figure 17-6), trade publication announcements, conventions, referrals by other salespeople and other employees, and college placement offices. Procter & Gamble uses a unique approach: It sends company representatives to visit college professors and ask for the names of students who might make good candidates.

The selection of a sales force is basically a matching process, and many means are used to evaluate potential salespeople—application forms, references, credit reports, psychological tests, physical examinations, and so on. All these and other devices help to screen out obviously unsuitable candidates, but the most common selection method is still the personal interview. This allows a company to evaluate such important qualities as a candidate's personality, drive, ability to meet and deal with people, and ability to think and react quickly. Few if any salespeople have been hired without first undergoing a personal interview.

Training the Sales Force

Once a sales force has been selected, training is required to turn the candidates into effective sales personnel. The methods of training vary widely. Some companies—especially those marketing products door to door—provide little formal training; rather, they expect new salespeople to learn by experience. But other companies invest thousands of dollars in initial training, and they provide frequent refresher courses to keep the sales force motivated and up to date.

Selling procedures are just one part of a salesperson's training. More and more companies are realizing the impact of computers on their business. Individual items at

Figure 17-5   (left) Sales management activities.

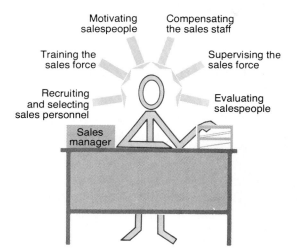

Motivating salespeople

Compensating the sales staff

Training the sales force

Supervising the sales force

Recruiting and selecting sales personnel

Evaluating salespeople

Sales manager

Figure 17-6   (right) Newspaper advertising is a popular method of recruiting used by small and large firms alike.

factory warehouses or at retail outlets can be tracked day by day; thus armed, corporate purchasing agents can shift buying patterns instantly. For the seller, the computer allows a constant monitoring of the pulse of a given market. Thus, modern salespeople must be as accomplished at reading computer printout as at reading sales manuals. Xerox and Standard Brands make computer education part of their sales training programs.

A training program should focus on providing (1) *product information,* which allows the sales staff to fit the product to the market's needs; (2) *sales techniques,* which enhance communication and the persuasiveness of the salespeople; and (3) *general information* about the employing organization—its history, policies, and general procedures—to help the salespeople conduct successful sales interviews. Eastman Kodak invests weeks in the initial training of its salespeople. Besides product information and the company's history, trainees are taught the various steps that help to close a sale.

Motivating Salespeople

The job of selling can be very frustrating. Customers can be unpleasant, the word *no* is frequently heard, traveling takes time and saps energy, and posttransaction problems often crop up and land in the salesperson's lap. In fact, sales are rarely completed after a single first call; research shows that about 80 percent of "new business" is obtained only after five sales calls.[3] In short, selling can be one big headache, and so sales managers must motivate the sales force constantly. This can take the form of both psychic and financial encouragement.

Like everyone else, salespeople respond favorably to many kinds of rewards other than money. For truly self-motivated salespeople, the greatest reward is knowing that they are doing a good job and helping their customers. For this reason, many companies establish a program for regularly communicating the various accomplishments of all salespeople and how they were achieved. They also encourage their sales forces by such means as formal sales meetings, conventions, bulletins in company publications, and various rewards such as trips and other prizes for top performers. Many real estate agencies designate a "Salesperson of the Month" and provide a highly visible parking space for that person's use for the month. Recognition is always appreciated.

Compensating the Sales Staff

Another method of motivating the sales staff, of course, is to offer financial rewards. An organization's compensation program can both motivate salespeople and keep them from leaving for greener pastures elsewhere.

There are many ways to compensate a sales staff, but they all tend to reward employees either for *time, productivity,* or both. If time is the main factor, salespeople receive a *salary;* productivity is rewarded most often by means of *commissions;* and bonuses are sometimes awarded for special efforts and achievements.

There is no perfect compensation plan for a sales staff, and most plans are tailored to meet the specific needs of the marketing organization. More than half of all marketing organizations compensate sales personnel through a plan that considers both time and productivity. Beginning salespeople usually receive a salary to assure them of a living wage until experience increases their productivity. A compensation plan that is based only on salary offers the most security because income is stable. After a period on salary, salespeople often become eligible for commission income, which depends on how many sales are generated. The amount of this income is uncertain, but there is no limit to how much can be made. Nearly all salespeople who earn over $20,000 a year are on some form of commission plan.

Any compensation plan, of course, should make the sales force feel reasonably compensated for their work. It should provide a strong incentive to work harder, and it should encourage sales personnel to identify with their organization. (See Application 17-2.)

Supervising the Sales Force

Salespeople are often isolated employees located far from an organization's headquarters. As a result, some means of supervising the sales force is needed to ensure that work is being carried out and that the salespeople know the organization cares about their work and productivity. In addition, the supervising activity can provide continuous training to the sales staff.

---

[3]Herbert L. Seeger, Jr., *Sales Promotion Planning, A Special Dartnell Sales and Marketing Service Report,* Dartnell Corporation, Chicago, 1970.

Application 17-2
Compensating Salespeople—
Making the Bumblebee Fly

"The reason our symbol is the bumblebee is that aerodynamically the bumblebee shouldn't be able to fly," says Richard Rogers, president and cofounder with his mother, Mary Kay Ash, of Mary Kay Cosmetics. "But the bumblebee doesn't know it, so it goes on flying anyway." Mary Kay's sales have shot from $54 million in 1978 to $167 million in 1980 and $250 million in 1981. By all standards, Mary Kay should not perform this well in that it competes with giants like Avon and Tupperware.

Mary Kay sells directly to the customer, using Tupperware-like parties in the home. More than 120,000 salespersons, working on commission, give free facials and beauty tips at these parties and manage to sell about $75 to $100 worth of merchandise per party. Motivation of sales personnel is in the hands of 2500 sales directors and Mary Kay, a blond-haired

(Courtesy Mary Kay Cosmetics, Inc.)

great-grandmother. According to *Forbes,* she conducts the company's annual inspirational sales meetings in Dallas and hands out free trips, diamond pins, mink coats, and pink Cadillacs that have been offered as incentives.

Recently the company faced a problem: the economy. "In 1970 our average sales director earned about $12,000 a year,"

Rogers told *Forbes,* "compared with $6,000 for an executive secretary. So we were getting a lot of proficient beauty consultants moving up to sales directors." But by the late seventies, sales directors were still making about $12,000 while executive secretarial salaries had jumped to $12,000 to $13,000. Mary Kay lost its competitive edge. It was decided to overhaul the compensation package. "We introduced the pink Buick Regal program. Prior to that, only the top people got Cadillacs. Now the whole middle structure can earn a car," said Rogers. In addition, the commission structure was overhauled, and, as a result, sales directors now average $25,000 per year. Mary Kay's competitive edge is back and the firm is experiencing a growth explosion.

Source of data: "The Flight of the Bumblebee," *Forbes,* June 22, 1981, pp. 104–106.

Lines of communication between the sales force and the company should be kept open. Memos, letters, reports, and various publications all help to accomplish this. Most important, however, is the personal supervision that brings a human element to the relationship between the organization and its sales force. The more personal and frequent the supervision, the better. Such supervision also helps the organization to detect problems that might otherwise be glossed over or missed in day-to-day reports. One large industrial products company in the East found its sales force too large for sufficient personal supervision, as the following tale illustrates. A new salesperson was hired and given a territory in the mid-Atlantic sales. His reports were religiously submitted, memos were sent in, and his salary was sent out for six months—until one customer called to report that he had never seen the salesperson. Investigation showed that the new employee had been fictionalizing his call reports while spending much of his time painting his home. So, close supervision is important.

Evaluating Salespeople

Strangely enough, many salespeople seem unaware that their performance is being evaluated continually by management. The information provided by sales reports, orders, and expense records is often used to assess the strengths and weaknesses of individual members of the sales force. These evaluation methods serve two purposes: They identify salespeople who need additional training, and they form the basis for promotions, transfers, pay raises, and terminations. Basically, each salesperson's performance is compared against some set of standards, usually centering on such factors as calls per day, sales per call, average order size, cost per call, cost per sales dollar, market share realized, sales by product line, or profitability by size or class of customer or product line. Salespeople must know which performance standards are being used for evaluation; otherwise, their efforts may be misdirected, and they may become dissatisfied with management.

Computers are also being used to help ease the task of evaluation. At Best Foods, for instance, 400 field sales people and managers make 45,000 calls per month on some 32,000 retail stores as well as on wholesalers, brokers, and retail chain headquarters. To keep track, after each sales call, the rep reports what was accomplished in terms of sales and promotional activity on a machine-readable form. Twice weekly these reports are mailed to the Englewood Cliffs, New Jersey, headquarters where they are read by an optical scanner and processed by computer. Five to seven working days later, the reps and managers receive a weekly productivity report appropriate to their level of activity.

Sales Promotion

While personal selling is the major promotional tool used by marketers, companies also commit large budgets to sales promotion. It was estimated that $40 billion was spent on this sales function in 1980—almost as much as was spent on mass-media advertising.[4] These figures must be interpreted with caution, however, for sales promotion expenditures are especially difficult to measure. Most firms count these expenses as part of advertising or selling costs.

---

[4]Louis J. Haugh, "Sales Promotion Grows to $40 Billion Status," *Advertising Age,* April 30, 1980, pp. 199–203.

Sales promotion activities
Calendars
Contests and sweepstakes
Coupons
Matchbooks
Pens
Point of purchase promotion
Premiums
Price-offs
Samples
Trade shows
Trading stamps

Figure 17-7 Sales promotion activities.

As explained earlier, sales promotion includes all those activities which we typically call advertising but which do not use the mass media. (See Figure 17-7.) Many people consider this a catch-all term, since it falls between advertising and personal selling. It is the third major means of promoting the product, and seems most effective when used in conjunction with advertising.

The main value of sales promotion can be seen at the point of purchase. It supports advertising and personal selling, but it is rarely used alone as the major promotional tool. Sales promotion techniques are designed to add something extra to promotion that will encourage an exchange. They can be used to attract new customers, to bring about repeat purchases, and to promote off-season products. In many highly competitive industries (such as those producing razor blades, chewing gum, and magazines) the quality of sales promotion may be the deciding factor in obtaining sales.

The success of many sales promotions is dependent upon channel support. The producer needs cooperation from retailers in accepting and locating promotional displays. With couponing promotion, success depends on retailers' willingness to manage the refunding process. Without reliable backing throughout the distribution channel, sales promotion is virtually useless. Procter & Gamble has been exceptional in gaining placement of its point-of-purchase displays at critical locations in retail outlets. When it introduced Wondra skin-care lotion with a large-scale sample program, it achieved 85 percent national distribution within six weeks. Because cooperation and conflict avoidance in the distribution channel go hand in hand with sales promotion effectiveness, marketers with firm, smooth-flowing channels have a substantial competitive edge when using sales promotion.

Sales promotion techniques are not used only by large consumer packaged goods companies. Services and not-for-profit concerns also employ sales promotion techniques. The Massachusetts Bay Transportation Authority (MBTA), the Massachusetts Department of Commerce, and the Greater Boston Convention and Tourism Bureau jointly promoted a coupon book to increase ridership on the financially troubled Boston MBTA. And colleges, experiencing rising costs and decreasing enrollments, have employed coupons in newspapers, discounts for courses beyond an initial fully paid one, and free frisbees distributed to high school students sunning themselves at the beach.

Many methods of sales promotion are used by marketers. In fact, their variety seems almost infinite. But some techniques are used more than others, and we will examine their advantages and disadvantages.

Free Samples

Sampling is the giving away of a product to consumers. It is often used to introduce a new product or to inform consumers about features of the product that cannot be conveyed adequately through advertising. It puts the product directly into the hands of the consumer. (See Figure 17-8.) But this technique is very expensive, and many samples will be given to consumers who are not in the target market. Even so, sampling is used widely by the marketers of coffee, soap, deodorants, household

Figure 17-8   The basic idea behind free samples rests on the marketer's belief that a high percentage of those who sample the product will then purchase it. (Randy Matusow)

cleaners, and some food products. Many cigarette manufacturers are major users of sampling, and new brands are sometimes given away to people passing on the street. In this case, the core market is not likely to be missed, since only people who smoke would have much interest in accepting the samples. In one of the most expensive campaigns ever, Brown & Williamson Tobacco Corporation's sampling reportedly spent $100 million on sampling its ultra–low tar Barclay. Cigarette manufacturers commonly pass out free minipacks when introducing a new cigarette, but B&W was the first to offer free *cartons*. During the fall of 1980, interested consumers had only to call a toll-free telephone number and state the name of their present brand. By return mail, they received a carton of B&W cigarettes and a coupon good for a second $6 carton of Barclay.

Sampling can result in widespread exposure and product trial. S. C. Johnson & Sons spent $30 million on promotion and advertising in 1978. To induce trial of its new shampoo Agree, the company spent $12 million on sampling. In August, 35 million samples, covering 60 percent of the households in the United States, were mailed. In September, an additional 5.3 million women on college campuses received samples. In total, the campaign called for issuance of 45.7 million packets of Agree shampoo. The end result: Agree grabbed a 6 percent market share of the $1 billion shampoo industry in 1980.

Coupons

A *coupon* is a certificate that consumers can bring to a retail store, receiving in return some indicated saving or cash refund. In 1971, it was estimated that 16.4 billion coupons were distributed; by 1980, the number of coupons had grown almost sixfold to 90.6 billion. Faced with inflation, more and more consumers are turning to coupon redemption as a means of saving. A 1981 study has shown that 36 percent of United States households participate in consumer-product refund offers. And marketers are responding with greater numbers of savings incentives.

Couponing is used to encourage product trial, to reach large numbers of prospects more economically than sampling, to ''trade up'' present users to larger sizes, and to hold current users against competitive activity. Couponing works best with a target market consisting of older, married, well-educated, high-income, and women consumers.

General Foods has used couponing to further its image as well as to support a good cause with its largest multibrand promotion in its history. GF, on behalf of some twenty brands, dropped 500 million coupons in the summer of 1981. The company estimated the coupons reached between 65 and 70 percent of all American households. For each coupon redeemed, General Foods donated 5 cents to the Muscular Dystrophy Association (up to $1 million). (See Application 17-3.)

Premiums

A *premium* is a reward that is offered to encourage an exchange. It is usually a product offered free or at less than the regular price in order to induce the consumer to buy another product. Banks have been using premiums heavily. Stuffed animals, snowblowers, even firewood have been used along with the old standbys of watches, clocks, and serving dishes. The East New York Savings Bank, for instance, ran a promotion in which depositors could choose between interest and merchandise worth the discount value of that interest. For early deposits, customers could choose to forgo their interest and receive such items as a 13-inch color television set for a two-year deposit of $1950, a week-long Caribbean vacation package for $1950 on deposit for four years, and perhaps the ultimate, a 1979 Rolls-Royce Silver Shadow II for a $160,000, eight-year deposit.

Like other incentives, premiums induce consumers to switch brands, to try larger sizes of the product, and to buy in the off season; they are also effective in countering competitors' prices. Finally, premiums are often offered to intermediaries in order to push products through the distribution channel. (Such premiums are called *push premiums,* in contrast with most consumer premiums, which are *pull premiums*

Application 17-3
Couponing—Triple Threat to Profits

(Ray Pfortner)

Manufacturer's coupons designed to hype movement of specific products often are getting out of hand at the retail level—particularly when the retailers attempt to capitalize by offering customers double or triple value.

Such is the case with Star Supermarkets of New York, which saw profits tumble by 10 percent when it tripled the value of coupons. Much the same story was repeated in Cleveland when thirty-four Stop-N-Shop supermarkets offered triple value in 1980. It took Stop-N-Shop six months to recover the losses incurred in four days of the promotion. But, the following January and February, Stop-N-Ship was offering double-value coupons.

Often, however, retailers find themselves between a rock and a hard place. They can't discontinue the practice for competitive reasons. Said a Stop-N-Shop executive, "I'm not going to give them up until my competitors do."

When retailers decide to double or triple the coupon value, the extra expense is theirs. Manufacturers redeem the coupons for face value only, plus 7 percent handling. Thus, any bonus is borne by the retailer. An industry consultant estimates the extra expense at 3 percent of a store's sales—a high figure in a thin-margin industry.

"It's a very destructive practice," the Stop-N-Shop executive told *The Wall Street Journal.*

Source of data: "Bonus Coupon Wars Produce Only Victims, Analysts Warn," *The Wall Street Journal,* June 4, 1981, p. 29.

designed to induce exchange.) Premiums are not especially useful for promoting products that are bought infrequently, such as refrigerators and air conditioners.

To offset the cost of this form of sales promotion, marketers use what are known as *self-liquidating* premiums. In this case, the consumers pay the marketer's cost for the premium. But, from their perspective, they pay far less than the item would cost them normally. Self-liquidating premiums can enhance a brand's image and reinforce advertising. They are also helpful in gaining the cooperation of intermediaries.

Many marketers are frequent users of self-liquidating premiums. Brown & Williamson's Kool cigarettes and J&B Scotch have both had their "cool as a summer breeze" and "sophisticated" images reinforced with, respectively, $699 catamaran sailboats and a $30 book, *Gold of Tutankhamen*. Marlboro has been powerfully reinforced with its Country Store, offering a range of items priced from $3.50 to $250. Yet self-liquidators have not been particularly good at getting initial trial of a brand. Less than 10 percent of households have *ever* sent for a premium.

Price-Offs

A *price-off* is a price reduction used to counter competition and to induce the trial of new, reformulated, or repositioned products. This promotional effort is aimed at people's desire to realize savings. While it can be useful in generating sales, it cannot save a declining product. In addition, most price-conscious consumers return to their usual brands once the price-off promotion is discontinued. Thus price-offs tend to help only temporarily. And to have any impact on the market, experts believe that a 15 to 20 percent price cut is necessary.

To avoid reducing the price of standard-sized products when offering price-offs, companies offer trial sizes, which are sold at a discount in small quantities. Trial sizes are usually employed for new products or for products that are being repositioned in the marketplace. Procter & Gamble offered Spic & Span in trial sizes when it repositioned the product from being a cleaner for floors and walls to one for sinks and tubs. Although manufacturers lose money on trial sizes, the loss is minimal, and consumers usually react favorably. The company can withdraw the trial-size offer at any time without suffering in the marketplace.

Contests and Sweepstakes

A *contest* offers prizes to consumers as a reward for doing some task—for instance, for showing creative thinking about a product. Contests have lost popularity in recent years, probably because they have come under serious legal examination and because they involve mental effort on the part of the consumer. In fact, only about 20 percent of the population have ever entered a promotional contest.

Meanwhile, *sweepstakes* are gaining in popularity. They encourage consumers to buy a product as part of the entry procedure, though purchase cannot be stipulated. Consumers are usually asked to signify their entry by mailing a postcard or entry blank, along with a label or a facsimile of it from the product.

Both contests and sweepstakes complement and reinforce point-of-purchase

Application 17-4
Contests—Taking the Fun Out of It

Some of McDonald's customers are cheating. The big hamburger chain uses contests as a means of keeping sales moving, but the company is finding that some people go out of their way to circumvent the rules.

McDonald's frequently runs national contests where the customers attempt to fill the blanks of a coupon book with stamps that make them eligible for prizes ranging from an order of fries to $100,000.

In order to win the big prizes, some customers are advertising for the illusive stamp, a practice clearly against the rules.

"It goes against the integrity of the game," a McDonald's official told *The Wall Street Journal*. But there is little that the company can do, since to police such activity would be virtually impossible.

Of course McDonald's would prefer that the contestants get their stamps at the counter—

preferably after buying a Big Mac. However, many are finding it cheaper and more efficient to simply run an ad.

One such winner of a $1000 prize ran an ad in a Detroit newspaper, and instantly got the missing stamp. He split his winnings with the original stamp owner.

Source of data: "The Fine Print Roils Contest at McDonald's," *The Wall Street Journal,* April 17, 1981, p. 23.

advertising. They encourage retailers to give the product better floor space and to exploit the marketer's promotional program. But such methods demand substantial financial and advertising support, and they usually do not result in mass trials of the product, as sampling does. For example, over 75 percent of contest and sweepstakes entries are accompanied by facsimiles of the product's label rather than by genuine proof of purchase. (See Application 17-4.)

Trading Stamps

This promotional device is used by retailers, while the methods discussed earlier tend to be used more often by producers. Trading stamps are owned by the stamp company (S&H or Gold Bond, among others) and are sold selectively to retailers— only one specific kind of retailer in an area will generally use a particular brand of stamps. The stamps are sold to the retailers for 2 to 3 percent of their total sales, and customers receive the stamps on the basis of how much they purchase. When they have saved up enough stamps, they can redeem them for various kinds of merchandise, either at a redemption center or through the catalog published by the trading stamp company.

Trading stamps require an effort on the part of everyone concerned. While they may encourage customers to be loyal, it is unlikely that they increase sales or lead to much store switching. Trading stamps have seen some lean years. In 1980, only 15 percent of the United States supermarkets distributed stamps—compared with 65 percent during the 1960s. But stamp companies are upgrading their gifts (Gold Bond offers a Chris-Craft motorboat for only 3914 books of stamps) and promoting them aggressively. For S&H, truck stops where drivers often pay more than $100 for a fill-up are a target. Truckers have been wooed by S&H with late-night radio commercials asking whether "those little green rascals don't make gettin' home a little better."

Point-of-Purchase Promotion

This promotional method is used at the retail level and is very effective at gaining consumers' attention. *Point-of-purchase promotions* include displays, signs, lights, and other attention-getting devices located at the place of actual purchase—at the checkout counter or the cash register. The importance of such displays and enticements has been magnified by the increase in self-service and by discount retailing, in which personal service is not provided. Thus, retailers must rely on other means to get attention for products.

The main limitation of point-of-purchase promotion is that it takes up space which could be used for other things. But such displays are helpful in introducing new products, in encouraging impulse sales, and in reinforcing a store's overall promotional program. In an industry that is extremely competitive—like the cigarette industry, with more than 170 brands on the market—point-of-purchase displays are extremely important.

Application 17-5
Trade Shows—Broadway, Move Over

Want to go to Manhattan and see a terrific show? It's 70 minutes long, has sixty singing and dancing cast members of all ages, and it stars Cyd Charisse, Ann Miller, and Phyllis Diller. There's a full house for every performance. Forty-five assistants help the cast through 250 costume changes. It's at the Waldorf-Astoria, and it's the Milliken Breakfast Show.

An annual event for the past quarter century, Milliken and Company's thirteen-show run draws 30,000 buyers, department store heads, and clothing manufacturers. Each Breakfast Show requires a year of planning. Twelve phone operators take special ticket requests.

The cast models Milliken fabrics made up into the latest styles of 100 manufacturers in the audience, and everyone there adores it. Says one Milliken man, "We have the absolutely undivided attention of our primary sales targets for roughly two hours."

Roger Milliken, president of the country's third-largest fabric manufacturer, said, "We did our first two shows at a little restaurant in our old offices at 1407 Broadway, with just two boys and two girls dancing. We found that buyers were standing in line to see them, so we decided to produce an important show."

Milliken's bill for this little once-over-lightly: $2 million a year.

Source of data: "What Milliken Gets for Its $2 Million Breakfast." *Business Week,* June 5, 1978, pp. 120–122.

Application 17-6
Creative Promotion—Hurry . . . Hurry . . . Hurry!

In a new promotion to move their 1980 inventory, some auto dealers discovered P. T. Barnum's marketing tactics. In Michigan, General Motors dealers joined forces for a circus.

Cars from various dealers were moved to the big top where they were displayed. The dealers brought 1300 cars to the show, and a 29-hour sale sold 827 of them. Arrangements for financing and licensing were made on the spot. "It proved there's still money out there," one dealer said. "People are looking for the right buy."

Dealers in other parts of the country are trying an array of new gimmicks. One Chevrolet dealer with too many Blazers and Chevettes on hand offered a two-for-one sale. If a customer would pay the $11,000 sticker price for a Blazer, he threw in a $4,000 Chevette for nothing.

"Everyone was dumbfounded," the dealer said, "but the promotion plan worked. "We had people arguing in the showroom—three different people who wanted the same Blazer at the same time." Within 48 hours, the dealer's inventory of seventeen Blazers was sold out. While the dealer broke even on the promotions, manufacturer rebate programs brought in some cash and the giveaway got a lot of publicity, increased traffic, and moved costly inventory.

Source of data: "Car Dealers Try Circus Atmosphere, Giveaways to Foster Buying Mood," *The Wall Street Journal,* Aug. 25, 1980, p. 17.

Other Sales Promotion Techniques

There are many other promotional techniques that marketers can use. Pens, calendars, and matchbooks are handed out by the millions, both to consumers and to intermediaries. Trade shows and conventions are also used to promote new products, particularly heavy industrial equipment. Footraces to promote Perrier and L'eggs products have gained a lot of brand visibility. T-shirts, billed caps, and men's ties have been used. Even the Goodyear blimp can be classified as sales promotion; hot-air balloons promote everything from Pepsi-Cola to the U.S. Navy. There appears to be no end to the inventiveness and imagination of sales promotion experts. In any case, it is crucial that sales promotion be meaningful and that it be tied to the marketer's entire communication program. (See Applications 17-5 and 17-6.)

Looking Back

This chapter has examined personal selling and sales promotion. We have explored the nature of these two major promotional activities and are now prepared to see how they fit into the overall marketing strategy. But before we do that in Chapter 18, review these important points:

1 Salespeople are more the marketing managers of their territories than they are pushers of products.

2 Personal selling requires the greatest investment of promotional expenditures and is not restricted to commercial exchanges.

3 Personal selling aids society by spreading innovations and raising the standard of living.

4 Salespeople can reap handsome financial rewards, but they are also motivated by means other than money.

5 Good salespeople must be recruited, trained, motivated, compensated, supervised, and evaluated.

6 Compensation of sales personnel tends to be based on payment for time or for productivity.

7 Expenditures for sales promotion are almost as large as those for mass-media advertising.

8 Sales promotion supports advertising and personal selling.

9 Coupons, premiums, contests, sweepstakes, trading stamps, and point-of-purchase displays are all familiar sales promotion techniques.

10 Successful sales promotion demands imagination and creativity.

Key Terms

If you aren't sure what each of the following words means, look back at the text. Numbers refer to pages on which the words are defined. Additional information can be found by checking the index and the glossary at the end of the book.

selling 533
salesperson 534
prospecting 539
lead 539
prospect 539
recruiting 544
sales promotion 548
sampling 549
coupon 550

push premium 551
pull premium 551
self-liquidating premium 552
price-off 552
contest 552
sweepstakes 552
trading stamps 553
point-of-purchase promotion 554

Questions for Review

1 What is perhaps the most important activity, other than bringing about exchange, that a salesperson performs for a company?

2 Briefly describe the major difference between a "lead" and a "prospect."

3 What must occur before any actual contact with the prospect can be made?

4 Briefly describe what is meant by the term *standing-room-only close.*

5 What is the first task of sales management? How do organizations achieve this?

6 At what point in the buying process is the use of sales promotion methods most valuable?

Questions for Thought and Discussion

1 Believe it or not, the door-to-door sales industry has become a booming $6 billion-a-year business. However, no longer are salespeople just knocking on doors and ringing bells. How do you think the industry has tried to change its image?

2 In an effort to drum up new business, moving companies use advertising campaigns to push brochures that give an overview of major cities. Do you think that the cost involved (usually a quarter-of-a-million dollars or so) is warranted?

3 Companies report that an increased percentage of their marketing budgets is being spent on sales promotion. Yet many feel that sales promotion is not getting the most effective and efficient results and that money is therefore being wasted. What would you suggest be done to ensure that sales promotion activities are successful?

4 You have probably often confronted someone giving out free product samples or redeemable cents-off coupons for a new product. Do you think it would be effective to use personnel from companies other than those connected with the product?

Suggested Project

Develop an album of the various sales promotion techniques described in this chapter. For each, indicate the type of sales promotion and what you believe the objective is.

Suggested Readings

Dodson, Joe A., Alice M. Tybout, and Brian Sternthal: "Impact of Deals and Deal Retraction on Brand Switching," *Journal of Marketing Research,* vol. 15, no.1 (February 1978), pp. 72–81. The authors provide some useful guidelines for couponing strategies.

Dubinsky, Alan J., Eric N. Berkowitz, and William Rudelius: "Ethical Problems of Field Sales Personnel," *Business Topics,* vol. 28 (Summer 1980), pp. 11–16. This article considers unethical behavior in field sales personnel.

Fouss, James H., and Elaine Solomon: "Salespeople as Researchers: Help or Hazard?" *Journal of Marketing,* vol. 44, no. 3 (Summer 1980), pp. 36–39. A study shows that it is difficult for salespeople to collect unbiased information.

Robertson, Dan H., and Donald W. Hackett: "Saleswomen: Perceptions, Problems and Prospects," *Journal of Marketing,* vol. 41 (July 1977), pp. 66–71. This study of 250 sales personnel in the real estate industry compares peer perceptions of female versus male salespeople.

Russell, Frederick A., Frank H. Beach, and Richard H. Buskirk: *Textbook of Salesmanship,* 11th ed., McGraw-Hill, New York, 1982. This highly readable textbook describes the selling process, with lively and often fascinating examples.

Shapiro, Benson R., and Ronald S. Posner: "Making the Major Sale," *Harvard Business Review,* vol. 54 (March–April 1976), pp. 68–78. An eight-step format is presented to help companies cope creatively with large and complex selling tasks.

Steinbrink, John P.: "How to Pay Your Salesforce," *Harvard Business Review,* vol. 56 (July–August 1978), pp. 111–122. The author sets out possible reasons for choosing a plan from among the alternatives of salary, commission, or a combination of them.

Strang, Roger A.: "Sales Promotion—Fast Growth, Faulty Management," *Harvard Business Review,* vol. 54 (July–August 1976), pp. 115–124. This article provides an excellent review of the status of sales promotion and the management of sales promotional activities.

Walker, Orville C., Jr., Gilbert A. Churchill, Jr., and Neil M. Ford: "Organizational Determinants of the Industrial Salesman's Role Conflict and Ambiguity," *Journal of Marketing,* vol. 39 (January 1975), pp. 32–39. This article stresses the importance of role playing in industrial sales.

Weitz, Barton A.: "Effectiveness in Sales Interactions: A Contingency Framework," *Journal of Marketing,* vol. 45, no. 4 (Winter 1981), pp. 85–103. A new approach for research on effectiveness in sales interactions is proposed.

Chapter
18

Strategic Marketing Planning— Putting the Marketing Program Together

Looking Ahead

We have now examined the major decision areas of the marketing mix. Such decisions are made by middle-level marketing managers. Next we survey the job of top management, looking at the strategic marketing planning process. We will see how the strategic plan provides the blueprint for all marketing decisions. In this chapter, we will find out how marketers implement and control the marketing mix to be integrated with the strategic plan.

Key Topics

How planning sets the stage for all marketing decisions

The strategic marketing planning process begins with organizational and marketing objectives

The situation analysis as an information base for strategic marketing planning

Deciding on a strategic marketing plan from one of many available alternatives

Different methods for organizing to develop a successful strategic plan

How the control process helps marketers adjust the strategic and tactical plans

The steps in the control process

What the marketing audit is

Chapter Outline

In the past seventeen chapters, we have carefully tracked the many tactical activities that constitute marketing. The complexities of getting a product or service to market involve many people and a wide variety of skills. We have seen the job of setting objectives; looked at information gathering, both the marketing information system and marketing research; and studied how marketers use their information to understand buyers, to segment markets, and to target their activities. We identified the 4 P's—product, price, place, and promotion—and the major decisions each one entails. In this chapter, we will look at the strategic marketing planning process and see how strategies drive the tactical decisions of the organization. We will also look at how marketing programs are coordinated, organized, executed, and controlled within the framework set by the overall marketing strategy.

The Nature of Planning

As we noted in Chapter 2, planning is the process of anticipating the future and determining courses of action to ensure that the organization achieves its goals. The environment that surrounds the organization constantly changes—new laws come into being, competitors become more aggressive, the economy changes, consumers' wants and needs shift, and so on. All such developments are beyond the control of the manager, and they impact on the success or failure of the organization. Effective planning prepares the manager for such changes and identifies alternative actions to reckon with these changes.

Marketing planning is the systematic analysis of the nature of the environment facing the organization and the designing and implementing of actions to accomplish the objectives of the firm in that environment. Successful planning continues through execution and includes monitoring the outcome of the organization's planned actions. Planning is not static. It is a continuing process; the monitoring of outcome allows decision makers to learn more about the environment and to adapt plans to meet unanticipated events. Planners and plans must be flexible so that managers can cope with the ever-changing environment.

The result of the planning process is a plan, a written document that communicates the desires of the planner to others. In this way, the plan is a crude blueprint for achieving stated objectives. Planning and plans are often categorized on the basis of scope or breadth. Long-range plans focus on organizational objectives over a time range of generally five or more years. Since such plans are usually broad and provide long-run guidelines for the organization, they are generally called *strategic plans*. Strategic plans chart the general path of the organization over an extended period of time. *Tactical plans* specify the specific activities necessary to carry out the strategic plans. Such tactical plans are generally short-term, more current in their time focus. By communicating the bigger picture and the reasoning behind it in a strategic plan, the top-level planners enable subordinates to develop their tactical plans to implement the overall goals and develop strategies for the many details not specifically discussed in the master plan. *Coordination* thus becomes more achievable. The written planning document permits others to evaluate the reasoning and assumptions of the plan and thus leads, it is hoped, to an improvement of the present effort or of future ones. The plan is also a *control* device. It states the objectives and the means to achieve them as they are seen at one point in time. Actual results can be compared with the expected results outlined in the plan and differences can be recognized and explained. Adjustments and changes can be made as needed. In this manner, the planning process itself is improved.

While planning is every manager's responsibility, planning is different at different levels in the organization. The top managers (corporate executive officer, president, senior vice presidents) in an organization spend greater time in planning than do people at lower levels—and their focus tends to be on long-run strategic plans. Middle managers focus on the tactical decisions to carry out the master plan. Thus, middle-management planning reflects the decision areas of the preceding chapters of this book. Middle managers (product or brand managers or regional sales managers) develop plans for specific products with desired price, distribution, and promotional decisions. At lower, more supervisory levels in an organization (district sales managers, salespeople), planning is performed to document how the goals of a specific responsibility area will be met. This book has focused on the decision areas of middle management. This chapter will look at higher-level, top-management strategic planning.

The Nature of Strategic Marketing Planning

Strategic marketing planning as we know it today has not always existed. In fact, it is a rather recently developed technique for marketers. The term has been used since the 1960s. During the early period, strategic planning meant five-year forecasts and budgets. The process was chiefly one of filling out forms to keep upper management happy; there was little true commitment to the process by middle managers. In many cases, this attitude was tolerable, since the 1960s were a positive time of economic growth, consumer affluence, and general optimism. In the 1970s, many organizations adopted the product management structure whereby each product had one or more managers responsible for its welfare. Here, marketing plans were devised for each of the product lines. And because a five-year time horizon became too unpredictable, the planning period was one to three years. But during the 1970s, marketers were shaken by some violent changes in their environment: shortages of natural resources, high inflation, high unemployment, a wave of consumer discontent, increased federal regulation, an environmental concern, and changing values and roles among women. Such environmental tremors sent shock waves through marketing planning and made top management much more aware of the need for properly forecasting and

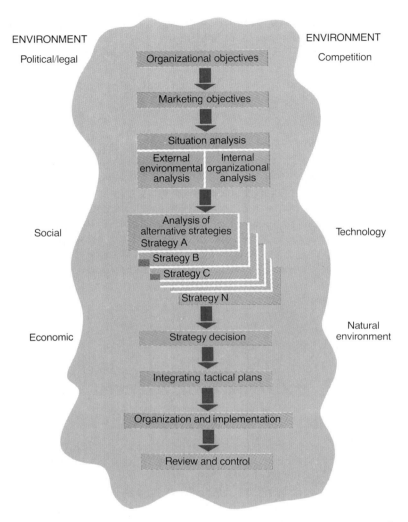

Figure 18-1   The strategic marketing planning process.

anticipating future changes in the uncontrollable environment. As a result, many contemporary marketers heavily focus on the strategic marketing process as a way of life.

The strategic process begins with the setting of objectives for the organization as a whole and then develops objectives for marketing that reflect the overall goals of the corporation or organization. (See Figure 18-1.) The organizational goals then provide top management's input to the strategic marketing planning process. On the basis of the organizational objectives, marketing's own objectives are set. Next, the strategic planner conducts a situation review which begins with an in-depth analysis of the environmental trends that affect the organization. Here, the planner is looking out of a ''strategic window,'' viewing the present and forecasted future of those uncontrollable influences on the firm. Then the planner looks inside the strategic window to analyze the strengths and weaknesses of the organization—and in particular, to assess the distinctive competencies of the firm. These two steps, external and internal analyses, are the cornerstone of effective strategic marketing planning. They provide the information base from which the remainder of the process follows. Additionally, such analyses may warrant an adjustment of inappropriate corporate or marketing objectives.

From these two fact-finding steps, the planner generates alternative master plans or strategic options. From these alternatives, the planner chooses that strategy which best matches the market opportunity with the strengths and weaknesses of the organization. This is a crucial step, for there are only limited times when the marketing organization's distinctive competencies are very closely aligned with those demanded by a dynamic external environment and market. Strategic planners want to be ready to seize upon these opportunities as they arise. Next, tactical action plans are developed from the overall strategy and integrated into the strategy to ensure that all the pieces work together. Finally, the entire program is monitored, reviewed, and modified so that the objectives of the organization are met.

Setting Strategic Objectives

As stated above, the strategic marketing planning process begins with the overall goals of the organization. Such goals must reflect an analysis of the organization's opportunities and distinct competencies. Marketing executives generally estimate the future of a market's size and opportunity and present their views to top management on how the organization can use its resources to capitalize on these opportunities. However, we will first look at some other considerations in the determination of the organization's goals before looking more specifically "outside" and "inside" the organization's "strategic window."

While we often think of the corporation or organization as simply setting goals for sales, profits, return on its investment and the like, organizations also exist to accomplish other, grander objectives. They are often guided by an invisible hand called their *purpose* or *mission*. We have seen in Chapter 9 how the market rationale drives diversification moves. In this sense, computer companies are information-providing companies and telephone companies are communication companies. And some organizations can reflect an even higher level of social purpose; consulting firms can be seen as educational or chaos-resolving firms, museums can be seen as culture-uplifting organizations. Such organizational purposes then guide the firms in determining their directions. Nabisco Brands, for example, is spending $250 million in the first five years of the 1980s to enter less-developed countries such as Venezuela, Mexico, and Nicaragua with its cookies and crackers. The company has stated that it sees itself as a company fighting world hunger. Such a corporate purpose is clearly more uplifting and socially responsible than one directed solely at profits.

The corporate mission depends on how the organization defines its business. Such a definition stems from answers to two questions: "What business are we in?" and "What business *should* we be in?" A business may be defined in one of two ways—in terms of the products or services offered or in terms of the market served. The marketing concept clearly favors a market-oriented business definition based on wants and needs satisfied, on benefits provided, or on customer problems solved. Thus Visa and MasterCard would not see themselves as credit card companies but rather as "value transfer" companies. Schaeffer-Eaton, the writing instrument company, becomes an "expression-producing" company. Sometimes too broad a definition can fog the path of an organization. To say that General Motors is a "transportation" company would open the door to such product diversification as intercontinental air freight, taxicab business, oil tanker shipping and the like—all of which really are outside the boundaries of the firm's present competencies. (See Application 18-1.)

Levi Strauss, for instance, is well known to be firmly entrenched in the apparel industry. The company added many new lines throughout the 1970s—sportswear, accessories such as belts and wallets, youth wear, and ski clothes as well as socks and shoes. However, in a 1979 talk to security analysts, the president stated that Levi Strauss should be looked upon "as a consumer-products company that just happens to be in the garment business."[1] As one worried analyst told *Fortune,* "If they ever really start to believe that, it's trouble."[2] Clearly, such a broad business definition would allow corporate management to focus on a whole range of possible strategic product additions the company has no business being in—cereals, automobiles, detergents, watches, and so on. And apparently the analyst was correct. In 1982, Levi Strauss began eliminating many lines and returned to its emphasis on mid-priced, middle-class-oriented apparel, most notably its jeans. That same president then told *Business Week,* "We've realized that just putting the Levi's name on something isn't enough to gain instant marketing acceptance."[3]

Sometimes an organization can define its business too narrowly. Anheuser-Busch, for instance, found that its primary emphasis on the domestic beer business did not provide any avenue for using its excess cash. As a result, the company redefined itself more broadly as a snack business and forged into the premium-priced Eagle brand of pretzels, corn curls, tortilla chips, and honey-roasted peanuts, which are complements for beer. Here the focus was on more highly utilizing the distinctive competence of its distribution system and developing products for its existing markets.

An organization's purpose or mission is determined by many influences. The accumulation of past experiences and accomplishments within the organization, the desires of the present top management, the changing environment that envelops the organization, as well as the unique set of resources and especially the talents of the personnel—all go together to forge the purpose of the firm. Recently, the notion has grown that organizations have a distinct culture, a set of values, such as aggressive-

---

[1] "Levi Strauss Is Stretching Its Wardrobe," *Fortune,* Nov. 19, 1979, p. 89.
[2] Ibid.
[3] "It's Back to Basics for Levi's," *Business Week,* March 8, 1982, p. 77.

Application 18-1
Defining and Redefining the Business—
Getting on the Right Track

(Courtesy Holiday Inns, Inc.)

"We are in the process of reshaping Holiday Inns into a different company," Roy E. Winegardner, the chairman of the Memphis-based motel company, told *Business Week.* At the direction of its founder, Kemmons Wilson, Holiday Inns had defined itself as a "travel company." The company acquired thirty diverse businesses ranging from furniture production to bus transportation. The rationale was based on being integrated fully into the travel process, from leaving home to

returning. But management did not have the proper skills. More important, the basic premise was faulty. For example, the company found that bus passengers would not stay in medium- to high-priced hotels. A change was obviously necessary. Now the approach is to "get into as few businesses as possible, and only those that have good growth, high returns, and are synergistic with our main business—hotels."

Winegardner intends fully to keep Holiday Inns in the lodging

business, but he is directing the giant company with 300,000 rooms into new market segments.

In redefining the Holiday Inns market, Winegardner is getting the company out of a number of businesses, and at the same time is directing the company into different lodging markets. For instance, Holiday Inns is becoming a major factor in the gaming arena and soon will be the only chain with facilities in such spots as Las Vegas, Reno, Lake Tahoe, and Atlantic City. (Harrah's is the gaming subsidiary of Holiday Inns.)

Being shelved are such properties as Trailways Inc., the bus company, and Delta Steamship Lines, both of which gave Holiday Inns more headaches than they did profits.

The new management has defined Holiday Inns as a lodging company, and will enter into new businesses only if they are compatible with its main products: food, lodging, and entertainment. Said a company official, "Wherever the customer is going, we are there."

Source of data: "Holiday Inns: Refining Its Focus to Food, Lodging—and More Casinos," *Business Week,* July 21, 1980, pp. 100–104.

ness, defensiveness, or flexibility, that form a distinct pattern for the company's activities, opinions, and actions. That pattern is instilled in employees by the examples provided by managers and is passed on to succeeding generations of new managers.

In fact, those influences on corporate purpose noted above are folded into the firm's corporate culture. The firm's purpose or mission, then, should reflect its corporate culture.

PepsiCo Inc. represents an example of a company whose corporate culture was preventing the company from meeting competitive threats and resulting in its stagnation—yet was consciously changed over two decades to become a much more aggressive corporate culture. At one time, the company was satisfied to be second best, offering Pepsi as a less expensive alternative to Coca-Cola. But, today, a new manager learns swiftly that beating the competition is the surest road to career success. Winning is the key at Pepsi. Losing has its definite drawbacks. Marketers and other managers know they must win merely to stay where they are—and must wipe out the competition to move ahead. Such an aggressive corporate culture is clearly translated into the corporate mission of toppling Coca-Cola from its market leadership position. (See Application 18-2.)

From the corporate purpose, the organization determines a set of objectives that direct the firm generally over a five- to ten-year period. Such goals reflect the expected achievements of the organization as a whole and generally are in terms of sales growth, market share improvements, profits, innovation, acquisitions, and risk reduction. Recently, because of inflation and the high cost of borrowing, many corporations set *cash flow* goals, wanting to improve the immediate amount of cash the firm has to spend on corporatewide improvements.

From overall corporate objectives flow more specific marketing goals. Although such objectives often focus on overall sales increases, more usually they are aimed at more precise targets, such as sales increases by geographic region, by product class, or by market segment. Recent studies have shown that increases in market share generally lead to higher profitability. Market share improvement translates into higher volume; higher volume means lower production costs and higher profits. So modern marketing objectives are often set in terms of improvement in market share, the measure of how well an organization is doing relative to competitors.

Since there are usually many objectives, the overall goals are generally set in some *priority ranking*. Some goals are clearly more important than others. Additionally, some goals are logically dropped when others are set. As best as possible, objectives should be measurable; that is, there should be a particular numerical goal so that management can measure progress and determine when the objective has been met. And goals must be *achievable;* unrealistic goals serve no purpose but to frustrate management. Finally, organizational goals must be *consistent;* they must follow from one another. To simultaneously set goals of maximizing sales and minimizing costs is not feasible. We all know it takes money to make money.

An elaboration of the Pepsi-Cola situation will help illustrate. As already noted, Pepsi-Cola was a distant second cousin to Coca-Cola. During World War II, both companies found growth as they both symbolized American patriotism around the world. Yet, after the war, Pepsi's market share declined. At that time, a dynamic, marketing-oriented Alfred N. Steele became president and recognized the problems facing the company:

—A very plain bottle with a paper label that dirtied during distribution and helped cause a tarnished image for Pepsi

—A clearly inferior taste amplified by poor quality control

—Its prior appeal of more Pepsi for its price ("Twice as Much for a Nickel, Too" advertising campaign) lessened by a rise in price following a rise in costs

—Poor employee morale

Application 18-2
Corporate Culture—
Matchmaker, Matchmaker . . .
"Make Me a Match"

A corporation's culture can be either a major strength or a pitfall.

International Business Machines Corporation's service philosophy is hard to match in any other corporation. IBM keeps a hot line open 24 hours a day, seven days a week, to service its products. This culture dominates the giant computer company, and it is credited with IBM's unparalleled success in the marketplace.

Delta Air Lines, Inc., has, since its founding, focused on customer service above all else. Delta employees frequently substitute in other jobs to keep planes flying and to make certain that baggage arrives with the customer.

But a culture that prevents a company from meeting competition or from adapting to changes in its environment can result in stagnation and failure unless the company takes action.

The American Telephone & Telegraph Company is again trying to alter its service-oriented operation to give equal weight to marketing. Its earlier attempts to do so ignored the company's culture and failed. For example, in 1961 AT&T set up a school to teach managers how to coordinate the design and manufacture of data products to create and sell custom services. When managers completed the course, however, they found that making noncustomized mass sales was what counted in the company. They were not given the analyses needed nor were they rewarded for their efforts. Consequently, 85 percent of the graduates quit, and AT&T disbanded the school.

In a break with tradition, AT&T is now going outside the company to hire executives. Archie J. McGill, a former IBM executive, was made vice president of business marketing. McGill is described by his associates as an innovator. He is in sharp contrast to the traditional "Bell-shaped man" because of his "combative, adversarial style." McGill's slogan, "I make the difference," is being hammered into each of his marketers to encourage them to become entrepreneurs. But this time, the new strategy is reinforced by incentives that pit salespeople against one another for bonuses. Clearly, AT&T internal culture has changed.

Source of data: "Corporate Culture, The Hard-to-Change Values That Spell Success or Failure," *Business Week*, Oct. 27, 1980, pp. 148–160.

From such problem recognition, Steele and his fellow top managers set a master plan to truly compete with Coke. It has two phases. The first phase (1950–1955) set up the following broad objectives:

—Improve Pepsi Cola's taste

—Develop a unified design for the bottle and other corporate symbols

—Develop an advertising campaign to upgrade Pepsi's image

—Make in-roads in Coca-Cola's "take-home" business

—Increase market share specifically in twenty-five major cities

By 1955, these goals had been met and sales had increased. The second phase was set in motion. Steele's phase 2 objectives were to:

—Make distinct market share in-roads on Coke's "on-premise" market, especially the vending machine and cold-bottle sales

—Introduce different-sized bottles to add convenience to the take-home and cold-bottle market segments

—Offer bottlers special financing to buy and install Pepsi vending machines

These major objectives all were consistent and apparently feasible. By 1960, Pepsi's sales had zoomed to 4 times their level in 1950. And this beginning has kept Pepsi on the competitive doorstep of Coca-Cola. In 1981, Pepsi-Cola commanded a 25 percent share of the soft-drink business while Coke stood at 35 percent. Share growth throughout the 1970s was 5 percent for Pepsi-Cola versus 3 percent for Coke. In the food stores where two-fifths of the soft drinks are purchased, Pepsi snatched the lead in 1977 and has stayed ahead.

The Situation Analysis

In the situation analysis phase, strategic marketing planners analyze information about the pertinent variables in the environment surrounding the organization. They look *outside* the organization. Such environmental scanning views the present state of the uncontrollable influences and forecasts their trends. The planners also turn *inside* and analyze their organization's strengths and weaknesses. Not only are tangible, observable resources assessed, but also the qualitative features, such as personnel expertise, goodwill, and corporate image. This analysis then brings to the surface the opportunities and threats that exist in the environment, the strengths and weaknesses residing in the firm. The outcome of this analysis is an understanding of how appropriate environmental opportunities can be matched with the distinctive competencies of the organization. This, then, is the crucial step in the strategic marketing planning process.

The Environment— Looking outside the Strategic Window

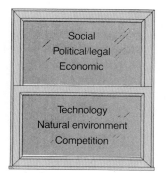

**Figure 18-2
Environmental
scanning—looking
outside the strategic
window.**

One of the strong imperatives of the strategic planning process is to monitor the environment that surrounds the organization and to forecast the direction and intensity of changes. The marketing environment represents all forces and institutions that lie outside the organization and at least potentially affect that organization. It is critical that marketers keep an alignment between these environmental variables and the organization's objectives, strategies, and marketing program. In Chapter 2 we discussed the major uncontrollable variables and their trends. Changes in these political, economic, technological, social, natural, and competitive environments can be both gateways and barriers to strategic success for a marketing organization. (See Figure 18-2.)

In some industries or firms, more than one of these environments have an impact. Consider the firearms industry. Such firms as Remington Arms Co., Smith & Wesson, and Colt Industries, Inc., have been mired in problems recently. The list of environmental threats and barriers is long and impressive: "skyrocketing product liability costs, highly restricted export markets, burgeoning labor and materials costs, foreign gunrunning scandals, the recurring threat of federal gun controls, diminishing hunting grounds and shorter hunting seasons, stiff competition from imports, and, recently, competition from foreign companies manufacturing firearms in the U. S."[4] These political, legal, economic, and competitive pressures have severely dampened enthusiasm within this industry's domestic competitors and motivated many, such as Smith & Wesson, Colt, and Winchester, to diversify out of the firearms business.

In other industries or firms, the main concern is with the impact of one overriding environmental factor. Consider Xerox Corporation. Its share of the United States copier revenues plummeted from 96 percent in 1970 to just 46 percent in 1980, largely because of Japanese competition. In the mid-1970s, a host of Japanese producers introduced low-price copiers in the United States and nearly eliminated Xerox from this market segment. In the 1980s, the Japanese are leveling their sights on the medium- and high-performance end of the copier market—the lucrative heartland of Xerox's business. Xerox has counterattacked in the small copiers field with a line of new models and additional marketing channels. It is also conducting a massive corporate overhaul in preparation for the battle heating up in larger machines.

Strategic planning, then, must include a sensing of the environment. Central to this task is the marketing information system (MIS) that we saw in Chapter 3. The marketing intelligence subsystem of the MIS has as its purpose the constant monitoring of the external forces that affect marketing efforts. Changes, even subtle ones, should be carefully and continually analyzed and this assessment incorporated into the strategic marketing plan.

Xerox has broadened its intelligence activity directed at the Japanese by linking

---

[4]"Why the Firearms Business Has Tired Blood," *Business Week,* Nov. 27, 1978, p.107.

up with a Japanese company, Fuji-Xerox. Xerox uses Fuji-Xerox through Rank-Xerox, its 51 percent-owned British subsidiary, which in turn owns 50 percent of the Japanese company. Fuji-Xerox is an extemely independent company, but the partnership has offered Xerox a valuable window on Japanese industry, especially its cost-cutting approach to manufacturing.

During an analysis of the environment, the organization should segment the market and determine whether different environmental variables have differing influences on the various segments. The changing family roles of women, for instance, have a much greater impact on younger market segments than on older ones, and, of course, on women more than on men. Once the segments are identified, the organization chooses those toward which it will target its strategic plans. Strategic plans, then, are target-segment specific. As such, they must reflect the appropriate environmental factors.

Midway Airlines, the short-haul service operating from Chicago's Midway Airport as a hub and with spokes into Cleveland, Detroit, and Kansas City provides a good illustration. In 1976, the then vice-president of a consulting firm and now president of Midway, Kenneth Carlson, heard from a Civil Aeronautics Board (CAB) official that the airline industry might become deregulated.

"I guess that's when the whole idea started," recalls Carlson. "This fellow from the CAB and I were talking about how someday soon the government would deregulate the airline industry.

"The airlines were resisting the movement and predicting that economic chaos would result from deregulation. But I envisioned deregulation as an opportunity."

"Then the CAB official started telling me about a problem his agency was having. He said CAB management was complaining because the major airlines refused to move out of Chicago's crowded O'Hare Airport and into dormant Midway Airport."

"Looking ahead a few years, I thought that if deregulation did occur and Midway was available, that would create the climate for a new airline company. It was just a gut reaction."[5]

Midway Airlines began business late in 1979 and became a thriving company because two environmental forces—political and competitive—created a new segment of the market at which Midway targeted its efforts.

The Organization— Looking inside the Strategic Window

Once the relevant external variables have been analyzed, planners next consider their available resources, both tangible and, often more important, intangible. Planners should thoroughly review the financial resources, production and distribution systems, and other easily observed resources. But they should also analyze the intangible resources, such as corporate image and culture, creative and administrative talent, employee attitudes toward the company, and vulnerability to competition. These intangibles, though difficult to monitor, often mean the difference between success

[5]"Midway Airlines Takes Off without Marketing Research," *Marketing News*, vol. 13, no. 15 (Jan. 25, 1980), p.1.

and failure. In short, evaluating resources determines the strengths and weaknesses on which the marketing strategy will capitalize. Two approaches to organizational analysis have become popular, and we will look at them right after advancing the notion of strategic business units.

Perhaps no company has made more advances in strategic marketing planning than General Electric, often referred to as the most diversified company in the country. In the 1970s, GE brought to strategic planning the concept of strategic business units (SBU). To add simplicity to its complex organization, the company reorganized its forty-eight divisions and nine product lines into SBUs. Each SBU comprises one or more products, brands, company divisions, or market segments that have something in common, such as the same distribution system, similar consumer benefits, or like technology. These SBUs have their own corporate mission and distinct set of competitors, and essentially each has its own distinct strategic plan. Many companies—International Paper, Ocean Spray, Union Carbide—have adopted this SBU approach; it is estimated that about 20 percent of the largest manufacturing firms in the United States have adopted this system. Just recently, as an example, the Campbell Soup Company overhauled its brand-management system and established eight separate strategic business units that operate independently, each with its own general manager. The eight SBUs are Soups, Beverages, Pet Foods, Frozen Foods, Fresh Produce, Main Meals, Grocery, and Food Service. Thus, the regular soup line, Manhandlers, and Chunky-style soups were combined into one SBU. Each SBU has been given both greater freedom than under the brand-management approach and the mission to become more aggressive—to seek new products and to create more of a marketing image than its past product orientation.

The BCG Portfolio Analysis

The Boston Consulting Group (BCG), a management consulting firm, has advanced the notion that, just as with personal investment securities, SBUs should be managed as a portfolio. Here, different SBUs have different purposes but they all fit together in a grand fashion to achieve the organization's overall objectives. Top management, then, strategically plans which business units to build, maintain, phase down, or get rid of. In short, the organization continually improves its portfolio by divesting itself of poor businesses and by acquiring promising new ones. In this way, all SBUs work as a team to achieve the organization's goals.

The BCG approach focuses on three factors: market growth, the SBU's *relative market share*, and cash flow. It defines a four-cell graph based on high and low industry growth and on high or low relative market share (See Figure 18.3.)

The definition of high growth, while somewhat arbitrary, is generally determined as having an annual rate of growth of 10 percent. This cutoff point comes from many industry and company studies conducted by the Boston Consulting Group. The focus on growth rate reflects the inclusion of concern for the product life cycle in the analysis. High-growth markets occur in the rapid growth and slow growth stages of the product life cycle.

The *relative market share* of an organization's SBU is determined by dividing the SBU's market share by that of its largest competitor. Thus, in 1980, Gillette's razors and blades SBU had a dominant 60 percent market share while Schick, its largest

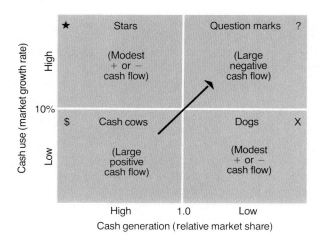

Figure 18-3 The BCG portfolio matrix.

competitor, had 22 percent, and Bic had 9 percent . Therefore, their respective relative market share positions would be as follows:

Gillette: 2.73 (60 ÷ 22)

Schick: 0.37 (22 ÷ 60)

Bic: 0.15 (9 ÷ 60)

The dividing line between high and low relative market share is generally set at "1." Thus only the market share leader will lie to the left of this point; only market leaders can be "stars" or "cash cows." And the higher an SBU's market share, the more it generates cash and, as studies have shown, the higher its profitability. Yet, in higher growth markets, the higher is the cash usage of the SBU.

Portfolio analysis is most concerned with cash flow, the disposable money generated by a SBU that is coming into an organization. Rather than profits or sales, as we have noted, many modern organizations see cash flow as the most important corporate objective, and the BCG approach reflects this.

SBUs are placed in the cells depending upon the amount of cash they give off (as in Figure 18-3). There are four types of SBUs:

Stars: These SBUs experience high growth rate and high relative market share. They are the leaders in their market. They need a continual shot of cash to maintain their growth. Eventually, their market growth will slow and stars will become cash cows.

Cash cows: Cash cows have a higher market share than competitors in a low growth market. Cash cows have high sales volume and low costs. Thus, they generate more cash than they need; that excess cash can be used to support other SBUs.

Question marks: These high-growth low relative market share SBUs are problems for management because their future direction is uncertain. While market growth

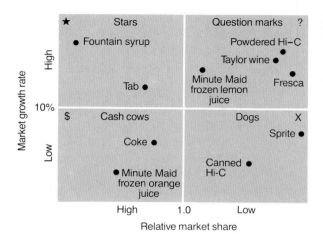

Figure 18-4   Coca-Cola Company's portfolio. (Adapted from Maurice I. Mandell and Larry J. Rosenberg, Marketing, 2d ed., Prentice-Hall, Inc., Englewood Cliffs, N.J., 1981, p. 104)

provides momentum, they need a lot of cash to *hold* their competitive position, and much more to *increase* their market share. Management must decide whether to infuse excess cash in the hope of making them into leaders; if not, these SBUs will likely be phased out of the portfolio.

Dogs: Dogs are low-growth, low-share SBUs. They may provide enough cash to support themselves, but do not promise to be a substantial cash resource. Such SBUs are often just entering a market or phasing out. Either way, their position is below average.

The distribution of an organization's SBUs in the different cells of the matrix, then, provides an internal profile of the health of the firm. Such an analysis of Coca-Cola'a SBUs was conducted in the late 1970s and is displayed in Figure 18-4.

But such a display needs to consider the future direction of each SBU. Figure 18-5 shows how SBUs might move over time. Organizations prefer that question marks be made into stars and then, as growth slows, that they become cash cows to

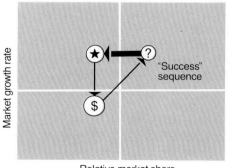
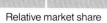
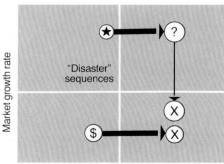

Figure 18-5   Changes in the portfolio over time.

fund other question marks. This is precisely the sequence at Gillette where the excess cash from the razor blade business was funneled into disposable lighters and resulted in its Cricket entry becoming a star.

In the worst situation, a star loses sufficient market share to become a question mark and, as growth slows, becomes a dog that is ready to be phased out of the portfolio. Such was the case with Adidas's American line of jogging shoes. Once the leader in the highly growing market, it lost market share to Nike's running shoe SBU and, as the jogging market became saturated in the early 1980s, dropped to the dog status. In still another scenario a cash cow, often through neglect or heavy competition, loses its leadership position and becomes a dog. This represents the sequence for the K2 line of skis which were displaced by Rossignol as the industry leader in a rather static growth market.

Analysis of the organization via the portfolio approach provides some future strategic direction, then, to the strategic planner. Basically, four strategies are available:

Build: This alternative is particularly appropriate for question marks if they are to be made to grow into stars. Here, the firm invests money to improve the product quality, develop promotional campaigns, or subsidize price reductions—all to beat the competition. But clearly, market share building is expensive.

Xerox has begun heavy investment to build a leading position in the small but exploding office-automation business unit. The company has moved boldly and quickly to establish its SBU. IBM has chosen the distributed processing, personal computer, and office automation businesses as its prime investment opportunity for the 1980s.

Hold: Cash cows and stars that are strongly entrenched are protected by this strategy. Here the market leader simply defends its market share and keeps its customer loyalty.

Until very recently, Coca-Cola has calmly sat back in a "hold" strategy and watched PepsiCo aggressively pursue market share. In 1981, the company's new chief executive, Robert C. Goizueta, openly admonished the company's stance of protecting its past successes and changed over to a "build" strategy, setting sights on a goal of 1 percent growth over and above the industry rate of 3 percent. However, building in such a low-growth market is expensive.

Harvest: When the future looks dim for a weak cash cow, a dog, or even a question mark, the strategy may well be to drain as much cash as possible before letting it go. Here, expenditures on marketing (especially promotional) and research and development (R&D) are curtailed, manufacturing economies are emphasized, customer services reduced—in short, all costs are lowered as the SBU is "milked" of its cash-generating opportunities.

Until recently, Standard Brands (now Nabisco Brands) had a well-earned reputation as one of the industry's slowest-growing companies because of an overall strategy based on harvesting. The company consciously squeezed every last cent out of such brands as Chase & Sanborn coffee, Curtiss candies, Planters nuts, and

Fleischmann's liquor and margarine brands. A "milking strategy" was employed by cheapening formulas, cutting marketing budgets, and raising prices for short-term profits. In the Standard Brands case, this strategy was poorly conceived since it weakened brands that had good long-term potential.

Once products are marked for harvest, they often remain on the market long after funds have been removed. Lifebuoy soap, for instance, has been distributed without advertising or promotional support for many years, yet provides sufficient profit to justify its continuation.

Divest: Once a dog or a question mark has no future, it is sold off or dropped from the portfolio because the cash needed to fund it can be used better elsewhere in the organization.

The divestiture of businesses happens frequently. International Telephone & Telegraph Corp., in the space of three years, divested itself of thirty-three businesses that the giant company considered poor performers in order to build a base around its primary business, telecommunications. Among its divestitures of 1980 alone were lighting, wire products, cosmetics, electrical parts distribution, television sales and rentals, timberlands business, and a South African telecommunications company.

The BCG approach has been a very popular one in analyzing the internal working of the organization. (See Application 18-3.) It supplies a simple map of where the organizational parts are and where they are going—and provides strategic direction. It emphasizes three key factors—market growth rate, relative market share, and cash flow. Yet, this approach has its limitations. In some instances, organizations are less concerned with their cash flow. And in some situtations, market share increases do not result in increased profitability because there is a point beyond which further increases in market share become prohibitively expensive. Also, the analysis hinges on the planner's definition of the market. For example, if Gillette's razor and blade SBU were further subdivided into two—one the regular replacement blade market and the other the disposable razor market—a different picture would emerge. In the replacement blade market, Bic does not compete. Gillette's market share percentage can be decomposed into 49 percent toward replacement blades and 11 percent toward disposables, where Bic has a 9 percent share. Thus in the disposable segment, Gillette's leadership position is highly challenged, an observation that is not apparent from a more global definition of the razor blade market. And from an internal resource analysis standpoint, the BCG approach lumps all of an organization's resources into one variable, relative market share. This does not provide much depth of analysis of the interworkings of the organization. So the BCG approach must be used with care; yet, it does provide a nice initial planning tool.

General Electric's Business Screen

Some critics of the BCG approach point to its emphasis on only two factors (industry growth and relative market share) to define an SBU's position. They believe that an analysis of the organization's resources should not be reduced to simply relative

Application 18-3
Employing the BCG Portfolio Analysis at Scott—
Shoot for the Stars and Shoot the Dogs

If a product has a chance of becoming a star, put your resources—meaning money—behind it, and let the dogs struggle along or get rid of them.

This strategy is simple to summarize, but not so simple to act on. Simply put, many companies are placing their big dollars behind products which display the greatest potential in the marketplace. At the same time, they're letting some old-name products die on the vine.

One firm following this course is Scott Paper Company, which has made the conscious decision

to give full attention and support to becoming the low-cost producer of consumer paper products and to let some old standbys fend for themselves.

Scott intends to "milk" some of its older products for whatever cash they're worth. Little advertising support will be given to them. A few older products will be repositioned and others will likely disappear from the supermarket shelves. Those rather well-known products singled out for this harvesting strategy include Cottonelle and Soft 'n' Pretty Tissues, Scotkins and Western Living Napkins, Confidets Sanitary Napkins, and Soft-Weave Tissue.

While these products slowly disappear, Scott will spend during the next five years about $2 billion on those products thought to have high prospects. The building strategy will be applied to lower-priced toilet tissue (ScotTissue, Family Scott, Waldorf), paper towels (ScotTowels, Viva, Job Squad), and facial tissues (Scotties), as well as some napkin products and a baby wipe.

Source of data: "Torn Up by Rivals, Scott Paper Draws Up Long-Term Strategy to Regain Stature," *The Wall Street Journal,* May. 11, 1981, pp. 29.

market share. They feel this oversimplification masks many factors besides the market's growth that make a business attractive and many other factors that identify a business's strength. We noted some of these at the beginning of this section. Such critics often prefer the investment opportunity chart or "business screen" developed by General Electric.

With the G.E. business screen approach, strategic business units are positioned according to how well they rate on certain success requirements, referred to as their *business strength,* within industries categorized by measures of opportunity, referred to as their *industry attractiveness.* Here, the BCG method is expanded from single measures of market share and growth to many measures of business strength and industry attractiveness. Such measures of business strength might include assessments of the SBU's product quality, price sensitivity, knowledge of the market, technological capability, image, and so on, while industry attractiveness might be measured by such factors as competitive intensity, seasonality of sales, legal constraints, importance of technological change, and the like. Clearly, not all these can be measured as objectively and thus as precisely as with the BCG approach. Yet, clearly, the G.E. method offers much greater flexibility and comprehensiveness to the analyst.

General Electric itself has experimented with many combinations of forty factors over the years to get the set of measures that most accurately represents what constitutes the best measure of industry attractiveness and business strength. Certainly, as the environment and the company's portfolio change, so does the importance of various industry and business measures. Furthermore, different companies would focus on different factors. In 1980, G.E. found the six measures of industry attractiveness and the nine measures of business position shown in Figure 18-6 to be those that best assessed its portfolio of SBUs. Notice the inclusion of inflation recovery and reflections of multinational markets in its factors. These would not have been included in the early 1970s.

The business screen is used in this way. The nine-cell matrix is divided into three zones; G.E. colored them green, yellow, and red (hence, it is often called the "stoplight" approach). The three zones at the upper left indicate those industries that are favorable in attractiveness and match the SBU's strengths. They have a *green* light

Figure 18-6   General Electric's business screen. (*Adapted from Charles W. Hofer and Dan Schendel*, Strategy Formulation: Analytical Concepts, *West Publishing Co., 1978, p. 32*)

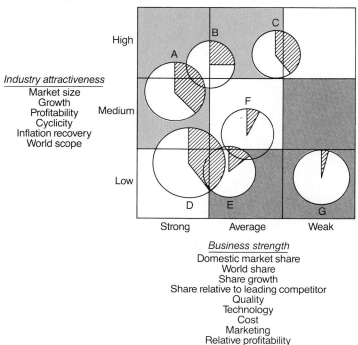

to "go" in investment to grow. Those three cells along the diagonal indicate industries medium in interest. They have a *yellow light* to denote "*caution*"; usually these businesses warrant a maintenance of share strategy. The three cells in the lower right show weak businesses where a harvesting or divesting strategy may be the best option.

The circles represent the SBUs; their size is in proportion to the size of the industries in which they compete. The pie slices represent the SBU's market share within that industry. Planners go a step further and project the expected future position of the SBU. Such trend analysis provides a clearer picture upon which to make strategic decisions.

As a result of the use of the business screen, General Electric has defined five investment groups in which its SBUs fall:

High growth businesses deserving the highest investment support (engineering plastics, transportation, and medical systems)

Steady reinvestiment businesses deserving high and steady investment (lamps, major appliances, and gas turbines)

Support businesses deserving steady investment support (meters and specialty tranformers)

Selective pruning or rejuvenation businesses deserving reduced investment

Venture businesses deserving heavy R&D investment (man-made diamonds and 10-ton aircraft engines)

Reevaluation of Objectives

The initial setting of corporate and marketing objectives guides strategic marketing planners through the situation analysis, the environmental scanning, and the resources evaluation. These goals, however, may be found to be inappropriate once the situation surrounding the organization has been analyzed. Often, marketers discover information that requires revision of the original objectives.

Recently, Warner-Lambert employed the GE business screen in conducting a massive two-year review of all phases of its business. The review resulted in a resetting of its major objectives. The company developed three major goals:

To strengthen its existing consumer and pharmaceutical businesses
To seek emerging high-technology health-care markets
To eliminate businesses that don't meet certain criteria for profitability and growth[6]

To meet these goals, the company produced the strategic plan shown in Figure 18-7.

---

[6]"Ad Dollars Flow in W–L Master Plan," *Advertising Age,* April 6, 1981, p. 82.

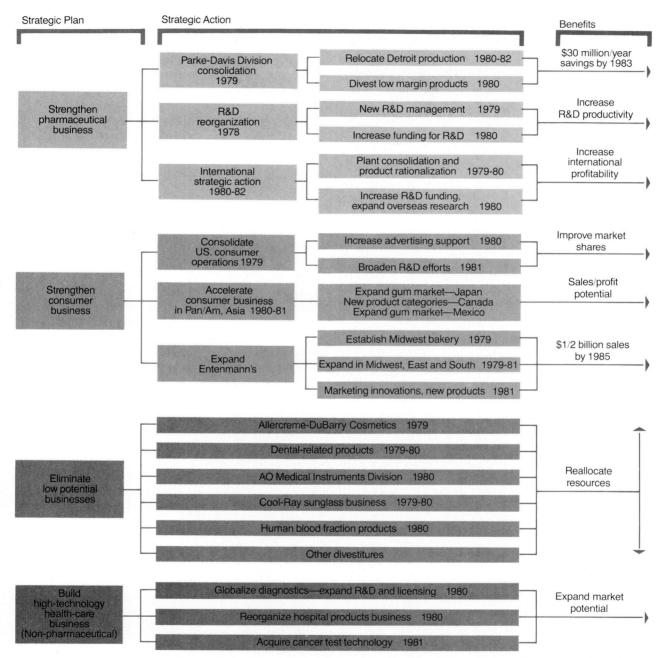

Figure 18-7   Warner-Lambert's strategic plan. (*Adapted from* Advertising Age, *April 6, 1981, p. 2*)

Strategic Alternatives and the Strategic Decision[7]

Once strategic marketing planners have analyzed information about both their environment and their internal resources, they are in a position to choose a strategy or game plan to meet their goals. A strategy provides some principles of competitive warfare that direct the activities of the marketing organization as it strives to reach its goals. Marketers do not pick a strategy at random. Instead, the situation review provides useful information upon which to make such a decision. Such information focuses on environmental factors such as competitive strategies, the target market's buying behavior, and the nature of the economy, while the internal analysis focuses on resources and the organization's position in the product life cycle. Perhaps most useful in determining an organization's strategy is its competitive size and market position. In the United States, there has been a continuing trend toward bigness within industries. Competitive power has been concentrated in the hands of a few companies. The beer industry provides a good example. In 1970, there were 92 breweries in this country; in 1980, there were only 41. The big get bigger by virtue of their aggressive competitive efforts. Some industry analysts believe that by the mid-1980s, Anheuser-Busch and Miller Brewing Company together will control 70 percent of the beer market. In the computer industry, some experts believe that by 1990 only three competitors will remain: IBM, AT&T, and the Japanese.

Some recent research by the Boston Consulting Group[8] and by a nonprofit organization called the Strategic Planning Institute[9] have found that industries tend toward a competitive equilibrium point. Called by the Boston Consulting Group the "rule of three and four," findings have shown that over time as markets become competitively stable, there are never more than three significant competitors. Any competitor with less than one-fourth the share of the largest competitor cannot effectively compete. These findings provide a nice framework for locating an organization's competitive position and identifying some alternative strategies. We will now look at strategic options of market leaders, market challengers, market followers, and market nichers.

Market Share Leader Strategies

Virtually every market has one organization with dominant market share that sets the innovative pace for other market competitors. Some well-known leaders include General Motors, Anheuser-Busch (with its "*King* of Beers"), Sears, Roebuck &

---

[7]Parts of this section have been adapted from Philip Kotler, *Marketing Management: Planning Analysis and Control,* 4th ed., Prentice-Hall, Inc., Englewood Cliffs, N.J., 1980), chap. 11.

[8]Boston Consulting Group, "The Rule of Three and Four," *Perspectives,* no. 187, Boston: Boston Consulting Group.

[9]Robert D. Buzzell, "Are There Natural Market Structures?" *Journal of Marketing,* vol. 45, no. 1 (Winter 1981), pp. 42–51.

Company, McDonald's, Procter & Gamble, IBM, Coca-Cola, and Gillette. Some leaders have highly dominant market shares (Gillette, with 60 percent market share, towers over its closest competitor, Schick, which has 22 percent market share), while others have lower shares (Hanes leads the panty-hose market with about 12 percent share). And, of course, the market leader is the only competitor that can be classified a star or a cash cow.

Basically, leaders must be constantly monitoring the competitive environment to avoid a competitive coup. The dominant firm's goal is to stay on top, but doing so is not easy. IBM, for instance, found its adherence to mainframe computers throughout the 1970s caused its overall market share to slip from 60 percent of the computer marketplace in 1970 to about 32 percent in 1981. Even giants can fall—and IBM is a giant. IBM's revenues were larger than the next seven United States computer companies combined, making it the nation's eighth largest industrial company. Market leaders can become weak by missing evolving market opportunities, becoming less cost-conscious, or being too conservative. IBM's problem was the first—it ignored such high-growth markets as distributed data processing and office automation.

Market leaders can take a defensive posture and protect their market share or take a more aggressive approach by increasing either the total market or their relative market share. Anheuser-Busch (A-B), with a 26 percent market share, provides an example of a protectionistic strategy used to hold on to its teetering crown. Miller Brewing Co. rose from 4.2 percent market share to 21 percent over the decade of the 1970s. To counter that competitive assault, Busch in 1980 began using a "flanking" strategy whereby each Miller entry in a particular category is bracketed by two or more A-B brands. In the premium beer segment, for instance, A-B reformulated and repackaged its formerly popular-price Busch Bavarian to accompany Budweiser. In the light beer caregory, A-B offered Michelob Light and Bud Light to combine with its Natural Light to compete against Miller's Lite. Such a "fortification" strategy helps to keep A-B before the eyes of the consumers and to hold on to shelf space at the dealer level.

Some leaders strategically improve their dominance by seeking expansion of the total market. Here, the strategy can be to get *new users* (Johnson & Johnson has expanded its baby products usage to adults and Nabisco Brands is moving into new geographical markets such as Asia and the Middle East with its Planters nuts, Curtiss candies, and Royal gelatin), by promoting *new uses* for a product (Arm & Hammer shows consumers that its baking soda can be used for brightening teeth, absorbing odors in the refrigerator, and improving the smell of kitty litter boxes), and by getting *greater usage* of the product (Campbell's offers many recipes incorporating its soups). To further expand on Campbell's, the company, with 80 percent market share in a 1 percent growth market, launched a new ad strategy simply to make people hungrier for soup. Unable in the past to stimulate great growth, the company spent $23 million on a "Soup is Good Food" campaign that emphasizes the nutritional value of soup.

Finally, market leaders can get aggressive and attempt to take market share from competitors. This confrontation strategy becomes more expensive as an organization's market share becomes higher; more money and effort must be spent to pull away loyal consumers. Such "holdout" consumers are difficult to convert. Some ways in which leaders have attempted to compete for expanded market share are through offering a product innovation (Hertz Rent-A-Car hurries customers along with its "People Express"), through market segmentation (Kellogg's appeals to adults and especially to women with its Nutri-Bran and Smart Start cereals), and through clever promotional efforts ("It's a miracle," exclaimed Brother Dominic for Xerox).

Market Share Challenger Strategies

Behind the leader in market share lies its enemy, the market share challengers. Challengers can take on the leader directly through what is called a *direct-attack strategy* (Pepsi, with its burning desire to be No. 1, goes toe-to-toe with Coca-Cola); they can take on other runners-up through a *backdoor strategy* (U.S. Time, with its low-price Timex watches, avoided the leaders by distributing through mass merchandisers rather than specialty jewelry stores); or they can aggressively pursue smaller firms by means of a *guppy strategy* (many beer brewers gained market share by buying up smaller regional competitors).

To be an effective challenger, the leader's weakness must be identified and exploited. Some ways in which challengers have been competitively successful include:

Price-reduction strategy: Datril challenged Tylenol by initially offering its equivalent brand of nonaspirin pain reliever at almost $1 less per 100 tablets.

Product extension strategy: Hunt went after Heinz's ketchup leadership by offering several new ketchup flavors and bottle sizes.

Product innovation strategy: Miller's meteoric rise to second place in the beer industry was due to its development of the low-calorie, less filling Lite beer.

Better service strategy: Avis challenged Hertz with the appeal "We try harder" and offered faster service and cleaner cars.

Distribution improvement strategy: Hanes outcompeted the then leader by bringing its panty hose to drug stores and supermarkets—and away from the conventional outlets of department stores and specialty stores. (See Application 18-4.)

Market Follower Strategies

In some industries, the leader is too strong to be challenged. In the competitor's judgment, the costs of the attack would be greater than the benefits that would likely result. Often the leader can humble a challenger by quickly reducing prices, improving services, or offering a strong promotional campaign. In short, from the perspective of the competitor, the leader has too much staying power to be toppled. In many cases, the better strategy is to avoid retaliation and simply to follow the market leader with a "me-too" type strategy. This approach is particularly appropriate in industries where the product is standardized (stationery, starch, paint remover), where there is little

Application 18-4
Competitive Strategies—Razors Getting Cutthroat

Gillette Company, after two decades of being pushed around by Bic, is finally shoving back. The competition between the pair is bloody. The chosen weapon is price slashing, and the prize is market share.

French-owned Bic entered the United States market in 1960 with its pens, but Gillette saw Bic only as a gnat. Ten years later, Bic again challenged Gillette in the disposable cigarette-lighter business, and Gillette's Cricket brand slid to second place. But Gillette wasn't overly concerned since pens and lighters accounted for only 15 percent of its sales. What did get Gillette's attention was Bic's entry into the razor business, the core of Gillette's market.

Bic holds a 9 percent share of the United States disposable blade market, only a shade less than the 11 percent carved out by Gillette's Good News. Bic paid dearly for that 9 percent. Its advertising

(Randy Matusow)

budget is running at about $7 million annually, compared with Gillette's $2 million budgeted for Good News. Moreover, between 1977 and 1980, Bic lost almost $25 million on its razor—or about one-half of its total pretax profits. During the same period, Gillette consistently made money on its disposable razor.

Gillette's strategy is to keep as much pressure as possible on Bic's profits, with the hope that its rival will be forced out of the razor market. To increase that pressure, Gillette is putting the squeeze on Bic's other businesses. In 1979, Gillette discounted its Cricket at a

price 10 percent below Bic's. While the attack did not appreciably harm Bic's market share, it did serve to hold profits that would have been put into Bic's razor business. And Gillette's Paper-Mate Division moved heavily into the low-price pen market. Low-price pens comprised 64 percent of unit volume in 1981, compared with 10 percent in 1972. Combined with the introduction of the erasable ink pen and a strong move into the office market, Gillette hit Bic again where it hurts—in its pocketbook. As a securities analyst told *The Boston Globe,* "Gillette finally hit on the idea of keeping Bic so occupied in the other businesses that it couldn't keep up the onslaught in shavers."

Source of data: "Sticking It to the Baron," *The Boston Globe,* Jan. 19, 1982, pp. 43, 48; and "Gillette Takes the Wraps Off," *Fortune,* Feb. 25, 1980, pp. 148–150.

opportunity to differentiate among competitive products, and where there is high price sensitivity. This latter characteristic can be crucial since it provides the opportunity for the leader to resort to a price war which can be disastrous for the less well-established follower.

The Seven-Up Company presents an interesting example of this. For years Seven-Up was a lackluster follower company that steadily held about a 6 percent market share in the soft-drink industry. The company was bought in 1978 by aggressive Philip Morris. The company's beverage had been positioned against other lemon-lime drinks which constitute 13 percent of all soft-drink sales while colas command 62 percent. When Philip Morris decided to reposition 7Up as a mainstream beverage, its "new" competitors were Coca-Cola Co. and PepsiCo Inc. To meet these big competitors, Philip Morris raised 7Up's advertising budget from $14.5 million in 1977 to $34.4 million in 1980.

However, Philip Morris did not anticipate Coca-Cola's strong reaction. After being hurt by the "Pepsi Challenge" advertising campaign, Coke was determined to regain its preeminence in the food stores. For a year and a half, Coke and Pepsi had been warring nationwide through furious couponing and heavy discounting. In the same combative nature, Coke took on Seven-Up by tripling its 1977 ad support for its competing lemon-lime drink, Sprite, to $11.5 million in 1980. This warfare defused 7Up's attempt for national attention and increased shelf space. In 1982, the Seven-Up Company again became aggressive with an advertising campagin stressing 7Up's lack of caffeine and also by bringing to market a noncaffeine cola called Like.

Market followers should, however, have a definite strategy of their own to move them along in a controlled fashion. Followers should choose specific market segments and develop specific advantages within those segments. Burroughs, for example, chooses not to compete head-on with IBM, but rather, to concentrate on marketing computers to the financial market segment it serves.

Market Nicher Strategies

Within almost every industry, there are a number of smaller firms that clearly avoid a direct clash with the larger competitors. These organizations have found a specialization that the majors have overlooked or consciously ignored. Nichers have found a match between their distinctive competencies and the requirements of the market. Ideally, a nicher serves a sufficiently large segment that has good growth prospects and where the nicher's specialized talents provide some measure of competitive advantage over majors. Often, simply goodwill can be a sufficient piece of ammunition to ward off attacking majors. Some ways that nichers have chosen to specialize include the following:

End-use specialist: Since the mid-1970s, Binney & Smith has broadened its product line substantially away from reliance on crayon and toward more products that are "fun to use and inspire creative self-expression."[10]

Specific customer specialist: When Oshkosh B'Gosh began in 1968 to sell children's denim overalls by mail-order catalog, the response was so great that by 1980, 44 percent of its sales of $42 million came from the children's line while its adult line was decreasing.

Product or product-line specialist: Los Angeles-based Mattel was one of the innovators in hand-held electronic toys but was outcompeted when the entry of many more advanced competitors eroded its market. Recently, the company has moved heavily into an expensive new adult product line, Intellivision, offering games involving lifelike

---

[10]"New Products Painting Rosy Future for Crayola," *Advertising Age,* Jan. 11, 1982, p. 4.

strategies and sport contests. From this, a keyboard attachment will convert it to a home computer and, with a new cable contract, Intellivision will be offered to cable subscribers.

Product-feature specialist: Tandem Computers was the first company to link two or more central processing units together. Thus, a failure anywhere in the system leads to a shift to another part of the system while the faulty parts are fixed. First Chicago Corporation uses thirty-one such units together in a worldwide network.

Quality price specialist: Rolex produces only 450,000 watches annually, 1 percent of the total Swiss watch production. Led by ultraconservative management and given to old-fashioned perfectionism, Rolex enjoys a place as an international status symbol while offering watches priced between $500 and $15,000.

Service specialist: Gould Manufacturing, making a bid to obtain part of the $2.5 billion replacement battery market, began a special service in the seven-county Chicago area. Anyone having battery trouble on the road could call 800-BAT-TERY and be serviced within an hour by one of the twenty-four leased vans operating around the clock.

Low-price specialist: MCI Communications Corp. has created a niche for itself by offering long-distance telephone service that costs 20 to 50 percent below AT&T, the industry giant.

Integrating Tactical Plans

Once a grand master plan has been set for the organization, it must support that decision with some specific tactical plans that combine to comprise the marketing mix. The strategy determines the overall plan; the tactics are the specific actions the organization undertakes to implement the strategy.

Minnetonka Softsoap provides a good example. When the company went national in 1980, it directly competed with market leaders such as Dial, the No. 1 brand with 15.6 percent market share, and P&G's Ivory, the No. 10 brand with 10.9 percent market share. How did this small company become a major challenger with more than 6 percent of the market in a little over six months? The firm's basic product innovation strategy was implemented with the following marketing-mix tactics:

Brand name: The name, Softsoap, clearly described both the product and its form.

Packaging: The package had an attractive wicker design on an unusual oval shape. Its see-through cap displayed the pump and helped the consumer see how the product was to be used.

Price: At a retail price of about $1.50, Softsoap, which the company maintains equals six bars of soap, was also economical.

Advertising: The company launched the product through television and consumer print media, spending $6 million to do so.

Sales promotion: Ads with 15-cents-off coupons ran in newspaper inserts in two widely separated months.

Distribution: The company used food brokers to sell to supermarkets and hired a national sales manager to work with the brokers.

Whatever tactical strategies a firm decides on, they must work together as an integrated whole rather than a set of isolated activities. In fact, all the parts *must* work harmoniously together in order to provide satisfaction. Marketing, after all, is a system composed of elements in a marketing mix designed to provide satisfaction to the market. Uncoordinated marketing systems give less satisfaction than they potentially could.

Assembling a total marketing program, a stategy, and a set of integrated tactics is very complicated. No one has ever discovered a foolproof plan to guarantee success for every product. Even the biggest and the most astute occasionally stumble. Procter & Gamble is widely considered one of the country's most talented marketers, but one of its biggest failures was a hair spray called Hidden Magic. Introduced right when women's hairstyles called for a fixative, Hidden Magic was a lucrative marketing opportunity. P&G seemed to have the distribution and promotional systems to turn Hidden Magic into a market leader. Yet the product was a bomb. Why? Hidden Magic bore the premium price of $2 at a time when competitive products were selling for about $1. Consumers didn't consider Hidden Magic 100 percent better than the competition. In short P&G's total marketing mix did not present the appropriate satisfaction. The price was an unsatisfactory component in an otherwise satisfactory marketing mix. As a consequence, some P&G executives refer to Hidden Magic as "Tragic Magic." (See Application 18-5.)

Organizing and Implementing

Organizing is the process of defining responsibilities and allocating authority to those who will implement the strategic and tactical plans. The various required tasks must be defined, differentiated, and matched to the appropriate people. The order of tasks must also be stated. Organizing usually culminates in an organizational chart to set the structure of the necessary tasks, the people who will carry them out, and their relationship to one another. Tasks are organized in four basic ways: by function, product, geography, and customer group. (See Figure 18-8.)

Another important aspect that must be organized is communication among decision makers in the marketing process. Executives at high levels in the structure set the procedures and policies necessary to ensure the proper implementation of the plan as well as the standards for performance that are expected at each level and for each task. Managers inform other managers about the details of the strategic and

Application 18-5
Integrating Strategy and Tactics—Putting the Pieces Together

"Pizzas today take too long to cook; these [Pizza Huts] aren't even fast-food restaurants," he says, slowly downing his ninth pizza slice of the afternoon. "And these breadsticks are a little oily, don't you think?" Cavatini, Pizza Hut's invention, is "a terrible product," says Donald Smith of Pizza Hut. Smith, the 40-year-old executive who has worked for such operations as McDonald's and Burger King, is now trying to salvage PepsiCo's Pizza Hut chain.

After six months of taste testing and inspecting 300 Pizza Hut's 4000-plus outlets, Smith is ready for the challenge. His plan: to test more than 100 changes, including new menu and decor

ideas, before starting a $100 million overhaul.

Smith wants to create two restaurants in one: a faster lunch place and an expanded-menu, "quality" dinner restautant.

A major feature of his plan will have to be an accelerated pizza cooking time, from 18 minutes to about 5 minutes. Pizza Hut then can classify as a truly *fast* food operation. To further speed up the lunch flow, Smith is experimenting with cafeteria-style ordering. Supper-menu changes, including pasta bars and sundae bars, are being tested. In addition to the menu and kitchen changes, repainting will be done, and landscaping and interiors will be

redesigned. For instance, the bright red roofs are being replaced with brown shingles, which Smith believes are more pleasing to the eye. No aspect of Pizza Hut is being overlooked.

Smith's goal is to increase the average Pizza Hut's annual sales by $100,000 and to raise the chain's return on assets from under 5 percent to more than 10 percent by 1983. Achieving these goals would add about $80 million to PepsiCo's pretax profits and should restore some of PepsiCo's prestige on Wall Street.

Source of data: "Pizza Hut's New Sales Strategy: Faster Service, Expanded Menus," *The Wall Street Journal,* Nov. 20, 1980, p. 29.

tactical plans and relay performance results. This communication flow, then, both supports and is dictated by the implementation of the strategic plan.

A strategic plan can be effective only if it is completely understood and accepted by everyone involved. Top management must make sure that information flows downward, and employees must feel that their ideas will be heard at the top of the organization. Good communications are vital for successful marketing. And execution of the plan does not always come easy. The strategic marketing planning process must include all activities, including proper organization and effective implementation, to be fully successful. (See Application 18-6.)

Review and Control

Strategic planners and marketers must exercise control in order to meet the organization's strategic objectives. In its simplest form, controlling compares actual with expected performance. If marketers find significant differences, they can take

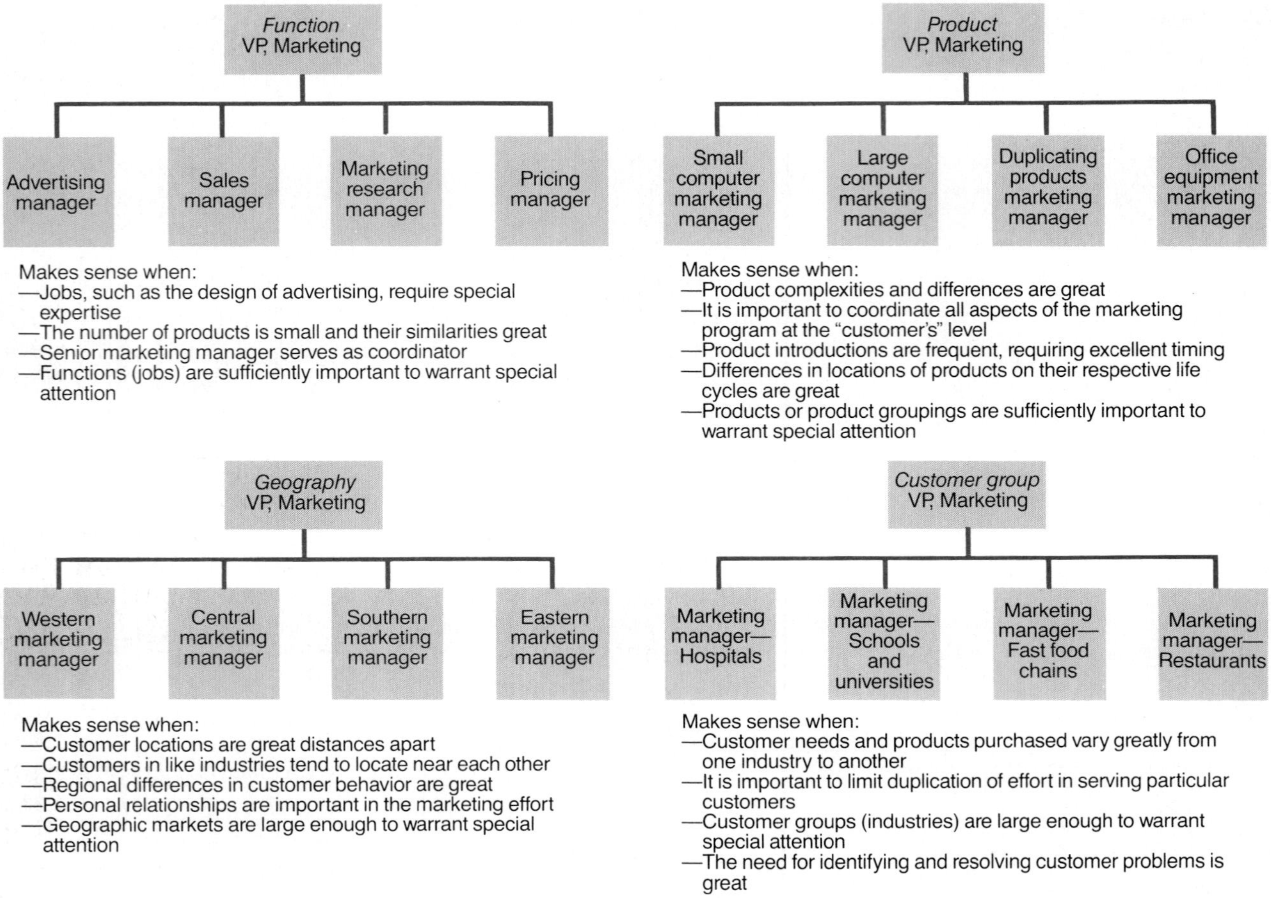

Function
VP, Marketing

| Advertising manager | Sales manager | Marketing research manager | Pricing manager |

Makes sense when:
—Jobs, such as the design of advertising, require special expertise
—The number of products is small and their similarities great
—Senior marketing manager serves as coordinator
—Functions (jobs) are sufficiently important to warrant special attention

Product
VP, Marketing

| Small computer marketing manager | Large computer marketing manager | Duplicating products marketing manager | Office equipment marketing manager |

Makes sense when:
—Product complexities and differences are great
—It is important to coordinate all aspects of the marketing program at the "customer's" level
—Product introductions are frequent, requiring excellent timing
—Differences in locations of products on their respective life cycles are great
—Products or product groupings are sufficiently important to warrant special attention

Geography
VP, Marketing

| Western marketing manager | Central marketing manager | Southern marketing manager | Eastern marketing manager |

Makes sense when:
—Customer locations are great distances apart
—Customers in like industries tend to locate near each other
—Regional differences in customer behavior are great
—Personal relationships are important in the marketing effort
—Geographic markets are large enough to warrant special attention

Customer group
VP, Marketing

| Marketing manager— Hospitals | Marketing manager— Schools and universities | Marketing manager— Fast food chains | Marketing manager— Restaurants |

Makes sense when:
—Customer needs and products purchased vary greatly from one industry to another
—It is important to limit duplication of effort in serving particular customers
—Customer groups (industries) are large enough to warrant special attention
—The need for identifying and resolving customer problems is great

Figure 18-8   Factors influencing the way in which organizations are structured to perform marketing tasks. (*Adapted from James l. Heskett,* Marketing, *Macmillan, New York, 1976, p. 445)*

corrective action. If they deem differences insignificant, they may decide against any corrective action. The MIS (marketing information system), used in the planning process, is also important and used more often for control purposes. MIS should provide information about performance so marketers can see whether they are meeting their objectives or whether they should make new decisions and take other actions. It is central to successful strategic marketing planning and to marketing.

Setting Performance Standards

For control purposes, organizational and marketing objectives must be measurable and feasible. Determining a set of criteria for control comes when marketers translate objectives into specific, measurable goals.

Application 18-6
Implementation—
A Strategy Is Only as Strong as the Weakest Link

Armed with a new strategy and a bevy of corporate planners, Standard Brands believed it was on the way to becoming a premier food marketer. When F. Ross Johnson became the company's chief executive in 1976, he installed as president a person steeped in a planning background. He then hired a coalition of planners to guide Standard Brands (SB) to success.

The grand plan was to push hard the company's established brands, make rapid acquisitions, and develop hot new products. SB stumbled, and hindsight revealed that the best strategy is worthless without good execution.

First, the idea of developing good new products met with disaster. Then a $20-million Mexican food acquisition was a failure. And while competitors were organizing their sales forces under strategic business units, SB continued with separate sales forces which managed only to bewilder buyers.

SB learned a tough lesson: good strategy, without equally good execution, doesn't solve any problems. The company had to put too much emphasis on the influence of planners and their strategy but had forgotten about the importance of implementation. As one critic of the president said, "Gutoff fell flat on his face because he didn't address himself to the day-to-day things that were required to make a business work." And Johnson himself assessed his president as having made a "tremendous contribution to the discipline of long-range planning. But we have had to adjust the kinds of skills we had in the company to accommodate to the new environment."

Finally, Johnson made the move that stopped the slide. In addition to planners, he brought in talented operating specialists who got SB back on the track.

Source of data: "When a New Product Strategy Wasn't Enough," *Business Week,* Feb. 18, 1980. pp. 142–146.

In marketing, there are two broad classes of measurement—effectiveness measures and efficiency measures. Effectiveness measures reflect the degree to which goals are reached, while the efficiency measures reflect the cost of reaching the goals. Table 18-1 shows the measures most commonly used as performance criteria.

Because sales figures reflect the marketer's effectiveness in satisfying market needs and wants, sales criteria are the most frequently used performance measures. Marketers use various sales figures to measure effectiveness—market share, percentage change in sales, and number of returned goods as well as sales broken down by product, salesperson, geographic region, type of customer, market segment, and so on. Other, more subtle measures of the degree of consumer satisfaction include the amount of product purchased, repeat purchasing, the consumer's perception of the quality of the product, its brand image, and even the volume of complaints. (Measuring the more subjective criteria requires the marketing research techniques discussed in Chapter 4.)

Efficiency measures focus on the costs of marketing activities. Costs, like sales, are viewed in the aggregate and are also broken down by product, by region, by

TABLE 18-1 Commonly Used Performance Standards

EFFECTIVENESS STANDARDS

A Sales criteria
  1 Total sales
  2 Sales by product or product line
  3 Sales by geographic region
  4 Sales by salesperson
  5 Sales by customer type
  6 Sales by market segment
  7 Sales by size of order
  8 Sales by sales territory
  9 Sales by intermediary
  10 Market share
  11 Percentage change in sales
B Customer satisfaction
  1 Quantity purchased
  2 Degree of brand loyalty
  3 Repeat purchases rates
  4 Perceived product quality
  5 Brand image
  6 Number of letters of complaint

EFFICIENCY STANDARDS

C Costs
  1 Total costs
  2 Costs by product or product line
  3 Costs by geographic region
  4 Costs by salesperson
  5 Costs by customer type
  6 Costs by market segment
  7 Costs by size of order
  8 Costs by sales territory
  9 Costs by intermediary
  10 Percentage change in costs

EFFECTIVENESS-EFFICIENCY STANDARDS

D Profits
  1 Total profits
  2 Profits by product or product line
  3 Profits by geographic region
  4 Profits by salesperson
  5 Profits by customer type
  6 Profits by market segment
  7 Profits by size of order
  8 Profits by sales territory
  9 Profits by intermediary

person, and so on. Marketers sometimes also use an index of both effectiveness and efficiency to measure profits. Profits are measured by sales (effectiveness measure) minus costs (efficiency measure).

Recently, various measures of profitability have been used to evaluate performance. While marketers are not in control of many of the costs on which profitability is based—such as R&D expenditures and manufacturing costs—recent efficiency emphasis has promoted the popularity of financial yardsticks such as return on investment (net profit ÷ investment), return on assets (net profit ÷ total assets), and profit margin (net profit ÷ sales). Such measurements are especially helpful in the analysis of specific aspects of marketing performance. Generally, such computations for an individual firm are compared with industry averages to determine their acceptability.

Forecasting

A vital task in control is forecasting—especially sales forecasting. To determine the appropriateness of the performance measures, marketers estimate what is expected for sales, costs, and profits at some future period. An inaccurate forecast will provide poor measures by which to judge the effectiveness and efficiency of the firm; it raises or understates expectations. Forecasts can be made for a short-term or long-term planning period.

Forecasting within organizations is performed in many different ways from sophisticated quantitative techniques to clear seat-of-the-pants guessing. Statistical techniques exist to analyze available data and provide reasonably accurate forecasts. Fundamentally, such techniques make the assumption that the future will be rather like the past that is reflected in the data used in the analysis. This assumption may be valid for, say, sales of bread and milk, but much less likely for sales of roller skates and specific record albums. At the same time, gazing into a crystal ball, flipping a coin, and such guides are all fraught with much greater problems. Marketers must use the best methods available to obtain the most accurate forecasts. The discussion of such techniques, however, is not within the scope of this text.

Evaluating Performance

Once the performance criteria have been set, actual performance is compared against them, as shown in Figure 18-9. Most organizations tolerate discrepancies between actual and expected performance. No salesperson, product, or territory can be expected always to perform up to ideal standards, and the evaluation process focuses on the severity of the discrepancies. What constitutes too large a difference is generally a matter of managerial policy, which varies for different marketers. Acceptable performance has a lower limit. For instance, when a product's sales are significantly below what is expected, marketers must analyze why and determine how to rectify this situation.

Marketers sometimes face the pleasant problem of dealing with deviations greater than the acceptable limit. A salesperson expected to sell $6,000 worth of product sells

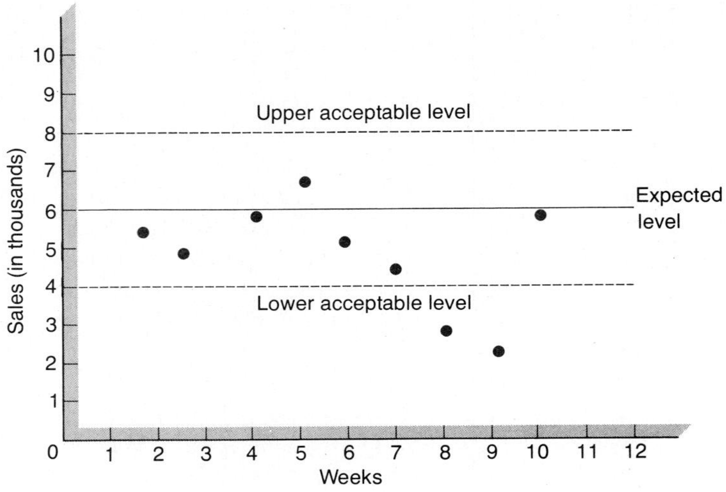

Figure 18-9 Control chart for evaluating performance.

$10,000 worth instead. The immediate reaction is that nothing needs to be done. Yet this is often a mistake, because overperformance can be symptomatic of problems too. Perhaps expectations are out of line or objectives faulty. Maybe the salesperson is offering illegal price cuts or kickbacks. In short, any significant deviation, negative or positive, deserves attention.

Taking Corrective Action

The evaluation process results in a decision either to take no action or to take corrective action. Nonsignificant differences between expected and actual performance generally require no changes. Important differences require corrective action, but it should not be immediate. First the underlying causes of the discrepancy need to be analyzed. Often deviations come about because of uncontrollable influences. Economic conditions take a turn for the worse, a competitor makes an amazing technological breakthrough, or the marketing organization has internal administrative difficulties. The salesperson who falls significantly below quota may be the victim of circumstances. Analysis of underlying causes, then, provides the necessary understanding of the deviation, why it occurred, and what to do about it. If the salesperson wasn't achieving because the competition came out with a truly revolutionary and improved product, the appropriate response would be for the company to shore up its research and development, rather than focus on the salesperson as the cause of the problem.

Objectives, as we've said, should be specific, measurable, and feasible. The evaluation process and the discovery of performance discrepancies may well point up the unfeasibility of the objectives.

The Marketing Audit

Marketing audits are an important responsibility of top management. A marketing audit has been defined as "comprehensive, systematic, independent, and periodic examination of a company's—or business unit's—marketing environment, objectives, strategies, and activities with a view of determining problem areas and opportunities and recommending a plan of action to improve the company's marketing performance."[11] The marketing audit is far more than simply the control process revisited. The audit requires a stepping back from the marketing system to determine its strengths and weaknesses. Too many marketing managers wait until problems arise before they evaluate their decisions. Marketing audits can benefit any organization and point to opportunities for it to improve its system.

The marketing audit should be comprehensive and review six aspects of the system: objectives, policies, organization, methods, procedures, and personnel.[12] Let's look at each one. Not all organizations know their objectives; marketers often end up pursuing objectives that have been modified in some way. Objectives should be reviewed for appropriateness and value to the organization. Policies are general guidelines to the achievement of goals, and auditors should determine whether policies do in fact help to achieve them. The audit should ensure that the organization structure appropriately coordinates tasks under prevailing circumstances. The methods and procedures, the rules to guide marketing action, must be effective. And the people who form the organization must be matched with the skills and talents needed to carry out the taks of the organization. In short, the audit should review every nook and cranny of the organization with an unbiased and objective eye. Table 18-2 shows some questions that might be raised in an audit.

How often audits occur depends on what is being audited. Audits of the simplest and cheapest marketing system components should be conducted the most frequently. There should also be frequent audits of those aspects that most benefit the marketing organization. Advertising agencies' greatest assets, for instance, are their personnel, so they should audit their human resources often. Markets that offer fast delivery should frequently audit relevant methods and procedures. Well-planned and well-executed marketing audits can help an organization provide satisfaction. An ongoing reappraisal cannot help but improve one's success in the marketplace.

Marketing audits should be systematically conducted, performed in an orderly fashion to ensure that every base is covered. Reviews should also be conducted by outside, unbiased, objective auditors. Generally, broadly experienced outside consul-

---

[11]Philip Kotler, *Marketing Management: Planning Analysis and Control,* 4th ed. Prentice-Hall, Inc., Englewood Cliffs, N.J., 1980, p. 651.

[12]Alfred R. Oxenfeldt, *Executive Action in Marketing,* Wadsworth Publishing Company, Belmont, Calif., 1966, pp. 745–757.

tants can provide the best unbiased assessment of the true situation confronting the audited organization. No organization is so effective that it cannot be improved. No organization—large or small, profit-oriented or nonprofit-oriented—should ignore the conduct of a marketing audit.

TABLE 18-2 Some Typical Marketing Audit Questions

THE MARKETING ENVIRONMENT AUDIT

1 What does the company expect in the way of inflation, material shortages, unemployment, and credit availability in the short run, intermediate run, and long run?
2 What major changes are occurring in product technology? In process technology?
3 What federal, state, and local agency actions should be watched? What is happening in the areas of pollution control, equal employment opportunity, product safety, advertising, price control, etc., that is relevant to marketing planning?
4 What changes are occurring in consumer lifestyles and values that have a bearing on the company's target markets and marketing methods?
5 What attitudes is the public taking toward business and toward products such as those produced by the company?
6 What is happening to market size, growth, geographical distribution, and profits?
7 How do current customers and prospects rate the company and its competitors, particularly with respect to reputation, product quality, service, sales force, and price?
8 Who are the major competitors? What are the objectives and strategy of each major competitor? What are their strengths and weaknesses? What are the sizes and trends in market shares?
9 What are the main trade channels bringing products to customers?
10 What is the outlook for the availability of different key resources used in production?
11 What is the outlook for the cost and availability of warehousing facilities?
12 How effectively is the advertising agency performing? What trends are occurring in advertising agency services?

THE MARKETING STRATEGY AUDIT

13 Are the corporate objectives clearly stated, and do they lead logically to the marketing objectives?
14 Are the marketing objectives appropriate, given the company's competitive position, resources, and opportunities? Is the appropriate strategic objective to build, hold, harvest, or terminate this business?
15 What is the core marketing strategy for achieving the objectives? Is it a sound marketing strategy?
16 Are the marketing resources allocated optimally to the major elements of the marketing mix, i.e., product quality, service, sales force, advertising, promotion, and distribution?

THE MARKETING ORGANIZATION AUDIT

17 Is there a high-level marketing officer with adequate authority and responsibility over those company activities that affect the customer's satisfaction?
18 Are there good communication and working relations between marketing and sales?
19 Is the product management system working effectively? Are the product managers able to plan profits or only sales volume?
20 Are there any problems between marketing and manufacturing that need attention?

THE MARKETING SUPPORT SYSTEMS AUDIT

21 Is the marketing intelligence system producing accurate, sufficient, and timely information about developments in the marketplace?

22 Is marketing research being adequately used by company decision makers?

23 Are sales quotas set on a proper basis?

24 Are the control procedures (monthly, quarterly, etc.) adequate to ensure that the annual plan objectives are being achieved?

THE MARKETING PERFORMANCE AUDIT

25 What is the profitability of the company's different products, served markets, territories, and channels of distribution?

26 Should the company enter, expand, contract, or withdraw from any business segments, and what would be the short- and long-run profit consequences?

27 Do any marketing activities seem to have excessive costs? Are these costs valid? Can cost-reducing steps be taken?

THE MARKETING TACTICS AUDIT

28 What are the product-line objectives? Are these objectives sound? Is the current product line meeting these objectives?

29 Are any products able to benefit from quality, feature, or style improvements?

30 What are the pricing objectives, policies, strategies, and procedures? To what extent are prices set on sound cost, demand, and competitive criteria?

31 Does the company use price promotions effectively?

32 What are the distribution objectives and strategies?

33 Are there adequate market coverage and service?

34 Is the sales force large enough to accomplish the company's objectives?

35 How is the company's sales force perceived in relation to competitors' sales forces?

36 What are the organization's advertising objectives? Are they sound?

37 Are the ad themes and copy effective? What do customers and the public think about the advertising?

Source: Adapted from Philip Kotler, William Gregor, and William Rodgers, "The Marketing Audit Comes of Age," *Sloan Management Review*, vol. 18 (Winter 1977), appendix A, pp. 39–43.

Looking Back

In this chapter, we have tied together the material from other sections of the text by means of the strategic marketing planning process. We have emphasized the need for gathering external and internal information to build a master plan, a strategy, for achieving the organization's goals. All marketing activities, the marketing mix, must be integrated and controlled to be in line with this strategy. Before we move on to more specialized areas of marketing in the next and final part, be sure you have mastered the following points.

1   Tactical plans must be coordinated with the strategic plan to ensure achievement of organizational goals.

2   Modern-day strategic marketing planning has evolved through numerous stages.

3   Environmental and internal analyses are the key to effective strategic marketing planning.

4   There are only limited times when the marketing organization's distinctive competencies are closely aligned with those demanded by a dynamic external environment.

5   Many organizations have a higher-level corporate objective than simply to make money and grow.

6   Corporate culture helps determine the organization's objectives.

7   Market share improvements are often set as goals because they result in improved profitability.

8   Strategic business units can be managed as a portfolio to achieve the organization's overall goals.

9   The BCG portfolio analysis focuses on market growth, relative market share, and cash flow; yet it has a number of limitations.

10 The GE business screen expands the measures used to analyze the company and its market.

11 Initial objectives may well be revised in light of information gained in the situation review.

12 The situation review provides the basis for a strategic choice.

13 A strategy choice depends on whether the organization is a market share leader, challenger, follower, or nicher.

14 Control involves discovering significant discrepancies between expected and actual performance and examining the magnitude of these discrepancies.

15 For controlling, there are two broad classes of performance standards: effectiveness measures and efficiency measures.

16 Most organizations do not expect actual and ideal performance to coincide precisely.

17 Even overperformance can indicate problems that need correcting.

18 Analysis of why expected and actual performances differ should precede corrective action.

19 Corrective action may force a revision of objectives.

20 The marketing audit identifies a marketing system's strengths and weaknesses to uncover opportunities for improvement.

Key Terms

If you aren't sure what each of the following words means, look back at the text. Numbers refer to pages on which the words are defined. Additional information can be found by checking the index and the glossary at the end of the book.

strategic plans 560
tactical plans 560

corporate mission 563
business definition 564
corporate culture 564
environmental scanning 568
strategic business unit 571
portfolio 571
relative market share 571
star 572
cash cow 572
question mark 572
dog 573

flanking strategy 581
direct-attack strategy 582
backdoor strategy 582
guppy strategy 582
market follower strategy 582
nicher strategy 584
organizing 586
controlling 587
performance standards 588
classes of measurement 589
marketing audit 593

Questions for Review

1 What determines an organization's purpose or mission?

2 What are some limitations of the Boston Consulting Group's portfolio analysis approach to looking inside the strategic window?

3 What is the "rule of three and four"?

4 What are the four basic ways that marketing tasks are organized?

5 Briefly describe the difference between effectiveness measures and efficiency measures.

6 Briefly define the term marketing audit.

Questions for Thought and Discussion

1 On the basis of information offered in the chapter, how would you classify Bic's disposable razors within the BCG portfolio?

2 What type of market share competitor in the razor blade business would you believe Schick is and what should its strategy be?

3 Do you believe that information within an organization flows upward or downward more easily? Why?

4 Within a given company, who should be chosen to conduct a marketing audit?

Suggested Project

Go to the library and research the strategies of one competitor in each of the four categories of leaders, challenger, followers, and nichers. Prepare a one-paragraph synopsis of the strategy employed in each category.

Suggested Readings

Abell, Derek, and John Hammond: *Strategic Market Planning,* Prentice-Hall, Inc., Englewood Cliffs, N.J., 1979. This book provides an overview of the process of strategic marketing planning.

Bloom, Paul,N. and Philip Kotler: "Strategies for High Market-Share Companies," *Harvard Business Review,* vol. 53 (November–December 1975), pp. 63–72. This article points out why gaining a higher market share may be more trouble than it's worth.

Day, George S.: "Diagnosing the Product Portfolio," *Journal of Marketing,* vol. 41 (April 1977), pp. 29–38. This article shows marketers how to avoid costly applications of the product portfolio approach resulting from incorrect measurements, unfeasible strategies, and violation of basic assumptions about market share dominance and the product life cycle.

Hall, William K.: "Survival Strategies in a Hostile Environment," *Harvard Business Review,* vol. 58 (September–October 1980), pp. 75–85. An in-depth study of sixty-four companies reveals success comes to those that achieve either the lowest cost or the most differentiated position.

Hamermesh, R. G., M. J. Anderson, and J. E. Harris: "Strategies for Low Market Share Businesses," *Harvard Business Review,* vol. 56 (May–June 1978), pp. 95–102. The authors offer four principles for firms that do not seek high market share.

Hulbert, James M., and Norman E. Toy.: "A Strategic Framework for Marketing Control," *Journal of Marketing,* vol. 41 (April 1977), pp. 12–20. This article presents a system designed to make it possible to assign responsibility, evaluate performance, and give credit

(or blame) where due. *Journal of Marketing,* vol. 47 (Winter 1983). This issue provides a set of articles on the theory and practice of strategic marketing planning.

Kotler, Philip: "From Sales Obsession to Marketing Effectiveness," *Harvard Business Review,* vol. 55 (November–December 1977), pp. 67–75. This article proposes a measure of marketing effectiveness in the form of a rating scale in each of five major functions.

———, William Gregor, and William Rodgers: "The Marketing Audit Comes of Age," *Sloan Management Review,* vol. 18 (Winter 1977), pp. 25–43. This article provides a complete guide to performing a marketing audit.

Mossman, Frank H., Paul M. Fischer, and W. J. E. Crissy: "New Approaches to Analyzing Marketing Profitability," *Journal of Marketing,* vol. 38 (April 1974), pp. 43–48. Marketing profitability analysis by control unit brings marketing and accounting together.

Schoeffler, Sidney, Robert D. Buzzell, and Donald F. Heany: "Impact of Strategic Planning on Profit Performance," *Harvard Business Review,* vol. 53 (March–April 1974), pp. 137–145. This article presents some of the results of the Strategic Planning Institute's research and emphasizes the importance of market share as an organizational goal.

Shanklin, William L.: "Strategic Business Planning: Yesterday, Today, and Tomorrow," *Business Horizons,* vol. 22 (October 1979), pp. 7–14. The author traces the evolution of strategic marketing planning.

Cases for Part Three begin on page 600.

Cases for Part Three concerning Product

Case 1 Cummins Engine Company

In the spring of 1982, Henry B. Schacht, chief executive officer of Cummins Engine Company, faced a number of decisions that would affect the future of his company, which had dominated the big diesel engine business for more than 50 years. Schacht's primary market, the heavy truck industry, had been hit hard by the recession. Scores of carriers had gone out of business, and subsequently new truck sales were adversely affected.

In 1980 Cummins posted a net loss of $10.9 million on revenues of $1.7 billion. On the bright side, Schacht boosted market share from 46.2 percent to 53 percent in 1980. The following year, after significantly boosting market share, cutting costs, and boosting industrial engine sales, the earnings of Cummins ballooned to $115.2 million on revenues of $2 billion.

Despite a financially successful 1981, Schacht saw total engine shipments fall 7 percent, to 109,000 units. To prepare for the future, Schacht decided to lead Cummins into engine markets he thought were potentially bigger than Cummins's traditional business. Schacht's new market included diesels for small and medium-sized trucks. Schacht believed this market was 20 times larger than that of the bigger engines for heavy trucks, and the

company looked for this segment to grow by a 15 percent compounded rate through the 1980s.

Schacht believed that he was taking some big risks to implement his strategy. First, to gear up to produce this new line of small diesel engines, Cummins would have to invest $1.3 billion by 1986. Additionally, Schacht assumed that gasoline prices will continue to rise, making diesels all that more appealing to the owners of small and medium-sized trucks. He estimated gasoline will cost $2.00 per gallon by the mid-1980s. The lower price of gasoline in Spring 1982 (average price $1.27 per gallon) caused some competitors to project that gasoline-powered engines will continue to dominate the market. Nonetheless, over 96 percent of the large trucks in the United States have changed over to diesels, since the cost efficiency for long hauls is extensive.

Cummins is preparing to enter a totally different type of market. Customizing is the rule with heavy-duty trucks, and price is a secondary concern. For buyers of small trucks, however, price is a major consideration. When Schacht enters this market, he will be competing with General Motors, which has years of pricing experience.

However, Schacht believed

that Cummins's reputation for quality will motivate customers to demand Cummins engines. Schacht hoped to initially market 75,000 small diesels annually.

To reduce Cummins's downside risk, Schacht has entered into a $350 million joint venture with J. I. Case Company, a subsidiary of Tenneco Inc. J. I. Case manufactures farm and construction vehicles. Under the agreement, two new small diesel lines (the 50- to 250-horsepower size) will be codeveloped. Both Case and Cummins will share development and manufacturing costs, and each will take half the expected 150,000 yearly output. J. I. Case will use its engines in its own vehicles. Cummins, on the other hand, expects to realize greater production economies of scale and to reduce its risk.

Schacht was convinced of the potential in the small truck market, but he wondered whether Cummins is prepared to compete in a different market.

1 Which pattern of diversification is Cummins following?

2 What recommendations would you have for Schacht?

Source of data: "Cummins: The Diesel Powerhouse Pins Its Future on Smaller Engines," *Business Week*, May 17, 1982, pp. 128–132.

Case 2 Campbell Soup Company

Improving Campbell Soup Company's lackluster performance has become Gordon McGovern's primary objective. McGovern became president and chief executive officer of the New Jersey-based company in 1980. For the past decade Campbell's earnings have grown by only 8 to 9 percent, come booms or recessions. This performance was a good 3 percent behind the rest of the food industry and significantly trailed H. J. Heinz—Campbell's arch rival—which had maintained a 16 percent growth rate.

It had thus fallen on McGovern to improve Campbell's fortunes. McGovern, who formerly headed Campbell's Pepperidge Farms subsidiary, assigned himself the objective of improving earnings growth by 16 percent—a challenging objective when circumstances are analyzed. Early in 1982, he was reviewing his situation and trying to figure out how he might succeed.

McGovern faced a number of challenges. Since joining Campbell, he had reorganized his staff, pushing aside a half-dozen executives, and had moved to hype Campbell's marketing operation with a line of new products. McGovern hoped to increase sales by $200 million every two years. New products would include such items as apple juice, low-sodium soups, low-calorie pickles, and convenience foods such as a ham-and-cheese pastry.

In pre-McGovern days, the company averaged 18 new products a year. It also registered a 98 percent failure rate. This high failure rate—McGovern believed—was the result of poor testing and haphazardly conceived products.

To succeed, McGovern will have to overcome Campbell's tradition of not gambling, as well as resistance within the company to any change. In the past, Campbell resorted to short-term solutions to keep earnings up. These short cuts included cuts in advertising and discouragement of expensive new products. One of McGovern's first new products was Prego, a home-style spaghetti sauce which the company spent $15 million to introduce and advertise.

In the past, product development often hinged on what's convenient for the company, for instance, a square omelet which was anything but a success. McGovern asked, Why square? Answer: This was the shape the machinery would make.

McGovern, however, brought to Campbell an enviable track record. Prior to coming to Campbell's, he increased Pepperidge Farms sales from $60 million to $300 million. Much of his success was the result of a flow of new products at premium prices.

Following his 12-year successful venture at Pepperidge Farms, McGovern broke Campbell into 40 units, each responsible for its own success. In 1982, McGovern increased advertising by 25 percent, to $260 million, and he planned to continue advertising the benefits of soup in an effort to increase consumption, which has been steadily dropping. After one year of advertising, Campbell's soup sales jumped by 2 percent.

1 What new product recommendations would you have for McGovern?

2 What product strategy would you advise for Campbell's line of soup?

Source of data: "After a Long Simmer, the Pot Boils Again at Campbell Soup Co.," *The Wall Street Journal*, July 16, 1982, pp. 1, 10.

Case 3 Quaker Oats Company

After finally selling Magic Pan, a restaurant chain which was losing $6 million annually, William D. Smithburg, president of Quaker Oats Company, was analyzing his options for building the company's direct-to-the-consumer business with Samuel Slade, Jr., president of Quaker's Direct to Consumer Division.

Although the restaurant business proved to be a costly

failure, Smithburg had not given up the concept of selling products directly to the consumer. In fact, his objective, he told Slade, was to make direct-to-the-consumer sales account for 20 percent of Quaker Oats business by the late 1980s. Smithburg was wondering, however, how to accomplish this goal.

Smithburg had admittedly set a tough objective for his company. In fiscal 1982, Quaker had revenues of $2.6 billion, and only 4 percent of this volume was attributable to direct-to-consumer operations. This direct sales segment had obvious appeal to Quaker since its profit margin was far higher than food processing operations.

Direct sales per se, however, are no sure ticket to success. Direct consumer sales are commonplace today, with at least half of the Fortune 500 companies engaged in the field in one way or another.

Smithburg appeared unperturbed by this strong competition and was setting out to acquire companies with specific product identification with solid customer bases. While searching for new acquisitions, Smithburg had his hopes high for three direct sales companies already in the Quaker fold—Jos. A. Bank Clothiers, Inc.; Herrschners, Inc., a needlepoint company; and Brookstone Co., a direct seller of high-quality tools.

Bank appeared to have the greatest potential. The company, which has retail and direct mail operations, had revenues of $58 million in 1982. Smithburg projected sales of $100 million by 1985.

Bank Clothiers is regarded as a poor relation to Brooks Brothers, but it is still recognized as a quality clothier. Bank's prices generally were 30 percent below stores like Brooks Brothers, which have expensive overhead costs. Bank stores traditionally were little more than factory outlets. Smithburg planned to boost advertising expenditures 30 percent to $1.2 million, greatly emphasizing direct order.

Although Bank was already considered a mail-order operation, 70 percent of its revenues were generated by 13 retail stores. Its lines were popular primarily with customers over 45. Smithburg was aiming to shift Bank's appeal to the affluent 20- to 30-year-old market and was attempting to reach this market with specialized mailing lists and ads in publications like *The Wall Street Journal* and *The New Yorker*. Smithburg hoped to gain loyalty of this younger group with Bank's line of "preppy" clothes. Yet the Bank appeal was to high-quality, traditional lines rather than to the faddish "preppy look."

Smithburg was wondering if the Bank retail stores were complementing its mail-order business. Two new stores opened in New York City and Houston in 1982. Mail-order customers received special invitations to visit the retail stores. Smithburg thought he had found the key to reaching his objectives and pointed to Brookstone and Herrschners as evidence.

Brookstone, which also operates retail outlets, had sales of $31 million in 1981 and projected $150 million in sales within 10 years. Herrschner, a direct sales operation, had maintained a 20.5 percent growth rate for the past 5 years, and had revenues of $30 million in 1981.

However, Smithburg wasn't looking for these three businesses to make his objective. He was on the prowl for new acquisitions— primarily small, well-managed companies with a myriad of products like modular furniture and home accessories. He was questioning Slade about the viability of these acquisitions.

1   What might be Quaker's rationale for such acquisitions?

2   What risks do Smithburg and Slade face with Jos. A. Bank Clothiers?

3   Do you agree with Quaker's product strategy planned for Jos. A. Bank Clothiers? Why?

Source of data: "Quaker Oats Tailors for Growth," *Business Week*, July 26, 1982, p. 79.

Cases for Part Three concerning Pricing

Case 4 Sensormatic Electronics Corporation

Ronald G. Assaf spent the early part of his business career as manager of a Kroger store in Akron, Ohio. The store was in a high-crime area where shoplifting was a way of life for a sizable segment of the population.

The position brought home the hard reality that shoplifting was a major crime problem, and it led Assaf to found Sensormatic Electronics Corporation in 1968. The company specializes in antitheft detection systems. While Assaf has built a successful company ($67 million in revenues in 1981), convincing the supermarket industry to use his system has not been easy.

Although few would argue that shoplifting is not a problem ($24 billion was lost by U.S. retailers to shoplifters in 1981), success has come slowly for Assaf. In 1973 his company had sales of only $3.8 million, and it nearly went bankrupt in the early 1970s as a result of a franchising scheme. And the failure rate has been high among competitors: fourteen have folded in recent years.

To date, Assaf has made his success by selling his innovation to retailers. If a shoplifter attempts to take goods, a sensor detects a magnetic tag attached to the merchandise and sets off an alarm. Almost completely untapped by Sensormatic is the supermarket industry, which is also one of the most shoplifter-prone industries in the country. It is estimated that the industry loses $1.2 billion to theft annually, a considerable cost since profit margins in the industry are only 1 percent. No doubt there is a need for shoplifting deterrents within supermarkets, but Assaf wondered whether his magnetic system was feasible in an industry which sells primarily small, inexpensive items. Some supermarket executives question whether it would be cost efficient to install the system. Tagging canned goods, obviously, would not be as easy as tagging a blouse or a coat, and the cost of tagging or marking could be prohibitive. Supermarkets are also wary of false alarms: the machines going off when they shouldn't and the store falsely accusing customers.

Assaf believed that even if his efforts to crack the supermarkets fail, his company's potential was rich. It is estimated that 96.4 percent of U.S. department stores, 90 percent of women's dress and specialty shops, and 98.2 percent of discount and variety stores have yet to install electronic theft deterrents. Adding the virtually untapped European market, Assaf saw a bright future.

But prospects for more growth are so bright that competition may be drawn to the field. Assaf has successfully beaten back a number of small companies, but a large corporation could pose problems.

Pricing had been a particularly difficult area for Assaf. In the past, prices were set by his subjective estimate of what he believed customers would pay. But Assaf was thinking that there must be a better way to approach this key marketing decision. He was wondering what he might do to be more successful at pricing.

1 What advice would you give to Assaf as he decides a pricing approach?

2 For Sensormatic to gain greater volume, would you recommend discounts to large chain store buyers?

Source of data: "Sensormatic: Out to Quadruple Revenue by Bagging Supermarket Thieves," *Business Week*, June 14, 1982, pp. 99–100.

Case 5 **Scripto, Incorporated**

A few years ago, Douglas Martin left a secure job with Gillette Company and assumed the task of trying to rescue Scripto, Inc., a company beset both with a decade or more of financial losses and with loss of its sales and marketing staffs.

Scripto's problems have been many, but primarily it had failed to build the marketing systems or products to compete against companies like Gillette, Bic, and other manufacturers of pens and lighters. Scripto, now a part of Allegheny Industries, has had a series of presidents, but Martin has already accomplished what many thought was impossible: Scripto has made money for the past two years. In 1982 the company earned $2.6 million on revenues of $55.4 million, and the year before it earned $614,000 on sales of $48.2 million.

Unfortunately for Martin, his primary competitors are formidable—Gillette and Bic. Both are powerhouses in pen and disposable lighters. Martin must quickly devise methods to compete with these companies in retail stores and discount chains.

In the past, Scripto survived by being regarded as a promotional manufacturer, producing pens and lighters at cheap prices. Retailers often stocked Scripto products, but only as promotional items. Martin is now trying to position Scripto into permanent distribution channels to have its product line displayed at checkout lanes and not just offered as an occasional gimmick.

Martin, to achieve this position, has committed $2 million to advertising a new product called Ultra Thin—a fancy disposable lighter positioned as a "fashion" item for women. It is scheduled to be priced at 99 cents, the same price as Gillette's Cricket and the Bic lighter. This is a dramatic departure for Scripto; in the past it has relied heavily on specials like three lighters for $1, thus undercutting Gillette and Bic in price. Martin looks for Ultra Thin to increase Scripto's 15 percent market share in the $200 million business, of which Gillette has a 30 percent and Bic has a 50 percent market share.

One major problem facing Martin is convincing retailers he is serious. The market is saturated with cheap lighters, and Scripto's products haven't gained a lot of quality confidence with either stores or consumers. While customers may gamble on a special, it remains to be seen if they will opt for an Ultra Thin over a Cricket or Bic.

Second guessers are numerous. Some observers feel Martin should continue to undercut Gillette and Bic, but most retailers would like to see pricing set in the $1.19 to $1.29 range—prices which would give them better margins, and also motivate them to provide Scripto with better store shelf position.

Others believe disposable lighters are a fad which are becoming a blur on the market place, and consumers are finding it difficult to differentiate between lines. Martin was wondering which would be the best way for Ultra Thin to be priced.

1 What pricing strategy would you recommend for Scripto?

2 How is the product life cycle affecting this decision?

Source of data: "A Hotter Scripto Bets on Lighters," *Business Week*, June 21, 1982, pp. 74–79.

Case 6 **Wachovia Corporation**

Wachovia Corp., the bank holding company based in Winston-Salem, North Carolina, and one of the Sun Belt's largest banks, managed to show significant growth during the late 1970s and early 1980s despite a period of extremely high inflation and high interest rates. Between 1970 and 1980 Wachovia reported a compounded growth in earnings of 10.6 percent, and the first quarter of 1981 saw earnings increase by 27 percent. This growth was accomplished during a period when many other financial institutions suffered severe decreases in earnings.

During the early 1980s, banks across the country—large and small—faced the problem of how to cope with interest rates in the 16 to 20 percent range. Interest rates devastated the real estate market since many lenders stopped making traditional long-term mortgage loans. All bankers know that when interest rates are volatile, what looks like a profitable loan rate today could be a disaster tomorrow. Bankers recall vividly the days when an 8 percent mortgage rate was regarded as almost excessive and economists were stating that rates would soon tumble. Today, there are thousands of homeowners with these 8 percent rates. In 1981, if mortgage loans were

made at all, bankers charged anywhere from 15 to 17 percent. In response to the problem of high interest rates, Wachovia came up with what is called the "variable interest rate." Variable interest rates are pegged to the prime rate (the interest rate which is available only to the most creditworthy customers and set weekly by the nation's largest banks); a person who obtains a loan agrees to have his or her payment float depending on financial conditions at the time. For instance, if a homeowner obtains a home loan at 2 points above the prime rate of 15 percent, he or she pays an interest rate of 17 percent. If the prime rate later goes up or down, the interest on the mortgage is adjusted accordingly. Thus the bank is spared the danger of

seeing rates soar and having its money locked up for years at the lower rate. The Wachovia plan is looked upon as more equitable to borrowers than existing variable interest rates, which are not tied to the prime rate but based largely on the discretion of bankers.

Wachovia executives were wondering whether this approach to pricing their loans would be an appropriate avenue to pursue.

1 What are some of the dangers of Wachovia's variable interest rate plan?

2 What other services could Wachovia augment its loans with?

Source of data: "Wachovia Has Other Bankers Taking Notice," *The Wall Street Journal*, April 27, 1981, pp. 1, 33.

Cases for Part Three concerning Distribution

Case 7   Carter, Hawley, Hale Stores, Incorporated

Shortly after World War II, the first shopping center in the United States was created by Broadway Stores in southern California. From this store sprung the massive Carter, Hawley, Hale (CHH) retailing empire, the fourth largest in the United States and parent of such names as John Wanamaker, Neiman-Marcus, and the Emporium Capwell stores in

northern California and fashionable Bergdorf Goodman in New York. From this beginning, CHH in 1982 consisted of six department store chains, including 41 Broadway units.

Philip M. Hawley, president and chief executive officer of CHH, projected in 1979 that his chain would double sales of $2.4 billion and earnings of $69 million

by 1985. By 1982, Hawley realized that to meet this goal, he would have to improve sales by 67 percent and triple earnings within the next three years. In 1981, earnings had dropped 21 percent to $44.7 million on sales of $2.9 billion. Hawley was trying to determine what strategy should be followed to reach his goal.

Hawley's problems can be

traced to 1978—the year he led the company into making a pair of costly, and now it appears very questionable, acquisitions. CHH that year absorbed the troubled Philadelphia-based Wanamaker chain and the Virginia-based Thalhimers operation. While these two chains were being acquired, Hawley decided to spend another $118.6 million to build and upgrade his existing chains. Upgrading proved particularly difficult, as reflected at the 41-store Broadway chain.

Some $35 million was spent upgrading Broadway merchandise and refurbishing stores. This was done to attract the more affluent shopper. Francis H. Arnone, chairman of the Broadway group, ignored its traditional moderate-price apparel as he upgraded merchandise in the early 1980s with trendy sportswear for the more affluent consumer. As a result, in 1981, Broadway had to take heavy markdowns to reduce inventory. Prior to the upgrading, moderate-priced lines was Broadway's main appeal. When Broadway shunned this merchandise, competitors like J. W. Robinson Co. and Bullock's rushed in to grab the market in moderate-priced clothes.

Another cause for concern had been Wanamaker's 16 stores, which had been losing up to $12 million annually. Hawley had been spending millions in an effort to streamline the Wanamaker stores, and the group had been hit by personnel changes and units in various stages of remodeling. Also, the economy had hit Wanamaker's eastern market. Meanwhile, Thalhimers faced stiff competition from Miller & Rhodes—an Allied Stores Corporation property. Thalhimers asked CHH for an infusion of $35 million for five new stores.

Hawley faced the prospect of having to spend massive amounts in the future, and he could not cut back for fear of losing market shares. His competitors were spending similar amounts and were apparently intent on taking business from CHH. Allied, for instance, committed $20 million in capital to go against Thalhimers, and others like Macy's/Bamberger's in the northeast took advantage of Wanamaker's problems. Hawley felt he was caught in the middle and was wondering what actions he should take.

1 What strategy should Hawley undertake?

2 What specific actions should Hawley take?

Source of data: "The Glamour Dims at CHH," *Business Week*, May 31, 1982, pp. 74–76.

Case 8 Emery Air Freight Corporation

For decades Emery Air Freight dominated the air freight business. So it is little wonder that John C. Emery, son of the founder and now chairman and chief executive officer of the company, gave little notice in the 1970s to a small company in Memphis called Federal Express, which promised to deliver small parcels overnight anywhere in the United States, "when it absolutely, positively has to be there overnight." In 1982, however, John Emery was facing some critical decisions to keep his company among the top in the freight industry.

When Federal Express made its debut, Emery was content to pick up freight and schedule its movement of goods on scheduled carriers. And self-satisfied Emery had every right to be. It had no debt and its stock was a must for almost all portfolios. By 1982 debt approached 63 percent of capital. Emery invested $77 million in a fleet of twenty-four Boeing 727-100s and built a new $50 million sorting center at the Dayton International Airport in Ohio.

The company's plight became painfully evident in 1977 after the Civil Aeronautics Board deregulated the airlines, a move that Emery had endorsed. Deregulation, however, resulted in airlines dropping many routes which Emery depended on for its freight movements. As a result, Emery diverted his company into head-to-head competition with Federal, setting up a light-package sorting center in Smyrna, Tennessee—an answer to Federal Express's center in Memphis. Emery's Smyrna center, however, was out of the way and hardly central to anything. John Emery then employed McKinsey & Co., a management consultant firm, to recommend plans that would make the Smyrna hub functional.

McKinsey had its own solution which was endorsed by John Emery—Smyrna was closed and a new hub built in Dayton, a city located within easy trucking distance of 13 cities. Now Emery had the capability of hauling both small and large parcels it had previously lacked. Its fleet of 53

planes and 20 trucks could unload 500 tons of freight large and small—and within hours it could be sorted and reloaded and enroute to 130 urban centers.

Emery was now well on the way to achieving rapid delivery. Emery claimed 98 percent of its afternoon packages and 95 percent of its morning deliveries were on time—quite an accomplishment considering the company was handling all sizes and weights, not just small packages and letters like Federal Express. (Federal claims 95 percent of its next-morning and 99 percent of its next-afternoon deliveries arrive on schedule.)

But Emery still faced hurdles. Foremost was the fact that Emery's payload was still 60 percent large packages (over 70

pounds each), and these shipments have decreased because of the recession. Also, the Federal Express method was being picked up by others like Northern Air Freight, United Parcel, Flying Tiger, Purolator, and the airlines themselves—to say nothing of the U.S. Post Office. John Emery was wondering what his next move ought to be if he was to keep pace with Federal Express.

1 What are the distinct benefits that Emery might focus on to gain customers over Federal Express?

2 What other specific actions might Emery consider taking?

Source of data: "Emery Returns Federal Express's Fire," *Fortune*, May 17, 1982, pp. 119–121.

Case 9   **Mitsubishi Motors Corporation**

When Chrysler purchased 15 percent of Mitsubishi Motor Sales of America (MMSA) in 1971, both companies saw only long-term benefits. MMSA would enjoy an instant dealer network for its automobile and truck line, and Chrysler would have the popular efficient imports for its dealers to sell. In 1982, the partnership faced difficult times as the Japanese U.S. subsidiary decided to distribute cars independently of Chrysler, and Richard D. Recchia, executive vice president of MMSA, saw Chrysler as a competitor. As Recchia commented, "I don't

think we should be worrying about whose toes we step on. We won't treat Chrysler any differently than Datsun or Toyota."

Mitsubishi Motors, the parent of MMSA, is no small factor in the automobile and truck business. In 1981 the company had sales of $5 billion worldwide, but its penetration in the United States lagged. It was the only one of seven Japanese car companies doing business in the United States without its own distribution system. Recchia's plans included changing this.

As part of the agreement

signed in 1971, Mitsubishi cars and trucks were to be sold through Chrysler dealers under the names of Plymouth Champ and Dodge Colt, and other Chrysler cars were to be equipped with Mitsubishi engines. Thus, it appeared that Mitsubishi would get an overnight dealer network, and Chrysler would have a hedge against imports.

But Chrysler fell on desperate times and Mitsubishi suffered as a result. In an effort to recoup, Mitsubishi negotiated a new contract to make sure that if Chrysler folded, it would not be totally out of the U.S. market. The new agreement required Mitsubishi to supply Chrysler through 1990, but allowed it to start its own dealer network.

Recchia has not been happy with Chrysler. In 1980, 192,000 Mitsubishi cars were sold by Chrysler, but only 145,000 were sold in 1981.

In 1982, Recchia planned to set up a dealer network in the face of a recession, import quotas, and heavy competition from other Japanese automobile makers. To find a niche in the market, Recchia was considering the introduction of upscale, stylish cars which would compete with the high-priced Japanese offerings.

Recchia's goal was set at selling 30,000 cars and 11,000 trucks the first year. The new dealerships would be backed by $10 million in advertising. If import quotas remained, Mitsubishi would consider pushing Chrysler to release some of its cars pledged to Chrysler. Chrysler had an annual allotment of 113,000 units from MMSA as part of their 1971 agreement.

Mitsubishi also must face the problem of parts centers, a move Recchia does not embrace but which may well cause him problems, since the availability of parts has helped make other Japanese autos popular.

Recchia was wondering how he might make Mitsubishi's distribution system competitive.

1 What other alternatives did MMSA have to overcome to channel conflict with Chrysler?

2 What suggestions would you make to reduce any further conflict with Chrysler as its channel member?

Source of data: "Mitsubishi Revs Up to Go Solo," *Business Week*, May 3, 1982, pp. 130–132.

Cases for Part Three concerning Promotion

Case 10 ITT Corporation

In 1982, International Telephone and Telegraph (ITT) was a $17.3 billion company and the world's 25th largest industrial company. But few people were aware of it. This was the problem facing executives of the massive conglomerate as they attempted to both improve ITT's image and gain the company an identity of its own through a sizable advertising campaign. Edward Gerrity, senior vice president of ITT and head of the company's public affairs, and John Lowden, vice president of ITT for corporate relations and advertising, had begun to set the wheels in motion and were evaluating their decisions. The need for such an advertising campaign became evident when a 1981 survey showed that 60 percent of the public confused ITT with American Telephone and Telegraph (AT&T). To those who did know ITT, there were other image problems. The company was closely linked to the Watergate scandal and was also remembered for its part in the overthrow of the Chilean government.

In 1972 and 1973, ITT's image was severely damaged.

First, a memo written by an ITT lobbyist became public. The document linked settlement of an antitrust suit against the company with a $400,000 pledge to help finance the 1972 Republican convention. Then in the following year, ITT was found to have contributed funds to the Central Intelligence Agency in its efforts to unseat the president of Chile, Salvador Allende.

The 1982 campaign was part of an eight-year effort to improve ITT's image. Gerrity and Lowden set ITT's advertising objectives as the follows: (1) to dispel confusion with AT&T, (2) to again clearly identify its businesses, and (3) to overcome a poor image caused by Watergate. Along the way, ITT dropped its old slogans: "Creating jobs is our most important responsibility" and "Serving people and nations everywhere." As Gerrity observed, "Perception is reality. You have to deal with perceptions."

The perceptions Gerrity referred to were uncovered by the 1981 survey conducted by Yankelovich, Skelly and White, Inc., a marketing research company. The results of the survey showed that although earlier campaigns had well defined in the public's mind what ITT did, confusion with AT&T still persisted and was the major problem to be dealt with.

To mark the distinction between the two companies, a TV commercial was designed portraying a character called Miss Elias who was depicted as a telephone operator. The commercial goes as follows.

The phone rings. "No, dear, you want AT&T, not ITT," Miss Elias tells a caller. "We are two totally different companies."

She then instructs the trainee: "Sometimes, Cheryl, you have to explain what ITT does. I mean, we make telecommunications equipment all over the world. But we also make Wonder bread." Her tone is reverent. "And we're Sheraton."

She clutches her heart. "And Hartford Insurance. And Scott's lawn products. And lots of other companies."

In addition to TV commercials, Gerrity and Lowden planned to use other media: magazines, newspapers, and direct-mail literature to schools, libraries, and scout troops. Material will also be distributed through its Sheraton hotels and via 10,000 agents of ITT-owned Hartford Insurance.

The target audience was to be the upward-mobile individuals which ITT describes as the "movers and shakers." The advertising budget was set at $10 million.

1 Evaluate this image campaign in terms of the advertising management process.

2 What changes would you suggest to Lowden and Gerrity?

Source of data: "How ITT Shells Out $10 Million or So a Year to Polish Reputation," *The Wall Street Journal*, April 2, 1982, pp. 1, 16.

Case 11   American Greetings Corporation

American Greetings Corporation has lived under the shadow of larger and better-known Hallmark for years, and despite a gallant effort to topple the number-one greeting card maker, it found itself a strong second in 1982—but second nevertheless. While American Greetings for the first nine months in 1981 reported earnings of $23.3 million on revenues of $458.2 million, it believed Hallmark, which is privately held and thus does not report earnings, was twice that size.

Morry Weiss, president and chief operating officer of American Greetings, left no doubt that Hallmark was his company's major concern, and Weiss intended to challenge Hallmark in all markets and in every product line. He was reflecting on his communications program and trying to decide what he could do to improve it.

American Greetings was founded by Jacob Sapirstein, and he saw as his market inexpensive cards for the masses. He succeeded in getting retailers to take his cards, partly with the agreement to buy back unsold cards. His marketing strategy was to get as many cards as possible before the consumer under the assumption that if they were available, people would buy them.

Perhaps Sapirstein's strategy was too good. While in 1982 American Greeting cards were sold in 50,000 stores—two and one-half times the number of stores that sold Hallmark—the cards were still perceived as inferior, and Hallmark's long-standing slogan, "When you care enough to send the very best," undoubtedly also helped make people perceive American Greetings cards as inferior. Despite American Greetings's edge in total outlets, Hallmark held 47 percent of the card market, versus 28 percent for American Greetings.

In the late 1970s, Weiss decided to close the gap on Hallmark. American Greetings correctly surmised that the key to growth was to cut into Hallmark's share since the two companies so dominated the market, and there was a general slowing in the overall card market.

But the challenge became one of overcoming Hallmark's perceived quality and almost generic name. Much to his chagrin in 1981, Weiss discovered that a well-done "sweetness and light" TV commercial was thought by a large segment of viewers to be a Hallmark production. American Greetings TV commercials were changed to hit hard at reinforcing the American Greetings name and stress humor rather than the "sweetness and light" commercials which were associated so closely to archrival Hallmark.

In an effort to gain more identification at retail outlets, American Greetings began installing signs, something Hallmark had long done. By the end of 1982, Weiss hoped to have 80 percent of the outlets carrying its cards appropriately identified. Hallmark had gotten the edge on American Greetings by appealing to the female shopper, who buys 90 percent of all cards. Hallmark stores and store sections offered a shopping atmosphere to appeal to women and offer a variety of other gift items.

From a creative standpoint, Hallmark also held the edge, employing 640 artists against American Greeting's 225. In its efforts to overcome Hallmark's dominance, American Greetings invested heavily in high-speed presses which could turn out nine million cards per day, and it retained researchers in an attempt to determine what kind of cards people wanted for different occasions.

American Greetings also began attempting to convert Hallmark retailers by offering faster and more efficient service.

Some felt that American Greetings's greatest asset was Strawberry Shortcake, a little girl with freckles, red hair, and a pink bonnet. Not only was Strawberry Shortcake a favorite card character, but American Greetings licensed her to other manufacturers for such items as sheets, lunch boxes, and sleeping bags. Strawberry Shortcake was to appear in 1982 on $500 million worth of merchandise, and American Greetings collected a royalty of between 5 and 10 percent of wholesale value. Strawberry Shortcake was preceded by characters Holly Hobby and Ziggy, and they too were later licensed to other companies.

1 Evaluate American Greetings Corporation's communication problems.

2 What should Weiss do to improve the company's communication program?

Source of data: "American Greetings Cares Enough to Try Its Very Hardest," *The Wall Street Journal*, March 17, 1982, pp. 1, 24.

Case 12 Goodyear Tire and Rubber Company

Goodyear Tire and Rubber Company, the only tire company in the world which can claim its products are sold in six continents, enjoyed unprecedented success in 1981 in face of strong competition and a worldwide recession. But 1982 found Goodyear Chairman Charles J. Pilliod, Jr., faced with

increased competition from abroad and fierce price cutting in almost all segments of the tire market. U.S. tire shipments hit 195 million in 1981, down from 250 million in 1978. And U.S. auto production declined 35 percent between 1978 and 1981.

In 1981 Goodyear had sales

of $9.2 billion and held a 30 percent share of the market in the United States; this hefty market share was accomplished against very formidable competitors like Firestone, Uniroyal, B. F. Goodrich, Michelin, and Bridgestone. Profits, however, had not kept pace at Goodyear. Pilliod decided in 1981 to look for bottom-line improvement. Goodyear reported earnings of $260 million in 1981, which represented only a 32 percent rise since 1972 when revenues were half those of 1981. Pilliod was confident of a resurgence of profit and believed that the company was poised for the future. As he told colleagues: "Through continued emphasis on manufacturing innovation, efficiency, and quality, we are in an excellent position to increase profitability by attacking both sides of the profit equation: lowering the cost of production and gaining market share."

Pilliod methodically built Goodyear into a marketing force. Through his efforts the company had made considerable strides in improving quality and met its foreign competitors head-on by expanding production facilities abroad. Domestically, Pilliod reorganized Goodyear's product development group, long a weak link in the organization. This group's biggest breakthrough was the heavy-duty radial truck tire, which enabled the company to dominate this market segment with a 40 percent share.

Another boon to Goodyear was its new all-weather tires, Tiempo and Arriva. With these tires, drivers use the same set year round, and don't have to change tires for cold-weather driving. All-weather tires accounted for 15 percent of all passenger tire sales in 1982 and were expected to account for a third of all tire sales by 1987.

The final element in Pilliod's success was advertising/promotional support for Goodyear's 6500 independent dealers and 1000 company-owned stores. In 1981 Goodyear spent $25 million in television advertising—a figure which represents nearly half of all dollars spent on TV tire commercials.

As Pilliod was planning for the future, a number of unsettling conditions were making it cloudy. In an effort to reduce inventories, most tire companies initiated price cutting, subsequently reducing profit margins. Michelin, long perceived as a quality tire maker, was one of the major companies meeting a slow market by cutting prices, and Japan's Bridgestone had plans to move aggressively into the truck tire business and was negotiating with Firestone for the purchase of its truck tire manufacturing facility in Nashville. Bridgestone already had a 12 percent share of the truck tire market, and with a domestic manufacturing plant it would undoubtedly strive to boost its share.

Pilliod wondered if he could maintain market share in the face of stiffer competition and a lackluster economy.

1 What kind of promotional mix would you suggest for Goodyear?

2 From an external and internal analysis of Goodyear, what strategy would you suggest to Pilliod?

Source of data: "Goodyear: Will Staying No. 1 in Tires Pump Up Profits?" *Business Week*, July 12, 1982, pp. 85–88.

Marketing Today

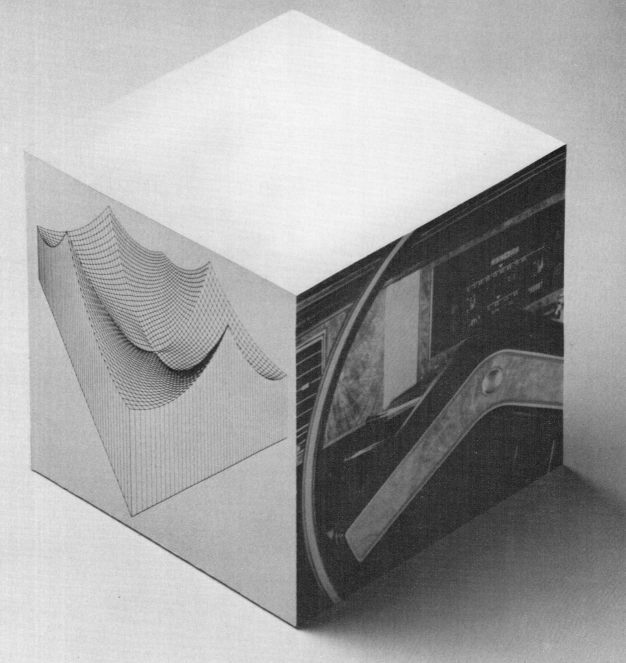

Cases

In Malaysia, the consumers do not have the protection Americans and people in other cultures have come to expect. Readily available on the Malaysian market are eyebrow pencils laden with lead; mosquito repellent loaded with DDT; baby bottles made of polyvinyl chloride that melt when sterilized; condensed milk with sugar sold as food for infants; candy with cherry color derived from Red Dye No. 2, a possible cancer-causing additive.

Obviously, consumer protection is needed in the third world. Malaysia is one of those developing nations rich enough to make or import an array of consumer products but not quite developed enough yet to be concerned with screening out dangerous products.

Life in Malaysia has grown much more complicated in recent years. Plastic wrap, with its problems of disposal, has replaced banana leaves. People now sit on chairs rather than their haunches, making low back pain a frequent ailment. The marketplace now is deluged with the new and the unknown, making the typical uninformed and unprotected consumer a sitting duck.

"We haven't reached affluence," says Mohammed Idris, Malaysia's counterpart to Ralph Nader, "but we already suffer from all its ills."

Idris is a founder and president of the Consumers' Association of Malaysia. The association tracks septic tanks and polluted waters, potholes and weevily rice. It monitors job agencies, unlicensed optometrists, and moonshine, and engages in product safety, ranging from investigation of flammable toys to broken glass in bottled drinks.

Consumer frauds are widespread. Counterfeiting of products is common; one example is Johnson & Johnson baby-powder containers filled locally with perfumed flour. Quite a few of the questionable products are genuine imports: drugs and pesticides banned in the West, high-priced protein sold as "health food," "recalled" electric gadgets like immersion coils and hair dryers.

The association has an annual budget of $75,000 and a staff of thirty which issues press releases and produces a weekly national newspaper column, a monthly newspaper (circulation 30,000), and a radio show. More than 2000 complaints a year are investigated.

Rising prices and a growing suspicion of technology's consumer spin-offs have helped spawn consumer groups in almost all developing countries, and concern has grown to the point where the United Nations Commission on Transnational Corporations is considering including an international consumer-protection clause in its proposed code of conduct.

Source of data: "Consumer Protection Is Underdeveloped in the Third World," *The Wall Street Journal,* April 8, 1980, p. 1.

Chapter 19

International Marketing

Looking Ahead

So far we have concentrated on domestic marketing. But many marketing operations take place from one country to another, and many take place entirely overseas. This chapter explores the special problems faced by international marketers.

Key Topics

Why marketers engage in international trade

The major international marketing strategies

Political, legal, and cultural influences on international marketing

The problems of conducting foreign marketing research and developing a marketing program

The expansion of domestic markets to global markets

Chapter Outline

World War II marked what many people consider the birth of international marketing. When United States forces fanned out across Europe and the Far East, they brought American-made products. These products were seen and used by other peoples, often for the first time, and soon a demand for them existed.

Before the war, countries tended to protect national industries from foreign competition by means of tariffs and other restrictive regulations. But at the end of the war, nations began tearing down trade barriers. Political leaders came to accept the idea that economic stability depends largely on the relatively free exchange of products across national borders. Immediately after the war, a number of international agreements were concluded to encourage trade among countries and preserve peace.

In 1947, the General Agreement on Tariffs and Trade (GATT) was negotiated to spur on international trade. This agreement among most Western countries sets a legal limit on the size of tariffs and forbids tariff discrimination among countries. Another boost to trade was the creation of the European Common Market, now called the European Community (EC). The idea behind the common market is to have no obstacles to trade among member countries. And all members are to impose the same tariffs and customs regulations on imports from nonmembers. The EC presently consists of Belgium, Denmark, France, West Germany, Ireland, Italy, Luxembourg, the Netherlands, the United Kingdom, and newly admitted Greece (1981). It has agreed to free movement of capital and labor within its boundaries, has common sales tax systems, common transportation regulations, even common antitrust legislation—and it also has the power to punish injustices. Recently, for instance, the EC levied a $280,000 fine, its heaviest to date, on Johnson & Johnson for restricting the availability of one of its pharmaceutical products. J&J had marketed the product to British buyers but refused sales to West German markets. There are economic organizations other than the EC (see Table 19-1), but they generally are not so well developed.

Technology has been very important to the growth of international trade. Today, marketers can reach Paris from the United States in less than four hours—less time than it takes for New Yorkers to travel to Los Angeles. Computers, satellites, and

---

TABLE 19-1   Some Multinational Economic Organizations

The Organization of Petroleum Exporting Countries (OPEC): Saudi Arabia, Kuwait, United Arab Emirates, Iraq, Iran, Algeria, Qatar, Libya, Venezuela, Nigeria, and Indonesia

The Latin American Free Trade Association (LAFTA): Brazil, Argentina, Mexico, Chile, Uruguay, Peru, Paraguay, Ecuador, and Colombia

The Central American Common Market (CACM): El Salvador, Honduras, Guatemala, Nicaragua, and Costa Rica

The Council for Mutual Economic Assistance (CMEA): Bulgaria, the German Democratic Republic, Poland, Hungary, Romania, and Czechoslovakia

The European Free Trade Association (EFTA): Sweden, Finland, Norway, Iceland, Portugal, Switzerland, and Austria

Figure 19-1   Pepsi Cola makes and bottles its products in Russia. (Burt Glinn/Magnum)

intricate data processing systems let marketers make instant foreign transactions. They no longer have to wait many days before enacting decisions.

We see evidence of international marketing every day. Bic Pen Corporation, the largest marketer of inexpensive pens and disposable cigarette lighters in the United States, is a French-owned company. McDonald's serves hamburgers around the world, from Paris to London to Munich to Perth. Russians drink Pepsi Cola; the French smoke Marlboros; and Toyotas clog the streets of Chicago as well as Tokyo. We could multiply such examples endlessly. (See Figure 19-1.)

But international marketing is risky. Even simple things can deter an organization from entering foreign markets. Consider, for example, what Pizza Hut went through when it entered the German market. The company admits that it rushed ahead after conducting only the basic studies, and its early experiences were disastrous. German labor costs were higher than expected, and German managers refused to help prepare and serve food, considering it beneath them. Pizza Hut discovered that Germans eat pizza with a knife and fork and not with their fingers, as American consumers do. The company had to rush supplies of knives and forks to all German units.

Along with cultural factors, marketers must also contend with political and legal factors. Let's see what's involved with international marketing and why it's so difficult.

Reasons For International Trade

Expanding a market and profits is the most compelling reason marketers can have for engaging in international trade. But they have other reasons. No country is completely self-sufficient. The United States could not possibly enjoy its high standard of living if it were restricted to domestically produced goods. Although it probably could produce its own coffee instead of importing it from Brazil and other countries, the United States could do so only at great expense. And though the nation could produce its own oil from coal or shale or other raw materials, such production would also be more costly. Fortunately coffee-rich Brazil needs the United States' more inexpensively produced industrial products (automobiles, appliances, machine tools), and the oil-producing countries of the Middle East need its efficiently produced food products, weapons, and machinery.

Because of differences in natural resources and the labor supply, one country is usually more efficient at making a particular product than others are. It seems logical, then, that a country which makes a product more efficiently should concentrate on that product and sell its surplus production to other countries. The income from such sales then can be used to buy needed products from other countries. This exchange pattern has been called the *principle of comparative advantage*. On the surface, it might seem that the world would function more efficiently if all countries strictly followed this principle. The theory sounds good, but it is actually unrealistic. The countries of Southeast Asia, for instance, produce textiles more cheaply than the United States does. But it clearly would be foolish and dangerous to shut down the American textile industry even if all its workers could be placed elsewhere. Indeed, what would people in the United States wear if another political situation led to world conflict and cut off United States trade with Southeast Asia? In short, the principle of comparative advantage doesn't work out all the time. Too many outside factors prevent the ideal distribution of world products in a way that satisfies world demand. In one form or another, cooperation in our complex world is crucial to success. (See Application 19-1.)

Application 19-1
China—Charting a New Course for International Trade

The Chinese have been adept for years in the art of placing billboards. But until recently these messages were of a political nature, more often than not quoting advice from Chairman Mao. Now, this talent has been directed toward our commercialism. Walls in China are today covered with posters advertising American products like Kodak film and Marlboro cigarettes.

幽美的音质,是从优越的技术和严格的量控制中产生的。

Better, newer sounds from ◆TDK 东京电气化学工业有限公司

(Gwendolyn Stewart)

These posters are solid evidence that trade between the United States and China is accelerating. Since relations were normalized in 1978, trade between the two countries has leaped from $1 billion to $4 billion in 1981. The Commerce Department estimates that by 1985 this trade will grow to at least $10 billion.

From the United States viewpoint, the most promising exports will be agricultural products and sophisticated technical equipment.

Evidence of this increasing trade abounds. Ships are unloading American cotton; in Sichuan province, a Hughes Tool Company plant is being built which will produce drill bits. In the Fujian province, R. J. Reynolds Tobacco Co. has joined with the China-owned Amoy Cigarette Co. to manufacture Camel cigarettes.

One of the biggest frustrations in marketing in China is dealing with its slow and inefficient bureaucracy. Making a deal can be frustrating. Chase Manhattan Bank experienced such problems when its agreement to finance a $250 million trade center in Peking fell through, seemingly because the Peking city government became involved in a

dispute with China's Ministry of Foreign Trade over the cost of the venture.

Despite the complications and the cost of doing business in China, American business is very much interested in that new market of roughly a billion people. The Chinese government's goal to improve its people's diet and standard of living affords the United States a major new outlet for both agricultural and high-technology products.

Source of data: "Traders Play the China Card," *Time,* Oct. 27, 1980, p. 91.

Strategies For International Marketing

The managerial philosophy and orientation toward marketing abroad generally evolve through various stages. Four phases have been noted:[1]

—*Ethnocentric stage:* At this early stage, the share of total revenue from outside a firm's national boundaries is inconsequential, and the firm treats international operations as secondary to domestic ones. Marketing abroad is carried on similarly to that at home, and planning generally is done at the home base.

—*Polycentric stage:* At this stage, each foreign country is treated as a separate market. Changes in local environments can be mirrored in changes in marketing strategies and actions. Most operations are handled by nationals within the host country. The approaches used in this stage are usually very effective.

—*Regiocentric stage:* At this point, national boundaries are somewhat ignored. Many countries are massed together to comprise a regional market. A coordinated strategy is set for the entire region. Marketing is standardized for all countries in that region.

—*Geocentric stage:* The entire world is treated as one big market. As with the regiocentric approach, this philosophy assumes different markets will adapt to the offering of the international marketer. Such an approach is difficult to coordinate and control.

Throughout these stages, an organization, when marketing its products to consumers in other countries, has a number of strategies from which to choose. Its main alternatives, which we'll examine next, are exporting, licensing, joint ventures, and foreign manufacturing.

Exporting

Traditionally, the first step in marketing products abroad is to export them. (See Figure 19-2.) Manufacturing, in such cases, is domestic, with the aim of export to a particular foreign market. For example, although many Volkswagens are manufactured in West Germany, they are aimed at the United States market and must meet American legal and safety standards. In its Allentown (Pennsylvania) plant, Mack trucks produces one line of trucks designed specifically for Middle Eastern nations. The trucks are exported in parts (called "knock-downs") and assembled upon arrival because of the high cost of exporting assembled units.

Sometimes, especially for smaller companies, exporting is a way to market surplus products and reduce costs through longer production runs. The manufacturing firm itself may handle export marketing, or the marketers may use export and

---

[1]Wind, Yoram, Susan P. Douglas, and Howard V. Perlmutter, "Guidelines for Developing International Marketing Strategies," *Journal of Marketing,* vol. 37 (April 1973), pp. 14–23.

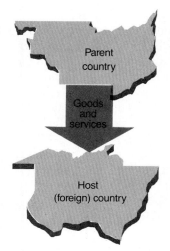

Figure 19-2 Exporting strategy.

import agents who specialize either in products or in geographical areas. As companies become larger and desire more aggressive marketing within the foreign country, they often develop company sales branches or other sales subsidiaries located directly in the foreign markets.

Exporting became big business in the 1970s. In 1970, United States exports amounted to only about 4 percent of the gross national product (GNP); in 1980 that amount more than doubled to 8.5 percent. Within the exporting field, the greatest growth has been seen in services—insurance, banking, consulting, accounting, transportation, and the like. While smaller than West Germany's (over 23 percent of its GNP) and Japan's (13 percent of its GNP), it is clearly growing in importance as part of the American economy and part of the revenue and profit mix of American firms. (See Table 19-2.) Philip Morris, R. J. Reynolds Industries, and other tobacco companies look to world tobacco-consumption growth rates of 2 to 3 percent (and 5 percent and more in developing countries) compared with a declining domestic rate as a means of corporate growth. And Weyerhaeuser Co. expects consumption of forest products overseas in the 1980s to increase at double the domestic rate of 2 to 3 percent. Exports accounted for 25 percent of its sales in 1980 but are projected to account for one-half Weyerhaeuser's total revenues by the year 2000.

TABLE 19-2 The Ten Leading Exporters

Rank 1980	Rank 1979	Company	Products	Exports (in thousands)	Sales (in thousands)	Exports as percentage of sales
1	1	Boeing (Seattle)	Aircraft	$5,503,800	$ 9,426,200	58.39%
2	*	General Motors (Detroit)	Automotive vehicles and parts, locomotives	$5,287,100	$57,728,500	9.16
3	2	General Electric (Fairfield, Conn.)	Generating equipment, aircraft engines	$4,265,000	$24,959,000	17.09
4	*	Ford Motor (Dearborn, Mich.)	Automotive vehicles and parts	$3,453,000	$37,085,500	9.31
5	3	Caterpillar Tractor (Peoria, Ill.)	Construction equipment, engines	$3,094,000	$ 8,597,800	35.99
6	5	E.I. duPont de Nemours (Wilmington, Del.)	Chemicals, fibers, plastics	$2,175,000	$13,652,000	15.93
7	6	United Technologies (Hartford, Conn.)	Aircraft engines, helicopters	$2,142,593	$12,323,994	17.39
8	4	McDonnell Douglas (St. Louis, Mo.)	Aircraft	$2,065,800	$ 6,066,300	34.05
9	*	International Business Machines (Armonk, N.Y.)	Information-handling systems, equipment, and parts	$1,615,000	$26,213,000	6.16
10	8	Lockheed (Burbank, Calif.)	Aircraft and related support services	$1,358,000	$ 5,395,700	25.17

*Not on the 1979 list.

Source: Adapted from "The 50 Leading Exporters," *Fortune*, Aug. 24, 1981, p. 86.

Licensing

Many small and medium-sized companies and some large ones that manufacture technologically sophisticated products license a foreign manufacturer to use a patent, a trademark, or a certain technological process. (See Figure 19-3.) The foreign firm (the *licensee*) produces and markets the product within its own country and pays the domestic firm (the *licensor*) a royalty fee. Lorillard Tobacco Company has made such a licensing agreement with British American Tobacco, the world's largest tobacco marketers, to sell its brands outside the United States. Lorillard benefits because it is relatively small and cannot manufacture or distribute products in some one hundred countries.

Licensing is a convenient way to enter a foreign market because it does not demand a large investment in manufacturing. Nor does it demand that the licensor learn how to market within particular foreign markets. The drawback, however, can be a lack of control over foreign sales and product development.

Joint Ventures

If a company wants to be present in the foreign market, it may enter into a joint venture with a foreign company. (See Figure 19-4.) Suppose that an American refrigerator manufacturer wanted to enter the Argentinian market. Exporting such heavy appliances would be too expensive, given transportation costs. And a licensing arrangement would not give the manufacturer enough control over the marketing and manufacturing. To minimize its risks and investment, the American manufacturer would seek an Argentinian company with the proper manufacturing and marketing capacity. These two companies would form a third company, each holding a percentage of this enterprise. (Such percentages vary from case to case, depending on capital resources, legal requirements, and so on.) Both would benefit because the Argentinian firm could manufacture the refrigerators relatively quickly, and the American firm could piggyback on an existing marketing operation.

It is difficult and expensive to build up a marketing organization in a foreign country. It also is time-consuming, another serious drawback. It may be next to impossible to use some countries' distribution networks. Many countries have only a few intermediaries, and these may already have exclusive contracts with competing marketers. Thus, in certain countries, joint ventures may be the only possible way to establish a market because foreign firms may be prohibited legally from operating facilities wholly owned by foreigners.

In 1981, Philip Morris bought 22 percent of British-based Rothmans International. The $350 million deal brings together the world's second- and fourth-largest tobacco companies. The agreement fosters each company's use of the other's production and distribution operations in markets where their shares widely differ. In Germany, Canada, parts of the Middle East, and Australia, both companies are among the top four manufacturers—and will continue to compete. But in India, the Philippines, and Pakistan, where Philip Morris is strong and Rothmans weak, and in Malaysia and Indonesia, where Rothmans is well entrenched and Philip Morris puny, the partners expect to share manufacturing and distribution facilities.

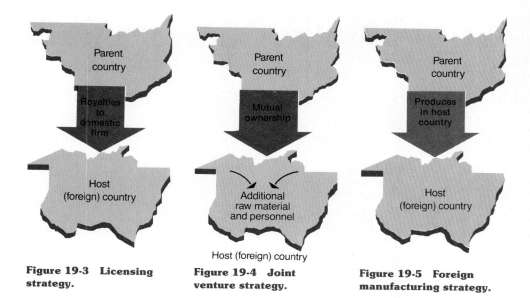

Figure 19-3   Licensing strategy.

Figure 19-4   Joint venture strategy.

Figure 19-5   Foreign manufacturing strategy.

Foreign Manufacturing

Foreign manufacturing is still another method of engaging in international trade. (See Figure 19-5.) Some products are better marketed if the manufacturer invests in foreign manufacturing facilities. Volkswagen, for example, opened a manufacturing plant in the United States after years of exporting its cars from Germany. Another advantage of foreign manufacturing is that governments tend to favor a foreign company that sets up local manufacturing facilities because it usually hires domestic labor and management. Many companies wish to reduce their image as a "foreign company," and domestic production helps to dispel it. Employing domestic labor shows a step toward integration into the domestic market.

Organizations, of course, are not limited to only one of these strategies. Rockwell International Corp., the multibillion-dollar automotive, aerospace, electronics, and machinery company, recently has set its goal to be a leading supplier of components to auto and truck manufacturers outside Detroit. To meet this goal, Rockwell (1) bought Wilmot-Breeden (Holdings) Ltd., a British auto parts company, (2) began negotiating a joint venture with IVECO (Industrial Vehicles Corp.), an Italian truckmaker, to obtain 80 percent control of a $500 million annual business in truck axles, and (3) signed a contract in Korea to license its truck axle technology. The result of these three activities of purchase, joint venture, and licensing: 20 percent of 1980 revenues were generated from foreign sales.

Multinational Corporations

When a company operates manufacturing and marketing facilities in any or all of the above ways in several countries and does a substantial share of its business outside the

TABLE 19-3   Ten Largest United States–Based Multinationals in 1979

Rank	Company	Foreign revenue (in millions)	Total revenue (in millions)	Foreign revenue as percentage of total
1	Exxon	$44,333	$60,335	73.5%
2	Mobil	20,481	34,736	59.0
3	Texaco	18,927	28,608	66.2
4	Ford	14,985	42,784	35.0
5	General Motors	14,172	63,221	22.4
6	Standard Oil of California	14,150	23,232	60.9
7	International Business Machines	11,040	21,076	52.4
8	International Tel. & Tel.	10,023	19,339	51.7
9	Gulf Oil	9,229	18,069	51.1
10	Citicorp	5,157	7,556	68.3

Source: Janet S. Ungerson, "A Game Any Number Can Play," *Forbes*, June 1979, p. 56.

border of the parent company, it qualifies as a *multinational corporation*. American corporations such as Exxon, IBM, Chesebrough-Pond's, Massey-Ferguson, and H. J. Heinz are multinationals. (See Table 19-3.) Multinational operations offer a number of advantages. Plants in different countries can specialize in different product lines. Production can be organized to minimize transportation costs of both raw materials and finished products. Marketing operations often become more efficient as promotional programs are utilized in more than one foreign country. And the experience gained in one foreign market often can be transferred to another. Yet multinational marketers must be careful to know when their marketing stategies and programs can be standardized and when they must be differentiated. The strategic marketing planning *process* is the heart of what drives successful multinational marketing.

But there are risks to operating plants abroad, especially in countries with unstable governments. A change in government, whether by election or coup, can produce sudden changes in attitudes toward the company. For instance, ITT lost millions when Chile nationalized its telephone system, and Iran was one of R. J. Reynolds's largest volume markets outside the United States until the late Shah's fall. Now it's zero. (See Application 19-2.)

Uncontrollable Variables of International Marketing

International marketers must be well aware of the uncontrollable environmental influences (such as those we discussed in Chapter 2) that affect their decisions, and they must pay particularly close attention to political, legal, and cultural influences. (See Figure 19-6.) Let's look at each in turn.

Application 19-2
Strategic Intelligence—
Tapping the Pulse of the Environment

A lack of sensitivity and understanding of local conditions can exact a high penalty from the unprepared marketer who enters the world of international trade.

To sidestep this problem, corporate managers are employing political risk analysts. Large oil companies and banks have always had in-house analysts to evaluate the stability of markets, and a 1980 survey by The Conference Board, a New York business-study group, revealed that smaller and less wealthy firms are seeking out specialists, too.

Analyses range from assigning an employee to monitor a potential hot spot to setting up an elaborate computerized system, as American Can Co. did, to rank investment risks in seventy countries. Outside consultants, like Chicago's Associated Consultants International and Boston's Arthur D. Little Inc., provide political risk assessments for smaller companies. American Ltd., headed by a former Arab League ambassador to the United Nations, was founded to advise companies on political conditions in the Middle East.

Risk Insights, Inc., a New York firm, tries to organize the subtle interplay of politics, economics, and social stress in various countries through computerized study. For $3000, it offers reports giving mathematical probabilities for business risks, such as war, expropriation, price controls, import restrictions, and labor strife for a particular country. Conrad Pearson, the firm's managing partner, says confidently: "Interest in risk analysis is so great these days that we are adding at least one client per week to our list."

Source of data: "In Search of Stable Markets," *Time,* May 25, 1981, p. 69.

The Political and Legal Environment

Politics abroad are often quite different from politics at home. Domestic politics are relatively stable. Our political leaders change, but the structure of government continues. Political change in the United States is relatively gradual. For instance, although the Federal Trade Commission affects the way companies conduct business, marketers usually have time to conform to new regulations. When cigarette advertising was barred from television and radio, tobacco companies had one year to adjust their marketing strategies.

In many foreign countries, and particularly in some developing nations, political leadership may change rapidly, and companies may discover that a new set of rules governing their operation has been put into effect overnight. What is acceptable one day may lead to a jail term the next. In short, international politics are among the most uncontrollable of variables, and international marketers must be prepared to meet almost any political situation and emergency.

In civil war–torn El Salvador, for example, government policy resulted in the central banks restricting the use of foreign currency to purchasing only vital products such as medicine and energy. Many companies were forced to purchase foreign exchange in the black market, where the exchange rate was at times 50 percent higher

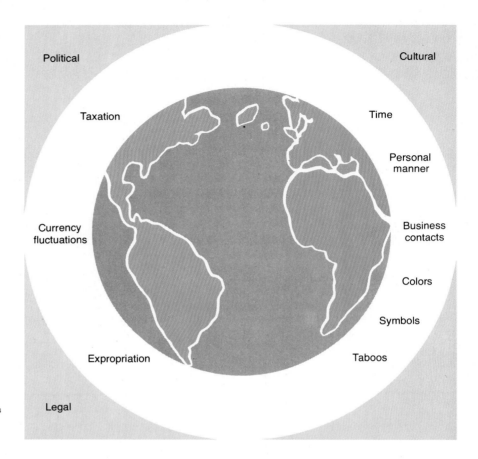

Political

Cultural

Taxation

Time

Personal manner

Currency fluctuations

Business contacts

Colors

Symbols

Expropriation

Taboos

Legal

Figure 19-6 Major uncontrollable variables of international marketing.

than normal exchange rates. Such regulations caused a 50 percent hike in prices to cover this unexpected cost—and thus limited sales.

Marketers must be especially sensitive to the regulations of the country in which they are operating. In the Soviet Union, for instance, privately held companies do not exist. United States marketers must deal directly with the government in order to engage in trade. Thus, Pepsi Cola oversees the operation of several bottling plants in the Soviet Union, but the government controls them, and it dictates where the beverage will be sold and for what price.

And consider the problems of Pringle's New-Fangled Potato Chips, a Procter & Gamble product, an instant success in Japan when it hit the shelves there. Sales reached $50 million, but suddenly Japanese customs regulations changed. Pringle's was converted from the ''processed foods'' classification, taxed at 15.5 percent import duty, to ''confection,'' subject to a 35 percent duty. P&G officials issued a complaint to a joint trade committee consisting of Japan's Ministry of International Trade and Industry and the U.S. Commerce Department, and Pringle's was again listed as processed food. But the sudden, unpredictable change took its toll on P&G profits.

It is often difficult to separate economic from political policy, and many marketers have found that economic conditions change as rapidly as political conditions in some parts of the world. Marketers must be well versed in the tax laws of host countries. They must be prepared for sudden changes in the value of currency and must face the possibility of nationalization or expropriation.

Taxation

When foreign marketers enter a developing country, they may be welcomed with such concessions as tax-free profits for a number of years or financial support from the government. But after a period of time, it is not uncommon for governments to change their rules and demand very high taxation on profits. In addition, foreign governments may forbid the transfer of profits to the marketer's country or set a time limit before which profits cannot be repatriated.

Currency Fluctuations

The exchange rate for currency— or the value of one country's money in terms of another's—is set by a country's government. The rate is established independently of the forces of demand and supply, which determine the general value of currency according to the prevailing economic situation. When a country's currency exchange rate is set very low compared with that of other countries, that country has to pay more for its imports. This situation makes the job of international marketers even more difficult, especially if they depend on other countries for raw materials and other production components.

Expropriation

One of the most serious problems international marketers face is linked both to nationalism and to political philosophy—expropriation. Many foreign companies have been taken over by foreign governments. For instance, Chile nationalized the operation of copper mines some years ago, and Venezuela nationalized the entire oil industry in 1977.

Many countries, notably in Latin America, now tell foreign marketers who seek permission to operate that they will have to be prepared for some form of nationalization within ten to fifteen years. The possibility of expropriation has forced many companies to enter into joint ventures or to license domestic companies to manufacture their products.

Indeed, international marketers are at the mercy of a host country. Although we read of international law and world courts, in reality neither is very effective. The only real law is the one in force in the country where marketers are operating. A good illustration is the case of Anaconda Company when the government of Chile seized its copper mines. Anaconda received $47.5 million in cash for its mines and a like amount in Chilean notes. Chile could have forced Anaconda to leave the country with nothing, but Anaconda was able to settle the dispute through arbitration. Of course, in some cases of expropriation, marketers may get help from the United States government, which can bring pressure to bear on the country involved. But there is no guarantee of government help and no assurance that the foreign government will respond favorably.

Two United States multinational corporations, IBM and Coca-Cola, joined fifty-five foreign corporations that recently decided to close down operations in India.

The ruling Janata Party turned to vigorous enforcement of a 1973 law that insisted on at least part Indian ownership of foreign companies that operate in India. IBM withdrew because of its strict 100 percent philosophy—total internal control of all operations from production to servicing. In a similar move, the Atlanta-based Coca-Cola Company faced an edict from India's Minister of Industry to end operations or relinquish 60 percent of its equity and its business know-how. Coca-Cola had originally agreed to 40 percent equity but insisted on not divulging certain trade secrets like the fabled Coke syrup formula. A company spokesperson noted that the Indian government seemed not to distinguish between "technological know-how" and "trade secret." (See Application 19-3.)

Application 19-3
Bribery—A Way of Business?

Bribery in business may be common in some circles, but it has always been frowned on by United States standards, and the jails are brimming with businesspeople who attempted this shortcut.

But in many foreign markets, what we would define as bribery is the way to do business. Americans doing business abroad find bribery a confusing issue. United States law makes it a criminal offense to pay bribes of any sort to foreign officials. The major problem of any law on bribery is that in some parts of the world, commercial corruption of government and business is looked upon as an inescapable fact of everyday life. Bribery is often a perfectly normal and legal method of operation under local law and custom.

The Persian Gulf has now become a playground of business corruption. In Saudi Arabia, a key government minister is widely reported to have collected over $500 million in "commission fees" on foreign business ventures for 1980 alone.

In Mexico, bribery is handled with flair. It typically starts with dinner at an expensive restaurant and ends with a weekend jet-jaunt to Punta Cancún or Acapulco. The beneficiary of this lavish hospitality is most likely the head of purchasing in one of the Mexican government's state ministries, whose role is to oversee procurement and importing.

While the purpose of bribery is the same in Asia, the style is different. In Malaysia, aspiring foreign business executives use the Malaysian mania for gambling as a vehicle for bribes. One common approach is to invite an official to play golf, bet heavily, and then carefully spend the next three hours swatting your ball into the sand traps. An only slightly more straightforward method is to join in an after-dinner poker game with a key civil servant and lose heavily.

In Germany, such expenditures, which can run into the millions of dollars on large engineering and construction projects, are completely tax-deductible as a necessary cost of business. Italy passed a law in 1980 stating that payments to foreign officials to procure business are perfectly legal, and France has no laws at all relating to foreign bribes.

The head of a medium-sized French company that does extensive business in the Middle East explains, "The French authorities know quite well that you cannot deal in those countries without payoffs."

Source of data: "Big Profits in Big Bribery," *Time,* March 16, 1981, pp. 58–67.

The Cultural Environment

Marketers who are going abroad with their products for the first time must also be sensitive to foreign cultures, and cultural differences are staggering. They are based, in large part, on religious, social, and economic tradition. Some of these differences may seem insignificant to the foreigner, but marketers who violate accepted practices in these areas are courting disaster.

Avon Products, Inc., had to reshape its marketing for Hong Kong. In the United States, the Avon saleswoman was accustomed to being greeted at the door by the woman of the house and led into the living room where she could sell over a cup of coffee. In Hong Kong, it is likely to be a servant who peers through a metal gate at vistors, and who is likely to announce that the mistress of the house is not at home. So Avon began recruiting special salespeople for Hong Kong. They tend to be well-to-do housewives or women at a certain professional level—like travel consultants or executive secretaries. The notion is that they can sell to their acquaintances or command access to women in their neighborhoods who will invite them to stop by.

Let's take a look at some of the areas where cross-cultural differences are most pronounced and where they complicate marketing most. Their implications are great for such marketing activities as advertising, personal selling, branding, and packaging.

Time

To Americans, punctuality and the setting of deadlines are normal business procedures. But to Latin Americans or Arabs, deadlines may be considered discourteous and uncivilized. In the United States, giving a person a deadline is a way of indicating the degree of urgency or relative importance of the work. But in the Middle East, an American can easily fall into a cultural trap. "Mr. Aziz will have to make up his mind in a hurry because my board meets next week and I have to have an answer by then" is considered undue pressure. To give someone a deadline in this part of the world is to be rude, pushy, and demanding.

Personal Manner

In some areas of the world, it is considered rude to sit with your legs crossed or, even worse, to put your feet on a table and display your soles. In Muslim countries, to show public affection—even for your spouse—can cause embarrassment. In some countries, it is even unlawful. Physical contact is regarded as a private matter. In other cultures, businesspeople may touch hands during a negotiation; and in Russia, men often greet one another by kissing.

Business Contacts

Many Westerners who negotiate with Russians or citizens of other socialist states don't understand that in socialist bureaucracies, plans and deals have to be approved by an endless string of committees. Negotiations may sometimes take years. In Japan, long periods of silence during negotiations are not uncommon. Unprepared Americans worry that something has gone wrong. But the silence is an excellent tactic, and the Japanese count on Westerners' impatience during negotiations.[2]

---

[2]Edward T. Hall, "The Silent Language in Overseas Business," *Harvard Business Review* (May–June 1960), pp. 87–96.

Also in Japan, *kosai-hi,* literally entertainment expenses, is the name of the business game. While the Japanese defense budget is 0.9 percent of the country's GNP, corporate wining and dining accounts for 1.2 percent of total national output. Top executives are expected to spend up to three or four nights a week entertaining— eating in posh restaurants or golfing on lush greens.

Colors

Colors mean different things in different cultures. Green, the national color of Egypt because religious leaders once wore it, is frowned upon as a packaging color. Similarly, black and white are the Japanese colors of mourning and should not show up on a product's package. And purple is unacceptable in many Hispanic countries because of its association with death.

An international manufacturer of water recreation products learned an expensive lesson in Malaysia. The company's Malaysian distributors sent an angry request to the home office to stop shipment of all products colored green. Many customers associated the color with the jungle and with illness. And in Hong Kong, Singer, the producer of sewing machines, halted an outdoor advertising campaign that used Prussian blue when it was found that the color signified death. Red and gold, on the other hand, were found to represent goodness.

Symbols

Advertisers in Japan should avoid the digit 4 because the word for four, *shi,* is also the word for death. For many years, a Swedish company (ASEA) used the swastika as a trademark. Originally, this symbol signified the sun on the old runestones, but in the 1930s the Nazis adopted the swastika as their party symbol, and the Swedish company had to change its trademark.

Taboos

All cultures forbid, or taboo, certain behavior. Marketers must observe these taboos. For instance, an American cleansing-product manufacturer worked up some commercials for the Hong Kong market that showed people tossing hats around in jest. One had a green hat landing on a male model's head. And that was the end of that creative strategy. The advertiser was shown that among Chinese, a green hat signifies that the male in question has an unfaithful wife.

Language

American marketers need to expand language knowledge beyond English to compete globally. In Latin America, the Chevy Nova wasn't doing well. The name was changed when someone realized that "nova" sounded like "no-go" to Spanish-speaking buyers. General Motors touts its "Body by Fisher," which was being translated as "Corpse by Fisher" in some countries. Pepsi's slogan "Come alive with Pepsi" was understood in the Taiwan market as "Pepsi brings your ancestors back from the grave." (See Figure 19-7.)

These are just a few of the kinds of cultural differences that marketers must recognize before they embark on an international marketing program. Potential pitfalls abound.

TABLE 19-4   Some Faux Pas to Avoid in Cross-Cultural Marketing

Americans usually smile as they shake hands. But some Germans consider smiles overly familiar from new business acquaintances. Americans shouldn't say *"Wie geht's?"* ("How goes it?"). It's also too informal for first meetings.

If you offer a compliment to a Chinese-speaking person, he or she will likely decline it because disagreeing is the polite way to accept praise.

Don't say *"Merci"* ("thanks") to a French person's compliment. You might be misinterpreted as making fun.

Italians wave goodbye as Americans beckon someone—with palm up and fingers moving back and forth; but in Oriental areas, waving with the palm down is not interpreted as goodbye but, rather, "Come here."

Offering gifts when you visit a home is expected in Japan, but in the Soviet Union it may be considered a bribe.

In Brazil and Portugal, businesspeople like to entertain foreigners in their homes. When it's time to go, the host may feel constrained to insist that the foreigner stay. Foreigners should politely take their leave.

Source: "Avoiding *Faux Pas* When Visiting a Foreign Country," *Business Week*, Dec. 12, 1977, pp. 115–116.

Figure 19-7   Breaking the language barrier: marketers must be certain that their message translates in foreign markets. *(Courtesy Deere and Company)*

Controllable Variables of International Marketing

The uncontrollable variables we've just mentioned affect the controllable variables of international marketing. Let's look at some of the things marketers must consider as they plan the product, price, place, and promotion activities. (See Figure 19-8.)

Marketing Research

In the United States, many businesses and private individuals are accustomed to answering questions. In most cases, we see nothing sinister about cooperating with most kinds of research, and sometimes we may even be proud to have the chance to state our opinion. But in some parts of the world, cultural barriers and social customs often interfere with marketing research, information about personal likes and dislikes may be considered private, and people may resist all inquiries. In some cultures, men are considered competent to discuss certain subjects, and women deal with other matters. In societies that keep the sexes strictly apart, housewives will not allow male interviewers into their homes or kitchens. In some cultures, men consider it beneath their dignity to discuss habits and preferences with female interviewers. Higher-status individuals may not feel obligated to answer an interviewer of lower status. Thus a person's sex and social class will affect the results of research conducted by interviews.

Another difficulty in conducting marketing research is the distrust some other cultures may bear toward business matters. Business habits, sales volumes, profits, and similar topics are considered private matters, and anybody inquiring about them is suspect. Concern about tax regulations or about the possibility of giving away business secrets can get in the way of research, and promises of anonymity will have little effect on people's willingness to cooperate.

In developing countries, research also may be impeded by low literacy levels and by the inability of respondents to express themselves. These impediments may be especially severe for products that are entirely new to an area. It is difficult for people

Figure 19-8 Major controllable variables of international marketing.

to express an opinion about an electronic calculator or a refrigerator if the product is totally unfamiliar. In addition, marketers who conduct research in several countries at once may find that the same questions elicit different answers.

Of course, one element of culture that interferes is language. It is often impossible to translate a question from one language to another and retain the right shades of meaning. In constructing a questionnaire in another language, it's a good idea first to develop an English version. After that has been translated into the foreign language, it should be given to another translator for conversion back into English. By comparing the original English version and the retranslated version, marketers can get a fairly good idea of which questions are likely to be misunderstood.

Researchers need reliable mailing lists, sometimes impossible to obtain in foreign markets. Nor can they always get statistical information to construct a reliable and valid sample. In many cases, marketers have to compromise and improvise, and they cannot be as confident of their results as they might be in domestic markets.

All in all, then, marketing research in foreign markets is more complicated than domestic research, but it certainly is not impossible, and it remains the cornerstone of successful marketing. (See Application 19-4.)

Product

When marketing a product abroad, the question that always arises is: Must the product be modified to meet the requirements of international markets? Differences in tastes, habits, and preferences often force such adjustments. For instance, when Duncan Hines introduced its rich, moist American-style cakes to England, the

Application 19-4
Marketing Research—
Learning Cultural Dos and Dont's

In the United States, soup is generally regarded as a dish served at noon or in the evening. If marketers assumed that this is universal, they would be in trouble in Japan where soup is a breakfast drink.

While soup manufacturers have done their homework in Japan, other United States businesses have stumbled by not learning their market. A candy company introduced a peanut-packed chocolate bar in Japan with the strategy of appealing to Japanese teenagers. Not until the campaign was launched did the company discover a Japanese old wives' tale that eating chocolate with peanuts gives one a nosebleed.

Keeping track of such tales and customs has become a growth industry for consulting firms. ASI Market Research, Tokyo, guides such United States marketers as Procter & Gamble and Levi Strauss.

"We not only gather primary data, but suggest what a company can do here," said William Hall, an officer with ASI.

Source of data: "Learning How to Please the Baffling Japanese," *Fortune,* Oct. 5, 1981, p. 122.

company soon found that the British prefer a dry cake. Moist pieces of cake are too messy to hold in one hand while sipping tea. And American refrigerator manufacturers have found that most foreign consumers prefer smaller models than the standard United States sizes for several reasons. Shopping trips abroad are often more frequent than in the United States, and the amount of food bought each time is less. Also, living accommodations tend to be smaller, and a large refrigerator won't fit. For some products, technological modifications are necessary. For example, in the United States the standard current voltage is 120 volts, 60 hertz (cycles) AC. In Europe, the standard is 220 volts, 50 hertz AC. In short, the key to success in product planning is to adapt to the culture of the foreign market.

Marketing strategy may also differ because a product's position in the life cycle may vary from country to country. A product that has reached the maturity stage in the United States, for example, may very well be in the growth stage in France and in the introductory stage in Nigeria.

Many foreign buyers are skeptical of imported goods because of problems with service and replacement parts. A company like Dunhill of London has been successful in marketing cigarette lighters around the world because it provides a network of special service centers. International marketers must learn how to provide such support for their products.

Price

Price is one element of the marketing mix that is very difficult to control in international markets. For some products such as grain, cotton, and cement, there is even a world price set by the forces of supply and demand, which are entirely outside the marketer's control. For an exporter selling through agents and intermediaries in a foreign country, the possibilities of affecting the ultimate consumer price are also small. And in many countries, it is illegal for the manufacturer to dictate or even advertise the consumer price.

Because the length of the channel of distribution varies and because intermediaries' margins differ from country to country, few companies can establish anything like a standardized pricing policy for the international market. Competitive pressures differ. The possibilities of supporting the product with promotion differ. The rates of currency exchange tend to fluctuate. All these conditions reduce the marketer's control of price.

Two other pricing issues complicate the pricing activity—bartering and dumping. Many marketers wanting to trade with other countries often find that the foreign country lacks hard currency to pay for the goods. Eastern Bloc nations, China, and developing countries in Asia and Africa often turn to *bartering* or trading their goods for American goods. PepsiCo, Inc., trades syrup and technology to the Soviet Union for vodka, while General Electric Company provides Poland with the technology and equipment to produce electrocardiogram meters which, in turn, Poland ships back to GE. Application 19-5 details additional bartering arrangements.

Dumping is the practice of selling your goods abroad at a price *below* that charged domestically. Recently, for instance, Florida tomato growers were charging that Mexican vegetables were being dumped across the border. And the United States

Application 19-5
Bartering Away the Price—
A Little of This for a Little of That

Bartering, by all accounts, is the oldest form of exchange and remains a common method in many parts of the world. In 1978, Hungary wanted to build a blue jeans plant but lacked the hard currency to pay for it. Levi Strauss wanted to expand its European operations. As a result, Hungary bought equipment and expertise from Levi Strauss, and Levi Strauss agreed to be the plant's biggest customer, buying 60 percent of the plant's annual output.

This agreement, called a countertrade, is not an isolated event. Similar deals account for 20 percent or more of all international trade in the 1980s.

Companies involved in bartering include General Motors, General Electric, PepsiCo, and McDonnell Douglas. And the number and size of the deals are so large that many companies have set up trading subsidiaries just to handle the bartering agreements.

General Motors Corporation has been involved in countertrades since the early 1970s. One GM deal involved the sale of $12 million in locomotive and diesel engines to Yugoslavia. In exchange, GM agreed to buy $4 million in Yugoslavian cutting tools. GM located a Detroit-based tool manufacturer to purchase the tools and thus completed the deal.

One of the more unusual

transactions involved Control Data and the Soviet Union. The Soviet Ministry of Culture needed a computer to catalog the artworks in the Hermitage Museum. Control Data agreed to ship a $3 million computer to the Hermitage if the Ministry would release some of its masterpieces for a two-year United States tour. The deal went through, and Control Data has recovered most of its investment from its exclusive rights to market reproductions and art books based on the tour.

Source of data: "Barter Becomes Big Business in World Trade," *The New York Times,* July 26, 1981, p. F15.

steel industry has been thunderously warning that cheap imports from Japan and Europe are endangering the structure of the steel industry. Higher import duties are one way to dampen dumping, but this political solution can lead to a reduction in trade between the countries involved. Throughout the 1970s, American television manufacturers have bitterly complained of lax enforcement of trade rules allowing Japanese dumping of television sets on the United States market and capturing 40 percent market share. In 1979, the U.S. Treasury Department, under pressure, moved to collect some $40 million in duties from thirty-eight importers that had brought sets into this country between 1971 and 1973.

Distribution

Selecting the right channel of distribution is an important element of marketing strategy. But, as with price, controlling the channels is limited in international markets. For many companies, particularly the smaller ones, it is often difficult to establish an effective channel arrangement. Channels similar to the ones used in domestic sales may simply not exist in another country. And if one does exist, it may not be available because competition often controls the channel (especially true in smaller countries). Generally, though, one can say that channels of distribution in most foreign countries tend to be longer and have more intermediaries. Margins tend to be larger, and the functions of wholesaling and retailing are often mixed, so that the same wholesalers sell their products both to retailers and to consumers. And the operations of many foreign intermediaries are very different from those of domestic ones. (See Table 19-5.)

The American shoe industry provides an example of problems arising from distribution differences. Recently, American footwear producers (Thom McAn, Sebago-Moc Company, Dexter Shoe Company, and others) had been trying to increase their European exports. The declining value of the United States dollar, European inflation, and the growing numbers of affluent young on the Continent had helped provide a market opportunity. But the biggest problem had been distribution. As a spokesperson for the industry noted, "Americans will have to adjust to distribution patterns that vary from one country to the next, the absence of many big chain department stores, and the large proportion of small independent retailers." United States manufacturers expected to counter these problems by pooling small shipments and hiring agents and brokers who really knew the outlets.

Promotion

Promotional activities, and particularly advertising, are among the most sensitive areas of international marketing. Cost and convenience dictate that a company use similar promotional tools in all markets. But what works in Philadelphia may not work in Paris or Tokyo. The main issue in international advertising, then, is the degree to which marketers can standardize their messages and promotional strategies, and here the major influence is the level of economic development. That is, an advertising campaign which was successful in the United States may go over well in West

---

TABLE 19-5 Retail Shopping Hours in Europe

West Germany: Shops are open from 8:30 or 9 A.M. to 6 or 6:30 P.M. They close Saturday afternoons—except the first Saturday of each month.

France: Some elegant Parisian boutiques and virtually all provincial stores close from 12:30 to 2 or 2:30 P.M. and again at 6:30 P.M. In Paris, small food shops close between 12:30 and 3:30 or 4 P.M., but department stores stay open Monday through Saturday from 9 or 9:45 A.M. until 6:30 or 7 P.M.

Holland: Shops generally are open from 8:30 or 9 A.M. to 5:30 or 6 P.M. on weekdays, but close at midday once a week (days vary locally). On Mondays, department stores and most shops do not open until 1:30 P.M., and many others close on Wednesday afternoons.

Sweden: Shops are usually open from 9 A.M. to 6 P.M., Monday through Friday. On Saturday and the day before a holiday, closing time varies between 1 and 4 P.M. Department stores and many other shops in larger cities are open until 8 o'clock one evening a week (usually Monday or Friday).

Spain: Shops open at 9 A.M., close at 2 P.M., reopen at 5 P.M., and close at 8 in the evening. Many close on Saturday afternoons, and in the summer, the afternoon closing hours tend to be longer.

Belgium: Stores are usually open from 9 to 6 or 6:30, but they must close for 24 consecutive hours once a week—and post a notice to say which day that will be.

Figure 19-9   The Marlboro Man has worked well as an advertising theme in some countries and not at all well in others. Name other campaigns which you suppose would "translate" differently in various cultures. (Ray Pfortner)

Germany or in Sweden, where standards of living are similar. Philip Morris was able to use its cowboy theme to promote Marlboro cigarettes in Germany, and the ads were considered extremely successful. But the same approach in Hong Kong produced negative results. Hong Kong Chinese, affluent and urban, did not see the charm of riding around alone in the hot sun all day. (See Figure 19-9.)

In the United States, marketers have more types of media available than anywhere else in the world. Radio, television, magazines, newspapers, and billboards are not universally found, however, and where they exist, they are not available to so many people. Many countries do not have television, and others forbid or restrict commercial advertising on radio and TV. No television advertising at all is allowed in Scandinavian countries. In Holland, commercials are allowed only on the news program but not at times that children might be watching and not at all on Sunday. In Italy, the use of jingles is not permitted.

By now American advertising agencies are spread throughout the world, and many have subsidiaries. American marketers thus can deal either with an American branch office or with a local agency. But the role of the agency tends to vary from country to country. Some are full-service agencies that offer everything from research to follow-up and evaluation but others may be little more than media buyers. (See Application 19-6.)

Application 19-6
Advertising Gears for Foreign Regulation

When cigarette commercials were banned in the United States in the late 1960s, the Marlboro cowboy simply galloped off to other countries. Those were the days when the rest of the free world did little or nothing to monitor what went into television commercials. However, the late 1970s and early 1980s have seen a marked change in advertising regulations, and marketers must now contend with regulation in almost every corner of the globe.

"In the good old days, advertising in the colony (Hong Kong) was almost unregulated," said one advertising head. "Now, if you make claims, you have to provide evidence of them."

Few would quarrel with standards which require truthful advertising, but the change has had a marked impact on marketers who now must learn different sets of regulations in almost every foreign market.

Just dubbing your United States commercial with another language is not enough. Marketers must be aware of the peculiarities of markets, and some claims of

ads don't "wash" abroad. Coke's slogan "Coke adds life" was forbidden in Thailand because the government says it is an exaggeration. In Malaysia, all foreign commercials and models are now banned. Even promotional jingles and music must be locally produced. And China outlawed blue jeans in ads as symbols of Western decadence.

Source of data: "Curbs on Ads Increase Abroad as Nations Apply Standards of Fairness and Decency," *The Wall Street Journal,* Nov. 25, 1980, p. 56.

The United States and the World as a Foreign Market

The United States is populous, wealthy, politically stable, and economically sound. Many foreign multinationals (see Table 19-6) view the United States as a logical target market for their growth. Nestlé, the world's largest food company, plans to expand its American share of business from 18 percent in 1981 to 30 percent; it considers the United States to be its most promising market. Mitsubishi, Japan's biggest industrial, trading, and banking conglomerate, is beginning a determined push into this country by exporting new corporate jet planes, drawing a bead on electronic products, and investing in everything from oil exploration and copper mining to manufacturing and restaurants, as well as expanding its banking network. The Mitsubishi group wants its name to be as much a household word in the United States as it is at home in Japan. The Japanese have clearly made their mark in consumer durables—electronic games, television sets, watches, automobiles. West Germany has made an impact within the automobile industry. And four Asian international competitors—South Korea, Taiwan, Hong Kong, and Singapore—are together beginning to rival Japan's impact on the world market. Many foreign companies and countries have found the United States market offers an opportunity they cannot overlook.

TABLE 19-6 Ten Largest European-Based Multinationals in 1979

Rank	Company and Country	Foreign revenue (in millions)	Total revenue (in millions)	Foreign revenue as percentage of total
1	Royal Dutch/Shell Group (Netherlands-Britain)	NA*	$45,246	—
2	British Petroleum (Britain)	$22,200	27,407	81.0%
3	Philips Gloeilampenfabrieken (Netherlands)	13,592	15,096	90.0
4	Unilever (Britain-Netherlands)	NA*	18,152	—
5	Nestlé (Switzerland)	NA*	11,798	—
6	Bayer (Germany)	8,030	11,369	70.6
7	Volkswagenwerk (Germany)	7,717	13,305	58.0
8	Siemens (Germany)	7,294	14,443	50.5
9	Compagnie Francaise des Pétroles (France)	NA*	10,876	—
10	B.A.T. Industries (Britain)	6,469	7,751	83.5

*Company does not report revenue outside the home country. Ranking is based on estimates of foreign revenues.

Source: Janet S. Ungerson, "A Game Any Number Can Play," *Forbes*, 25 (June 1979), p. 62.

Among the foreign competitors being lured to the American market, none is as aggressive and effective as the Japanese. Over the decade of the 1970s, Japan's Ministry of International Trade and Industry has proclaimed high-technology businesses ranging from genetic engineering to semiconductors as the nation's top targets for increased international trade. Japan's strategy is rather simple. Armed with strong ability and determination, the Japanese first secure their home market, then use long production runs to invade at an advantage. Their strategy is to provide technology comparable to that of the United States; they often upgrade the export product's quality, cut domestic prices for a while at least, and then cut away profits of the United States companies, making investment for expansion more difficult. This aggressive strategy has worked well. At home, Japanese computer companies have taken the lead in market share (52 percent) over competitors (predominantly IBM); and they are launching into this country's computer market with new technologies. In semiconductors, they have captured large chunks of the American chip manufacturers' business and secured 40 percent of the world market for the popular 16,000-bit memory chip.

Foreign marketers use the same means of entering the United States as American marketers use when going abroad. For instance, consider the Japanese invasion of the semiconductor industry. Nippon Electric Company, Japan's largest electronics firm, first started a sales branch in 1974, then grew through purchasing its own semiconductor maker. Fijutsu has a disk memory plant in Santa Clara, California, and owns 36 percent of the American computer maker Amdhal. The Toyo Electronics Industry Corporation founded Exar Systems of Sunnyvale, California. So a wide variety of entry techniques are used.

In marketing in the United States foreign competitors also face the same set of uncontrollable environmental influences. As foreign imported automobiles ate away at Detroit's market share (imports hit 27 percent), heavy lobbying in Washington resulted in a voluntary import quota being enacted by the Japanese automobile manufacturers. Rather than face explicit legal restraints on trade, the Japanese competitors chose self-regulation to reduce criticism of their impact on the cornerstone industry of the American economy.

American marketers can fully expect increased competition from abroad on the domestic battleground. Trade barriers to the United States are minimal, the affluence of Americans is attractive, and within many product categories—automobiles, china, fabrics, furniture—the allure of foreign-made is substantial.

Many international marketers today are looking beyond and operating in a new era of business. American businesspeople know they must meet the threat of foreign competition. Many also realize that there is great opportunity in markets overseas. To capitalize on these opportunities, many multinational corporations are becoming *global* enterprises.

Multinational corporations view each of their businesses around the world as an independent entity, fairly much on its own to serve a national market where it is situated. *Global enterprises,* by comparison, set their sights on selling a fairly uniform product in markets all over the earth, and coordinate their international activities accordingly. They may make or buy components on several continents and then transport them to a country with low labor costs to be partially assembled and finally finished in plants close to the ultimate customer. The result may be a Sony television set or an IBM computer.

On the downside, global enterprises are particularly vulnerable to political and other environmental risks. To conventional multinational corporations, a revolution may mean the loss of one country's market. To a global company with world-scale assembly operations, a coup in one country may result in shutting down operations everywhere. To avoid such a catastrophe, backup assembly systems and careful environmental intelligence are needed.

Clearly, the orchestration of a global enterprise calls for massive doses of coordination and heavy reliance on the methods of strategic marketing planning. The intercountry transfer of parts and products is highly complicated and can be fraught with delays, stockouts, and stoppages. Certainly, a master plan is needed to guide such actions. More and more companies are turning toward this global perspective and setting their strategies accordingly. At S. C. Johnson, the marketer of household and personal care products, 60 percent of its 1980 sales were derived from outside the United States. In an interview with *Advertising Age,* the company's president and chief operating officer reflected the thinking of many internationally inclined top management people when he said:[3]

Strategic planning is crucial to us. As the business grows internationally, we have to think strategically and more on a total worldwide basis. We have to begin to think globally.

---

[3]"U.S. Fuels World Goal of Johnson," *Advertising Age,* March 9, 1981, p. 4.

Looking Back

Basically, marketing's concepts are applicable everywhere. Whether the organization markets in Peoria or Paris, the marketing program should be built around a product that is properly priced, appropriately distributed, and promoted to a market that has been well researched. We have noted some of the major considerations in cross-cultural marketing. Before looking at the social responsibilities of marketers in the next chapter, be sure you have learned the following points:

1 World War II marked the birth of international marketing.

2 World trade has helped improve our standard of living.

3 Strict adherence to the *principle of comparative advantage* is not practical.

4 International marketing usually evolves through four stages of managerial philosophy and orientation.

5 Multinational corporations pose both advantages and disadvantages.

6 Foreign politics are often less stable than domestic politics.

7 Marketers must pay close attention to cultural differences among nations, particularly differences in time, personal manner, business contacts, colors, symbols, and taboos.

8 Conducting marketing research poses many cross-cultural problems.

9 Products must be adjusted for cultural differences.

10 Prices are not easily controlled by the marketer in international settings.

11 Channels of distribution tend to be longer in foreign countries than in the United States.

12 Promotion, particularly advertising, is one of the most sensitive areas of international marketing.

13 American marketers are finding greater competition at home from foreign firms.

14 Global enterprises are reflecting a broadened view of doing world business.

Key Terms

If you aren't sure what each of the following words means, look back at the text. Numbers refer to pages on which the words are defined. Additional information can be found by checking the index and the glossary at the end of the book.

General Agreement on Tariffs and Trade 615
European Community 615
principle of comparative advantage 616

ethnocentric stage 618
polycentric stage 618
regiocentric stage 618
geocentric stage 618
exporting 618
licensing 620

joint venture 620
foreign manufacturing 621
multinational corporations 621
uncontrollable variables of
   international marketing 622

controllable variables of
   international marketing 630
international bartering 632
dumping 632
global enterprises 638

Questions for Review

1 Of the strategies for international marketing, which is usually the marketer's first strategy to gain access to markets abroad?

2 What are the positive and negative aspects of a licensing arrangement between countries?

3 What are some of the advantages of being a multinational corporation?

4 Many businesses are warmly welcomed when they enter foreign markets. What are at least two uncontrollable variables that can drastically change this situation?

5 If a United States marketer uses a green package to sell its product domestically, should the same package be used in foreign countries? Why?

6 What is the key to developing successful products in international settings?

Questions for Thought and Discussion

1 Kentucky Fried Chicken used large pictures of Colonel Sanders in West Germany for promotion. The German response was very negative. Can you guess why?

2 In 1977 the Bendix Corporation and the Soviet Union agreed to produce and sell Bendix spark plugs in Russia. According to the terms of the agreement, the spark plugs would carry the Bendix name but would be stamped "Made in the U.S.S.R." Why would the Soviets insist upon such a stamp?

3 If the United States dollar loses value or is devalued in relation to other currencies, what effect does that have on our foreign trade?

4 Brazil had been one of the leading importers of Scotch whiskey until the military government recently began taxing heavily all imported brands it considered "superfluous." Brands like Chivas Regal and Passport rose to unprecedented prices of over $50 and $30, respectively. How do you think such a tax has affected Brazilian consumers and liquor marketers?

Suggested Project

Go to the library and research three unique customs that have relevance to international marketers wanting to enter three different countries. Choose three countries in widely separated parts of the world.

Suggested Readings

Bartels, Robert: "Are Domestic and International Marketing Dissimilar?" *Journal of Marketing,* vol. 32 (July 1968), pp. 56–61. The author of this article emphasizes the similarities rather than the differences in international marketing.

Douglas, Susan, and Bernard DuBois: "Looking at the Cultural Environment for International Marketing," *Columbia Journal of World Business,* vol. 12 (Winter 1977), pp. 102–109. This article illustrates the need to consider cultural factors in planning international marketing strategies.

Doz, Yves L., and G. K. Prahalad: "How MNCs (Multinational Corporations) Cope with Host Government Intervention," *Harvard Business Review,* vol. 58 (March–April 1980), pp. 149–157. This article classifies types of restrictions and shows strategies for matching corporate response to these government demands.

Hall, Edward T.: "The Silent Language in Overseas Business," *Harvard Business Review,* vol. 38 (May–June 1960), pp. 87–96. This classic article stresses the importance for American business executives of having a solid understanding of social, cultural, and economic differences when attempting to do business in foreign countries.

Igal, Ayal, and Z. F. Jehiel: "Market Expansion Strategies in Multinational Marketing," *Journal of Marketing,* vol. 43 (Spring 1979), pp. 84–94. The authors analyze the product and market factors that favor market concentration versus market diversification.

Keegan, Warren J.: "Multinational Product Planning: Strategic Alternatives," *Journal of Marketing,* vol. 33 (January 1969), pp. 58–62. Five strategies involving combinations of product and communications activities are presented.

Killough, James: "Improved Payoffs from Transnational Advertising," *Harvard Business Review,* vol. 56 (July–August 1978), pp. 102–110. A study shows how advertising ideas and presentations can be transferred across geographic boundaries.

Narayana, Chem: "Aggregate Images of American and Japanese Products: Implications on International Marketing," *The Columbia Journal of World Business,* vol. 16 (Summer 1981), pp. 31–35. This article reports the results of research comparing United States and Japanese consumers' perceptions of products made in this country and Japan and discusses their implications on international and domestic marketing strategies.

Terpstra, Vern: *International Marketing,* 2d ed., Dryden Press, Hinsdale, Ill., 1978. This standard textbook treats the areas of cross-cultural marketing.

Chapter
20

Consumer Issues in Marketing

Looking Ahead

Throughout this book we have emphasized the idea that marketing is concerned with providing satisfaction. When consumers perceive that an exchange does not meet their expectations, they are dissatisfied. From such dissatisfaction springs one of the most significant external, uncontrollable variables that affects contemporary marketing: the consumer movement.

Key Topics

What consumerism is

The roots of the consumer movement

The role of consumer advocates

The present consumer movement and why it has flourished

The reactions of industry and individual companies to the consumer movement

How marketers might best react to consumer issues in the future

Chapter Outline

The Nature and History of Consumerism
The First Wave of the Consumer Movement
The Second Wave of the Consumer Movement
The Third Wave of the Consumer Movement

The Consumer Movement until the 1980s
Consumer Advocates
Government and the Consumer Movement
Consumer Protection Laws

Business Reactions to Consumerism
Industrywide Reactions
Company Reactions

Consumerism in the 1980s

Looking Back

Why is the subject of consumers' dissatisfaction covered in a marketing textbook? After all, isn't the consumer movement made up simply of a vocal group of activists looking to find fault with our economic system? Such thinking characterized early attitudes toward the consumer movement among many business leaders. In fact, the business community coined the word *consumerism* to refer negatively to the actions of dissatisfied consumers during the early 1960s. (See Application 20-1.)

But today, marketers cannot ignore consumerism. Marketers must recognize the consumer movement as an external, uncontrollable influence on their decisions about product development, pricing, distribution, and promotion. No longer can this movement be dismissed as radical or frivolous. Consumerism will not go away.

Application 20-1
Consumer Dissatisfaction— Caveat Emptor?

Are consumers becoming more aggressive, or are more firms producing shoddy goods?

Arguments could be presented on both sides, but the fact remains that consumers are making more complaints about poor products and poor services.

Evidence of this consumer militancy is reflected at the Denver Better Business Bureau. In August 1981, the office received 14,300 inquiries about business practices. A year before, only 5000 calls per month were coming into the office.

"People are becoming a lot more careful," said the BBB head. "We're getting back to the buyer-beware society."

Small fly-by-night operators continue to fleece the public, as the transmission shop did when it advertised it would rebuild a car's transmission for $149.50. One customer took the shop up on the offer and received a bill for $450. When the customer refused to pay, the shop took out the transmission and returned it in pieces with a bill for $200!

Mail-order purchases are the source of most complaints to the Better Business Bureau. Recently, a Roseville, Michigan, woman answered an ad promising big money—$350 to $700 a week—for stuffing envelopes at home. She mailed $20 for the initial supply of envelopes, then found that she was required to advertise to obtain customers. When she asked for a refund, she was told that the money-back period of 30 days had expired.

And a Detroit firm offered to mail a quarter-point faceted diamond for $5. When the gem arrived, the purchaser found it was the size of a speck of dust. An Oregon consumer sent $10 to a mail-order house for a "valuable engraved picture of Abraham Lincoln" and got a Lincoln penny by return mail.

In Nashville, a member of the state legislature bought a $25 watch from a local Woolco store. The watch stopped and he took it back to the shop for repairs. He was told to send the watch back to the factory—that the store wasn't responsible. Perhaps Woolco isn't responsible today, but if the legislator has his way, all retailers in Tennessee in the future will be liable for the goods they sell. He is introducing legislation to make this the law.

Sources of data: "Why Consumers Gripe Louder than Ever," *U.S. News & World Report,* Oct. 5, 1981, pp. 56–57; "Malfunctioning Watch Brings Consumer Bill," *The Nashville Tennessean,* Dec. 16, 1981, p. 35.

Throughout this book, we have emphasized that the marketing process does not end merely because an exchange takes place. In a sense, an organization's responsibility begins when consumers take possession of the product. The failure of many marketers to recognize this important fact led consumers to demand not only quality products that live up to their stated use but also fair and nondeceptive advertising. (See Table 20-1.)

As evidence of the consumer movement's impact during the early 1970s a new executive position began to appear on corporate organizational charts: the Department of Consumer Affairs. Most companies did not create consumer affairs departments of their own free will. Rather, the departments were established as a result of a wave of consumerism that swept the country in the late 1960s. And the business community reluctantly recognized consumerism only after it was apparent that the movement had a widespread social base. The consumer affairs manager in a marketing organization is the person who represents the customers. The responsibilities of the position vary. Some companies, like Coca-Cola, offer strong representation to consumers. Others provide only superficial service, often using form letters in an attempt to pacify concerned consumers.

Despite initial resistance, most companies have found that the consumer affairs position is effective and can head off expensive problems. For example, at RJR Foods, the consumer affairs department keeps track of each letter from consumers (complaining or otherwise) and daily passes this information on to the quality control unit and to the marketing department. Depending on the severity of complaints, RJR Foods may call a consumer directly or, in extreme cases, may send a representative to meet with the complaining party. In every case, consumers who write to RJR Foods are provided routinely with coupons that can be exchanged for free products.

TABLE 20-1   The Main Targets of Consumers' Complaints in the First Half of 1981

	Complaints
Mail-order companies	39,701
Auto dealers	8,549
Home-furnishings stores	6,056
Mail-ordered magazines	5,030
Home maintenance firms	4,920
Auto repair shops	4,772
Department stores	4,563
Other automotive firms	3,829
TV repairers	3,480
Insurance companies	3,325

Source: Council of Better Business Bureaus, "Why Consumers Gripe Louder than Ever," *U.S. News & World Report*, Oct. 5, 1981, p. 56.

Figure 20-1   Each product made by Procter & Gamble includes in its packaging telephone numbers which consumers can call toll-free. Does this seem to you to be an effective way to handle customer relations? What other kinds of products are likely candidates for such direct producer access? (Randy Matusow)

And at Procter & Gamble, each of its eighty or so brands carries a toll-free phone number on the package or label so that consumers can immediately call in their thoughts on or problems with the brand in question. (See Figure 20-1.) In 1980, P&G received 250,000 calls and letters—half of them requesting information, a sixth expressing praise, and a third consisting of complaints of all kinds. The company employs a staff of sixty people in its consumer services department to handle inquiries and problems. Said the department head: "If people have a problem with one of our products, we'd rather they tell us about it than switch to a competitor's product or say bad things about ours over the backyard fence."[1]

The Nature and History of Consumerism

Consumerism in the United States is associated with a search for gaining better treatment for consumers—and with a disdain for those who intentionally or unintentionally hinder this quest. Today, the consumer movement is made up of a loose coalition of private and public agencies that have evolved to influence public policy and alter the way business operates (often by getting legislation passed to control business).

Figure 20-2 shows that the consumer movement consists of interest groups that include a wide variety of individuals and organizations. There are four main sources of influence on business: consumer interest groups, government groups, public policy, and buyers. At the top of Figure 20-2 is shown a variety of *consumer interest groups*

---

[1]"At Procter & Gamble, Success Is Largely Due to Heeding Consumer," *The Wall Street Journal,* April 29, 1980, p. 35.

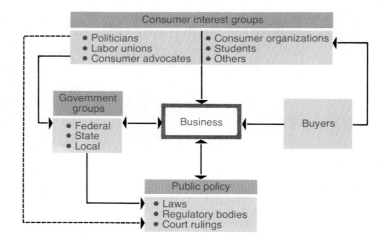

Figure 20-2 Influences on the consumer movement.

that are only loosely affiliated with one another. This coalition of groups and individuals exerts influence directly on both business and government. *Buyers* directly influence business by voicing dissatisfaction. *Government groups* directly and indirectly affect business by influencing the enforcement of *public policy* (laws and regulations). The focal point of all these influences is business. And, as the most visible element of business, marketing has become the most frequent target of these groups. The issues involved, of course, are as varied as the people who make up the movement.

Before asking why the consumer movement has grown so much in recent years, we should examine its background. The consumer movement is not unique to our times. In fact, the development of consumerism in the United States can be divided into the following well-defined periods (see Figure 20-3):

First wave—late 1800s to World War I

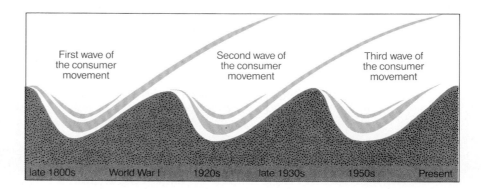

Figure 20-3 The waves of the consumer movement.

Second wave—late 1920s to late 1930s

Third wave—late 1950s to the present

The First Wave of the Consumer Movement

The beginning of the consumer movement came after the industrial revolution and the Civil War period in the United States. During the late 1800s, buyers and sellers were separated to the point that a buyer's power and ability to judge products were hindered. In earlier times, when someone needed a pair of shoes, a local artisan would produce them. The shoemaker had a local reputation; a buyer could see the materials that went into the shoes; and if a problem arose with the product, the buyer could resolve it personally with the shoemaker.

Contrast that with the process of buying a pair of shoes through a catalog in the late 1800s. Buyers no longer knew personally how the shoes were made or who made them or what materials went into them. They could no longer get the kind of satisfaction from a complaint that had been possible when dealing with a local shoemaker. Mail-order abuses were so widespread that a law was passed in 1872 to reduce attempts to defraud by mail. This was one of the first laws to protect consumers. In 1901, the National Bureau of Standards was established to help assure consumers that when they bought a pound of meat, a quart of milk, or a yard of cloth, they would receive the quantity they had paid for.

Between 1879 and 1905, more than 100 bills dealing with consumer protection in the sale of food and drugs were introduced to Congress, but they did not pass. Consumers were not vocal enough to force Congress to act on abuses. Finally, a vocal and influential group of "muckrakers" brought to bear enough pressure to trigger legislative action. For instance, Upton Sinclair, author of *The Jungle* (1905), was in part responsible for mobilizing political support against abuses in the food and drug industries. His book dramatically exposed the practices of meat-packing houses in Chicago.[2]

There would come back from Europe meat that had been rejected, and that was moldy and white—it would be dosed with borax and glycerine, and dumped back into the hoppers, and made over again for home consumption. There would be meat that had tumbled out on the floor, in the dirt and sawdust, where workers had tramped and spit uncounted billions of consumption germs. There would be meat stored in great piles in rooms; and the water from leaky roofs would drip over it, and thousands of rats would race about on it. It was too dark in these storage places to see well, but a man could run his hand over these piles of meat and sweep off handfuls of dried dung of rats.

If this description of conditions is revolting to you now, imagine the impact that *The Jungle* had on motivating people to take action at the time that it was written.

In 1906, a year after *The Jungle* was published, the federal government passed the Pure Food and Drug Act. This law prohibited misbranding and adulteration of

---

[2]Upton Sinclair, *The Jungle,* Viking, New York, 1946, pp. 134–135; original copyright 1905.

food and drugs to be transported across state lines. In 1907 the Meat Inspection Act further regulated the sanitation of food. [In addition to such consumer-oriented activity at the turn of the century, a variety of antitrust laws were enacted, including the Sherman Act (1897), the Clayton Act (1914), and the Federal Trade Commission Act (1914). But these laws were aimed more broadly at protecting competitors than at protecting consumers.]

Grass-roots consumer organizations were also emerging. The American Home Economics Association (1908) and the Chicago Housewives League (1910) advised buyers how to spend their dollars more wisely and how to speak out against shoddy products. Though *The Jungle* was the most successful book in gaining public support, others—like Thorstein Veblen's *Theory of the Leisure Class* and Wesley Mitchell's *The Backward Art of Spending Money*—showed consumers how business led them into unwise purchases. Magazines like the *Ladies' Home Journal* and *Colliers Weekly* were particularly vocal in criticizing patent medicines and helped to alert the public to fraudulent practices in that industry.

The momentum of the young consumer movement slowed in 1907 with the passage of laws concerning the inspection of food, drugs, and meat. These issues, which had aroused greatest public attention, were at least partially resolved. Not until other serious problems developed did the second wave of activity begin.

The Second Wave of the Consumer Movement

The second wave began in the late 1920s. In 1927, Stuart Chase and Frederick J. Schlink wrote a book entitled *Your Money's Worth.* They painted a picture of bewildered consumers who were unable to make logical economic decisions. This book sold 100,000 copies and touched off other exposés. In 1933, Schlink and Arthur Kallet wrote *100,000,000 Guinea Pigs,* and its contents shocked readers. Some examples:[3]

A girl, aged seven, killed by arsenic fumes from dye in moldy wall paper. . . . Six persons poisoned in California in 1931 by greens sprayed with lead arsenate. . . . A four-year-old Philadelphia girl dead in August 1932 from eating sprayed fruit. . . . Willingly or not, if you eat apples, pears, cherries and berries, celery and other fruit and vegetables, you are also eating arsenic, and there is good reason to believe that it may be doing you serious, perhaps irreparable injury [p. 47].

At its best, the patent medicine industry is guilty only of the economic fraud of selling necessary drugs under meaningless or fantastic names with absurd claims of special merit, at five to a thousand times their ordinary value. These drugs, with some exceptions, are injurious only to the extent that they drain from slim purses the dimes and quarters needed for bread and meat and milk. At its worst, the patent medicine industry is guilty of murder: murder through selling medicines containing poisons; murder through persuading the poor and ignorant to rely upon worthless nostrums for the treatment of diseases as dangerous to the individual and to the race as cancer and tuberculosis and syphilis [p. 116].

In what precedes, the reader will have seen control of foods and drugs in America has been characterized by inexcusable official indifference and negligence; . . . such control has been

---

[3]Arthur Kallet and F. J. Schlink, *100,000,000 Guinea Pigs,* Vanguard, New York, 1933.

hamstrung by a weak and nearly useless body of laws, state and national; . . . there has been a progressive weakening of official activity and concern for the public health through the pressure of concealed commercial forces [p. 195].

We suggest that in general you set yourself the task of making it less and less comfortable for your state and local health and food officials. Give your Congressman and senators, and your State legislators no rest until they sit in judgment on the work of the national food and drug administration and the local health and food control authorities [p. 302].

These excerpts will give you a feeling for the kind of issues that the second consumer movement dealt with. Other similar books outraged large numbers of consumers. It was a time when the Depression was raging, and people were receptive to criticism of business.

Many groups, including labor unions, educational institutions, business and government agencies, and women's organizations, helped to channel the frustrations of the public into constructive political pressure. Though this loose coalition of groups failed to unify into a national organization, it did succeed in forcing congressional action. In 1938, Congress passed both the Food, Drug and Cosmetic Act and the Wheeler-Lea Amendment. The former helped to bolster the 1906 Pure Food and Drug Act by including cosmetics and prohibiting "false and misleading labeling." The Wheeler-Lea Amendment changed the FTC Act of 1914, strengthening the power of the Federal Trade Commission over deceptive practices affecting consumers and preparing the way for the strong regulatory role that the FTC plays today.

During this period, the practice of testing products became widespread. Private companies, such as General Motors and Sears, Roebuck, developed programs to test products, and *Good Housekeeping* magazine ran a laboratory to test the products of its advertisers (those that passed were awarded the now-famous Good Housekeeping Seal of Approval). Consumers Union, the organization that publishes *Consumer Reports,* was established in 1935.

But the consumer movement was made up largely of middle- and upper-income people. A poll conducted by George Gallup in 1940 revealed that only 12 percent of lower-income families had even heard of the consumer movement. Without this important mass support, and with the country facing World War II in the 1940s and the Korean War in the 1950s, the second wave of the consumer movement vanished.

The Third Wave of the Consumer Movement

During the late 1950s and throughout the 1960s and 1970s, Congress began to discover that consumer issues attracted votes. Legislative action picked up again in 1958, with the Automobile Information Act and the Textile Fiber Products Act, both of which require manufacturers to disclose specific product information. In 1965, an aggressive young lawyer named Ralph Nader wrote a book called *Unsafe at Any Speed,* which focused heavily on the dangers of the Chevrolet Corvair. Publicity received from the book—along with abortive attempts by General Motors to discredit it—propelled Nader into the national limelight, and he became the focal point that had been missing from earlier consumer movements. (See Figure 20-4.) Momentum now was beginning to build. Nader has characterized his role as bringing issues into the open, where they cannot be ignored. He has consistently and methodically criticized

Figure 20-4 Ralph Nader became the catalyst for the consumer movement during the 1960s, and his position as a consumer advocate remains strong today. (*Wide World Photos*)

the ability of business and government to regulate their activities on behalf of consumers.

Another major factor that bolstered the consumer movement was a speech by President John F. Kennedy to the House of Representatives in 1962, in which the following "rights of consumers" were outlined:[4]

1 The right of safety—to be protected against the marketing of goods which are hazardous to health or life

2 The right to be informed—to be protected against fraudulent, deceitful, or grossly misleading information, advertising, labeling, or other practices, and to be given the facts needed to make an informed choice

3 The right to choose—to be assured, wherever possible, access to a variety of products and services at competitive prices and, in those industries in which competition is not workable and government regulation is substituted, to be assured satisfactory quality and service at fair prices

4 The right to be heard—to be assured that consumer interests will receive full and sympathetic consideration in the formulation of government policy and fair and expeditious treatment in its administrative tribunals

---

[4]Message from the President of the United States Relative to Consumers Protection and Interest Program, Document No. 364, House of Representatives, 87th Cong., 2d Sess., March 15, 1962.

During this period when support for consumerism became politically attractive, agencies and legislation emerged to help consumers. Some forty agencies of the federal government now have some responsibilities in this area, including the Environmental Protection Agency, the Food and Drug Administration, the Product Safety Commission, and the Federal Trade Commission (FTC). Created in 1914, the FTC was often considered a "toothless" agency, but a series of court rulings gave it more power. In 1965, the court ruled against Colgate-Palmolive in a significant test case for the FTC. The case concerned a television commercial which left viewers with the impression that Rapid Shave could soften even sandpaper to the point that it could be shaved. But the truth was that sand had been applied carefully to Plexiglas for this demonstration.

The Consumer Movement

During the current wave of consumerism, extraordinary pressure has been brought to bear on marketers and business in general. Consumer advocates and a variety of private and public agencies, court rulings, and new legislation have shaped the marketer's environment. Let's take a look at them and their effects.

Consumer Advocates

Ralph Nader helped to focus attention on the consumer movement during the early 1960s. Since then, other advocates—including Betty Furness and Bess Myerson— have succeeded in capturing national public attention. On the local level, television stations have hired consumer reporters, and newspapers and magazines have created regular features to cover consumer issues. Marketers today must take note of the issues raised by such established and strong advocates of consumers' rights. (See Application 20-2.)

Government and the Consumer Movement

During the 1960s and 1970s, government became increasingly concerned about consumers. We can see this in the increased power given to old agencies and the establishment of new agencies, in the many new laws, and in the enforcement of old laws designed to aid consumers. Between 1965 and 1978, more than twenty pieces of federal consumer legislation were passed by Congress and signed into law. In the 1970s, the powers of existing agencies, such as the Food and Drug Administration and the Federal Trade Commission, were expanded. Passage of the Truth-in-Packaging Law (1966), the Truth-in-Lending Law (1968), and the Magnuson-Moss Act (1975), among others, greatly extended the power of the FTC. The increase in the number of government agencies and laws and the greater frequency of enforcement affected marketing in at least three broad areas: promotion, product, and pricing.

Application 20-2
Consumer Advocates—
Giving Consumers a Fighting Chance

(Wide World Photos)

Laboratory tests used by marketers to validate claims made in their television commercials are sometimes too perfect, David Horowitz, host of a syndicated consumer advocate show, told *Advertising Age.* Horowitz, who challenges a selected TV claim each week as the highlight of his show, has gotten the attention of companies who make these product claims.

How do the commercials fare in the challenges? One out of four fail.

One failing ad was an Oxydol commercial that claimed the product did wonders in cleaning soiled white garments. The "Fight Back" test showed its claims to be overstated. Procter & Gamble, the manufacturer, took strong issue with the use of a laundromat washing machine to test the advertising claims.

"Most advertising claims of P&G products are tested in a laboratory and results are determined to be statistically significant through retesting," said P&G spokesperson Robert Norrish. "You can't get that kind of environment in the Horowitz show."

Horowitz countered, "When we challenge a commercial, we use the kinds of situations that people face in everyday life."

Source of data: "Consumerist Earns Grudging Respect," *Advertising Age,* March 16, 1981, pp. 12, 63.

Effects on Promotion

Promotion is a highly visible marketing activity and a closely scrutinized one. In particular, the FTC has actively regulated the content of advertising by demanding more truth in advertising. Tactics such as advertising lower-priced items with the intent of selling higher-priced ones are illegal under the FTC's bait-and-switch guidelines. The FTC has forced advertisers to substantiate their claims and to disclose the ingredients of products and the proper methods of using them.

The FTC has forced certain advertisers to devote time or space to corrective advertising that informs the public about deceptive features in previous advertising. Thus, Ocean Spray was forced by the FTC to explain that "food energy," a phrase used in the company's early advertising, simply means "calories." Profile Bread was obliged to disclose that the reason its bread had "fewer calories per slice" was that the slices themselves were thinner than those of competing brands. Listerine was ordered to mount a campaign denying over fifty years of advertising that the mouthwash "kills germs on contact." American Home Products was ordered to spend $24 million on advertising to disclose that "Anacin is not a tension reliever," as early ads had falsely proclaimed.

Another aspect of FTC rulings revolves around the issue of *affirmative disclosure,* which requires advertisers not only to list ingredients but to state how the ingredients or use of the product can affect consumers. (See Application 20-3.)

Effects on Products   As a result of pressures from consumer interest groups, an army of new federal agencies has been created. Two of the most important have been the Environmental Protection Agency (EPA) and the Consumer Product Safety Commission. Both agencies focus on the areas of product safety and liability, and product packaging.

In 1978, another federal agency, the National Highway Traffic Safety Administration (NHTSA), compiled impressive evidence that Firestone 500 steel-belted radial tires were particularly prone to blowout, blister, or crack and were suspect in auto accidents that killed forty-one people and injured sixty-five others. Firestone conceded that the NHTSA might have a case and agreed to recall an estimated 10 million tires made during a twelve-month period in 1975–1976, and also included such Firestone-made models as Montgomery Ward's Grappler 8000 and Shell Oil Co.'s Super Shell steel radials. Firestone had 60 days to begin notifying owners by mail, television, radio, and print; customers turning in their tires had them replaced free of charge with Firestone 721 steel-belted radials or any other Firestone tire. The cost to

Application 20-3
Product Labeling—Menu Misdeeds

Several local and state consumer protection agencies have formed special "truth-in-menu" teams in response to the many complaints from consumers. The head of Washington, D.C.'s Environmental Health Administration put it simply: "The consumer would like to eat what he or she is paying for." A survey of 141 popular area restaurants and 350 menus turned up distressingly frequent cases of bamboozling the patron. More than 75 percent of all restaurants surveyed put cheaper turkey in the "chicken" salad. All "fresh" shrimp were frozen.

"Colorado" trout came from Japan, "African" lobster tails from Florida.

More serious to some were findings that menus exaggerated the size of portions. A lobster weighed in 12 ounces lighter than promised, steaks up to 2 ounces light. Half the D.C. restaurants advertised as "kosher" used products that had not been correctly prepared or certified.

In Los Angeles, a similar survey disclosed that of 125 area restaurants, 75 percent misstated items, and 50 percent of the false claims were considered "serious"

by investigators. The enforcers' arsenal includes fines and lawsuits. When the menu at L.A.'s Hungry Tiger restaurant told Dale Reeves that "the fish you eat tonight slept last night in Chesapeake Bay," the assertion cost $4000 in fines. The fish had come—frozen—from Nova Scotia, and Reeves directs the county menu-sleuthing team.

Sources of data: "The Menu Sleuth,' *Newsweek,* Oct. 18, 1976, pp. 100–101; "A Capitol Idea Gives Some Restaurants Food for Thought," *The Wall Street Journal,* March 29, 1978, p. 1.

Firestone? In sum, $230 million (more than double its 1977 net profits!), consumer and class action suits seeking damages of up to $2 billion, and a slippage in market share from 22 percent in 1978 to 15 percent in 1981.

Effects on Pricing

Pricing directly affects the consumer's pocketbook. Excessively high prices have caused consumers to boycott meat in 1973, sugar in 1975, and coffee in 1977. Some states have passed laws to prevent stores from raising prices of products already on the shelves. Deceptive pricing practices have been undercut by *unit pricing.* Many states require stores to display both the total price of an item and its cost per ounce or pound, making it far easier for consumers to compare the prices of competing brands in various packages. The government has also cracked down on price collusion or price fixing, both of which affect consumers.

In Pittsburgh, a consumer hotline was set up to allow people to report possible consumer-oriented price fixing. In its first six weeks in 1977, 125 calls were received and 15 cases were reported to the FTC. The mere presence of the hotline is designed to deter price fixing. And with the free 30-second TV spots and the publicity generated by the program, there is hope that the problem of consumer-oriented price fixing will be cut to a minimum.

Consumer Protection Laws

We can get a good perspective on the consumer movement if we look at the number of federal laws that have been enacted to protect consumers. Table 20-2 makes it clear that the tremendous legislative reaction affects marketing deeply.

TABLE 20-2 Growth of Federal Consumer Legislation			
	Areas affected by each law		
Product	Pricing	Distribution	Promotion
1st wave of consumer movement			
Mail Fraud Act (1872) ×			×
National Bureau of Standards Act (1901) ×			
Pure Food and Drug Act (1906) ×			
Meat Inspection Act (1906) ×			
Federal Trade Commission Act (1914)			×
2d wave of consumer movement			
Federal Alcohol Administration Act (1935) ×			×
Wheeler-Lea Act (1938) (Amendment to FTC Act)			×
Federal Food, Drug and Cosmetic Act (1938) (Amended Pure Food and Drug Act) ×			×

	Areas affected by each law			
	Product	*Pricing*	*Distribution*	*Promotion*
Wool Products Labeling Act (1939)	×			
Fur Product Labeling Act	×			
Flammable Fabric Act	×			
3d wave of consumer movement				
Textile Fiber Products Identification Act (1958)	×			×
Automobile Information Disclosure Act (1958)		×		
Federal Hazardous Substances Labeling Act (1960)	×			
Kefauver-Harris Drug Amendments (1960) (Amended Food and Drug Act)	×			
Fair Packaging and Labeling Act (1966)	×			
Cigarette Labeling Act (1966)	×			
Wholesome Meat Act (1967)	×			
Consumer Protection Credit Act (1968)				×
Child Protection and Toy Safety Act (1969)	×			
Public Health Smoking Act (1970)				×
Poison Prevention Labeling Act (1970)	×			
Federal Deposit Insurance Act (1970) (Amendment for credit cards)				×
Consumer Product Safety Act (1972)	×			
Consumer Product Warranty and Federal Trade Commission Improvement Act (1975)	×	×		×
Fair Billing Credit Act (1975)	×	×		
Magnuson-Moss FTC Extension Act (1975)	×	×	×	×
Consumer Goods Pricing Act (1975)		×		
Consumer Leasing Act (1976)		×		
Consumer Education Act (1978)	×	×		×

Besides the increased number of laws, the prosecution of violations has been enhanced by a concept known as the *class-action suit*. This allows a case to be filed on behalf of a group, or a class, of individuals on a local, state, or national basis. Thus, instead of each individual's having to file a case against a company, all individuals who have the same complaint can become part of the class or group of people filing the lawsuit. The extent of a class action is still subject to court interpretation, but consumer groups are pressing for more liberal guidelines.

Business Reactions to Consumerism

The consumer movement has raised issues that have wide-ranging effects on marketing activities. Table 20-3 enumerates consumers' complaints, most of which relate directly to the marketing mix (product, price, distribution, and promotion).

Perhaps the most accurate statement that can be made about the reaction of businesses and marketers to consumerism is that it has been mixed. But let's examine both industrywide and company reactions.

Industrywide Reactions

Historically, trade associations have reacted defensively to consumerism. This reaction has changed, under pressure, to be responsive to the increasing threat of government regulation. Many industries are taking a variety of actions to deal with consumers' problems. The National Association of Broadcasters (NAB) has established strict guidelines that govern the type of products advertised and the amount, and sometimes even the type, of advertising permitted. The Council of Better Business Bureaus, the Association of American Advertising Agencies, and the American Advertising Federation have established self-regulatory bodies in the form of the National Advertising Review Board (NARB) and the National Advertising Division (NAD) to examine claims made in advertising.

In the automobile industry, where historically there have been many complaints about dealers, automobile service, and performance, progress was made by the establishment of AUTOCAPs around the country. AUTOCAP (Automotive Consumer Action Panel) was suggested as a means to bridge the gap between dealers and customers. Complaining auto owners can call a toll-free number. AUTOCAP mails the consumer a form that is filled out, mailed back, and answered by AUTOCAP within 15 days. AUTOCAP conducts an investigation and, if necessary, intercedes with insurance and finance companies and car manufacturers. AUTOCAP's opinions and decisions are voluntary and not binding, and thus leave the consumer free to pursue other remedies.

In the past, self-regulation by industries has tended to be ineffective because trade members' interests took precedence over enforcement. But increased pressure from consumers and the desire to avoid legislative intervention have begun to

TABLE 20-3   Specific Complaints of Consumers

Marketing area	Complaints
Pricing	Unfair pricing practices
	High prices
Selling	Unfair tactics in selling
	Impersonal selling
Advertising	Promotion of superficial values
	Deceptive advertising
	Exploitation of children
	Bait-and-switch practices
Public relations	Lack of communication with business
	Failure to handle complaints properly
Sales promotion	Exploitation of children
	Phony contests
	Substitution of other merchandise for that promoted
Product development	Deceptive packaging
	Growth of too many packages
	Growth of too many products
	Lack of product information
	Unsafe products
	Junk products
	Selling of used for new products
	Exploitation of children
	Poor services
	Stress on quantity, not quality
	Inadequate product guarantees
	Misleading warranties
	Products too technically complex
	Planned obsolescence
Marketing research	Violation of information privacy
Other	Debt-collection deception
	Refusal to make refunds
	High credit costs
	Lack of competition
	Cheating the poor

Source: Portions adapted from Robert J. Holloway and Robert S. Hancock, *Marketing in a Changing Environment*, 2d ed., Wiley, New York, 1973, pp. 564–565.

produce industrywide programs for handling complaints, for educating consumers and dealers, for disseminating research, and for establishing standards and codes.

Company Reactions

Within individual firms, we can note a wide variety of reactions to consumerism. Some companies, including Coors, have attempted to anticipate the inevitable and have urged the Environmental Protection Agency (EPA) to go ahead with a national bill affecting beverage containers, even while much of the industry opposes such a law. Coors executives like to call themselves realists and are helping to shape an equitable bill. In anticipation of such a bill, Coors has even developed a can-eating machine to recycle cans at the retail level.

Other companies, such as Bristol-Myers and Procter & Gamble, have attempted to develop programs of consumer education. Bristol-Myers offered a free "Consumer Guide to Product Information." Hunt-Wesson Foods offered computerized menus to help homemakers budget their food expenses. Ralph's and Pantry Pride food chains placed representatives in their stores to function as "shoppers' guides." Toll-free telephone lines have been leased by a number of companies. Du Pont developed a 24-hour service to answer consumers' questions and complaints and to give product information. In one of the earliest consumer programs, Whirlpool established a "cool line" to handle consumers' problems.

Many consumer affairs departments have tried to respond positively to consumer pressure. The Zayre Corporation, a large Eastern department store chain, began using its consumer affairs department in an active public relations campaign. Booklets telling the history of Zayre's consumer affairs outlined ways in which the firm attempted to carry out its orientation. A Zayre Consumer Bill of Rights was even offered in the booklet.

Another reaction to consumer pressure has been to try to patch up poor corporate images through advertising. When ITT (International Telephone and Telegraph) had such an image problem, it developed an advertising campaign that strongly emphasized the positive aspects of its products and the improved quality of the life they have brought.

Most companies, of course, do not believe that all consumer issues are valid, and some firms have taken aggressive positions against specific proposals embodied in the consumer movement. The American Electric Power Company has engaged in a hard-hitting campaign against the EPA's policies requiring expensive pollution "scrubbers" on smokestacks. The company went so far as to take out full-page magazine advertisements in national publications to arouse public opinion against the EPA's position. (See Application 20-4.)

Consumerism in the 1980s

Throughout history, social causes—like people and products—have gone through life cycles. The burning issues of the 1960s faded and gave way to the hue and cry of issues of the 1970s—ecology and consumerism. While still very much a part of our social and political fabric, these issues now seem to be moving into the maturity stage of their life cycle.

Throughout the 1970s, consumerism moved from a few organizations heavily promoting legal reaction to marketplace wrongdoing to an enormous network of organizations and institutions, each attempting to serve the interests of consumers by advancing its own set of protectionist actions. But some recent occurrences suggest a

Application 20-4
Social Responsibility—P&G Goes a Step Beyond

Procter & Gamble prides itself on marketing products that are thoroughly tested. So it came as a major setback to the company when its Rely tampons were singled out in the 1980s as being associated with toxic shock syndrome, a disease that had struck women during their menstrual cycle.

The product was voluntarily recalled (with a little pressure from the Food and Drug Administration) from the supermarket and drug store shelves. The cost to P&G was $75 million.

Most companies who find themselves in P&G's position generally recall the product and allow the issue to be forgotten. But P&G, feeling itself treated poorly, is intent on finding out whether Rely was a contributing factor. Of course, P&G hopes to prove that Rely was not at fault, but its immediate objective is to discover the causes of the disease. The company is both doing its own research and financing fourteen major outside research projects in the hope of finding out what causes the disease and what can be done to prevent it.

"We wouldn't know half of what we do about toxic shock if P&G hadn't been willing to make the financial commitment," says Dr. James K. Todd of Denver, one of the first to describe the disease.

P&G's corporate pride is at stake. By clearing up the Rely issue, P&G hopes to drive away the dark clouds the unfortunate incident created and reinforce its reputation for product testing and safety.

Source of data: "P&G Is Going All Out to Track Toxic Shock and Exonerate Itself," *The Wall Street Journal,* June 26, 1981, pp. 1, 14.

consumer and general public backlash against the possible overreaction of consumerists. In the late 1970s, the need for seat-belt interlock systems and air bags, as well as bans on advertising on children's television programs, met with challenges by individuals known by the public to be sensible and responsible. Ralph Nader himself was criticized for his vocal and public denouncement of former colleague Joan Claybrook when, as head of the National Highway Traffic Safety Administration, she delayed the requirements for auto air bags. In 1978, Congress voted down a federal agency that, if established, would have represented the concerns of consumers within the federal bureaucracy. And in the spring of 1980, Ralph Nader and his allies organized "Big Business Day" to demonstrate in 150 cities around the country against such generally hot issues as pollution, consumer price gouging, and governmental corruption—but they met with sparse rally attendance and general public apathy. These events point to a definite public disenchantment with the basic concerns of consumerism that, only a few years before, had been so strongly supported. The 1980 elections further indicated a reversal of public sentiment and a shift in popular attitudes.

Building on the Carter Administration's approach to ridding the federal government of unnecessary regulation, the Reagan Administration worked quickly to speed up the deregulation process. In what consumer activists saw as a catastrophe, Ronald Reagan championed a revival of a free market economy where the emphasis on regulation of injustices is pushed from the stringent laws of the federal government back into the hands of local municipalities and the people. Americans had turned the focus of their attention to the woes of inflation, interest rates, and economic recovery—and away from consumerism issues. Deregulation was selected by the new administration as a vehicle for reviving the economy.

As a result, the Reagan Administration reviewed existing regulations and eliminated many which affected the consumer. By so doing, the administration changed the entire concept of the federal government as guarantor of the four basic consumer rights spelled out by President John Kennedy—to be informed, to be protected from dangerous products, to choose goods and services freely, and to be heard. Some of the principles that were immediately compromised in 1981 were the following: The White House canceled regulations that made drug firms describe the possible risks of each of their medicines. The Car Book, a popular 68-page pamphlet that lists the safety features and maintenance costs of eighty-one United States and foreign automobiles, was not reprinted even though it was one of the most successful government publications ever issued. The funding and powers of the FTC were cut back and regulation of unfair trade practices (especially antitrust) was relaxed. For example, FTC charges of shared monopoly against the three major breakfast cereal manufacturers were suddenly dropped in 1981 after nine years of litigation and $27 million in legal costs for the cereal companies. The FTC also backed away from plans to regulate nonprescription drugs, to require used-car dealers to issue warranties, and to restrict advertising for sugared cereals and other products aimed at children. Table 20-4 shows the major deregulation effects on the automobile industry alone—and only within the first ten months of the Reagan Administration. The elimination of air-quality and safety regulations was estimated to save auto makers $1.3 billion and consumers $8 billion over a five-year period. Looked at another way, federal regulations require 26,000 full-time employees at General Motors alone. Moreover, GM estimates that meeting emissions standards adds $725 to the price of a new car while meeting safety standards adds $400. (See Application 20-5.)

In sum, as the 1980s began, the mood and mechanics of consumerism had changed dramatically from the heydays of the mid-1970s. As we stated at the beginning of this chapter, consumerism is still quite alive, but now its form and function seem to have changed. Consumers still feel dissatisfactions in the marketplace and still have a desire for the protectionism offered by the consumerism movement. But such interest seems to blossom only when the consumer does *not* feel "inconvenienced" and *does* feel endangered. The seat-belt interlock system, for example, was judged to be too much trouble to operate and was rejected by the populace. More and more, the costs of consumer protection agencies were weighed against the benefits they provide—and found less desirable by the American public. The end result should be a quieter, but still active, consumer movement in the 1980s.

TABLE 20-4 Major Changes in Auto Deregulation, January–November 1981

Subject	Description	Action
Air bags and seat belts	To protect occupants in crashes, the air bag inflates on impact and the "passive" seat belts envelop passengers automatically on entering car. These devices were scheduled for 1983.	Rescinded
Air pollution	Environmental Protection Agency seeks to soften emission standards. GM seeks a roll back to 1980 permissible emission levels.	Congress must act through revision of Clean Air Act
Bumpers	Rules now require protection from damage at speeds up to 5 miles an hour. Proposal would lower speed to 2.5 m.p.h.	Safety agency considering 9 proposals
Crash ratings	The results of crash tests at 35 miles an hour would have been required to be displayed on window price stickers on the various car models.	Rescinded
Fuel economy	Federal standards on gas mileage expire in 1985. Officials were planning advance notice of proposed rule making beyond that date.	Rescinded
Speedometers	Proposed speedometer standards would have included calibration in miles per hour and kilometers. Measure also called for tamper-resistant odometers.	Rescinded
Visibility	A ruling had been proposed to require minimum fields of direct view through the windshields of passenger cars and trucks.	Rescinded

Source: "What Deregulation Means for GM," *The New York Times,* Nov. 1, 1981, p. F1.

Application 20-5
Consumerism Matures—The Auto Industry on the Offensive

The auto industry has been on the ropes since the 1960s over safety and pollution regulations for cars. Now, the industry sees some signs that it may have gotten Washington's ear.

Spurred on by the industry's staggering losses and mounting layoffs, Washington is loosening the regulatory grip a bit. Seizing the opportunity, industry officials are making a major effort to rid themselves of the many regulations they consider unnecessary and too costly.

Most of all, the auto makers want to roll back certain car and truck pollution rules, get rid of requirements for automatic crash-protection devices, and reduce existing standards for bumpers.

Previous industry pleas have fallen on deaf ears, but the disastrous financial condition of the industry in recent years has gotten the legislators to listen. "People are really scared about the industry's survival," says one legislative aide in Washington. "Nobody knows what to do to help the auto industry, but everybody wants to do something."

"There does seem to be a new mood in Washington," says Roger B. Smith, the chairperson of General Motors Corp. Adds Betsy Anoker-Johnson, the GM vice president for environmental affairs: "It's like the difference between night and day."

Source of data: "Auto Companies Press for More Deregulation in Safety and Pollution," *The Wall Street Journal,* Aug. 14, 1981, p. 1.

Looking Back

It now should be clear that consumerism is a potent external force affecting marketers. Only through conscious effort can marketers expect to create satisfaction that is acceptable both to consumers and to society in general. The following points are important for marketers concerned with consumer issues:

1 Marketing is a focal point for consumers' complaints and for activities aimed at redressing them.

2 The consumer movement has evolved through several stages since the late 1800s.

3 The third wave of the consumer movement was more active than past consumer movements.

4 The consumer movement has become institutionalized at federal, state, and local levels of government.

5 The consumer movement has effects on marketing decisions, especially in promotion, product development, and pricing areas.

6 Consumerism in the 1980s is taking on a new shape—a still active but quieter one.

Key Terms

If you aren't sure what each of the following words means, look back at the text. Numbers refer to pages on which the words are defined. Additional information can be found by checking the index and the glossary at the end of the book.

consumerism 643
muckrakers 647
Pure Food and Drug Act 647
Meat Inspection Act 648
Sherman Act 648
Wheeler-Lea Amendment 649
Automobile Information Act 649

Magnuson-Moss Act 651
affirmative disclosure 653
Consumer Product Safety
  Commission 653
unit pricing 654
class-action suit 656

Questions for Review

1 What does the term *consumerism* mean?
2 What are the four main interest groups within the consumer movement?
3 What two factors gave the third wave of the consumer movement such force with the American public?
4 Which marketing activity has come under the closest scrutiny by government bodies?
5 What is a class-action suit?
6 What has contributed to the maturing of the consumer movement in America?

Questions for Thought and Discussion

1 *The Thing* could be driven on beaches, *Volkswagen* ads claimed, so a couple from Massachusetts purchased the jeeplike vehicle to use as a dune buggy. *The Thing* was turned away from three Massachusetts beaches because the vehicle had neither four-wheel drive nor wide, treadless sand tires. *The Thing* was allowed on a fourth beach, but it quickly bogged down. After receiving little satisfaction, the owners were forced to take the complaint of deceptive VW advertising to the Consumer Protection Division of the Attorney General's office. Do you believe they had a legitimate complaint?

2 Do you believe that consumer advocates such as Ralph Nader always help the consumer?

3 In 1978, the Federal Trade Commission won a settlement against Pat Boone for endorsing a facial blemish product by offering false product claims. The settlement called for Mr. Boone to pay a share of any consumer refunds if the FTC charges were upheld. Do you believe endorsers should be held responsible for actions of the firm whose products they help advertise?

4 With the third wave of the consumer movement reaching maturity, consumerism experts believe the 1980s will be still active but quieter than earlier times. What specific actions in the consumerism area might you expect during this period?

Suggested Project

Interview three consumers you know rather well, and uncover one dissatisfaction each has had in his or her buying experiences. Write up the details of each experience and suggest what would remedy the problem.

Suggested Readings

Andreason, Alan R., and Arthur Best: "Consumers Complain: Does Business Respond?" *Harvard Business Review,* vol. 55 (July–August 1977), pp. 93–101. This survey shows that fewer than one-half of consumers having complaints took those complaints to the seller or maker—and only about one-third of those who did felt the outcome was unsatisfactory.

Barksdale, Hiram C., and William D. Perreault: "Can Consumers Be Satisfied?" *MSU Business Topics,* vol. 28 (Spring 1980), pp. 19–30. This article catalogs changes in consumer dissatisfaction throughout the 1970s.

Berry, Leonard L: "Marketing Challenges in the Age of the People," *MSU Business Topics,* vol. 20 (Winter 1972), pp. 7–13. This article asserts that value changes in society are leading us into a period unlike any other in history. These changes will affect marketing philosophy, practices, and education.

———, and James S. Hensel (eds.): *Marketing and the Social Environment,* Petrocelli Books, New York, 1973. This work deals with the changing social environment of marketing, its challenges, and its opportunities. The authors present pro- and anti-marketing arguments.

Bloom, Paul N., and Stephen A. Greyser: "The Maturing of Consumerism," *Harvard Business Review,* vol. 59 (November–December 1981), pp. 130–139. The consumer movement is shown to be moving into the advanced phase of its product life cycle.

Cohen, Dorothy: "The FTC's Advertising Substantiation Program," *Journal of Marketing,* vol. 44 (Winter 1980), pp. 26–35. This article describes the program's genesis and current status, offers suggestions for managerial policies designed to meet the regulatory requirement, and raises questions relevant to an evaluation of the program from a public policy perspective.

Hise, Richard T., Peter L. Gillette, and J. Patrick Kelley: "The Corporate Consumer Affairs Effort," *MSU Business Topics,* vol. 26 (Summer 1978), pp. 17–26. Several recent studies suggest that most consumer affairs offices operate with allegiance to their companies first and their customers second.

Kelley, William T. (ed.): *New Consumerism: Selected Readings,* Grid, Columbus, Ohio, 1973. This book traces the historical evolution of the consumer movement.

Kotler, Philip: "What Consumerism Means for Marketers," *Harvard Business Review,* vol. 50 (May–June 1972), pp. 48–57. The author challenges marketers to convert problems raised by consumers into opportunities.

Nader, Ralph (ed.): *The Consumer and Corporate Accountability,* Harcourt Brace Jovanovich, New York, 1973. This book takes a very combative view of the business and marketing community. It presents abuses and inequities as the norm and develops new agenda for change.

Chapter

21

Planning Your Career in Marketing

Looking Ahead

Throughout the preceding chapters we have emphasized the importance of the marketing mix in selling products and services. Yet you yourself are marketable, and marketing your skills is precisely what you're doing when you set out to find a job. You must sell yourself and you need a marketing plan to help you make the sale. It's a process that deserves your best efforts, careful planning, and a positive attitude.

You must "package" your abilities, experiences, education, objectives, and unique achievements, just as businesses package their products and services. Your ability to make your personal package attractive to prospective employers will enable you to land interviews and job opportunities. Developing your skills will aid your progress through the ranks of an organization, but you may not get a chance to develop those skills unless you can get that first job. Shoddy preparation—misspelled words on your letter and résumé, a negative attitude, an unkempt appearance—will detract from your chances. The first half of this chapter will help you to prepare a marketing plan that will set you off to your best advantage. In the second half of this chapter, we'll describe some of the entry-level positions that exist in the field of marketing.

Chapter Outline

How to Find a Job
Plan Your Career Path
Research the Company and the Job
Prepare an Effective Letter of Introduction
Prepare a Distinctive Résumé
Prepare for Interviewing
Follow Up on Interviews

Jobs in Marketing
Sales
Brand or Product Management
Marketing Research
Public Relations
Advertising
Sales Promotion
Retailing
Information Sources

It's scary to realize all of a sudden that you've got to go out and find a job. But if you approach the job search with a plan, if you know what kind of job you want, you can manage—and even enjoy—the experience. You should understand right away that you won't start out as a vice president (unless, of course, a close relative controls the company, but few of us are in that position). It is important to think ahead and form long-term career goals. What do you want to do in five or ten years? At the same time, plan a path to that career; consider your short-term goals. It's likely that your first job will be as an assistant or a trainee. You'll probably have less responsibility than you'd like, but remember that to a new employer you're an unknown quantity. Make clear when you interview that you are ready to help out, work hard, and learn. Your job is to demonstrate and develop the skills you have, to acquire new skills while you're on the job, and to prove to your employer that you've mastered the tasks that make up your job.

How to Find a Job

In a way, planning your job search *is* your first marketing job. The tasks you must master in order to develop your personal marketing plan are as follows:

1 Plan your career path.

2 Research the company and the job.

3 Prepare an effective letter of introduction.

4 Prepare a distinctive résumé.

5 Prepare for interviewing.

6 Follow up on interviews.

Plan Your Career Path

The first step should be to plan your career path. In Chapter 18 we discussed the strategic planning process. This approach to marketing has relevance to you and your career. You should begin by determining your own *mission,* what you want to accomplish in terms of your own career. Where do you want to be five and ten years from now? To get some idea, you can begin now to *scan the environment.*

To obtain a firm understanding of career opportunities, you can start by talking to people who are knowledgeable. Arrange for a discussion about careers with your professors. Contact company personnel offices, ask for brochures on jobs, and, if the company is willing, arrange for an introductory interview. Review newspaper advertisements (*The Wall Street Journal* and *The New York Times* are excellent in this regard) and check the job descriptions. Talk to friends of your parents. In short, turn on your "career information sensors."

Once you have defined a targeted position, work backward. Consider the logical sequence of steps needed to reach that job goal. If it's a brand manager position in a large packaged-goods firm, consider getting an M.B.A. degree and some sales experience with a related product. If you want an industrial position with a high-technology company, don't waste your time being a sales representative for Procter & Gamble. Think ahead and plan your route to success.

Once you have defined your mission and scanned the job environment, turn inward and *analyze* your *strengths* and *weaknesses*. You are good, no doubt, at some things and less skilled at others. Some of us are analytical, others more person-oriented. Be honest and write down where you really believe you shine—but don't neglect to note your shortcomings. Good marketers try to improve their deficiencies; they rightfully avoid emphasizing their weaknesses.

Additionally, think hard about what you like to do in life. Your career will be successful when you find it enjoyable. A job decision should reflect your own interests. If you enjoy playing with computers, consider careers in that field. If getting to know people is important to you, consider sales-oriented careers. You should really love doing what you do. And don't choose a job because it offers more money at the entry level. Accepting that inducement often is shortsighted. If you enjoy your occupation, your long-term rewards will be much greater.

Research the Company and the Job

How do you go about looking for companies that might have the kind of job you want? Start at your college. Most schools have listings of career opportunities at various companies. Most colleges host company recruiters who come to campus to interview. Find out when the interviewers will arrive, and decide which ones you want to meet.

Look in the business press. *The Wall Street Journal* carries pages of help-wanted ads that run the gamut from chairperson to trainee. These ads usually refer applicants to a post office box or directly to a company. They may ask for résumé and salary requirements. Other newspapers to check are *The New York Times* (Sunday edition), *The Los Angeles Times,* and *The Chicago Tribune*. Regional newspapers, such as *The Atlanta Constitution* and *The Denver Post,* are also important. They carry ads for local companies and divisions of national concerns.

Specialized trade papers and magazines are also good sources for job leads. For marketing jobs, check *Advertising Age, Marketing News,* and *Sales Management Magazine*. There are hundreds of trade magazines, and a day in your library reviewing them is time well spent.

You can also go to employment agencies. Try to sign up with those that do not require a fee, or inquire only about "fee paid" positions. Some large corporations pay employment agency fees.

Some students entering the job market have met with success by systematically poring over Standard & Poor's *Register;* they select companies that interest them and write to the personnel or marketing vice president in each one. The *Register* provides company name, mailing address, and a list of key corporation officers.

Many job applicants don't really know enough about the company to which they're applying. This ignorance is inexcusable considering the mounds of material published on United States companies. Most of this material is available in your college or public library.

Standard & Poor's Corporation is a primary source for company data. It publishes *Corporate Records,* which provides financial histories and corporate histories of major firms. For instance, if you were applying for a position with American Safety Razor Company and wanted to know more about the company, you would find that the company was sold by Philip Morris in 1977 and is now independent.

For current facts on a certain company, your best bet would be to use the *Business Periodicals Index,* which will provide you with a list of news stories that have been published on the company. For example, you would find that *Business Week* carried a cover story on Sears Roebuck and Company in its Nov. 16, 1981, issue and that the story started on page 140. And ask reference librarians where else to look.

Another source of information is the company itself. Public corporations are required by law to publish annual reports, which are available from any stock brokerage company or from the individual company. See also the list of information sources that begins on p. 679.

Research serves two purposes. First, it makes you better informed for interviews, and second, you just might discover that you don't want to work for a particular company. It might be too big, have a history of firing personnel, or appear to lose money consistently. Look into the particular job as well as the company. Talk with people in similar positions. You'll be able to find out what different positions require and whether you are really interested in them.

Opportunities exist in the summer intern programs that many major corporations offer. A select group of students—usually college juniors—get to work in a corporate environment for the summer. A bonus is that many colleges give course credit for these programs. Many summer interns have the inside track on full-time employment with these companies later on. In addition, intern experience is a plus in the job market.

As you can see, it's really never too early to start thinking about a career. As Ronald Sustana, vice president of R. J. Reynolds Industries, Inc., says:[1]

Finding that first job is one of the most difficult things a young man or woman faces, and my advice is to start early while still in college. Get a feel of the business world during your college days. You may find that the profession you thought was appealing isn't all that enchanting, and there is still time to readjust. I would begin writing letters while in college and making the rounds of local companies which often provide summer employment to college students. This exercise will give you experience in how to write your résumé and how to interview. If you religiously do this, by the time you graduate you will be steps ahead of many of your colleagues.

Prepare an Effective Letter of Introduction

Once you know the nature of the companies to which you plan to apply and the nature of the job you seek, you should prepare a cover letter, a letter of introduction, like the one shown in Figure 21-1. It's your first contact with a prospective employer, and it has all the force of any first meeting. Most personnel directors recommend that a

---

[1] Personal communication, January 1982.

40 Highland Avenue
Andrews, MA 01588
April 15, 1982

Ms. Elizabeth Grisetti
Vice President, Marketing
Northern States Bank
8420 Charles Street
Boston, MA 02151

Dear Ms. Grisetti:

As a graduating college senior about to embark on a career, I have
researched the banking industry extensively--especially in the greater
Boston area. All sources indicate the Northern States Bank to be New
England's most competitive institution. Your foresight in providing such
services as Insta-Credit and Phone-4-Cash have certainly established
Northern States as the leading bank in Boston. This is just the
environment in which I feel I can make the most effective contribution.

To work in banking has always been my career objective--so much so that I
have taken two summer jobs in the field. As my resume shows, I have also
worked part time while at the University of Massachusetts in the
financial area. My minor field of economics, I feel, adds still another
valuable dimension to my career preparation. I also put particular
emphasis on money and banking in my course work, but my real interest
lies in marketing, particularly marketing planning and strategy. I don't
know of any industry that has adopted the marketing orientation as
enthusiastically as the contemporary banking industry.

My resume is enclosed to give you a more in-depth look at my background.
I would like very much to meet with you to discuss how I might be of
service to Northern States Bank. I will contact your office within the
next two weeks to see whether such an interview could be arranged.

Thank you for your consideration. I look forward to speaking with you.

Sincerely,

Robert J. Hannah

Robert J. Hannah

Enclosure

Figure 21-1   Sample letter of introduction.

simply worded letter be brief and clearly composed. The letter should stimulate the reader to want to know more about you and to want to read your attached résumé. The cover letter should point out your particular qualifications for the job sought and the company involved. Use a *benefits* approach, emphasizing what you have to offer, not what you want from the company.

"The cover letter is frequently more important than the résumé," comments Donald Dunn, a columnist with *Business Week* magazine who follows the employment market for executives. "This is the first impression that a prospective employer has of you."[2]

The letter is your representative. Make sure it doesn't have any grammatical or spelling errors. A sloppy letter nearly guarantees that you won't get an interview, much less a job.

Prepare a Distinctive Résumé

Like the letter of introduction, the résumé reflects on you. Your résumé, therefore, is one of the most important documents you may ever write, says Guy L. Smith IV, vice president of The Seven-Up Company:[3]

The résumé is an essential part of your job-hunting mission. The good letter of introduction leads the prospective employer to the résumé, and if it's sound, then you have a good chance of being granted that all-important interview. Remember that the résumé represents you; it is a brief history of your life.

The résumé is a short history of your life. As shown in Figure 21-2, it includes biographical information; full name, address, telephone number, and if you wish, your sex and birth date. Include your educational record; the name of the school, class standing, honors and awards, majors and minors, even a selected list of courses you've taken. List your work experience, including summer and part-time jobs. State your assignments and responsibilities, any innovations you brought to the job, and contributions you made. You may list either experience or education first, depending on which you feel is stronger or more relevant to the field you're exploring. You may want to add outside interests (clubs, sports participation, hobbies, and special skills). This section is less important to employers, but it shows that you're versatile and can get along well with people. Finally, prepare a list of references, people who know you well enough to vouch for you when questioned by a prospective employer. References can be included on the résumé if space permits, or you may prepare the list on a separate page and state on your résumé that references are available on request or attached. Personal and professional references are necessary, so be sure to have them "ready." Contact references first to ask permission, and make sure you know whether they'll give you a good recommendation. If they won't, don't use their names. Former employers, college professors, high school teachers, and businesspeople are all good reference sources.

---

[2]Personal communication, January 1982.
[3]Personal communication, January 1978.

ROBERT J. HANNAH

40 Highland Avenue
Andrews, MA 01588
617-234-2997

PROFESSIONAL
OBJECTIVE

To work within the marketing environment in a
position which would prove challenging to me and
worthwhile to my employer.

EDUCATION

University of Massachusetts, Amherst, May 1982
  graduate
Bachelor of Business Administration
Major: Marketing   Minor: Economics
Cumulative average: 3.8 on a 4.0 scale

Northbridge High School, 1978 graduate

EXPERIENCE

Blackville Valley National Bank, Andrews, MA
Bank Teller, summers of 1980 and 1981

Phillips Market, Andrews, MA
Stock Clerk, July 1977 - August 1979

Stanley Woolen, Uxbridge, MA
Woven Hanger, summer of 1978

ACTIVITIES AND
ORGANIZATIONS

Proctored a Financial Statistics course.
Part-time teller and a senior member of the
  Marketing Committee for University of
  Massachusetts Student Federal Credit Union.
Member of University of Massachusetts Honors Program.
Member of University of Massachusetts Undergraduate
  Business and Marketing clubs.
Selected to attend Boy's State in the summer of 1977.
Captain of basketball and softball teams in the
  Northbridge Summer Recreation Program.
Peer counselor for prospective honor students in the
  School of Business Administration.

ACADEMIC
AWARDS

Chosen Outstanding Scholar of the University of
  Massachusetts School of Business Administration,
  spring 1981, awarded a $500 scholarship.
Member of Phi Eta Sigma, Beta Gamma Sigma, and Phi
  Kappa Phi honor societies.

REFERENCES

Dr. William Ames, Professor of the Marketing
  Department, School of Business Administration,
  University of Massachusetts, Amherst, MA 01003

Mr. John Martin, Vice President, Administration,
  Blackville Valley National Bank, Andrews, MA 01588
  Telephone: 617-234-7446

Ms. Anne Staples, Manager, Phillips Market,
  Walker Street, Andrews, MA 01588
  Telephone: 617-234-5350

Figure 21-2 Sample résumé.

Remember that your résumé should be honest and well organized. Treat it like one of the most important exams you've ever had to pass, and it will reward you well. Don't allow a single mistake in spelling or grammar. Don't inflate your claims. On the other hand, don't sell yourself short. False modesty on a résumé can be disastrous.

Prepare for Interviewing

If you've researched the company and the job and have prepared a letter of introduction and a résumé, you will be ready for the interview should the company select you as a likely job candidate. Initial interviews are often with a representative of the company's personnel department. It is the personnel department's responsibility to select a group of candidates to be interviewed by the manager who actually needs the new employee and who will ultimately make the hiring decision.

A first interview with the personnel department will cover a lot of ground. Keep in mind always that you are on trial—harsh words, but accurate. The best advice from personnel executives is to be yourself. You are not expected to be entirely relaxed, so don't worry if you reflect some apprehension, particularly in your first job interview. The days of intentionally creating stress in interviews are largely over.

"When interviewing a person for an entry level position, I don't expect the candidate to be a polished professional. If this was my objective, I would be interviewing someone with experience," says Reynolds's Sustana. "I look for a young man or woman to be inquisitive—willing to learn."[4]

Be prepared to discuss the reasons why you want to work for the company and why you think you will excel at the job. The personnel representative is likely to probe your academic record and ask you such questions as "What are your long-term career objectives?" or "Why do you feel you are qualified for this job?" Be truthful. If you have a C average in mathematics, admit that you are no math genius. Don't make alibis, but don't put yourself down, either.

The problem of discrimination against women and minority groups is a serious one. If you're a woman, be aware that it is illegal for interviewers to ask questions about your child-rearing or other personal plans. Ambitious women are much in demand at some companies, but others may present female graduates with a wall of prejudice. Interviewers may imply that women are poor hiring risks because, they believe, women work only until they start raising a family. Discrimination on the basis of sex, race, or national origin is against the law, but laws don't always change human behavior as fast as they might. Check to see whether the company you're interviewing with has a history of promoting women, whether it has an affirmative action program, whether there's any evidence of discrimination. You should also know that, conversely, in some companies, candidates who are women or from minorities actually have an edge. And men who are applying for jobs would do well to be able to offer such beginner's skills as typing, especially in highly competitive job markets.

The interviewer will also look for other features—your dress and grooming habits. Although jeans, T-shirts, and running shoes may be great for the campus, they

---

[4]Personal communication, January 1982.

Figure 21-3 The personnel executives' advice to "be yourself" is sound, whether you're playing the role of the student, as shown on the left, or the job applicant, shown on the right, who aspires toward a professional career. (Randy Matusow)

hardly fit in a business environment. You want to leave the impression that you are now ready for a career, even if this means investing in a new wardrobe. Although longer hair for men may be acceptable in some companies, looking like a sheepdog isn't. A personnel officer of one major corporation even looks at a candidate's shoes. If the heels are worn down, he concludes that the person is not attentive to details. So make sure you're as neat as the proverbial pin, and try to dress in the style appropriate to the company. (See Figure 21-3.)

Don't be tempted to get overly familiar with the personnel interviewer. Should he or she call you by your first name, don't reciprocate until asked to do so. And don't smoke, period. Remember that your initial objective is to be among the select group that finally makes its way into the office of the hiring manager. The same rules follow at this stage of the interview, but be prepared to answer questions in more depth and to know more about what the company does.

Application 21-1
Do Gimmicks Work?

As a general rule, the tried-and-true methods are the best for the job seeker. But when the job market grows tight, some searchers rely on the unorthodox.

During the early 1980s, jobs with advertising agencies were extremely hard to come by as advertising expenditures by major companies were pared. The agencies found themselves dealing with a new type of job hunter.

One applicant for a position with a New York agency sent a résumé printed on a T-shirt and delivered in a Brooks Bros. box. Another equally imaginative applicant named Randy Rensch sent several agencies wrenches with this note: "When it's a copywriter, it's spelled Rensch."

While an occasional gimmick may work, agency heads advise that the more traditional approach is the most effective way of landing a job. "A good cover letter makes all the difference to me," Norman Stahl, creative director of the Ted Bates agency, told *The Wall Street Journal.*

And Burt Manning, chairman of giant J. Walter Thompson, warned: "If you're willing to risk a 99 percent chance of being totally wrong, do something off-the-wall."

Source of data: "Landing a Job in Advertising Often Requires Unusual Skills," *The Wall Street Journal,* Feb. 26, 1981. p. 25.

Follow Up on Interviews

After you've gone through the interviewing process, write to the people who conducted the interviews. Simply thank them for their time, express your hope that you will be selected, and restate a particular qualification and your interest. This letter, if nothing else, leaves a good impression, and if you miss out on the job, perhaps you will have a head start when there is another opening.

If you don't get the job, don't take it personally. It may merely mean that someone else is better qualified. But, if you're not getting any second interviews, you may be coming across badly. Have a friend or teacher interview you and evaluate you. Observe *others* in mock interviews and practice your communication skills. (See Application 21-1.)

Jobs in Marketing

Marketing is one of the broadest fields of business and, as a result, needs people with diverse skills and personalities. As we discussed in the preceding chapters, marketers are found in most companies and organizations. The titles, of course, may differ, but marketers are the key to any successful enterprise—from IBM and General Motors to the Boy Scouts and the Red Cross. The marketing umbrella is a big one. It covers marketing research, product management, advertising, public relations, and sales. Within each of these categories are scores of subcategories.

The lines of reporting often differ from corporation to corporation. But many are structured along lines that call for all marketing people to report to a vice president or chief executive officer. We will not cover all the job opportunities within marketing, but we will describe positions which are open for the new employee who has limited or no experience.

Sales

Figure 21-4   Selling is the most common job in marketing, and it's also characterized by a wide diversity of needed backgrounds and skills. *(Grant Compton)*

Far and away, the sales job is the most common of all marketing positions. But to say you are a salesperson would give your audience no clue about what you really do. The clerk at Woolco is a salesperson, as is the engineer who preaches the virtues of IBM computers. Few would argue that these two selling jobs are the same. Sales jobs demand specialization and different kinds of preparation. A successful salesperson at a discount store can accomplish assignments with perhaps a high school education, while an IBM salesperson may have to earn an advanced college degree. (See Fig. 21-4.)

Most large companies look for sales representatives from the college ranks. Different criteria are used by different companies when choosing sales representatives, but as a rule they all seek outgoing individuals who are comfortable meeting and working with others.

Few companies, once they have made a hiring decision, expect their new sales representatives to go out and begin selling immediately. Most have some form of training, and some have extensive training facilities and courses. Eastman Kodak, for instance, spends months training its new sales representatives. When sales trainees emerge from the Kodak training center, they have a good understanding not only of the corporation but also of its products and how they work and compare with those sold by competitors. But even at this point, the trainee is not released from the company's watchful eye. For weeks thereafter, a trainee works with an experienced Kodak sales representative to observe customer calls.

Persons entering the sales field are generally assigned to small territories where, in effect, they are tested. At this level, the sales representative's job includes clerical work, such as taking orders and handling routine correspondence for senior sales representatives, in addition to selling. Good sales representatives are on the move constantly, and many work out of their homes rather than company offices.

Brand or Product Management

The most common entry-level position in brand management is assistant brand manager. At this level, the trainee learns how a brand makes its way into the marketplace, from conception to test market to national distribution. Michael Sheets, president of Airwick Consumer Products, defines what is expected of a young brand manager.[5]

---

[5]Personal communication, January 1978.

I look for a commitment to business by the candidate and a sincere interest in devoting an important part of his or her life toward achievement of success in business. The candidate must have integrity. He or she must also have ambition, a high level of intelligence, and an inquiring mind. He or she should be self-motivated, well-organized, thorough, and willing to work hard without getting bogged down in details or side issues. We believe in learning by doing. We give new people responsibility early and do everything possible to continually challenge and stretch them. We expect our people to become productive quickly, with emphasis on outstanding personal performance and results for the enterprise.

Brand managers, or product managers as they are called in some organizations, are involved in decisions from product research through product inventory. They decide what kinds of research techniques to use in measuring the market for a particular product. A brand manager may even develop ideas for new products and work with the research and design department to produce a model of the new product. Advertising, sales promotion, and packaging decisions get special attention from brand managers. They must also consider the legal aspects of marketing a product, the optimum price at which the product is sold (its profitability), and the appropriate inventory levels of the product in the company's warehouse. If a person succeeds in the assistant brand manager position, logical promotions are to brand manager, group brand manager, and on up the marketing ladder.

Marketing Research

Another entry-level position, although one with perhaps the fewest openings, is the marketing research assistant. Here a person with a bent toward research practices the methodology discussed in Chapter 4. Research assistants must be inquisitive and analytical, objective and rational, and, above all, organized. They must be problem solvers, ready to analyze data and present recommendations to marketing management.

Marketing research positions are available in marketing companies, in marketing research consulting companies, and in advertising agencies. In a marketing company, such as Procter & Gamble or General Foods, the researcher usually focuses on the problem and its managerial implications and directs an outside research team. In a research consulting firm, the researcher implements techniques and conducts research projects that supply information to client companies. In advertising agencies, the research emphasis falls on testing copy appeals.

Public Relations

Although public relations is a part of the marketing function, the background for positions in this field differs sharply from that for positions in brand management and marketing research. The public relations segment draws many of its recruits from communication and journalism schools.

Public relations is the department that is called upon to deal directly with the news media—editors and reporters. Practitioners must break down marketing and other management jargon into everyday language so that the media can convey stories on corporate and product events to the public.

A well-run marketing operation keeps its public relations department fully advised of product development, changes in marketing strategy, and new advertising campaigns.

Entry-level positions within public relations are numerous both at the corporate level and within agencies. Generally, persons entering public relations obtain jobs as assistant writers, monitoring product development and preparing press releases.

In addition to working directly with brand management, marketing research, and advertising, public relations executives are generally responsible for internal communication, including management newsletters and employee newspapers.

Advertising

Entry-level positions in advertising occur in advertising agencies and company advertising departments. Here, trainees generally begin their careers as account executives, media buyers, or copywriters. Some companies do not create their own advertising but leave this responsibility to agencies whose representatives work directly with company marketing managers. The company devises the overall marketing plan for a product, and the agency, with guidance from the marketing department, creates an advertising program.

The account executive in the typical advertising agency reports to the account supervisor, who in turn reports directly to the corporate client's upper management. The account executive must be familiar with the client's marketing objectives, personal tastes, sales problems, and budget. Often, the account executive sits in with the copywriter during creative sessions and is there to make sure that the client's thoughts on the program are reflected in the advertising copy.

Another entry-level position is media buyer, and it is ideal for the candidate who is good with figures. The media buyer must become familiar with the various advertising rates of newspapers, radio, and television. It is the media buyer's responsibility to determine which medium will carry the client's ad. The media buyer generally reports to the media supervisor, who in turn answers to the media director—the executive who makes the final determination of how a client's money will be spent.

Sales Promotion

Another area of marketing is sales promotion. As competitive pressures in all fields have mounted, the need for specialists in sales promotion has become obvious. This fact has given rise to sales promotion houses.

Operating similarly to advertising agencies, sales promotion houses oversee the merchandising needs of their clients. They are involved in almost everything beyond media advertising that prompts sales. They understand the promotional objectives of the marketer and translate these goals into promotional devices—coupons, sweepstakes, contests, T-shirts, trade shows, samples, sales meetings, and other kinds of promotion. The boundaries of this position lie only in an individual's creative limits. (See Figure 21-5.)

To be successful in sales promotion, a person should be innovative and

Figure 21-5 Sales promotion is one of the fastest growing areas in marketing. *(Arthur Tress/Photo Researchers, Inc.)*

imaginative, have a sound grasp of marketing principles, and have some background in graphic arts. Sales promotion promises to be a growth area in marketing as companies look for better ways to call attention to their product lines.

Retailing

Retailing, too, provides opportunities for the marketer, and this field has changed greatly in recent years so that it now uses most of the marketing techniques found in consumer products companies. In the past, retailers were regarded as merchandisers who just hoped the public would buy their goods. Now, however, many retailers carefully study the market to determine customer needs and wants. Retailing offers positions to buyers (those who must buy the goods that you see on the shelves and on the racks), to the section managers who oversee buyers, and to sales clerks who meet the customers and keep inventories in line.

Information Sources

Did any of the preceding job descriptions interest you? Or did you find that none quite described the job you want? Many organizations publish information that describes careers in marketing. The following source list is published by the American Marketing Association.[6] Gathering material can help you learn more about job opportunities in

---

[6]Neil Holbert, "Careers in Marketing," Monograph Series no. 4, American Marketing Association, Chicago, 1976, pp. 25–28.

marketing. It can also help you to examine the field for other opportunities. While specific titles are listed with many sources, all the sources have bibliographies that show all their publications. Just write to the organization and request a specific title or ask for the organization's bibliography. You might also check your school's placement office; many have these publications available.

Administrative Research Associates, Inc., Irvine Town Center, Box 4211, Irvine, California 92664 ("Choosing Your Career," $1.00).

Advertising Education Publications, 3429 55th Street, Lubbock, Texas 79413.

Advertising Research Foundation, 3 East 54th Street, New York, New York 10022.

Alpha Kappa Psi, 3706 Washington Boulevard, Indianapolis, Indiana 46206 ("Careers in Business," $.10; "Planning Your Career," $.10).

American Association of Advertising Agencies, 200 Park Avenue, New York, New York 10017 ("Advertising: A Guide to Careers in Advertising," $.50).

American Bankers Association, 1120 Connecticut Avenue, N.W., Washington, D.C. 20036.

American Collegiate Retailing Association, Rochester Institute of Technology, c/o Dean Raymond F. Von Deken; College of Business, 1 Lomb Memorial Drive, Rochester, New York 14623 ("Careers in Retailing," free).

American Management Association, 135 West 50th Street, New York, New York 10020 ("Your Career in Management," $.50).

American Marketing Association, 222 South Riverside Plaza, Suite 606, Chicago, Illinois 60606.

American Psychological Association, 1200 17th Street N.W., Washington, D.C. 20036 ("Careers in Psychology," free).

American Statistical Association, 806 15th Street N.W., Washington, D.C. 20005 ("Careers in Statistics," free).

Association of Industrial Advertisers, 41 East 42d Street, New York, New York 10017.

Association of National Advertisers, 155 East 44th Street, New York, New York 10017.

Bank Marketing Association, 309 West Washington Street, Chicago, Illinois 60606.

Business and Professional Women's Foundation, 2012 Massachusetts Avenue, N.W., Washington, D.C. 20003 ("Women in Management," $.50)

Chemical Marketing Research Association, 100 Church Street, New York, New York 10007.

Chronical Guidance Publications, Inc., Moravia, New York 13118.

Industrial Marketing Associates, 516 Pleasant Street, St. Joseph, Michigan 49085.

Institute of Life Insurance, 277 Park Avenue, New York, New York 10017 ("A Life Career," free).

Life Insurance Marketing and Research Association, 170 Sigourtney Street, Hartford, Connecticut 06105 ("The Life Insurance Career," $.30).

Market Research Association, P.O. Box 145, Grand Central Station, New York, New York 10017.

National Association of Bank Women, 111 East Wacker Drive, Chicago, Illinois 60601 ("A Career for Women in Banking," free).

National Association of Broadcasters, 1771 N Street, N.W., Washington, D.C. 20036 ("Careers in Television," free; "Careers in Radio," free).

National Association of Business Economists, 888 Seventeenth Street, N.W., Washington, D.C. 20006, Suite 208 ("Business Economics Careers," $.25).

National Association of Purchasing Management, 11 Park Place, New York, New York 10007 ("Purchasing as a Career," $.50; "Your Career in Purchasing Management," free).

National Association of Wholesalers, 1725 K Street, N.W., Washington, D.C. 20006 ("Career Opportunities in Wholesaling," free).

National Automobile Dealers Association, 2000 K Street, N.W., Washington, D.C. 20006 ("Your Career in the Retail Car and Truck Business," free).

National Food Brokers Association, NFBA Building, 1916 M Street, N.W., Washington, D.C. 20036 ("Job Previews," free).

Sales and Marketing Executives—International, 380 Lexington Avenue, New York, New York 10017 ("Opportunities in Selling," free).

Sales Promotion Executives Association, 2130 Delancey Street, Philadelphia, Pennsylvania 19103.

Savings Institutions Marketing Society of America, 111 East Wacker Drive, Chicago, Illinois 60601.

U.S. Department of Education, Washington, D.C. 20202.

U.S. Department of Labor: Bureau of Labor Statistics, Washington, D.C. 20212 ("Occupational Outlook Series," free); Bureau of Labor Statistics, New York Office, 1515 Broadway, New York, New York 10036; Employment Standards Administration, Washington, D.C. 20210; Manpower Administration, Washington, D.C. 20402; Office of Information, Washington, D.C. 20210.

Cases for Part Four

Case 1   Hoover Ltd.

When the world suffers in a recession, multinational companies suffer apace. One company that felt the full impact of the European recession was Hoover Company, which long depended on foreign operations to produce 50 percent of its sales. Hoover's primary problem rested with its British subsidiary, Hoover Ltd., which had been set back by both the European recession and aggressive low-priced competition in the home-appliance industry. In 1982 Hoover Ltd. offered both vacuum cleaners and washing machines for sale. Foreign (non-British) operations have been so important to Hoover Ltd. that the British subsidiary's problem was adversely hurting its U.S. parent. Hoover Ltd. lost $40 million in 1981 and resulted in a $20 million loss for Hoover Company, completely wiping out profit in the U.S. operations. Comparing this with Hoover's $30 million profit in 1980, the company clearly saw the need for action.

To meet the challenge, Merle R. Rawson, chairman of Hoover, was trying to devise a plan to restore order to his company. First, to avoid high labor costs, some manufacturing was to be moved out of England to France, where costs were lower and the labor force more stable. Since 1972, Hoover had spent $40 million renovating manufacturing plants in Britain while reducing its work force from 13,000 to 9,800. At the same time, Rawson invested $11 million in a plant in Dijon, France. The strength of the British pound and continually high inflation kept the landed cost of British-made vacuums very high—29 percent higher than the French-made vacuums in 1980 alone.

Second, Rawson planned to introduce a series of new vacuum cleaner lines in Europe called the Sensotronic. Offered in eleven models, these cleaners would be priced between $60 and $300 and would thus be competitive in all segments of the market.

Third, Rawson decided to largely restrict washing machine sales to England, where its market share was 25 percent in 1982, down from 32 percent in 1976. The drop in market share was partly the result of an aging product line, and so the company began offering new models. At the same time, Rawson began withdrawing products from a large part of the European market in face of competition from Italian manufacturers, who were able to offer washers at prices Hoover could not match.

Hoover also faced problems in the United States, where Rawson was witnessing a fall-off in vacuum sales. Sales in 1981 were off 1 million units from peak sales of 9.3 million vacuum cleaners in 1977.

To counter, Rawson began looking for a U.S. acquisition outside of vacuum cleaners in an effort to strengthen the company. Efforts to capitalize on the Hoover name with other appliances for the U.S. market had failed in the past, and such a strategy appeared remote.

To strengthen British operations, Rawson stepped up his efforts to make and sell a line of security products like smoke detectors, fire extinguishers, and burglar alarms. Security products sales amounted to only $10 million in 1981, but Rawson looked for 25 percent of this $380 million market in Britain and 15 percent of the large European market. Rawson was wondering if his actions were the correct ones and where he ought to go from here.

1 What advice would you offer Rawson?

2 Should the foreign and domestic operations be run differently?

Source of data: "Hoover: Revamping in Europe to Stem an Earnings Drain at Home," *Business Week*, February 15, 1982, pp. 144–146.

Case 2   IAPA

In 1960, the Airways Club of New York was chartered as the air travelers' answer to the AAA for drivers, and in 1982 it was still promoting itself as a consumer advocate.

Having changed its name to the International Airline Passengers Association (IAPA), the organization owned by James Dunn of Louisville, Kentucky, evolved into much more of a business enterprise than a public-spirited organization. Although the IAPA claimed credit for helping to temporarily ground DC-10s following a series of crashes and periodically issued statements and positions on public issues affecting air travel, in recent years the IAPA expanded its services. In early 1982, Dunn was reviewing the organization's operations and thinking about its future.

The organization had been service-oriented. For instance, for $40 per year IAPA members were entitled to services ranging from discount car rentals to baggage tracing. Membership fees generated $4.4 million in 1982, enough to pay 100 employees to work out discount programs, deal with airlines, and flood the membership with direct-mail advertising. Most of the services offered to members, however, were readily available to almost anyone with or without IAPA membership. But one of the IAPA's most lucrative ventures was insurance.

The association offered its members travel insurance for premiums of between $45 and $540 per year with death benefits of up to $1.5 million. Insurance coverage is optional, but 70 percent of the IAPA membership elect the coverage. The risk for the IAPA is minimal, with a claim payout ratio of only 9 percent. The chances of being in an airplane crash and dying are one in a million, and the average member buys $200,000 worth of coverage for $90.

In 1981, insurance premium income was $5.6 million. The IAPA reportedly paid its underwriter, Lloyds of London, $4 million to assure risks, which means $1.6 million was left over. Insurance now represents more than half of the IAPA's $10 million in gross revenues.

Dunn wondered whether he should continue to direct the IAPA into new commercial ventures.

1   Do you think it's socially irresponsible for the IAPA to proclaim it is a consumer advocate while it sells such insurance?
2   What other products might IAPA add?

Source of data: "Let the Flier Beware," *Forbes,* July 19, 1982, p. 65.

GLOSSARY

Adaption is the process by which one adjusts to changes in one's environment.

Adaptive replacements are new products with significant changes that replace existing products.

Administered vertical marketing systems are vertical marketing systems where integration is achieved by means of the power held by one channel member.

Advertising agencies are firms that are specialists in performing the tasks of advertising.

Agents are wholesaling intermediaries, sometimes called middlemen, who do *not* take title to goods they help distribute.

Area (cluster) samples are probability samples in which the population is divided into areas by means of maps; a random sample of areas is then selected.

Assimilation is the process by which the individual selects material to be remembered (sharpened) and material to be eliminated (leveled).

Attitudes are feelings, the liking or disliking of objects in one's environment.

Auction companies are establishments that bring buyers and sellers together at one location to inspect merchandise before purchasing it.

Augmented products are products with a set of features not anticipated by potential buyers that exceed the customer's expectation.

Average fixed costs are the allocation of total fixed costs over the quantity of products produced.

Average total costs are the sum of average fixed costs and average variable costs.

Average variable costs are the per-unit direct costs associated with producing a given quantity.

Bait pricing is pricing a product below normal to entice a customer into the store—and then trying to get the customer to trade up to a higher-quality product or brand.

Basing point is the geographical location from which the freight rate charge is computed.

Benefit segmentation is the breaking down of a market into groups based upon the benefits purchased, the values received, and the needs or wants matched.

Biogenic needs are physiological states of deprivation such as the needs for food, drink, sex, or bodily comfort.

Brand is a name, term, symbol, or design, or a combination of them, which is intended to identify the goods or services of one seller or group of sellers and to differentiate them from those of competitors.

Brand labels are the brands alone applied to the product or to the package.

Brand marks are those parts of the brand which are in the form of a symbol, design, or distinctive coloring or lettering.

Brand names consist of words, letters, and/or numbers that may be vocalized.

The breakeven point is that volume of sales at which total revenue equals total costs.

Brokers are agent intermediaries whose primary task is to bring buyers and sellers together.

Bundle of utility is the total satisfaction coming to a consumer from the sum of the components of a product—the sum of its form, time, place, and possession utilities.

Business definitions set the boundaries within which the organization will take competitive action.

Buying centers consist of the individual or groups of individuals within an organization who are responsible for a purchase decision.

Cannibalization is the act of adding a new product to an

existing line and thereby taking sales and profits away from existing products.

A cash-and-carry wholesaler is a limited-service wholesaler who offers no credit and no transportation.

Cash cows are strategic business units with high relative market shares in low-growth markets.

A cash discount is a price reduction offered for payment of a bill within a stated period of time.

Centrality is the quality of attitudes which are closely related to the consumer's self-concept and basic values.

Chain stores are retail organizations consisting of two or more units with common ownership.

A channel captain is the channel member who exerts the greatest influence over other channel members.

The channel of distribution is the route taken by the title to a product as it moves from the producer to the ultimate consumer or end user.

Class action is court action taken on behalf of a segment (class) of individuals or organizations.

Commission merchants are agricultural agent intermediaries who take possession of goods when they are shipped to a central market for sale and then act as the producer's salesperson in negotiating an exchange.

Common carriers are businesses that serve the general public

by transporting goods at established rates and with standard practices set by regulatory bodies or by company rules.

A common market is formed when countries group together in order to do away with obstacles to trade—particularly tariffs.

Communication is the function that consists of the transmittal of information and messages between the buyer and seller to the end that the most favorable climate for the seller is created in the marketplace.

Concentrated marketing is the strategy of market segmentation but with only one market segment being served.

Conclusive research is the investigation that provides the manager with information to make a rational decision.

A consumer advocate is an individual who acts in an official or unofficial role as a spokesperson for consumer rights.

Consumer affairs marketing is a level of marketing that blends sensitivity of issues raised by the consumer movement with the traditional marketing concept.

Consumer goods are those goods and services which are destined for the ultimate consumer.

Consumerism is the label for the consumer movement in the United States since the early

1960s and refers today to a social movement aimed at placing consumers on an equal footing with business.

Contests offer prizes to consumers as a reward for doing some task—often, for showing creative thinking about the product.

Contract carriers are those businesses that ship on a contractual basis.

Contractual vertical marketing systems are vertical marketing systems where integration is achieved by contracts between channel members.

Controlling is the comparison of actual performance with expected performance.

Convenience goods are those goods which people want to buy with a minimum of shopping effort.

A convenience sample is a nonprobability sample, composed of respondents who come in to the sample by accident; they happen to be *where* the study is being conducted *when* it is being conducted.

Convenience stores are retail stores located near the residences or places of work of their target customers.

A cooperative is an organization initiated by retailers who come together to own their own wholesaling operation.

The copy is all of the written or spoken material in an advertising message, including the headline, coupons, and advertiser's name and address, as well as the main body of the message.

The core market is that part of the market where the match between market wants and needs and the product offered is perfect.

Corporate culture is the set of values within an organization that set a distinct pattern for the company's activities, opinions, and actions.

Corporate purpose or mission is an organization's statement of what it would like to accomplish in its environment.

Corporate vertical marketing systems are vertical marketing systems where integration of channel members is by ownership.

Cost-per-thousand is a formula for calculating the cost efficiency of an advertising medium in reaching consumers.

A coupon is a certificate that the consumer takes to a retail store, receiving in return some previously indicated saving or a cash refund.

Criteria are measures used by decision makers to determine when they have reached an objective.

Culture is a complex of values, ideas, attitudes, and other meaningful symbols created by humans to shape human behavior.

A cumulative quantity discount is a quantity discount applied to purchases over a period of time.

Customary pricing is the pricing policy that sets prices according to what has been traditionally acceptable.

Data are recorded observations, usually in statistical form.

Dealer selection is a controlling method in a distribution channel whereby the manufacturer tries to select those dealers to whom the company will sell—and to prohibit selling to others.

A decision is the chosen alternative.

Decision making is the commitment to a specific alternative solution.

Decision rules are the guidelines for choosing a solution from the alternatives available.

Decoding is the process by which the signs of the message are interpreted by the receiver.

Demarketing is the activity of reducing or discouraging exchanges of goods and services.

Demographics are descriptor variables that define the population.

A department store offers a wide range of product lines and is organized into departments based on those product lines.

Descriptive labels and informative labels are labels which give written or illustrative objective information about the use, construction, care, performance, or other features of the product.

Determinant buying attributes

are evaluative criteria that are highest in importance and also perceived differently among competing products.

The difference threshold is the smallest increment of change in stimulus intensity that will be noticed by an individual.

Direct-action advertising has as its purpose the gaining of immediate behavior or action by the market.

A direct channel of distribution is one in which no intermediaries are used.

Disassociative reference groups are groups that an individual avoids.

A discount is a reduction from the list price.

Discount stores are self-service, general merchandise stores that combine low prices and high-unit volume to achieve profits.

Distribution is the act of moving goods and services closer in time and place to the buyer.

A distribution center is a streamlined storage facility geared to taking orders and delivering goods; it is a fully integrated system for the efficient flow of goods.

A distributor is a wholesaler.

Diversification is the process of adding different products to an already existing line of products.

Dogs are strategic business units with low relative market shares in low-growth markets.

Door-to-door retailing is any

exchange in which the transaction occurs in the consumer's home.

A drive is a strong motivating tendency or instinct that prompts activity toward a particular end.

A drop shipper is a limited-service wholesaler who does not take physical possession of the goods he or she distributes.

Dual distribution is the use by a manufacturer of two different channels of distribution to move goods.

Dumping is the international pricing practice of selling goods abroad at a price below that charged to domestic consumers.

Ego involvement is the psychological commitment that an individual has to any given object, group, idea, or value.

Elastic demand is the condition where a percentage change in price (an increase or decrease) brings about a greater percentage change (an increase or decrease) in quantity purchased.

Emergency goods are convenience goods that are purchased when the need is even more urgent for them than for impulse goods and that solve a current crisis.

Encoding is the process by which the source translates the meaning or idea that is to be conveyed into signs.

Environmental scanning is the information-gathering activity aimed at monitoring the external uncontrollable variables of marketing.

Ethical pricing is the pricing policy that sets prices with social-responsibility guidelines.

The ethnocentric stage of the evolution of international marketing management thought is the stage at which international operations are considered secondary to domestic operations.

Evaluative criteria are the group of product features or performance characteristics, such as size and dependability, that consumers value and expect to find in a particular product, brand, retail store, or organization.

Exchange involves the offering of a product with the expectation of receiving payment—something having utility—in return.

Exchange rate is the ratio applied when changing one country's money into another's.

Exclusive dealing is a controlling method used by manufacturers that prohibits dealers from carrying competitive products.

Exclusive distribution is the use of only one intermediary in a given territory.

Exclusive territories are areas established by controlling agreements between producer and dealer ensuring that dealers sell only to customers within their territory.

Exempt carriers are those shippers exempt from state and federal regulations.

Expected products are those that must meet minimal purchase conditions by products before they will be bought.

Experimentation is a scientific investigation by which an investigator manipulates and controls one or more independent variables, observes the dependent variable, and infers cause and effect relationships.

Exploratory research is the preliminary investigation of a problem with major emphasis on gaining ideas and insights.

Express warranties are those warranties stated in written or spoken words.

Expropriation is the taking over of a company by the government of the country in which that company is doing business.

Extended family includes the nuclear family plus other relatives—aunts, uncles, grandparents, etc.

Family brand is the use of the same brand name for all the items handled by one company or produced by one manufacturer.

Family of orientation is the family into which we are born or by which we are adopted.

Family of procreation is the family one begins by marriage.

Feedback is the means by which

the source checks whether—and to what extent—the message was correctly conveyed.

A flexible price policy is a pricing approach where the marketer offers the same products in the same quantities to different customers at different prices.

F.O.B. means "free on board" and refers to the point when the buyer actually takes title to the goods (i.e., owns them).

Form utility is the satisfaction that comes from the shape, function, or style of the product.

A franchise is a legal, contractual relationship between a supplier (either a manufacturer or a wholesaler) and several (sometimes many) small, independent retailers.

Freight absorption is the tactic whereby sellers take part or all of the actual freight charge out of their profits.

Freight forwarders are transporters of goods who serve small shippers by pooling the small shipments of many shippers in order to lose the less-than-carload or less-than-truckload rate.

The fringe market is that part of the market where the match between market wants and needs and the product offered is less than perfect but not totally imperfect.

A full-line competitor is one who offers broad assortments of products to match all the varying needs of the marketplace.

A full-service wholesaler is one who provides almost all of the services that a wholesaler can provide.

A full warranty is one which includes the following provisions: Any defect must be fixed without charge and within a reasonable time; customers cannot be required to incur undue expense or go to great trouble to have defective products fixed; and if the manufacturer or seller fails to correct a defect after a reasonable number of attempts, the buyer is entitled to either a refund or a replacement.

A general merchandise, full-service wholesaler is one who handles a broad line of nonperishable items.

A general merchandise retailer is one who carries a wide range of products for his or her customers.

Generics are no-name, unbranded products.

The geocentric stage in the evolution of international marketing management thought is the stage where the entire world is treated as one big market.

Geographical pricing is the approach that adjusts the list price to meet differences in locational patterns of the buyers.

Global enterprises are companies that sell a fairly standard product in markets all over the earth and that coordinate their manufacturing in many different countries.

A grade label is a label which identifies the quality of a product by a letter, number, or word.

Heredity is the transmission of characteristics from parents to offspring.

Horizontal cooperative advertising is advertising whose cost is shared by a group of marketers at the same level in the distribution channel.

Ideal self-image is the way we would *like* to see ourselves and/or have others see us.

The illustration is the photograph, graph, chart, drawing, painting, reproduction, cartoon, or any other pictorial feature of the advertisement.

Imitative products are products that may be new to the marketer but not new to the market.

Implementing is the carrying out of a plan.

Implied warranties are promises legally in effect even though they are not actually stated.

Impulse items are convenience goods which the consumer does not plan to buy but which he or she buys because of some strongly felt immediate need or want.

An independent retailing operation is one which consists of a single store that has no affiliation with any other retail unit offering similar lines of merchandise.

Indirect-action advertising is aimed at gaining recognition and developing favorable attitudes as a prerequisite to purchase action.

The indirectness of a *channel* refers to the degree to which intermediaries are used in that channel; the more indirect the channel, the more intermediaries that are used.

An individual brand is a brand name applied to only one product or brand.

Industrial goods are those goods and services which are destined for use in producing other goods and services.

Inelastic demand is the condition where the percentage change (the increase or decrease) in price brings about a smaller percentage change (the increase or decrease) in quantity purchased.

Information is knowledge communicated by others or obtained by study and investigation.

Innovative products are those new products which are unique.

Institutional advertising is advertising designed to build a favorable image of the advertiser rather than of individual products.

Intensive distribution is the utilization of many intermediaries to obtain wide market coverage.

Intention is commitment to a course of action.

An intermediary is a buyer of goods who resells them rather than consumes them. Intermediaries bring goods closer in time and place to the ultimate consumer.

Inventory is the amount of finished goods that exist at a given point in the distribution system.

Joint venture is an undertaking in which two or more companies share ownership.

A judgment sample is a nonprobability sample where respondents are hand-picked by someone regarded as knowledgeable about how well they represent the population being studied.

The label is that part of the product which carries verbal information about the product or the seller.

The layout is the overall structure or the way that the various design elements in an advertisement are positioned.

A lead is any organization or individual that may be a potential customer for the product.

Leasing is a form of pricing where the user does not take title to the goods but, rather, rents the functions of the product.

Leveling is the process by which an individual makes what is retained in memory shorter, more concise, and easier to grasp.

Lifestyle segmentation is the breaking down of the market on the basis of distinctive modes of living, thus grouping segments based upon similarities in activities, interests, and opinions.

A limited-line, full-service wholesaler is one who carries only a few product lines but offers a full range of services.

A limited-line retailer is one who offers only one line or several similar lines to his or her customers.

A limited-service wholesaler is one who provides less than a full complement of services.

A limited warranty is one which states clearly what it does and does not cover, provides guidelines on how to use and maintain the product in order to qualify for the warranty, and tells you where and how you can have the warranty fulfilled.

The list price is the price that the buyer is normally asked to pay for the product.

Long-range plans focus on objectives over a five-year or longer time period.

Mail-order retailers are those that sell by description (without the consumer's actually seeing the goods) and deliver the product by mail.

A mail-order wholesaler is a limited-service wholesaler who sells through the mail.

Manufacturers' agents are independent intermediaries who do not take title to goods and who distribute related but noncompeting products for a number of manufacturers.

Manufacturers' brands are owned

by the producers and are frequently called "national" brands.

Manufacturers' sales branches are manufacturer-owned wholesaling operations.

Marginal cost is the extra cost of producing one more unit of a good.

Marginal revenue is the extra revenue that comes from selling one more unit of the product.

A market consists of people with specific, similar needs and/or wants.

Market aggregation is the strategy of producing a single product and offering it to all consumers with a single marketing program.

Market atomization is the strategy of treating each consumer as though he or she was unique.

Market delineation is the process of determining potential purchasers and their identifying characteristics.

The market rationale is the focusing on the marketer's knowledge of the market as a basis for convergence in adding products.

Market segmentation is the strategy of breaking a heterogeneous market into groups, each of which is homogeneous in some way. This allows the development of a unique marketing program for each segment.

Market share is the percentage of a total industry's sales that is held by a particular company.

A market audit is a systematic, critical, and impartial review and appraisal of the total marketing operation: the basic objectives and policies of the operation and the assumptions which underlie them as well as the methods, procedures, personnel, and organization employed to implement the policies and achieve the objectives.

The marketing concept is the philosophy of management that recognizes that the focal point of all activity within the organization lies within the consumer.

A marketing information system is a structured, interacting complex of persons, machines, and procedures designed to generate an orderly flow of pertinent information collected from both intra- and extraorganizational sources for uses as the bases for decision making in specified responsibility areas of marketing management.

A marketing manager is any person who makes any decisions about marketing activities.

The marketing mix is that unique combination of activities that a given firm undertakes to provide satisfaction to the market.

A marketing program is a list of the tasks of marketing necessary to provide satisfaction.

Marketing research is the systematic, objective approach to the development and provision of information for the marketing management decision-making process.

Marketing strategy is a specific plan for the allocation of marketing resources to reach the marketing objectives.

Marketing tactics are the specific decisions and actions necessary to carry out the strategy.

Markup is the difference between the quoted sales price and the cost of the goods to be sold.

Mass media are the vehicles for disseminating messages to large numbers of people; they include newspapers, magazines, television, radio, billboards, and direct mail.

Merchandising is the procedure whereby companies plan for products that are to be marketed.

Merchant intermediaries or middle men are those who take title to goods they help distribute.

The message is a sign or set of signs transmitted over a message channel.

A message channel is the means by which the message is transmitted.

Middlemen, or intermediaries, are buyers and resellers of goods who stand between the producer and consumer.

Middlemen's brands are brand names owned by intermediaries (middlemen) and are referred to as "private" brands.

Missionary salespeople are not expected or permitted to solicit an order—but, rather, set out to promote goodwill toward the marketing organization, help customers in their promotional activities, and provide other services for customers.

A model is a representation of something.

Modified rebuys are routine industrial purchases that involve some modification, such as a change in price, terms, product specification.

The most favored nation principle extends to a country that has been designated to receive tariff concessions.

Motives are stimulated needs that consumers look to satisfy.

A multinational company is one that operates manufacturing and marketing facilities in at least five countries.

Need is something that is lacking but is necessary for a person's physical and psychological well-being.

New task purchases refer to first-time industrial purchases.

Noise is any interference in the communication system that reduces effectiveness.

A noncumulative quantity discount is a quantity discount offered to a buyer on each individual order.

A nonprobability sample is a sampling procedure in which the selection of a member of

a population as part of the sample is based in some part on the judgment of the researcher or field interviewer.

Norms are standards or rules that define the limits of acceptable behavior for group members.

The nuclear family consists of the family members that one lives with—father, mother, and children.

The objective is the desired goal.

Observation is the method of data collection in which the situation of interest is checked and the relevant facts, actions, or behaviors are recorded.

Odd-even pricing is the pricing approach which focuses on the setting of the price to make it an odd number or a price just under a significant round number (99, 98).

A one-price policy is the approach to pricing where the marketer assigns one price to the product and offers that same price to all customers who purchase the same quantity of the item under the same conditions.

Organizing is the process of defining responsibilities and allocating authority to members of the organization for the carrying out of those responsibilities.

Packaging consists of the activities in product planning which involve designing and producing the container or wrapper for a product.

Penetration pricing is a pricing policy that sets the price low in the hope that the volume sold will be high.

Perception is the process by which one attributes meaning to what one senses.

Personal selling is one of the three major promotional activities which provides individual-to-individual communication between the marketer and members of the market.

Personality is an individual's most consistent pattern of responses.

Phantom freight is that part of the freight rate charged to the buyer which is greater than the freight cost actually paid by the seller.

Physical distribution is concerned with the movements of goods from points of production to points of consumption.

Place utility is the satisfaction that comes from moving the good closer in terms of geographical distance to the consumer.

A plan is a set of guidelines for action that is in anticipation of the future.

Planned obsolescence is the strategy of forcing a product in a line to be out of date, thus increasing the replacement market.

Planning is the activity of determining goals or objectives and developing a procedure for future activity to reach this goal.

Point-of-purchase promotion refers to the displays, signs, lights, and other attention-getting devices located at the place of actual purchase.

Policies are a manager's guidelines to bring day-to-day activities in line with objectives.

The polycentric stage of international marketing management thought is the stage where each foreign market is treated as a separate market.

A population is the aggregate of the elements defined prior to selection of the sample.

Portfolios are sets of strategic business units that work together as a team to achieve an organization's overall goals.

Possession utility is the satisfaction that comes from owning and having the right to consume the product.

Posttransaction consists of the activities which ensure satisfaction with the product in use and the follow-through activities which provide feedback for more effective performance of marketing operations.

The pre-approach is the process in which the salesperson accumulates facts that will be helpful in approaching and appealing to a prospect.

A premium is a product that is usually offered free or at less than the normal price in order to induce the consumer to purchase another product.

Prestige pricing is a pricing policy that aims the price high to convey a high-quality, high-status product image.

Price is what the buyer gives up to receive a bundle of utility in the exchange.

Price administration is the adjustment of prices as they move through the channel of distribution and are confronted with certain market conditions.

Price elasticity of demand is a measure of the responsiveness of consumers in terms of quantity demanded compared with changes in price.

A price leader is a product priced below the usual full markup.

Price-leader pricing is the pricing policy whereby the company attempts to set the price for all competitors in the industry.

Price lining is the setting of a limited number of prices for products or brands within a product class.

Price off is a reduction in price from the regular price.

Primary data consist of information collected specifically for the purpose of the investigation at hand.

Primary demand is the demand for a product class.

Primary-demand advertising promotes the demand for the generic product.

Primary reference groups are aggregates of individuals small enough and intimate enough that all members can communicate with one another face to face.

Private carriers are shippers that own the goods being shipped. The goods are related to the company's principal business, the company employs the drivers, and the company owns or leases the equipment used.

A private warehouse is one that is owned and controlled exclusively by the user.

A probability sample is a sample in which each element of the population has a known chance of being selected for the sample.

A problem is the difference between an actual and an ideal state.

Problem solving is the process of searching for a solution to a problem.

A product is the set of tangible and intangible attributes of the good, service, person, place, or idea that is being exchanged.

Product adjustment includes those activities which are conducted to match the product with the market in which it is to be purchased and consumed.

Product depth is the number of variations offered within a basic product line.

Product differentiation is the strategy of market aggregation where the marketer produces a single product and marketing program.

The product life cycle is the set of stages that a product's sales go through from the product's commercialization to its being taken off the market.

The product line is the broad group of products intended for essential similar uses and possessing reasonably similar physical characteristics.

The product mix is all the different products offered by a company.

Product position is the image that a product projects in relation to images projected by (1) competitive products and (2) other products in the line.

Product relaunching is the strategy of moving products from stagnant markets by initiating product mix changes to attract new users and to obtain increased usage from existing users.

Product width is the number of product lines contained in the product mix.

A program is a listing of the order of events.

Programmed decisions are those that are routine and are made to meet recurring problems.

Promotion is the all-inclusive term representing the broad field of sales communication—advertising, personal selling, and sales promotion.

Promotional discounts are price reductions made to

intermediaries to pay them for carrying out promotional activities.

Promotional pricing is a pricing technique that utilizes prices lower than normal to make products more attractive.

A prospect is an organization or an individual who can both afford to purchase the product and benefit from using it.

Prospecting is the process by which the salesperson locates and classifies potential buyers of the product.

Psychogenic needs are psychological states of deprivation, such as when one needs prestige, a sense of belonging, pride, recognition, and the like.

Psychological pricing is the adjusting of the list price so that it is psychologically appealing to the buyer.

Public relations is any communication created primarily to build prestige or goodwill for an individual or an organization.

Public service advertising is directed at changing attitudes or behavior for the good of the community or the public at large.

A public warehouse is one owned by an independent contractor where space is rented to suit the needs of the user.

Publicity is communication through mass media for which no payment is made by the sponsor.

A pull strategy is one where demand for the product is created in the market by advertising and where the product is drawn through the channel by customer requests.

Purchasing motivation is the assessment of those direct and indirect factors which underlie, impinge upon, and influence purchase behavior.

A push strategy is one where the product is moved through the channel by personal selling and by incentives to intermediaries.

A quantity discount is a price reduction made to encourage the purchase of larger amounts of goods than would be expected otherwise.

Question marks are strategic business units with low relative market share in high-growth markets.

A quota sample is a nonprobability sample in which the interviewer is assigned a quota which specifies the characteristics of the people to be contacted but is allowed to select the sample members at his or her discretion.

A rack-jobber is a limited-service wholesaler who focuses on selling items that are sold in food stores or in-store display racks.

Real self-image is the way we see ourselves and/or believe other people actually see us.

A reference group is any interacting aggregation of people that influences an individual's attitudes or behavior.

The regiocentric stage of the evolution of international marketing management thought exists where many countries are massed together to comprise a regional market.

Reinforcement is the reward derived from a response.

Response is the outcome of or reaction to a given stimulus.

Retailer is someone who buys goods and sells them to ultimate consumers.

Retailing includes all those business activities associated with selling goods and services to an ultimate consumer or a final user for personal consumption.

Retention is remembering what is learned.

Return on investment is the ratio of profits to invested capital.

The sales approach consists of the salesperson's first few minutes of conversation with the prospect prior to the actual sales presentation.

The sales presentation is that part of the sales process between the approach and the time that the prospect has heard the story and begins to ask questions and raise objections.

Sales promotion consists of those marketing activities, other than personal selling, advertising, and publicity, that stimulate consumer purchasing and dealer effectiveness, such as displays, shows and expositions, demonstrations, and various nonrecurrent selling efforts not in the ordinary routine.

A sample is the subset of the elements of the population.

Sampling is the giving of a sample of the product to the consumer.

Sampling error is the likely extent of the difference between the sample value and the population value of interest.

A scale is the means by which numbers are ascribed to abstract things such as beliefs, attitudes, and intentions.

The scientific method is the approach to conducting research that emphasizes objectivity and accuracy throughout the process.

Scrambled merchandising is the addition to a store's product line of products that are not traditionally found in that line.

Seasonal discounts are price reductions made to encourage orders for goods when they are out of season.

Secondary data are statistics gathered not for the immediate study at hand but for some other purpose.

Secondary reference groups are aggregates of individuals with whom an individual has only indirect contact.

Selective demand is the demand for a brand within a product class.

Selective demand advertising promotes the demand for a brand.

Selective distribution is the use of a limited set of intermediaries to distribute goods.

Selective perception is the process by which an individual chooses from all available stimuli those stimuli that will be given attention.

Selling is the personal or impersonal process of assisting and/or persuading a prospective customer to buy a commodity or service or to act favorably upon an idea that has commercial significance to the seller.

Selling agents are non-title-bearing intermediaries who are responsible for the entire marketing program of their principal's product line.

Sensory discrimination is the ability to distinguish between two or more similar stimuli presented to one sense mode.

Services are intangible, perishable bundles of utility exchanged in the marketplace to satisfy consumers' wants and needs.

Sharpening is the process by which an individual makes what is retained in memory and not forgotten (leveled) more prominent and of greater importance.

Shippers cooperatives are groups of shippers who band together to pool shipments of similar items, thereby gaining advantageous freight rates.

Shopping centers are groups of retail units that are planned, developed, and controlled by one organization.

Shopping goods are items which are compared for price and quality before being bought.

Shopping stores are retail outlets that seem to be favored by consumers shopping for certain types of products.

A simple random sample is a probability sample in which each population element has a known and equal chance of being included in the sample.

Skimming policy is the pricing approach that initially prices the product at the high end of the acceptable range, then lowers the price in stages.

Social classes are relatively permanent and homogenous divisions in a society into which individuals or families sharing similar values, lifestyles, interests, and behavior can be categorized.

Social-responsibility marketing is a level of marketing that considers profit, consumer satisfaction, and societal well-being of equal value.

Sorting is the process of concentration and dispersion of goods in a channel of distribution.

Specialty goods are goods for which there is an intense demand and which buyers insist upon having.

Specialty-line stores are those which offer only one or two product lines but with substantial depth within those lines, and which offer a greater expertise than the limited-line stores.

Specialty stores are those retail stores for which consumers develop a strong allegiance and preference.

Staple items are convenience goods which consumers usually make advance plans to buy.

Stars are strategic business units with high relative market shares in high-growth markets.

Status is an individual's rank in society.

A stimulus is anything causing or regarded as causing a response.

Straight rebuys are simple reorders of industrial products already purchased.

Strategic business units are combinations of one or more products, brands, company divisions, or market segments that have something in common, such as the same distribution system, similar consumer benefits, or like technology.

Strategic plans are long-range plans that chart competitive courses of action for an organization over an extended period.

A stratified sample is a probability sample that is distinguished by a two-step procedure where (1) the population is divided into subgroups called "strata" and (2) a simple random sample is chosen independently from each subgroup or stratum.

The structure of distribution is made up of the routes or channels along which goods move on their way from producer to ultimate consumer.

A subculture is a smaller group within the large society or culture.

Substantiation is a program first undertaken by the Federal Trade Commission in 1971 to ensure that claims made by advertisers are based on fact.

Supermarkets are large self-service stores which carry a full line of food products and, more often than not, a number of nonfood products.

A super store is a mass-merchandise retailer that combines a general merchandise discounter with a supermarket and offers an extremely wide product line.

The supply rationale is the focusing on the marketer's source of supply as the basis for convergence in adding products.

Survival pricing is the pricing policy that attempts to price low enough to compete in the short run but to stay in the market in the long run.

Sweepstakes are used to encourage consumers to buy a product as part of the entry requirement—though, by law, purchase cannot be mandatory.

Tactical plans specify short-term activities that are necessary to carry out a strategic plan.

A target market is a particular group of people with specific needs and wants that a marketer attempts to serve.

Telephone selling is retailing in which the sale of goods and services takes place over the telephone.

Test marketing is the marketing of a product in a limited geographic area and the projecting from this sample of the company's sales potential (market share) over a larger area.

Time utility is the satisfaction that accrues from moving the product closer in time to the consumer.

Total costs are the sum of total fixed costs and total variable costs.

Total fixed costs are those costs which do not change in the short run with the volume of goods produced.

Total variable costs are those costs that fluctuate depending upon the number of items produced.

Trade advertising is advertising directed toward producers or intermediaries.

Trade discounts are price reductions offered to intermediaries for services rendered.

A trademark is essentially a legal term and refers to a brand which is given legal protection because, by law, it has been appropriated exclusively by one seller.

Trading down is the adding of products of lower price and quality to products already existing in the line.

Trading up is the adding of prestigious products of higher price and quality to products already existing in the line.

Traits are relatively enduring and distinctive ways in which consumers differ from one another.

Transaction includes those activities which must be performed between the time a meeting of minds occurs among the parties concerned and the actual transfer of ownership.

Tying agreements force a dealer to buy additional products from a producer to secure the purchase of one highly desired product—or at least restrain the buyer from buying the said product from some other source.

Uniform delivered pricing is the approach under which all buyers within a specified area are charged the same price regardless of location and transportation charges.

Unit pricing is the approach whereby the price of a package is indicated in a standard measure, such as dollars and cents per ounce, pound, pint, or some other measure.

Unitary elasticity is the condition in which a percentage change (increase or decrease) in price brings about an equal percentage change (decrease or increase) in quantity sold.

Unprogrammed decisions are those decisions that happen infrequently and that are usually more complex and unstructured than programmed decisions.

Unsought goods are goods buyers don't yet realize they want.

Utility is the satisfaction that the consumer receives from a product.

Vending-machine retailing is the nonpersonal form of selling to consumers from machines conveniently located for the customer.

Venture teams are ongoing groups responsible for new-product development.

Vertical cooperative advertising is advertising whose cost is shared by marketers at different levels in the channel of distribution.

Vertical marketing systems are the integration of channel members into a unified channel.

A voluntary is a wholesaler-initiated organization of retailers who pledge purchases through the wholesaler.

A wagon or truck wholesaler is a limited-service wholesaler who sells goods directly from a vehicle.

Want is something that is lacking

which is desirable or useful.

A warranty is a manufacturer's promise that the product is fit for the purpose intended.

Waste circulation occurs when a medium is exposed to audience members not in the marketer's target market.

Wholesalers are merchant intermediaries primarily engaged in selling to retailers, to individual, commercial, institutional, or professional users, or to other wholesalers.

Wholesaling intermediaries are those involved in exchange for the purpose of resale or business use.

The zone of indifference market is that part of the market in which match between market wants and needs and product offered is totally lacking.

Zone pricing is the geographical pricing approach wherein areas are set off and any buyer in the area is charged the same freight charge.

Index